WITHDRAWN

Parallel Paths:
Fiduciary Doctrine and the Crown–Native
Relationship in Canada

In a landmark decision in 1984, the Supreme Court of Canada declared that the Crown is bound by fiduciary, or trust-like, obligations to Canada's aboriginal peoples. By holding the Crown's duty to be legal, rather than merely political or moral, the Supreme Court blazed a new path in Canadian aboriginal rights jurisprudence. Yet, more than a decade later, many of the outstanding issues arising from that decision have yet to be answered or adequately addressed. This is, in part, because the Supreme Court provided little guidance as to the nature and extent of the Crown's duty.

Leonard Rotman explores the unanswered questions that plague the Crown–Native fiduciary relationship. He begins by looking at the politics underlying Crown–Native relations and the effects of colonialism on Native peoples. Legislation and case law are then surveyed to reveal the historical and current status of fiduciary doctrine. By examining its fundamental characteristics and principles, Rotman formulates a functional rather than a categorical interpretation of fiduciary law. Finally, he discusses the effects of applying fiduciary law to the Crown–Native relationship.

Considering the present status of aboriginal rights issues in Canada, it is striking that the Crown–Native fiduciary relationship remains the subject of so much confusion and uncertainty. With this principled treatment of fiduciary doctrine and its impact upon Crown–aboriginal relations in Canada, Rotman bridges a significant gap in legal writing.

LEONARD IAN ROTMAN teaches in the Faculty of Law at the University of Alberta. He has also acted as a consultant to aboriginal law practitioners and the Indian Claims Commission.

LEONARD IAN ROTMAN

Parallel Paths: Fiduciary Doctrine and the Crown–Native Relationship in Canada

UNIVERSITY OF TORONTO PRESS
Toronto Buffalo London

© University of Toronto Press Incorporated 1996
Toronto Buffalo London
Printed in Canada

ISBN 0-8020-0821-6 (cloth)
ISBN 0-8020-7813-3 (paper)

Printed on acid-free paper

Canadian Cataloguing in Publication Data

Rotman, Leonard Ian
  Parallel paths : fiduciary doctrine and the
  Crown–Native relationship in Canada

  Includes index.
  ISBN 0-8020-0821-6 (bound)   ISBN 0-8020-7813-3 (pbk.)

  1. Native peoples – Legal status, laws, etc. – Canada.*
  2. Native peoples – Canada – Government relations.*
  I. Title.

  KE7709.R67 1996   342.71'0872   C96-930806-X
  KF8205.R67 1996

University of Toronto Press acknowledges the financial
assistance to its publishing program of the Canada Council
and the Ontario Arts Council.

This book has been published with the help of a grant from
the Social Science Federation of Canada, using funds
provided by the Social Sciences and Humanities Research
Council of Canada.

Brothers: We have heard the talk of our Great Father; it is very kind. He says he loves his red children ...

When the first white man came over the wide waters, he was but a little man ... very little. His legs were cramped by sitting long in his big boat, and he begged for a little land ...

When he came to these shores the Indians gave him land, and kindled fires to make him comfortable ...

But when the white man had warmed himself at the Indian's fire, and had filled himself with the Indian's hominy, he became very large. He stopped not at the mountain tops, and his foot covered the plains and the valleys. His hands grasped the eastern and western seas. Then he became our Great Father. He loved his red children, but he said: 'You must move a little farther, lest by accident I tread on you.'

With one foot he pushed the red men across the Oconee, and with the other he trampled down the graves of our fathers ...

On another occasion he said, 'Get a little farther; go beyond the Oconee and the Ocmulgee [Indian settlements in South Carolina and Georgia] – there is a pleasant country.' He also said, 'It shall be yours forever.'

Now he says, 'The land you live upon is not yours. Go beyond the Mississippi; there is game; there you may remain while the grass grows and the rivers run.'

Will not our Great Father come there also? He loves his red children, and his tongue is not forked.

Brothers! I have listened to a great many talks from our Great Father. But they always began and ended in this – 'Get a little farther; you are too near me.' I have spoken.

Speckled Snake, aged Cree chief, speaking in 1829 when the Creeks were considering the advice of President Andrew Jackson, who was urging them to move beyond the Mississippi, as quoted in Frederick W. Turner III, ed., *The Portable North American Indian Reader* (New York: Viking, 1974), at 249–50.

This book is dedicated to the memory of Joseph Mendlovitz, whose wisdom and sacrifices remain an inspiration to all who knew him

Contents

PREFACE ix
ACKNOWLEDGMENTS xi
TABLE OF CASES xiii

Part One: The Juridical Understanding of the Crown–Native Fiduciary Relationship
1 Introduction 3
2 The Politics Underlying the Crown–Native Fiduciary Relationship in Canada 19
3 The Incidents of Colonialism 50
4 The Legislative and Jurisprudential History of the Crown–Native Relationship in Canada 66
5 The Characterization of the Crown–Native Fiduciary Relationship by the Courts: *Guerin v R* 88
6 Judicial Characterizations of the Crown's Fiduciary Duty after *Guerin* 111
7 The Status of the Crown's Fiduciary Duty 139

Part Two: General Principles of Fiduciary Doctrine
8 A Re-examination of Fiduciary Doctrine 149
9 Fiduciary Theories 164
10 A 'Back to Basics' Approach to Fiduciary Doctrine 176

Part Three: The Crown's Fiduciary Duty towards Aboriginal Peoples in Canada
11 The British Crown's Obligations 203

viii Contents

12 The Canadian Crown's Obligations 221
13 Aboriginal Understandings of 'the Crown' and the Nexus between Governmental Power and Fiduciary Responsibility 244
14 Characteristics of the Crown–Native Fiduciary Relationship 255
15 The Practical Application of Fiduciary Doctrine in the Native Law Context: A Reappraisal of *Kruger v R* 273
16 Prospects for the Future 281

APPENDICES 291
 1 Statement of the Government of Canada on Indian Policy, 1969 291
 2 The Bull *Romanus Pontifex*, 8 January 1455 309
 3 Treaty of Albany, 1664 311
 4 Report of the Lords of Trade, 23 November 1761 313
 5 Royal Proclamation of 1761 316
 6 Governor Belcher's Proclamation, Nova Scotia, 1762 318
 7 Royal Proclamation of 1763 320
 8 Mi'kmaq Treaty of 1752 323
NOTES 327
REFERENCES 455
INDEX 477

Preface

This book marks the culmination of a number of years of research, writing, and thinking about a complex topic existing within an even more complicated area of law.

From my first reading of the Supreme Court of Canada's decision in *Guerin v R*,[1] which judicially sanctioned the Crown's fiduciary duty to aboriginal peoples, I could not help but think that the decision, while noteworthy for what it said, was equally noteworthy for what it left unsaid: Which emanations of 'the Crown' owed the duty to aboriginal peoples? What was the extent of the duty? What was 'the Crown' required to do in order to discharge its fiduciary obligations? What was it required not to do? The existence of these unanswered questions initiated my search for answers and ultimately resulted in this book.

This work centres on the premises that the relationship between the Crown and aboriginal peoples in Canada cannot properly be characterized as fiduciary in the absence of an adequate understanding of fiduciary doctrine and its application to that *sui generis* relationship. It is not enough to describe a relationship as fiduciary if the ramifications of such a description are not readily evident or forthcoming. Indeed, Equity's requirement that its doctrines, including fiduciary law, be tailored to the needs of specific situations – what I have referred to as the *situation-specific* nature of fiduciary doctrine – insists that fiduciary principles be applied to particular relationships only where the nature of the relationships warrant their application. Even then, fiduciary doctrine is applicable only to the extent that its general characteristics and principles are relevant to the relationship under scrutiny.

1 (1984), 13 D.L.R. (4th) 321 (S.C.C.).

The goal of this book is to address the unanswered questions that plague the development of the Crown–Native fiduciary relationship in Canadian aboriginal rights jurisprudence within an appropriate contextual framework. This process is initiated by examining the politics underlying Crown–Native relations and the effects of colonialism on the Native peoples. Legislation and case law is then surveyed to reveal the historical and current status of fiduciary doctrine as it is applied to the Crown–Native relationship. An exposition of the fundamental characteristics and principles of fiduciary law, achieved through a critical examination of its conceptual background, is the second step of the process, culminating in the formulation of a functional rather than categorical understanding of fiduciary doctrine. Finally, the effects of applying fiduciary law to the Crown–Native relationship, juxtaposed against the questions left unanswered by *Guerin* and subsequent decisions, will be discussed.

The intended purpose of proceeding in this manner is to foster a greater understanding and appreciation of the fiduciary nature of the relationship between the Crown and aboriginal peoples in Canada. Cementing the understanding of Crown–Native fiduciary relations requires a firm demonstration of the nexus between fiduciary doctrine and Crown–Native relations and its implications that is thus far lacking in existing juridical treatments. Once this is achieved, the fiduciary nature of the Crown–Native relationship may be placed within an appropriate context in the sphere of Canadian aboriginal rights jurisprudence.

Leonard I. Rotman
Toronto, Ontario

Acknowledgments

I owe a number of people and organizations a great deal of appreciation. I thank the Department of Justice Canada for providing me with a Duff-Rinfret Graduate Scholarship in Law, and the Osgoode Hall Law School and University of Toronto Graduate Programmes in Law for financial assistance over the years that the ideas that germinated into this book were formed. I also appreciate the financial help of the Social Science Federation of Canada in providing a grant for the publication of this book.

Thanks go to the many people whose paths I crossed and who offered their insight and support during the research, writing, and publishing of this study. Helpful commentary and criticism of some chapters came from Jim Phillips and Deborah Blumenthal, as well as from the three anonymous reviewers of the manuscript. Deserving of special thanks for their contributions to what became this book are Noel Lyon, Brian Slattery, and Mary Ellen Turpel. I appreciate the support of Virgil Duff, Executive Editor of University of Toronto Press, who started me on the path to publication.

The members of my family have provided me more support and encouragement than anyone could reasonably expect. They have each given of themselves, in their own, inimitable ways, through the various stages leading to the completion of this work. Without the unwavering faith, encouragement, and tremendous patience of my wife Tammy, from the earliest stages of my work in this area through to her review of my final manuscript, this book would simply not be.

Table of Cases

Aberdeen Railway Co v Blaikie Brothers (1854), [1843–1860] All E.R. Rep. 249 (H.L.).
Air Canada v M & L Travel Ltd (1993), 108 D.L.R. (4th) 592 (S.C.C.).
Alberta Government Telephones v Canada (CRTC) (1989), 61 D.L.R. (4th) 193 (S.C.C.).
Alexandra Oil & Development Co v Cook (1908), 11 O.W.R. 1054 (C.A.).
Allcard v Skinner (1887), [1886–90] All E.R. Rep. 90 (C.A.).
Amodu Tijani v The Secretary, Southern Nigeria, [1921] 2 A.C. 399 (P.C.).
Apsassin v Canada (Department of Indian Affairs and Northern Development), [1988] 3 F.C. 20 (F.C.T.D.), aff'd [1993] 2 C.N.L.R. 73 (F.C.A.), rev'd (14 Dec. 1995), File No. 23516 (S.C.C.).
Armstrong Growers v Harris (1924), 1 D.L.R. 1043 (B.C.C.A.).
Attorney-General v Nissan, [1970] A.C. 179 (H.L.).
Attorney-General for Quebec v Attorney-General for Canada, Re Indian Lands (The Star Chrome Case) (1920), 56 D.L.R. 373 (P.C.).
Attorney-General of Canada v Giroux (1916), 30 D.L.R. 123 (S.C.C.).
Attorney-General of Ontario v Mercer (1883), 8 A.C. 767 (P.C.).
Bastien v Hoffman (1867), 17 L.C.R. 238 (Q.B.).
Beatty v Guggenheim Exploration Co, 225 N.Y. 380 (N.Y.C.A. 1919).
B(J) v B(R), File No. 1862-89, 11 Feb 1994 (Ont. Gen. Div.).
Bombay (Province of) v Bombay (City of), [1947] A.C. 58 (P.C.).
Bown v West (1846), 1 E. & A. 117 (U.C. Exec. Council).
Bray v Ford, [1896] A.C. 44 (H.L.).
Bruno v Canada (Minister of Indian Affairs and Northern Development), [1991] 2 C.N.L.R. 22 (F.C.T.D.).
Burns v Kelly Peters & Associates Ltd (1988), 41 D.L.R. (4th) 577 (B.C.C.A.).
Caffrey v Darby (1801), 31 E.R. 1159 (Ch.).

Calder v Attorney-General of British Columbia (1973), 34 D.L.R. (3d) 145 (S.C.C.).
Campbell v Hall (1774), 1 Cowp. 204, 98 E.R. 1045 (K.B.).
Canada Safeway Ltd v Thompson, [1952] 2 D.L.R. 591 (B.C.S.C.).
Canada Trust Co v Lloyd (1968), 66 D.L.R. (2d) 722 (S.C.C.).
Canadian Aero Service Ltd v O'Malley (1973), 40 D.L.R. (3d) 371 (S.C.C.).
Canson Enterprises Ltd v Boughton & Co (1989), 61 D.L.R. (4th) 732 (B.C.C.A.); aff'd [1991] 3 S.C.R. 534.
Cardinal v R (1991), 4 E.T.R. 297 (F.C.T.D.).
Carl B. Potter Ltd v Mercantile Bank of Canada (1980), 8 E.T.R. 219 (S.C.C.).
Carlsen v Gerlach (1979), 3 E.T.R. 231 (Alta. Dist. Ct.).
Carruthers v Carruthers, [1896] A.C. 659 (H.L.).
Carter v Boehm (1766), [1558–1774] All E.R. Rep. 183 (K.B.).
Central Trust Co v Rafuse (1986), 31 D.L.R. (4th) 481 (S.C.C.).
Chase Manhattan Bank v Israel British Bank, [1981] Ch. 105.
Chisholm v The King, [1948] 3 D.L.R. 797 (Exch.).
Church v Fenton (1878), 28 U.C.C.P. 384, aff'd (1879), 4 O.A.R. 159, (1880), 5 S.C.R. 239.
City of Kamloops v Nielsen (1984), 10 D.L.R. (4th) 641 (S.C.C.).
Coleman v Myers, [1977] 2 N.Z.L.R. 255 (C.A.).
Corbiere v Canada, [1994] 1 C.N.L.R. 71 (F.C.T.D.).
Corinthe v Seminary of St Sulpice (1910), 38 Que. S.C., aff'd (1911), 21 Que. K.B., (1912), 5 D.L.R. 263 (P.C.).
Courtright v Canadian Pacific Ltd (1983), 5 D.L.R. (4th) 488 (Ont. H.C.), aff'd (1985), 18 D.L.R. (4th) 639n (Ont. C.A.).
Coy v Pommerenke (1911), 44 S.C.R. 543.
Cramer v United States, 261 U.S. 219 (1923).
Cree Regional Authority v Robinson, [1991] 4 C.N.L.R. 84 (F.C.T.D.).
Daniels v R. [1968] S.C.R. 517.
Davis v Duke of Marlborough (1819), 2 Swan 108 (Ch.).
Davis v Kerr (1890), 17 S.C.R. 235.
Day v Mead, [1987] 2 N.Z.L.R. 443 (C.A.).
Deglman v Guaranteed Trust Co and Constantineau, [1954] S.C.R. 725.
Delgamuukw v British Columbia (1991), 79 D.L.R. (4th) 185 (B.C.S.C.), var'd (1993), 104 D.L.R. (4th) 470 (B.C.C.A.).
Derrickson v Derrickson (1986), 26 D.L.R. (4th) 175 (S.C.C.).
Dick v The Queen (1985), 23 D.L.R. (4th) 33 (S.C.C.).
Dominion of Canada v Province of Ontario (Treaty No. 3 Annuities Case) (1907), 10 Ex. C.R. 445; rev'd (1909), 42 S.C.R. 1; aff'd [1910] A.C. 637 (P.C.).

Dreaver v The King (1935), 5 C.N.L.C. 92 (Exch.).
Dudley v Dudley (1705), 24 E.R. 118 (Ch.).
Dunlop Pneumatic Tyre Co v Selfridge & Co, [1915] A.C. 847 (H.L.).
Easterbrook v R [1931] S.C.R. 210.
Eastmain Band v Robinson, [1992] 1 C.N.L.R. 90 (F.C.T.D.), rev'd *Eastmain Band v Canada (Federal Administrator),* [1993] 3 C.N.L.R. 55 (F.C.A.).
Entick v Carrington (1765), 19 St. Tr. 1029, 95 E.R. 867 (K.B.).
Erlanger v New Sombrero Phosphates Ltd (1877–78) 3 A.C. 1218 (H.L.).
Esquimalt & Nanaimo Railway Co v Wilson, [1920] A.C. 358 (P.C.).
Ex parte Lacey (1802), 6 Ves. 625, 31 E.R. 1228 (Ch.).
Ex parte James (1803), 8 Ves. 337, 32 E.R. 385 (Ch.).
Farrington v Rowe McBridge and Partners, [1985] 1 N.Z.L.R. 83 (C.A.).
Fibrosa Spolka Akcyjna v Fairbairn Lawson Combe Barbour Ltd, [1943] A.C. 32 (H.L.).
Fine's Flowers Ltd v General Accident Assurance Co. (1974), 5 O.R. (2d) 137 (H.C.), aff'd (1977), 81 D.L.R. (3d) 139 (Ont. C.A.).
Fitzroy v Gwillim (1786), 1 Term Rep. 153 (Ch.).
Follis v Albemarle TP, [1941] 1 D.L.R. 178 (Ont. C.A.).
Fonthill Lumber v Bank of Montreal (1959), 19 D.L.R. (2d) 618 (Ont. C.A.).
Four B Manufacturing v United Garment Workers of America (1979), 102 D.L.R. (3d) 385 (S.C.C.).
Frame v Smith (1988), 42 D.L.R. (4th) 81 (S.C.C.).
Friends of the Oldman River Society v Canada (Minister of Transport) (1992), 88 D.L.R. (4th) 1 (S.C.C.).
Gardner v The Queen in Right of Ontario (1984), 45 O.R. (2d) 760 (Ont. H.C.).
Gilbert v Abbey, [1992] 4 C.N.L.R. 21 (B.C.S.C.).
Girardet v Crease & Co (1987), 11 B.C.L.R. (2d) 361 (S.C.).
Goldex Mines Ltd v Revill (1975), 7 O.R. (2d) 216 (C.A.).
Goodbody v Bank of Montreal (1974), 47 D.L.R. (3d) 335 (Ont. H.C.).
Greenhalgh v Arderne Cinemas Ltd, [1950] 2 All E.R. 1120 (C.A.).
Greenwood Shopping Plaza Ltd v Beattie (1980), 111 D.L.R. (3d) 257 (S.C.C.).
Gros-Louis v Société de Développement de la Baie James, [1974] R.P. 38 (Que. S.C.).
Guerin v R (1981), 10 E.T.R. 61 (F.C.T.D.), with additional reasons (1981), 127 D.L.R. (3d) 170 (F.C.T.D.), rev'd, [1983] 143 D.L.R. (3d) 416 (F.C.A.), rev'd (1984), 13 D.L.R. (4th) 321 (S.C.C.).
Harrison v Harrison (1868), 14 Gr. 586 (P.C.).
Hawrelak v City of Edmonton, [1972] 2 W.W.R. 561 (Alta. S.C.); aff'd [1973] 1 W.W.R. 179 (Alta. C.A.); rev'd [1976] 1 S.C.R. 387.

Hayward v Bank of Nova Scotia (1984), 7 D.L.R. (4th) 135 (Ont. H.C.).
Henry v The King (1905), 9 Ex. C.R. 417.
Hereford Railway Co v The Queen (1894), 24 S.C.R. 1.
Hodgkinson v Simms (1994), 117 D.L.R. (4th) 161 (S.C.C.).
Hospital Products Ltd v United States Surgical Corp (1984), 55 A.L.R. 417 (H.C. Aust.).
Huff v Price (1991), 76 D.L.R. (4th) 138 (B.C.C.A.).
Huguenin v Baseley (1807), 33 E.R. 526 (Ch.).
Hunter v Mann, [1974] Q.B. 767.
Hunter Engineering Co v Syncrude Canada Ltd (1989), 57 D.L.R. (4th) 321 (S.C.C.).
Hyde v United States, 225 U.S. 347 (1911).
In re Gulbenkian's Settlement; Whishaw and Another v Stephens and Others, [1970] A.C. 508 (H.L.).
In re Vernon, Ewens, & Co (1886), 33 Ch.D. 402 (C.A.).
In re West of England and South Wales District Bank, Ex parte Dale and Co (1879), 11 Ch.D. 772.
Inglis v Beaty (1878), 2 O.A.R. 453.
Isaac v Davey (1977), 77 D.L.R. (3d) 481 (S.C.C.).
Island Realty Investments Ltd v Douglas (1985), 19 E.T.R. 56 (B.C.S.C.).
Jirna Ltd v Mister Donut of Canada Ltd (1973), 40 D.L.R. (3d) 303 (S.C.C.).
Joe v John (1990), 34 E.T.R. 280 (F.C.T.D.).
Johnson and Graham's Lessee v M'Intosh, 8 Wheat. 541 (U.S. 1823).
Jones v Meehan, 175 U.S. 1 (1899).
Keech v Sandford (1726), 25 E.R. 223 (Ch.).
Kinloch v Secretary of State for India in Council, [1881–82] 7 A.C. 619 (H.L.).
Kitchen v Royal Air Forces Ass'n, [1958] 2 All E.R. 241 (C.A.).
Knox v Gye (1872), L.R. 5 H.L. 656.
Knox v Mackinnon (1888), 13 A.C. 753 (H.L.).
Krendel v Frontwell Investments Ltd, [1967] 2 O.R. 579 (H.C.).
Krueger v San Francisco Forty Niners, 234 Cal. Rep. 579 (C.A. 1987).
Kruger v R. (1981), 125 D.L.R. (3d) 513 (F.C.T.D.), aff'd (1985), 17 D.L.R. (4th) 591 (F.C.A.).
Kruger and Manuel v R (1977), 75 D.L.R. (3d) 434 (S.C.C.).
LAC Minerals v International Corona Resources Ltd (1988), 62 O.R. (2d) 1 (Ont. C.A.); aff'd (1989), 61 D.L.R. (4th) 14 (S.C.C.).
Laskin v Bache & Co (1971), 23 D.L.R. (3d) 385 (Ont. C.A.).
Lavigne v Robern (1984), 51 O.R. (2d) 60 (C.A.).
LeMesurier v Andrus (1986), 54 O.R. (2d) 1 (C.A.).
Lindsay Petroleum Co v Hurd (1874), L.R. 5 P.C. 221.

Table of Cases xvii

Lloyd's Bank v Bundy, [1975] 1 Q.B. 326 (C.A.).
Logan v Styres (1959), 20 D.L.R. (2d) 416 (Ont. H.C.).
Lower Kootenay Indian Band v Canada (Federal Administrator), [1992] 2 C.N.L.R. 54 (F.C.T.D.).
Lyell v Kennedy (1889), 14 A.C. 437 (H.L.).
M(K) v M(H) (1992), 96 D.L.R. (4th) 289 (S.C.C.).
Mabo v Queensland [No. 2] (1992), 175 C.L.R. 1 (H.C. Aust.).
Manuel and Others v Attorney General, [1982] 3 All E.R. 786 (Ch.), aff'd [1982] 3 All E.R. 118 (C.A.).
McInerney v MacDonald (1992), 93 D.L.R. (4th) 415 (S.C.C.).
McLeod and More v Sweezey, [1944] 2 D.L.R. 145 (S.C.C.).
MacMillan Bloedel Ltd v Binstead (1983), 14 E.T.R. 269 (B.C.S.C.).
Meinhard v Salmon, 164 N.E. 546 (N.Y.C.A. 1928).
Midcon Oil & Gas Limited v New British Dominion Oil Company Limited (1958), 12 D.L.R. (2d) 705 (S.C.C.).
Miller v The King, [1948] Ex. C.R. 372, rev'd (1950), [1950] 1 D.L.R. 513 (S.C.C.).
Mitchell v Homfray (1881), 8 Q.B.D. 587 (C.A.).
Mitchell v Peguis Indian Band, [1983] 5 W.W.R. 117 (Man. Q.B.), aff'd [1986] 2 W.W.R. 477 (Man. C.A.), (1990), 71 D.L.R. (4th) 193 (S.C.C.).
Molchan v Omega Oil and Gas Ltd (1988), 47 D.L.R. (4th) 481 (S.C.C.).
Moore v Royal Trust Co, [1956] S.C.R. 880.
Morley v Loughnan, [1893] 1 Ch. 736.
New Zealand Maori Council v Attorney-General, [1987] 1 N.Z.L.R. 641 (N.Z.C.A.).
New Zealand Netherlands Society 'Oranje' Inc v Kuys, [1973] 2 All E.R. 1222 (H.L.).
Nixdorf v Hicken, 612 P. 2d 348 (S.C. Utah 1980).
Nocton v Ashburton, [1914] A.C. 932 (H.L.).
Noltcho and Others v Attorney General, [1982] 3 All E.R. 786 (Ch.).
Norberg v Wynrib (1992), 92 D.L.R. (4th) 449 (S.C.C.).
Nowegijick v The Queen (1983), 144 D.L.R. (3d) 193 (S.C.C.).
Olson v Gullo (1994), 17 O.R. (3d) 790 (C.A.).
Ontario and Minnesota Power Co v The King, [1925] A.C. 196 (P.C.).
Ontario (Attorney-General) v Bear Island Foundation (1984), 15 D.L.R. (4th) 321 (Ont. H.C.), aff'd (1989), 58 D.L.R. (4th) 117 (Ont. C.A.), (1991) 83 D.L.R. (4th) 381 (S.C.C.).
Ontario Mining Company Ltd v Seybold (1899), 31 O.R. 386 (Ch.); aff'd (1900), 32 O.R. 301 (Div. Ct.); (1901), 32 S.C.R. 1; [1903] A.C. 73 (P.C.).
Orapko v Manson Investments Ltd., [1978] A.C. 95 (H.L.).

Oyekan v Adele, [1957] 2 All E.R. 785 (P.C.).
Parfitt v Lawless (1872), 2 L.R. P.& D. 462.
Pasco v C.N.R. (1985), 69 B.C.L.R. 76 (S.C.).
Paul v Canadian Pacific Ltd (1989), 53 D.L.R. (4th) 487 (S.C.C.).
Pawis v The Queen (1979), 102 D.L.R. (3d) 602 (F.C.T.D.).
Pawlett v Attorney-General (1668), 145 E.R. 550 (Exch.).
Peso Silver Mines Ltd v Cropper (1965), 56 D.L.R. (2d) 117 (B.C.C.A.), aff'd (1966), 58 D.L.R. (2d) 1 (S.C.C.).
Peter v Beblow (1993), 101 D.L.R. (4th) 621 (S.C.C.).
Pettkus v Becker (1980), 117 D.L.R. (3d) 257 (S.C.C.).
Phipps v Boardman, [1967] 2 A.C. 46 (H.L.).
Pre-Cam Exploration and Development Ltd v McTavish (1966), 57 D.L.R. (2d) 557 (S.C.C.).
Province of Ontario v Dominion of Canada and Province of Quebec: In re Indian Claims (Robinson Treaties Annuities Case), [1896] 25 S.C.R. 434; aff'd [1897] A.C. 199 (P.C.).
Quirt v The Queen (1891), 19 S.C.R. 510.
R v Agawa (1988), 65 O.R. (2d) 505 (C.A.).
R v Big M Drug Mart, [1985] 1 S.C.R. 295.
R v Bombay, [1993] 1 C.N.L.R. 92 (Ont. C.A.).
R v Derriksan (1976), 71 D.L.R. (3d) 159 (S.C.C.).
R v Francis (1956), 3 D.L.R. (2d) 641 (S.C.C.).
R v Gentile (1993), 81 C.C.C. (3d) 541 (Ont. Prov. Div.).
R v George (1966), 55 D.L.R. (2d) 386 (S.C.C.).
R v Gladstone, [1993] 5 W.W.R. 517 (B.C.C.A.).
R v Horse, [1988] 1 S.C.R. 187.
R v Horseman, [1990] 1 S.C.R. 901.
R v Jones (1993), 14 O.R. (3d) 421 (Ont. Prov. Div.).
R v Joseph, [1990] 4 C.N.L.R. 59 (B.C.S.C.).
R v Kelly (1992), 92 D.L.R. (4th) 643 (S.C.C.).
R v Koonungnak, [1963–64] 45 W.W.R. 282 (N.W.T. Terr. Ct.).
R v Lewis, [1994] 5 W.W.R. 608 (B.C.C.A.).
R v Litchfield (1993), 86 C.C.C. (3d) 97 (S.C.C.).
R v Morley, [1932] 4 D.L.R. 483 (B.C.C.A.).
R v NTC Smokehouse Ltd, [1993] 5 W.W.R. 542 (B.C.C.A.).
R v Oakes (1986), 26 D.L.R. (4th) 200 (S.C.C.).
R v Secretary of State for Foreign and Commonwealth Affairs, ex parte Indian Association of Alberta and Others (Alberta Indian Association Case), [1982] 2 All E.R. 118 (C.A.).
R v Sikyea (1964), 43 D.L.R. (2d) 150 (N.W.T.C.A.), aff'd [1964] S.C.R. 642.

Table of Cases xix

R v Sioui (1990), 70 D.L.R. (4th) 427 (S.C.C.).
R v Sparrow (1990), 70 D.L.R. (4th) 385 (S.C.C.).
R v Sutherland (1980), 113 D.L.R. (3d) 374 (S.C.C.).
R v Syliboy, [1929] 1 D.L.R. 307 (N.S. Co. Ct.).
R v Symonds (1847), N.Z.P.C.C. 387 (N.Z.S.C.).
R v Taylor and Williams (1981), 62 C.C.C. (2d) 227 (Ont. C.A.).
R v Vanderpeet, [1993] 5 W.W.R. 459 (B.C.C.A.).
R v Vincent, [1993] 2 C.N.L.R. 165 (Ont. C.A.).
R v White and Bob (1964), 50 D.L.R. (2d) 613 (B.C.C.A.), aff'd (1965), 52 D.L.R. (2d) 481n (S.C.C.).
Rae v Meek (1889), 14 A.C. 558 (H.L.).
Rawluk v Rawluk (1990), 65 D.L.R. (4th) 161 (S.C.C.).
Re Consiglio Trusts (No. 1) (1973), 36 D.L.R. (3d) 659 (Ont. C.A.).
Re Craig, [1971] Ch. 95.
Re Diplock, [1948] Ch. 465; aff'd (*sub nom. Min. of Health v Simpson*), [1951] A.C. 251 (H.L.).
Re Eskimo, [1939] 2 D.L.R. 417 (S.C.C.).
Re Gabourie; Casey v Gabourie (1887), 13 O.R. 635 (Ch.).
Re Gosman, (1880), 15 Ch. D. 67, rev'd 17 Ch. D. 771 (C.A.).
Re Howlett, [1949] Ch. 767.
Re Kane (1939), [1940] 1 D.L.R. 390 (N.S. Co. Ct.).
Re Poche (1984), 6 D.L.R. (4th) 40 (Alta. Surr. Ct.).
Re Vandervell's Trusts (No. 2), [1974] 1 Ch. 269.
Reading v Attorney-General, [1949] 2 K.B. 232 (C.A.), aff'd [1951] A.C. 507 (H.L.).
Reference re Amendment of the Constitution of Canada, [1981] 125 D.L.R. (3d) 1 (S.C.C.).
Reference re Offshore Mineral Rights of British Columbia, [1967] S.C.R. 792.
Regal (Hastings) Ltd v Gulliver, [1942] 1 All E.R. 378 (H.L.).
Roberts v Canada (1989), 57 D.L.R. (4th) 197 (S.C.C.).
Ronald Elwyn Lister Ltd v Dunlop Canada Ltd (1982), 135 D.L.R. (3d) 1 (S.C.R.).
Rose v Rose (1914), 22 D.L.R. 572 (Ont. C.A.).
Rowe v Grand Trunk Railway Co (1866), U.C.C.P. 500.
Rustomjee v The Queen (1876), 2 Q.B. 69 (C.A.).
RWDSU Local 580 v Dolphin Delivery, [1986] 2 S.C.R. 573.
Saunders v Vautier (1841), 4 Beav. 115 (Ch.).
Securities & Exchange Commission v Chenery Corp. 318 U.S. 80 (1943).
Sero v Gault (1921), 50 O.L.R. 27 (H.C.).
Sheldon v Ramsay (1852), 9 U.C.Q.B. 105.

Simon v The Queen (1985), 24 D.L.R. (4th) 390 (S.C.C.).
Sinclair v Brougham, [1914] A.C. 398 (H.L.).
Skerryvore Ratepayers' Ass'n v Shawanaga Indian Band (1993), 16 O.R. (3d) 390 (C.A.).
Smith v R (1983), 147 D.L.R. (3d) 147 (S.C.C.).
Soar v Ashwell, [1893] 2 Q.B. 390 (C.A.).
Sorochan v Sorochan (1986), 29 D.L.R. (4th) 1 (S.C.C.).
Spector Motor Service v Walsh, 139 F.2d 809 (C.A. Conn. 1944).
St Ann's Island Shooting and Fishing Club v The King, [1949] 2 D.L.R. 17 (Exch.), aff'd (1950), [1950] 2 D.L.R. 225 (S.C.C.).
St Catherine's Milling and Lumber Co v The Queen (1885), 10 O.R. 196 (Ch.), aff'd (1886), 13 O.A.R. 148, (1887), 13 S.C.R. 577, (1888), 14 A.C. 46 (P.C.).
Standard Investments Ltd v CIBC (1983), 5 D.L.R. (4th) 452 (Ont. H.C.). rev'd (1985), 22 D.L.R. (4th) 410 (Ont. C.A.).
Stein v The Ship 'Kathy K,' [1976] 2 S.C.R. 802.
Tannock v Bromley (1979), 10 B.C.L.R. 62 (S.C.).
Tate v Williamson (1866), 2 L.R. Ch. App. 55.
Taylor v Davies, [1920] A.C. 636 (P.C.).
Taylor v Wallbridge (1879), 2 S.C.R. 616.
The King v Cowichan Agricultural Society, [1950] Ex. C.R. 448.
Theodore v Duncan, [1919] A.C. 696 (P.C.).
Three Affiliated Tribes of Fort Berthold Reservation v United States, 390 F.2d 686 (U.S. Ct. Cl. 1968).
Tito v Waddell (No. 2), [1977] 3 All E.R. 129 (Ch.).
Tombill Gold Mines Ltd v Hamilton (1956), 5 D.L.R. (2d) 561 (S.C.C.).
Toronto (City of) v Bowes (1858), 14 E.R. 770 (P.C.).
Totten v Watson (1858), 15 U.C.Q.B. 392.
Turner v Corney (1841), 5 Beav. 515 (Ch.).
United Scientific Holdings Ltd v Burnley Borough Council, [1978] A.C. 904 (H.L.).
United Services Funds (Trustees) v Richardson Greenshields of Canada Ltd (1988), 48 D.L.R. (4th) 98 (B.C.S.C.).
United States v Santa Fe Pacific Railroad Company, 314 U.S. 339 (1941).
United States v Sioux Nation of Indians, 448 U.S. 371 (1980).
Vandepitte v Preferred Accident Insurance Co, [1933] 1 D.L.R. 289 (P.C.).
Walker v Baird, [1892] A.C. 491 (P.C.).
Weisenger v Mellor (1989), 16 A.C.W.S. (3d) 260 (B.C.S.C.).
Williams v Johnson, [1937] 4 All E.R. 34 (P.C.).
Worcester v Georgia, 6 Pet. 515 (U.S. 1832).
Wyman v Patterson, [1900] A.C. 271 (H.L.).
Zamet v Hyman, [1961] 3 All E.R. 933 (C.A.).

PART ONE

The Juridical Understanding of the Crown–Native Fiduciary Relationship

1

Introduction

In the 1984 landmark case of *Guerin v R*,[1] the Supreme Court of Canada unanimously declared that the Crown[2] is bound by fiduciary obligations to the aboriginal peoples[3] of Canada. By determining that the nature of the Crown's obligation to aboriginal peoples is fiduciary, hence, legal rather than merely political or moral, the Supreme Court of Canada blazed a new path in Canadian aboriginal rights jurisprudence. Yet, more than ten years later, the Canadian judiciary remains poised at the perimeter of the Crown's duty, refusing to venture into its core.

The implementation of fiduciary doctrine to simultaneously describe and monitor the Crown–Native relationship has created difficulties both for the judiciary and legal scholars. Unlike many other areas of the law, such as contracts, the fiduciary relation – and its concomitant duties, obligations, rights, and benefits – is not very well understood. As one jurist has commented, 'It is striking that a principle so long standing and so widely accepted should be the subject of the uncertainty that now prevails.'[4] Ironically, the confusion surrounding fiduciary doctrine has neither hampered the tremendous increase in the use of fiduciary arguments by litigants nor their acceptance by the judiciary in recent years.[5]

Fiduciary relationships are similar to trust relationships. However, whereas a finding of a trust relationship results in the existence of fiduciary duties, it is not the same thing as a fiduciary relationship. A trustee is a type of fiduciary, but a fiduciary is not necessarily a trustee. A trust creates a legally binding obligation in which the party or parties controlling the property of the trust (the *trustees*) hold that property for the benefit of a party or parties (the beneficiaries or *cestuis que trust*[6]) and not for themselves in their roles as trustees.[7] The actors in a fiduciary relationship (the fiduciary and beneficiary) are governed by virtually identical laws to those governing the relationship between trustee and beneficiary. However, whereas a fiduciary relationship is similar in nature to a trust relationship, the former does not depend on the existence of a property interest for its sustenance.[8] Rather, its existence depends on the quality and character of the relationship between the parties which gives rise to equitable obligations[9] on the part of some, or all, of the parties in that relationship.[10]

The Crown's fiduciary duty to the aboriginal peoples applies to virtually every facet of the Crown–Native relationship.[11] It has its basis in the historical relationship between the parties dating back to the time of contact,[12] which describes the period ensuing immediately after the first meeting of Europeans and indigenous peoples in North America. It may also be noted in the terms of various treaties, compacts, and alliances between the groups. In addition to being judicially sanctioned in the *Guerin* case, the Crown's fiduciary duty to Native peoples has been constitutionally entrenched in Section 35(1) of the Constitution Act, 1982.[13]

Although fiduciary law has enjoyed its position as one of the most significant facets of Canadian aboriginal rights jurisprudence for a decade, it is largely misunderstood and misapplied by the judiciary and legal scholars alike. The *Guerin* decision provides little guidance as to the nature and extent of the Crown's duty and its implications for the parties affected by its existence. Subsequent aboriginal rights cases have provided ample opportunities for the judiciary to discuss the ramifications of applying fiduciary principles to the relationship between the Crown and Native peoples, yet it has been content to fall back on the Supreme Court's findings in *Guerin* without much in the way of elboration. Outstanding issues, including such fundamental questions as who owes the fiduciary duty to Native peoples,[14] have yet to be answered or adequately addressed. With the present status of aboriginal rights in Canada, it is striking that these fundamental issues remain the subject of such confusion and uncertainty.

Native rights in Canada currently enjoy a greater level of recognition and visibility than at any time since the British Crown's assertion of suzerainty over North America's indigenous peoples and their lands. Much of this recognition may be linked directly to the Supreme Court of Canada's recognition of the special relationship between the Crown and Native peoples in *Guerin*. Recent events, such as the constitutional proposals regarding aboriginal self-government contained within the failed Charlottetown Accord,[15] the Oka crisis in Quebec, and the Manitoba Aboriginal Justice Inquiry, together with the tremendous media attention that they have generated, have resulted in greater public awareness of the status of Native peoples and Native issues in Canada.

In August 1991 a Royal Commission on Aboriginal Peoples was established with the mandate to investigate the evolution of the relationship among Indian, Inuit, and Métis peoples, the Canadian government, and Canadian society. To fulfil its mandate,[16] the commission held cross-Canada hearings which received significant media attention. However, the high profile enjoyed by Native rights issues in Canada is a relatively recent phenomenon. Many of the issues that still exist today predate any significant degree of public awareness. In fact, Native rights have been the subject of litigation in Canada since the early stages of the nineteenth century.[17] A prime illustration of the public's distorted perception of the aboriginal rights controversy in Canada may be seen in the Oka crisis that occurred in the spring of 1990. The dispute over land which led up to the Oka crisis had been the subject of litigation as early as 1910 in the case of *Corinthe v Seminary of St Sulpice*.[18] Moreover, the dispute over the land in question had existed for some time prior to the commencement of even that litigation.[19]

Judicial recognition of the Crown–Native fiduciary relationship came at a point in Canadian history when Native rights and issues had only started to achieve a higher public profile. Shortly before the *Guerin* decision was released by the Supreme Court of Canada, aboriginal and treaty rights had been enshrined in Sections 25 and 35 of the Constitution Act, 1982.[20] Until the final draft of the Constitution was approved, however, the constitutional protection and affirmation of Native rights that ultimately came into being was by no means guaranteed. During the constitutional patriation process, Native rights had been omitted entirely from the initial set of resolutions presented to Parliament and were later dropped from the second set that had been reached by Prime Minister Pierre Elliott Trudeau and the nine provincial premiers on 5 November 1981. If not for the organization of an ongoing and highly visible campaign initiated by aboriginal groups – which included lobbying at the domestic and international levels and litigation in the courts of England[21] – aboriginal and treaty rights may not have been included in the repatriation package at all.[22] As the Supreme Court of Canada acknowledged in *R v Sparrow*: 'It is clear, then, that s. 35(1) of the Constitution Act, 1982, represents the culmination of a long and difficult struggle in both the political forum and the courts for the constitutional recognition of aboriginal rights. The strong representations of native associations and other groups concerned with the welfare of Canada's aboriginal peoples made the adoption of s. 35(1) possible.'[23]

In an ironic twist of events, the strength of the Indian lobby during the constitutional repatriation process owed much to the federal government's own initiative to eliminate the special status of Indians in Canada[24] – the *Statement of the Government of Canada on Indian Policy, 1969,* more commonly known as the 'White Paper.' The White Paper advocated the complete assimilation of Canada's Native population by removing all vestiges of difference between them and non-aboriginals.[25] The federal government's rationale for taking such action was its professed desire to remove the negative effects of discrimination from hampering Canadian Indians:

The policies proposed recognize the simple reality that the separate legal status of Indians and the policies which have flowed from it have kept the Indian people apart from and behind other Canadians ...

The treatment resulting from their different status has been often worse, sometimes equal and occasionally better than accorded to their fellow citizens. What matters is that it has been different ...

The discrimination which affects the poor, Indian and non-Indian alike, when compounded with a legal status that sets the Indian apart, provides dangerously fertile ground for social and cultural discrimination ...

...

The Government does not wish to perpetuate policies which carry with them the seeds of disharmony and disunity, policies which prevent Canadians from fulfilling themselves and contributing to their society. It seeks a partnership to achieve a better goal. The partners in this search are the Indian people, the governments of the provinces, the Canadian community as a whole and the Government of Canada.[26]

The result of the White Paper was a tremendous backlash against the government by aboriginal peoples across the nation.[27] The Prime Minister, Pierre Trudeau, fueled aboriginal discontent by stating that the federal government could not recognize aboriginal rights because 'no society can be built in historical "might have beens."'[28] The National Indian Brotherhood, the major national Indian organization at that time, maintained that the implementation of the White Paper's proposals would 'lead to the destruction of a Nation of people by legislation and cultural genocide.'[29]

Paradoxically, the federal government's ambition of removing all distinctions between Indians and non-Indians in the White Paper served to reinforce those very distinctions. The mass opposition to the White Paper by aboriginal peoples resulted in the creation and politicization of Native interest groups to oppose the government's proposed initiatives: 'The White Paper became the single most powerful catalyst in the Indian nationalist movement, launching it into a determined force for nativism – a reaffirmation of a unique cultural heritage and identity. Ironically, the White Paper had precipitated "new problems" because it gave Indians cause to organize against the government and reassert their separateness.'[30] Because of the tremendous reaction against the White Paper by Native groups, it was never implemented. Instead, in an attempt to patch over its ill-fated policy initiative, the federal government began to provide funding for Indian political bodies. This resulted in the rapid creation of a network of federal and provincial Native organizations representing Indian, Inuit, and Métis peoples.

The aboriginal political activism that arose as a direct result of the White Paper foreshadowed the changes in Canadian aboriginal rights jurisprudence that were initiated in 1973 by the Supreme Court of Canada's judgment in *Calder v Attorney-General of British Columbia*.[31] The *Calder* decision transformed aboriginal rights litigation in Canada and marked a transition in the legal understanding of aboriginal rights. *Calder* directly overruled the Privy Council's characterization of aboriginal title in *St Catherine's Milling and Lumber Co v The Queen*[32] – which had been the benchmark of Canadian aboriginal rights jurisprudence since its determination in 1888 – by holding that aboriginal title is not dependent on any treaty, executive order, or legislative enactment.[33] Beginning with *St Catherine's Milling*, aboriginal rights were recognized by the judiciary only if they could be documented in positive acts of the Crown, such as a Crown grant or treaty. Consequently, aboriginal peoples were deemed not to possess any rights that existed independently of their recognition or affirmation by the Crown. Until *Calder*, the reasoning in *St Catherine's Milling* regarding the nature of aboriginal rights had not been seriously questioned, much less challenged in its entirety.

The *St Catherine's Milling* decision had determined that any aboriginal rights which existed in Canada were created by the Royal Proclamation of 1763.[34] The proclamation had been issued by King George III upon Britain's formal acquisition of Canada from France under the Treaty of Paris, 1763. Lord Watson, on behalf of the Privy Council, stated that the Indian possession of land 'can only be ascribed to the general provisions made by the royal proclamation in favour of all Indian tribes then living under the sovereignty and protection of the British Crown.'[35] In making that assertion, Lord Watson viewed the Proclamation as a grant of rights to aboriginal peoples rather than a recognition and affirmation of their pre-existing rights.[36] In refuting the Privy Council's determination, the *Calder* decision initiated a process which, over twenty years later in *Guerin*, would result in a complete overruling of the principles which had shaped judicial considerations of aboriginal rights in Canada for almost a hundred years.

At the time of *Calder*, the Privy Council's decision in *St Catherine's Milling and Lumber Co v The Queen*,[37] was still the most significant judgment in Canadian aboriginal rights jurisprudence.[38] However, cases dealing with aboriginal rights in the nineteenth and into the early twentieth centuries were entirely different than their more recent counterparts. Major Indian rights cases in the nineteenth century were based primarily on the competing legislative and commercial interests of the federal and provincial governments, or of the governments and/or private enterprise, rather than the interests of Native peoples. In *St Catherine's Milling*, which was the first major case in Canadian aboriginal rights jurisprudence, the Saulteaux band of Ojibway, whose land interests were the subject matter of judicial deliberation, was not even a party to the proceedings.[39] The real matter to be determined in that case was whether the Dominion of Canada or the Province of Ontario was entitled to ownership of the lands which had been surrendered to the Crown by the Saulteaux Indians under the terms of Treaty No. 3.

The issues raised in *St Catherine's Milling* formed the basis of the prominent judicial decisions made in *Province of Ontario v Dominion of Canada and Province of Quebec: In re Indian Claims* (the *Robinson Treaties Annuities* case),[40] *Ontario Mining Company Ltd v Seybold*,[41] and *Dominion of Canada v Province of Ontario* (the *Treaty Number 3 Annuities* case)[42] between 1897 and 1910. Like *St Catherine's Milling*, these three cases all centred around competing federal and provincial interests which were themselves based on Indian rights. Among the early major Native law cases, litigation conducted on behalf of aboriginal peoples and focused primarily on aboriginal interests was rare. In fact, aboriginal rights-focused litigation was almost eliminated altogether by the Indian Act, a federal statute regulating the activity of status Indians[43] in Canada, in the early stages of the twentieth century.

In 1927 a special joint committee of Parliament was established to consider the question of Indian land claims in British Columbia.[44] Ultimately, the joint committee's recommendations led to an amendment of the existing Indian Act[45] which made the raising of funds for the purposes of commencing legal action for Indian land claims an offence. This was accomplished by the addition of Section 149A to the Indian Act in 1926–7, under which Indian bands were effectively prohibited from retaining solicitors to commence legal actions against the Crown without the written consent of the superintendent-general of Indian Affairs.[46] Section 149A read as follows: 'Every person who, without the consent of the Superintendent General expressed in writing, receives, obtains, solicits or requests from any Indian any payment or contribution or promise of any payment or contribution for the purposes of raising a fund or providing money for the prosecution of any claim which the tribe or band or Indians to which such Indian belongs, or which he is a member, has or is represented to have for the recovery of any claim or money for the benefit of the said tribe or band, shall be guilty of an offence and liable upon summary conviction for each offence to a penalty not exceeding two hundred dollars and not less than fifty dollars or to imprisonment for any term not exceeding two months.' Thus, aboriginal peoples were both denied their claims in the political process and effectively prohibited from raising them in the legal realm by parliamentary action.

Even after Section 149A was repealed in 1951[47] until *Calder* few cases sought the determination of major aboriginal rights issues on behalf of Indian bands or groups. After that decision aboriginal issues could not be ignored by governments and the courts as they had been previously. In response to the *Calder* decision the Trudeau government issued a new statement of Indian policy in 1973. Its purpose was to 'signify the Government's recognition and acceptance of its continuing responsibility under the British North America Act for Indian lands and lands reserved for Indians.'[48] The statement also indicated the federal government's willingness to negotiate claims of aboriginal title in the primary areas of the country not covered by treaty: British Columbia, Northern Quebec, and the Northwest Territories.

With its suggestions regarding the inherent nature of aboriginal rights, *Calder* set the stage for Native groups to lobby for the recognition and protection of their rights in the political forum and in the courts. The political and social effects of the *Calder* decision had a major impact on the James Bay hydroelectric project in Quebec and the Mackenzie Valley Pipeline project, both of which threatened to adversely affect Native rights. The James Bay project had been initiated without regard to the rights of the aboriginal inhabitants of the areas affected, even though these rights were explicitly protected by the terms of the Quebec Boundary Extension Act, 1912.[49] Eventually, the dispute between the aboriginal peoples affected by the project and the federal and Quebec governments was resolved by agreement in 1975.[50] Meanwhile, in 1974 the federal government instituted a public inquiry into the Mackenzie Valley Pipeline project.[51] After extensive hearings and substantial media coverage, the report of the inquiry, published in 1977,[52] recommended a ten-year moratorium on the construction of the pipeline to permit the resolution of outstanding Indian and Inuit land claims. The pipeline proposal was ultimately rejected by the National Energy Board in 1977.

The increased public attention and awareness of aboriginal rights generated by these issues resulted in the adoption of greater respect for those rights by government and the judiciary. In 1981 the federal Crown's report, *In All Fairness – A Native Claims Policy*, outlined its policy on comprehensive land claims[53] which implicitly recognized the existence of Aboriginal title.[54] This was followed, in 1982, by *Outstanding Business – A Native Claims Policy*,[55] which outlined the federal Crown's specific claims process.[56] The growing sensitivity towards aboriginal rights was also reflected in the Canadian judiciary's treatment of Native rights cases. In 1983 the Supreme Court of Canada's decision in *Nowegijick v The Queen* affirmed a special doctrine of Indian treaty and statutory interpretation which recognized the injustice that often resulted from judicial failures to consider aboriginal viewpoints and understandings relating to Indian treaties and statutes relating to Indians. The Supreme Court held that 'treaties and statutes relating to Indians should be liberally construed and doubtful expressions resolved in favour of the Indian.'[57] The *Nowegijick* interpretive principles, which were based on the earlier decision of the Ontario Divisional Court in *R v Taylor and Williams*,[58] were a complete about-face from previous judicial determinations in the aboriginal rights sphere.[59]

After the inclusion of aboriginal and treaty rights in Sections 25 and 35 of the Constitution Act, 1982, the House of Commons Special Committee on Indian Self-Government (the Penner Committee) recommended that the right of aboriginal peoples to self-government be explicitly stated and entrenched in the Canadian constitution.[60] Although this recommendation never came to fruition, a bill designed to recognize aboriginal self-government – Bill C-52, entitled 'An Act Relating to Self-Government for Indian Nations' – was placed before the House of Commons. It received first reading in June, 1984, but was stalled because of the end of the parliamentary session and never revived.

Aboriginal rights case law also flourished after 1982. It is doubtful, however, if any of these advancements, including the Supreme Court of Canada's legal sanctioning of the Crown's fiduciary duty in *Guerin*, would have arisen if not for the combined effects of the Native reaction against the White Paper and the *Calder* decision.

In *Guerin*, Dickson J, as he then was, expanded on *Calder*'s findings – just as he stated in *Guerin* that *Calder* had expanded on those in *St Catherine's Milling* – by holding that *Calder* recognized the existence of aboriginal title as a legal right derived from Indians' historic occupation and possession of their tribal lands.[61] Wilson J, meanwhile, suggested in *Guerin* that *Calder*'s discussion of aboriginal title was one of the roots of the Crown's fiduciary duty.[62] Whereas *Calder*'s finding that aboriginal title was not dependent on positive actions of the Crown exhumed the judicial treatment of aboriginal rights from its nineteenth-century, *St Catherine's Milling*-based approach, *Guerin*'s recognition and affirmation of the Crown's fiduciary duty towards aboriginal peoples brought Native rights into the forefront of issues of national importance.

Unfortunately, in a number of judicial considerations since *Guerin*,[63] Canadian courts have neither questioned the application of fiduciary doctrine to Native law nor have they attempted to explain the nature and extent of its application. Academic commentaries written in this area have been similarly plagued.[64] As with existing judicial commentaries, these scholarly attempts to explain the application of fiduciary principles to the Crown–Native relationship have invariably been more descriptive than analytical.[65] Even with all of these shortcomings, the application of fiduciary principles in Native law has become axiomatic. They are now presumed to exist as self-evident truths without ever having been put through any thorough examination of their applicability or appropriateness to the Crown–Native relationship. Indeed, the ramifications flowing from the existence of this relationship have yet to be fleshed out.

The longer this phenomenon continues, the more comfortable others become with it, and its precedential value increases. Whereas a system of precedent may be effective where judicial decision-making is well-reasoned and logically deduced, it can also proliferate the effects of misapplied judgments and render them more difficult to challenge or overturn in the future. The law's emphasis on tradition, stability, and continuity – as contained within the legal principle of *stare decisis* on which the common law is predicated[66] – connotes the approval of a precedent merely through the passage of time.[67] To overturn a long-established precedent, therefore, requires something more than the dismissal of one argument in favour of another. Instead, it brings into question the entirety of judicial reasoning in every case in which the precedent has previously been upheld.

The continued application of fiduciary principles to the Crown–Native relationship based on the *Guerin* precedent may be seen to be inversely related to the perceived need to explain its application to that relationship. The more often *Guerin* is cited, without elaboration, for its proposition that the Crown owes fiduciary obligations to aboriginal peoples, the perceived need to explain the basis of the Crown's duty is reduced. Indeed, since *Guerin* has been used as the springboard for the imposition of fiduciary duties upon the Crown towards aboriginal peoples, judicial and academic analysis of the basis of the Crown's duty and its effects has decreased.[68] However, it is of little benefit to state that a fiduciary relationship exists or that it has been breached without illustrating what the relationship encompasses or the ramifications of such a breach.[69] Indeed, the portrayal of a relationship as fiduciary is only an initial step; the explanation of the resultant obligations arising by virtue of the relationship's existence is much more onerous.[70]

The marriage of fiduciary law and Native law is, at first glance, an unlikely one. Fiduciary law is, traditionally, a part of private law,[71] but Native law, insofar as such an area of the law actually exists,[72] encompasses the legal relationship between aboriginal peoples and the Crown in Canada, which is a part of public law.[73] However, Crown–Native fiduciary relationships are neither traditionally public nor private relationships,[74] but *sui generis* ('of their own kind or class').[75] Ultimately, all Crown–Native fiduciary relations are rooted in the historical, political, social, and legal interaction of the groups from the time of contact, and this unique background creates the *sui generis* character of the Crown–Native fiduciary relationship. As will become evident, the unique circumstances giving rise to individual fiduciary relations render each and every one of them *sui generis*.

The theory of fiduciary doctrine and its application to the Crown–Native relationship in Canada suggested in this book differs significantly from commonly held notions. Traditionally, accounts of fiduciary relations between the Crown and Native peoples in Canada have regarded aboriginal peoples as being subordinate to the Crown.[76] This is unfortunate, because it leads to patently unreasonable decisions that patronize Native peoples and mocks the nature of their historical relationship with the Crown. The notion that fiduciary relationships exist only between inherently unequal parties is a widely held, but nevertheless entirely incorrect assumption. Nothing in fiduciary relations inherently necessitates that they exist only between dominant and subordinate parties. As will be discussed in greater detail in Part Two, beneficiaries are, by virtue of their participation in fiduciary relationships, vulnerable to the actions of their fiduciaries. However, excessive judicial categorization of inherently unequal forms of fiduciary relationships, such as parent and child or guardian and ward, and an overemphasis on the vulnerability of beneficiaries have combined to create the mistaken impression that all fiduciary relationships exist between parties that are unequal.[77]

The adherence to this incorrect view of fiduciary relationships in Canadian aboriginal rights jurisprudence has further reinforced the mistaken notion that aboriginal peoples are subordinate to the Crown. Such an understanding, moreover, is a purely colonialist vision of Crown–aboriginal relations and has no foundation in historical reality. The Crown–Native fiduciary relation has its origins in the interaction between the groups in the immediate, post-contact period.[78] During the formative years, which roughly covers the period from contact until the removal of France as a major colonial power in North America in 1760–1, Crown–Native relations were based on mutual need, respect, and trust.[79] Furthermore, when the fiduciary character of these relations was crystallized, the participants conducted themselves on a nation-to-nation basis. Consequently, the nature of the Crown's fiduciary obligations is founded on the mutually recognized and respected sovereign status of the Crown and aboriginal peoples.[80] This fact was recognized by the Royal Commission on Aboriginal Peoples, which stated: 'When Europeans first came to the shores of North America, the continent was occupied by a large number of sovereign and independent Aboriginal peoples with their own territories, laws, and forms of government. These nations entered into relations with incoming European nations on a basis of equality and mutual respect, an attitude that persisted long into the period of colonization.'[81] Whereas there have been many changes in the nature of Crown–Native relations in the more than three hundred years that have passed since they were solemnified in the Treaty of Albany, 1664,[82] their initial foundation forms the basis of the fiduciary aspect of their interaction.

Although the *Guerin* case may have been the first overt judicial recognition of the fiduciary nature of that relationship, it did not create a form of relationship that did not exist previously. *Guerin* merely gave a title and method of analysis for the subsequent treatment of the reciprocal rights, duties, and responsibilities existing between the groups. Therefore, in the nation-to-nation relationship between the Crown and aboriginal peoples, the interaction of the parties being governed by fiduciary law is not the product of an acceptance of the legitimacy of colonialism in Canada,[83] but, rather, the rigorous, yet malleable principles of fiduciary law which are contextually appropriate to monitor the special needs of this *sui generis* situation.

The use of fiduciary doctrine is valuable as a tool to ensure that the Crown performs the duties it owes to aboriginal peoples. It is rigorous in its demands of the Crown, protecting of the interests of the aboriginal peoples, and, as part of the common law, binding upon the Crown and enforceable in Canadian courts.[84] Just as fiduciary doctrine is a part of the common law, though, it is also a part of the special, *sui generis* Crown–Native relationship.[85]

The specific nature of a relationship and the situation under which it germinated is what renders it fiduciary, not the actors involved or whether it fits neatly into an already-established category of fiducial relations.[86] Fiduciary doctrine, therefore, may be described as being *situation-specific*. Its situation-specificity insists that fiduciary principles be applied to a relationship only where the nature of the relationship warrants it.[87] Even then, fiduciary doctrine is applicable only to the extent that its general characteristics and principles are relevant to the relationship under scrutiny.[88]

The Crown–Native fiduciary relationship, in actuality, is comprised of two distinct types, or genres, of fiduciary relationships. The Crown owes a general, overarching fiduciary duty to aboriginal peoples as a result of the historical relationship between the parties dating back to the time of contact. In addition, the Crown also owes specific fiduciary duties or obligations to particular Native groups stemming from its relationships with those groups or from specific treaties, agreements, or alliances that it entered into. Depending on individual circumstances, it is possible for the Crown to owe both a general and one or more specific fiduciary duties to an aboriginal nation as a result of its intercourse with those people. As the Crown's fiduciary obligation may be recognized in the totality of its relationships with aboriginal peoples or in specific events or circumstances, such as treaties, initiatives, or legislation, an aboriginal nation's claim against the Crown for a breach of fiduciary obligation may be based either on the totality of the events giving rise to the

Crown's general fiduciary duty or on the obligations arising out of any one particular event or occurrence.

The discussion herein purposely refers to the Crown's fiduciary duty to aboriginal peoples in a general, doctrinal fashion so that the principles underlying the analysis may be applied to all Crown–Native relationships in Canada. For this reason, the Crown's general duty is the primary topic of focus. The rationale for this approach is twofold. Unless general guidelines are established, the judicial treatment of Crown–Native fiduciary relationships will continue in the haphazard fashion that has characterized post-*Guerin* jurisprudence. Moreover, in the absence of context, it is not possible to discuss specific fiduciary relationships between particular Indian bands and the Crown in a meaningful way.

What is needed in individual circumstances is for the historical, political, social, and legal aspects of the specific Crown–Native relationship under scrutiny to be fleshed out sufficiently to document the nature of the intercourse between the parties which gives rise to its fiduciary status. This is what the situation-specificity of fiduciary doctrine requires. Once the specifics of particular Crown–Native relationships are ascertained, they will modify the general theory and principles discussed herein to render them applicable to the specific situation under consideration. What is proffered to the reader in the pages that follow may be straightforwardly applicable to the Crown's general fiduciary duty to aboriginal peoples, or a conduit for specific application to individual circumstances.

Because of the situation-specific basis on which fiduciary doctrine is premised, the unexplained application of fiduciary law to the Crown–Native relationship may clearly be seen to be detrimental to the understanding of that relationship. What is sorely needed before the Crown–Native fiduciary relationship may truly be understood is an explanation of why the relationship is a fiduciary one, who owes the obligations to the Native peoples, and what the ramifications of applying fiduciary doctrine to the Crown–Native relationship are. Thus far, no such commentary exists. It is not surprising, then, that the Crown–Native relationship is not more fully understood in the absence of any thorough examination of its fiduciary basis and effects.

The comfort exhibited by the juridical use of fiduciary rhetoric to characterize Crown–Native relations – and one of the inevitable questions raised as a result of its indiscriminate application – is illustrated in the Supreme Court of Canada's recent decision in *Ontario (Attorney-General) v Bear Island Foundation*.[89] It is insufficient to state, as the Supreme Court of Canada did in *Bear Island*, that 'the Crown ... breached its fiduciary obligations to the Indians'[90] without revealing which personifications of the Crown are bound by those obligations. In a juridical context, the phrase 'the Crown' has a multitude of meanings which refer to a variety of personae. It may refer to the historical constitutional notion of the single and indivisible Crown, the British Crown in its various personalities, or, domestically, to the Crown in right of Canada or the Crown in right of a particular province.[91]

The failure of the court in *Bear Island* to pinpoint whom it meant by its indiscriminate reference to 'the Crown' is the result of an overly rigid judicial adherence to acontextual, 'black-letter' law in the manner of the *St Catherine's Milling* decision.[92] This approach to understanding the Crown–Native fiduciary relationship has resulted in judicial attempts to root it in the Royal Proclamation of 1763,[93] in legislative enactments such as the Indian Act,[94] in the Constitution Act, 1982,[95] in legislative requirements such as the necessity for aboriginal bands to surrender their interests in land to the Crown before the land may be alienated to a third party,[96] or in recognized legal entities such as aboriginal title.[97] Although these various 'roots' of the Crown's fiduciary obligation do, in different ways and to various extents, entrench the Crown's duty to the aboriginal peoples, they do not create the duty on their own; rather, they only affirm its existence or spell out some of its requirements.

These black-letter law-based attempts to understand the basis of the relationship are improperly focused as they concentrate on its concrete manifestations rather than its inherent nature and characteristics. This methodology is fundamentally incompatible with fiduciary doctrine. The situation-specificity of fiduciary doctrine requires that the relationship be the primary focus of judicial scrutiny; the concrete results of that relationship are secondary.[98] That is not to suggest that the latter ought to be ignored, but that they must be viewed within their proper historical, political, social, or legal context.

Despite the manner in which it presents itself and is often regarded, the law is not acontextual. Laws come into being in response to external stimuli, not as a result of a priori assumptions. Consequently, any legal entrenchment of fiduciary obligations upon the Crown towards aboriginal peoples must also arise in response to particular events, circumstances, or requirements. In and of themselves, the Royal Proclamation of 1763, the Indian Act, and the Constitution Act, 1982 each provide one basis for ascertaining the nature of the Crown–Native relationship.

However, a different light is shed on the legal entrenchment of the Crown's duty once these various components are placed within the context in which they originated.

Focusing exclusively on the legal effects of the Royal Proclamation of 1763, for example, provides only one element of the Crown's duty. Recognizing that the Proclamation affects the Crown's responsibilities to the aboriginal peoples renders another component of the Crown's duty. Examining the process by which the Proclamation was promulgated and the underlying rationale for its institution in law is a third component that provides additional information on which the fiduciary character of the Crown–Native relationship may be determined. The result of placing the concrete recognition of the Crown's fiduciary duty in context, then, is a multitiered view of the effect of any one component of the Crown–Native fiduciary relationship on that relationship.

By examining the entirety of events and documents that comprise various elements of the Crown's fiduciary duty, a much richer understanding of the nature of that duty may be obtained. Unless these events and documents are scrutinized for their effects on the legal entrenchment of the Crown's obligations, only a limited understanding of the Crown's duty may be achieved. To avoid this result, a proper accounting for these happenings must itself be well rounded. This includes a consideration of these events as understood by both the Crown and aboriginal peoples.

Traditionally, aboriginal understandings of the Crown–Native relationship are among the most neglected aspects of any examination of the applicability of fiduciary law to that relationship. One of the inherent flaws which has historically plagued the development of Canadian aboriginal rights jurisprudence has been its inability to account for or pay heed to Native perspectives.[99] From an aboriginal standpoint, the nature of the Crown–Native relationship appears fundamentally different than it does from a strictly common law perspective, which is based on colonialist attitudes and the subjugation of aboriginal rights and claims to those more consistent with the common law's European origins and biases. Through the teachings of aboriginal elders and scholars, aboriginal understandings of the nature of their relationship with the Crown and the effects of various documents, events, alliances, and treaties on that relationship may begin to be more fully understood.[100]

By examining the relationship between the Crown and aboriginal peoples in context, it is possible to address the untreated questions and issues arising from previous treatments of the Crown's fiduciary duty to aboriginal peoples. These range from the fundamental issues of the principles applicable to the Crown–Native fiduciary relationship and who is bound by the fiduciary duty to aboriginal peoples to the more specific issues of how the Crown is to discharge its duty and how it may avoid situations of conflict of interest. Only after these issues have been addressed may the full implications and ramifications of the imposition of fiduciary doctrine upon the relationship between the Crown and aboriginal peoples in Canada begin to be truly understood.

2

The Politics Underlying the Crown–Native Fiduciary Relationship in Canada

When the white man first seen us, when they first said, 'Well, there's something wrong with these people here. They don't have no religion. They have no judicial system. We have to do something for these people.' I guess that must have been what they thought because they totally screwed up what we already had.

They introduced new religion and there was nothing wrong with our old religion. They just didn't understand it. We had our own ways of teaching our children, like the Elders and everything. There was nothing wrong with that way of teaching children. They just didn't understand it.

The same thing with our judicial system. We had that judicial system and the white people, when they came here, they didn't see that. They said, 'These guys have nothing. We have to introduce all these different things to them so they can be one of us.' That's exactly the problem that we have.

Chief Philip Michel, Brochet[1]

Until the Supreme Court of Canada's decision in *Guerin v R*,[2] the relationship between the Crown and Native peoples in Canada was customarily characterized by the courts as a relationship between unequals. In 1852, in the case of *Sheldon v Ramsay*, the Upper Canada Court of Queen's Bench said of aboriginal peoples in Canada that 'the Crown should be in a situation to protect their interest and treat them as a people under its care, not capable of disposing of their possessions.'[3] The court's characterizations were based, in part, on the Crown's own, colonialist attitude towards its relationship with the aboriginal peoples. Indeed, in the trial level decision in *Guerin*, Collier J's description of the relationship between the Musqueam band and the Department of

Indian Affairs[4] in the 1950s indicates that the Crown's attitude had remained relatively unchanged one hundred years after the decision in *Sheldon v Ramsay*: 'At that time, and for many years before, according to the evidence, a great number of Indian Affairs personnel, vis-à-vis Indian bands, and Indians, took a paternalistic, albeit well-meaning, attitude: the Indians were children or wards, father knew best.'[5]

The paternalistic attitude adopted by the Department of Indian Affairs towards Native peoples stems from the approach taken by the Crown and its representatives in Canada following the solidification of British claims to North America in the late eighteenth and early nineteenth centuries.[6] The traditional description of the Crown–Native relationship by Canadian courts prior to *Guerin* was that of guardian and ward.[7] This characterization dates from the early nineteenth-century case of *Cherokee Nation v State of Georgia*, the third in the series of prominent aboriginal rights decisions rendered by the United States Supreme Court under Chief Justice John Marshall.[8] In guardian–ward relationships, the guardians are invested by law with the authority and duty to take care of their wards who, by virtue of defect of age or understanding, are deemed incompetent to administer their own affairs. The interests of the wards are determined entirely by their guardians, who have complete and total control over those interests.

By being characterized as wards, Native people were viewed as persons completely incapable of managing their concerns whom the Crown felt an obligation to protect.[9] This obligation, however, was understood to be moral rather than legal and certainly not binding. As Taschereau J explained in the Supreme Court of Canada's judgment in *St Catherine's Milling*: 'The Indians must in the future ... be treated with the same consideration for their just claims and demands that they have received in the past, but, as in the past, it will not be because of any legal obligation to do so, but as a sacred political obligation, in the execution of which the state must be free from judicial control.'[10] This view was typical of that shared equally by governmental officials and reflected in Indian legislation. In 1824 Attorney-General of Upper Canada Sir John Beverly Robinson, later a distinguished judge, wrote a letter to Robert Wilmot Horton, under secretary of state for war and colonies, in which he described the Mohawk Indians as peoples who did not need to be treated with, since they already reaped the rewards of the Crown's benevolence: 'To talk of treaties with the Mohawk Indians, residing in the heart of one of the most populous districts of Upper Canada, upon lands purchased for them and given to them by the British Government, is much the same, in my humble opinion, as to talk of making a treaty of alliance with the Jews in Duke street, or with the French emigrants who have settled in England.'[11]

These perceptions of Native peoples continued into the twentieth century, often with unfortunate and inappropriate results. In 1929 the trial judge in *R v Syliboy*[12] characterized aboriginal peoples as 'uncivilized people' and 'savages' with no rights of sovereignty or ownership over the land they had used and occupied since time immemorial. It was not until 1985, in the case of *Simon v R*, that the Supreme Court of Canada condemned the rhetoric implemented in *Syliboy*. As Dickson CJC stated in *Simon*, the language used in *Syliboy* 'reflects the biases and prejudices of another era in our history. Such language is no longer acceptable in Canadian law and, indeed, is inconsistent with a growing sensitivity to native rights in Canada.'[13]

Since the *Simon* case Canadian courts have expressed some remorse for the Crown's historical treatment of aboriginal peoples in Canada. In the same year that the *Simon* decision was released, MacDonald J stated, more generally, in *Pasco v CNR*: 'We cannot recount with much pride the treatment accorded to the native people of this country.'[14] MacDonald J's comment was later cited with approval by the Supreme Court of Canada in *R v Sparrow*, where Dickson CJC and La Forest J discussed the Crown's historical treatment of Native peoples at some length.[15] The courts have also seen fit to criticize the Crown's treatment of aboriginal peoples and their rights. Such criticism is demonstrated by the statements made in *Sparrow* that 'there can be no doubt that over the years the rights of the Indians were often honoured in the breach' and that 'for many years, the rights of the Indians to their aboriginal land – certainly as *legal* rights – were virtually ignored.'[16]

The Historical Origins of Aboriginal Policy in Canada

Canadian Indian policy has its origins in the fifteenth-century colonialist policies implemented by the first seafaring European states to make contact with the indigenous peoples of the New World. These nations generally believed themselves to be intellectually and morally superior to the peoples whose lands they invaded. To justify their incursions into these new lands, their right to reap its rewards and, in some instances, to enslave their indigenous populations, these nations initially relied on a variety of papal bulls, grants, and royal charters which presumed to grant religious or royal authority to conquer their 'barbarian' populations and to claim their lands and treasures as Europeans possessions.[17]

These European nations often made claims to territories in the New World without ever having explored the lands claimed or having achieved any degree of control over them. Their claims were based solely on the purported authority of bulls, grants, and royal charters. Papal bulls were the earliest documents which purported to grant authority to European nations to seek out and colonize lands in the New World in the middle of the fifteenth century. Originally intended only to authorize the conquest of enemies of the faith from the Holy Land, these bulls were later expanded to justify European colonialist incursions into the New World.[18] Initially, papal authority to conquer and enslave all pagan nations, wheresover located, even those 'situated in the remotest parts unknown to us,'[19] was an exclusive right granted to King Alfonso V of Portugal. Spain's defiance of this restriction by way of Columbus's voyage to the New World resulted in 1493 in Pope Alexander VI granting both Portugal and Spain the right to conquer pagan nations.[20] Shortly thereafter, in 1495, Henry VII defied the papacy when he commissioned John Cabot, by royal charter, to seek out New World territories in the name of Britain.

In addition to these bulls and charters, European colonizing nations attempted to vindicate their claims through various acts of discovery, conquest, and settlement,[21] all of which were European-based notions of colonial acquisitions that had been legitimized by the European-initiated 'Law of Nations.'[22] They also made use of symbolic acts, such as the planting of crosses or the recitation of words of conquest.[23] A typical example of these symbolic acts was Jacques Cartier's erection of a cross on the point of the entrance to Gaspé Bay in July 1534:

Upon the 25 of the moneth, wee caused a faire high Crosse to be made of the height of thirty foote, which was made in the presence of many of them, upon the point of the entrance of the sayd haven [Gaspé Bay], in the middest whereof we hanged up a Shield with three Floure de Luces in it, and in the top was carved in the wood with Anticke letters this posie, Vive le Roy de France. Then before them all we set it upon sayd point ... So soone as it was up, we altogether kneeled downe before them, with our hands towards Heaven, yeelding God thankes: and we made signes unto them, shewing them the Heavens, and that all our salvation dependeth onely on him which in them dwelleth ... And after wee were returned to our ships, their Captaine clad with an old Beares skin, with three of his sonnes, and a brother of his with him, came unto us in one of their boates ... there he made a long Oration unto us, shewing us the crosse we had set up, and making a crosse with two fingers, then did he shew us all the Countrey about us, as if he would say that all was his, and that wee should not set up any crosse without his leave ... Then did we shew them with signes, that the crosse was but onely set up to be as a light and leader which wayes to enter into the port, and that wee would shortly come againe ...[24]

Symbolic acts such as this were performed to deter other European nations interested in laying claim to the territory; they were not intended to demonstrate to the aboriginal peoples that the European nation thereby claimed the land.[25] As Cartier's explanation to the Indians demonstrates, the Europeans were not concerned with what the aboriginals thought or were told of the meaning or purpose of these symbolic acts. Not surprisingly, these actions, as well as other European claims based on discovery, conquest, or settlement – whether fictional or actual – were meaningless to the indigenous inhabitants and were not recognized by them as conferring authority over their lands. Moreover, the claims of these European nations to New World territories were often in conflict with the claims advanced by rival European powers.[26]

European claims to New World territories, to the extent that they were in accordance with and sanctioned by the *jus gentium*, or Law of Nations, could only bind those nations who were themselves bound by it. The Law of Nations, a precursor to modern international law, comprised a loosely set grouping of rules formulated by European nations that were not always prepared to follow its dictates. The theoretical, if not practical, premise of the Law of Nations was to have its customs and practices be binding upon those nations.[27] As indigenous nations in the New World were not a part of the group of nations that generated the governing rules of the Law of Nations and were not recognized as 'nations' under it, they could not be bound by its dictates.

Any claims made by European nations which they attempted to legitimize under the Law of Nations were binding only upon those nations that were recognized by, and ascribed to, its laws. It is difficult to sustain the argument that the indigenous nations 'lost' their sovereignty over their lands by the invocation of customs and practices which they were unfamiliar with and did not recognize,[28] but which were legitimized by a vague body of law that did not even recognize their status as nations. The legitimacy of European claims to New World territories is further questioned by the fact that the very nations which made grandiose claims to those territories by discovery, conquest, settlement, or symbolic acts paid little or no attention to the similar claims made by their competitors where it was against their interests to do so. As Brian Slattery explained in 'Aboriginal Sovereignty and Imperial Claims': 'Any balanced survey of European state practice reveals that although most imperial powers indulged on occasion in lofty claims based on discovery, symbolic acts and occupation, these same powers often poured scorn on such claims when advanced by their European rivals. In short, they were not prepared to grant others the benefit of principles claimed on their own behalf.[29]

Soon after the first encounters between European nations and indigenous peoples in the New World, the legitimacy of European assertions of sovereignty to New World territories and the legal and political rights of their indigenous populations became an issue of debate in European circles. There were sharp divisions among European theorists over the nature and extent of aboriginal rights. As one of the first European nations with a significant New World presence, Spain was the hub of these early deliberations. Heated debate raged between Spain and its colonial outposts over how the indigenous peoples in New Spain[30] ought to be treated. In 1511 the Dominican friar Antonio de Montesinos delivered a sermon in Hispaniola condemning Spanish treatment of the indigenous peoples. This resulted in the promulgation of the Laws of Burgos in 1512, by which the indigenous peoples of New Spain were declared to have the right to freedom and humane treatment, yet they would remain subject to religious coercion and kept close to the Spaniards in order to facilitate their conversion.[31]

Spanish theologian Francisco de Vitoria, who held the *prima* chair of theology at the University of Salamanca, was another strong supporter of the rights of indigenous peoples in the New World. However, he also shared the belief that the indigenous peoples ought to be converted to Christianity, by force if necessary.[32] His views were expressed in his lectures *De Indis et De Jure Belli* in the first half of the sixteenth century.[33] Vitoria's support of indigenous rights was proliferated by his pupil Dominic Soto, Confessor of Charles V of Spain. The harsh treatment of the indigenous peoples in New Spain was later the subject of a public debate between the Dominican friar Bartolomé de las Casas[34] and Juan Ginés de Sepúlveda, the theologian of Córdoba, at Valladolid in 1550–1.[35] By this time the debate over aboriginal rights had extended beyond Spain.[36]

One noteworthy twist on the discussion of indigenous peoples and their lands is contained in Sir Thomas More's novel *Utopia*, a social commentary on European corruption and vice, published in 1516. In the novel the peninsula of Sansculottia (meaning 'without pants' and hence connoting savagery) had been conquered by a person named Utopos (meaning 'no person'). Once Utopos had obtained control of the peninsula, he transformed it into an island by digging out a channel in the fifteen-mile isthmus which connected it to the mainland. Raphael Nonsenso, More's guide, explained that Utopos was also responsible for 'transforming' the indigenous inhabitants of Utopia from 'a pack of ignorant savages into what is now, perhaps, the most civilized nation in the world.'[37] The result of the physical and social transformation of the formerly indigenously owned lands was the creation of a world described as being 'like Plato's *Republic*, only better.'[38] If the island became overpopulated, a certain number of people from each town would start up a new colony on uncultivated land on the mainland. The mainland's indigenous population would be invited to join the new colony;[39] if they refused, they would be forcibly expelled and their land annexed: 'If the natives won't do what they're told, they're expelled from the area marked out for annexation. If they try to resist, the Utopians declare war – for they consider war perfectly justifiable, when one country denies another its natural right to derive nourishment from any soil which the original owners are not using themselves, but are merely holding on to as a worthless piece of property.'[40]

Of the various discussions of the rights of indigenous peoples in the New World, some sought to rationalize European marginalization of the indigenous populations by espousing the latter's inferiority. One such example was the report from the Dominican Tomas Ortiz before the Council of the Indies in 1525:

On the mainland they eat human flesh. They are more given to sodomy than any other nation. There is no justice among them. They go naked. They have no respect either for love or for virginity. They are stupid and silly. They have no respect for truth, save when it is to their advantage. They are unstable. They have no knowledge of what foresight means ... They are incapable of learning. Punishments have no effect upon them. Traitorous, cruel, and vindictive, they never forgive. Most hostile to religion, idle, dishonest, abject, and vile, in their judgments they keep no faith or law ... They exercise none of the humane arts or industries. When taught the mysteries of our religion, they say that these things may suit Castilians, but not them, and they do not wish to change their customs ... I may therefore affirm that God has never created a race more full of vice and composed without the least mixture of kindness or culture ... the Indians are more stupid than asses and refuse to improve in anything.[41]

26 Juridical Understanding

A number of specific grounds have been raised as bases of justification for the dispossession and subjugation of indigenous peoples over the past four hundred years: the 'heathenism' of indigenous peoples;[42] theories of racial inferiority[43] and natural slavery,[44] describing aboriginal peoples as 'barbarians,'[45] and theories on the 'proper' use and development of land.[46] Others, meanwhile, attempted to promote or defend indigenous rights.[47] For the most part, though, these groups of thought shared a common belief, which was later to be reflected in each of the Imperial, British, and Canadian Crowns' practices in Canada: the necessity for European colonizers to facilitate and oversee the transition of the indigenous peoples to a European, and hence civilized, way of life.[48]

To accomplish this, European colonizing nations deemed it necessary to afford the indigenous peoples the special protection of the European sovereigns who asserted suzerainty over them. Perhaps not coincidentally, this European 'protection' of aboriginal peoples also provided the colonizing nations with yet another justification for the implementation of their colonialist ambitions. To protect the aboriginal peoples, it was first necessary to acquire and maintain control over their territories. This was accomplished by a variety of means: treaties of peace, purchases of land directly from their aboriginal owners, and other, less scrupulous methods, such as simply denying the existence of aboriginal rights. Once control over aboriginal territories was obtained, 'civilized' government, religion, and other institutions could be sufficiently entrenched to extol the beliefs and values of European society.

This common belief in the need to protect indigenous peoples in order to ease their transformation to European modes of existence was adhered to by the British Crown as much as by its colonialist competitors. The British Crown's desire to protect aboriginal peoples was a fundamental part of British Indian policy from the beginning. It was reflected in the terms of early Indian treaties, including the Treaty of Albany in 1664 and the treaties entered into with the Native peoples of the Maritimes. Furthermore, this principle eventually found its way into British political documents, such as the Treaty of Utrecht, 1713, the Articles of Capitulation at Montreal of 8 September 1760, and into what has been referred to as the Aboriginal Bill of Rights, the Royal Proclamation of 1763.[49]

Early Political Documents Bearing on British Indian Policy in Canada

The Treaty of Utrecht, 1713, ended the battles between Britain and France as a result of their participation in the War of the Spanish Succession. Its effect on Canada was twofold. Geographically, it resulted in the cession of Acadia[50] by France to Britain. In addition, Article 15 contained special provisions for the protection of the Native allies of both Britain and France in North America: 'The subjects of *France* inhabiting *Canada*, and others, shall hereafter give no Hindrance or Molestation to five Nations or Cantons of *Indians*, subject to the Dominion of *Great Britain*, nor to the other Natives of *America*, who are Friends to the same. In like manner, the Subjects of *Great Britain* shall behave themselves peaceably towards the *Americans* who are Subjects or Friends to *France*.'[51]

More than forty years later, under Article 40 of the Articles of Capitulation at Montreal,[52] France surrendered its North American outpost. That document also made provisions for France's Indian allies to be maintained in the lands that they inhabited and remain unmolested by the British: 'The Savages or Indian allies of his most Christian Majesty, shall be maintained in the Lands they inhabit; if they chuse to remain there; they shall not be molested on any pretence whatsoever, for having carried arms, and served his most Christian Majesty. They shall have, as well as the French, liberty of religion, and shall keep their missionaries.'[53] The effect of Article 40 was to grant to France's Indian allies the same protection under British authority as had been afforded them under the authority of the French Crown.

Building on the protectionist policy underlying Article 15 of the Treaty of Utrecht and Article 40 of the Articles of Capitulation was the most prominent document pertaining to British Indian policy in Canada in the eighteenth century, the Royal Proclamation of 1763. It was issued by King George III of Britain following the formal cession of New France to Britain under the Treaty of Paris that same year. Rather than solidifying British interests in North America, the conquest of France rendered those interests even more precarious than they had been previously. The defeat of France created a situation in which Britain's hold on its North American possessions, as well as on its commercial interests, was threatened by the Thirteen Colonies' expansionist desires, the defeated French in Quebec, and deteriorating British-Indian relations. The Proclamation was Britain's response to these potential threats to its newly acquired North American empire.

Until the British conquest of the French in 1760–1, aboriginal groups had played a vital role in maintaining the delicate military balance between Britain and France in the struggle for supremacy in North America in the seventeenth and eighteenth centuries. With both Britain and France present as military powers in North America, aboriginal

28 Juridical Understanding

groups utilized the opportunity to serve their own interests by playing one nation off against the other for their own political, military, and commercial benefit. Indeed, as long as Britain and France were preoccupied with each other, their attention was diverted from the Indians. The Indians were well aware of their unique role and the potential repercussions which would befall them if either the British or French were defeated. In the aftermath of the British triumph over France, relations with the Indians became strained, to the point that wars with them loomed as distinct possibilities.[54]

To guard against the threats to its newly acquired position in North America, Britain deemed it necessary to curb American territorial expansion, establish legal and political control over the newly acquired colony of Quebec, and prevent the outbreak of politically and economically costly Indian wars. The Royal Proclamation of 1763 attempted to single-handedly address Britain's multifarious concerns. It designated as Indian hunting grounds an immense tract that included all land bordered to the north by Rupert's Land and resting between the Thirteen Colonies to the east and the Mississippi River to the west, save for the newly expanded colony of Quebec, Florida, and Newfoundland.[55] Under the sole pretence of protecting Indian interests, the Proclamation prevented these hunting grounds from being trespassed on or purchased from the Indians without the express permission of the Crown:

And whereas great Frauds and Abuses have been committed in purchasing Lands of the Indians, to the great Prejudice of our Interests, and to the great Dissatisfaction of the said Indians; In order, therefore, to prevent such Irregularities for the future, and to the end that the Indians may be convinced of our Justice and determined Resolution to remove all reasonable Cause of Discontent, We do, with the Advice of our Privy Council strictly enjoin and require, that no private Person do presume to make any purchase from the said Indians of any Lands reserved to the said Indians, within those parts of our Colonies where, We have thought proper to allow Settlement; but that, if any Time any of the Said Indians should be inclined to dispose of the said Lands, the same shall be Purchased only for Us, in our Name, at some public Meeting or Assembly of the said Indians.[56]

This provision enabled Britain to monitor the activities of the Americans, French, and Indians while keeping them separate and apart. Although Britain did not necessarily want settlement of the Indian hunting grounds permanently closed, by temporarily halting settlement in the area it established a buffer zone between the American colonists and

Quebec, thereby quelling fears of an alliance between them.[57] The temporary nature of the ban on settlement in the area was intended to appease the expansionist American colonies that had set their territorial sights west of the Appalachians under the pretext of restoring order to the area in the aftermath of seven years of British–French warfare. Meanwhile, the Proclamation's protection of the Indians and their lands enabled them to continue to serve the needs of the fur trade rather than fighting to protect their land from usurping American colonists. This provision was consistent with Britain's mercantilist ambitions. It wished to ensure the continuation of economically thriving colonies in North America which had sufficient funds to purchase British manufactured goods while supplying all-important raw materials such as fur, timber, and fish to the mother country.[58]

Ultimately, the Royal Proclamation of 1763 failed in its intentions. There were numerous violations of the restriction upon the settlement and purchase of lands within the Indian hunting grounds. British relations with the French in Quebec deteriorated significantly in response to British attempts to remove all vestiges of French rule in the colony.[59] The Thirteen Colonies became increasingly consumed with the notion of independence and eventually waged war with Britain.[60] Despite its failure on these fronts, the Proclamation had a lasting effect on Crown–Native relations in Canada which remains to this day.[61] It recognized and affirmed the existence of the special relationship between the Crown and Native peoples. Moreover, through its protection of aboriginal peoples and their lands, the Proclamation spelled out the basic principle of Crown–Native relations in Canada and was the harbinger of subsequent Indian legislation in Canada.[62]

The Paradox of British Indian Policy in Canada: The Coexistence of Colonialism and the Recognition of Aboriginal Sovereignty

Although the policy reflected in the Treaty of Utrecht, the Articles of Capitulation, 1760, and the Royal Proclamation of 1763 denotes the British Crown's protection of aboriginal peoples in Canada, these documents also recognize the latter's independent and sovereign status. The protection of the aboriginal peoples contemplated in these documents is merely a continuation of the mutual protection arising out of the sovereign alliances entered into between the Crown and the Native peoples in the course of their unique relationship. Equally unique, however, is the fact that the British Crown simultaneously embraced the notion of North

American colonialism while recognizing and affirming aboriginal sovereignty throughout its relations with the aboriginal peoples from the Treaty of Albany in 1664 to the early part of the nineteenth century. The paradox of the coexistence of British colonialism with the Crown's affirmation of aboriginal sovereignty is a reflection of the unique circumstances that shaped Crown–Native relations in North America from the time of contact.

From the early stages of its presence in North America, the British Crown was interested in establishing a colonial presence in North America. That desire was by no means unique to the British, however. Virtually all of the European nations who maintained a significant presence in North America from the sixteenth century onward[63] possessed some interest in establishing and maintaining colonies on the continent.[64] This was largely the result of the popularity of the mercantile system, whereby raw materials would be shipped from colonies to the mother land, processed, and sold back to the colonies as manufactured goods. This system provided a guaranteed overseas market for the home country's manufacturing sector while supplying the colonies with the finished goods they required.[65] However, it meant that the European nations first had to acquire colonies to provide the markets to be supplied. In spite of these grandiose schemes,[66] the desire of these nations to establish North American colonies and their ability to do so in the presence of powerful and numerous aboriginal nations were two entirely different matters.

In the early stages of British–aboriginal contact in North America, the British were few in number and militarily inferior to the Native peoples.[67] Moreover, they were faced with the difficult task of adjusting to strange new surroundings, with little or no knowledge of the continent's topography or the presence and edibility of its vegetation. Relying entirely on supplies from home was not feasible because of the great distance involved and the length of time for travel between Britain and North America. The would-be colonizers were thus forced to rely for survival on the benevolence of the Indian nations they encountered.[68] Under such circumstances the notion of colonization remained a theoretical goal, though an impracticable reality.

The Indians shared their food with the new European arrivals and taught them how to plant and cook new crops.[69] They introduced the Europeans to the peculiar geography of their lands and showed them how to survive in the North American climate. They shared their knowledge relating to such necessities as clothing, shelter, modes of transportation, and medicine.[70] Most important, they shared their lands with the newcomers. Once the British had acclimatized themselves to their new surroundings, they began trading with the Indians and entered into a variety of friendship treaties and alliances with them. The British soon discovered that they were able to entrench themselves in particular geographical areas without the necessity of continuous warfare with their European competitors by enlisting powerful aboriginal allies occupying strategic positions. These alliances foreshadowed the historic turn of events that culminated in the conquest of French North America by Britain in the second half of the eighteenth century. If one European nation could establish and later strengthen its Indian economic and political ties without interference from its European rivals, it could gain a position of military and economic superiority *vis-à-vis* its colonial competitors. Once one European nation had assumed economic and military superiority, it was then, at least in theory, in a position to challenge the other contenders for North American supremacy.

It was obvious to Britain that if it was to obtain these necessary Native alliances, it was not going to acquire them by treating the Native peoples as objects of colonial domination. Rather, these alliances were to be secured by gaining the trust of the aboriginal nations and entering into agreements with them on mutual terms. The agreements that were ultimately entered into between Britain and Native peoples in North America were, in fact, sovereign-to-sovereign unions which reflected historical reality as well as the intention of the parties concerned at the time.[71] They established peace and friendship, provided Britain and the Indian nations with partners in trade, and supplied them with political and military allies that could be used against their rivals. These agreements also provided for the mutual protection of the parties, ensuring military and economic support in times of war, and acting as deterrents to their enemies in times of peace.[72]

In addition to the more tangible results that these agreements produced, they also reflect the precarious political tightrope traversed by Britain, which wanted to solidify its North American colonies, but was forced by numerical inferiority and military powerlessness relative to the aboriginal nations to play a waiting game until its desires could be realized and acted upon.[73] Britain's success in accomplishing these ends, though, was ultimately dependent on its recognition of aboriginal groups as sovereign and independent nations: 'From the time of the earliest European explorations of the North American continent, relations between Indians and non-Indians were shaped by mutual needs of self-preservation and survival; military alliance, commercial enterprise and the disposition of land and its resources were preoccupations of all participants. The relative success of the countries which emerged in the eighteenth century as the most persistent and prosperous New World colonizers depended upon how well these nations were prepared to recognized the importance of this basic principle and to adapt their policies and actions accordingly.'[74]

The alliance entered into between Britain and the Five Nations of the Iroquois Confederacy (now Six Nations)[75] that resulted in the Treaty of Albany, 1664 is one of the earliest, and most noteworthy, examples of how Britain recognized aboriginal peoples as sovereign nations and treated with them in an appropriate manner.[76] Indeed, at the time, the Iroquois were both more numerous and powerful than the British in North America.[77] Under the treaty, the Iroquois were to receive 'such wares and commodities from the English for the future, as heretofore they had from the Dutch.' In addition, the treaty provided for separate British and Iroquois jurisdiction in criminal matters involving their own citizens and promised to the Iroquois British military assistance against certain Indian enemies of the former.[78] The alliance between the nations was preserved on a wampum belt made from beads fashioned out of shells, which were pierced and sewn into patterns on animal hides.[79] The Iroquois delivered and explained the significance of the belt to the British at the signing of the Treaty of Albany.[80] This marked the commencement of formal, sovereign relations between them.[81]

Because of the pattern of the wampum belt, the Treaty of Albany became known as the Two-Row Wampum treaty. The belt showed two parallel rows of purple wampum on a background of white wampum. The white wampum symbolized the purity of the agreement. The two purple rows denoted the spirit of the nations' ancestors and the separate, but parallel paths which they would each take in their respective vessels. One vessel, a birch-bark canoe, was for the Iroquois people, their laws, customs, and way of life; the other, a ship, was for the British, their laws, customs, and way of life. Three beads of wampum – symbolizing peace, friendship, and respect – separated the two rows. The three rows were the links between the nations, but just as their paths never cross on the wampum belt, neither was to attempt to steer the other's vessel.[82] The independence of the nations established in the Treaty of Albany is still cited today as an example of British recognition and affirmation of aboriginal sovereignty:

Our belief and faith that we are still an independent nation go back to the first treaty signed in North America, in 1664, when the original European settlers came to confer with our people in Albany, New York. What came out of that was the Two Row Wampum Treaty, in which conditions for our collaboration were agreed to by the two sides.

...

The Europeans at the 1664 conference said that their King would be a father to us, but the Haudenosaunee replied that there is only one father for us, and we call him Sonkwaiatisen, the Creator. The Iroquois said, this is how it will be: You and I are brothers. We will not make laws for you, but we will look after you, help you settle in this land, give you the medicines you will need to survive, and show you what you can plant, what animals you can hunt, and how to use this land. When the white men and their nations were weak with various sicknesses, it was the Native Americans who offered them medicines and food. Staples in our diet, such as 'the three sisters' – corn, beans, and squash – were food types introduced to the Europeans at that time that improved their diets and health.

The original Two Row Wampum agreement stipulated that each side would refrain from interference in the other's government. Because we feel that this agreement is still binding, Akwesasne has steadfastly refused to vote in Canada's elections.[83]

On the heels of the Treaty of Albany came the notion of the Covenant Chain, a military, political, social, and economic alliance initially between the Dutch and River Indians of the Hudson River region, but later forged between the British and Iroquois Confederacy and expanded to encompass other aboriginal nations.[84] The Covenant Chain was described symbolically as a ship tied to a tree, first with rope, later with an iron chain, and, ultimately, by a silver chain.[85] The chain was representative of this strong and lasting alliance in which the groups were considered by the others as equals. The chain itself was a gestalt – the parties individually were not as strong as they were when joined together as links: 'The Covenant Chain was a mutual protectorate, in which the individual nations were like links in a chain, each gathering strength from its connection with the others while maintaining its individual existence as a nation.'[86]

Whereas the Covenant Chain was designed as a permanent alliance, it was expected that the nations would regularly renew its undertakings, lest it be taken for granted, neglected, and left to weaken.[87] Sir William Johnson, in a speech shortly after his appointment as superintendent-

34   Juridical Understanding

general of Indian Affairs in 1755, discussed the renewal of the Covenant Chain more than a hundred years after its creation:

You well know and these Books testifie that it is now almost 100 years since your Forefathers and ours became known to each other – That upon our first acquaintance we shook hands & finding we should be useful to one another, entered into a covenant of Brotherly love and mutual friendship – And tho' we were at first only tied together by a Rope, yet lest this Rope should grow Rotten and break, we tied ourselves together by an iron Chain – lest time and accidents might rust and destroy this Chain of iron, we afterwards made one of Silver; the strength and brightness of which would but eject to no decay – The ends of this Silver chain we fixt to the immoveable mountains, and this in so firm a manner, that the hands of no mortal Enemy might be able to remove it. All this my Brethren you know to be Truth; you know also that this Covenant Chain of love and friendship, was the dread and envy of all your Enemies and ours, that by keeping it bright and unbroken, we have never spilt in anger one drop of each other's blood to this day – You well know also that from the beginning to this time we have almost every year strengthened and brightened this Covenant Chain in the most publick & solemn manner. You know that we became as one body, one blood & one people, the same King our common Father, that your Enemies were ours, that whom you took into your Alliance and allowed to put their hands into this Covenant Chain as Brethren, we have always considered and treated as such.[88]

The notions of peace, friendship, and mutuality that characterized the Covenant Chain also found their way into the alliance between Britain and the aboriginal peoples living in the Maritimes in a number of treaties between 1693 and 1752.[89] These treaties attempted to provide for peace and friendship between the nations in a period marred by constant warfare and raids across what is now the eastern Canada–United States border, and fluctuating aboriginal alliances between Britain and France. Interestingly, the rhetoric used by the Native peoples to characterize their eighteenth-century relations with the British in the Maritimes is strikingly similar to that used to describe the Covenant Chain:

The eighteenth century agreements between the Mi'kmaq nation and Britain were, and still are, regarded by us as a form of brotherhood. When there was some injury or threat of conflict we met to exchange reassurances and renew our engagements. That is why, over several decades, one finds half a dozen or more seemingly separate treaties between the Mi'kmaq and the British Crown. The surviving documents are often incomplete summaries of meetings that typically required many days and were repeated every few years as necessary. By themselves, the documents are fragments; considered together, they constitute a great chain of agreement. In other words, the treaty documents ... should be seen not as distinct treaties but as stages and renewals of a larger agreement or pact that developed during the 1700s between the Mi'kmaq and the British.[90]

The alliance between Britain and the Mi'kmaq nation was seen by the latter as a form of kinship, or the joining together of the nations: 'By entering into treaty, Britain joined our circle of brother nations, the Wabanaki Confederacy, and we joined its circle of nations, later known as the British Commonwealth. The Mi'kmaq symbolized this important relationship by adding an eighth point – Great Britain – to the seven-pointed star representing the seven districts of our nation.'[91] In a manner similar to the effect of the Treaty of Albany upon the Covenant Chain, the Mi'kmaq saw the series of treaties and alliances as renewing the original bond and commitment made between the groups. Although the treaty signed at Boston in 1725 followed the tenor of earlier agreements, it acted as the catalyst for future negotiations and alliances. Subsequent agreements between the nations were simply viewed as affirmations and renewals of the 1725 compact.[92]

Throughout the time the British Crown was entering into these treaties and alliances with aboriginal nations on a nation-to-nation basis, promising to keep them secure in their lands and rights, Britain maintained its desire to eventually subjugate them and take their lands. Yet, the political sleight of hand implemented by Britain in its dealings with the Native peoples was by no means one-sided. The Indians engaged in similar manoeuvres against both the British and French in order to obtain the greatest possible benefits for themselves.[93] They also attempted to undercut established Indian–European alliances. Similarly, the European nations attempted to circumvent or dissolve established alliances forged between their rivals and the Natives. 'The mother countries [Great Britain and France] did everything in their power to secure the alliance of each Indian nation and to encourage nations allied with the enemy to change sides. When these efforts met with success, they were incorporated into treaties of alliance or neutrality. This clearly indicates that the Indian nations were regarded in their relations with the European nations which occupied North America as independent nations ... Further, both the French and the English recognized the critical importance of alliances with the Indians, or at least their neutrality, in determining the outcome of the war between them and the security of the North American colonies.'[94] As the Royal Commission on Aboriginal Peoples has recognized, 'Relations between the British colonies and aboriginal peoples were complex and diverse, with elements of contradiction and paradox.'[95]

In general, treaty negotiations and alliances between European powers and aboriginal peoples in North America in the seventeenth and eighteenth centuries resembled a chess match, with each manoeuvring to gain strategic positions while waiting for a corresponding weakness in their rivals. This political manoeuvring reached its apex during the battle between Britain and France for North American supremacy from the latter stages of the seventeenth century, culminating in the British conquest of New France in 1760–1.

With Britain and France competing to achieve predominance in North America, the Indians were able to play the two European powers off against each other for their own benefit. They were shrewd negotiators who knew full well that they were the catalysts in the European struggle in North America.[96] They also knew that their precarious interests were best served by maintaining the delicate balance of power between the two European nations. This enhanced their bargaining position *vis-à-vis* Britain and France and necessitated that they be treated with respect and diplomacy. Aboriginal peoples were crucial to the existence and proliferation of the fur trade, which was one of the fundamental tools in the early economic development of North America.[97] Moreover, their military strength and numbers were far superior to that of any European nation's presence in North America. They were, therefore, potentially dangerous enemies to the Europeans as well as much sought-after allies. The threat of exclusive aboriginal alliances with either Britain or France enabled the aboriginal peoples to command superior terms in their dealings with both European powers. The crucial value of the Indians as allies in the conflict between Britain and France was recognized by the Supreme Court of Canada in *R v. Sioui*: 'Following the crushing defeats of the English by the French in 1755, the English realized that control of North America could not be acquired without the co-operation of the Indians. Accordingly, from then on they made efforts to ally themselves with as many Indian nations as possible. The French, who had long realized the strategic role of the Indians in the success of any war effort, also did everything they could to secure their alliance or maintain alliances already established.'[98]

The removal of France as a major power in North America forever changed the relationship between the Crown and Native peoples. The Indians could no longer occupy the enviable position of holding the balance of power between Britain and France and derive advantage from forcing the two European nations to compete for their favour. Disease, war, and colonial expansion had decimated the aboriginal population. These factors limited their numbers and military effectiveness, in addition to hampering their ability to hunt, trap, and fish. Moreover, their role in the fur trade had altered their traditional ways of life and made them heavily dependent on European manufactured goods.

Having abandoned their traditional methods, Native peoples became increasingly more reliant on European trade to obtain guns, pots, kettles, blankets, and other implements.[99] By virtue of their heavy reliance on European manufactured goods, the Native peoples devoted more and more time pursuing pelts and other commodities for trade with the Europeans and less time to their more traditional practices. Eventually, the combination of their desire for manufactured goods and their disuse of the skills necessary to produce their own implements manifested in their dependency on the British. What had once been a relationship controlled entirely by the aboriginal peoples had now come full circle:

Indian–White relationships in North America have passed through several well-defined stages. In the first contacts the Europeans were in a subordinate position, dependent on the sufferance of the Indians for advice, guidance, and survival. The newcomers had to accommodate to the natives' way of doing things and to accept their control of the relationship. However, the newcomers inadvertently introduced diseases that wreaked devastation on the receiving society and undermined its self-sufficiency. Paradoxically, those who survived this first onslaught were able to live better than before because they acquired European tools that allowed them to do what they had always done, only more efficiently: Iron replaced stone, the cooking pot superseded the hollowed-out tree stump. Gradually, the traditional artifacts fell into disuse, along with the knowledge that produced them. The Indians became dependent on imported goods that they could not duplicate, and as their dependence grew, so the importance of the supplier increased. The tool that was servant became the master.[100]

Aboriginal leaders insisted that Britain's defeat of the French had no effect on the sovereign nature of their relations with Britain. As the Ojibway Chief Minavavana explained to English trader Alexander Henry at Michilimackinac in the fall of 1761, 'Englishman, although you have conquered the French, you have not yet conquered us. We are not your slaves. These lakes, these woods and mountains, were left to us by our ancestors. They are our inheritance; and we will part with them to none.'[101] As John Borrows explains, the complete text of Minavavana's speech[102] is important for its indication of how the Ojibway people regarded power relations between themselves and the British around the time of conquest: 'This speech is notable in many respects as a statement of the government to government relationship which First Nation peoples were proposing to the British. Minavavana recounted some of the principles of peace and co-existence being formulated by First Nations. First, it is significant that the Ojibway stated unequivocally that they were "not yet conquered." They considered their allegiance as being to the Great Spirit, and not to any European power. Second, it is important to note that the Ojibway regarded themselves and the English as being reliant on one another for trade and peace, and therefore their power relationship was regarded as being parallel. Finally, the Ojibway stated that the British had to fulfil certain obligations, such as the giving of gifts, in order to attain even a state of co-existence with them.'[103]

In spite of their assertions of sovereignty and expectations that their nation-to-nation relationship with Britain would continue unchanged by the defeat of France, the increasing disparity in military and economic power between aboriginal peoples and the Crown did, in fact, alter the nature of these relationships from their pre-conquest form.[104] The increasing differential in power between the Crown and aboriginal peoples rendered the latter more heavily dependent on the Crown. With their political and military clout gone and their absolute reliance on Britain for manufactured goods, the First Nations were inescapably caught up in the Crown's colonialist ambitions. The process of entrenching its position in North America initiated in the Royal Proclamation of 1763 was now underway.

In setting out its intentions to solidify its North American possessions in the Royal Proclamation of 1763, however, the Crown did more than recognize and protect aboriginal land interests and the rights which flow from those interests.[105] The Proclamation served the dual function of denoting the Crown's assertion of suzerainty over Canada and affirming the inherent sovereignty of the aboriginal peoples: 'Thus, while the Royal Proclamation asserted suzerainty over Aboriginal peoples living "under Our Protection" it also recognized that these people were "Nations" connected with the Crown by way of treaty and alliance ... The Proclamation acknowledged the retained sovereignty of Aboriginal peoples under the Crown's protection, and adopted measures to secure and protect their Territorial rights. This arrangement is the historical basis of the enduring constitutional relationship between Aboriginal nations and the Crown and provides the source of the Crown's fiduciary duties to those nations.'[106] It should be noted, however, that in recognizing and affirming aboriginal rights, including aboriginal sovereignty, rights to land and the rights that flow therefrom, the Proclamation did not create any rights which were not already in existence. It was merely a document that affirmed the status quo with respect to aboriginal peoples and their interaction with the Crown.[107] Aboriginal rights of sovereignty were well entrenched by 1763, as were their rights to land. Indeed, these were recognized as far back as 1664 with the signing of the Treaty of Albany.

The Proclamation recognized that the exploitation of Indian land interests by European settlers posed a threat to the continued good relations between the Indians and the Crown that the Crown desperately wanted and needed to maintain: 'Britain was well aware in 1763 of the precarious nature of its relations with the old Indian allies of France, and the growing dissatisfaction of its own native allies and trading partners. Since mid-century, the British government had been increasingly occupied with Indian affairs, and the war with France had emphasized the importance of native friendship and support.'[108] The Proclamation characterized the relationship between the Crown and aboriginal peoples as one between sovereign entities coexisting in a peaceful, reciprocal, and mutually beneficial manner. Its description of 'the several Nations or Tribes with whom we are connected, and who live under our Protection' indicates that the aboriginal peoples were not subjects of the Crown, but allied nations. By simultaneously asserting British suzerainty while affirming the inherent sovereignty of the aboriginal peoples, the Proclamation was consistent with the symbiotic nature of the Crown–Native relationship. The Proclamation sought to maintain the integrity of this relationship by prohibiting the exploitation of aboriginal peoples and their lands. The Proclamation recognized the importance of the Indian interest in land and sought to protect the aboriginals from being taken advantage of by the Crown's subjects as a result of the different understandings each had with relation to the use of land.[109]

The idea of property rights in law stems from cultural understandings of land and land use.[110] These understandings, meanwhile, emanate from particular conceptions of humans' place in the universe. Consequently, when these conceptions diverge, conflicts between different notions of property rights arise. One Western perception of land rights

40 Juridical Understanding

finds its origins in the Book of Genesis. Verses 1:27 and 1:28 describe the role of humankind in the following manner:

And God created man in His image, in the image of God He created him; male and female He created them.
God blessed them and God said to them, 'Be fertile and increase, fill the earth and master it; and rule the fish of the sea, the birds of the sky, and all the living things that creep on earth.'

In contrast, Anishnawbe, or Ojibway, thought stresses that instead of holding dominion over the earth and its inhabitants, humankind is the least important of all living beings:

Creation came about from the union of the Maker and the Physical World. Out of this union came the natural children, the Plants, nurtured from the Physical World, Earth, their Mother. To follow were Animalkind, the two-legged, the four-legged, the winged, those who swim and those who crawl, all dependent on the Plant World and Mother Earth. Finally, last in the order came Humankind, the most dependent and least necessary of all the orders.[111]

Whereas humans are the masters of the earth under the Genesis formulation, under the Anishnawbe formulation, they are its caretakers or stewards with the responsibility to maintain it for future generations.[112] From these diametrically opposed notions of the relative positions of humans in their physical surroundings, equally diverse understandings of land and property rights in land exist between aboriginal and non-aboriginal societies.

Common law notions of property focus on the exclusivity of possession and the creation of a bundle of reciprocal rights and obligations which flow from that exclusivity of possession. The notion of land ownership under the common law begets the concept of title, which represents the legally recognized and entrenched ownership or interest in the land. In simplified terms, the concept of absolute land ownership under the common law – as represented by the fee simple interest – entails the authority of landowners to determine the use of the land. It also creates a set of legal relations between persons that recognizes and entrenches a landowner's exclusive rights to the land in question.

For example, if person A possesses a fee simple interest in a piece of land, that person has the exclusive legal right to it and a corresponding right, which is also legally enforceable, to prevent others from using it without permission. Subject to any restrictions imposed by law, A possesses rights to the land against the world, including the ability to dispose of it, alter its character, or destroy it.[113] The fact of ownership endows landowners with certain ownership 'rights' or 'powers' which are protected by law.[114] The common law recognizes and entrenches A's rights through the promulgation of laws such as the law relating to trespass.

Conversely, many aboriginal notions[115] of land stress that land cannot be 'owned' in the English common law understanding of the term.[116] Under these aboriginal conceptions of property, land is something whose fruits may be reaped and which may be used, possessed, cultivated, and cared for, but not owned or sold in the common law understandings of those terms. This is illustrated by a statement made by a Cree hunter testifying before Malouf J in *Gros-Louis v Société de Développement de la Baie James*.[117] When the hunter was asked if he believed that the land in question belonged to his people, he said, 'We say that in your language. In our language, we say that we belong to the land.'[118]

In most traditional aboriginal cultures, then, in return for the privilege of using the land, the aboriginal peoples agree to share it with all living beings and undertake its stewardship. Thus, whereas aboriginal peoples may use the land to hunt, fish, or grow crops, they may not engage in activities which will spoil the land for future generations. They must leave the land in a condition which will enable future generations to reap similar benefits from it.[119] Moreover, the sale of land by an aboriginal tribe or group is prohibited, because it belongs to the Creator. Even if a tribe or group could sell land, it could only transfer its own limited interest; it would be unable to transfer the equal interests belonging to other living beings or to future generations.

In addition to recognizing and protecting aboriginal land interests, the Royal Proclamation of 1763 recognized and affirmed the pre-existing, sovereign relationship between the Crown and Native peoples. For this reason, it became known as the Indian 'Bill of Rights.'[120] The entrenchment of the aboriginal rights clauses of the Proclamation stems from the Crown's continuation of the mutuality of respect, trust, and the recognition of sovereignty previously embodied in the Treaty of Albany, the Covenant Chain, and the Maritime peace and friendship treaties. The Proclamation was also a declaration of the Crown's exclusive rights *vis-à-vis* other European nations in North America,[121] which included the exclusive right to obtain land from the aboriginal peoples at such time as they desired to dispose of it.[122] The protection of aboriginal rights in the Proclamation denotes the qualifications on the Crown's rights, namely, the pre-existing sovereignty and rights of the aboriginal peoples.

The Proclamation was not based entirely on the Crown's recognition and affirmation of its historical relationship with the aboriginal peoples. As detailed earlier, the protection of aboriginal lands through the creation of the Indian hunting grounds served the Crown's own interests as well as those of the Indians. This is reflected in the Proclamation itself, which states that not only is the protection of the aboriginal peoples and their interests 'just and reasonable,' but that its provisions are 'essential to Our Interest and the Security of Our Colonies': 'And whereas it is just and reasonable, and essential to our Interest, and the Security of our Colonies, that the several Nations or Tribes of Indians with whom We are connected, and who live under our Protection, should not be molested or disturbed in the Possession of such Parts of Our Dominions and Territories as, not having been ceded to or purchased by Us, are reserved to them, or any of them, as their Hunting Grounds.'[123] While recognizing, protecting, and affirming aboriginal interests, the Proclamation also sowed the seeds for the onslaught of colonialism that was soon to become the dominant characteristic of Crown–Native relations.[124]

The Proclamation may be clearly seen as a major turning point in Crown–Native relations. Shortly after it was issued, relations between the Crown and its Indian allies began to take on a new character. With the conquest of France leaving Britain as the sole major European power in Canada, the Crown's long-standing goal of widescale colonization was set to begin. Once Britain had achieved its position of predominance in North America, it developed and implemented Indian policies to govern its relations with the Native peoples and allow for the continued infusion of British settlers. The promulgation of Indian legislation and the continued use of treaties were the means by which this was accomplished.[125] Although legislative initiatives were made entirely at the behest of the Crown, the nature of Indian treaties changed drastically from their pre-Proclamation form.

Over time Indian treaties became increasingly more one-sided in favour of the Crown. Just as the nature of the relationship between the Crown and Native peoples had not remained static, treaties between the Crown and Native groups mirrored the change in power relations between the two groups. Indian treaties were gradually transformed from agreements entered into between sovereign nations, which were equally beneficial to all parties concerned, into documents whose terms the Indians attempted to make as favourable as they could, but which were ultimately dictated by the Crown. Indeed, the terms and conditions of treaties could be unilaterally altered by legislative initiatives after their ratification without recourse by the treaty signatories. The Crown's ability to alter the terms of Indian treaties remained until the repatriation of the Canadian Constitution in 1982.[126] With the constitutional protection of aboriginal and treaty rights in Section 35(1) of the Constitution Act, 1982, legislative abrogation of aboriginal and treaty rights was prohibited.[127]

These 'new-look' treaties were gradually transformed from the treaties of peace and friendship characteristic of the Maritime Indian treaties to treaties whose primary goal was to obtain the surrender of Indian land rights.[128] These land surrender treaties[129] were prevalent in more desirable geographical areas where increased settlement necessitated the Crown's acquisition of additional lands. In exchange for these surrenders of land, the Crown offered a variety of goods to the aboriginal peoples: reserves, money, annuities, guns and ammunition, alcohol, tools, blankets, hatchets, pots, pans, knives, beads, and a variety of other implements. The changes in the intent of these treaties from that of their peace and friendship predecessors, not coincidentally, mirrored the change in the power relations between the Crown and the Indians.

Despite the changes in the terminology employed in Indian treaties, the Crown's representatives continued to make representations to the aboriginal peoples that their sovereignty and rights were never ignored and continued even after the Royal Proclamation of 1763 was issued. Indeed, instructions to General Murray, commander in chief of British forces in North America on 7 December 1763, exactly two months after the Proclamation was issued, indicate that, in spite of the Crown's assertion of suzerainty over Canada in the Proclamation, the Crown still considered the aboriginals as sovereign peoples whose friendship required cultivation:

60 And whereas Our Province of Quebec is in part inhabited and possessed by several Nations and Tribes of Indians, with whom it is both necessary and expedient to cultivate and maintain a strict Friendship and good Correspondence, so that they may be induced by Degrees, not only to be good Neighbours to Our Subjects, but likewise themselves to become good Subjects to Us; You are therefore, as soon as you conveniently can, to appoint a proper Person or Persons to assemble, and treat with the said Indians, promising

44 Juridical Understanding

and assuring them of Protection and Friendship on Our part, and delivering them such Presents, as shall be sent to you for that purpose.
61 And you are to inform yourself with the greatest Exactness of the Number, Nature and Disposition of the several Bodies or Tribes of Indians, of the manner of their Lives, and the Rules and Constitutions, by which they are governed or regulated. And You are upon no Account to molest or disturb them in the Possession of such Parts of the said Province, as they at present occupy or possess; but to use the best means You can for conciliating their Affections, and uniting them to Our Government, reporting to Us, by Our Commissioners for Trade and Plantations, whatever Information you can collect with respect to these People, and the whole of your Proceedings with them.
62 Whereas We have, by Our Proclamation dated the seventh day of October in the Third year of Our Reign, strictly forbid, on pain of Our Displeasure, all Our Subjects from making any Purchases or Settlements whatever, or taking Possession of any of the Lands reserved to the several Nations of Indians, with whom We are connected, and who live under Our Protection, without Our especial Leave for that Purpose first obtained; It is Our express Will and Pleasure, that you take the most effectual Care that Our Royal Directions herein be punctually complied with, and that the Trade with such of the said Indians as depend upon your Government be carried on in the Manner, and under the Regulations prescribed in Our said Proclamation.[130]

These instructions to General Murray indicate that the Native peoples were not yet subjects of the Crown, but nations to be treated with and won over to British allegiance. It also indicates that the aboriginal peoples were not to be molested or otherwise interfered with (as laid out in the Proclamation of 1763), and that the terms of the Proclamation (including its references to trade with the Indians) be respected and fulfilled.

It stands to reason that if the aboriginal peoples were not British subjects, as article 60 makes clear, and were peoples to be treated with and won over to British allegiance, they had to be independent nations. If they were not the subjects of any foreign potentate and were bound only by their own dictates, they were, by necessity and logical implication, sovereign.

Later, in 1774, Sir Guy Carleton, who succeeded General Murray as commander in chief (and who, in 1786, became Lord Dorchester), affirmed to the Algonquin people that unless they had relinquished their land rights, those rights continued to exist.[131] Lord Dorchester once

Politics Underlying the Relationship   45

again attempted to quiet aboriginal concerns about their rights in 1791 when he made the following comments:

Brothers: You have told me, there were people who say that the King your father when he made peace with the United States gave away your lands to them. I cannot think the government of the United States would hold that language, it must come from ill-informed individuals. You will know, that no man can give what is not his own ...

The King's rights with respect to your territory were against the nations of Europe; these he resigned to the States. But the King never had any rights against you but to such parts of the country as had been fairly ceded by yourselves with your own free consent by public convention and sale. How then can it be said that he gave away your lands?

So careful was the King of your interests, so fully sensible of your rights, that he would not suffer even his own people to buy your lands, without being sure of your free consent, and of ample justice being done you ... The King has not forgot your friendship, he never forgets his friends.

You desire the King's protection, you desire his power and influence may be exerted to procure your peace and to secure your rights.[132]

In the latter part of the eighteenth century growing concerns over trade and commerce with aboriginal peoples resulted in a dispute between Canada and the United States. During the dispute – which ultimately led up to the conclusion of the Treaty of Amity, Commerce, and Navigation in 1794, better known as the Jay Treaty, 1794 – the Crown's instructions to its Canadian representatives suggest that the Indians were autonomous, sovereign peoples with whom it was necessary to curry favour. Draft instructions to Lord Dorchester in 1786[133] relating to American trade with aboriginal peoples once again indicated that the aboriginal peoples were independent and sovereign nations:

4th ... you are also to Obtain the most authentick Information, whether any of the Nations of Indians in alliance and Friendship with Us, continue to reside within the Territories of the United States of America, and the Boundaries thereof, as settled by the Treaty of Peace; and whether those Indians, or any others within Our Territories, are supplied with goods from the subjects of the said United States, or have any commercial or other Intercourse with them; and You are to transmit the same to Us thro one of our Principal secretaries of State as before directed, together with any Information, or proposition, by which you may think, proper and effectual Measures may be taken,

46   Juridical Understanding

to Induce those Indians to remove within Our Territories, and to discontinue any Intercourse with the subjects or Inhabitants of the said United States, which may Lessen Our Influence with them, and be prejudicial to Our Service, and the Interest and Commerce of Our Subjects.[134]

Article III of the Jay Treaty dealt specifically with the issue of aboriginal peoples' mobility rights between Canadian and American territorial jurisdictions. It stipulated:

It is agreed that it shall at all times be free to His Majesty's subjects, and to the citizens of the United States, and also to the Indians dwelling on either side of the said boundary line, freely to pass and repass by land or inland navigation, into the respective territories and countries of the two parties, on the continent of America, (the country within the limits of the Hudson's Bay Company only excepted,) and to navigate all the lakes, rivers and waters thereof, and freely to carry on trade and commerce with each other ...

...

No duty of entry shall ever be levied by either party on peltries brought by land or inland navigation into the said territories respectively, nor shall the Indians passing or repassing with their own proper goods and effects of whatever nature, pay for the same any impost or duty whatever. But goods in bales, or other large packages, unusual among Indians, shall not be considered as goods belonging bona fide to Indians.

...

As this article is intended to render in a great degree the local advantages of each party common to both, and thereby to promote a disposition favorable to friendship and good neighborhood, it is agreed that the respective Governments will mutually promote this amicable intercourse, by causing speedy and impartial justice to be done, and necessary protection to be extended to all who may be concerned therein.[135]

Even after the Jay Treaty was signed relations between Britain and the United States remained tenuous. In 1812 full-scale war broke out between the two countries. A negotiated end to these hostilities came on 24 December 1814, with the signing of the Treaty of Ghent.[136] Article 9 of that treaty was a provision by which both nations also agreed to end all hostilities with the aboriginal nations:

The United States of America engages to put an end, immediately after the ratification of the present treaty, to hostilities with all the tribes or nations of Indians with whom they may be at war at the time of such ratification; and forthwith to restore to such tribes or nations, respectively, all the possessions, rights and privileges which they may have enjoyed or been entitled to in one thousand eight hundred and eleven, previous to such hostilities: Provided always that such tribes or nations shall agree to desist from all hostilities against the United States of America, their citizens and subjects, upon the ratification of the present treaty being notified to such tribes or nations, and shall so desist accordingly. And His Brittanic Majesty engages, on his part, to put an end immediately after the ratification of the present treaty, to hostilities with all the tribes or nations of Indians with whom he may be at war at the time of such ratification, and forthwith to restore to such tribes or nations respectively all the possessions, rights and privileges which they may have enjoyed or been entitled to in one thousand eight hundred and eleven, previous to such hostilities: Provided always that such tribes or nations shall agree to desist from all hostilities against His Brittanic Majesty, and his subjects, upon the ratification of the present treaty being notified to such tribes or nations, and shall so desist accordingly.[137]

From these various instructions and treaties occurring subsequent to the passage of the Royal Proclamation of 1763, it may be concluded that the Proclamation did not terminate the sovereignty of the aboriginal peoples, either in the document itself or in the minds of the British Crown. What the document did accomplish, however, was to entrench the fiduciary nature of the Crown–Native relationship and set the stage for the full-scale onslaught of British colonialism in the nineteenth century.

Throughout its tenure in North America, British colonialist ambitions in North America continued strongly, even while it engaged in sovereign relations with aboriginal nations. Indeed, the Crown engaged in a precarious balance of internally promoting its colonialist ideas while externally recognizing and respecting the independence and sovereignty of the Native peoples. Thus, it may be fairly said that Britain was prepared to recognize, and did, indeed, recognize, aboriginal sovereignty either out of necessity or political opportunism, depending on the circumstances. However, when aboriginal military power waned *vis-à-vis* that of the British, Britain became less and less willing to recognize aboriginal sovereignty. Once the aboriginals lost their coercive edge, Britain even became unwilling to acknowledge that it had recognized aboriginal independence in the past. Britain adopted this cavalier attitude towards its historical undertakings despite the fact that one of its European colonial rivals could just as easily have become dominant in Canada.

For Britain to have emerged from the European colonial free-for-all that began in the late fifteenth century as the last significant European colonial power left in North America in the second half of the eighteenth century necessitated a number of events that could not possibly have been envisaged when Henry VII granted his charter to John Cabot in 1495. First, Britain had to establish a colonial presence in North America, which meant that it had to attain some degree of self-sufficiency. The British settlers desperately needed the aboriginal peoples to teach them how to cope in surroundings that they were completely unfamiliar with. They relied wholeheartedly on the benevolence of the aboriginal peoples for their very survival. Had the aboriginals not given food and other aid to the British, their initial attempts at colonization would have quickly resulted in disaster.

Next, Britain had to vie with the several other European nations for the favour of the Native peoples. Without obtaining at least some alliances with powerful aboriginal nations, Britain would have been unable to maintain its presence in North America, either militarily or economically. The aboriginals were the most powerful military force on the continent for some two hundred years after contact. Their military might made them essential for successful endeavours in trade – in fish and timber, but especially in fur. They were successful trappers who knew the topography of the land far better than the new European arrivals. Moreover, the most powerful aboriginal nations controlled trade routes. Britain therefore had to secure alliances with enough powerful aboriginal nations to resist the military and economic might of rival European nations and their aboriginal allies, or that of politically neutral nations such as the Iroquois.

Third, Britain had to count on the devastating effects that disease would have on the aboriginal peoples, decimating their population and rendering them far less of an opposition to Britain's colonialist ambitions. In addition, Britain would have had to have foreseen the aboriginals' heavy reliance on manufactured goods that resulted in increasing aboriginal dependence on their relations with the British. Although disease and warfaring had irrevocably devastated the aboriginal population, thereby reducing their military strength and advantage over the British, it was their reliance on manufactured goods that had the effect of rendering them ultimately dependent on the British: 'Even those who did not participate directly in the fur trade obtained European goods from Indian middlemen, while those Indians who did participate, blending a subsistence living with the pursuit of furs for trade, became particularly dependent upon European goods: guns, ammunition, traps, hardware of all sorts, and manufactured cloth. One Indian, while expressing antipathy towards the Hudson's Bay Company, said that the Indians would die if the Company went away.'[138]

Finally, if predicting this chain of events was not outlandish enough, Britain had to count on the fact that none of its other European competitors would have been equally able to rely on these events for their own benefit or end up in a better position than Britain as a result. Had this chain of events not occurred, each building on the other in Britain's favour, Britain would have by no means been assured of its ultimate place in North American affairs in the second half of the eighteenth century. Therefore, it is clear that, regardless of its initial colonialist ambitions – which all other European seafaring nations who came to North America shared – Britain could not possibly have predicted the outcome of its North American endeavours, nor could it have planned each event in the chain to have occurred in precisely the fashion that it did. What the British perhaps should have anticipated, though, was that their relations with the aboriginal peoples carried with them obligations of a binding nature which, like the alliances they had entered into, were designed to be perpetual.

3

The Incidents of Colonialism

In law, with law, and through law, Canada has imposed a colonial system of government and justice upon our people without due regard to our treaty and Aboriginal rights. We respect law that is fair and just, but we cannot be faulted for denouncing those laws that degrade our humanity and rights as distinct peoples.

Ovide Mercredi, Berens River[1]

... Our object is to continue until there is not a single Indian in Canada that has not been absorbed into the body politic and there is no Indian question, and no Indian Department.

Duncan Campbell Scott, Deputy Superintendent of Indian Affairs, 1920[2]

After defeating France and proclaiming its intentions for its new colonial possessions in the Royal Proclamation of 1763, Britain was set to finally fulfil its long-standing colonialist ambitions in North America. Before it could embark on such an endeavour, however, the unrest among the American colonies came to a head and the American Revolution was under way. With Britain's attention focused on maintaining its hold on the American colonies, it had little time to implement plans for the colonization of Canada. After Britain's defeat in the Revolutionary War, hostilities between the newly formed American nation and its former colonial overlord resulted in periodic raids, warfare, and continuing ill-will between the two nations. This distraction kept the Crown from engaging in much in the way of further colonization in Canada until into the nineteenth century.

The aboriginal peoples adopted a new version of a familiar role in the battle between Britain and the American colonies during this period. Through the course of its disputes with the United States after the Revolutionary War had ended, Britain maintained that some aboriginal nations were sovereign and independent and did not come under either British or American jurisdiction. At the same time, Britain attempted to win the alliance of these nations and turn them against the Americans. The role played by the Native peoples in the hostilities between Britain and the United States mirrored their role in the British–French battles during the seventeenth and eighteenth centuries, only this time in a more symbolic fashion. The significant decrease in the Natives' power attributable to disease, lengthy warfare, and their dependency on European manufactured goods, prevented them from maintaining as prominent a position as they had had in earlier times. Once the political benefits of recognizing the aboriginal peoples as independent nations waned in the nineteenth century, Britain, who had treated with them as equals and described them as 'nations' when it was to Britain's advantage to do so, began to describe and view them as 'tribes' or 'bands.'[3]

As a result of the American Revolution, there was an influx of new settlers into Canada who either sought refuge from the war or were loyal to the Crown and wanted to remain under its dominion. This new wave of immigration greatly increased the population of the British colonies of Quebec and Nova Scotia and eventually resulted in the division of Quebec into Upper and Lower Canada, and the creation of New Brunswick. The swell in population created by this northward migration created the need for greater tracts of land. In response to the demands of settlers for land, Britain initiated negotiations with aboriginal nations for the surrender of their lands through treaty.[4] It was not unusual for the Crown to use coercion to obtain these surrenders. For example, a letter written by Lieutenant-Governor Adams G. Archibald during the negotiations of Treaties No. 1 and 2 stated that: 'We told them that whether they wished it or not, immigrants would come in and fill up the country; that every year from this one twice as many in number as their whole people there assembled would pour into the Province, and in a little while would spread all over it, and that now was the time for them to come to an arrangement that would secure homes and annuities for themselves and their children.[5]

Just as the intention behind Indian treaties began to change in emphasis from compacts of peace and friendship to terms of land surrender, British interaction with the aboriginal peoples also adopted a new form.

52 Juridical Understanding

The treaties and compacts that Britain had entered into with the aboriginal peoples dating from the Treaty of Albany – and, more importantly, the obligations that existed under them – were no longer regarded or upheld in the same way. For example, the Covenant Chain, which had been regularly polished for well over a hundred years through the regular giving of presents and renewing of sovereign agreements, began to rust from neglect once Britain ceased these practices. Meanwhile, legislation, which once had been promulgated to continue the policy of protecting aboriginal lands specified in the Royal Proclamation of 1763,[6] underwent a change in emphasis from the protection of aboriginal peoples to the subjugation of them. Whereas Native land rights had once been affirmed and protected by having the Crown be a requisite intermediary in all sales of Indian lands in order to discourage unscrupulous dealings by settlers and land speculators, Native rights to land soon failed to be protected or recognized by the Crown.

The increased use of land surrender treaties and the change in the nature of Crown–Native relations, not surprisingly, coincided with another significant change – the Crown's new policy of aboriginal assimilation. A key factor in this new policy was the implementation of the reserve system. In exchange for their surrenders of land, aboriginal nations received reservations on which they had exclusive rights of occupancy. Although the reservations were supposed to provide a place for aboriginal peoples free from non-aboriginal incursion (at least in theory), more importantly, from the Crown's perspective, the reservation system allowed the Crown to simultaneously satisfy the increasing demand for land by non-aboriginal settlers while playing a role in its assimilationist policy:[7]

[T]he most effectual means of ameliorating the condition of the Indians, of promoting their religious improvement and education, and of eventually relieving His Majesty's Government from the expense of the Indian department, are – 1st. To collect the Indians in considerable numbers, and to settle them in villages, with due portion of land for their cultivations and support. 2d. To make such provision for their religious improvement, education and instruction in husbandry, as circumstances may from time to time require. 3d. To afford them such assistance in building their houses, rations, and in procuring such seed and agricultural implements as may be necessary, commuting where practicable, a portion of their presents for the latter.[8]

In addition to providing the scenario for assimilation, the reserve system

Incidents of Colonialism 53

also provided a perspicacious means with which to remove the threat of aboriginal military strikes against the Crown: '[T]he Canadian system of band reserves has a tendency to diminish the offensive strength of the Indian tribes, should they ever become restless.'[9]

Legislation was increasingly used in the nineteenth and twentieth centuries as a means of controlling Native peoples through the control of their land and resources.[10] The Crown's use of legislation to control the aboriginal peoples was most evident through the creation of the federal Indian Act in 1876.[11] The imposition of the Indian Act was intended to codify the dominion government's regulation of aboriginal peoples in Canada as well as provide for Canadian governmental control over aboriginal peoples and their affairs. By way of the Indian Act, virtually all aspects of aboriginal existence came under governmental authority.

The Indian Act had no respect for aboriginal peoples or their institutions, whether governmental or cultural. It eliminated traditional forms of aboriginal governments, at least in an official sense, and replaced them with an artificial, non-aboriginal form which neither reflected the cultures nor the requirements of the peoples whom they were intended to govern.[12] It ignored aboriginal understandings of identity and group membership by creating and imposing its own categorization of aboriginal peoples and groups. The Indian Act determined who was to be considered as 'Indian' for the purposes of the Act, through its description of aboriginal persons as either 'status' or 'non-status' Indians. Under the Indian Act only those persons who were entitled to be registered under the Act were 'Indians.'[13] Aboriginal persons who did not fulfil the government's terms of registration were simply not recognized as aboriginal by the Canadian federal government. Not only did the term 'Indian' apply only to certain peoples, it excluded the Métis entirely, and was held to include the Inuit only after a Supreme Court of Canada decision in 1939.[14]

The Indian Act is a wide-ranging, 'cradle-to-grave set of rules, regulations and directives.'[15] It directly or indirectly governs matters ranging from wills and estates[16] and family law matters [17] to taxation[18] and the ability of an aboriginal person or band to secure finances using reserve property as collateral:[19] 'From the time of birth, when an Indian child must be registered in one of seventeen categories defining who is an "Indian," until the time of death, when the Minister of Indian Affairs acts as executor of the deceased person's estate, our lives are ruled by the Act and the overwhelming bureaucracy that administers it.'[20] In addition to determining who was and who was not an 'Indian,' the

54 Juridical Understanding

Indian Act also established regulations for group identity and membership through the imposition of the band system. Under the current Act,[21] an Indian band is not defined by notions of group identity or integrity. Rather, a band is defined as a body of Indians: '(a) For whose use and benefit in common, lands, the legal title to which is vested in Her Majesty, have been set apart before, on or after September 4, 1951, (b) for whose use and benefit in common, moneys are held by Her Majesty, or (c) declared by the Governor in Council to be a band for the purposes of this Act.'[22] Membership in a band is determined by the band list, which is maintained in accordance with the dictates of the Act. As well as determining who was considered to be an Indian and what constituted a band, the Indian Act also instituted rules regarding the structure and election of band governments[23] and the powers that may be exercised by a band council.[24]

By determining who was or was not entitled to be recognized as an 'Indian,' what constituted a 'band,' who was entitled to membership in a particular band, and the powers that may lawfully be exercised by a band council, the imposition of the Indian Act rendered customary aboriginal governments extinct.[25] In other words, rather than allowing the aboriginal peoples to determine the composition of their own governments, as they had for centuries, the Crown decided that these people were either no longer capable of making such determinations or wanted to prevent them from doing so. In eliminating the ability of Native peoples to be self-determining and with that their traditions and choices, traditional aboriginal identities were destroyed and replaced by statutory ones.

The imposition of Indian Act governments upon aboriginal peoples with their own forms of government has resulted in conflicts between Indian Act and traditional governments, some of which have been referred to Canadian courts for adjudication.[26] The Indian Act created aboriginal disdain for the imposed system of government that was forced on them. Whatever the intentions behind its initial promulgation may have been, the Indian Act is, quite clearly, about control – control of aboriginal peoples, their lands, governments, and welfare. It renders status Indians subject to a massive bureaucracy which is not in touch with the realities of day-to-day Indian life. In bygone days, Indian agents resided near or on reserves. Although they may not have been any more sensitive to the needs of the Native peoples, there was, at least, some human contact that accompanied the governmental directives. Regardless whether governmental directions come with a face attached, the Indian Act kept Native peoples in a state of dependency by removing control over their own lives from them and suppressing their cultures.

A prime illustration of the Indian Act's use as a tool to suppress aboriginal peoples and ensure their dependency on the Crown was the addition of Section 149A to the Act in 1927.[27] Section 149A made the raising of funds for the purposes of commencing legal action against the Crown an offence. It thereby prevented aboriginal peoples from having their claims against the Crown heard in the courts without any determination of whether or not those claims were legitimate. The suppression of aboriginal religious and cultural identity was effectuated by the Indian Act's prohibition on traditional Native practices, such as various forms of dance, the wearing of ceremonial dress, and the potlach, which was effectively banned by an amendment to the Indian Act in 1884[28] that made participating in the potlach or even encouraging another person to participate an offence punishable by imprisonment:[29]

Every Indian or other person who engages in or assists in celebrating the Indian festival known as the 'potlach' or in the Indian dance known as the 'tamanawas' is guilty of a misdemeanor, and shall be liable to imprisonment for a term of not more than six nor less than two months in any gaol or other place of confinement; and any Indian or other person who encourages, either directly or indirectly, an Indian or Indians to get up such a festival or dance, or to celebrate the same, or who shall assist in the celebration of the same is guilty of a like offence, and shall be liable to the same punishment.[30]

The banning of the potlach is discussed by Ovide Mercredi and Mary Ellen Turpel in *In the Rapids: Navigating the Future of First Nations*: 'The potlach is a highly symbolic and formal sharing of identity and material wealth. It is all about extending the circle of friendships and gratefulness. The gift is important. The pleasure and honour of giving represents how highly our people value the principles of caring and responsibility. It instilled cultural values, spiritual values and social values. Why was the potlach banned? Because it violated, in the opinion of some missionaries and government officials, the values of the dominant society. It offended the idea of maximizing individual wealth or greed. The great sharing of the potlach was seen as pagan, ungodly, because too much was given away.'[31]

In 1914 what had been Section 149 of the Indian Act was altered by increasing its list of banned aboriginal practices to include the wearing of ceremonial dress: 'Any Indian in the province of Manitoba, Saskatchewan, Alberta, or British Columbia, or the Territories who par-

56 Juridical Understanding

ticipates in any Indian dance outside the bounds of his own reserve, or who participates in any show, exhibition, performance, stampede or pageant in aboriginal costume without the consent of the Superintendent General of Indian Affairs or his authorized Agent, and any person who induces or employs any Indian to take part in such dance, show, exhibition, performance, stampede or pageant, or induces any Indian to leave his reserve or employs any Indian for such a purpose, whether the dance, show, exhibition, stampede or pageant has taken place or not, shall on summary conviction to liable to a penalty not exceeding twenty-five dollars, or to imprisonment for one month, or to both penalty and imprisonment.'[32] These prohibitions remained until they were removed in 1951.[33]

As well as banning customary practices and traditions, the Crown took other measures to assert control over Native peoples through the Indian Act. One of the most significant, and shameful of these was the residential school system. Under the pretence of education, the residential school system had a far more basic motive underlying its creation – the removal of Native children from their people, languages, and traditions, and their forced assimilation into non-aboriginal society. Associate Chief Judge Murray Sinclair of the Manitoba Provincial Court, later one of the commissioners of the Manitoba Aboriginal Justice Inquiry, described the residential school system in the following manner: 'In the 1880's the Federal Government enacted amendments to the Indian Act in which Indian children were legally required to attend schools as established or directed by the Minister of Indian Affairs. This was some time before compulsory education existed for the rest of Canada. The only schools established by the Minister at that time were residential schools patterned on the industrial school model then popular in the United States for Indian children and juvenile delinquents. Indian children were taken from their parents (and from their influence), the Minister was appointed their legal guardian and they were educated in schools run sometimes by the Department, but generally by missionary societies.'[34]

Residential schools were generally located far from reserve communities geographically and even further socially and culturally. Their function was to instil Christian values into the young Native children that were brought through their doors at the expense of their own religious and cultural heritages. At the residential schools, Native languages, religion, customs, and forms of dress were forbidden. Those who disobeyed these rules were punished. As one former residential school student told the Manitoba Aboriginal Justice Inquiry: 'The elimination of language has always been a primary stage in a process of cultural genocide. This was the primary function of the residential school. My father, who attended Alberni Indian Residential School for four years in the twenties, was physically tortured by his teachers for speaking Tseshaht: they pushed sewing needles through his tongue, a routine punishment for language offenders ... The needle tortures suffered by my father affected all my family (I have six brothers and six sisters). My Dad's attitude became "why teach my children Indian if they are going to be punished for speaking it?" so he would not allow my mother to speak Indian to us in his presence. I never learned how to speak my own language. I am now, therefore, truly a "dumb Indian."'[35]

The legacy of the residential school system is its devastating results on Native languages[36] and individuals. What often occurred was the removal of young, impressionable children from their communities, only to return as older, Western-educated people who had lost the ability to converse in their own languages and were left with no sense of aboriginal identity. When they returned to their communities, they could not communicate with the older community members, and they no longer identified with their ways. Those who were less fortunate were left with various degrees of physical and emotional scarring from abusive instructors.

The Indian Act is, in many ways, a throwback to the notions of religious, moral, and intellectual superiority espoused by the European colonizing nations to justify their dispossession and subjugation of indigenous peoples in the New World.[37] If aboriginal peoples truly were intellectually inferior to Europeans, as these theories insisted, then legislating the mandatory placements of Native children into European run schools where they would learn useful European information and skills was seen to be not only just, but honourable.[38] Moreover, if aboriginal peoples were uncivilized and had no government or culture, then it was deemed equally legitimate and necessary to impose government and culture upon them through statutory means.

As well as being the underlying bases of the Indian Act, these notions of aboriginal inferiority also found their way into the *Statement of the Government of Canada on Indian Policy, 1969* – the White Paper. Through its attempt to eliminate the so-called Indian problem, the White Paper sought the assimilation of aboriginal peoples by eliminating what made them distinct in law: 'The Government believes that its policies must lead to the full, free and non-discriminatory participation of the Indian people in Canadian society. Such a goal requires a break with the past. It requires that the Indian peoples' role of dependence be replaced by a role of equal status, opportunity and responsibility, a role they can share with all other Canadians.'[39] By proposing to treat aboriginal peoples in the same manner as other members of Canadian society, the White Paper was proposing that the uniqueness of aboriginal peoples and cultures, or their 'aboriginalness,' be ignored. Equally, the White Paper's suggestions ignored the history of Crown–Native relations in Canada, as well as the duties and obligations assumed by the Crown in the various treaties, compacts, and alliances it had entered into with them from the time of contact.

On a much grander scale, the governmental policy behind both the Indian Act and the White Paper is predicated upon the validity of the granting of land via papal bulls and royal charters, or under the theories of discovery or conquest that were promoted by European colonizing nations in the sixteenth through eighteenth centuries and legitimized under the Law of Nations. Reliance on papal bulls or royal charters as granting rights to land were dismissed as ridiculous in early American aboriginal rights jurisprudence in the case of *Worcester v State of Georgia*, where Chief Justice John Marshall held that 'these grants asserted a title against Europeans only, and were considered a blank paper as far as the rights of the natives were concerned.'[40] Earlier in his judgment, Marshall CJ had explained: 'The extravagant and absurd idea, that the feeble settlements made on the sea coast, or the companies under whom they were made, acquired legitimate power by them to govern the people, or occupy the lands from sea to sea, did not enter the mind of any man ... The Crown could not be understood to grant what the crown did not affect to claim; nor was it so understood.'[41]

Theories of discovery and conquest, meanwhile, could only be binding upon aboriginal peoples if they either agreed to their formulation or accepted the theories as binding upon them. Neither of these situations ever occurred. The aboriginal peoples were never consulted about these theories as this aspect of the Law of Nations was designed exclusively to sort out competing European claims to aboriginal lands.[42] Even if aboriginal nations agreed to the application of the principles of discovery and conquest, an examination of their requirements demonstrates that they could not have granted rights to aboriginal lands in North America.

The doctrine of discovery is premised on the notion that a nation obtains title to land by virtue of its 'discovery' of land that is *terra nullius* – uninhabited land belonging to no one. Clearly, discovery could not have applied to North America. As was duly evident to the European colonizing nations, lands in North America were far from *terra nullius* upon their arrival. The only way, then, to have discovery grant rights to aboriginal lands in North America was for the Europeans to have deemed aboriginal use and possession of those lands as unimportant or as not constituting 'ownership' in the subjective and self-serving European definition of the term.

A bastardized form of discovery was popularized in aboriginal rights jurisprudence by its use in the early American case of *Johnson and Graham's Lessee v M'Intosh*.[43] In the *Johnson* case, Marshall CJ described a different version of discovery that he stated was applied, out of necessity, by European nations in order to regulate their competing claims to North American lands: 'But, as they were all in pursuit of nearly the same object, it was necessary, in order to avoid conflicting settlements, and consequent war with each other, to establish a principle, which all should acknowledge as the law by which the right of acquisition, which they all asserted, should be regulated as between themselves. This principle was, that discovery gave title to the government by whose subjects or by whose authority it was made, against all other European governments, which title might be consummated by possession.'[44]

As Marshall CJ's comments indicate, this form of discovery granted only partial rights to land. It was valid only against other European governments who subscribed to and were bound by the Law of Nations. It required that possession be consummated before it granted full rights. Most importantly, it did not give actual title to the 'discovered' lands; it merely gave a pre-emptive right to the discovering nation to acquire title from the Native inhabitants: 'The exclusion of all other Europeans, necessarily gave to the nation making the discovery *the sole right of acquiring the soil from the natives*, and establishing settlements upon it. It was a right with which no Europeans could interfere. It was a right which all asserted for themselves, and to the assertion of which, by others, all assented'[45] (emphasis added). Indeed, as Marshall CJ later explained in *Worcester v State of Georgia*: 'This principle, acknowledged by all Europeans, because it was in the interest of all to acknowledge it, gave to the nation making the discovery, as its inevitable consequence, the sole right of *acquiring* the soil and of making settlements on it. It was an exclusive principle which shut out the right of competition among those who had agreed to it; not one which could annul the previous rights of those who had not agreed to it. *It regulated the right given by discovery among the European discoverers; but could not affect the rights of those already in possession*, either as aboriginal occupants, or as occupants by virtue of a discovery made before the memory of man'[46] (emphasis added).

It is evident that the reason for this modified form of discovery was based on the inability to properly describe North American lands as *terra nullius*, combined with Marshall CJ's reasoning that some method of precluding competing claims for the right to obtain title from the Native inhabitants was needed. But, as Marshall CJ made clear, this 'title by discovery' was not the same as the title granted under the principles of discovery sanctioned by the Law of Nations; it gave the European discoverer only a right to purchase the title possessed by the aboriginal peoples. However, like the notion of discovery sanctioned by the Law of Nations, Marshall CJ's modified doctrine of discovery could only have dispossessed the aboriginal peoples if their rights were deemed by the Europeans to be somehow less than those of the European nations who asserted rights to their lands.

Conquest theory is also ineffective in granting European nations title to aboriginal lands. In its true form, conquest theory requires that a people be conquered militarily before sovereignty over them and their lands could be acquired. Even after such a conquest, the rights of the conquered nation remain until such time as the conquering nation explicitly abrogates or eliminates them entirely through executive action, such as the passing of laws or the issuing of a proclamation.[47] As Canada was neither conquered, nor, even if it was conquered, were aboriginal rights extinguished through executive action, conquest theory cannot demonstrate the existence of a valid title to land in Canada.

Despite their evident invalidity when scrutinized for their effects upon aboriginal lands in North America, these theories of discovery and conquest provide the basis for colonialist attitudes which underlie some of the most important cases in Canadian aboriginal rights jurisprudence. In particular, the landmark decisions in *St Catherine's Milling and Lumber Co v The Queen*[48] and *R v Sparrow*,[49] which were decided more than a hundred years apart, are each based, in different ways, on accepting the colonialist rhetoric espoused through the doctrines of discovery and conquest.

In *St Catherine's Milling* the Privy Council's decision that the aboriginal interest in land amounted only to a 'personal and usufructuary right, dependent upon the goodwill of the Sovereign'[50] is a straightforward indication of the judiciary's acceptance of colonialist theory. By holding that aboriginal rights were dependent on their recognition and acceptance by the Crown, as indicated in a Crown grant, the Privy Council was affirming the Crown's right to sovereignty over both Canada and the aboriginal peoples. The Privy Council's explanation of how the Crown acquired its sovereignty over Canada focused exclusively on Britain's acquisition of the rights belonging to France upon the latter's conquest.

Additionally, in accordance with the adherence to legal positivism at the time of the *St Catherine's Milling* decision, in which legal rights could only be derived from the state, the Privy Council held that aboriginal rights could only exist insofar as they had been explicitly recognized by legislative or executive recognition: 'Their possession, such as it was, can only be ascribed to the general provisions made by the royal proclamation in favour of all Indian tribes then living under the sovereignty and protection of the British Crown.'[51] The positivistic bias in the Privy Council's decision in *St Catherine's Milling* may also be found in the Supreme Court of Canada's decision in the very same case, particularly in the judgment rendered by Taschereau J:

Now when by the treaty of 1763, France ceded to Great Britain all her rights of sovereignty, property and possession over Canada ... it is unquestionable that the full title to the territory ceded became vested in the new sovereign, and that he thereafter owned it ... in as full and ample a manner as the King of France had previously owned it ... To exclude from the full operation of the cession by France all the lands then occupied by the Indians, would be to declare that not an inch of land thereby passed to the King of England, as, at that time, the whole of the unpatented lands of Canada were in their possession in as full and ample a manner as the 57,000 square miles of the territory in dispute can be said to be in possession of the 26,000 Indians who roam over it.

Now, when did the Sovereign of Great Britain ever divest himself of the ownership of these lands to vest it in the Indians? When did the title pass from the Sovereign to the Indians? Not by any letters patent.

...

The words 'for the present,' in this and the next clause [of the Royal Proclamation of 1763], are equivalent to a reservation by the king of his right, thereafter or at any time, to grant these lands when he would think it proper to do so ... Is that, in law, granting to these Indians a full title to the soil, a title to those lands? Did the sovereign thereby divest himself of the ownership of this territory? I cannot adopt that conclusion, nor can I see anything in that proclamation that gives to the Indians forever the right in law to the possession of any lands as against the crown. Their occupancy under that document has been one by sufferance only.[52]

In the Supreme Court of Canada's decision in *Sparrow*, an aboriginal fishing rights case, the Supreme Court was thrust headlong into an examination of the rights contained within Section 35(1) of the Constitution Act, 1982.[53] This required the court to examine the historical background to the promulgation of Section 35(1), beginning with British policy on aboriginal affairs. In the very first sentence of the judgment dealing with this issue, the court stated: 'It is worth recalling that while British policy towards the native population was based on respect for their right to occupy their traditional lands, a proposition to which the Royal Proclamation of 1763 bears witness, there was from the outset never any doubt that sovereignty and legislative power, and indeed the underlying title, to such lands vested in the Crown.'[54] The colonialist underpinnings of such a bold, uncircumscribed statement leap off the page.

By holding that 'there was from the outset never any doubt' of the Crown's sovereignty in Canada, the *Sparrow* decision firmly entrenched itself in colonialist jurisprudence. Like *St Catherine's Milling* more than one hundred years previously, *Sparrow* rooted its most basic assumptions in the fact that aboriginal rights could only exist through Crown grant. By necessary implication, then, aboriginal rights were deemed by the *Sparrow* court to have no independent existence of their own. In line with the reasoning provided in *St Catherine's Milling*, before the British Crown obtained sovereignty over Canada, aboriginal rights were dependent on their recognition by the French Crown. The obvious flaw in this reasoning is illustrated by the query which inevitably flows from the argument – 'Did aboriginal rights exist prior to the arrival of France in Canada and, if so, on what basis?' Neither the *Sparrow* nor the *St Catherine's Milling* decisions are equipped to deal with this logical extension of their own arguments.

On a macroscopic level there are two primary theories of aboriginal rights in Canada. One is a contingent rights approach, the other an inherent rights approach.[55] The contingent rights approach is an extension of positivism. Under this approach aboriginal rights exist only where they are explicitly recognized, such as in the constitution, by legislative or executive action, in treaties, or via judicial recognition. It takes as fundamental the notion that the Canadian state is the fountain of rights from which all others flow. Inherent rights theory, on the other hand, holds that aboriginal rights pre-existed any European assertions of sovereignty in Canada. Consequently, aboriginal rights exist independently of such sovereignty or its logical extensions. The inherent rights approach adopts the position that aboriginal rights 'inhere in the very meaning of aboriginality.'[56]

The *St Catherine's Milling* decision adheres entirely to the contingent rights approach. The *Sparrow* decision, although showing strong elements of inherent rights theory,[57] ultimately betrays this position through its assertion that ultimate sovereignty and rights emanate from the Crown.[58] Both decisions do, however, share the same underlying basis: the unquestioned acceptance of the Crown's sovereignty over Canada and aboriginal peoples. They each accept the proposition that the Crown possesses ultimate sovereignty and title to all lands in Canada, though the latter is subject to the aboriginal 'burden' on that title.[59] In making these findings, the court in each instance adopted the instruments of colonialist legal theory. The judiciary's adherence to colonialist theory is not restricted to these two decisions, though.[60] Aside from the implications on these particular cases and the precedents they created, the judiciary's adherence to colonialist legal theory in these cases has given legitimacy to governmental legislative initiatives, such as the Indian Act and the residential school system, by treating aboriginal peoples as inferiors who are unable to manage their lands or govern their own affairs.

Summary

The effects of colonialism have resulted in serious social costs to aboriginal peoples. It almost lost them the use of their languages and cultures. It took away their control over their lands and resources by requiring that surrenders only be made to the Crown. It attempted to take away their identities by removing their ability to determine their membership and method of government. The cumulative effect of British colonialism was to weaken Native peoples and their communities: 'Long-standing policies of assimilation and diminution of First Nations spirituality and values – through such vehicles as the residential school system – have undermined First Nations individuals and weakened communities. These experiences have resurfaced in First Nations communities in the form of alcoholism and substance abuse, family violence, depression and suicide. Skyrocketing rates of diabetes, heart disease, fetal alcohol syndrome and mental disorders have created a health care crisis that is a by-product of the assimilation mentality that has insisted on changing First Nations lifestyles to suit southern Canada's industrial society. The social, health and economic problems of those living in urban areas are equally apparent.'[61] This is the backdrop against which any discussion of aboriginal issues, including the notion of the Crown–Native fiduciary relationship, must take place.

Although overt policies of assimilation, such as the residential school system and the White Paper, have been shelved in favour of the recognition and protection of aboriginal rights through Sections 25 and 35 of the Constitution Act, 1982, the effects of British colonialism on aboriginal peoples in Canada are still being felt. Even with the federal government's pilot project of dismantling the Department of Indian Affairs in the province of Manitoba, colonialist attitudes continue to deeply affect aboriginal peoples. The Indian Act and its forcible imposition of foreign concepts and governments upon the Native peoples is still in force. Aboriginal rights, though constitutionalized, remain vague and ill-defined. The notion of aboriginal land interests, as understood by the common law, remains subordinate to that of the Crown. More important, the notion of absolute Crown sovereignty, as espoused in *St Catherine's Milling* and *Sparrow*, remains a source of contempt for native peoples within the Canadian legal system.

The process of colonialism meant that the Crown's sovereign relations with the aboriginal peoples that had been honed over centuries were left to decay in mere decades. The Crown renounced responsibility for the sovereign alliances that it had voluntarily entered into and the resultant responsibilities that it had undertaken through the terms of various Indian treaties and compacts in favour of achieving its long-standing colonialist goal in North America. Yet, in the process of the decay of their unique relationship, the Crown continued to enter into treaties with the aboriginal peoples and to affirm to them the sovereign nature of their rights and status in Canada.[62] The Crown's justification of its activities under the rule of law, however, was as faulty as the very foundations of the colonialist doctrines on which its claim to absolute sovereignty over Canada was based.

The Crown's justifications of discovery or conquest as the basis of its sovereignty in Canada were not only invalid under the principles of the Law of Nations in effect at the time, but its repudiation of the solemn commitments, responsibilities, and obligations that it incurred in its interaction with the Native peoples – such as by the Indian Act's disempowerment of aboriginal peoples – offended the principles of fiduciary doctrine embodied in the Crown's own laws which it was bound to obey. Whereas fiduciary law may not have been understood to govern the formative years of Crown–Native relations,[63] its principles and rules were part of the jurisdiction belonging to the law of Equity prior to the origins of those relations.[64] As will become clear in the ensuing chapters, the Crown's colonialist actions were inconsistent with the dictates of fiduciary law. Rather, the Crown's activities were governed by its desire for land, minerals, and increased settlement at the direct expense of the aboriginal peoples. Therefore, the assertion that the Crown invoked the rule of law as the basis for its colonialist activities is false.

With the de facto, if not de jure, sovereignty of the Crown existing as a Canadian reality, the application of common law and equitable doctrines within Canada is legitimate under the rule of law.[65] Therefore, when the Crown enters into relationships with the aboriginal peoples that are of a fiduciary nature, the Crown is bound by the dictates of fiduciary doctrine. This is the basis on which the application of fiduciary doctrine to the Crown–Native relationship in Canada ought to be reflected in Canadian legislation and jurisprudence relating to Native peoples.

4

The Legislative and Jurisprudential History of the Crown–Native Relationship in Canada

The British Crown's balancing of its colonialist ambitions with its recognition and affirmation of aboriginal sovereignty that characterized Britain's relations with the aboriginal peoples of Canada from contact through to the late eighteenth century is also reflected in Canadian legislation and jurisprudence relating to Native peoples. Prior to the *Guerin* decision, though, contemplation of the relationship between the Crown and Native peoples in legislative and jurisprudential spheres focused entirely on trust law, not fiduciary doctrine.

Aside from its position as a major turning point in Canadian aboriginal rights jurisprudence, the shift from trust law to fiduciary doctrine in the Supreme Court of Canada's decision in *Guerin* marked a significant departure from previous judicial analysis of the legal nature of Crown–Native relations. The Musqueam band's arguments and the treatment of the matter by the courts at trial and on its initial appeal regarded *Guerin* as a trust case. Indeed, only eighteen months prior to *Guerin*'s release, a major research report entitled 'The First Nations and the Crown: A Study of Trust Relationships' was prepared for the Special Committee of the House of Commons on Indian Self-Government.[1] There was no discussion of fiduciary relationships and their distinction from trust relationships anywhere in the report.[2] Based on the jurisprudential and legislative history of the Crown–Native relationship, however, the exclusive focus on trust law prior to the Supreme Court's decision in *Guerin* is hardly surprising.[3]

The Legislative History of the Crown–Native Relationship

Once Britain had assumed a greater degree of control over North America, it sought to establish a new Indian policy to replace the haphazardness that characterized previous Crown–Native relations. However, the implementation of this new Indian policy was limited primarily to what eventually became Upper and Lower Canada. In the rest of Canada, pre-Confederation Indian policy, where it existed, took on a vastly different character.

In Rupert's Land pre-Confederation government rested in the hands of the Hudson's Bay Company. Whereas in the Rupert's Land Charter, 1670,[4] Charles II of Britain granted the Hudson's Bay Company exclusive rights of trade and commerce over all lands lying between the rivers and lakes flowing into Hudson Bay, as a commercial enterprise, during the 200 years that it reigned supreme in the territory the Hudson's Bay Company was more interested in the proliferation of trade than in aboriginal rights. in 1869 Rupert's Land was surrendered by the Hudson's Bay Company to the Crown. The territory was then admitted into Confederation via the Rupert's Land and North-Western Territory Order, 1870.[5]

Aboriginal rights were virtually ignored in the Maritimes prior to Confederation, despite the fact that most Indian bands in the region had signed treaties of peace and friendship with the Crown following the Treaty of Utrecht. Britain did not believe that it needed to enter into many land cession treaties with Native peoples in the region as it had acquired Acadia by cession from France under the treaty in 1713. It remains open to question, then, why Britain entered into these peace and friendship treaties if the aboriginal peoples were not sovereign nations who were independent of Britain?[6]

The major pre-Confederation Indian policy initiative in the Maritimes occurred in 1762, when Lieutenant-Governor Jonathan Belcher of Nova Scotia issued a proclamation which protected the aboriginal peoples and their lands, and recognized their rights to hunt and fish over much of the colony. It was issued in response to the Royal Proclamation of 1761, a precursor of the Royal Proclamation of 1763, with substantially the same content regarding Native peoples.[7]

Shortly after its issue, Belcher's Proclamation was annulled, and the terms of the earlier peace and friendship treaties[8] largely ignored, leaving Crown–Native relations in the region dubious at best. When Cape Breton and Prince Edward Island were acquired by Britain under the Treaty of Paris, 1763, indigenous rights in those areas were simply ignored. No significant Indian legislation was promulgated in the Maritimes until 1842, when Nova Scotia passed legislation which appointed a commissioner for Indian affairs.[9] Later, both Nova Scotia and New Brunswick implemented legislation governing Indian reserves which remained in effect until superseded by federal Indian legislation.[10] On the whole, the Maritime provinces did not take the issue of aboriginal rights seriously, providing little legislative instruction or guidance and leaving the Native peoples on their own to combat the effects of colonialism on their lands and rights.[11]

Even prior to British Columbia's entrance into Confederation in 1871, its Indian policy was more firmly established than that in the Maritimes. This occurred for two distinct reasons. Unlike in other regions, Indian policy in British Columbia was an entirely local concern, as Britain had relinquished control over Indian affairs to the local administration. More importantly, the colonial administration rested in the hands of the Hudson's Bay Company, which had been granted the colony of Vancouver Island by royal charter in 1849. As with the situation in Rupert's Land, the Hudson's Bay Company was more interested in the proliferation of trade than in aboriginal rights. The combination of the Hudson Bay Company's preoccupation with commercial rather than colonizing interests and the colony's lack of attraction to potential colonists resulted in sparse settlement until the second half of the nineteenth century.

The essence of Indian policy in British Columbia was straightforward: the local administration consistently and vehemently denied the existence of aboriginal title to land. The colonial administration set aside some Indian reserves, but not as a result of its recognition of aboriginal title. Moreover, little or no financial support was provided to the aboriginal peoples. Not surprisingly, few Indian treaties were ever negotiated and signed in British Columbia, even after the influx of settlers in the middle of the nineteenth century. The reason for the vastly different treatment of aboriginal peoples in British Columbia was largely the result of its geographical position and late settlement. By the time the colony possessed a sizeable population, Britain was well entrenched in North America, and the Native peoples had been marginalized militarily and politically through the incidence of colonialism.[12]

The greater part of structured Indian policy and legislation in what was to become Canada was centred in the geographic centre of the country, which would become Upper and Lower Canada in 1791. In 1755 Sir William Johnson was appointed as superintendent-general of Indian affairs in the north district of British North America in an attempt to consolidate and develop a unified Indian policy.[13] Prior to this various Indian agents appointed to oversee specific regions of British control were more or less responsible for formulating their own Indian policies with the groups occupying those regions. The appointment of Johnson centralized and solidified Crown–Native relations, while expanding the number of Britain's Indian allies.

In 1837 the report of the Select Committee on Aborigines, which had been convened to discuss British practices regarding the indigenous inhabitants of its various colonial possessions, arrived at the following conclusions: 'This, then, appears to be the moment for the nation to declare, that with all its desire to give encouragement to emigration, and to find a soil to which our surplus population may retreat, it will tolerate no scheme which implies violence or fraud in taking possession of such a territory; that it will no longer subject itself to the guilt of conniving at oppression, and that it will take upon itself the task of defending those who are too weak and too ignorant to defend themselves.'[14] One of the primary recommendations of the select committee was the centralization of Indian affairs in order to protect the aboriginals from adverse local interests. This recommendation was later adopted by the province of Canada on the recommendation of the Bagot Commission, which had been established to investigate Indian policy in the province.[15] Until around 1850 the increasing centralization of responsibility over Indian affairs was the only truly significant change to the Crown's Indian policy in Canada.

Beginning in the middle of the nineteenth century, Indian legislation which made extensive use of trust and fiduciary terms was enacted in the province. In 1849 legislation entitled, 'An Act for the Protection of the Lands of the Crown in this Province from Trespass and Injury and to Make Further Provision for that Purpose,' was promulgated to apply to all lands in Upper Canada 'whether the same be held in trust or in the nature of a trust for the use of the Indians or of any parties whomsoever.'[16] The following year the first piece of legislation providing for the management and control of Indian lands was passed. It expressly used trust terminology in describing the Crown's holding of Indian lands in Lower Canada on behalf of Indian bands: 'That it shall be lawful for the Governor to appoint from time to time a Commissioner of Indian Lands for Lower Canada, in whom and in whose successors by the name aforesaid, all lands or property in Lower Canada which are or shall be set apart or appropriated to or for the use of any Tribe or Body of Indians, shall be and are hereby vested, in trust for such Tribe or Body.'[17]

When the Imperial government relinquished its control over Indian affairs to the province of Canada in 1860, legislation passed to deal with

70 Juridical Understanding

the management of Indian matters included a recognition of the Crown's obligations to manage Indian lands, moneys, and properties in the manner of a fiduciary: 'The Governor in Council may, subject to the provisions of this Act, direct how and in what manner, and by whom, the monies arising from sales of Indian lands and from the property held or to be held in Trust, for the Indians, shall be invested from time to time, and how the payments to which the Indians may be entitled shall be made, and shall provide for the general management of such lands, monies, and property, and what percentage or proportion thereof shall be set apart, from time to time, to cover the cost of such management under the provisions of this Act.'[18] By Confederation, it was not unusual to find the use of trust or fiduciary terminology in Indian legislation in the province of Canada.

Upon Confederation the special relationship between the Crown and Native peoples in the newly created Dominion of Canada was given constitutional recognition. Under the British North America Act, 1867, absolute legislative authority over 'Indians, and Lands reserved for the Indians' was given to the Dominion of Canada by Section 91(24) of the Act. Recognition of Section 91(24)'s continuation of the Crown's special duty to the aboriginal peoples was exemplified by the statement made by Gwynne J in *Ontario Mining Company v Seybold*, where he stated that the lands in question in that instance '[S]hould be regarded ... as lands vested in Her Majesty in trust for the sole use and benefit of the Indians upon the terms and conditions agreed upon as those upon which the trust was accepted by Her Majesty; and, as I have already said, it was, in my opinion, for the purpose of maintaining unimpaired a continuance of that condition of things that the subject "Indians and lands reserved for the Indians" was placed under the exclusive legislative authority of the Dominion Parliament.'[19]

Shortly after Confederation the Crown embodied is historical obligations to the aboriginal peoples in the Rupert's Land and North-Western Territory Order, 1870,[20] and the British Columbia Terms of Union, 1871,[21] which respectively admitted Rupert's Land and British Columbia into the Dominion of Canada. In each of these documents trust or fiduciary language was used to denote the Crown's responsibility for the Native peoples residing in the areas affected. The preamble to the Rupert's Land and North-Western Territory Order notes the Crown's approval of the terms and conditions contained in resolutions made by the Canadian Parliament on 28 May 1869 regarding the transfer of the territories.[22] The resolutions included the following undertaking: '[U]pon transference of the territories in question to the Canadian Government, it will be our duty to make adequate provision for the protection of the Indian tribes whose interests and well-being are involved in the transfer.'[23] Meanwhile, Clause 13 of the British Columbia Terms of Union, which transferred the responsibility for Indians and Indian policy in British Columbia to Canada, stated: 'The charge of the Indians, and the trusteeship and management of the lands reserved for their use and benefit, shall be assumed by the Dominion Government, and a policy as liberal as that hitherto pursued by the British Columbia Government shall be continued by the Dominion Government after the Union.'

The trust-like nature of the Crown's duty towards the aboriginal peoples was once again highlighted in federal legislation promulgated in 1912 to extend the geographical boundaries of Ontario and Quebec. Section 2 in each of the respective Acts, commonly referred to as the Ontario and Quebec Boundary Extension Acts, states: "That the trusteeship of the Indians in the said territory, and the management of any lands now or hereafter reserved for their use, shall remain in the Government of Canada subject to the control of Parliament.'[24]

In 1930 the Natural Resource Transfer Agreements between the federal government and the provinces of Manitoba, Saskatchewan, and Alberta again contained provisions that highlighted the Crown's responsibilities towards Native peoples. These agreements, which transferred the beneficial ownership of land and natural resources from the federal Crown to the provincial Crowns, specifically employed language that indicated the special relationship between the Crown and Native peoples:

All lands included in Indian reserves within the Province, including those selected and surveyed but not yet confirmed, as well as those confirmed, shall continue to be vested in the Crown and administered by the Government of Canada for the purposes of Canada, and the Province will from time to time, upon the request of the Superintendent General of Indian Affairs, set aside, out of the unoccupied Crown lands hereby transferred to its administration, such further areas as the said Superintendent General may, in agreement with the appropriate Minister of the Province, select as necessary to enable Canada to fulfill its obligations under the treaties with the Indians of the Province, and such areas shall thereafter be administered by Canada in the same way in all respects as if they had never passed to the Province under the provisions hereof.[25]

Ultimately, the Crown's constitutional responsibility to protect 'Indians' in Section 91(24) was further strengthened by the inclusion of the Crown's duty and the concomitant obligations flowing from it in the Constitution Act, 1982. The constitutional guarantee of aboriginal and treaty rights is contained within Section 35 of the Constitution Act, 1982, which reads as follows:

35(1) The existing aboriginal and treaty rights of the aboriginal peoples of Canada are hereby recognized and affirmed.
 (2) In this Act, 'aboriginal peoples of Canada' includes the Indian, Inuit and Métis peoples of Canada.
 (3) For greater certainty, in subsection (1) 'treaty rights' includes rights that now exist by way of land claims agreements or may be so acquired.
 (4) Notwithstanding any other provisions of this Act, the aboriginal and treaty rights referred to in subsection (1) are guaranteed equally to male and female persons.

Section 25 of the Act modifies and explains the rights guaranteed by Section 35(1) as well as constitutionally entrenching the rights contained in the Royal Proclamation of 1763 and 'any other rights or freedoms that pertain to the aboriginal peoples of Canada.' It also protects those rights from being abrogated or derogated from by the Charter of Rights and Freedoms:

25 The guarantee in this Charter of certain rights and freedoms shall not be construed so as to abrogate or derogate from any aboriginal, treaty, or other rights or freedoms that pertain to the aboriginal peoples of Canada including
 (a) any rights or freedoms that have been recognized by the Royal Proclamation of October 7, 1763; and
 (b) any rights or freedoms that now exist by way of land claims agreements or may be so acquired.

The combination of the entrenchment of aboriginal and treaty rights in the Constitution Act, 1982, and the history of Crown–Native relations which precipitated the constitutionalization of those rights illuminates both the unique nature of the Crown–Native relationship and the former's duty to the latter.

Despite these references to the *sui generis* nature of the Crown–Native relationship, the central legislative area where the Crown's duty to aboriginal peoples has been highlighted most vividly is in the Indian Act. In 1876 all post-Confederation Indian legislation was consolidated

Legislative and Jurisprudential History 73

into the very first Indian Act.[26] The 1876 Indian Act remained relatively unchanged until the next major consolidation of Indian legislation in 1951. Until 1951 the act made extensive use of trust and trust-like terminology. However, all trust references were removed in the 1951 Indian Act[27] and omitted in all subsequent versions of the act. Curiously, the removal of these references coincides with the last of the major Indian trust cases decided by the Supreme Court of Canada prior to the *Guerin* decision in 1984, in which the trust-like wording of the Indian Act played a major role.[28]

The elimination of trust terminology in the Indian Act may be seen by juxtaposing the 1951 act with its predecessors. Section 4 of the 1876 Indian Act and Section 18(1) of the 1951 Indian Act, for example, both deal with the holding of Indian reserve lands. Section 4 of the 1876 Act clearly makes use of trust terminology: 'All reserves for Indians or for any band of Indians, *or held in trust* for their benefit, shall be deemed to be reserved and held for the same purposes as before the passing of this Act, but subject to its provision' [emphasis added]. Section 18(1) of the 1951 Act eliminated the use of trust terminology, yet retained the use of fiduciary terms to describe the Crown–Native relationship: 'Subject to the provisions of this Act, reserves *shall be held by His Majesty for the use and benefit of the respective bands* for which they were set apart; and subject to this Act and to the terms of any treaty or surrender, the Governor in Council may determine whether any purpose for which lands in a reserve are used or are to be used is for the use and benefit of the band' [emphasis added].

This brief history of Indian legislation in Canada indicates that there has long been an acknowledgment of the Crown's historical duty to the aboriginal peoples in most of the country. This duty was recognized, at the very latest, by the Royal Proclamation of 1763, which itself codified the Crown's assumption of responsibility dating back to the time of contact. The numerous treaties entered into between the Crown and its representatives and Native peoples in Canada further highlight the Crown's assumption and assertion of a fiduciary responsibility towards Native peoples.[29]

The Jurisprudential History of the Crown–Native Relationship

Judicial recognition of the Crown's duty to aboriginal peoples, if not in its explicit, post-*Guerin* form of understanding, has existed from the early stages of Canadian aboriginal rights jurisprudence. In the 1846 case of *Brown v West*, Robinson CJ[30] expressly recognized the Crown's role as protector of Native peoples: 'The government, we know, always made it their care to protect the Indians, so far as they could, in the enjoyment of their property, and to guard them against being imposed upon and dispossessed by the white inhabitants.'[31] Twelve years later, Robinson CJ again affirmed the historical nature of the Crown–Native relationship in *Totten v Watson*: 'From the earliest period the Government has always endeavoured, by proclamation and otherwise, to deter the white inhabitants from settling upon Indian lands, or from pretending to acquire them by purchase or lease.'[32]

In the latter part of the nineteenth century, the judiciary began to have greater opportunities to consider the legal effect of the Crown's undertaking to protect aboriginal peoples, their rights, and their lands through instruments such as the Royal Proclamation of 1763, Indian legislation, and the terms of Indian treaties. This resulted from an increase in the number of cases which raised the question of the Crown's duty towards Native peoples as a subsidiary issue.[33] In some of these cases the Crown was said to possess distinct trust or trust-like obligations to Native peoples.[34] In others the Crown was held either to have only a moral or political duty to the aboriginal peoples or no obligations to them whatsoever.[35]

A notable characterization of the Crown's duty to aboriginal peoples came in *Re Kane*, an otherwise minor case which discussed that duty as a subsidiary issue.[36] Eleven Indians from the Caughenewaga reserve in Quebec, who worked in Sydney, Nova Scotia, in the summer of 1939, had been jailed for their failure to pay a municipal poll tax imposed under the Sydney City Charter. The issue before the court was whether the Indians should have been made subject to the poll tax and to imprisonment on their failure to pay it. In finding that the Indians were not subject to the poll tax, McArthur J based his conclusion on the nature of the relationship of the Crown and aboriginal peoples, which he found to be of a fiduciary or trust-like quality: 'For reasons which are quite apparent, the Indian has been placed under the guardianship of the Dominion Government. He is its ward, so long as he remains unenfranchised, and the Minister of the Interior, as Superintendent General of Indian Affairs, is given the control and management of all lands and property of Indians in Canada. *They are looked upon and treated as requiring the friendly care and directing hand of the Government in the management of their affairs.* They and their property are, so to speak, under the protecting wing of the Dominion Government, and I do not think in such circumstances, it was

Legislative and Jurisprudential History 75

ever contemplated that the body of an Indian should be taken in execution under a civil process pure and simple'[37] (emphasis added). The limited discussion of the specific nature of the Crown's duty to Native peoples in the majority of pre-*Guerin* jurisprudence is not particularly helpful or insightful. The nature and effects of the Crown's duty are not discussed in any detail in most of these cases as these were raised only as subsidiary elements of other issues. There are five cases, however, in which the precise nature of the Crown's duty to the aboriginal peoples and the effects of that duty was the central issue.

Henry v The King[38]

The *Henry* decision, released in 1905, was the first major case which centred around the legal definition of the relationship between the Crown and Native peoples in Canada. The Mississaugas of the Credit Indian band sought a declaration, by petition of right, that band moneys which had incorrectly been paid into the general accounts of the dominion government be repaid or restored, with interest thereon, to band funds held in trust by the Crown. The moneys claimed by the band had been promised to it under the terms of a surrender dated 28 February 1820. They were to be used for the maintenance and religious instruction of the band out of profits from the Crown's sale or lease of the surrendered lands. The band also sought the enforced payment of an annuity owing under a land surrender treaty dated 28 October 1818 which the Crown had ceased paying in the 1889–90 fiscal year.

Upon Confederation, the debts of the province of Canada, including the amounts owed to the band,[39] were assumed by the Dominion of Canada through the operation of Section 111 of the British North America Act, 1867.[40] In 1883, by virtue of the conclusions contained in an 1858 report authored by a special commission appointed to investigate Indian matters in the province of Canada, the band was credited with additional money. However, although the Department of Indian Affairs spent the additional money on the band's behalf under the authority of an Order in Council authorizing the transfer of funds from the dominion's consolidated revenue fund to the band's trust fund, the matter had not yet been finalized.[41]

A second Order in Council authorized the inclusion of the additional sum in the items of account to be considered in the settlement of pre-Confederation debts between the treasurers of Ontario and Quebec and the Dominion of Canada rather than charging it to the consolidated revenue fund.[42] When a third Order in Council was passed ten years later, on 26 October 1894, charging Indian Affairs' expenditure of interest against the band's capital account, the balance of the account had already been paid out to the band or on its behalf. Some of the money that had been distributed to the band for its maintenance on an annual basis between 1884 and 1894 had been taken from the band's capital funds rather than from the income obtained under the treaties. The band claimed that the federal Crown's actions were in breach of its trust obligations to the band.

The band claimed that the Crown was a trustee in respect of Indian lands and moneys on the basis of the provisions contained in pre- and post-Confederation Indian legislation. As the band's trustee, the Crown was alleged to be responsible to replace the moneys wrongfully taken out of the band's capital account and to continue to pay the annuity. The Crown denied the existence of any trust relationship between it and the band. The Crown submitted that the statutes governing the administration of Indian trust funds by the Crown did not create a trust or other equitable obligation on the Crown, but were to be read merely as 'statutes relating to the administration.'[43] Moreover, the Crown argued that the surrender documents neither constituted a declaration of trust nor otherwise imbued it with a trustee's obligations.

The Crown's argument was premised on the notion that it could not be a trustee unless it explicitly and voluntarily assumed such a role or had that function imposed on it by an act of Parliament. Absent such an occurrence, the Crown insisted that it could not be held in law to be a trustee. The Crown's argument was based on the 'political trust' doctrine, which became prominent during the latter part of the nineteenth century[44] and states that the Crown may be a trustee, with responsibilities that may be similar or identical to those of a normal trustee, but only of a morally binding political trust which is unenforceable in the courts. In the absence of the necessary circumstances to render it a trustee of a legally enforceable trust, the Crown claimed that any obligation to the band existed only at the Crown's pleasure.

As a preliminary matter the Exchequer Court had to determine whether it had jurisdiction to entertain the band's claim. Initially, Burbidge J determined that the moneys arising from the sale of the surrendered lands were held in trust for the band: '[W]ith regard to the moneys arising from the sale of the lands surrendered by the Mississaugas of the Credit, it is clear, I think, that the Crown holds them in trust for that band of Indians. By the terms of the surrender of the 28th of February,

Legislative and Jurisprudential History 77

1820, to which reference has been made, the lands were to be held upon the trust therein mentioned.'[45] Despite this finding, Burbidge J determined that the many legislative references to lands or moneys being held in trust by the Crown for Indian bands did not provide the Exchequer Court with jurisdiction to enforce those trusts or to make a declaration as to the rights of the parties.

Under Section 15 of the Exchequer Court Act,[46] the court only possessed jurisdiction in cases where a 'demand was made or relief sought which might in England to be the subject of an action against the Crown'; where the Crown held land, goods, or money of the subject; or where the claim arose from a contract entered into by or on behalf of the Crown.[47] Under the limits imposed by the Exchequer Court Act, Burbidge J determined that there were three possible bases on which the Exchequer Court could have jurisdiction to hear the band's claim under Section 15 of the Act: that the Crown was a trustee for the band; that the Crown was in possession of the moneys claimed by the band; and that the band's claim rested on the terms of the 1818 and 1820 surrenders.

Burbidge J denied jurisdiction to hear the band's claim that the Crown was its trustee as there had been no case in England in which relief was given against the Crown as trustee. Burbidge J also denied the court's jurisdiction on the basis that the Crown still had possession of band moneys. He found that the relief sought by the band was in respect of *moneys which were no longer in the Crown's possession*, even if, as alleged, the moneys ought to have been in the Crown's possession.[48] Burbidge J did determine, however, that the court possessed jurisdiction to hear the band's claim on the basis of the 1818 and 1820 surrenders, as the claim was analogous to the court's jurisdiction over contracts entered into by or on behalf of the Crown. Additionally, Burbidge J held that Section 16(d) of the Exchequer Court Act, which granted jurisdiction to hear any claim against the Crown arising under any law of Canada, conferred jurisdiction on the court to hear the band's claim as it was based on Section 111 of the British North America Act, 1867, and acts of the Legislature of the Province of Canada and the Parliament of Canada.

Despite his earlier finding that the moneys arising from the sale of the surrendered lands were held in trust for the band, Burbidge J concluded that the Crown was not an ordinary trustee and could not be bound to the responsibilities of an ordinary trustee. He based his conclusion on the grounds that (1) the Crown did not execute the trust personally, but through the Parliament of Canada, which, in turn, subdelegated the

78 Juridical Understanding

responsibility to the superintendent-general of Indian affairs; (2) that Parliament alone had the authority to review any decisions made or actions taken on behalf of the Crown;[49] (3) that the Crown was not bound by estoppels[50] and could not have laches[51] imputed to it; and (4) that the Crown ought not to be penalized by the negligence of its officers.[52]

Burbidge J also determined that the Crown was not responsible for replacing the moneys expended by the Crown on the band's behalf out of the band's capital fund rather than from the income obtained under the 1820 indenture as the Crown's actions were neither in violation of the terms of the indenture nor of any statute. Burgidge J did find that the Crown was responsible to pay the annuity under the 1818 treaty, but that the Crown's obligation to pay the annuity rendered it a debtor of the band, not a trustee. As the Crown's obligation was based on the terms of the treaty and Section 111 of the British North America Act, 1867, Burbidge J found that the Exchequer Court had jurisdiction to enforce the payment of the annuity.

The *Henry* case is an early judicial indication that, under certain circumstances, the Crown owes equitable obligations[53] to Native peoples in Canada and may be in the position of a trustee *vis-à-vis* the latter. Jurisdictional problems surrounding the court's ability to hear actions against the Crown at the time prevented it from enforcing the existence of a trust between the Crown and the band rather than any lack of basis in trust law. Indeed, the court acknowledged that the Crown held the moneys arising from the sale of the surrendered lands in trust for the band.[54] Meanwhile, the jurisdictional difficulties which plagued the resolution of the *Henry* case have since been removed by the Federal Court Act.[55] In any event, there are other problems with the *Henry* decision which bring into question its authority as a precedent.

The jurisdictional obstacles to a judicial finding in favour of Crown trust obligations to the band could easily have been eliminated by relying on the provisions of the Petition of Right Act[56] then in force. Section 7(1) of that Act would have removed any difficulty resulting from the fact that the moneys which were held in trust by the Crown for the band had already been paid out.[57] The section stated: 'If the petition is presented for the recovery of any real or personal property, or any right in or to the same, which has been granted away or disposed of by or on behalf of Her Majesty, or her predecessors, a copy of the petition ... shall be served upon ... the person in the possession or occupation of such property or right.' Meanwhile, Burbidge J's misinterpretation of Section

15 of the Exchequer Court Act created another unnecessary obstacle to a finding of Crown trust liability. The requirements of Section 15 were satisfied by demonstrating that the band's request for a declaration that the Crown was a trustee of its moneys might, in England, be the *subject* of an action against the Crown. The section did not necessitate the demonstrated existence of cases in England in which relief had been granted against the Crown as trustee.[58]

The problems associated with the *Henry* decision all lead to the conclusion that, had the case been decided according to a straightforward interpretation of all relevant statutory authorities at the time, it should have enforced the existence of a Crown trust rather than merely indicating its existence. It was not until thirty years later, in the *Dreaver* case, that the judiciary was again faced squarely with the question of the legal nature of the Crown's obligations to Native peoples.

Dreaver v The King[59]

The *Dreaver* decision, which was released in 1935, but not reported until the 1970s, was the second major Indian trust case in Canadian aboriginal rights jurisprudence. The Mistawasis band claimed that the federal Crown owed it moneys which had been improperly charged against funds received by the band under the terms of three deeds of surrender.

The deeds of surrender were signed after the band's adhesion to a treaty it signed in 1876. Under the treaty the band surrendered its land interests in exchange for a reserve. By the deeds of surrender the band relinquished some of its reserve lands set aside under the treaty to the Crown to be held in trust and disposed of for the band's welfare. The band was to receive the proceeds of disposition, minus the Crown's management expenses associated with the sale of the lands. Under two of the deeds band members resident on the reserve were to be paid a fixed amount of money from the net proceeds, with the remainder being distributed between the band's capital account and other enumerated purposes.[60]

The band brought an action against the Crown, alleging that the conditions attached to the three surrenders were not properly fulfilled and that certain charges to the band's capital account were improperly made. For instance, the band alleged that the Crown charged its capital account for drugs, education, and other treaty items that were supposed to be provided free of charge; that the Crown overcharged for other items received by the band, such as horses; and that other charges imposed were improperly made to the band's account, including the charges to the band for the salary and maintenance of government officials carrying out the Crown's duties under the terms of the treaty.[61] The band also alleged that the superintendent-general of Indian Affairs permitted his Indian agent on the Mistawasis reserve to farm over one hundred acres of reserve land for his own purposes without the band's consent. The Crown denied any impropriety regarding the accounts submitted to the band. It also maintained that any claims for moneys expended prior to 6 August 1926 were statute-barred.[62] In its reply the band claimed that the Crown stood in a fiduciary position to it and therefore could not rely on a limitations defence.

Angers J determined that the accounts rendered by the Department of Indian Affairs from 1911 to 31 March 1931 were only received by the band in or about 1932. Therefore, he ruled that the Crown's claim that the band's action was statue-barred must fail. Angers J awarded the band a portion of the monetary relief it had sought and restrained the Indian Affairs agent from farming on the band's reserve without its permission.

The band's contention that the Crown was its fiduciary was not directly addressed in Angers J's judgment. However, he ordered the return of moneys inappropriately charged to the band by the Department of Indian Affairs on the basis of the Crown's obligations to the band stemming from the terms of the 1876 treaty, the three deeds of surrender, and the provisions of the Indian Act. The basis of Angers J's award, although not explicitly endorsing the band's claim that the Crown was its fiduciary, upholds the existence of some form of legally enforceable obligation owed by the Crown to the band which is entirely consistent with either a trust or a fiduciary relationship.

Chisholm v The King[63]

Unlike the two earlier trust cases, the *Chisholm* case, handed down in 1948, was based entirely on the construction of the Indian Act rather than the terms of treaties or indentures. The critical issue in *Chisholm* was whether the Dominion Crown, as trustee of Indians by virtue of the Indian Act, was personally liable for legal services rendered to an Indian band, at the band's request, in connection with its claims against the Crown.

Between 1915 and 1942 lawyer Andrew Gordon Chisholm provided legal services to the Six Nations Indians[64] in connection with the prepa-

Legislative and Jurisprudential History 81

ration and prosecution of a claim by them against the Crown. Chisholm's fees for the services rendered remained unpaid at the time of his death in January 1943. His widow, the executrix and sole beneficiary of his estate, brought an action against the Crown for the payment of the outstanding fees out of the band's funds, which the Crown held in trust under the terms of the Indian Act.

Mr Chisholm had earlier applied to the Crown for payment of the outstanding fees, but failed to obtain a settlement. At the time of his death he was owed $5,034.70. By a resolution dated 8 February 1943 the Six Nations had approved and recommended that $1,500 be paid to Mr Chisholm's estate in partial payment of his services rendered. At the time that the action was commenced, no payment had been received by the estate.

O'Connor J held that as the Crown had not retained Mr Chisholm's services, it was only liable for the moneys owed to Mr Chisholm in its position as trustee of the band's funds. O'Connor J determined, however, that the Crown's position as trustee did not impose any liability on it to pay the moneys owed to Mr Chisholm out of the band's trust funds or otherwise. In addition, he held that the superintendent-general of Indian Affairs' decision not to pay the band's debt was beyond the court's jurisdiction to review. O'Connor J also denied the existence of Crown liability on the basis of Section 90(2) of the Indian Act,[65] which stated that no contract or agreement which purported to bind an Indian band or which dealt with Indian moneys was of any force or effect unless it had been approved in writing by the superintendent-general of Indian Affairs. As the estate's claim did not allege the existence of written approval from the superintendent-general to pay the moneys owed, its claim of liability was denied.

A noteworthy, but generally ignored, element of the *Chisholm* case is that it did not deny that the Crown may be liable to an Indian band as its trustee under appropriate circumstances. Indeed, the court acknowledged that 'the Minister of Mines and Resources is and has been at all times material the trustee of the Indians.'[66] Moreover, had the estate obtained the written approval of the superintendent-general of Indian Affairs to pay the band's debt, the court would have held the Crown liable to pay the moneys due and owing. In addition, the Indian Act's interposition of the requirement to obtain the superintendent-general's authorization for the purposes enumerated in Section 90(2) is consistent with the Crown's assumption of its position as a requisite intermediary in any alienation of Indian lands, as contained in the Royal Proclamation

82 Juridical Understanding

of 1763, and which, as will be seen in Chapter 5, was later held in *Guerin* to be an element of its fiduciary duty to the aboriginal peoples.

Miller v The King[67]

A contemporary of the *Chisholm* case, and heard by the same judge at trial, *Miller* is one of the most celebrated and often-cited of the pre-*Guerin* cases concerned with the nature of the Crown's obligations to Native peoples. The cause of action in *Miller* stemmed from an alleged breach of trust and breach of contract arising from a land surrender to the Crown on 5 February 1798 by Captain Joseph Brant under a power of attorney from the Six Nations of the Grand River (who were, at the time that the cause of action arose, the Five Nations). The Six Nations were to receive the proceeds from the sale or lease of the surrendered lands under the terms of the treaty.

Three events gave rise to the claim by the Six Nations. In 1826 the construction of a dam flooded and permanently destroyed approximately 1,800 acres of the land that had been surrendered in 1798. The Crown failed to collect compensation on the Indians' behalf from the company constructing the dam, even though the statute incorporating the company provided that compensation be paid to any band whose lands were damaged by the construction. Around 1833, without the knowledge or consent of the Six Nations, Upper Canada agreed to purchase $160,000 worth of shares from the Grand River Navigation Company from the moneys realized from the sale of the surrendered lands. The shares were paid for, without further authority, by the Province of Canada after the union of Upper and Lower Canada in 1840. They ultimately became worthless as a direct result of a mortgage on the company's assets authorized by an act of Parliament in 1851. Finally, on 20 October 1836 Upper Canada authorized a free grant of 369 acres of the surrendered land to the Grand River Navigation Company. No money or other compensation for the value of the land was ever provided to the Six Nations, in direct contravention of the terms of the 1798 surrender.

As a result of these events, the Six Nations sought compensation for the value of the lands destroyed by the flooding, repayment of the $160,000 paid for the shares of the Grand River Navigation Company, and payment for the value of the lands contained in the free grant. The Six Nations alleged that the 1798 surrender rendered the Crown an express trustee on their behalf and that its failure to collect money for the lands destroyed by the flooding and the value of the lands contained in the free grant amounted to a breach of trust. They also claimed that the surrender created a contract and that the purchase of the shares out of the moneys realized from the sale of the surrendered lands without their authorization constituted a breach of contract.

O'Connor J determined that the Crown was not a trustee in respect of the surrendered lands under the 1798 treaty other than for the purpose of granting the lands to purchasers. Moreover, O'Connor J found that the Crown did not receive the moneys realized from the purchase of those lands, but that the money had been received by trustees appointed by the aboriginals.[68] His conclusions were derived primarily from the contents of a letter from the president of the Executive Council of Upper Canada, Peter Russell, to the Duke of Portland, the secretary for the colonies, which was set out in the minutes of the meeting of the Executive Council on 5 February 1798. The letter specifically noted that the then-Five Nations had appointed the acting surveyor general, the superintendent of Indian Affairs in the district, and lawyer Alexander Stewart as their trustees to receive and distribute payments from the sale of the surrendered lands.

On the appeal by the Six Nations to the Supreme Court of Canada, Kerwin J, Rand J concurring, broke down the substance of the appeal into three separate claims: (1) the value of the surrendered lands destroyed by flooding; (2) the value of the lands contained in the free grant to the Grand River Navigation Company; and (3) repayment of the moneys paid out of the Six Nations' funds for shares in the Grand River Navigation Company. He disposed of the first two claims on the basis that the federal Crown could not be held responsible for incidents that occurred prior to the union of Upper and Lower Canada in 1840. Kerwin J distinguished the third claim on the basis of its allegation that Upper Canada, and the province of Canada after 1840, purchased the shares from the proceeds of the sale of the surrendered lands. He ordered the third claim to be remanded for trial, subject to a determination as to whether the claim was statute barred by the Exchequer Court Act[69] and the Ontario Limitations Act.[70]

Kellock J, with Taschereau J concurring, disposed of the appeal in the same manner as Kerwin J, but with additional reasons. In opposition to the determination made in the *Henry* case, Kellock J found that, in appropriate circumstances, a declaration could be made which stated that moneys held by the Crown were trust moneys belonging to aboriginal peoples. However, he ruled that the court was without jurisdiction to

84 Juridical Understanding

enforce the terms of such a trust.[71] Despite the court's inability to enforce the trust, Kellock J stated, on the basis of earlier precedents, that 'it is inconceivable that at this date ... the Crown, as the fountain of justice, would not do justice.'[72]

In further opposition to the *Henry* decision, Kellock J determined that the court had jurisdiction to enforce an order against the Crown for payment of moneys it held in trust. He determined that if land, goods, or money belonging to a subject, to which no trust existed and which found their way into the Crown's possession, could be the subject of a petition of right against the Crown, then so too could money which had come into the possession of the Crown which was impressed with a trust in favour of the subject.[73] The fact that the Crown had already spent the money was of no consequence to the Six Nations' right of action against the Crown, as recognized by Section 7 of the Petition of Right Act[74] and the case of *Re Gosman*.[75] Moreover, in opposition to the trial judge's findings, Kellock J determined that the Crown was to receive, and did, in fact, receive the money paid for the surrendered lands, rather than the trustees named in the letter from Russell to the Duke of Portland.[76]

In remanding the appeal by the Six Nations with respect to their third claim back to the Exchequer Court for determination, Kellock J highlighted the legal nature of the Crown's obligations to the Six Nations,[77] the Crown's contentions that the claim of the Six Nations should be restricted to a claim arising prior to 1840, and the Crown's alternative argument that any Crown obligations rightfully belong to the Imperial Crown[78] as issues which required the presentation of further evidence to enable their proper adjudication. Locke J's judgment agreed with Kerwin and Kellock JJ's disposition of the matter.

Although the case was to be retried before the Exchequer Court, no subsequent decision was ever handed down. The legacy left by the *Miller* decision, then, is its finding that the Crown, in appropriate circumstances, may be a trustee on behalf of aboriginal peoples and have its obligations enforced by the courts. The case is also noteworthy for its clarification and refutation of the jurisdictional problems which plagued the *Henry* decision.

St Ann's Island Shooting and Fishing Club v The King[79]

The *St Ann's Island* case is often discussed together with any analysis of *Miller* as it was decided within a few months of the *Miller* decision. The primary issue in *St Ann's Island* was the Crown's obligations regarding

Legislative and Jurisprudential History 85

the disposition of lands that had been surrendered by the Chippewa and Pottawatomie Indians[80] of Walpole Island to the Crown on 8 February 1882. The St Ann's Island Shooting and Fishing Club ('the club') sought a declaration of its right to renew a lease of the lands pursuant to a renewal clause contained within a lease it had signed with the superintendent-general of Indian Affairs on 19 May 1925. The club had leased the lands in question since 1881 and had expended substantial sums of money in erecting a clubhouse and other buildings and by opening up ditches and canals.

In response to the club's concern over the validity of the original 1881 lease, the Crown had obtained a formal surrender of the land on 8 February 1882. An Order in Council accepting the surrender and authorizing the lease to the club followed on 3 April 1882. Upon the expiration of the 1882 lease, new leases were entered into in 1884, 1892, 1894, 1906, 1915, and 1925. Beginning in 1894 each lease provided for one renewal of ten years. The club indicated its intention to exercise the renewal clause in the 1925 lease – which expired on 1 October 1944 – by letters dated 12 April 1944 and 1 September 1944 to the superintendent-general of Indian Affairs, who refused to grant the renewal or to admit that the club was legally entitled to demand a renewal. The lease expired and the matter was referred to the Exchequer Court for adjudication. At that time an agreed-upon statement of facts was filed for the purpose of determining whether the club was entitled to renew its lease on the same terms as the 1925 lease – save as to the amount of rent payable – for a further ten-year period.

Based on the terms of the surrender, Cameron J determined that the Crown had full power to vary the terms and conditions of any lease of Indian lands, subject only to the dictates of Section 51 of the Indian Act, which stated: 'All Indian lands which are reserves or portions of reserves surrendered, or to be surrendered, to His Majesty, shall be deemed to be held for the same purpose as heretofore; and shall be managed, leased and sold as the Governor in Council directs, subject to the conditions of surrender and the provisions of this Part.'[81] The surrender itself stated that the island could be leased to the club for the purposes of shooting and fishing 'for such term and on such conditions as the Superintendent-General of Indian Affairs may consider best for our advantage.'[82] Cameron J interpreted the surrender to be absolute, without any rights being reserved to the Indians.

Cameron J determined that without a direction of the governor in council, any lease executed by the superintendent-general was invalid.[83]

Therefore, he held that the 1882 Order in Council, even under the broadest possible interpretation, could only retroactively authorize the 1881 lease, not any of the subsequent leases. Although the club had argued that the Crown was legally prohibited, or estopped, from denying the validity of the club's tenancy owing to the superintendent-general's execution of further leases after 1881,[84] Cameron J held that an estoppel cannot cure any defect in formality required by a statute.[85] He also determined that the superintendent-general's non-compliance with the conditions imposed by Section 51 of the Indian Act rendered the 1925 lease and its renewal provision void.

Cameron J's judgment was unanimously affirmed on the club's appeal to the Supreme Court of Canada. Each of the three judgments rendered dismissed the club's appeal, but Rand J's judgment has drawn particular attention from judges and commentators. In finding that Section 51 of the Indian Act required a direction by the governor in council in order to validly lease the surrendered lands, Rand J based his conclusion on the language of the section: 'The language of the statute embodies the accepted view that these aborigines are, in effect, wards of the state, whose care and welfare are a political trust of the highest obligation. For that reason, every such dealing with their privileges must bear the imprint of Governmental approval, and it would be beyond the power of the Governor in Council to transfer that responsibility to the Superintendent General.'[86]

Rand J's suggestion that the care and welfare of aboriginal peoples in Canada amounted only to a political trust has been seized upon to assert that the nature of the Crown's obligation is neither binding in law nor enforceable in the courts.[87] One must be mindful, however, of the fact that Rand J determined that the language of the Indian Act, or at least its Section 51, embodied the Crown's obligation. This determination brings into question the effect of statutorily embodying obligations previously characterized as exclusively morally or politically based. If Rand J's political trust assertion is correct, his finding that it was embodied in Section 51 of the Indian Act rendered the Crown's obligations under such a trust statutorily enforceable. But what does this mean in practical terms?

A political trust, as we have seen, is neither legally binding nor enforceable in the courts. Its contents are, however, unclear. Rand J's characterization of a political trust required the Crown to undertake the 'care and welfare' of Native peoples and to oversee their 'privileges.' Based on the context within which his comments originated, his understanding of a political trust would appear to be akin to the aboriginal rights delineated in the Royal Proclamation of 1763, the terms of various Indian treaties, and the Indian Act, under which the Crown has accepted or recognized its responsibility to the aboriginal peoples. A legally enforceable trust or fiduciary obligation, simply requires that the Crown act in the best interests of aboriginal peoples, which includes the protection and promotion of their aboriginal and treaty rights.[88]

Based on these characterizations, by even the most conservative appraisal there would appear, prima facie, to be little or no difference between the content of the Crown's obligations under a political trust under Rand J's formulation and a legally enforceable trust or fiduciary obligation aside from the former's unenforceability in the courts. However, the statutory embodiment of the Crown's political trust by Section 51 of the Indian Act, as asserted by Rand J, renders such a trust, *ipso jure*, enforceable by the courts. By logical implication, then, Rand J's characterization of the Crown's political trust to Native peoples in *St Ann's Island*[89] blurs the distinction between that duty and that of a legal trust or fiduciary obligation by rendering them of similar content and enforceability.[90] Indeed, more than thirty years later, in *Roberts v Canada*, the Supreme Court of Canada characterized the Crown's fiduciary duty to aboriginal peoples in a similar manner by holding that the Indian Act codifies some of the Crown's legally enforceable fiduciary duties to aboriginals.[91]

What may be gathered from these five pre-*Guerin* cases is that they either explicitly indicate the existence or possibility of legally enforceable Crown trust or fiduciary obligations to aboriginal peoples or, at the very least, indicate the presence of political trust obligations which, based on the reasons outlined above, are essentially similar in substance, effect, and enforceability to legal trust or fiduciary obligations. These cases are the first noteworthy judicial expositions of the Crown's equitable obligations[92] to Native peoples. Nevertheless, there was no authoritative settlement of the legal nature of the Crown's obligations to aboriginal peoples until the *Guerin* decision, more than thirty years later.

5

The Characterization of the Crown–Native Fiduciary Relationship by the Courts: *Guerin v R*

The significance of the *Guerin* case transcends its position as the first Canadian case to judicially sanction the Crown's fiduciary duties and responsibilities towards aboriginal peoples. Through the divergent application of equitable doctrines and principles to the facts of the *Guerin* case at trial and on appeal, *Guerin* reveals the judiciary's lack of comfort in applying those doctrines and principles to a relationship whose ground rules had long been judicially characterized as existing at the pleasure of the Crown.[1] *Guerin*, therefore, not only changed the way in which the Crown–Native relationship was to be perceived in the future, but it also laid to rest the Canadian courts' working conception of that relationship which had been the foundation of its decisions in Canadian aboriginal rights jurisprudence for well over a hundred years, since the Privy Council's judgment in *St Catherine's Milling and Lumber Co v the Queen*.[2]

The issues arising in *Guerin* revolved around a dispute between the Musqueam Indian band, which occupied an Indian reserve of 417 acres situated within the charter area of the City of Vancouver (Musqueam Indian Reserve No. 2), and the Department of Indian Affairs, the agency of the federal Crown responsible for discharging the Crown's obligations to Native peoples in Canada.

Although *Guerin* was the first Canadian case that judicially characterized the relationship between the Crown and Native peoples as fiduciary in nature, it, like its predecessors, began as a case in which the existence of a trust relationship between the Crown and aboriginal peoples was alleged by the latter. To create a legally valid trust, three essential characteristics, known as the three certainties, must exist. The subject matter of the trust, also known as the *corpus* or *res*, must be clearly and readily identifiable and legally recognizable as property.[3] This is known as the *certainty of subject*. The person who seeks to establish the trust – the *settlor* – must use explicit language in creating the trust so that there is no doubt as to the purpose or function of the trust. This is known as the *certainty of object*. Finally, the intention of the settlor to establish the trust must itself be beyond question. This is known as the *certainty of intent*.[4] The judicial consideration of these concepts in *Guerin* underlies its transformation from a trust case to one which recognized and affirmed the fiduciary relationship between the Crown and Native peoples in Canada.[5]

The Musqueam band sued the federal Crown in December 1975 for damages, alleging that the Crown was a trustee of lands surrendered by the band for lease to a golf club and that the Crown acted in breach of trust through its conduct in negotiating and signing the lease. The band alleged that many of the terms and conditions of the finalized lease were different than those that had been disclosed to and approved of by it prior to the surrender. Moreover, it maintained that some of the terms included in the lease had not been disclosed to the band at all.

The events leading up to the band's suit against the federal Crown commenced some twenty years before the action was initiated. In the mid-1950s Indian Affairs branch officials in Vancouver had received many applications for the sale or lease of Musqueam reserve lands and were concerned about how to develop the Musqueam reserve for the band's financial benefit. Under the provisions of the Indian Act, Indian bands are prohibited from selling, leasing, or otherwise alienating title to their lands other than to the federal Crown.[6] For private interests to purchase or lease Indian reserve land, it is necessary for the band whose land is being sought to surrender the land to the Crown. The Crown, in turn, may then sell or lease the land to the private party for the benefit of the band.[7] Surrenders obtained in this fashion may either be conditional surrenders – that is, subject to certain conditions imposed by the band prior to surrender which may restrict the use of the land or the length of any lease – or they may be unconditional. The distinction between conditional and unconditional surrenders, the explicitness of any conditions to be imposed upon a surrender, and the manner and form in which any conditions to a surrender must be made are all vital questions raised in the judicial consideration of the *Guerin* case.

On 11 October 1955 Frank Anfield, the district superintendent of the Indian Affairs branch in Vancouver, detailed some suggestions for the development of the Musqueam reserve in a letter to William Arneil, the Indian commissioner for British Columbia. Anfield suggested that the zoning of the reserve be altered from agricultural use to allow for a use such as a golf course, with an eventual change to residential occupation. In a report to Arneil on 17 September 1956 Anfield recommended having an expert appraisal of the reserve land and retaining an expert estate planner to advise on the best manner of developing the reserve. On 1 October 1956 the Musqueam band council approved a resolution to have a land appraisal made at the band's expense to determine the total value of the land for leasing purposes. Shortly thereafter Anfield wrote a memorandum to Arneil detailing the possibility of leasing 232 acres of the upper level of Musqueam Indian Reserve No. 2 to the Shaughnessy Heights Golf Club.

An appraisal of the reserve lands was conducted by Alfred Howell, an appraiser with the Veterans' Land Act Administration, but not a land use expert. Howell's report concluded that the upper level land was a first-class residential area worth approximately $5,500 per acre. Howell placed a total value on the land of $1,360,000, which assumed a rate of return of 6 per cent. A contemporaneous report on the adjacent University Endowment Lands belonging to the University of British Columbia pegged the value of those lands at $13,000 per acre.[8] Anfield shared the Howell report's conclusions with representatives of the golf club, but not with the Musqueam band. The band was only informed of some of the report's contents and did not receive a copy of the report until December 1975, after it had launched its lawsuit. On 4 April 1957 the president of the Shaughnessy Heights Golf Club proposed a lease of approximately 160 acres of the upper level reserve lands on the following terms:

1 The club was to have the right to construct on the leased area a golf course and country club and such other buildings and facilities as it considered appropriate for its membership.
2 The initial term of the lease was to be for fifteen years commencing May 1, 1957, with the club to have options to extend the term for four successive periods of fifteen years each, giving a maximum term of seventy-five years.
3 The rental for the first fifteen year term was to be $25,000 per annum.
4 The rental for each successive fifteen year period was to be determined by mutual agreement between the Department and the club and failing agreement, by arbitration, but the rental for any of the fifteen year renewal periods was in no event to be increased or decreased over that payable for the preceding fifteen year period by more than 15% of the initial rent.

Characterization by the Courts: *Guerin v R*   91

5 At any time during the term of the lease, and for a period of up to six months after termination, the club was to have the right to remove any buildings and other structures it had constructed or placed upon the leased area, and any course improvements and facilities.[9]

The Musqueam band was first informed of the negotiations between the Indian Affairs branch and the golf club at a band council meeting on 7 April 1957. At that meeting Anfield put forward some of the terms of the golf club's proposal, but he did not present copies of the actual proposal itself nor was it read out in its entirety, either at that meeting or at any time thereafter. Anfield did mention that the proposal was to lease the land for fifteen years with options to renew for successive fifteen-year periods on terms to be agreed upon by the band and the golf club. Anfield then presented the band council with a formal application to lease 160 acres for fifteen years at $25,000 per annum, with options for four additional fifteen-year periods on terms to be agreed upon. Based on the information given by Anfield and the terms of the lease presented, the band council passed a resolution approving the lease of the 160 acres of their reserve to the golf club and to surrender such land to the Crown for that purpose.

Following the band council meeting, the superintendent of reserves and trusts of the Indian Affairs branch in Ottawa, William Bethune, questioned whether the golf club's proposal, in particular the $25,000 annual rental payment to the band for the initial fifteen-year lease, provided an adequate return for the band. Bethune noted that Howell's appraisal had indicated that a return of 5 to 6 per cent was appropriate, while the golf club's proposal only yielded an annual return of approximately 3 per cent. Bethune suggested that Anfield obtain Howell's opinion of the adequacy of the golf club's proposal prior to proceeding any further in the negotiations.

Anfield sought Howell's opinion on the proposed lease, but neglected to provide him with all of the details of the proposal. Howell was not advised that the golf club retained the right to remove any buildings or improvements it had made to the land up to six months after the lease's termination. Howell was also not informed that any rental increase for subsequent fifteen-year rental periods was limited to 15 per cent of the initial $25,000 rent, or $3,750. On the basis of the incomplete information, Howell revised his earlier position and advocated accepting the golf club's proposal. He based his conclusion on the assumption that any improvements made by the golf club would

92   Juridical Understanding

revert to the band upon the termination of the lease and that after the initial fifteen-year term, the Indian Affairs Branch would be in a stronger position to renegotiate a more favourable lease.[10] As he stated in a letter to Anfield:

The improvements to the property which will be made by the lessee must be considered. This has been discussed with the secretary of the Club, and ... he felt that in the course of the lease, they will spend close to $1,000,000 in buildings and improvements. Clearing alone will be around $100,000 and the club house may cost over $200,000. These improvements will revert to the band at the end of the lease.

...

Another point ... is that there is a limit to the amount the Club can afford to pay, and while their present offer may not be up to that limit ... if their offer is accepted, the Department will be in a much sounder position to negotiate an increase in rental in fifteen years' time, when the Club will have invested a considerable amount of capital in the property, which they will have to protect.[11]

At no time was the band informed that Anfield had sought the appraiser's opinion as to the adequacy of the golf club's proposal.

Based on Howell's revised opinion, Arneil recommended that the Indian Affairs branch in Ottawa accept the golf club's lease proposal and prepare appropriate surrender documents. On the basis of Arneil's recommendation and Howell's revised opinion, the director of Indian Affairs in Ottawa recommended approval of the golf club's terms to the deputy minister. Final approval of the golf club's proposal was granted on 13 June 1957. When Bethune sent the surrender documents to Arneil, he stated that the 15 per cent limitation on rental increases for renewals of the initial lease was inadequate and suggested that Arneil attempt to remove it, if at all possible. When Musqueam Chief Edward Sparrow asked for information concerning the valuation of the reserve lands, Anfield informed him of the $1,360,000 appraised value, but also stated that the $25,000 per year rental figure proposed by the golf club 'is considered by the appraiser to be a very high return for such land use,' and that 'the land in its improved state will eventually revert to the Band.'[12]

A second band council meeting was held on 25 July 1957 to discuss the terms of the proposed lease and accompanying surrender. The two band councillors present stated that the initial terms of the lease and its subsequent renewal periods should be ten rather than fifteen years in duration. Anfield confirmed the ten-year lease and renewal periods in a letter to Chief Sparrow on 29 July 1957. At its meeting on 9 September 1957 the band council resolved that the proposed rate of rent for the initial period of the lease ought to be renegotiated.

Another band council meeting was convened on 27 September 1957 to discuss the lease proposal. Anfield, William Grant, the officer in charge of the Vancouver agency, and representatives of the golf club were all in attendance. Chief Sparrow insisted on a return of 5 per cent of the value of the land to be surrendered, or approximately $44,000 per annum. The golf club representatives refused to agree to those terms. The representatives were then asked to leave so that the others could conduct a private discussion. During that discussion Anfield told the band council that 5 per cent was unreasonable. After considerable discussion the band council reluctantly agreed to the suggested amount of $29,000 per year, $4,000 per year more than the initial golf club proposal.[13]

On 6 October 1957 a meeting of all of the band members was called to vote on the surrender. Prior to this meeting the band did not receive any independent legal advice nor any independent expert advice regarding land appraisal and development. The only information they had received regarding the surrender and lease was that obtained through Anfield. The Musqueam were under the impression that the lease agreement would be according to the terms and conditions specified by the band council at the meeting of 27 September 1957. Based on this understanding, the band approved and signed a surrender document, which had been read aloud by Anfield, that contained the following terms:

TO HAVE AND TO HOLD the same unto Her said Majesty the Queen, her Heirs and Successors forever in trust to lease the same to such person or persons, and upon such terms as the Government of Canada may deem most conducive to our Welfare and that of our people.

AND upon the further condition that all moneys received from the leasing thereof, shall be credited to our revenue trust account at Ottawa.

AND WE, the said Chief and Councillors of the said Musqueam Band of Indians do on behalf of our people and for ourselves, hereby ratify and confirm, and promise to ratify and confirm, whatever the said Government may do, or cause to be lawfully done, in connection with the leasing thereof.[14]

After the surrender meeting, Anfield sent the Indian Affairs branch in Ottawa a copy of a draft lease prepared by the golf club's solicitors. The draft lease retained the fifteen-year initial period and renewals as originally proposed by the golf club. Commenting on the use of the fifteen-year terms, Anfield wrote: 'There has been discussion with the Indians that this term should be reduced, possibly to 10 year periods. In this regard it should be stated that it is going to take 3 years to get this site into operable condition, in addition to which the Club is going to have to make a million dollar investment in a Club House and the cost of constructing and perfecting the golf course. It would hardly seem fair to expect a review of rentals, presumably upward, in as short a space of time as 10 years and we are inclined to recommend that the 15 year period is fair and equitable.'[15] Regarding the 15 per cent cap on rent increases for subsequent renewal periods, Anfield wrote: 'The Directors point out ... that this 15% limitation be retained; that they will be turning back to the Musqueam Indian Band property of terrific value and with vast improvements.'[16] The statements included in Anfield's letter were never disclosed to the band council. Further correspondence between Anfield, Bethune, Arneil, the golf club, and the Indian Affairs branch in Ottawa continued after the surrender meeting to work out the details of the golf club's lease. At no time was the band ever informed of these post-surrender negotiations or consulted as to the terms being discussed. The Musqueam surrender was accepted by the Crown on 6 December 1957.

A letter detailing the golf club's lease proposal was read at a band council meeting on 9 January 1958. The letter indicated renewal periods of fifteen years. After objecting to this condition, the band was told that it was stuck with the fifteen-year terms. The band council subsequently passed a resolution agreeing to have the first term of the lease be fifteen years, but insisting that subsequent renewal periods must be based on ten-year periods.[17] The lease was signed on 22 January 1958. Included among its terms were the following:

1 The term is for 75 years unless sooner terminated.
2 The rent for the first 15 years is $29,000 per annum.
3 For the succeeding 15-year periods, annual rent is to be determined by mutual agreement, or failing such agreement, by arbitration, such rent to be equal to the fair rent for the demised premises as if the same were still in an uncleared and unimproved condition and used as a golf course.
4 The maximum increase in rent for the second 15-year period (January 1, 1973 to January 1, 1988) is limited to 15% of $29,000, that is $4,350 per annum.
5 The golf club can terminate the lease at the end of any 15-year period by giving 6 months' prior notice.

6 The golf club can at any time during the lease and up to 6 months after termination, remove any buildings or other structures, and any course improvements and facilities.[18]

The Department of Indian Affairs agreed to these terms and signed the lease on behalf of the band. The department did not seek the band's consent to these terms and only provided the band with a copy of the lease in March 1970, twelve years after its execution, despite numerous requests by the band for a copy in the interim.

The Formulation of the Crown's Obligations at Trial

At trial[19] the Crown countered the Musqueam's claims of breach of trust by arguing that if a trust indeed existed, it amounted to nothing more than a political trust which was not legally binding and was unenforceable in the courts. Because of procedural irregularities, Collier J held that the Crown was not entitled to rely on its political trust argument.[20] The Crown then altered its position, insisting that if a legally enforceable trust existed, the terms of that trust were contained exclusively in the surrender document signed by the band. As the surrender document was unconditional, the Crown maintained that it was entitled to lease the surrendered lands to anyone for any purpose and on any terms which, at its absolute discretion, it deemed to be favourable to the band. In addition, the Crown maintained that the band's action was barred by the lapse of statutory limitations or by the equitable doctrine of laches.[21]

A number of important discoveries were revealed by the evidence obtained at trial. Alfred Howell stated that had he known that the golf club's improvements to the land would not become the property of the Musqueam band upon the termination of the lease, he would have recommended a rate of return of 4 to 6 per cent. He expressed shock at finding out about the cap of 15 per cent of the initial annual rental payment on annual increases. Moreover, he had assumed, in providing his opinion of the proposal, that at the end of the initial fifteen-year lease the rental agreement would be renegotiated based on the improved condition of the land rather than in its previous form.[22]

William Guerin, a band councillor in attendance at the 27 September 1957 meeting, testified at trial that the band council only agreed to the $29,000 rental figure because they were led to believe that the first lease period would be ten years, subsequent renegotiations would take place every five years, and the band council believed that it would be able to

96 Juridical Understanding

negotiate for 5 per cent of the subsequent value of the land upon the expiry of the initial lease term.[23] Guerin also testified that Anfield had said that if the band's conditions and requirements were unreasonable, Indian Affairs could lease the land without obtaining a surrender and on such terms as it desired.[24]

William Grant, the officer in charge of the Vancouver agency, testified that there was 'absolutely no question that the vote at the September 27 meeting was for a specific lease to a specific tenant on specific terms' and that Anfield was not authorized by the band council to alter those terms.[25] Grant also stated that the lease ultimately entered into by the Department of Indian Affairs on behalf of the band bore little resemblance to what had been discussed at the meeting of 6 October 1957, when the lease and surrender were voted on and approved by the band. Finally, Andrew Charles Jr, the band council secretary, testified that Anfield had informed the band council that it was 'not in a position or allowed to engage professional people outside the Department of Indian Affairs.'[26]

Based on the evidence presented Collier J found that the band members who attended the meeting had not received full disclosure of the lease negotiations and were under a number of mistaken impressions regarding the lease's terms. For instance, Collier J determined that the band members at the meeting believed that the initial term of the lease would be for ten years rather than the fifteen years contained in the lease. The band members were also not aware that there was a cap of 15 per cent of the initial annual rental payment on annual rent increases. Additionally, those band members present at the meeting were not informed that the golf club intended to reserve the right to remove any buildings, structures, or other improvements until six months after the lease was terminated.[27]

In addition to these facts Collier J determined that two matters which were neither raised at the surrender meeting nor included in the golf club's initial proposal to Anfield appeared in drafts of the lease agreement after the surrender had been voted on and approved. An additional proviso to the arbitration clause provided that the new rent would be equivalent to a fair rate of rent calculated on the basis that the land was still uncleared and unimproved and used as a golf club. More importantly, the termination clause was altered to give the golf club and not the Crown, the right, at the end of each fifteen-year lease agreement, to terminate the lease on six months' notice.[28] These two matters were never raised with the band council or band members for approval or discussion, but simply incorporated into the terms of the lease agreement.

Characterization by the Courts: *Guerin v R* 97

From these discoveries, Collier J concluded that the majority of the band members who had voted in favour of the surrender would not have done so had they been aware of all of the terms of the lease as signed on 22 January 1958.[29]

Collier J determined that the Crown chose to act as trustee for the Musqueam when it accepted the surrender of land on 6 October 1957. Further, he found that the Crown was bound to lease the land on the terms specified by the band. He declared that the Indian Act contemplated that the Crown, by virtue of the surrender requirements contained therein, would become a trustee in a legally binding sense for any Indian band which surrendered land for lease or sale.[30] Collier J concluded that the Crown breached its duty to the Musqueam band by (1) failing to employ land use experts or advertise the availability of the land in order to obtain the best possible offer, (2) not advising the band of other parties' interests in and proposals regarding the Musqueam's land, (3) failing to negotiate adequate lease terms, and (4) entering into a lease which bore little resemblance to what had been discussed at the band council meeting of 6 October 1957.

By acting contrary to the band's interests, Collier J held that the Crown was in breach of its trust responsibilities to the band and liable to it in damages in the amount of ten million dollars. He determined that the Crown's failure to deliver a copy of the lease to the band until 1970 was unconscionable and amounted to equitable fraud. Where fraud conceals the existence of a cause of action, a statutory limitation period does not begin to run until the fraud is discovered or ought reasonably to have been discovered – unless the limitation statute specifically holds otherwise. As the band did not receive a copy of the lease until 1970 and had commenced its action in 1975 – and the British Columbia limitation statute was silent on the matter – the band was entirely within the applicable six-year statutory limitation. Moreover, the Crown's equitable fraud prevented it from invoking a defence of laches.[31]

The Crown appealed the trial court's decision to the Federal Court of Appeal. It raised a variety of arguments to dispute the trial judge's finding of a legally enforceable trust obligation owing to the Musqueam. Meanwhile, the Musqueam cross-appealed for a higher award of damages and interest.

The Rejection of the Crown's Legal Obligations on Appeal

A number of new arguments were raised for the first time on appeal by

98 Juridical Understanding

both the Crown and the Musqueam band. The Crown insisted that no legal trust could exist with regard to the surrendered reserve lands because the Indian interest in reserve lands existed at the pleasure of the Crown and could be revoked at any time. The Crown contended that, because of the ephemeral nature of the Indian interest in land, the Musqueam interest in their reserve lands could not constitute the subject, or *res*, of a trust.[32] Alternatively, if the Musqueam interest could constitute the *res* of a trust, the Crown maintained that the terms of that trust were restricted to those contained in the surrender document alone.

Under the requirements of the Indian Act in effect at the time of the surrender,[33] a surrender had to be voted on and approved by a majority of electors of a band, certified on oath by the superintendent or other officer who attended the meeting and the chief or other member of the band council, and submitted to the governor in council for acceptance or refusal to be binding on the Crown. The Crown insisted that as the oral terms and conditions found by the trial judge to comprise the essence of the trust were not included in the surrender document accepted by the governor in council, they could not bind the Crown. In any event, the Crown maintained that the trust found to exist at trial was merely a political trust.

The Musqueam asserted that the Indian interest in land was entirely sufficient to constitute the *res* of a trust. It claimed that the provisions of the Indian Act regarding the management and disposition of reserve lands imposed a statutory trust upon the Crown that existed separate and apart from the trust found to exist at trial. The band alleged that this statutory trust provided the basis for the Crown's breaches of trust that occurred prior to the surrender surrounding the negotiations with the golf club, as well as the Crown's lack of disclosure of such to the band. The band also maintained that the oral terms and conditions were an integral element of the surrender and, but for those conditions, there would have been no surrender. Based on the precedents contained in *Dreaver v The King*,[34] *Miller v The King*,[35] and *Kruger v R*,[36] the band insisted that the nature of the Crown's trust obligations were legally, not politically, based, thereby rendering the courts the proper forum for their enforcement. The Musqueam also disputed the Crown's ability to raise the political trust argument on appeal.

On behalf of the court, Le Dain JA stressed that the court's consideration of the Crown's appeal was restricted to the issue of breach of trust and whether the Crown was a trustee, in the private law sense, of the

Musqueam reserve land leased to the golf club.[37] The Musqueam's statutory trust argument was held to be merely another consideration which arose within the context of determining the nature and extent of the Crown's duties to the Musqueam relating to the surrendered reserve lands.[38] Meanwhile, Le Dain JA determined that the Crown's political trust argument was only another manner of referring to the concept of a trust 'in the higher sense' and did not raise any new issue of fact.

Le Dain JA noted that there was nothing in law preventing the Crown from acting as a trustee – a point that was conceded by the Crown and which helps to differentiate *Guerin* from the cases discussed in the previous chapter. He focused his attention on two primary issues: whether the trust found to exist at trial was based on the oral terms as determined by Collier J or by the written terms of the surrender document, and whether the Indian title or interest in the surrendered reserve land was sufficient to constitute the *res* of a trust. Le Dain JA determined that the oral terms of the surrender afforded no basis in law for a finding of liability on the part of the Crown, as they were neither voted on and approved by a majority of the band, nor accepted by the governor in council as required by the Indian Act.[39] He did find, however, that the Indian interest in reserve land was of the nature of a right of property and could, therefore, be the subject of a trust.

To bolster its argument that the provisions of the Indian Act create a legally enforceable trust between the Crown and an Indian band regarding the surrender of reserve lands, the Musqueam relied heavily on the decision in *Miller v The King*.[40] The band relied in particular on Kellock J's judgment in the Supreme Court of Canada's disposition of the case.[41]

Le Dain JA disagreed with the Musqueam's contention that Kellock J's judgment in *Miller* found the existence of a true trust created by the act of surrender or under the Indian Act and its precursors.[42] Le Dain JA distinguished Kellock J's comments in *Miller* by emphasizing that Kellock J's observations were made within the context of Crown obligations concerning the application of Indian moneys. Consequently, he concluded that they did not relate to the issue in *Guerin* of whether a conditional surrender or the provisions of the Indian Act concerning the surrender of reserve lands imposed trust obligations upon the Crown.[43] Le Dain JA concluded that the discretion conferred upon the governor in council by Section 18(1) of the Indian Act rendered the Crown's trust obligations a matter to be determined by the Crown, not the courts: 'The extent to which the government assumes an administrative or management responsibility for the reserves of some positive scope is a matter of governmental discretion, not legal or equitable obligation. I am, therefore, of the opinion that s.18 of the *Indian Act* does not afford a basis for an action for breach of trust in the management or disposition of reserve lands.'[44]

Le Dain JA determined that Section 18(1) did not create an obligation to deal with reserve lands in any particular fashion. He held that the discretionary authority contained within the Musqueam surrender was not a statutory discretion created by the Indian Act, but 'may be regarded as a statutorily authorized qualification of the power of control and management under the Act.'[45] He stated that the use of the phrase 'in trust' in the surrender document was not a significant fact 'except possibly to emphasize the importance of the political or governmental responsibility for such land.'[46] Le Dain JA founded this conclusion on his assertion that while the phrase 'in trust' had been used in Indian surrenders for over a hundred years as well as in general use when referring to the Crown's responsibility for Indian lands, the Crown never intended to have its use impose anything other than political, or moral, obligations on it – and certainly not the obligations of a trustee in the legal sense.[47] On this basis, Le Dain JA concluded that the band's claim against the Crown must fail: '[T]he words "in trust" in the surrender document were intended to do no more than indicate that the surrender was for the benefit of the Indians and conferred an authority to deal with the land in a certain manner for their benefit. They were not intended to impose an equitable obligation or duty to deal with the land in a certain manner. For these reasons I am of the opinion that the surrender did not create a true trust and does not, therefore, afford a basis for liability based on a breach of trust.'[48]

The Crown's appeal was allowed and the trial judgment set aside. The Musqueam's cross-appeal was dismissed. The Musqueam then sought and obtained leave from the Supreme Court of Canada to appeal the Federal Court of Appeal's decision.

The Finding of a Fiduciary Obligation by the Supreme Court of Canada

Before the Supreme Court of Canada the Musqueam argued that the Federal Court of Appeal's decision to allow the Crown to use its political trust defence was in error. In any event, the Musqueam maintained that the political trust argument was part of the act of state doctrine and could not be invoked by the Crown against its own citizens.[49] The band

Characterization by the Courts: *Guerin v R* 101

also disputed the Federal Court of Appeal's interpretation of the case law raised in argument, especially the case of *Miller v The King*.[50]

The Supreme Court unanimously held[51] that the political trust idea found to exist by Le Dain JA was not an accurate depiction of the relationship between the Musqueam band and the Crown. It overturned the Federal Court of Appeal's decision and reinstated the trial court's judgment, including its award of ten million dollars in damages. The Crown's duty to the Musqueam was determined to be equitable rather than political and therefore rooted in law rather than moral obligation. Whereas the decision to reinstate the trial court's judgment was unanimous, there were three separate judgments in *Guerin*, none of which garnered the support of a majority of the eight participating justices.

Estey J based his judgment on his assertion that the Indian Act, by requiring that Indians surrender their land interests to the Crown rather than being able to alienate those interests on their own behalf, created a statutory agency between the Crown and aboriginal peoples regarding the surrender of reserve lands. Although he determined that the Crown's obligations to the Musqueam were those of an agent, Estey J insisted that the Crown's obligations as agent were no different than if the Crown was deemed to be a fiduciary of the band. The theoretical basis of Estey J's decision was predicated upon his belief that the law of agency provided the same results, but in a simpler manner than what he described as 'the more technical and far-reaching doctrines of the law of trusts and the concomitant law attaching to the fiduciary.'[52]

Despite Estey J's rationale, the Crown–Native relationship cannot be properly characterized as one of agency. Unlike the relationship created by the Indian Act land surrender requirements, an agency relationship is a voluntary one. The principal in an agency relationship voluntarily delegates authority to another who acts on the former's behalf. Moreover, the principal possesses absolute authority, unless it provides otherwise, over the agent's actions and may remove the agent at any time. Although the Crown must act in accordance with any conditions imposed on an Indian surrender of land, it otherwise possesses absolute discretion to negotiate the terms of any sale or lease of the land and may not be removed from this position by an Indian band or group. Quite obviously, then, the Crown does not occupy the role of an agent on behalf of aboriginal peoples.[53]

The judgment rendered by Dickson J, as he then was,[54] insisted that the Crown's Indian Act-imposed obligation to act in the interests of the Musqueam band imposed liability on the former. In direct contradiction of Le Dain JA's conclusions, Dickson J found that the Indian Act created an equitable obligation by which the Crown must deal with reserve lands for the benefit of Indians. Moreover, this obligation was legally valid and enforceable in the courts. According to Dickson J, the governor in council's discretion to dispose of surrendered reserve lands had the effect of transforming the Crown's duty into a legally enforceable one.[55] However, unlike the decisions below, Dickson J based this obligation in the law of fiduciaries rather than the law of trusts.

Dickson J's finding in favour of a fiduciary obligation had the same results as if he had found the existence of a legal trust relationship between the Crown and the Musqueam. The nature and extent of the Crown's obligations to the Musqueam band and the remedies which flow from a breach of those obligations are essentially the same, regardless of whether the relationship is characterized as fiduciary or trust.[56] A trustee is a type of fiduciary and, consequently, owes virtually identical duties as the latter.[57] Despite the similarities between trust and fiduciary relations, Dickson J's analysis of the factual background to the *Guerin* case, particularly the nature of the Indian interest in land, led him to conclude that whereas a fiduciary obligation existed as a result of the Crown's actions, a legal trust relationship did not.[58]

The third judgment, rendered by Wilson J, also found the existence of a Crown fiduciary obligation to aboriginal bands which arises pursuant to the uses to which reserve lands may be put.[59] She determined that Section 18 of the Indian Act was a statutory acknowledgment of the Crown's fiduciary obligation, which was rooted in the nature of aboriginal title.[60] She held that the discretion conferred upon the governor in council by Section 18 must be exercised for the use and benefit of the band, subject to the terms of any applicable treaty or surrender.[61] Therefore, the terms and conditions stipulated by the Musqueam band during its negotiations with the Department of Indian Affairs pre-empted any discretion that the governor in council may otherwise have possessed in negotiating the terms of the golf club lease: '[I]n the circumstances of this case as found by the learned trial judge the Crown was compelled in equity upon the surrender to hold the surrendered land in trust for the purpose of the lease which the band members had approved as being for their benefit. The Crown was no longer free to decide that a lease on some other terms would do. Its hands were tied.'[62] As the governor in council's discretion under Section 18 was not unfettered and could not be arbitrarily invoked, Wilson J concluded that the band was entitled to legal recourse against the Crown if the governor in council failed to properly exercise its discretion. The availability of legal recourse by the band could only be provided for by a legally based Crown duty, not by a political trust (as the latter existed at the Crown's discretion and had no basis in law).[63]

In addition to finding the existence of the Crown's fiduciary duty to Native peoples with respect to Indian reserves, Wilson J determined that the facts in *Guerin*, especially the Crown's failure to negotiate the golf club lease on the terms and conditions stipulated by the Musqueam, despite its equitable obligation to do so, rendered the Crown's duty a trust obligation rather than a fiduciary one. Under Wilson J's assessment, the Musqueam's surrender of their reserve lands did not create the Crown's fiduciary duty; that duty was already in place by virtue of the nature of aboriginal title. Because of the specific terms on which the surrender was effected and the concomitant obligations of the Crown to carry out those terms, the Crown's fiduciary duty was transformed into a trust obligation: 'What effect does the surrender of the 162 acres to the Crown in trust for lease on specific terms have on the Crown's fiduciary duty under the section? It seems to me that s.18 presents no barrier to a finding that the Crown became a full-blown trustee by virtue of the surrender. The surrender prevails over the s.18 duty but in this case there is no incompatibility between them. Rather the fiduciary duty which existed at large under the section to hold the land in the reserve for the use and benefit of the band crystallized upon the surrender into an express trust of specific land for a specific purpose.'[64] Wilson J agreed with the trial judgment in finding the Crown, by failing to carry out the terms of the surrender in the manner agreed to by the Musqueam, to be in breach of trust.[65]

When juxtaposing the judgments of Dickson and Wilson JJ, it is interesting to note that Dickson J's key ingredient for the existence of the fiduciary obligation in *Guerin* – the surrender requirement – is the very same element which Wilson J found to create a trust relationship. These different conclusions are arrived at because of the fundamental differences in their respective notions of the basis of the trust and in their understandings of the nature and extent of aboriginal title. One of the more important points to be gleaned from the *Guerin* decision, though, is that regardless of whether the relationship between the Crown and Musqueam is described as fiduciary *or* trust-like in nature, there is no difference in the nature, scope, or extent of the Crown's obligations.

Dickson J suggested that the nature of Indian title is not accurately described by common law conceptions of property, but is *sui generis*. He stated that aboriginal title does not, strictly speaking, amount to beneficial ownership,[66] but it is not entirely caught by the concept of a personal right either.[67] Its vital characteristics are its existence independent of any treaty, executive order, or legislative enactment,[68] its general inalienability[69] and that, upon its surrender, the Crown is under an obligation to deal with the land on the Indians' behalf.[70] He deemed anything beyond these three[71] features to be unnecessary and potentially misleading.

Because of his determination that the Indian interest in land was not beneficial in nature, Dickson J found that it was insufficient to constitute the *res* of a trust.[72] He found that the basis of the fiduciary relationship in *Guerin* was the Crown's duty to act in the best interests of the Musqueam band in the leasing of the surrendered reserve lands. The legally enforceable nature of the duty existed to regulate the manner in which the Crown exercised its discretion over the surrendered Musqueam land pursuant to the surrender requirements contained in the Indian Act.

In holding that the act of surrender created the trust relationship between the Crown and the Musqueam,[73] Wilson J contended that Indian bands do possess a beneficial interest in their reserves.[74] Although she also held that the Indian interest in land is limited, she determined that it is sufficient to constitute the *res* of a trust in a situation where a band surrenders land to the Crown on specified terms for the purpose of alienation to a third party. In the absence of a surrender, however, Wilson J declared that the nature of the Indian title does not give rise to a trust. Instead, where there is no surrender, she determined that the nature of the Indian interest in reserve lands combines with the Crown's duty to protect that interest to create a fiduciary relationship.[75]

The significance of the *Guerin* case lies in its recognition of the Crown's legal duty and the obligations which emanate from it, not whether the Crown's duty is rooted in fiduciary doctrine or the law of trusts. Upon a judicial determination that an Indian band or organization is owed equitable obligations by the Crown to act in its best interests, it is ultimately immaterial to the court whether those obligations are derived from fiduciary or trust law. However, from an evidentiary point of view, the distinction between classifying the Crown as a fiduciary, as opposed to a trustee, is quite significant. The evidentiary requirements for demonstrating a fiduciary relationship are substantially lower than those necessary to prove a trust. There are no 'certainties' in fiduciary law as there are in trust law.[76] Moreover, the existence of a fiduciary relationship is not dependent on the existence of a property interest, or *res*, as is a trust relationship.[77] It is the nature and scope of a relationship which renders it fiduciary, not the actors involved or the subscription to particular rules or regulations.[78]

The *Guerin* decision, therefore, imposes the strict demands of a trustee's duties on the Crown without imposing the onerous task of establishing the existence or maintenance of a trust on aboriginal peoples. As a result, the nature of the Crown's obligations to the Musqueam are the same under both Dickson and Wilson JJ's judgments in *Guerin*, despite having the circumstances under which the Crown's duty arises differ in their respective formulations. The nature of the Crown's obligations entails its responsibility to act in the best interests of the aboriginal peoples concerned and renders it liable for any failure to do so. In *Guerin* the oral conditions attached to the surrender document were a vital part of the surrender agreement, representing the wishes of the Musqueam regarding the lease of their land. The Crown, in accordance with the nature of its obligations to the Musqueam, could not ignore those obligations without breaching its duty, as Dickson J explained. 'The oral representations form the backdrop against which the Crown's conduct in discharging its fiduciary obligation must be measured. They inform and confine the field of discretion within which the Crown was free to act. After the Crown's agents had induced the band to surrender its land on the understanding that the land would be leased on certain terms, it would be unconscionable to permit the Crown simply to ignore those terms ... The existence of such unconscionability is the key to a conclusion that the Crown breached its fiduciary duty. Equity will not countenance unconscionable behaviour in a fiduciary, whose duty is that of utmost loyalty to his principal.'[79]

After the *Guerin* decision was released by the Supreme Court of Canada, debate ensued over whether the Crown's fiduciary duty was restricted to the surrender of Indian reserve lands or whether it was of wider applicability within the ambit of the Crown–Native relationship. Dickson J's judgment soon became the focus of the debate. Many judicial and academic considerations of the *Guerin* decision incorrectly determined that the Crown's fiduciary duty was limited to situations involving the surrender of Indian reserve lands.[80] It should be noted, though, that these considerations fail to penetrate the surface of Dickson J's judgment because of an overly rigid adherence to acontextual, 'black-letter' legal analysis. As fiduciary doctrine is premised entirely on its contextual application, an adherence to this strict interpretation of Dickson J's judgment in *Guerin* is not only unhelpful, but derogates from the very basis of his analysis in the case.[81]

Under the strict interpretation of Dickson J's judgment the Crown's fiduciary obligation to the Musqueam regarding their reserve lands stems from three sources: the nature of aboriginal title,[82] the requirements of the Royal Proclamation of 1763 and the Indian Act,[83] and the Crown's discretionary power to manage and dispose of aboriginal lands.[84] Whereas the latter source is an independent progenitor of the Crown's fiduciary obligation, the first two sources must be combined for a fiduciary obligation to result. As Dickson J stated in his judgment: 'The conclusion that the Crown is a fiduciary depends upon the further proposition that the Indian interest in land is inalienable except upon surrender to the Crown.'[85]

Although this narrow view of Dickson J's judgment grounds the Crown's fiduciary duty in these three sources, its determination of the fiduciary nature of the Crown's obligation to Native peoples is entirely dependent on the surrender of Indian reserve land. Although the nature of aboriginal title and the requirements of the Royal Proclamation of 1763 and the Indian Act are necessary elements of the Crown's fiduciary obligation, they do not impose that duty in and of themselves. The act of surrender is the catalyst which creates the Crown's fiduciary obligation.[86] The nature of the Indian interest in land requires its surrender before it may be alienated to a third party. Similarly, the Crown's discretion to deal with the land does not arise until after the act of surrender. The second source, the requirements of the Royal Proclamation of 1763 and the Indian Act, simply mandates the surrender.

The necessity of the act of surrender to the existence of the Crown's fiduciary obligation, under the strict interpretation of Dickson J's judgment, is underscored by Dickson J's statement: 'When, as here, an Indian band surrenders its interest to the Crown, a fiduciary obligation takes hold to regulate the manner in which the Crown exercises its discretion in dealing with the land on the Indians' behalf.'[87] Under this method of analysis, it follows that in the absence of a situation where the Crown is entrusted with the alienation of surrendered Indian reserve lands for the benefit of an Indian band, the Crown cannot owe a fiduciary duty to Indian bands. The apparent result of adhering to this strict interpretation of Dickson J's judgment is that it imposes more limited and less onerous obligations on the Crown than what had been intended in *Guerin*. There are two fundamental flaws inherent in the strict interpretation of Dickson J's judgment, however, which render its use dubious at best.

The strict interpretation of Dickson J's decision overlooks the precise and deliberate use of language in his judgment. In particular, he stated that upon surrender, the Indians' *sui generis* interest in land gives rise to 'a distinctive fiduciary obligation on the part of the Crown to deal with the land for the benefit of the surrendering Indians.'[88] Later in his judgment, Dickson J again explained that when a band surrenders its interest to the Crown, 'a fiduciary obligation takes hold to regulate the manner in which the Crown exercises its discretion in dealing with the land on the Indians' behalf.'[89] In neither instance does Dickson J state that the Crown's general fiduciary *duty* arises upon surrender, only that a *particular* fiduciary *obligation* is created.[90] As suggested earlier,[91] the Crown's general fiduciary duty towards Native peoples is the result of the relationship between the parties from the time of contact and both builds on and informs the specific fiduciary obligations which arise within the context of particular relationships between the Crown and Indian bands. The Crown's obligation regarding surrendered reserve lands is merely one constituent element of its overall duty.

Because of the context in which it arose, the *Guerin* case only illustrated one particular aspect of the fiduciary relationship between aboriginal peoples and the Crown in Canada – the procedure by which aboriginal peoples may sell, lease, or otherwise dispose of their lands. Accordingly, the findings in *Guerin* concentrate exclusively on that particular facet of the Crown–Native relationship. The strict interpretation of Dickson J's judgment, therefore, is incorrect on yet another ground. It fails to take into account that his discussion of the Crown's duty in *Guerin* is limited to the duty of the Crown in relation to surrendered Indian reserve lands *because of the facts of the case, not as a result of the limited scope of the Crown's equitable obligations* to Native peoples.[92] Dickson J expressly contextualized the scope of his examination of the Crown's fiduciary duty in the *Guerin* case by stating that the relevance of the Crown's fiduciary duty 'in the present appeal ... is based on the requirement of a "surrender" before Indian land can be alienated.'[93] Had he wanted to indicate that the Crown only possessed fiduciary obligations to Native peoples within the limited context of the surrender of reserve lands, he would have specifically limited the application of the Crown's obligations to that context.

The foundation of Dickson J's judgment illustrates that his understanding of the Crown's duty towards aboriginal peoples is more deeply rooted and far-reaching than the strict interpretation of his judgment indicates. The historical and political basis for the Crown's imposition of the surrender requirement, which he recognized in his judgment, suggests that the strict interpretation's portrayal of the surrender requirement's role in creating the Crown's fiduciary obligation is, in fact, the mirror-image of reality. It is the fiduciary duty assumed by the Crown which gives rise to the surrender requirement, not vice versa.

Dickson J's emphasis on the Crown's historical obligation to Native peoples demonstrates that the Crown's duty predates the Indian Act and, therefore, exists independently of the Act. The Indian Act, as he stated, merely confirms the 'historic responsibility which the Crown has undertaken, to act on behalf of the Indians so as to protect their interests in transactions with third parties.'[94] He determined that the Crown's responsibility originated from the Royal Proclamation of 1763[95] and has been continuously maintained since that time, initially by the British Crown, subsequently by the governments of the colonies once they became responsible for the administration of Indian affairs and, after Confederation, by the federal Crown.[96]

The Royal Proclamation of 1763 mandated that any purchases of aboriginal lands were to be made only from the Crown. Purchases of land directly from the aboriginal peoples were strictly prohibited.[97] However, despite Dickson J's statements to the contrary in *Guerin*, the origins of the requirement that aboriginal peoples not surrender their lands other than to or with the permission of the Crown or its representatives predates both the Indian Act and the Royal Proclamation of 1763. The intention of the Crown and its representatives in North America to be a requisite intermediary in any transactions of Indian lands originated in the practice of the American colonies in the seventeenth century. One such example is an act passed by the Grand Assembly of Virginia on 10 March 1655, which stated: 'What lands the Indians shall be possessed of by order of this or other ensuing Assemblys, such land shall not be alienable by them the Indians to any man de futuro, for this will putt us to a continuall necessity of allotting them new lands and possessions and they will be allwais in feare of what they hold, not being able to distinguish between our desires to buy or inforcement to have, in case their grants and sales be desired; Therefore be it enacted, that for future no such alienation or bargaines and sales be valid without the assent of the Assembly.'[98] Virginia was not the first American colony to

Characterization by the Courts: *Guerin v R* 109

enact legislation of this type to effect a similar purpose. The 1655 Virginia Act was predated by two Acts of similar tenor in the colony of Maryland in 1638 and 1649.[99]

The Royal Proclamation of 1763, then, simply continued a long-standing practice 'to interpose the Crown between the Indians and prospective purchasers or lessees of their land, so as to prevent the Indians from begin exploited.'[100] The purpose of the surrender requirement to protect aboriginal land interests from exploitation is only one element of the Crown's desire to protect the aboriginal peoples' peaceful occupation of their lands and the concomitant rights which flow from those interests.[101] The Crown's protection of Native interests – one facet of which limits the alienation of Indian lands exclusively to the Crown – denotes its affirmation of the Crown's fiduciary responsibility towards Native peoples.[102] Therefore, the surrender requirement documented in the Royal Proclamation of 1763 is a requirement which *flows from* the Crown's fiduciary undertaking; it is not, as the strict interpretation of Dickson J's judgment suggests, a prerequisite for the founding of the Crown's fiduciary duty.

The Musqueam's commencement of their action in *Guerin* predated the passage of the Constitution Act, 1982. Accordingly, the Supreme Court of Canada's decision in *Guerin* did not incorporate or refer to the affirmation and protection of aboriginal and treaty rights contained within Sections 25 and 35 of the Act.[103] However, just as *Guerin*'s particular facts do not restrict the application of its precedent to the relationship between the Crown and aboriginal peoples within the context of the disposal of Indian reserve land, the temporal placement of the case does not render it inapplicable to an analysis of the rights and protections contained within Sections 25 and 35.[104] To do so strays from the very basis of the common law, which both promotes and is dependent on the gathering of principles and guidelines which provide a foundation for future judicial decision making.

To buttress the assertion that the Crown's fiduciary obligations to Native peoples extend beyond situations involving the surrender of reserve lands, one need only consider the historical basis on which the Crown protected aboriginal peoples and their interests. The duty which arose from this undertaking was not initially restricted to the protection of aboriginal lands. It extended to a protection of the aboriginal peoples in the enjoyment of their pre-existing rights *in rem*,[105] such as the right to hunt, trap, and fish, as well as to exercise religious, cultural, and linguistic freedom, and to practice self-government.[106] To limit the application of the legally enforceable Crown duty affirmed by *Guerin* to something less than the initial intention behind the Crown's undertaking of that duty is inappropriate. Consequently, the Crown's fiduciary obligation found in *Guerin* cannot be restricted in its application to Indian land interests, but extends to all aboriginal interests; in its broadest form, it is a general, all-encompassing duty.[107]

6

Judicial Characterizations of the Crown's Fiduciary Duty after *Guerin*

Fiduciary law currently enjoys a high profile within the confines of Canadian aboriginal rights jurisprudence. Its application to virtually every aspect of relations between the Crown and aboriginal peoples and its corresponding importance to the future of Crown–Nature relations in Canada has made it a topic of significant judicial and academic discussion. This high profile, however, cloaks the fact that the first Canadian judicial characterization of the relationship between the Crown and aboriginal peoples as fiduciary in nature occurred slightly more than ten years ago in the Supreme Court of Canada's landmark decision in *Guerin v R*.[1] Meanwhile, the casual manner in which the judiciary and academic commentators have discussed the application of fiduciary doctrine to the Crown–Native relationship after *Guerin* implies a sophisticated understanding of the ramifications of applying fiduciary theory to that relationship. This picture painted by existing judicial and academic commentaries on the subject is misleading.

The application of fiduciary doctrine to the Crown–Native relationship is neither a finished work nor even a nearly completed one. Rather, it remains a project in its infancy. There is still a considerable lack of judicial confidence and understanding in applying fiduciary principles to Crown–Native relations. The problems that continue to surround the implementation of fiduciary doctrine to the Crown–Native relationship are clearly evident in the aboriginal rights case law decided since the legal understanding of the relationship was permanently changed by *Guerin*.

One difficulty faced by post-*Guerin* cases dealing with the legal nature of the Crown–Nature relationship is *Guerin*'s paucity of suggestions as to the application of the Crown's fiduciary duty beyond that related to aboriginal lands.[2] Although both Dickson and Wilson JJ based the Crown's duty in its historical relationship with the aboriginal peoples,[3] post-*Guerin* courts and commentators have been uncertain about the precise nature and scope of the Crown's obligations. This confusion and uncertainty remain to the present day. As Donovan Waters, a noted trust law expert, has commented: '[A]s a self-contained, quasi-trust relationship the *Guerin* fiduciary association is of uncertain application or scope. It may refer in the instance of the Crown and the Indian peoples to the lands (reserve or reserve and tribal) of the Indians or to the total relationship between the Crown and the Indians.'[4]

Judicial discussion of the nature and extent of the Crown–Native fiduciary relationship after *Guerin* has been mixed. It took a few years for the judiciary – as well as for aboriginal peoples and their legal advisers – to fully comprehend the impact of the *Guerin* decision and its ramifications upon Canadian aboriginal rights jurisprudence. Although there was a definite lack of significant fiduciary case law in the immediate post-*Guerin* period, the number of cases in which fiduciary arguments have been raised has increased steadily since that time.[5]

The decision by the Federal Court of Appeal in *Kruger v R*[6] was one of the first fiduciary cases handed down after the Supreme Court's judgment in *Guerin*. The trial decision in *Kruger* was contemporaneous with the trial judgment in *Guerin*. Like its predecessors – including *Guerin* at the pre-Supreme Court of Canada level – *Kruger* was initially an action for breach of trust against the Crown. The Crown had expropriated two parcels of land from the Penticton Indian Reserve No. 1 for use as an airport. One parcel was expropriated without obtaining its surrender from the Penticton band. Compensation was paid to the band three years after the expropriation. The other parcel was also expropriated without obtaining a surrender, although a surrender was obtained two years after the fact upon the payment of compensation to the band.[7] The band alleged that in expropriating the land, the Crown failed to exercise the degree of care, stewardship, and prudent management required of a trustee.[8]

A trial, Mahoney J determined that the Crown held the reserve lands in trust for the band and that the trust was a legal, rather than politically based, trust. However, Mahoney J found that the Crown's actions in taking the parcels were not in breach of its trust obligations to the band. Although he held that the Crown was obligated to provide proper compensation to the band, the compensation issue was not reviewable because of the lapse of the applicable limitation period. The band's appeal of the trial judgment was dismissed. The Federal Court of Appeal did find, though, that the fiduciary duty discussed in *Guerin* extended beyond the limited context of surrenders of Indian reserve lands. As Heald JA explained: 'I do not think, however, that what was said by Mr Justice Dickson relative to the fiduciary relationship existing between the Crown and the Indians can be construed in such a way as to be authority for the proposition generally that the fiduciary relationship arises only where there is a surrender of Indians [sic] lands to the Crown ... Accordingly, I think it clear that the fiduciary obligation and duty being discussed in *Guerin* would also apply to a case such as this as well.'[9]

Far from being confined to reserve surrenders, the appellate judgment in *Kruger* determined that the Crown's fiduciary obligations were a fundamental part of the special, *sui generis* relationship between the Crown and Native peoples. Despite this finding the court made no attempts to elaborate on the nature and extent of the Crown's duty to the aboriginal peoples. As Stone JA indicated in his judgment, the judicial understanding of the Crown's duty sanctioned by *Guerin* was still in its initial stages: 'The doctrine of fiduciary duty enunciated by the Supreme Court of Canada in *Guerin et al. v The Queen et al.* will, of course, require elaboration and refinement on a case-by-case basis.'[10]

The trial judgment in *Apsassin v Canada (Department of Indian Affairs and Northern Development)*[11] was released two years after the final decision in *Kruger* and four years after the Supreme Court of Canada's decision in *Guerin*. The Dunne-Za Cree[12] had surrendered their traditional lands to the Crown in 1900 under the terms of Treaty No. 8. A reserve was set aside for them by Order in Council in 1916 and designated as Indian Reserve No. 172 (IR 172). In 1940 the Crown obtained a surrender of the Dunne-Za Cree's mineral rights to the reserve for the purposes of leasing them for the Dunne-Za Cree's benefit.

Near the end of the Second World War minister of mines and resources, J Allison Glen whose portfolio included Indian Affairs as well as acquiring land for returning war veterans – expressed interest in obtaining the surrender of IR 172 for the purposes of non-aboriginal settlement.[13] Glen initiated a series of events which culminated in the surrender of the reserve in September 1945.[14] Although the reserve was appraised at $93,000, negotiations between the Department of Indian Affairs and Northern Development (DIAND) and the director, the Veterans' Land Act[15] (DVLA), who had assumed the responsibility of acquiring lands for the returning veterans, resulted in only $70,000 being paid for the reserve.[16] Title to IR 172 was then transferred to DVLA by letters patent,[17] whereupon it was subdivided and sold. In September 1978 the Dunne-Za Cree commenced an action against the Crown alleging negligence, breach of fiduciary obligation, and fraud.

The interpretation of the Crown's fiduciary duty to aboriginal peoples adopted by Addy J at trial was based on the strict interpretation of Dickson J's judgment in *Guerin*. Addy J determined that the Crown's fiduciary duty applied to surrenders of Indian reserve lands, but it only arose upon surrender. He held that the duty did not arise upon the surrender of reserve mineral rights, though. Once the reserve lands were disposed of, the Crown's duty then attached to the proceeds of disposition. Any other duties – aside from what Addy J described as the Crown's onerous, and legally enforceable, duty to take reasonable care in offering advice or taking action on behalf of Indians 'the breach of which will bring into play the appropriate legal and equitable remedies'[19] – were only of a political or moral character:

With the exception of any special obligations which might be created by treaty, there is no special fiduciary relationship or duty owed by the Crown with regard to reserve lands previous to surrender, nor *a fortiori*, is there any remaining after the surrendered lands have been transferred and disposed of subsequently. The duty from that moment attaches to the proceeds of disposition. There might indeed exist a moral, social or political obligation to take special care of the Indians and to protect them (especially those bands who are not advanced educationally, socially or politically) from the selfishness, cupidity, cunning, stratagems and trickery of the white man. That type of political obligation, unenforceable at law, which the Federal Court of Appeal in the *Guerin* case (*supra*) felt should apply to the Crown following surrender (which concept was, of course, rejected by the Supreme Court), would be applicable previous to surrender.[20]

Addy J held that all of the male Dunne-Za Cree members had given their fee and informed consent to the surrender of the reserve, thereby exonerating the Crown of any wrongdoing in that regard. He did find, on the basis of the *Kruger* decision, that the dealings between DIAND and DVLA over IR 172 resulted in a conflict of interest.[21] He also found that DIAND was under an onerous fiduciary duty to ensure that it made all reasonable efforts to secure the best possible price for IR 172 at the time of the sale.[22] That duty charged DIAND with the onus of demonstrating that it had obtained a full and fair purchase price from DVLA. By failing to discharge that onus at trial, DIAND was found to have breached its duty. DIAND was not held liable for the breach, however, because of the lapse of the statutory limitation period for such a claim.

Under Addy J's formulation the Crown's duty with respect to IR 172, which was administered by DIAND, ceased once the letters patent had been issued to DVLA in 1948. The fiduciary duty attached to the reserve was then transformed into a duty attached to the proceeds, which remained with DIAND; it did not follow the title to the reserve into DVLA's hands. In any event, Addy J determined that DVLA was a corporation sole,[23] in which capacity it obtained and held the land for the purposes set forth in the Veterans' Land Act, 1942.[24] As a result, he concluded that the sale from DIAND to DVLA was, in effect, a sale from the Crown to an independent third party, thereby removing any appearance of self-dealing on the part of the Crown. He also exonerated DIAND from having committed, or intending to commit, fraud or wilfully concealing its actions from the Dunne-Za Cree.

Addy J's characterization of the Crown's fiduciary duty misses the mark on a number of grounds. He improperly applied the strict interpretation of Dickson J's judgment in *Guerin* to support his general finding that the Crown's fiduciary duty to Native peoples does not exist until the act of surrender.[25] Additionally, his characterization of the Crown's duty was based on his mistaken understanding that fiduciary relationships exist only between unequal parties.[26] In a manner consistent with traditional descriptions of the Crown–Native relationship prior to *Guerin*, Addy J denied the existence of a general fiduciary duty of the Crown towards Native peoples on the basis that the latter would only be owed such a duty if they were incapable at law of protecting their rights: 'Indians are not to be treated at law somehow as if they were not *sui juris* such as infants or persons incapable of managing their own affairs, which would cause some legally enforceable fiduciary duty to arise on the part of the Crown to protect them or to take action on their behalf.'[27]

Ultimately, however, Addy J's view that the Crown's fiduciary duty to the Dunne-Za Cree was attached to particular objects – first to IR 172 upon surrender and, once it was disposed of, to the proceeds from its disposition – is based on a fundamental misconception of the basis of fiduciary relationships. The Crown's duty is rooted in its relationship with the Dunne-Za Cree, not in the reserve land or the moneys obtained from its sale. Fiduciary relationships are people-specific rather than object-specific. The nature and scope of the relationship between parties is what renders a relationship fiduciary, not the existence of a legally recognizable property interest.[28]

The Dunne-Za Cree appealed the trial court's decision, alleging that the Crown breached its fiduciary obligations arising both prior and subsequent to the 1945 surrender. They also claimed that the Crown's fiduciary obligations relating to IR 172 were not extinguished by the transfer of title to the reserve to DVLA, but remained outstanding until the divided parcels of the reserve were deeded to individual purchasers. Furthermore, they insisted that their claims were not statute-barred or prohibited by laches. The Crown cross-appealed the trial judge's finding that it had breached its fiduciary duty by failing to obtain the highest possible price for the sale of IR 172.

The Federal Court of Appeal's decision in *Apsassin* was not rendered until February 1993. Stone JA's majority decision concluded that the relationship between the Crown and the Dunne-Za Cree was fiduciary in nature prior to the surrender of IR 172. He characterized the nature of the Crown's duty as an obligation to advise the Indians whether it was in their best interests to surrender their reserve for sale or lease. That duty stood ahead of the Crown's own desire to obtain the reserve lands for distribution to returning war veterans. Nevertheless, on the basis of the evidence presented and the precedent established by the Supreme Court of Canada in *Stein v The Ship 'Kathy K'*,[29] – which held that an appellate court should not reverse a trial judge's finding of fact absent 'palpable and overriding error' which affected the judge's assessment of the factual evidence presented – Stone JA found that the Crown did not breach its duty to the Dunne-Za Cree prior to and including the 1945 surrender.

Stone JA also agreed with Addy J's determination that the Crown's duty regarding IR 172 ceased once the reserve was vested in DVLA in 1948. He found that DVLA was an agent of the Crown only in relation to what the Veterans' Land Act authorized it to do and for no other purpose, including the continuation of the Crown's fiduciary duty. In addition, he determined that DVLA had no notice of the Crown's fiduciary duty relating to IR 172 and, therefore, could not be bound by it. Stone JA also upheld Addy J's finding that DIAND breached its duty to the Dunne-Za Cree by failing to obtain the highest possible price for the land, but was not liable for the breach because of the lapse of the relevant statutory limitation period.

In his additional reasons for judgment, Marceau JA outrightly rejected the Dunne-Za Cree's allegation of the Crown's conflict of interest as a result of the competing interests of DIAND and DVLA. He stated that the Crown could only be placed in a conflict of interest in 'very exceptional circumstances,' as 'the essence of the Crown is to serve the public and satisfy various public interests rather than to make acquisitions for itself.'[30] Marceau JA also agreed with Addy J's characterization of the Crown's fiduciary obligation. He concluded that the Crown's fiduciary duty could not attach to DVLA; rather, the duty remained with DIAND, which administered the proceeds of disposition after the sale. Marceau JA said that to hold that DVLA also held fiduciary obligations to the Dunne-Za Cree would have resulted in the 'ridiculous and inconsistent' situation of having fiduciary obligations attach to both the land and the proceeds of disposition.[31]

In a radical departure from the trial and majority judgments, Isaac CJ determined that the Dunne-Za Cree's surrender of mineral rights in 1940 was the catalyst of their claim. Pursuant to his determination that the mineral rights surrendered in 1940 were not included in the 1945 surrender, Isaac CJ insisted that the Crown breached its fiduciary duty relating to the mineral rights in either of two ways: by failing to inform the Dunne-Za Cree that the 1945 surrender was intended to include the mineral rights, if that was indeed the case and that it intended to sell rather than lease those rights, contrary to the terms of the 1940 surrender. Isaac CJ also determined that the transfer of title to IR 172 by DIAND to DVLA was not a sale from the Crown to an independent third party, but an administrative transfer between Crown agencies pending the sale of the land to the returning war veterans.[32]

As Isaac CJ held that the Crown retained the mineral rights to IR 172 after the 1945 surrender, he found that it did so under an equitable obligation to lease them for the benefit of the Dunne-Za Cree.[33] However, regardless of whether the mineral rights had been included in the 1945 surrender, Isaac CJ maintained that the Crown's fiduciary obligations in that regard, as well as those *vis-à-vis* the surface rights, remained intact after the 1948 letters patent, but ceased upon DVLA's conveyance of title to the veterans between 30 May 1952 and 4 April 1977.[34] The veterans purchasing from DVLA were not bound by the Crown's duty as Section 5(2) of the Veterans' Land Act statutorily gave the veterans a new title to the lands purchased. Furthermore, they could not be held legally bound by any pre-existing fiduciary duty attached to the land because they were 'bona fide purchasers for value without notice' of the Crown's duty.[35]

As a result of the Crown's actions, Isaac CJ held that it breached its fiduciary duty to the Dunne-Za Cree as of the date of conveyance and was liable for the damages flowing from the breach. Unlike the determinations reached at trial and by the majority on appeal, Isaac CJ found that the Dunne-Za Cree's action was not statute-barred.[36] Citing the case of *M(K) v M(H)*,[37] he favourably analogized the applicability of statutory limitation periods in the *Apsassin* situation with their application to victims of childhood sexual abuse.[38] Moreover, on the basis of Dickson J's judgment in *Guerin*,[39] he determined that the Crown's actions constituted equitable fraud. In finding that the Crown had breached its fiduciary duty to the Dunne-Za Cree, Isaac CJ dismissed the Crown's cross-appeal.

The judgment of the Federal Court of Appeal in *Apsassin* is plagued by fundamental errors. The majority's rooting of the Crown's fiduciary duty in property interests rather than the relationship between the Crown and the Dunne-Za Cree illustrates its misunderstanding of fiduciary doctrine.[40] That misunderstanding resulted in its failure to recognize the Crown's conflict of interest regarding the transfer of IR 172 from DIAND to DVLA. The majority also failed to appreciate the effect of a fiduciary's inequitable conduct on the application of statutory limitation periods and laches.[41]

Additionally, although the restrictions resulting from the *'Kathy K'* decision prohibited the Court of Appeal from reviewing Addy J's findings of fact absent 'palpable and overriding error,' the trial judge's decision was arguably blemished by such error. Addy J's judgment did not include any discussion of evidence of governmental policy contemporaneous with the surrender of IR 172 regarding the sale of Indian lands raised at trial which supported the Dunne-Za Cree's allegations.[42] It is arguable that Addy J's failure to deal with this evidence affected his assessment of the factual evidence presented before him, resulting in 'palpable and overriding error.' Both Stone JA and Isaac CJ explicitly noted Addy J's failure to discuss this evidence.[43] Indeed, Isaac CJ went so far as to state that 'the Crown's self-assumed policy of earning the maximum revenue from unused Indian lands while at the same time ensuring that Indian title was not extinguished is of considerable relevance.'[44] Despite these admonitions of Addy J's treatment of the governmental policy evidence, none of the judgments in the Federal Court of Appeal's treatment of *Apsassin* mention the possibility that this failure may have amounted to 'palpable and overriding error.'

The Supreme Court of Canada's disposition of *Apsassin* departed largely from the rationales underlying the judgments rendered by the courts below.[45] The court was divided over whether the 1940 surrender of mineral rights for lease was subsumed under the 1945 surrender of IR

172 for sale or lease. Gonthier J, for the majority, held that it was, while McLachlin J, with Cory and Major JJ concurring, determined that the two surrenders were mutually exclusive. Despite their disagreement, the court unanimously held, in contrast to Stone JA's majority decision at the Federal Court of Appeal, that the Crown did not hold any fiduciary duty to the Dunne-Za Cree prior to the surrenders.[46] McLachlin J found, instead, that the Crown only owes Indian bands a duty to prevent them from being exploited in the surrender of their lands.[47] The court agreed, however, with the trial judge's assessment that the Crown did not breach any duty to the band by way of the 1945 surrender.[48]

The Supreme Court found that the Crown was under a fiduciary obligation to deal with both the surface and mineral rights in the best interests of the Dunne-Za Cree once they had been surrendered. This duty encompassed both the monetary aspects of the transaction and whether the surrender was conducive to the Dunne-Za Cree's best interests at large.[49] The court overturned the earlier decisions in *Apsassin* by finding that the Crown had not breached its duty with regard to the surface rights to IR 172. It found that the $70,000 price obtained for the reserve was not unreasonable in the circumstances.[50] However, the court held that the Crown breached its fiduciary duty to the band when it transferred the mineral rights to IR 172 to DVLA for no consideration in 1948 since that action was inconsistent with the band's best interests.[51]

Although the court held that the transfer of mineral rights from DIAND to DVLA constituted a breach of fiduciary duty, the court held that the transfer of rights to IR 172 was not accompanied by a transfer of the former's fiduciary duty to the latter.[52] Consequently, DVLA could not be held responsible for a breach of fiduciary duty to the Dunne-Za Cree since it never possessed such a duty. Meanwhile, due to applicable provincial limitations legislation, DIAND could not be held liable for its breach of duty relating to the transfer of mineral rights to DVLA. The Supreme Court did find the Crown liable for a second breach of fiduciary duty, however, on grounds not considered by the lower courts. It determined that DIAND's transfer of the mineral rights to DVLA was an error or mistake. Meanwhile, section 64 of the 1927 Indian Act allowed the Crown to revoke any sale or lease issued in error or mistake, even against bona fide purchasers. The court determined that DIAND was under a fiduciary duty to use this statutory power to correct its error once the error and the potential value of the minerals that it had transferred were discovered.[53]

Since DIAND never used this statutory power, even after acquiring the requisite knowledge of the situation on 9 August 1949, it was in breach of its fiduciary duty. The Crown was not relieved of liability for this breach since the Dunne-Za Cree had filed their action on 18 September 1978, which was within the applicable statutory limitation period. However, while the Dunne-Za Cree were awarded damages for DIAND's breach of duty, their recovery was limited to sales of mineral rights by DVLA occurring after 9 August 1949, or only 6.75 sections of the 31 that had been transferred by DIAND to DVLA in 1948.

The Supreme Court of Canada's decision in *Apsassin* avoids some of the difficulties plaguing the earlier judgments in the case, most notably the rooting of fiduciary doctrine in property interests rather than in the nature of the relationship between the Crown and the Dunne-Za Cree. It nevertheless falls prey to a number of fundamental errors. For instance, McLachlin J's finding that the Crown was under no greater obligation to Indian bands in the context of surrender negotiations than to ensure that a band was not exploited by a surrender is inconsistent with the existence of the Crown's general fiduciary obligation towards Native peoples. The Crown's fiduciary obligation requires that it act in the aboriginal peoples' best interests, not merely to see that they are not exploited. In such a situation, the Crown is under a duty to put the band's interests foremost in its consideration in negotiating, securing, and perfecting a surrender. Moreover, McLachlin J's assertion that the band had the freedom to accept the surrender or not fails to account for the power relationship between the parties or the fact that the band was not free to negotiate a surrender on its own behalf.[54]

The very fact that the Crown must be a party in all alienations of Indian lands and that aboriginal interests in such lands must be surrendered to it prior to their release to third parties creates a fiduciary obligation on the part of the Crown. This obligation, insofar as it encompasses not just the act of surrender, but the general management of Indian lands whose title rests with the Crown, arises prior to surrender. Just as the Crown's involvement with Indian land interests arises prior to surrender, so, too, does its fiduciary duty in that respect. It is unseemly that the Crown be involved in all aspects of the surrender negotiations, act as liaison between Indian bands and interested purchasers, negotiate on behalf of the bands, and draft the terms of the surrender, only to be burdened with the less-than-onerous chore of ensuring that the bands are not exploited in the manner suggested by the Supreme Court in *Apsassin*. Moreover, the Supreme Court's reaffirmation of the trial judge's finding that the Crown owes no duty prior to surrender improp-

Judicial Characterizations after *Guerin* 121

erly adheres to the strict interpretation of Dickson J's judgment in *Guerin* and ignores the historical basis of the Crown's obligations to the aboriginal peoples.

The Supreme Court of Canada's first opportunity to consider the Crown–Native fiduciary relationship after *Guerin* arose only after the decisions in *Kruger* and the trial judgment in *Apsassin*. It briefly mentioned the existence of the fiduciary relationship between the Crown and aboriginal peoples in the cases of *Paul v Canadian Pacific Ltd*[55] and *Roberts v Canada*.[56] Although neither case dealt specifically with the question of the Crown's fiduciary duty, they are early, albeit brief, illustrations of the Supreme Court's understanding of the nature of the Crown's obligation that it had initiated in *Guerin*.

The primary issue to be decided in the *Paul* case was whether Canadian Pacific was entitled to a permanent injunction to restrain the Woodstock Indian band from interfering with the operation of a railway which ran along a right of way through the band's reserve. In 1975 the Woodstock band had blocked the right of way, whereupon Canadian Pacific initiated an action to restrain the band from interfering with the railway's operation. The injunction was granted at trial, but was reversed on appeal. In overturning the appeal court's judgment, the Supreme Court adopted the restrictive view of Dickson J's judgment in *Guerin* by holding that the Crown's duty applied only to reserve lands. As the court stated, 'In *Guerin* ... this Court recognized that the Crown has a fiduciary obligation to the Indians with respect to the lands it holds for them.'[57]

The *Roberts* case centred around a dispute between two Indian bands competing for the exclusive use and occupation of a reserve. Technically, it took the form of a trespass action brought by the Wewayakum Indian band[58] against the Wewayakai Indian band.[59] The Wewayakum band also sought a permanent injunction against the Wewayakai band to keep the latter off the land in dispute. Like *Paul*, *Roberts* did not expand upon the understanding of the Crown–Native fiduciary relationship illustrated by the Supreme Court of Canada in *Guerin*. It did suggest, however, that the Crown's duty is rooted in something more than just aboriginal title: '[T]he provisions of the *Indian Act* which, while not constitutive of the obligations owed to the Indians by the Crown, codify the pre-existing duties of the Crown toward the Indians. Still another source is the common law relating to aboriginal title which underlies the fiduciary nature of the Crown's obligations.'[60] The *Roberts* decision is also noteworthy for its statement, reminiscent of Rand J's comments in the *St*

Ann's Island case,[61] that the Crown–Native fiduciary relationship was incorporated into federal law by the terms of the Indian Act: 'While, as was made clear in *Guerin*, s. 18(1) of the *Indian Act* did not create the unique relationship between the Crown and the Indians, it certainly incorporated it into federal law by affirming that "reserves are held by Her Majesty for the use and benefit of the respective bands for which they were set apart."'[62]

Interestingly, although both *Paul* and *Roberts* seem to have adhered to the land-based conception of the Crown's duty in its most restrictive sense, in neither case does the Supreme Court state that the Crown's fiduciary obligations exist only where there is a surrender of Indian lands. It should be remembered, though, that the nature of the Crown's duty is merely mentioned by the court in each case as a consideration within its determinations of the main issues in question. It was not until the case of *R v Sparrow*[63] that the Supreme Court grappled more extensively with the implications of the *Guerin* decision.

The *Sparrow* decision is one of the most prominent in modern Canadian aboriginal rights jurisprudence. Its lofty position is derived from its discussion of the aboriginal and treaty rights contained in Section 35(1) of the Constitution Act, 1982, the nature of the Crown–Native fiduciary relationship, and the impact of the latter on the former. Although *Sparrow* is not a fiduciary case *per se*, its imposition of restrictions on the Crown's ability to pass legislation which impinges on aboriginal and treaty rights is rooted in the Crown's historical fiduciary obligations to Native peoples.

The primary issue in *Sparrow* was the determination of the nature and scope of aboriginal fishing rights and the ability of the Crown to interfere with those rights. The appellant, Ronald Sparrow, was charged under the federal Fisheries Act[64] with fishing with a drift net longer than that permitted by the terms of his band's food fishing licence.[65] Section 4 of the British Columbia Fishery (General) Regulations[66] specifically prohibited anyone from fishing without a valid licence and imposed restrictions on the areas, times, and the manner in which fishing could take place.[67] Sparrow admitted using a net longer than the licence allowed, but contended that he was exercising his aboriginal right to fish under Section 35(1) of the Constitution Act, 1982. He maintained that the legislation was repugnant to his aboriginal right to fish and that he should not be limited in his right because of the conflict with Section 35(1).

To determine the fundamental issue in dispute, the Supreme Court was faced with the task of 'explor[ing] for the first time the scope of s.35(1) of the Constitution Act, 1982, and to indicate its strength as a promise to the aboriginal peoples of Canada.'[68] From the court's assessment of the terms included within Section 35(1), the power of Parliament to regulate the aboriginal and treaty rights contained within it, and the historical relationship between the Crown and aboriginal peoples in Canada, it determined that Section 35(1) afforded aboriginal peoples with constitutional protection against provincial legislative power, the basis of which was rooted in the precedent established by *Guerin*.[69] However, there is no discussion in *Guerin* of the ability of provincial governments to legislate in respect of Native rights. This finding by the court in *Sparrow* demonstrates its understanding of the breadth of the *Guerin* decision and rejection of the strict interpretation of Dickson J's judgment in that case. It also indicates that the precedent established in *Guerin* is unaffected by the constitutional protection of aboriginal and treaty rights in Section 35(1).

The *Sparrow* decision should have put to rest the argument in favour of restricting the Crown's fiduciary duty to situations involving the surrender of reserve lands. Based on the precedents in *Guerin*, *Nowegijick v The Queen*,[70] and *R v Taylor and Williams*,[71] the Supreme Court determined that Section 35(1) embraced the notion of a general Crown fiduciary duty that extended to all situations involving aboriginal and treaty rights.[72] In so doing, *Sparrow* did not ignore *Guerin's* finding that the basis of the Crown's duty rested in the historical relationship between the Crown and aboriginal peoples in Canada.[73] Instead, *Sparrow* determined that section 35(1) itself included the existence of a Crown responsibility to act in a fiduciary capacity with respect to aboriginal peoples.[74] The court determined that the combination of the Crown's fiduciary duty and its entrenchment in Section 35(1) 'import some restraint on the exercise of sovereign power.'[75]

Whereas the Crown's exercise of sovereign power was held to be restrained by its fiduciary duty,[76] the court found that such a limitation did not entail the Crown's inability to regulate aboriginal rights. The effect of Section 35(1)'s constitutionalization of the Crown's fiduciary duty rendered the Crown's legislative authority over 'Indians and Lands reserved for the Indians' in Section 91(24) of the British North America Act, 1867, subject to the restraint on that power contained in Section 35(1). As the court stated in arriving at this conclusion, the existence of Section 35(1) entailed that 'federal power must be reconciled with federal duty and the best way to achieve that reconciliation is to demand the justification of any governmental regulation that infringes upon or denies aboriginal rights.'[77]

The result of combining the federal Crown's exclusive power over aboriginal rights with its fiduciary duty to the Native peoples was the establishment of a justificatory scheme in *Sparrow* through which any legislation affecting an aboriginal right must pass to be constitutionally valid.[78] Prior to the implementation of the *Sparrow* justificatory test, there were a number of different interpretations of the meaning and extent of Section 35(1) rights. The most reasonable understanding of those rights prior to *Sparrow* was that the guarantee of rights in Section 35(1) was dependent on the sovereignty of the Constitution Act, 1982,[79] and subject to the necessary balancing of rights and competing interests that exist in democratic societies.[80] This notion is reflected by Section 1 of the Charter of Rights and Freedoms, which allows for the infringement of rights guaranteed under the Charter if such infringements are 'demonstrably justified in a free and democratic society.' The limitation of Charter rights in accordance with this principle is further explained by the imposition of what has become known as the *Oakes* test.[81] In accordance with this notion, Blair JA suggested in *R v Agawa*: 'Indian treaty rights are like all other rights recognized by our legal system. The exercise of rights by an individual or group is limited by the rights of others. Rights do not exist in a vacuum and the exercise of any right involves a balancing with the interests and values involved in the rights of others. This is recognized in s.1 of the *Canadian Charter of Rights and Freedoms*.'[82] What did not exist, however, was any explicit explanation of how Section 35(1) rights ought to be limited where necessary.

Unlike rights enshrined in the Charter, Section 35(1) rights, although subject to being balanced with competing interests, had no explicit limitation placed on them prior to *Sparrow*.[83] The rights guaranteed by Section 35(1) are not affected by the limitations clause in Section 1 as Section 35(1) exists outside of the Charter. Section 35(1) protects and constitutionally entrenches all aboriginal and treaty rights which had not been extinguished prior to 17 April 1982, including rights which had been infringed, but not terminated, prior to that date.[84] Before *Sparrow* Section 35(1) rendered any legislation that was inconsistent with the dictates of Section 35(1) invalid to the extent of that inconsistency, subject only to an amorphous balancing of Section 35(1) rights with competing interests.

Prior to entering into a discussion of the *Sparrow* test, it is necessary to point out a contentious issue relating to the test's application. From the *Sparrow* decision itself, it is unclear whether the *Sparrow* justificatory test

Judicial Characterizations after Guerin 125

applies to both aboriginal and treaty rights contained in Section 35(1). Although the *Sparrow* case dealt only with aboriginal rights, it did not restrict the application of its justificatory test to those rights. It could be argued that limiting the test's application to aboriginal rights would improperly abridge its application in a manner akin to the limitation of the Crown's fiduciary duty to Native peoples seen in the restrictive interpretation of Dickson J's judgment in *Guerin*. However, there is a significant difference between the *Guerin* and *Sparrow* scenarios that requires clarification.

In *Guerin* there was no compelling reason to restrict the scope of the Crown's fiduciary duty to the surrender of land for leasing purposes. The court limited its discussion of the Crown's duty to the Crown's specific obligation relating to the surrender of Indian lands owing to the facts in the case and for no other reason.[85] In relation to the application of the justificatory test described in *Sparrow*, however, there is a significant distinction between the application of the test to aboriginal rights versus its application to treaty rights.

Aboriginal rights are inherent rights, whereas treaty rights may be obtained only through negotiation with the Crown. Therefore, it could be argued that as compacts between the Crown and aboriginal peoples, treaties cannot be limited in the manner contemplated by the *Sparrow* test because, as negotiated rights, they may take any form which is agreed to by the parties (in a manner similar to arguments in favour of freedom of contract). In any event, as with the opposition to the notion of freedom of contract, the fact that rights existing in a democratic society cannot be absolute means that the *Sparrow* test, or some other form of limitation, be applied to treaty rights. Yet, because treaties are negotiated instruments, the Crown's fiduciary duty to uphold the integrity of treaty rights that it has guaranteed and put its name to requires that it be able to infringe upon treaty rights only under the most urgent of circumstances. On those rare occasions where it is able to derogate from its guarantee of treaty rights to Native peoples, the Crown must act in accordance with fiduciary obligations of the highest order.

In some recent cases the *Sparrow* justificatory test has been held to apply equally to aboriginal and treaty rights.[86] With deference to those decisions, it appears as though the significant distinction between aboriginal and treaty rights was not given its proper due therein. For example, in *R v Bombay*, Austin JA dealt with the issue in the following manner. 'The *Sparrow* case dealt with the Aboriginal rights. The language of the decision of the Supreme Court of Canada in that case, however, is equally applicable to treaty rights. In *R v Joseph*, [1990] 4 C.N.L.R. 59 (B.C.S.C.) Murphy J held that the framework provided by the Supreme Court in *Sparrow* "applies also to treaty rights." I agree.'[87] Clearly, there was no consideration given in the written judgment in *Bombay* to the significant distinction between aboriginal and treaty rights. It appears as though the lumping together of those rights in Section 35(1) is solely responsible for the joint application of the *Sparrow* test to those rights rather than because of any reasoned analysis of why aboriginal and treaty rights should be treated equally with respect to their limitation by governmental legislative initiatives. Consequently, and for the reasons detailed above, this point is in need of clarification by the Supreme Court of Canada.[88] However, in consideration of the present status of the law regarding the *Sparrow* test's application, the discussion of the test herein will focus on both aboriginal and treaty rights.

To avoid the misunderstanding of Section 35(1) rights as being absolute, *Sparrow* imposed a test which acts in the place of the Section 1 justificatory test, or *Oakes* test, for the purpose of limiting the rights contained within Section 35(1) where it is deemed both legitimate and necessary to do so.[89] In the aftermath of *Sparrow* Section 35(1) rights may only be abrogated or derogated from in three ways: (1) by voluntary consent of the aboriginal peoples concerned; (2) by constitutional amendment; or (3) by passing the *Sparrow* test. The first method is straightforward. The second is somewhat less so. It requires that the onerous amending procedure outlined in Section 38 of the Constitution Act, 1982, be followed. The less stringent amending procedure in Section 43 cannot be used because it applies only to amending constitutional provisions which apply to one or more, *but not all* of the provinces, whereas aboriginal and treaty rights apply to all provinces and territories, albeit to varying degrees and extents.

The third method of limiting Section 35(1) rights applies only to legislation, not to private action.[90] Although the Supreme Court of Canada has held in a number of cases that the Charter applies only to public, not private, activity,[91] Section 35(1), existing outside of the Charter, arguably applies to both public and private activity. The importance of this distinction is that Section 35(1) rights cannot be interfered with by a private party without breaching Section 35(1) and requiring the balancing of these competing interests. Whereas public activity prior to *Sparrow* could also not interfere with Section 35(1) rights without being subjected to the same amorphous balancing of rights, the *Sparrow* test allows for the infringement of aboriginal rights by legislative initiatives which pass its justificatory standards. Unless and until the *Sparrow* test is broadened to include all infringements of Section 35(1) rights, or some other limitation is created, private interference with Section 35(1) rights will remain subject to the pre-*Sparrow* balancing of rights test discussed above.

The *Sparrow* test, as emphasized by the court, must be implemented on a case-by-case basis because of the generality of Section 35(1) and the 'complexities of aboriginal history, society and rights,' which necessitate that 'the contours of a justificatory standard must be defined in the specific factual context of each case.'[92] The test itself may be summarized in five parts:

1 There must be a *legislative* objective for the test to be applied (that is, the objective must be supported by legislation).
2 If a legislative objective exists, it must be determined whether that objective interferes with Section 35(1)'s guarantee of aboriginal and treaty rights.[93] A three-part approach is implemented to determine whether there is a prima facie interference with a Section 35(1) right:
   i Is the limitation imposed by the legislation unreasonable?
   ii Does the legislation impose undue hardship on the aboriginal peoples?
   iii Does the legislation deny aboriginal peoples their *preferred* means of exercising their Section 35(1) rights?[94]

   The onus of proving a prima facie infringement remains with the person or group challenging the legislation.[95] An infringement exists if the purpose or effect of the limitation unnecessarily infringes the interests protected by the Section 35(1) right. An example of such an infringement would be where a regulation makes fishing much more difficult, time consuming, and costly to aboriginal peoples.[96]
3 If a legislative objective exists which interferes with a Section 35(1) right, does it amount to a legitimate regulation of a constitutional right?[97] To determine this point, the legislative objective must be deemed to be *valid*.[98]
4 If the legislative objective is valid, it must be consistent with the Crown's fiduciary obligation towards Canada's aboriginal peoples.[99] In keeping with the Crown's fiduciary duty, any legislative interference with Section 35(1) rights must infringe those rights as little as possible in order to effect the desired result.[100]

   The onus of proving that the infringement of Section 35(1) rights is justifiable rests on the government enacting the legislation.[101] To demonstrate a justifiable infringement, the legislation must not have an underlying unconstitutional objective and must be 'absolutely necessary to accomplish the required limitation.'[102]

5 Other factors to be considered within this context include an obligation to pursue other feasible options for producing the same net effect which do not infringe Section 35(1) rights. It is only where there is no other viable option to the infringement of Section 35(1) rights that a legislative objective, having passed the requirements set out above, may be upheld by the courts. Even where legislation is upheld in this way, there exists an obligation to consult with the aboriginal peoples affected with regard to the legislative initiative to be implemented.[103] Moreover, in circumstances which involve the expropriation of aboriginal lands, fair compensation must be made available.[104]

The *Sparrow* court's final comments regarding its justificatory test reemphasize the fiduciary nature of the Crown–Native relationship. Should any considerations arise under circumstances which were not contemplated by the court, any measures to be implemented must be consistent with the terms of Section 35(1) itself. This requires 'sensitivity to and respect for the rights of aboriginal peoples on behalf of the government, courts and indeed all Canadians.'[105] Moreover, the Crown's fiduciary obligation to aboriginal peoples necessitates that the *Sparrow* test pass only those valid legislative objectives which are deemed sufficiently necessary to warrant their intrusion upon the aboriginal enjoyment of Section 35(1) rights: 'By giving aboriginal rights constitutional status and priority, Parliament and the provinces have sanctioned challenges to social and economic policy objectives embodied in legislation to the extent that aboriginal rights are affected. Implicit in this constitutional scheme is the obligation of the legislature to satisfy the test of justification. The way in which a legislative objective is to be attained must uphold the honour of the Crown and must be in keeping with the unique contemporary [fiduciary] relationship, grounded in history and policy, between the Crown and Canada's aboriginal peoples.'[106]

The fiduciary duty described in *Sparrow* may, therefore, be seen to be derived from a different, although not contrasting, source than the duty established in *Guerin*. Whereas the Crown's fiduciary obligation to Native peoples in *Guerin* was ultimately based on the historical relationship between the groups and the Crown's undertakings to protect Native interests, the *Sparrow* duty is rooted in Section 35(1) of the Constitution Act, 1982. However, the historical, political, social, and legal factors which gave rise to the Crown–Native fiduciary relationship in

Judicial Characterizations after *Guerin* 129

Guerin form the backdrop of Section 35(1). Therefore, in rooting the Crown's fiduciary duty in Section 35(1), *Sparrow* did not ignore the historical genesis and background of the Crown–Native fiduciary relationship.

The *Sparrow* decision marked a significant advance in the judicial understanding of the Crown–Native fiduciary relationship. One of its least familiar effects is its direction regarding the interpretation of the Crown's duty to Native peoples. Whereas previous decisions treated the Crown's duty as they would any other obligation, the Supreme Court in *Sparrow* suggested that the Crown's fiduciary duty be purposively applied: 'The nature of s. 35(1) itself suggests that it be construed in a purposive way. When the purposes of the affirmation of aboriginal rights are considered, it is clear that a generous, liberal interpretation of the words in the constitutional provision is demanded.'[107] The implications of this conclusion in subsequent decisions are yet to be observed.[108] In the interim, the purposive application of the governmental duty in *Sparrow* forms the basis for speculation as to its future implementation and resultant effects on the Crown–Native relationship.[109]

Although the Supreme Court of Canada has had few opportunities to consider the fiduciary nature of the Crown–Native relationship since *Sparrow*,[110] the use of fiduciary arguments in aboriginal rights cases has increased substantially since the *Sparrow* decision was handed down in 1990. Unfortunately, few of these decisions demonstrate any advances in the judicial understanding of the nature and extent of the Crown's duty beyond that displayed by the Supreme Court in *Sparrow*. Nevertheless, a number of these judgments are worthy of analysis for their illustrations of the disparate judicial characterizations of the Crown's fiduciary duty.

The Federal Court, Trial Division's consideration of the Crown's fiduciary responsibilities in *Bruno v Canada (Minister of Indian Affairs and Northern Development)*[111] adhered to the strict interpretation of Dickson J's judgment in *Guerin*. Pursuant to a jointly agreed-upon statement of facts, the parties applied for the determination of a Special Case[112] to ascertain whether the Crown was under any duty to pass the Indian Oil and Gas Regulations[113] earlier than 22 April 1977. If it was determined that there was such a duty upon the Crown, the parties sought a ruling as to whether that duty was breached and, if so, whether the breach caused damages to the plaintiff, the Alexander Indian Band No. 134 (the Alexander band).

The band had surrendered all petroleum and natural gas rights on its Alberta reserve to the Crown for lease in exchange for production royalties. In 1973 world oil and gas prices increased substantially. Certain Alberta Indian bands whose production was provincially regulated realized substantial increases in their royalties as a result of the higher prices. Because it was under federal regulation, the Alexander band did not receive similar royalty increases. It finally obtained an increase in its royalties in 1977. The band asserted that the Crown was under a fiduciary duty to take timely action to raise its royalties to a level equivalent to that realized by the provincially regulated bands during the period from 1973 to 1977.[114]

On behalf of the court, Strayer J determined that the Crown was under no obligation to adopt the Indian Oil and Gas Regulations earlier than April 1977. He reasoned that the regulations involved the exercise of a general legislative power granted to the governor in council that transcended any possible fiduciary obligation owed by the Crown to the band in the particular facts of the case. He held that the enactment of the Indian Oil and Gas Regulations was to be viewed primarily as the performance of a political duty which was unenforceable by the courts.[115] Despite Strayer J's statement that the nature of the Crown's fiduciary duty, after *Guerin*, amounted to 'a general fiduciary obligation owed by the Crown in right of Canada towards each Indian band in respect of the reserve land of each band,'[116] the court's ruling was much more restrictive. Strayer J's findings concord entirely with the strict interpretation of Dickson J's decision in *Guerin*: 'One can deduce from the protective stance taken by the Crown ever since the *Royal Proclamation, 1763* that the Crown kept to itself the exclusive right to acquire and dispose of Indian title because it had the unique power and responsibility to act as an appropriate protector of the interests of the people who inhabited this land before the arrival of Europeans. It is wholly consistent with this view that the Crown should exercise these governmental powers which only it has, where this may reasonably and lawfully be done to perform adequately the specific fiduciary obligation it owes to a given band *whose Indian title has been surrendered to the Crown.*'[117]

Although Strayer J recognized the Crown's historic desire to protect aboriginal interests, in accordance with the strict interpretation of Dickson J's judgment in *Guerin*, he restricted the scope of the Crown's protection to Indian land interests which have been surrendered to the Crown. There is a logistical leap in reasoning from his explanation of why the Crown retained the exclusive right to acquire and dispose of Indian title to the limit he placed on the application of the Crown's duty. In particular, he failed to explain why, given his recognition of the Crown's unique power and responsibility to act as the protector of aboriginal interests, the Crown must only exercise that power and responsibility where there has been a surrender of Indian title.

One reason why the Crown has retained the exclusive right to acquire and dispose of Indian lands for a lengthy period is its desire to protect aboriginal interests from the encroachment of non-aboriginal settlers.[118] Indeed, this fact has been recognized by the Canadian judiciary for well over one hundred years.[119] However, the necessity of the Crown interposing itself between aboriginal peoples and prospective purchasers of their lands, at least within the context of protecting aboriginal interests,[120] is based on the intermeshing of aboriginal spiritual, cultural, and other interests with their land interests. These spiritual, cultural, and other interests are inextricably linked with aboriginal interests in land and have long been protected by the Crown.[121] In order to fulfil its general fiduciary obligations to Native peoples, the Crown's duty to monitor and protect aboriginal interests must be continual and all-encompassing; it cannot arise only upon the surrender of land in respect of that land. Strayer J's curtailment of the Crown's duty in *Bruno* is, therefore, fundamentally incompatible with his own conceptual understanding of the basis of the Crown's duty.

Of further note is the court's determination that it is 'the Crown in right of Canada,' that owes the fiduciary duty to the aboriginal peoples. This determination is contextual rather than conclusive, because the issue of provincial fiduciary responsibilities was irrelevant to the *Bruno* situation. It is similar to the situation in *Guerin*, whereby the Crown's fiduciary duty was restricted to situations involving the surrender of aboriginal land interests as a result of the nature of the issues before the court. In the absence of any explicit limitation on the application of the Crown's fiduciary duty to Native peoples, it cannot be inferred that the extent of the Crown's duty is limited to situations in which it has been found to exist,[122] including previous judicial determinations of which emanation of 'the Crown' owes the duty. There is no such limitation in *Bruno*.

The case of *Cree Regional Authority v Robinson*[123] was decided almost one year after the *Bruno* decision. The central issue to be judicially determined in the case was the obligation of the federal administrator appointed pursuant to the James Bay and Northern Quebec Agreement (JBNQA)[124] and its implementing legislation[125] *vis-à-vis* conducting an environmental assessment of the Great Whale River Hydroelectric Project in Northern Quebec. Specifically, the court had to decide whether the federal administrator was obligated to conduct federal environmental and social impact assessment and review procedures pursuant to the JBNQA or whether the federal and Quebec Crowns could jointly conduct a single environmental assessment study of the project similar to that provided for by the Environmental Assessment and Review Process Guidelines Order (EARP guidelines).[126]

The court determined that the federal administrator had to follow the procedure mandated by the JBNQA's requirements, as any review carried out pursuant to the EARP guidelines would be of no force or effect to a provincial undertaking. Although the court agreed with the decision in *Bruno* that *Guerin* is authority for imposing fiduciary obligations on the federal Crown where a band has surrendered its land interest to the Crown,[127] it implied that provincial Crowns may also hold fiduciary obligations towards Native peoples. The court held that the *Sparrow* decision did not distinguish between the federal and provincial Crowns and, therefore, that 'the provincial authorities are also responsible for protecting the rights of the Native population.'[128] As a result, it was not open to the federal and Quebec Crowns, in the absence of seeking the Cree's consent, to subvert the only method of protecting the Cree's rights under the JBNQA. Had the court ruled otherwise, it would have sanctioned the federal and Quebec Crowns' ability to unilaterally implement an alternative assessment process which was unable to prevent the Great Whale project from proceeding even if it failed to pass the EARP guidelines.[129]

The facts in *Eastmain Band v Robinson*[130] are virtually identical to those in the *Cree Regional Authority* case. The plaintiff sought to have the federal administrator of the JBNQA carry out the federal environmental and social impact assessment and review procedures provided for in the JBNQA with respect to the proposed Eastmain 1 Hydroelectric Project (EM1) in Northern Quebec. Alternatively, it sought to have the ministers of Transport, Indian Affairs and Northern Development, and Fisheries and Oceans comply with the assessment procedures under the EARP guidelines. Although the EM1 project was found to be exempt from the JBNQA's review requirements, the court held that the minister of Indian Affairs and Northern Development was responsible for discharging the Crown's fiduciary duty to aboriginal peoples. That obligation was found by the court to include a duty to apply the EARP guidelines.[131]

The trial judgment in *Eastmain* was reversed on appeal.[132] The Federal Court of Appeal held that the federal Crown's fiduciary duty to the band did not render the EARP guidelines applicable to the EM1 project, as no federal law or other affirmative duty imposed an obligation on the minister of Indian Affairs and Northern Development to make a decision with respect to the carrying out of the project. The court also held that the possibility of environmental impact on matters relating to the exclusive federal jurisdiction over 'Indians, and Lands reserved for the Indians' was insufficient to render the EARP guidelines applicable to the project.[133]

Although the Federal Court of Appeal overturned the trial court's finding of fiduciary duty, it attempted to place the Crown's duty within context: 'When the Crown negotiates land agreements today with the Aboriginals, it need not and cannot have only their interests in mind. It must seek a compromise between that interest and the interest of the whole society, which it also represents and of which the Aboriginals are part, in the land in question.'[134] The court's discussion of compromise is similar in sentiment to that suggested by Blair JA in *Agawa*.[135] Of particular note in the appellate judgment was the court's recognition of the purposive application of the Crown's fiduciary duty found to exist in *Sparrow*. Interestingly, the court did not cite *Sparrow* on this point, but quoted from the New Zealand Court of Appeal's decision in *New Zealand Maori Council v Attorney-General*, where Cooke P stated: '[T]he duty of the Crown is not merely passive but extends to active protection of Maori people in the use of their lands and waters to the fullest extent practicable. There are passages in the Waitangi Tribunal's Te Atiawa, Manukau and Te Reo Maori reports which support that proposition and are undoubtedly well-founded.'[136]

One of the most recent treatments of the Crown's fiduciary obligations to Native peoples by the Supreme Court of Canada is that court's decision in *Ontario (Attorney-General) v Bear Island Foundation*.[137] At trial, the case focused on the claim of the Teme-Augama Anishnabai – referred to as 'the Temagami' by the trial judge – to ownership of their traditional lands by virtue of aboriginal title. Ontario sought to prevent the Temagami band from maintaining cautions[138] which had been registered against certain tracts of unceded lands. Meanwhile, the band sought a declaration that it possessed aboriginal title to its traditional lands. Until the Supreme Court of Canada's judgment was handed down, there had been no mention of fiduciary duty in the case, either at trial or in the Ontario Court of Appeal level.

The pivotal issue in the Supreme Court's consideration of *Bear Island* was whether or not the Teme-Augama Anishnabai adhered to the Robinson-Huron Treaty, 1850, either expressly or by implication.[139] In an exceedingly brief judgment for a case of its magnitude, the Supreme

Court held that the Temagami people surrendered their rights to the land by arrangements subsequent to the Robinson-Huron Treaty, 1850, by which they adhered to the treaty in exchange for annuities and a reserve. The Supreme Court did find, however, that 'the Crown' breached its fiduciary obligations to the Temagami by failing to comply with its obligations under the treaty. The court did not elaborate on how the Crown breached its obligations, what the extent of those obligations was, or the ramifications of the breach.

Interestingly, the court stated that, at the time its decision was handed down, the breach was the subject of negotiations between the parties involved. The court did not divulge the identity of the parties involved. However, the only parties to the negotiations mentioned by the court were the Teme-Augama Anishnabai and the Province of Ontario; the federal Crown was not involved. The obvious implication to be garnered is that the province was, itself, bound by the fiduciary obligations of 'the Crown.' If the province was not bound by those obligations, what would be the purpose of its involvement in negotiations over the breach of duty to the Temagami by 'the Crown' without that of the federal Crown?[140] The implications arising from this statement are significant for their ramifications upon the understanding of who is bound by the Crown's fiduciary obligations towards Native peoples in Canada.[141]

The facts in *Lower Kootenay Indian Band v Canada (Federal Administrator)*[142] gave the Federal Court, Trial Division, a golden opportunity to dive headlong into a reasoned consideration of the nature and extent of the Crown's fiduciary duty to Native peoples. The Lower Kootenay band sought a declaration that the Crown breached its fiduciary obligations to the band regarding two surrenders of land as well as damages resulting from the Crown's failure to fulfil its fiduciary duty.

In 1934 a surrender of uncultivated land was made by the band and a fifty-year lease signed between the Crown and a local reclamation company. The company began work on the lands after the band assented to the surrender, but prior to the signing of the lease. The band never received a copy of the lease.[143] In 1948 it was discovered that the band's surrender had never been perfected by Order in Council, as required under Section 51 of the 1927 Indian Act.[144] This omission was only made known to the band in 1974. The band had been applying pressure on the Department of Indian Affairs for a number of years to terminate the lease.[145] The lease was terminated in 1982 when the band had commenced an action against the Crown (which was ultimately discontinued).[146]

Judicial Characterizations after *Guerin* 135

The band claimed that it was not properly consulted about the lease, that its terms were unfavourable, and that a collateral agreement which was to provide it with additional lands was not fulfilled.[147] It maintained that the lease should have been terminated no later than 1948, when the failure to perfect the surrender was discovered. The Crown contended that the failure to perfect the surrender did not harm the band as the band still received benefits under the lease. More importantly, the Crown insisted that it did not have to obtain a surrender of uncultivated lands under Section 93 of the Indian Act, thereby rendering the surrender gratuitous and not in need of perfection. The band objected to the Crown's contention, asserting instead that because the Crown had obtained a surrender of the land, it was duty-bound to fulfill the Indian Act's requirement of perfection.

In finding that the Crown had, indeed, breached its fiduciary duty to the band, Dube J adhered, for the most part, to the understanding of the Crown's duty formulated by Addy J in the trial level decision in *Apsassin*. However, Dube J strayed from that formulation by finding that the Crown's duty was not transferred to the proceeds of the lease after surrender, but attached to the lease for its duration.[148] As for the issue of perfection, he agreed with the band's assertion that the Crown had to perfect the surrender it had obtained, even though the surrender itself was not necessary under the circumstances: 'In my view, it is clearly irrelevant whether the Department could have proceeded by way of s. 93. In fact it did not. It chose the surrender route but failed to follow it through. The surrender was never approved by cabinet and the Indians were therefore denied a protection to which they were entitled by law.'[149]

As the surrender had not been perfected it was void *ab initio*, as was the lease.[150] Dube J found that the Crown breached its fiduciary duty by not informing the band of the failure to perfect the surrender upon its discovery of that fact, much less waiting for thirty-four years to disclose that information.[151] He also found the Crown to have breached its duty to the band for failing to negotiate the lease in the band's best interests[152] and for not taking action to renegotiate the lease once it had discovered, in 1938, that the terms were inadequate.[153] The Crown was not held liable for failing to enforce the collateral agreement alleged by the band because of a lack of evidence.[154] The band was awarded damages of just under one million dollars, plus accrued interest from 1982 to the date of judgment and costs.

An obscure, but noteworthy, case that touches on the Crown's fiduciary duty is *R v Vincent*.[155] The appellant was a status Indian convicted of breaching the Customs Act[156] by being in possession of illegally imported tobacco. She maintained that the terms of the Jay Treaty, 1794, by which the free passage of aboriginal peoples between Canada and the United States was specifically addressed in Article III, and other international treaties, as well as the protection of treaty rights in Section 35(1) of the Constitution Act, 1982, exempted status Indians from the payment of customs duties on goods imported from the United States into Canada. The appellant was supported in her claim by the Chiefs of Ontario. Article III of the Jay Treaty entered into between Britain and the United States stipulated: 'No duty of entry shall ever be levied by either party on peltries brought by land or inland navigation into the said territories respectively, nor shall the Indians passing or repassing with their own proper goods and effects of whatever nature, pay for the same any impost or duty whatever. But goods in bales, or other large packages, unusual among Indians, shall not be considered as goods belonging bona fide to Indians.'[157]

The Court of Appeal upheld her conviction on the basis of the precedent established by the Supreme Court of Canada in *R v Francis*,[158] in which a status Indian lost his bid to avoid paying customs duties on three large appliances he had purchased and brought back from the United States. Citing the cases of *Rustomjee v The Queen*[159] and *Civilian War Claimants Association Limited v The King*,[160] the court stated that in an international treaty between sovereign states, the Crown cannot be the fiduciary or agent of a subject, nor can a subject be the beneficiary of a trust.[161] In the course of its judgment, the court enlarged the judicial understanding of the Crown's fiduciary duty to Native peoples by determining that the interpretive principles enunciated in *Nowegijick v The Queen* were a part of the Crown's fiduciary duty.[162]

The Court of Appeal's inclusion of the *Nowegijick* principles of treaty and statutory interpretation as a part of the Crown's fiduciary obligations was not arbitrarily done. Although no basis for this inclusion was made explicit in the *Vincent* judgment, it would appear to be an extrapolation from the Supreme Court of Canada's statement in *Sparrow* that 'the principles ... derived from *Nowegijick, Taylor and Williams* and *Guerin* should guide the interpretation of s. 35(1).'[163] As Section 35(1) was found by the court in *Sparrow* to include the Crown's fiduciary obligation to Native peoples, the guiding principle in *Nowegijick* was held by the Court of Appeal in *Vincent* to be, itself, a part of the Crown's duty.

In contrast to the important principle found in the otherwise insignificant *Vincent* case, the Crown's fiduciary duty in *Delgamuukw v British Columbia*[164] was a very minor element of a highly publicized and widely anticipated judgment. The *Delgamuukw* case was widely anticipated for its pronouncement on many prominent aboriginal rights issues. The Gitksan and Wet'suwet'en hereditary chiefs had commenced an action seeking a declaration that they possessed jurisdiction over and ownership of their traditional lands. Alternatively, they maintained that they possessed aboriginal rights to use the land. Their claim was founded on the occupation, use, and enjoyment of the land by the plaintiffs, their people, and ancestors since time immemorial; the terms of the Royal Proclamation of 1763; and the further confirmation of their rights by the Constitution Act, 1982. The province maintained that the lands in dispute, as well as jurisdiction over them, belonged to it.

In finding in favour of the province at trial, McEachern CJBC, as he then was, addressed many issues of importance to Canadian aboriginal rights jurisprudence. Unfortunately, his lengthy judgment was plagued by numerous errors and fundamental misunderstandings of vital aboriginal rights issues and precedents which negate its jurisprudential value. Although he denied the plaintiffs' claims, McEachern CJBC held that the Crown had a fiduciary duty to the plaintiffs. The extent of that obligation was to permit the plaintiffs, subject to the general laws of the province, to use unoccupied or vacant Crown lands for subsistence purposes until such lands were dedicated to another purpose.[165] The Crown was further prevented from arbitrarily limiting the aboriginals' use of vacant Crown land or else be found in breach of its duty.[166] He did not specify the ramifications of such a breach upon the Crown.

What McEachern CJBC characterized as the Crown's fiduciary duty is in no wise such a thing. Rather, it was an allowance for Native peoples to use something which belonged to the Crown while it was of no use to the Crown. This 'right' is not at all consistent with fiduciary doctrine. The 'fiduciary' right of the aboriginal peoples to use the land, as he characterized it, is not protected by Section 35(1) and is, therefore, not subject to the *Sparrow* justificatory test. The right may simply be legislated away by the province at any time, subject only to the provision that any such legislation must not arbitrarily limit the aboriginal use of vacant Crown land. Moreover, as McEachern CJBC determined that the Crown's fiduciary duty 'should be confined to issues which call the honour of the Crown into question with respect to the territory as a whole,'[167] that duty is merely a political one. It is, essentially, no different than Le Dain JA's characterization of the Crown's duty in the Federal Court of

Appeal's judgment in *Guerin*, which was subsequently overturned by the Supreme Court of Canada.

McEachern CJBC's portrayal of the Crown's fiduciary duty is incapable of being enforced as it may be eliminated simply by dedicating vacant Crown land to some use. Its presence in the *Delgamuukw* trial judgment is more symbolic than real. What is interesting about the *Delgamuukw* trial decision, however, is that it indicates that the Crown's fiduciary duty belongs to both the federal and provincial Crowns. In dismissing the province's counterclaim, which sought a declaration that the aboriginals' cause of action could seek compensation only from the federal Crown, McEachern CJBC held that as the aboriginals had the Crown's promise that it would permit them to use vacant Crown land and as that promise could only be enforced against the province because of the operation of Section 109 of the British North America Act, 1867,[168] the province was bound by it.[169] When the *Delgamuukw* case was appealed, the fiduciary obligation that McEachern CJBC found to exist at trial was neither raised by the parties nor fleshed out by the British Columbia Court of Appeal. The case is now to be heard by the Supreme Court of Canada.

These post-*Guerin* cases demonstrate that the judiciary has been entirely inconsistent in its application of fiduciary principles. Furthermore, no clear judicial understanding of the nature and extent of the Crown's fiduciary obligation towards Native peoples may be derived from the sum of the post-*Guerin* case law. The majority of cases offer few insightful points within their individual judgments. A significant number blindly apply the strict interpretation of Dickson J's judgment in *Guerin* without attempting to understand the basis or the actual breadth of the *Guerin* decision. Moreover, their individual assertions are often incompatible with each other and inconsistent with fiduciary doctrine. The legacy of these post-*Guerin* cases, then, is short on substance and abundant in confusion. Not surprisingly, this situation is not entirely different than what the Supreme Court of Canada initially left after its decision in *Guerin*.

7

The Status of the Crown's Fiduciary Duty

As the discussion in the previous chapter of post-*Guerin* case law on the Crown's fiduciary duty demonstrates, there is no common thread to the judicial reasoning which underlies these judgments. Part of the legacy of misunderstanding and confusion which arises from these jurisprudential considerations of the Crown–Native fiduciary relationship is the result, in part, of the deficiencies inherent in the Supreme Court of Canada's decision in *Guerin*.

One of the peculiar aspects of the *Guerin* decision is that it details the grounding of the relationship between the Crown and aboriginal peoples without actually discussing the specifics of either the relationship or its resultant obligations. Nevertheless, judicial considerations of fiduciary law within the confines of Native rights have followed *Guerin*'s precedent by similarly imposing fiduciary obligations on the Crown in its dealings with aboriginal peoples without discussing or detailing the specifics of the Crown's duty. What may be gathered from *Guerin* and subsequent considerations of the Crown–Native relationship, then, is that the Crown owes a fiduciary duty to aboriginal peoples, but fundamental questions, such as which personifications of the Crown owe the duty or the effects of the duty on the parties affected by it, remain unclear.

Of the judicial considerations of the Crown's duty since *Guerin*, the Supreme Court of Canada's decisions in *Roberts v Canada*,[1] *R v Sparrow*,[2] *Ontario (Attorney-General) v Bear Island Foundation*,[3] and *Apsassin v Canada*[4] are worthy of special attention. Of these, *Sparrow* provides the most insightful analysis. Nevertheless, it possesses the very same basic flaws as *Guerin*; it neither addresses the question of who owes the Crown's duty nor what is actually encompassed within it. Although the

Sparrow judgment judicially entrenched the Crown's fiduciary obligations in Section 35(1) of the Constitution Act, 1982, and determined that the Crown's duty must be acted upon purposively – both of which are significant advances beyond the duty discussed in *Guerin* – the decision fails to elaborate any further on the integral aspects of the duty itself.

The Supreme Court of Canada's considerations of the Crown's fiduciary duty after *Guerin* provide little aid to future judicial determinations as to whether the Crown's fiduciary obligation in a particular scenario has been fulfilled. The *Bear Island* decision is emblematic of that court's unquestioned application of fiduciary doctrine. It illustrates the Supreme Court's comfort in applying fiduciary doctrine to the Crown–Native relationship without explaining what its application to that relationship entails. Based on the Supreme Court of Canada's treatment of the Crown's fiduciary duty to aboriginal peoples, it is perhaps less surprising that the federal and provincial courts have also failed to significantly advance the judicial understanding of the Crown's obligations.

The judiciary's handling of the fiduciary question within the field of Native law and the content of its judgments have had two effects. The most obvious has been to entrench fiduciary law as a vital element of Canadian aboriginal rights jurisprudence. However, in securing a place for fiduciary law in the law of aboriginal rights, the judiciary has managed to add an additional, unexplained piece to the aboriginal rights puzzle. The judiciary's failure to elaborate on the implications of the legal sanctioning of the Crown's duty in *Guerin* points to the existence of a significant problem which the judiciary has thus far been unwilling to address. This problem revolves around the courts' inability to understand or characterize the historical relationship between the Crown and Native peoples in Canada in an appropriate context.

Understanding this historical relationship within a conceptual framework befitting its many facets is the key to understanding the nature of modern Crown–aboriginal relations and the fiduciary obligations which are an integral part of them. A number of post-*Guerin* cases acknowledge that the Crown's fiduciary obligation is ultimately rooted in this relationship, which dates from the time of initial British contact in North America. However, whereas *Guerin* was the first case to designate the Crown–Native relationship as fiduciary, the existence of that relationship as a fiduciary one did not begin with *Guerin*. By recognizing that the relationship from which the Crown's fiduciary obligations originate predates the judicial recognition of the relationship's fiduciary nature, the courts implicitly acknowledge this fact.

Describing a relationship as fiduciary does not change or alter its dynamics. After all, the dynamics of a relationship cause it to be described as fiduciary by the courts in the first place. A court's description of a relationship as fiduciary, therefore, does not transform it into something other than what it has always been. Rather, the only effect of such a designation is to afford it the protection of the law. This protection provides beneficiaries with the ability to enforce their fiduciaries' obligations in the courts and furnishes remedies for breaches of those obligations. At their most basic level, then, legally sanctioned fiduciary relationships are those which are neither rooted in nor created by law, but are merely affirmed and protected by law.

Fiduciary relationships exist on two independent, but interconnected planes – the legal and the extralegal. The legal plane of fiduciary relationships includes all relationships which are recognized by law as fiduciary. The extralegal plane is comprised of relationships that may be designated as 'pure' fiduciary relationships in the scientific or mathematical sense. Pure fiduciary relationships include relationships which are properly recognized by law as fiduciary, as well as other relationships which are fiduciary in nature because of their facts and circumstances, but have yet to be recognized by the law as such. Their place on the second plane emanates from the fact that they are fiduciary by reason of the interaction of the parties involved.

In contrast to pure fiduciary relationships, 'applied' fiduciary relationships include only those relationships which are deemed to be fiduciary by the judiciary. They include relations which are properly declared to be fiduciary as well as those deemed to be fiduciary without any sound basis for such a determination. Unfortunately, the distinction between 'pure' and 'applied' fiduciary relationships is not always recognized. Only the former are appropriately classified as fiduciary. Meanwhile, the latter are largely responsible for much of the confusion which presently surrounds fiduciary doctrine.

The independence of these two planes of fiduciary relationships is reflected in the fact that some relationships which are fiduciary on one plane may not be fiduciary on the other. A relationship which is wrongfully characterized by law as fiduciary – that is, merely to facilitate the equitable remedy of tracing[5] – exists only on the legal plane. A relationship which, by its nature and circumstances, is fiduciary, but has yet to be recognized as such by law – such as the Crown–Native relationship prior to the *Guerin* decision – exists only on the extralegal plane. It is entirely possible, however, for a relationship to exist simultaneously on both planes – which is what happened to the Crown–Native relationship in the aftermath of *Guerin*. In accordance with this understanding, it may be seen that the fiduciary relationship between the Crown and aboriginal peoples was not 'created' by the Supreme Court of Canada in *Guerin*. *Guerin* only marks the first judicial recognition and protection of this historical relationship.

As the autonomy of the two planes of fiduciary relationships illustrates, mere recognition by law does not render any relationship a pure fiduciary relationship. Pure fiduciary relationships exist only as a result of the facts and circumstances unique to the intercourse between two or more persons or groups. In this sense, pure fiduciary relationships are extralegal. Their purity becomes more evident by contrasting them with those judicially sanctioned, or 'applied' fiduciary relationships which are not fiduciary by nature, but only by judicial decree.

The distinction between pure and applied fiduciary relationships is significant. The difference between a duty which is recognized and affirmed by law and one which is created by law is that the latter, as a positive creation of law, relies entirely on the law for its existence and vitality. The former, meanwhile, is merely a positive affirmation of a pre-existing duty. As such, it does not depend on the law for its existence, although its existence without legal affirmation provides no legal protection or remedy for wronged beneficiaries. Where the former does depend on the law is for its implementation and protection against competing interests by legal mechanisms and forums such as civil rights of action and the courts.[6]

The notion that pure fiduciary relationships depend on the law only for the enforcement of fiduciaries' equitable obligations is illustrated by the recent decision of the High Court of Australia in *Mabo v Queensland [No. 2]*.[7] The Meriam people, the Aboriginal plaintiffs in *Mabo*, sought declarations as to their Aboriginal rights to their traditional lands in the Murray Islands. The Murray Islands had been formally annexed to Queensland in July 1879 pursuant to Letters Patent issued by Queen Victoria in October 1878 and thereafter were created as Crown lands. The islands had been considered by the government of Queensland to be reserved for the use of the Meriam people, subject to specific exceptions. In their action, the Meriam people asserted that the islands remained subject to their unextinguished Aboriginal title and did not belong to the Crown.

The majority decision of the court held that the Murray Islands were not Crown lands, but remained subject to the unextinguished Aboriginal title of the Meriam people. Accordingly, the Meriam people were entitled to the possession, occupation, use, and enjoyment of their traditional lands *in rem*, or against all potential claimants.[8] Their title to the islands, however, was held to be subject to extinguishment by the valid exercise of power by the Queensland Parliament or its governor in council. In the course of his analysis, Brennan J found what whereas Aboriginal title is recognized by English common law, it is neither an institution of the common law, nor alienable under the common law. Accordingly, he determined that the rights existing under Aboriginal title could not be enforced under the common law, but only under the customary laws from which they were derived: 'The common law cannot enforce as a proprietary interest the rights of a putative alienee whose title is not created either under a law which was enforceable against the putative alienor at the time of the alienation and thereafter until the change in sovereignty or under the common law.'[9] Brennan J did find, however, that the common law principle of recognizing customary title only where it is consistent with the common law is subject to an exception in favour of traditional aboriginal title.

An essentially similar determination about the enforceability of aboriginal title under the common law was made by the United States Supreme Court in one of its earliest decisions on aboriginal rights, *Johnson and Graham's Lessee v M'Intosh*.[10] The case centred around a dispute over the ownership of former Indian land situated within the Indian territory designated in the Royal Proclamation of 1763 and the original boundary of the Virginia colony established by royal charter in 1609. Johnson was the successor-in-title of a colonist, who, in contravention of the proclamation's prohibition on the private purchase of Indian lands, had obtained the land from its original Indian owners shortly before the American Revolution. M'Intosh had obtained his title from the United States government, which had obtained it from Virginia after the Revolutionary War had ended.

In finding in favour of M'Intosh, Marshall CJ did not dispute the validity of Johnson's title under Indian law. He held, however, that it was unenforceable by American courts, as it was the creature of a separate legal system and thereby governed by its laws:

If an individual might extinguish the Indian title for his own benefit, or, in other words, might purchase it, still he could acquire only that title. Admitting their power to change their laws or usages ... still it is a part of their territory, and is held under them, by a title dependent on their laws. The grant derives its efficacy from their will; and ... the courts of the United States cannot interpose for the protection of the title. The person who purchases lands from the Indians, within their territory, incorporate himself with them, so far as respects the property purchased; holds their title under their protection, and subject to their laws ... [T]he plaintiffs do not exhibit a title which can be sustained in the courts of the United States.[11]

The Crown's ability to alter the nature and extent of any pre-existing right belonging to the aboriginal peoples – or any pre-existing duty owed to them by the Crown – which is merely recognized or affirmed by the law is less than what it would possess if the right or duty had been created by the law. Where a right is made by the law, it can also be entirely undone by the law. The same cannot be said for pre-existing rights or duties that exist independently of the law. All that a legal system can do in such a circumstance is to refuse to recognize or enforce those rights or duties.

The law need not always recognize a pre-existing, extralegal duty. However, in situations where a pre-existing duty is known, especially where the Crown has been directly involved, the law is obliged to recognize it. One such example is the fiduciary nature of the Crown–Native relationship. The law's obligation to recognize known, pre-existing duties stems from the nature and origins of the relationships which give rise to the duties as well as the law's own duty to protect those relationships. In the Crown–Native situation, the law's duty to protect that relationship and its concomitant obligations is, by virtue of the *Guerin* decision, expressed by fiduciary doctrine. The fact that fiduciary doctrine has been used to describe and govern the Crown–Native relationship does not render that relationship subservient to the common law or denote an acceptance of British colonialist practices. Rather, it merely indicates the existence of a mechanism to both illustrate and monitor the special, *sui generis* relationship between the Crown and aboriginal peoples which is adequate to the task.

The fiduciary character of the Crown–Native relationship, as we have seen, has its origins in the formative years of Crown–Native interaction. Elements of the general fiduciary nature of the relationship may be seen in documents ranging from the Treaty of Albany through to the Royal Proclamation of 1763 and beyond. As a result of its basis in the formative years of their relationship, the existence of the Crown–Native fiduciary relation is not dependent on the continued recognition of aboriginal sovereignty by Britain or affected by the change in the intent of Indian treaties. Fiduciary law's concern with these events lies solely in determining whether these changes are consistent with the fulfilment of fiduciary obligations by the Crown (that is, whether they constitute a breach of the Crown's duties to Native peoples).

If the Crown entered into these sovereign alliances with the Native peoples, but did not, in fact, recognize such status in the aboriginal peoples, it would still be bound by these same fiduciary obligations. The content and context of Crown–Native relations from the time of contact demonstrate that, even if the Crown never believed in the notion of aboriginal sovereignty or equality, its representations acknowledging that status are sufficient to render it a fiduciary of the Native peoples. As will become evident in later chapters, the intention, or lack thereof, of a fiduciary (or beneficiary, for that matter) to enter into a fiduciary relationship is irrelevant to the ultimate determination of whether or not a fiduciary relationship exists.[12] The important consideration to be weighed is whether the nature of the interaction of the parties is such as to render their relationship a fiduciary one.

The Crown's general fiduciary duty is derived from a number of historical, political, social, and legal events and occurrences which date from the time of contact. This duty is rooted primarily in the formative years of Crown–Native relations, but hovers over the totality of Crown–aboriginal relations. The Crown's general duty may also be accounted for in a number of documentable events, including the reciprocally enriching, interdependent relationship between the Crown and aboriginal peoples characterized by the recognition of the independence of its actors, mutual respect, need, and political expediency (especially in the immediate post-contact period);[13] the military and political alliances forged between the Crown and aboriginal peoples; the ongoing process of treaty negotiations; the Royal Proclamation of 1761[14] and the Royal Proclamation of 1763, which reflect the Crown's recognition and affirmation of its fiduciary responsibility towards the Native peoples;[15] the further assertion of this fiduciary responsibility in Section 91(24) of the British North America Act, 1867; the promulgation of specific legislation to govern aboriginal peoples, which eventually became consolidated as the Indian Act in 1876;[16] and Section 35(1) of the Constitution Act, 1982.

The various forms of the Crown's fiduciary duties to Native peoples may arise in any of four different ways. They may arise from the Crown's unilateral assumption of specific duties for a Native group's benefit, including, for example, the constitutional entrenchment of aboriginal and treaty rights in Section 35(1) of the Constitution Act, 1982.

The voluntary entering into of an arrangement between the Crown and Native peoples, such as by way of treaty or agreement, may also result in the creation of fiduciary duties. The nature of the relationship between the Crown and Native peoples itself may result in the imposition of fiduciary duties. This may be seen in the context of the Crown's general fiduciary duty to the aboriginals – resulting from the historical intercourse between them – or in more specific fiduciary obligations arising from particular Crown–Native relationships. Finally, the Crown may be found to hold fiduciary responsibilities to aboriginal peoples by way of the judiciary's imposition of such duties on it.[17]

The Crown's fiduciary obligations to the aboriginal peoples, which began when the Crown was subordinate in power to the aboriginal peoples and has continued to exist throughout all of the changes in the nature of that relationship over time, remain despite the drastic change in the nature of the Crown–Native relationship. It is the product of historical relationships, the actions of the Crown and its representatives, British and Canadian governmental practice, treaties, and legislative recognition.[18] However, since the early stages of the twentieth century, the aboriginal peoples have become more dependent on the Crown's fulfilment of its duty than at any other stage of their relationship. It is arguable that the Crown's obligations have become even more stringent as a result of the ascent of the Crown in the political and economic structure of Canada at the expense of the aboriginal peoples and in direct contravention of its fiduciary duty to them.[19]

In spite of the long-standing history and importance of the Crown–Native fiduciary relationship, judicial expression of the Crown's duty since *Guerin* has been limited, incomplete, and desperately in need of elaboration. To remedy this fundamental deficiency, it is necessary to examine the general principles of the law of fiduciaries in order to obtain a solid working knowledge of its basic tenets. Moreover, by examining the constituent elements of fiduciary relationships in general, the more complicated, *sui generis* nature of the Crown–Native fiduciary relationship may be more adequately understood.

PART TWO

General Principles
of Fiduciary Doctrine

8
A Re-examination of Fiduciary Doctrine

Fiduciary doctrine is an elusive concept. It has a lengthy existence, dating back over 250 years to the celebrated case of *Keech v Sandford*.[1] Before that, it had been a well established part of Roman law. The duration and frequency of fiduciary law's application to a wide variety of relationships fosters the impression that the fiduciary concept is one of the most well understood of legal doctrines. Indeed, within the past thirty years, the Supreme Court of Canada has discussed the existence of fiduciary relationships between senior officers/directors and a corporation,[2] custodial parent and non-custodial parent,[3] solicitor and client,[4] federal government and Indian band,[5] doctor and patient,[6] father and daughter,[7] and financial adviser and client.[8] On closer scrutiny, however, the frequent judicial application of fiduciary principles is only a thin veneer concealing the uncertainty which plagues fiduciary theory.[9]

The law reports abound with descriptions of relationships as fiduciary when they actually bear little or no resemblance to such relationships.[10] In fact, the judiciary has misapplied fiduciary law in a variety of instances: for remedial purposes in instances where there has been no demonstrated existence of a fiduciary relationship or where such a demonstration would prove impossible,[11] or where heads of obligation exist independently of the fiducial relation.[12]

Despite, or perhaps because of, the general confusion surrounding fiduciary doctrine, it has recently experienced a tremendous growth in use.[13] Fiduciary arguments have become something of a 'catch-all' – if all other claims are meritless or no other cause of action exists, a claim of breach of fiduciary duty is often resorted to.[14] In *Burns v Kelly Peters & Associates Ltd*, Lambert JA highlighted the potential problem stemming from the indiscriminate use of fiduciary doctrine's malleable principles in this fashion: 'The danger, of course, which such a flexible remedy, is that it should be used as a catch-all for cases which offend against some of the more exacting standards of commercial morality. So the extra flexibility should promote a sense of caution in determining whether the fiduciary relationship exists. Or, as Viscount Haldane said in *Nocton v Ashburton*, at p. 596: "... the special relationship must ... be clearly shown to exist."'[15]

The increase in the use of fiduciary arguments has not escaped notice by the judiciary. In *Girardet v Crease & Co*, Southin J, as she then was, noted that the word 'fiduciary' is flung around now as if it applied to all breaches of duty by solicitors, directors of companies and so forth.'[16] In *LAC Minerals v International Corona Resources Ltd*, La Forest J stated, 'There are few legal concepts more frequently invoked but less conceptually certain than that of the fiduciary relationship.'[17] Judicial notice of the misapplication of the fiduciary concept illustrates the existence of a serious problem. What have often purported to be applications of fiduciary principles by the courts have too often been an amalgamation of unrelated rules, only some of which may be a part of fiduciary doctrine.

Some of the confusion surrounding fiduciary doctrine may be traced to judicial tendencies to incorrectly view the labeling of a person or relationship as fiduciary as the end of their investigatory process. The judiciary has often acted as though the mere description of a relationship as fiduciary was sufficient to enable it to apply a remedy.[18] As the American jurist Oliver Wendell Holmes once stated, 'It is one of the misfortunes of the law that ideas become encysted in phrases and thereafter for a long time cease to provoke further analysis.'[19] Rather than denoting the end of judicial investigation, describing a person or a relationship as fiduciary creates the need for further inquiry. As Mr Justice Felix Frankfurter explained in *Securities & Exchange Commission v Chenery Corp*: '[T]o say that a man is a fiduciary only begins analysis; it gives direction to further inquiry. To whom is he a fiduciary? What obligation does he owe as a fiduciary? In what respect has he failed to discharge these obligations? And what are the consequences of his deviation from duty?'[20]

The judicial desire to describe relationships as fiduciary cannot ignore the ramifications of such a description *en route* to the imposition of one of fiduciary doctrine's desirable remedies.[21] Without knowing what it is that renders a person or relationship fiduciary, that description is meaningless. The explanation of the obligations arising by virtue of the relationship's existence is what breathes life into the fiduciary characterization. This necessitates, however, an investigation into the nature of the interaction giving rise to the fiduciary relation: 'It is pointless to describe a person – or for that matter a power – as being fiduciary unless at the same time it is said for the purposes of which particular rules and principles that description is being used. These rules are everything. The description "fiduciary" nothing.'[22]

The examination of fiduciary doctrine in Part Two rests upon twin premises: Fiduciary doctrine is both a valuable tool for the control and regulation of socially valuable or necessary relationships and it has often been wrongfully characterized and misunderstood.[23] Fiduciary law is not only 'law's blunt tool' for the control of a fiduciary's discretion,[24] but shapes the parameters of the ability of beneficiaries to rely upon their fiduciaries' exercise of that discretion in good faith. Fiduciary relationships ought to be understood both for the duties and obligations possessed by fiduciaries as well as the benefits that flow to beneficiaries from the existence of such relationships. This necessitates a contextualization of fiduciary doctrine, something that has been omitted far too frequently from juridical examinations.

There is a need for a different approach to fiduciary doctrine, one that can avoid the pitfalls that have resulted in its inconsistent application by the judiciary. Such an approach ought to begin by looking to the theoretical basis and origins of fiduciary doctrine for guidance in the proper method of understanding and applying fiduciary principles. By discovering the rationale behind the imposition of fiduciary doctrine, it may then look to existing theories and commentaries to ascertain their key aspects, including their limitations. What is needed, then, is an explication of the underlying purpose of fiduciary doctrine, what it aims to promote, and how it attempts to do so, through an examination of its theoretical underpinnings. Once these are understood, it is possible to apply the principles of fiduciary doctrine in a manner consistent with the doctrine's fundamental purpose.

A Functional Approach to Fiduciary Doctrine

Traditionally, fiduciary relationships have been defined according to categories. Where questions of the fiduciary nature of particular relationships arose, juridical examinations would focus on whether the relationship under scrutiny belonged to the list of relationships that were generally understood to be fiduciary in nature, such as trustee and beneficiary, parent and child, and guardian and ward. The nature of the particular relationship itself or the interaction of the parties involved in it was a secondary matter. Accordingly, there were no established guidelines for determining what constituted a fiduciary relationship: '[I]n times gone by we really were not troubled by the absence of a coherent definition. When pushed to answer the question of who a fiduciary is, we simply rattled off the standard categories of fiduciaries: trustee–beneficiary, agent–principle [sic]; director–company; guardian–ward and solicitor–client. The traditional approach, in other words, was that although we could not define "the beast," we could recognize one when we saw it so lack of a definition was not a problem.'[25]

The use of categories to determine the fiduciary nature of a relationship runs counter to the very basis of fiduciary doctrine. Fiduciary law has its origins in public policy, specifically the desire to protect certain types of relationships that are deemed to be socially valuable or necessary.[26] The common elements to the relationships which come under its protection are the trust and confidence placed by one person in another within a given context. This reposing of trust by one person in the honestly, integrity, and fidelity of another, as well as the former's reliance upon the latter's care of the trust, is the basis for the creation of legal mechanisms such as fiduciary law and the law of trusts.[27] These laws seek to protect those who trust in the ability of others from having that trust abused.[28]

The policy underlying the law of fiduciaries is focused on a desire to preserve and protect the integrity of socially valuable or necessary relationships which arise from human interdependency. Fiduciary law's preservation of relationships that come under its auspices requires that fiduciaries adhere to a high standard of conduct. This is achieved through the imposition of certain restrictions on fiduciaries' fulfilment of their special office, a requirement necessitated by virtue of the inherent inequality of the parties created by the nature of their interaction.[29] Meanwhile, the ever-increasing degree of interdependency in societies governed by English common law or its derivatives has resulted in the commensurately broadened mandate of fiduciary law within those spheres. Fiduciary doctrine has expanded its application to fill the increasing need to protect those who are dependent on others for particular tasks and to ensure that relationships created by the push towards interdependency remain viable. As Ernest Weinrib has suggested: 'A sophisticated industrial and commercial society requires that its members be integrated rather than autonomously self-sufficient, and through the concepts of commercial and property law provides mechanisms of

A Re-examination of Fiduciary Doctrine 153

interaction and interdependence. The fiduciary obligation ... constitutes a means by which those mechanisms are protected.'[30]

Without the need of individuals to rely on others, there would be no need for fiduciary law. Maintaining the viability of an interdependent society requires that that interdependency is closely monitored to avoid the potential for abuse existing within such relations. Individuals are far more apt to subject themselves to situations of dependence or reliance upon others if they can be assured that their interests and consequent vulnerability are protected.[31] Fiduciary law satisfied this additional need by providing protection for beneficiaries who are involved in fiduciary relations from the potential for indecorous activities against their interests by unscrupulous fiduciaries. Therefore, the existence of fiduciary law protects the interest of individuals who rely on others and allows for the continuation and proliferation of interdependent relationships which carry the possibility for mala fide activity by one party against the other.

What is truly important, then, and what fiduciary law is designed to protect, is the integrity of a wide variety of socially valuable or necessary relationships.[32] Therefore, fiduciary law ought to be applied on the basis of its inherent purpose rather than through the application of 'established' categories of fiduciary relations. Protecting the integrity of these relationships requires that those who possess the ability to affect the interests of others be prevented from abusing their powers for personal gain. Because individual beneficiaries or external factors such as existing social mores or the marketplace cannot completely eliminate the potential for fiduciaries to abuse their positions, Equity filled this gap through its imposition of fiduciary doctrine.[33]

In addition to augmenting the constraints of social mores and the rules of the marketplace, Equity's imposition of fiduciary doctrine also ensures that the spirit, as well as the intent, of interdependent relations is maintained. In *McLeod and More v Sweezey*,[34] the defendant was to stake and record some asbestos mineral claims on behalf of the plaintiffs as part of a profit-sharing agreement. The defendant reported that there was no asbestos, whereupon the plaintiffs allowed the claims that had been staked under the agreement to lapse. When the defendant was no longer associated with the plaintiffs, he returned to the area – which had no asbestos, but which he knew was rich in chrome – and staked his own claims. The plaintiffs brought an action against the defendant for their share of the profit earned from the sale of his claims.

In finding in favour of the plaintiffs, the Supreme Court of Canada imposed a constructive trust on the proceeds from the defendant's sale of the claims, with 75 per cent to go to the plaintiffs as per the agreement. In determining the nature of the defendant's undertaking pursuant to the agreement, the court held that the defendant's obligations were not limited to asbestos claims, but covered all minerals found in the area staked out:

> They had bargained for his mature judgment and for that not only on the possibility of asbestos. The expression in the memorandum agreement, 'asbestos mineral claims,' was description [sic] of what had been originally staked. The plaintiffs desired an expert opinion on those claims in the totality of their possibilities and not on one of them only. That, therefore, was the measure of the defendant's duty as the fiduciary of the plaintiffs in acting upon the disclosure of all the plaintiffs had of value; he undertook to apply his experience to everything found in the area of the claims ... He, therefore, owed to the plaintiffs the utmost good faith in his examination of the structure, formation, and other evidence of the land to which he was directed, and a duty to give them an unreserved account of what he had found and what, in his judgment, the mineral prospect was.[35]

In the *McLeod* case the existence of the defendant's fiduciary duties to the plaintiffs prohibited him from being able to take advantage of a technicality – no asbestos, but chrome – for personal gain at the expense of others. Had the defendant not entered into the agreement with the plaintiffs, under which they reposed their trust and confidence in him and gave him key information, the defendant would not have known of the existence of the claims and, consequently, would not have discovered the chrome deposits. Essentially, the defendant's duty of utmost good faith to the plaintiffs entailed an obligation to live up to the spirit of the agreement – that is, an obligation to report on the existence of all minerals, not just asbestos – and not merely its technical terms. Of course, the defendant's duty in this sense was not unlimited. Had he found the existence of an underground spring or a rare breed of truffle on the claimed lands and kept that information to himself for his own benefit, it is arguable that he would not have been found liable for a breach of fiduciary duty – such information would be too far removed from his obligation to the plaintiffs for him to have to share it with them.[36]

Two basic themes becomes evident from the theoretical basis of fiduciary doctrine. Initially, it is apparent that the fiduciary nature of any relationship arises from circumstances peculiar to that relationship and

A Re-examination of Fiduciary Doctrine   155

the interaction of its participants and not as a result of belonging to 'traditional' categories of fiduciary relations. Second, as fiduciary relationships ought not be confined to already established categories and should be determined by a more functional approach, the categories of relationships that may be described as fiduciary should be viewed as open ended.

The Situation-Specific Nature of Fiduciary Doctrine

The most vital aspect of fiduciary doctrine, and what ought to receive the bulk of juridical attention, is its focus on the specific characteristics of individual relationships. In its own milieu, the basis of fiduciary theory is quite general and deliberately so. However, to be consistent with its theoretical basis, the facts specific to the relationship being examined must provide the necessary guidelines for the application of fiduciary doctrine's general principles. A priori assessments are therefore completely inappropriate within the realm of fiduciary law. Because of its implementation on a case-by-case basis, fiduciary doctrine is most appropriately described as *situation-specific*. What this means is that the law of fiduciaries is not properly implemented without regard for the context within which it is to be applied.

The situation-specific nature of fiduciary doctrine renders the judiciary's implementation of fiduciary doctrine a much more proactive endeavour than the application of most legal principles. The tremendous importance of this characteristic is reflected in the notion that a relationship ought to be described as fiduciary only if its nature and the circumstances under which exists warrant its classification as fiduciary: 'What must be shown ... is that the actual circumstances of a relationship are such that one party is entitled to expect that the other will act in his interest in and for the purposes of the relationship. Ascendancy, influence, vulnerability, trust, confidence or dependence doubtless will be of importance in making this out, but they will be important only to the extent that they evidence a relationship suggesting that entitlement.'[37]

Because the determination of the fiduciary nature of any relationship is situation-specific, it follows that it is not possible to authoritatively determine the totality of relationships which may be deemed to be fiduciary.[38] For these reasons, any attempt to create a taxonomic definition of fiduciary relations in the absence of context is impossible or, at the very least, unwise: 'Everything depends on the particular facts, and such a relationship has been held to exist in unusual circumstances as between purchaser and vendor, as between great uncle and adult nephew, and in other widely differing sets of circumstances. Moreover, it is neither feasible nor desirable to attempt closely to define the relationship, or its characteristics, or the demarcation line showing the exact transition point where a relationship that does not entail that duty passes into one that does.'[39]

The situation-specific nature of fiduciary doctrine also has a tremendous effect on the nature of the duties and obligations which fiduciaries may owe to their beneficiaries, the rights and entitlements of the beneficiaries, and the application of fiduciary rules to specific relationships. None of these considerations may be determined in the absence of contextual analysis of the particular relationship under scrutiny: 'So much varies in the application of fiduciary principles in particular contexts that the conception of fiduciary obligation itself is unable to justify its applicability, as a general matter and irrespective of context. This view, however, does not deny that the concept of fiduciary obligations has content, or that the content is cogent and intelligible; any general theory of fiduciary obligations that ignored this content would lack integrity and persuasiveness.'[40] The situation-specific nature of fiduciary doctrine stresses that fiduciary law is not capable of being boiled down into a simplified theory capable of precise and identical application to all relationships. To do so would eliminate the flexibility that is one of the most valuable attributes of fiduciary theory. Therefore, whereas the situation-specific nature of fiduciary doctrine prevents the fiduciary relation from being precisely defined in the absence of context, that does not prohibit a general understanding of fiduciary theory.

In spite of fiduciary doctrine's need for contextual analysis, common core principles of fiduciary doctrine are capable of being isolated and scrutinized in the absence of context. Indeed, fiduciary principles cannot be properly implemented unless they are first understood in a general fashion and then given contextual application through their adaptation to individual relationships. After all, without an awareness of the underlying theory upon which fiduciary doctrine is premised and the goals that it seeks to achieve, it is difficult to see how the various aspects of fiduciary theory work together to achieve their objectives when the objectives remain unknown. It should be noted, however, that the application of these principles to various relationships will differ to the same degree as the relationships differ from each other.[41] Just as not all fiduciary relationships are identical, the application of fiduciary principles to

A Re-examination of Fiduciary Doctrine 157

those relationships is not identical. Consequently, recognizing that fiduciary doctrine is situation-specific ought to be both a primary consideration and a precursor to its application to particular relationships.[42]

The Categorical Open-Endedness of Fiduciary Relationships

The open-ended nature of fiduciary doctrine holds that no relationship may be precluded from being classified as fiduciary because it does not fit into established classes of fiduciary relationships or the actors involved are not traditionally associated with fiduciary relations.[43] It maintains that the only relevant consideration is whether the nature of the relationship is such that it ought to be considered fiduciary.

Although a relationship is fiduciary if it possesses certain characteristics, the limits of fiduciary relations ought not be absolutely defined by those characteristics. To do so offends the situation-specificity of fiduciary doctrine. As Sir Eric Sachs J explained in *Lloyd's Bank v Bundy*, '[T]he relationships which result in such a duty must not be circumscribed by reference to defined limits.'[44] Being mindful of fiduciary law's focus on the unique attributes of individual relationships ought to prevent the creation of exhaustive lists or categories of fiduciary relations that arise at the expense of the underlying purposes for their institution: 'The existence of a list of nominate relationships dulls the mind's sensitivity to the purposes for which the list has evolved and tempts the court to regard the list as exhaustive and to refuse admittance to new relations which have been created as a matter of business exigency.'[45]

Even where particular types of relationships have been described by the courts as fiduciary, that does not necessarily entail that every instance of those relationship is fiduciary. Furthermore, not every aspect of a fiduciary relationship is fiduciary.[46] Along this same line of reasoning, La Forest J held in *LAC Minerals v International Corona Resources Ltd* that it is far more important to look at the particulars of a relationship to ascertain whether it is fiduciary rather than simply to observe who the parties to it are: 'The imposition of fiduciary obligations is not limited to those relationships in which a presumption of such an obligation arises. Rather, a fiduciary obligation can arise as a matter of fact out of the specific circumstances of a relationship. As such it can arise between parties in a relationship in which fiduciary obligations would not normally be expected.'[47] What is truly meant by the open-endedness of the fiduciary relation, then, is that the categories of fiduciary relations are never closed and neither are their limits.

Implementing the Functional Approach

Whereas the integrity of fiduciary relations may be preserved by prescribing acceptable standards of fiduciaries' conduct, the success of such a regime is ultimately dependent on a proper balance being struck between the desire to protect the interests of beneficiaries and the sanctioning of the behaviour of fiduciaries. The fiduciary office will remain vacant if the cost to prospective fiduciaries is so high that they are discouraged from accepting the position. Fiduciary doctrine attempts to provide an equitable balancing of the need to preserve the integrity of fiduciary relations by imposing strict standards of conduct on fiduciaries which are sufficiently stringent to protect the interests of the beneficiaries,' yet not so strict as to discourage others from accepting the fiduciary office.[48]

Using a functional approach to understanding fiduciary doctrine differs significantly from category-based modes of analysis. It provides a sound theoretical basis for the imposition of fiduciary principles rather than resorting to a list of relationships previously described as fiduciary on some level. However, this type of approach differs from the adherence to categorical analysis in a far more significant way. It insists that fiduciary doctrine should be applied only where its application is consistent with the doctrine's theoretical foundations. Under a functional approach, fiduciary theory provides solid guidelines for determining the application of fiduciary principles to specific relationships as well as parameters for the application of fiduciary principles to relationships at large. Thus, promoting a functional understanding of fiduciary doctrine also requires providing some boundaries for the application of fiduciary doctrine.

Numerous relations between persons within any given society entail some form of dependence or potential for one person to positively or negatively affect the interests of another. These relationships take a variety of forms. Not all of them involve the reposing of trust, however. Moreover, not all of them ought to be treated as fiduciary in nature. The potential for one person's interests to be affected by the actions of another varies in degree according to a number of criteria. These include, among other things, the nature and scope of the relationship, and the degree of trust and reliance involved. Although the determination of the types of relationships that come under the protective sheath of fiduciary law ought to be made according to the facts and requirements of the specific relationship under scrutiny and not be limited by

A Re-examination of Fiduciary Doctrine   159

general rules, that does not entail that all relationships involving degrees of dependency, reliance, or trust ought to be characterized as fiduciary. There are other reasons why fiduciary doctrine ought not to be implemented as freely as it has been in the past. The duties and penalties imposed on fiduciaries are quite onerous. Fiduciaries must ascribe to high standards of morality and selflessness, as reflected in the concept of utmost good faith, or *uberrima fides*, discussed *infra*. Moreover, the wide range of remedies available for breach of fiduciary duty reflect, in part, Equity's desire to punish fiduciaries in breach of their duties as well as discouraging other fiduciaries from engaging in acts of breach. Consequently, applying fiduciary standards of loyalty, disclosure, and so on should not be applied haphazardly, but, as under a functional approach, these standards ought to be based on a careful consideration of the particulars of the relationship being examined and imposed only where necessary, not simply where their application would provide a convenient resolution to a problematic situation.[49] Indeed, in *Hodgkinson v Simms*, Sopinka and McLachlin JJ warned that courts and commentators have used phrases like 'unilateral exercise of power,' 'at the mercy of the other's discretion,' and 'has given over the power' when describing fiduciary relationships because of their concern for the need to clarify what gives rise to a fiduciary relationship and, more importantly, because of the 'Draconian consequences of the imposition of a fiduciary obligation.'[50]

The unprincipled application of fiduciary doctrine, as is the case with the categorical approach, may result in the imposition of unwarrantedly harsh sanctions on persons who ought not to be made subject to them. Moreover, it also allows persons who would not otherwise be entitled to fiduciary remedies to be availed of them. Aside from acting as punishments or deterrents for fiduciaries and serving to maintain the integrity of fiduciary relations, fiduciary remedies exist to protect the interests of beneficiaries by correcting fiduciaries' abuse of their positions in ways that go beyond ordinary remedies.[51] Beneficiaries are only entitled to fiduciary remedies by virtue of their positions *vis-à-vis* their beneficiaries and the perception in fiduciary doctrine that such onerous penalties are required to ensure that fiduciaries live up to the high standards required of them. The reason parties to a contract, for example, are neither imposed with the same high degrees of loyalty or availed of similarly far-ranging remedial aid is that the moral standards applied to contracting parties are far less exacting than those required of fiduciaries.

The category-based approach used in the past never imposed restric-

160 General Principles of Fiduciary Doctrine

tions on the scope of the application of fiduciary doctrine because it never looked to the basis of fiduciary doctrine's reason for being. Although the variety of relationships that are capable of being described as fiduciary are not circumscribed, they are, in fact, limited by the purpose and intent of fiduciary doctrine. Simply put, if a particular relationship is inconsistent with the desire in fiduciary doctrine to protect certain forms of interactions, then it is outside of the types of relationships that ought to properly be described as fiduciary. In general terms, fiduciary law exists to monitor the intercourse between those who give their trust and those who care for that trust.[52] It ensures that fiduciaries live up to the high expectations required of them, provides beneficiaries with the means to enforce their fiduciaries' duties, and imposes remedies where fiduciaries fail to discharge their obligations. In all, fiduciary law seeks to ensure the equitableness of dealings between parties to relationships which, by their nature, are particularly susceptible to fraud, undue influence, and other activities which run afoul of public policy.[53] Unfortunately, as a result of the tremendous scope of activity that fiduciary doctrine was designed to monitor, it has been particularly susceptible to incorrect usage which has hampered its theoretical development.

The Misapplication of Fiduciary Doctrine

Despite the complex nature of fiduciary doctrine, the judiciary has avoided serious theoretical analysis of fiduciary doctrine in favour of haphazard and often ill-fitting applications of its most general principles. The failure of the judiciary to engage in serious analysis of fiduciary theory has prevented it from recognizing the limits of the application of fiduciary doctrine. The judiciary's use of fiduciary doctrine in inappropriate scenarios has, in turn, produced a multitude of decisions which only further confuse the issue of the proper scope of the application of fiduciary law.

One of the most notorious examples of the misapplication of fiduciary doctrine occurred in *Chase Manhattan Bank v Israel British Bank*.[54] In that case the plaintiff had transferred two million dollars to the defendant's account. As a result of a clerical error, a second payment in the same amount was made by the plaintiff to the defendant that same day. On discovering its error, the plaintiff gave instructions to stop the second payment but the instructions were not received in sufficient time to prevent the defendant from receiving the funds. The defendant bank was put into receivership shortly thereafter.

A Re-examination of Fiduciary Doctrine 161

As the plaintiff's money was indistinguishable from the other monies belonging to the defendant, it could not be recovered through common law remedies. To trace property at common law, title to the property being followed must be readily identifiable.[55] The commixture of the plaintiff's funds with those of the defendant prevented identification and, consequently, the ability to trace. Tracing in Equity, however, places a charge on the asset to be traced, thereby allowing a claimant to follow the asset into a mixed fund or into property purchased with money obtained from such a fund.[56]

In finding for the plaintiff, Goulding J held that a fiduciary relationship existed between the parties as a result of the incorrect payment of money to the defendant arising from the second transfer. Before the mistaken payment, there had been no existing fiduciary relationship between the parties. Nevertheless, in arriving at his conclusion, Gould J determined that to allow for the tracing of the funds mistakenly forwarded, it was necessary to find 'a continuing right of property recognised in equity or what I think to be its concomitant, "a fiduciary or quasi-fiduciary relationship."'[57] Clearly, the fiduciary relationship found to exist in *Chase Manhattan* was imposed merely to allow for the equitable remedy of tracing and deny the defendant bank the benefit of the plaintiff's error. The fiduciary relationship was used instead of the more obvious action of unjust enrichment because the latter was not recognized as an independent head of action in England.[58]

A similar judicial 'creation' of a fiduciary relationship occurred in *Goodbody v Bank of Montreal*,[59] where the Ontario High Court of Justice declared that the bank of a thief had a fiduciary relationship with the thief's victim to enable the tracing of proceeds from stolen property. A number of a company's share warrants were alleged to have been stolen from the plaintiff's premises. The alleged thief, Lester, claimed to be a bona fide purchaser of the warrants. He claimed to have purchased them from another individual without knowing that they had been stolen. Lester then sold the warrants, opened a bank account under an assumed name, and deposited the proceeds from the sale of some of the shares in it. Although the court declared that the bank had a fiduciary relationship with the plaintiff, it did not discuss the fiduciary nature of the parties' relationship. Rather, it demonstrated the existence of an unjust enrichment which was deserving of remedy. As Lacourciere J explained, 'To permit Lester to retain the proceeds of his fraud in such circumstances would be to allow him to benefit from his fraudulent activities, to become unduly enriched at the expense of the plaintiffs.'[60]

Once again, the court's inability to use the principle of unjust enrichment resulted in the artificial creation of a fiduciary relationship in order to provide a remedy. The basis of the court's finding of such a relationship was, again, explained by necessity rather than its actual existence: 'On the authority of *Sinclair v Brougham et al*, [1914] A.C. 398 ... the Court will establish a fiduciary relationship to enable the plaintiffs to follow their property in equity into Lester's bank account.[61]

Perhaps the prime example of the judicial creation of a fiduciary relationship in an attempt to right an obvious wrong occurred in the case of *Reading v Attorney General*.[62] Reading, a British Army sergeant in Egypt during the Second World War, assisted smugglers in transporting illicit alcohol by riding in their civilian vehicle in military uniform to avoid inspection by the police. At the time of his arrest, a substantial amount of money in his possession earned from assisting the smugglers was seized. Reading was tried by court-martial, found guilty of conduct prejudicial to good order and military discipline, and sent to prison for two years. On his release, he commenced an action to have the seized money returned.

In finding that Reading was not entitled to have the seized money returned, the Court of Appeal held that he occupied the position of a fiduciary to the Crown by virtue of his position in the British Army.[63] The money Reading received from the smugglers was deemed to have constituted a secret profit earned through the breach of his fiduciary duties in favour of his own pecuniary interests. His breach of duty required him to disgorge the amount of his profit to his beneficiary, the Crown.[64] Consequently, Reading was unable to have the money returned to him, because it properly belonged to his beneficiary. The Court of Appeal's findings were unanimously upheld by the House of Lords.[65]

Cases such as *Chase Manhattan*, *Goodbody*, and *Reading v Attorney General* illustrate exactly how far courts have been willing to stretch the fiduciary concept in order to find a basis of liability. Although just and equitable results were obtained in each of these cases, the manner in which they were obtained resulted in the extrapolation of fiduciary doctrine far beyond its intended limits.[66] Whereas it may be arguable that Reading was in breach of his fiduciary obligations by using his uniform for unauthorized and fraudulent purposes, the finding of fiduciary relationships in both the *Chase Manhattan* and *Goodbody* cases has no basis in fiduciary doctrine. The latter two cases are the unfortunate products of well-intentioned attempts to provide wronged innocent parties with remedies. However noble the intentions behind such attempts may be, the precedents they created have clouded the perception of fiduciary relationships and the attendant role of fiduciary doctrine therein.

Although the situation-specific nature of fiduciary doctrine presupposes that it possesses sufficient flexibility to be applied to a wide range of relationships, that does not entail its application in situations that are inconsistent with its underlying purpose. Through its unprincipled application by the judiciary, fiduciary doctrine is prone to being imposed in places where it simply does not belong, as evidenced by the illustrations above. Confining fiduciary doctrine to its proper sphere of influence has become increasingly more important in the face of the tremendous increase in the use of fiduciary arguments. The problem is how to prevent its future misapplication. It is suggested that a greater knowledge and awareness of fiduciary theory is needed if fiduciary doctrine is to be kept within its own backyard. This necessitates examining the various fiduciary theories that currently exist.

9
Fiduciary Theories

A number of commentators have attempted to define the fiduciary relation. Some have tried to define it through taxonomy.[1] Others argue that the fiduciary relation cannot be generally encapsulated, but may be rendered precise by classes for which particular rules may be devised.[2] There are those who suggest that the fiduciary relation cannot be defined at all.[3] Still others insist that the fiduciary relationship cannot be delimited because it is an illogical creature created by loosely tied or entirely unrelated principles which have been improperly grouped together for the sake of jurisprudential convenience.[4] Finally, there are those who believe that fiduciary doctrine cannot be understood in the absence of context.[5]

Traditional definitions of the term 'fiduciary' have tended to focus on the similarity of the fiduciary and the trustee and of the fiduciary relationship with the trust relationship.[6] Indeed, 'fiduciary' is derived from the Latin words *fiducia*, which means trust, or reliance, and *fiduciarius*, which translates to something that is entrusted or given in trust. Moreover, the latter two are derivative of the verb *fido*, which means 'to trust.'[7] In the legal context, the notion of fiduciary relations was first conceived of by Equity in relation to trustees, and was later expanded to include the actions of any person who occupies a position of trust or is entrusted by another for a particular purpose.[8]

Both the fiduciary and trust relationship entail similar duties, benefits, and liabilities. The fiduciary relation involves the beneficiary's reposing of trust and confidence in the fiduciary to act – with the utmost good faith, integrity, candour, and fidelity – in the former's best interests. The fiduciary is bound, meanwhile, to act selflessly for the benefit of the beneficiary and must not take unfair advantage of the beneficiary so as to

Fiduciary Theories   165

prejudice the latter's interests. This basic definition has been refined and expanded over time by judges and legal scholars. Their definitions may be organized into a number of theoretical categories, including property theory, reliance theory, inequality theory, contract theory, unjust enrichment theory, utility theory, and power and discretion theory.[9]

It should be noted at the outset that this list is not meant to include all possible theories of fiduciary doctrine.[10] Moreover, the following discussions of each of these various theories are not exhaustive. Rather, their inclusion is intended to highlight the various elements that have most often been raised as constituting the basis of fiduciary relations. From these considerations, the core elements of fiduciary doctrine may be ascertained by the theories' commentaries upon the doctrine's most vital elements.

Property Theory

The essential proposition underlying the property theory of fiduciary doctrine holds that a fiduciary relationship exists only where a person possesses de facto[11] or de jure[12] control over property belonging to another. Consequently, where no property interest – in the traditional common law understanding – exists, there can be no fiduciary relationship. Property theory is the starting point of most economic analyses of fiduciary doctrine. Cooter and Freedman, for example, describe a fiduciary relation as existing in any situation where 'a beneficiary entrusts a fiduciary with control and management of an asset.'[13] Property theory has also been used in the Native law context to describe the Crown's fiduciary obligation to First Nations.[14]

This theory of fiduciary doctrine may be seen to have its origins in trust law, where the existence of a trust *corpus*, or *res*, is a prerequisite for the existence of a trust relationship. However, although the finding of a trust relationship results in the existence of fiduciary duties, it is not the same thing as a fiduciary relationship. A trustee is a type of fiduciary, but a fiduciary is not necessarily a trustee.

In simple terms, a trust creates a legally binding obligation in which the party or parties controlling the property of the trust – the trustees – hold that property for the benefit of a party or parties – the beneficiaries or *cestuis que trust* – and not for themselves in their roles as trustees.[15] The actors in a fiduciary relationship – the fiduciary and beneficiary or *cestui que trust* – are governed by virtually identical principles as those governing trust relationships. However, a fiduciary relationship does not depend on the presence of a property interest for its sustenance.[16] Its existence depends on the quality and character of the relationship between parties which gives rise to equitable obligations.

Many fiduciary relationships exist which do not have a property component to them, or not a property interest in the traditional legal sense. Indeed, La Forest J noted in *Canson Enterprises Ltd v Boughton & Co*, 'There is a sharp divide between a situation where a person has *control* of property which in the view of the court *belongs* to another, and one where a person is under a fiduciary duty to perform an obligation where equity's concern is simply that the duty be performed honestly and in accordance with the undertaking the fiduciary has taken on.'[17] Perhaps the prime examples of relationships which are understood to be fiduciary in nature, yet do not possess a property component are those between a doctor and patient or between a religious leader (such as a rabbi or other clergyman) and a congregation member. Whereas both the health of the patient and the spiritual well-being of the congregation member may loosely be defined as property – insofar as they are possessions which belong to a person – they are not property as it is traditionally defined by the common law. Nevertheless, this fact has not prevented these relationships from being classified as fiduciary.[18] The fundamental problem inherent in the property theory of fiduciary doctrine, then, is that its emphasis upon the property component of a fiduciary relationship is misplaced.[19]

Reliance Theory

The reliance theory of fiduciary doctrine is the most straightforward of the various theories. It is also the most often-used theory, both on its own and in conjunction with elements of others.[20] Reliance theory insists that a relationship is fiduciary where one person reposes trust and confidence in another. It has been held to apply in relationships as diverse as those between an investor and a stockbroker[21] or promoter,[22] to those between doctor and patient[23] and parent and child.[24] Where one person reposes confidence in another, that person relies upon the other's honesty, integrity, fidelity, and good faith not to breach that confidence. Sir Eric Sachs J illustrated this notion in *Lloyd's Bank v Bundy*, where he stated that many cases in which fiduciary relationships have been found to exist 'arise where someone relies on the guidance or advice of another ... and where the person on whom reliance is placed obtains, or may well obtain, a benefit from the transaction or has some other interest in it being concluded.'[25]

Under this theory, it is the entrustor's reliance on the entrustee that provides the impetus for fiduciary doctrine to ensure that the former's reliance is not abused: 'Broadly, it may be said that a fiduciary relationship exists, giving rise to obligations of that character, where the relationship is one of confidence, in which equity imposes duties upon the person in whom confidence is reposed in order to prevent the abuse of the confidence.'[26] In this sense, reliance theory is theoretically similar both to trust relationships and to so-called traditional definitions of fiduciary relations, such as those existing between parent and child and guardian and ward.[27]

The basis of reliance theory may be seen to be intrinsically morally or public policy oriented. Its origins may be traced back to Equity's jurisdiction to provide remedies for abuses of trust and confidence reposed by one person in another.[28] Yet, although reliance is an important facet of a fiduciary relation, many non-fiduciary relationships also contain various degrees of reliance, such as the relations between freely contracting parties. As Waters argues, '[N]ot all relationships will be held to be fiduciary, even though they involve reliance upon integrity and the presumption that a party will fully disclose his position.'[29] Whereas reliance may be an element of many fiduciary relationships, its existence is not sufficient, on its own, to warrant labeling a relationship as fiduciary. Reliance, therefore, is more properly viewed as a determinant, rather than determinative, of the fiduciary character of a relationship.[30]

Inequality Theory[31]

In equality theory is premised upon the notion that beneficiaries are generally inferior in power *vis-à-vis* their fiduciaries. As a result, the theory stresses that fiduciary law functions to temper this inequality by imposing strict duties on fiduciaries to act in their beneficiaries' best interests. A common illustration of inequality theory's characterization of fiduciary relationships is the relationship between guardian and ward.

Although inequality theory highlights the power imbalance between fiduciaries and beneficiaries within the confines of their fiduciary relationships, it has been improperly expanded beyond those confines. Adherence to this bastardized form of inequality theory has led many to believe that all fiduciary relationships exist only between dominant and subservient parties. This premise is simply untrue. Fiduciary relationships are as prevalent among parties on an equal footing – such as partners in a business venture, spouses, directors of corporations, and partners in a professional services firm (that is, law, accounting, architecture) – as to parties in an unequal relationship – such as employer and employee. Although the nature of any given fiduciary relationship may result in an inequality in power between the fiduciary and the beneficiary *within that relationship*, there is no requirement or need for any inequality to exist *outside* of that relationship.

One possible reason for the misunderstanding that an inequality must exist between parties to a fiduciary relationship in all circumstances, including those beyond the fiduciary aspect of their relationship, may be the excessive juridical categorization of acceptable classes of fiduciary relationships. In an unfortunate wave of circularity, many attempts to explain the nebulous fiduciary relation have actually resulted in its perversion. These attempts have not only failed to explain what comprises a fiduciary relation, but they have led many to believe that fiduciary relations are restricted to the paradigms established in their illustrations, which tend to be patently unequal relationships.[32]

Indeed, the most common illustrations of fiduciary relationships used by judges and scholars are more akin to those of parent–child, doctor–patient, and employer–employee rather than those between partners in a professional services firm. The Supreme Court of Canada has been a prime culprit in perpetuating the myth that fiduciary relations exist only between unequal parties.[33] Its recent decision in *Hodgkinson v Simms*[34] continues the court's internal debate over the appropriate place of vulnerability as necessary characteristic of fiduciary relations.

An inherent aspect of fiduciary relationships is that fiduciaries possess the ability, by virtue of their positions, to positively or negatively affect the interest of their beneficiaries. Fiduciary law mandates that the fiduciary's actions adhere to the former; when they result in the latter, the beneficiary has legal recourse to seek appropriate sanctions against the fiduciary. The fiduciary's ability to affect the beneficiary's interest creates a situation of unequal power relations between the two within the confines of that relationship.[35] However, the power of the parties *vis-à-vis* each other outside of the boundaries of their fiduciary relationship is irrelevant to the determination of whether any relationship is fiduciary: 'It cannot be the *sine qua non* of a fiduciary obligation that the parties have disparate bargaining strength ... The fiduciary relation looks to the relative positive of the parties that results from the agreement rather than the relative position that precedes the agreement.'[36]

In 'The Vulnerable Position of Fiduciary Doctrine in the Supreme Court of Canada,'[37] I suggest that the best way to understand the relative positions of the parties in fiduciary relationships is to think of the fiduciary relationship as a transfer of powers from the beneficiary B to the fiduciary F. The powers transferred by B to F originally belonged to the former and, in fact, still do. B has merely *loaned* the powers to F within the ambit of their fiduciary relationship; they do not become F's own possession. F is duty-bound to use these powers in the same manner as B would, subject to any constraints B imposes in their use. F may not exceed these imposed limits or else be liable for breach of duty; the purpose of F's duty is to act within the parameters established by B through the latter's transfer of powers, not to exceed them.[38] When the fiduciary relationship is terminated, the powers return to B. A similar method of understanding the relative positions of fiduciaries and beneficiaries in fiduciary relationships was espoused by McLachlin J in the Supreme Court of Canada's decision in *Norberg v Wynrib*, where she explained: 'It is as though the fiduciary has taken power which rightfully belongs to the beneficiary on the condition that the fiduciary exercise the power entrusted exclusively for the good of the beneficiary.'[39]

The inequality in the relationship between fiduciary and beneficiary results from the transfer of powers from B to F. The inequality of this position is illustrated by the change in power relations between B and F within the boundaries of their fiduciary relationship. Originally both had complete and equal powers – Q. Upon the transfer of prescribed powers P from B to F, the fiduciary relationship came into being. However, within that fiduciary relationship, F's powers now amount to $Q + P$, whereas B only possesses $Q - P$, thereby resulting in a power inequality that did not exist prior to the creation of the fiduciary relation. Although the beneficiary's interests are protected by the law of fiduciaries, this protection serves only as a check on the fiduciary's ability to abuse the power transferred from the beneficiary.

Contract Theory

The contract theory of fiduciary doctrine holds that the fiduciary relationship is quasi-contractual, in that one person undertakes to act in the best interests of another.[40] The beneficiary in this transaction transfers certain powers to the fiduciary in return for the latter's promise of fidelity to the former's best interests. In accordance with this theory, one recent article has argued that a fiduciary relation is nothing more than a contractual relationship with uncommonly high costs of specification and monitoring: 'The duty of loyalty replaces detailed contractual terms, and courts flesh out the duty of loyalty by prescribing the actions the parties themselves would have preferred if bargaining were cheap and all promises fully enforced.'[41]

The use of contract law as an analogy for understanding the fiduciary obligation may be the result of an attempt to attach the nebulous principles which underlie the law of fiduciaries to the more concrete understanding of contract law. However, the analogy has some rather obvious flaws. Whereas a contract necessarily requires an offer and acceptance, a fiduciary relationship may arise in situations entirely devoid of such formalities. For example, a fiduciary relationship may arise by the unilateral actions of a would-be fiduciary,[42] by voluntary and mutual arrangements,[43] as a result of the nature of the intercourse between parties,[44] or by its imposition by the courts. Also, although a gratuitous undertaking is unenforceable in contract law, it is enforceable under fiduciary law.[45] Moreover, a fiduciary relationship may be found to exist where neither party intended to create such a relationship.[46]

In addition to these problems, the methods by which parties are bound to a contract do not at all coincide with the obligations of fiduciaries to their beneficiaries. In the former, the contract or agreement is the centre of judicial attention to determine the adherence or lack thereof to the bargain made between parties.[47] On the other hand, fiduciary law places greater emphasis on the relationship of the parties to each other, their respective undertakings, and the degree of reliance by the beneficiary on the fiduciary. Finally, and perhaps most importantly, contract law monitors the activities of all parties to the contract, whereas fiduciary law regulates fiduciary relations by focusing exclusively upon the actions of fiduciaries.

There are other important differences between theories of contract and fiduciary law. The ideological underpinnings of contract law are closely tied to the morals of the marketplace. Historically, the freedom and sanctity of contract were put forward as self-evident truths, as evidenced by the remarks of Jessel MR in *Printing & Numerical Registering Co v Sampson*: '[I]f there is one thing which more than another public policy requires it is that men of full age and competent understanding shall have the utmost liberty of contracting, and that their contracts when entered into freely and voluntarily shall be held sacred and shall be enforced by Courts of justice.'[48] Although the unfettered notion of freedom of contract may no longer hold the place that it once did, commercial standards of reasonableness and market pressures still play an important role in determining acceptable standards for contracting parties.

Fiduciary Theories 171

Fiduciary law, on the other hand, has always been premised upon principles which are not limited or dictated by the actions of its participants. Moreover, it prescribes acceptable manners of conduct that are based on a higher moral standard than that of the marketplace.[49] The basis of the fiduciary standard is the mirror image of contract's reliance upon the self-interest of the parties. As Cardozo J explained in *Meinhard v Salmon*: 'Many forms of conduct permissible in a work-a-day world for those acting at arm's length are forbidden to those bound by fiduciary ties. A trustee is held to something stricter than the morals of the marketplace. Not honesty alone, but the punctilio of an honour the most sensitive, is then the standard of behavior. As to this there has developed a tradition that is unbending and inveterate. Uncompromising rigidity had been the attitude of courts of equity when petitioned to undermine the rule of undivided loyalty by the "disintegrating erosion" of particular exceptions ... Only thus has the level of conduct for fiduciaries been kept at a level higher than that trodden by the crowd.'[50] This aspect of fiduciary doctrine is also reflected in La Forest J's majority judgment in the Supreme Court of Canada's recent decision in *Hodgkinson v Simms*.[51]

Because of the significant differences between contract and fiduciary principles, it is suggested that the former's usefulness as a tool to aid in understanding fiduciary doctrine is outweighed by the dangers inherent in its use. Consequently, the use of contract principles, even in the limited form of analogy, ought to be abandoned. As Deborah DeMott has suggested, 'Resorting unreflectively to contract rhetoric is insidiously misleading and provides no rationale for further development of the law of fiduciary obligation ... [E]ven considering the obligation's elusive nature, descriptions drawn exclusively from contract principles are surely mistaken.'[52]

Unjust Enrichment Theory

Unjust enrichment theory states that fiduciary relationships exist where beneficiaries may obtain remedial aid from their fiduciaries when the latter use their powers for their own ends rather than those of their beneficiaries. The unjust enrichment arises where the fiduciaries, who receive powers from their beneficiaries to use in the latter's best interests, obtain personal benefit by using those powers to their own advantage. In such instances, the fiduciaries are in breach of their duties to their beneficiaries and are liable for the amount of their unjust enrichment, or the unjust enrichment of third parties whom they have wrongfully benefited. The foundation of this theory is illustrated by Fry J in *Re West of England and South Wales District Bank, Ex parte Dale and Co*: 'What is a fiduciary relationship? It is one in respect of which if a wrong arise, the same remedy exists against the wrong-doer on behalf of the principal as would exist against a trustee on behalf of the *cestui que trust*.'[53]

Unlike the other theories illustrated herein, unjust enrichment theory may be seen to be remedy driven. It reasons from the remedy to the breach of duty instead of from the breach of duty to the remedy. The remedy is that fiduciaries must disgorge any benefits they receive by virtue of their unjust enrichment; the duty is that fiduciaries must not take advantage of their acquisition of dominance over their beneficiaries or be liable to disgorge any proceeds thereby obtained. Unjust enrichment theory does nothing, then, to assist in the determination of whether a particular relationship is fiduciary. Rather, its focus rests on the finding of a remedy where a fiduciary is unjustly enriched.[54]

A fundamental problem with unjust enrichment theory, then, is that it is circular in its reasoning.[55] The duty cannot be defined without reference to the remedy. This creates a logistical problem in that in a workable theory of fiduciary doctrine 'one cannot both define the relation by the remedy and use the relation as a triggering device for remedy.'[56] The circularity of unjust enrichment theory may be contrasted with reliance theory, for example, where beneficiaries' reliance on their fiduciaries provides the basis for the fiduciaries' liability. Under reliance theory, fiduciaries' duties are based on their utmost good faith, integrity, and fidelity to the best interests of their beneficiaries, who rely on the fulfillment of their fiduciaries' duties. The remedy is derived from the fiduciaries' failure to carry out their obligations in this manner.

A second problem with unjust enrichment theory is that it often treads dangerously close to the jurisdiction possessed by the equitable doctrine of unjust enrichment.[57] As an independent head of action, unjust enrichment does not necessarily indicate the existence of a fiduciary relationship; it merely indicates that a person has been unjustly enriched at the expense of another.[58] Because of the ideological proximity of actions based on fiduciary doctrine and those based on unjust enrichment, the use of unjust enrichment theory within the ambit of fiduciary doctrine requires careful monitoring so that situations of unjust enrichment which do not give rise to fiduciary relations are kept within their own independent sphere.

In summation, whereas a fiduciary relationship may result in an

Fiduciary Theories 173

unjust enrichment, an unjust enrichment does not create a fiduciary relationship. Therefore, while unjust enrichment theory is a useful determinant in ascertaining whether a particular relationship is fiduciary, it, like reliance theory, is illustrative rather than indicative of the existence of fiduciary relations.

Utility Theory

The basis of utility theory is closely related to the underlying purpose of fiduciary law.[59] It holds that fiduciary relationships will be found by the courts in situations where there is a determined need to protect the integrity of particular types of relationships. This may arise in a number of situations, whether because of the relative status of the parties, such as in the relationship between guardian and ward, or because of a perceived commercial utility, such as where directors or employees seize corporate opportunities for themselves.[60] In other words, the utility of the relationship to society at large is what renders it sufficiently important to warrant its placement under the protective auspices of fiduciary doctrine.

The application of utility theory is widespread. It covers the entire range of relationships which may be deemed to be fiduciary – from the public relationship between elected officials and their constituents[61] to the private relationship between doctor and patient.[62] The primary drawback to this theory is that it is particularly susceptible to incorrect usage. More specifically, utility theory may be improperly applied to all socially valuable relationships, whether or not they are fiduciary in nature. For utility theory to be a useful aid in determining what relationships are fiduciary, it cannot overstep its boundaries. Whereas some socially valuable relationships are, indeed, fiduciary, the fact that a relationship is socially useful does not necessarily render it fiduciary.

Power and Discretion Theory

There are many similarities between power and discretion theory, reliance theory, and inequality theory. Essentially, power and discretion theory holds that a fiduciary relationship exists where one person possesses power and discretion over the interest of another: '[T]he fiduciary obligation is a device that enables the law to respond to a range of situations in which, for a variety of reasons, one person's discretion ought to be controlled because of characteristics of that person's relationship with another.'[63] Another formulation of power and discretion theory holds that the fiduciary 'is likely either to have stewardship of some of the assets of the person to whom the duty is owed, or will hold an office in which there are uniquely-available opportunities for self-interested activity or, the relationship is likely to be one in which the fiduciary has considerable authority or influence over the individual to whom the duty is owed.'[64]

Like many of the other theories discussed herein, power and discretion theory is closely related to its counterparts. It is, for example, the theoretical complement of reliance theory. Where reliance theory puts emphasis on the beneficiary's reliance on the fiduciary's power and discretion, power and discretion theory emphasizes the fiduciary's exercise of power and discretion on which the beneficiary relies. Power and discretion theory also underlines the inequality of the relationship between fiduciary and beneficiary.[65] In addition, the power and discretion basis of the theory may exist within the realm of property theory – such as though the power and discretion of the fiduciary over property belonging to the beneficiary – or it may be completely devoid of any relationship to property interests.

Although one person's power and discretion over another's interest is necessarily a part of fiduciary relationships, power and discretion theory overstates the case. Clearly, not all relationships where one person possesses power and discretion over the interests of another may be properly characterized as fiduciary. For example, a judge possesses power and discretion over civil litigants and criminally accused persons, but the judge's position *vis-à-vis* those parties does not entail the existence of fiduciary obligations to act in their best interests.

Summary

What may be drawn from the above discussion of the various theories of fiduciary doctrine is that no single one, in and of itself, provides a satisfactory basis for understanding fiduciary doctrine. Indeed, not one of these theories is adequate to the task of addressing all of the multifarious relationships that ought to properly be considered fiduciary. The various theories of fiduciary doctrine discussed provide different points of emphasis for the determination of whether a relationship ought to be described as fiduciary. However, even in situations where their respective criteria are satisfied, that fact does not necessarily indicate that a relationship is fiduciary, as Finn explains:

Fiduciary Theories 175

It is obviously not enough that one is in an ascendant position over another: such is the invariable prerequisite for the unconscionability principle. It is obviously not enough that one has the practical capacity to influence the other: representations are made, information is supplied (or not supplied) as of course with the object of, and in fact, influencing a host of contractual dealings. It is obviously not enough that the other party is in a position of vulnerability: such is the almost inevitable state in greater or lesser degree of all parties in contractual relationships. It is obviously not enough that some degree of trust and confidence are there: these are commonly placed in the skill, integrity, fairness and honesty of the other party in contractual dealings. It is obviously not enough that there is a dependence by one party upon the other: as the good faith cases illustrate, a party's information needs can occasion this. Indeed elements of all of the above may be present in a dealing – and consumer transactions can illustrate this – without a relationship being in any way fiduciary.[66]

10

A 'Back to Basics' Approach to Fiduciary Doctrine

The primary difficulty with existing fiduciary theories, as noted earlier, is that they are all subject to exception and qualification. A workable general theory of fiduciary doctrine ought not be subject to exceptions, but should be capable of application to all relationships which may be properly described as fiduciary. Accordingly, a viable theory must be flexible enough to provide feasible and practical guidelines, yet simultaneously allow for the situation-specificity required by fiduciary doctrine. It must also be consistent with the fundamental premises upon which fiduciary doctrine is based.

The *Chase Manhattan*, *Goodbody*, and *Reading* cases discussed earlier demonstrate how the judiciary has strayed from the boundaries within which fiduciary law was intended to operate. Not all relationships in society are fiduciary relationships.[1] Accordingly, relations which are not fiduciary in nature ought not be labeled as fiduciary merely to enable the application of a remedy to a wronged party. Any new theory of fiduciary doctrine must recognize this fact in order to avoid the wrongful application of fiduciary doctrine that has plagued judges and theorists alike.

The fashioning of a new theory of fiduciary doctrine that meets all of these criteria is not an insurmountable task. The ingredients with which to create such a theory already exist, explicitly or implicitly, in the theories discussed in Chapter 9. Once the fundamental aspects of fiduciary doctrine are identified and fleshed out of these theories, they provide a recipe for the sanctioning and monitoring of a wide variety of relationships as fiduciary existing in an infinite number of contexts. However, the determination of whether a particular relationship is fiduciary is only the first in a three-step process.

The Three-Step Application of Fiduciary Doctrine

As discussed earlier, the principles of fiduciary doctrine apply only to particular types of relationships, not to any relationship in which a disadvantaged or dependent party is wronged or taken advantage of by another party. Although fiduciary doctrine applies to all relationships properly described as fiduciary, its remedial aspects take effect only once the integrity of those relationships disappears, as in the face of a breach of duty. The active role taken by fiduciary doctrine in the face of a breach of duty is the cumulative effect of a three-step process.

The initial step is the determination of whether a particular relationship is fiduciary. The determination of whether a particular relationship is fiduciary is a matter of fact which, although scrutinized in accordance with general precepts, may be determined only by reference to the particular circumstances in question.[2] If a fiduciary relationship is found to exist, the focus shifts from the existence of the duty to the nature of the relationship under scrutiny, as Shepherd explains: '[O]nce we have found the duty, we must forget about it. It is after all only a foundation for liability. It provides the bedrock on which we build our finding of a breach. But, like the foundation of a house, it does not determine either the form or the existence of the breach. It will, of course, again like the foundation of a house, limit in many respects the superstructure built upon it.'[3]

Any relationship which is deemed to be fiduciary proceeds to the second step, in which it is subjected to the general principles of fiduciary doctrine. This second step determines whether a breach has occurred by applying only those fiduciary principles germane to the relationship under scrutiny. The determination of applicable fiduciary principles is a question of law which, like the determination made in step one, is based on the specifics of the relationship under scrutiny. If a breach is found to have occurred, the application of an appropriate remedy forms the third and final step. Once again, the remedy to be applied is considered in light of the specific nature of the relationship, the precise form of breach, and the effects of the breach on the beneficiary or beneficiaries in the relationship. This three-step procedure identifies a fiduciary relationship, applies only pertinent principles of fiduciary doctrine to it in order to determine the existence of a breach, and furnishes an appropriate remedy where necessary.

Is the Relationship Fiduciary?

In order to determine whether a relationship is fiduciary, it is necessary to isolate the fundamental aspects of fiduciary relationships. To accommodate the need for a workable general theory, these fundamental aspects must be applicable to all relationships that may be classified as fiduciary. From a review of the various theories of fiduciary doctrine discussed, four basic elements appear.

(1) One or more person (X) possess the ability to affect – positively or negatively – the interests of one or more others (Y).

The notion that one person has the ability to affect the interests of one or more others is the most fundamental of these four criteria. That fiduciaries have the ability to affect the interests of their beneficiaries is drawn from power and discretion theory. The fiduciaries' power and discretion – and resultant ability to affect their beneficiaries' interest, at the latter's expense – is drawn from inequality theory. Without the ability to affect one or more others' interests, it is simply not possible for a person to be a fiduciary.

(2) Y's interests *within the confines of the particular relationship* may only be served – directly or indirectly[4] – through the actions of X.

The idea that beneficiaries' interests are dependent on the actions of their fiduciaries complements the notion that fiduciaries possess the power to affect their beneficiaries' interests. This element also draws from power and discretion theory and inequality theory. Just as one cannot be a fiduciary without the ability to affect another's interests, one cannot be a beneficiary unless that person is somehow dependent on the actions of another.

The premise that beneficiaries' interest may be served either directly or indirectly through their fiduciaries' actions is based on the fact that fiduciaries may possess obligations to their beneficiaries even where they do not have any direct contact with their beneficiaries or where their actions only indirectly affect others' interests. One such example is the relationship between directors of a corporation and the shareholders of that corporation.[5]

(3) X has an obligation to act in Y's best interests.[6]

Although fiduciaries' obligations to act in the best interests of their beneficiaries are particularized or defined by the imposition of fiduciary duties on them, they arise by the nature of their relationship with their beneficiaries. As noted earlier, fiduciaries need not voluntarily assume these obligations to their beneficiaries in order for them to arise.[7]

Fiduciaries' obligations may be seen to arise through one or more factors derived from the various theories of fiduciary doctrine discussed earlier. For example, these obligations may arise as a result of fiduciaries' control over beneficiaries' property; by way of beneficiaries' reliance on their fiduciaries' actions; from the inequality of the parties within the confines of their relationship; because of the undertaking of such obligations by fiduciaries; where fiduciaries are unjustly enriched at the direct expense of others' interests; because of the socially valuable nature or necessity of the relationship in question; and/or as a direct consequence of fiduciaries' power and discretion over their beneficiaries' interests.

(4) Y relies upon the honesty, integrity, and fidelity of X towards Y's best interests as a result of their relationship.

This element stems primarily from reliance theory, but it is also drawn from inequality theory and power and discretion theory. In addition, it is a by-product of the second and third elements set out herein.

Because beneficiaries' interests within the confines of the relationship under scrutiny may only be served by their fiduciaries, it is logical that the former rely on the latter to act in accordance with those interests. Similarly, fiduciaries' obligations to act in beneficiaries' best interests gives a direct impetus for the latter to rely wholeheartedly on the former.

These four criteria illustrate what aspects of individual relationships render them fiduciary. If all four are found to exist on an examination of the facts particular to a specific relationship, then that relationship is properly described as fiduciary. Underlying these general propositions is the situation-specificity of fiduciary doctrine. It is the catalyst which extracts these criteria from their abstract origins and places them firmly in context, plugging the particulars of any relationship into this theory.

The Consequences of Finding a Fiduciary Relationship

Where a fiduciary relationship is found to exist, a number of consequences necessarily arise. The initial description of a relationship as fiduciary is significant in that it brings the relationship into the domain of fiduciary law. However, once inside, the focus shifts to a determination of the effects of fiduciary doctrine on the relationship under scrutiny. The fiduciary nature of the relationship describes both the law governing its existence as well as the character of the bundle of rights, duties, and obligations that stem from such a relationship.

The notion that law is merely the amalgamation of the rights, duties, and obligations stemming from a particular situation was pioneered by Wesley Newcomb Hohfeld in the early part of the twentieth century. In two landmark articles,[8] Hohfeld described and illustrated the proposition that law is merely the description and enforcement of the bundle of rights and duties that are possessed by the participants in various situations and which govern the relationships that stem therefrom. Using Hohfeldian theory to animate fiduciary doctrine creates a situation whereby after beneficiaries' transfer of powers to their fiduciaries, certain rights are bestowed on the beneficiaries, and concurrent obligations are imposed on their fiduciaries to act in the former's best interests. Where both the beneficiary and fiduciary in any given fiduciary relation act in accordance with their respective entitlements and responsibilities, the integrity of the relationship is maintained through the balancing of those reciprocal rights and obligations.

In its attempt to preserve the integrity of these types of relationships, fiduciary law has seen fit to impose certain duties on fiduciaries. Fiduciaries have a duty to act with honesty, integrity, and the utmost good faith (*uberrima fides*) towards their beneficiaries' best interests. The correlative of this duty is beneficiaries' right to rely entirely on their fiduciaries' honesty, integrity, and fidelity without having to inquire into their fiduciaries' activities.[9] The restraints imposed on fiduciaries in order to preserve the integrity of fiduciary relationships described above may be broken down into three essential subduties from which all other fiduciary duties emanate:

1 Fiduciaries must not act in conflict of interest – that is, fiduciaries: (i) must not benefit from their positions; (ii) must provide full disclosure of their actions; and (iii) may not compromise their beneficiaries' interests.

A 'Back to Basics' Approach 181

2 Fiduciaries may delegate or transfer authority over their beneficiaries' interests, but may not delegate absolute responsibility for those interests.
3 Fiduciaries are personally liable for their breach of duty to their beneficiaries or the wrongful action of their appointees which results in a breach of duty.[10]

Meanwhile, the correlative benefits conferred upon beneficiaries which flow from their beneficiaries' duties may also be subdivided into three subcomponents as a result of their delegation of powers to their fiduciaries:

1 Beneficiaries may commence legal action for any breach of fiduciary duty once the cause of action is discovered.[11]
2 Beneficiaries need not prove a breach of fiduciary duty, but only allege it; the onus of discharging an allegation of breach of fiduciary duty rests with their fiduciaries.[12]
3 Beneficiaries may obtain remedial aid upon a finding of breach of duty by their fiduciaries.

Where fiduciaries' duties to their beneficiaries are properly fulfilled, the integrity of the fiduciary relationship to which they attach remains intact. Once they are deviated from, however, there is a breach of that integrity and a corresponding need to bring in the remedial aspects of fiduciary theory.

Determining whether a Breach Has Occurred

In order to determine whether a breach of fiduciary duty has occurred, only the actions of the fiduciary are relevant.[13] The common, core obligation pertaining to all fiduciaries within the scope of their fiduciary positions is to act in the best interests of their beneficiaries. To ensure that fiduciaries fulfil this obligation, fiduciary doctrine requires that they act with the utmost good faith, or *uberrima fides*, towards their beneficiaries.

The Fiduciary Standard of Utmost Good Faith (*Uberrima Fides*)
The necessity of *uberrima fides*, or utmost good faith, is the foundation of fiduciary doctrine.[11] It is not only the fundamental premise around which fiduciary law is built; it is the hallmark of the fiduciary relation. In

order to allow the proper functioning of the fiduciary relation, the utmost good faith of the parties, in particular that of the fiduciary, must be strictly observed.

The requirement of *uberrima fides* insists that fiduciaries carry out their duties to a high, objective standard.[15] It entails the fiduciaries' duty to act in the best interests of their beneficiaries whose interests the fiduciaries both hold and serve.[16] Whereas fiduciaries possess the autonomy to determine for themselves what is in their beneficiaries' best interests, their discretion is, nevertheless, subject to the governing principles of fiduciary doctrine and their application by the judiciary. A court's function upon a claim of fiduciary breach is to scrutinize the fiduciary's conduct and to impose appropriate sanctions for any deviation from an acceptable standard.[17]

The fiduciary standard of *uberrima fides* also allows beneficiaries to rely on their fiduciaries' fidelity. Beneficiaries are under no compulsion or duty to inquire into their fiduciaries' actions to ensure that the fiduciaries are not in breach of their obligations. As Rand J explained in *Midcon Oil & Gas Limited v New British Dominion Oil Company Limited*, fiduciary law strictly prohibits fiduciaries' deviation from its accepted standard of conduct so that beneficiaries need not monitor their fiduciaries' activities: 'The loyalty of a fiduciary ... means that he must divest himself of all thought of personal interest or advantage that impinges adversely on the interest of the beneficiary or that results from the use, in any manner or degree by the fiduciary, of the property, interest or influence of the beneficiary. Equity, in applying the rule as one of fundamental public policy, does so ruthlessly to prevent its corrosion by particular exceptions; by an absolute interdiction it puts temptation beyond reach of the fiduciary by appropriating its fruits.'[18]

Where fiduciaries deviate from the standard of *uberrima fides*, they are prima facie, in breach of their duties to their beneficiaries. For the limited purpose of determining whether a breach has occurred, fiduciary doctrine is not concerned with why or how a fiduciary departed from this standard; rather, it concentrates on the fact that a departure took place. The circumstances giving rise to the departure may come into play in the appraisal of a remedy, but it has no effect on the initial determination of breach.[19] The requirement of *uberrima fides* therefore serves two purposes. It simultaneously protects beneficiaries' interests while deterring and/or sanctioning fiduciaries who seek to deviate from the fiduciary standard of fidelity. To discipline those fiduciaries who fail to live up to the standard of good faith required of them, fiduciary law may impose such onerous penalties as accounting for profits or punitive damages.[20] Because of the existence of these harsh measures, fiduciary doctrine has been described as 'the law's blunt tool for the control of [the fiduciary's] discretion.'[21]

The Reverse Onus
In addition to requiring that fiduciaries act with the utmost good faith in fulfilling their beneficiaries' best interests, fiduciary doctrine makes it easier for beneficiaries, as a result of their positions *vis-à-vis* their fiduciaries, to allege breaches of duty by the latter. As a result of the difficulties that beneficiaries may face in attempting to demonstrate a breach of fiduciary duty,[22] fiduciary doctrine presumes the existence of the fiduciary's breach of duty upon its allegation by a *cestui que trust*.[23] The basis of this reverse onus was described by Lord Penzance in *Erlanger v New Sombrero Phosphates Ltd*: 'The relations of principal and agent, trustee and *cestui que trust*, parent and child, guardian and ward, priest and penitent, all furnish instances in which the Courts of Equity have given protection and relief against the pressure of unfair advantage resulting from the relation and mutual position of the parties, whether in matters of contract or gift; and this relationship and position of unfair advantage once made apparent, the Courts have always cast upon him who holds that [fiduciary] position, the burden of shewing that he has not used it to his own benefit.'[24]

As a result of this reverse onus provision, the courts are inclined to accept beneficiaries' allegations of fiduciary breach once the fiduciary nature of their relationships has been accepted. Beneficiaries need only demonstrate, prima facie, the existence of a fiduciary relationship between the parties. The prima facie inference of breach is made by juxtaposing the beneficiary's allegation of its occurrence against the nature of the intercourse between the parties. Once a court accepts that a relationship is fiduciary and that a breach may have occurred, the burden of proof shifts to the fiduciary to disprove the existence of a breach.[25]

Fiduciaries may only rebuff allegations of breach by demonstrating that they did not act in any manner other than the best interests of their beneficiaries. In other words, fiduciaries may not satisfy their onus by illustrating that their actions also benefited their beneficiaries: 'Thus, if a fiduciary acts with the object or effect of deriving an improper advantage, he cannot validate an invalid act by showing that the act benefitted the beneficiary. Where the actions may be deciphered as motivated by the fiduciary's self-interest, the onus falls upon him to disprove the rebuttable presumption.'[26] The notion that fiduciaries may only disprove an allegation of breach by demonstrating their fidelity to their beneficiaries' interests holds true regardless of whether the actions were entered into in good or bad faith.[27] As long as fiduciaries place their interest before or on par with those of their beneficiaries, they may be found liable for breaching their fiduciary duties. This notion was approved by the House of Lords in *Regal (Hastings) Ltd v Gulliver*: 'The rule of equity which insists on those, who by use of a fiduciary position make a profit, being liable to account for that profit, in no way depends on fraud, or absence of *bona fides*: or upon such questions or considerations as whether the profit would or should otherwise have gone to the plaintiff, or whether the profiteer was under a duty to obtain the source of the profit for the plaintiff, or whether he took a risk or acted as he did for the benefit of the plaintiff, or whether the plaintiff has in fact been damaged or benefited by his action. The liability arises from the mere fact of a profit having, in the stated circumstances, been made. The profiteer, however honest and well-intentioned, cannot escape the risk of being called upon to account.'[28] Fiduciaries may also not be relieved of liability for breaching their duties by demonstrating that any loss suffered by their beneficiaries would have occurred notwithstanding the former's wrongful actions.[29]

Even after a breach has been found to have occurred, the nature of a fiduciary breach must be revealed prior to discussing the appropriateness of a remedy. A remedy for a breach of fiduciary duty may only be properly fashioned after considering both the nature of the fiduciary relationship in question and the manner of the breach committed. To ascertain whether the integrity of a fiduciary relationship has been breached, the particulars of the relationship under scrutiny must be subjected to the general principles of fiduciary doctrine. These principles exist to govern fiduciaries' activities and protect beneficiaries' interests so that the integrity of any given fiduciary relation may be preserved. Subsequently, to be in a position to determine whether there has been a breach of fiduciary duty, it is first necessary to outline the principles from which the determination is properly made.

General Principles Governing Fiduciary Relations[30]

There are four general principles designed to protect beneficiaries and preserve the integrity of fiduciary relationships. They are all derived or adapted from the fiduciary standard of *uberrima fides* discussed earlier, under which fiduciaries must fulfil the obligations owed to their beneficiaries in accordance with objective standards of the utmost good faith.[31] These four principles require that fiduciaries (1) must not benefit from their positions; (2) must provide full disclosure of their actions; (3) may not compromise their beneficiaries' interests; and (4) may not delegate absolute responsibility over their beneficiaries' interests.

Fiduciaries Must Not Benefit from Their Positions

The most basic of these fiduciary principles is that fiduciaries may not benefit from their positions as fiduciaries.[32] This notion is often described as the rule against conflict of interest. Where fiduciaries obtain benefits from their fiduciary positions, regardless of whether their beneficiaries suffer any harm from such occurrences, they must disgorge the entirety of the benefit thereby obtained: 'So strict is the obligation that it requires the disgorging of a profit even when that profit is not made at the expense of the trusting party.'[33] Although the rule against conflict of interest played a vital role in *Keech v Sandford*, the rule was not clearly articulated in that case or for quite some time afterwards even though it was well used.[34] One of the first enunciations of the conflict rule came in *Aberdeen Railway Co v Blaikie Brothers*, in which it was said that 'it is a rule of universal application that no one having such duties to discharge shall be allowed to enter into engagements in which he has or can have a personal interest conflicting or which possible may conflict with the interests of those whom he is bound to protect.'[35] One of the earlier affirmations of the conflict of interest prohibition in Canada was made by Taschereau J more than 100 years ago in the Supreme Court of Canada's decision in *Davis v Kerr*: '[N]o one having duties of a fiduciary character to discharge shall be allowed to enter into engagements or assume functions in which he has or can have a personal interest conflicting or which possibly may conflict with the interests of those he is bound to protect.'[36]

Not only may fiduciaries not benefit personally, but they may not benefit a third party at the direct expense or in lieu of their beneficiaries' interests.[37] The prohibition against personal gain also applies to situations where there is an *opportunity* for personal gain or third-party gain.[38] The reason for prohibiting fiduciaries' personal gain while in their fiduciary offices is twofold: to prevent any semblance of shady dealings or improper activities and to pre-empt the courts' need to investigate the nature of fiduciaries' dealings by forbidding these occurrences before they arise.[39]

186 General Principles of Fiduciary Doctrine

The rigour with which the judiciary continues to enforce the rule against conflict of interest demonstrates how essential it is to the continued efficacy of fiduciary doctrine.[40] If fiduciaries were allowed to place other concerns above or on par with those of their beneficiaries, the very basis of fiduciary relationships – that fiduciaries must selflessly act in the best interests of their beneficiaries – would cease to exist. The Ontario High Court highlighted this notion in its decision in *Standard Investments Ltd v CIBC*: 'Equity then imposes a duty on the fiduciary to act in good faith and with due regard to the interests of the one imposing the confidence. It is the undertaking to act for and on behalf of another which imports the fiduciary responsibility. The conflict of duty and interest rule applies not simply because of the placing of trust and confidence, but, in my view, because of the undertaking of the fiduciary to act for or on behalf of his principal.'[41]

The Requirement of Full Disclosure

A corollary to the rule that fiduciaries must not benefit from their positions is the notion that fiduciaries *must* fully disclose their fiduciary activities to their beneficiaries.[42] The *raison d'être* of both the general conflict rule and the rule requiring full disclosure is to protect the integrity of interdependent relationships from the unsavoury elements of human nature.[43] This rationale is consistent with the basis for the determination of a breach of fiduciary obligation, namely, that a breach occurs simply by way of the fiduciary's departure from the beneficiary's best interests and does not require malevolent action or improper motive on the part of the fiduciary.[44]

The requirement of full disclosure is well illustrated by the case of *Harrison v Harrison*,[45] where a trustee was required to invest trust funds in a particular bank stock. In good faith, the trustee sold some of his own such stock to the trust. The beneficiary had consented to the purchase of the bank stock, but had not been informed that the trustee was also the vendor of some of the stock being purchased. The bank failed, resulting in a loss to the beneficiary. The court ordered that the sale of the stock be set aside and placed the loss resulting from the failure of the bank on the trustee/vendor. Not surprisingly, the court also ordered the appointment of new trustees. In rendering his judgment, Viscount Mowat held that in potential conflict-of-interest situations the presumption of fraud or wrongdoing is so high that all transactions occurring under such auspices, though perhaps completely innocent and free of conflict, must be rendered void by law.[46]

Fiduciaries Must Not Compromise Their Beneficiaries' Interests

The rule that fiduciaries must not compromise their beneficiaries' interest is also closely related to the general rule against conflicts and the requirement of full disclosure. This rule applies regardless of the number of beneficiaries which exist in relation to the same, or different, fiduciary duties. Where, for example, directors of a corporation owe fiduciary duties to the corporation's shareholders, they owe that same duty to each and every shareholder within a particular class, regardless of their number or the amount of shares they own, and must act fairly as between classes of shareholders.[47] These duties are derived from the directors' ability to affect the shareholders' interests through their control over the corporation that the shareholders collectively own.[48]

Fiduciaries may not compromise their beneficiaries' interests for personal gain or for the benefit of a third party or another *cestui que trust*.[49] Where more than one beneficiary exists, fiduciaries must treat them all fairly and equally or risk being found in breach of their obligations. Fiduciaries may also not be relieved of liability for breaching their fiduciary duties to one or more beneficiaries by citing competing fiduciary responsibilities.[50]

In addition, fiduciaries may not compromise or ignore their beneficiaries' wishes where those wishes are expressly known. In *Guerin v R*,[51] the failure of the Crown, through its agents, to secure lease arrangements according to the terms specified by the Musqueam band constituted a breach of the Crown's fiduciary duty to not compromise the band's interests. The *Guerin* scenario also illustrates how fiduciaries may be in breach of their duties for not obtaining optimum benefits for their beneficiaries where they sell their beneficiaries' properties at lower prices than could have legitimately been obtained.[52]

Other situations in which fiduciaries may be seen to compromise their beneficiaries' interests occur where fiduciaries are availed of exculpatory clauses in contracts or wills which propose to insulate them from personal liability for breaching their duties. To allow fiduciaries to invoke such clauses is tantamount to allowing them to contract out of their equitable responsibilities. Such a notion offends the fundamental basis of fiduciary doctrine.[53] Moreover, it marginalizes the existence of fiduciary relations to the point of extinction.

Fiduciary obligations are only kept in check through fiduciaries' legal liability for their breach of duty. If fiduciaries are entitled to escape this liability, their beneficiaries' rights are effectively rendered meaningless, thereby terminating the functional existence of the fiduciary relation.

For this reason, where exculpatory provisions exist which allow fiduciaries to escape liability to their beneficiaries, they should be struck down by the courts as contrary to public policy.

In *Re Poche* a trustee's attempt to invoke an exculpatory clause contained in a will to insulate herself from liability for negligence was prohibited. In denying the trustee the protection of the clause, the court determined that 'a trustee must be held responsible for any loss resulting from his gross negligence, regardless of any provision in the trust instrument relieving him from such liability.'[54] The principle affirmed in *Re Poche* is well established in fiduciary jurisprudence.[55] Unfortunately, it has not always been followed. In some instances, courts have upheld provisions in agreements which attempt to exclude fiduciary obligations in order to deny the rightful existence of fiduciary liability.[56]

A circular situation arises in the fiduciary's attempt to escape liability for breach of duty through an exculpatory clause. By invoking such a clause, a fiduciary is, by the act of invocation, in breach of duty before the clause may be taken advantage of.[57] Any fiduciary who attempts to escape liability for the non-commission of fiduciary duties contravenes the duty to act selflessly and in the beneficiary's best interests. Therefore, by attempting to avoid liability for a breach by exercising an exculpatory clause, the fiduciary is actually instigating a breach.

Fiduciaries' Delegation of Authority

A general rule of fiduciary doctrine holds that fiduciaries may not absolutely delegate their fiduciary authority to others. Although fiduciaries may delegate the entirety of their fiduciary *powers* to act in their beneficiaries' best interests, they cannot divest themselves of the totality of their fiduciary *obligations* to their beneficiaries. This distinction allows fiduciaries to transfer fiduciary powers where such a transfer is consistent with or in support of their beneficiaries' best interests, yet protects the beneficiaries in such a situation by not allowing the fiduciaries to be absolved of ultimate liability relating to the exercise of those powers.[58] The basis of the non-delegation rule stems from the maxim *delegatus non potest delegare* – a delegate is not able to re-delegate.[59]

As mentioned above, the idea that a fiduciary who has been delegated a duty may not re-delegate it to another is not, and should not be, absolute. In certain circumstances, it may be to the beneficiary's advantage for a fiduciary to delegate decision-making authority to another. One such situation may exist where a financially unsophisticated fiduciary

A 'Back to Basics' Approach 189

delegates authority over the beneficiary's investments to an investment broker or financial specialist. Where a delegation is legitimately in the beneficiary's best interests, it will not automatically result in a breach of fiduciary duty.[60] Nevertheless, upon an allegation of breach of duty by a beneficiary, the courts retain the authority to determine whether a fiduciary's delegation amounts to a breach.

The reason why a fiduciary remains responsible for the results of any delegation of powers, even where a delegation is made in a beneficiary's best interests and does not constitute a breach of duty, is to protect the beneficiary's interests and to ensure that the fiduciary is careful in choosing an appointee. In situations where there is more than one fiduciary, each fiduciary holds joint and several liability for any breach of duty towards common beneficiaries caused either by the fiduciaries or their appointees.[61] Any one fiduciary in such a scenario may not be absolved of liability for the actions of a co-fiduciary by being unaware of the other fiduciary's actions. Because the act of delegation itself does not remove a fiduciary's responsibility, a fiduciary should only delegate with great caution.

Summary

These four general rules of fiduciary doctrine illustrate some of the more profound duties that are vital to the continued existence, vitality, and integrity of fiduciary relationships. The common theme behind these rules is the attempts of fiduciary doctrine to ensure that beneficiaries may rely on their fiduciaries' fidelity. If fiduciaries are prohibited from using their office for personal gain or the benefit of parties other than their beneficiaries, required to disclose all of their fiduciary activities, forbidden from compromising their beneficiaries' interests, and remain ultimately responsible for all exercise of fiduciary powers, even where those powers have been delegated to another, there are few avenues left by which fiduciaries may depart from acting in the best interests of their beneficiaries without being held accountable.

Now that the general rules of fiduciary doctrine have been illustrated, the circumvention of which will result in a breach of fiduciary duty, the last of the three steps of fiduciary doctrine – the imposition of a remedy – may be examined. Only once a relationship has been deemed to be fiduciary and a breach of fiduciary obligation is found to have occurred through the application of the general rules of fiduciary doctrine should the appropriateness and availability of a remedy be discussed.

Fiduciary Relations: Limitation Periods, Laches, Acquiescence, and Fraud

The great advantage to pursuing the fiduciary route in litigation is the avoidance of many troublesome restrictions evident elsewhere in law. Perhaps the most obvious of these is the avoidance of limitation periods in a number of instances. This ability to avoid the defence of a lapse of statutory limitation or laches, where appropriate, stems from the twin premises which allow beneficiaries to rely on their fiduciaries' honesty, integrity, and fidelity and not inquire into the fiduciaries' activities. As a result, beneficiaries in those circumstances are entitled to commence legal action for any breach of fiduciary duty owed to them once they discover the cause of action.

The notion that fiduciaries need not inquire into the actions of their fiduciaries was settled by the Supreme Court of Canada in *Carl B. Potter Ltd v Mercantile Bank of Canada*.[62] The court came to this conclusion by being unable to find an authority for the proposition that a beneficiary owes a duty to its trustee to ensure that the terms of the trust are observed.[63] The *Potter* decision superseded the inference made by the Ontario Court of Appeal in *Inglis v Beaty* that the passage of time may assist in demonstrating a beneficiary's acceptance of a fiduciary breach.[64] It also dispelled the notion that, in some instances, beneficiaries must inquire into the actions of their fiduciaries. As the English Court of Appeal explained in *In re Vernon, Ewens, & Co*: 'the *cestui que trust* is entitled to trust in and place reliance upon his trustee, and is not bound to inquire whether he has committed a fraud against him unless there is something to raise his suspicion.'[65] Similar sentiments are expressed by Tamar Frankel, who explains that 'the law entitles the entrustor to rely on the fiduciary's trustworthiness. The entrustor is therefore not required to show that he actually relied on the fiduciary.'[66]

Statutory Limitations

As beneficiaries are not bound to inquire into their fiduciaries' activities and may rely on their fiduciaries' good faith exercise of their fiduciary duties,[67] it would appear to be difficult to sustain an argument which allows a beneficiary's ability to commence an action to be barred by a lapse of a statutory limitation period. The essential starting point for any consideration of the commencement of a statutory limitation period is the Supreme Court of Canada's decision in *City of Kamloops v Nielsen*. In

Kamloops the Supreme Court held that a statutory limitation period begins to run only once the beneficiary discovers, or ought reasonably to have discovered through reasonable diligence, the cause of action.[68] It should be noted, however, that the principle enunciated in *Kamloops* does not apply to 'ultimate limitation periods,' which impose a set period beyond which no claim may be made (in the absence of fraudulent activity by the person against whom the claim is to be made) regardless of whether the cause of action was known.[69] In any event, the analogy of *Kamloops*, a tort case, to a situation of a breach of fiduciary duty is not at all straightforward because of the differences between fiduciary doctrine and tort law.

Unlike the tort scenario, it cannot be plausibly judged at what date a beneficiary should have reasonably discovered the existence of a breach of fiduciary duty, because the beneficiary is under no duty to inquire into the actions of the fiduciary. Therefore, it would be logical to deduce that a limitation period would only begin to run, if at all, once the beneficiary has actually discovered that a breach of fiduciary duty has occurred. This entails that the beneficiary had knowledge of the fiduciary obligations owed to it, the breach of those obligations by the fiduciary, and that the breach gives rise to a cause of action. This three-tiered requirement is particularly relevant within the context of the Crown–Native relationship.

In a great many instances aboriginal groups only discover, or are advised by their legal counsel, that they are owed specific fiduciary duties by the Crown one hundred or more years after the signing of a treaty or agreement which created those specific obligations. It must also be remembered within this context that the fiduciary nature of the Crown–Native relationship was not judicially sanctioned until 1984 in *Guerin*. Under these circumstances, it would, prima facie, be inequitable to have an action by a band against the Crown for breach of fiduciary obligations stemming from a mid-nineteenth century treaty deemed to be statute-barred. This statement holds true even where a limitation statute provides for an 'ultimate limitation period.' The presence of an ultimate limitation period is irrelevant to a claim for breach of fiduciary duty, though, where the limitation statute does not explicitly apply to equitable actions.

In Supreme Court of Canada's recent judgment in *M(K) v M(H)*, the court held that there was no statutory limitation period for a breach of fiduciary obligation in Ontario.[70] The case concerned the ability of a woman who had been sexually abused by her father while she was a child to bring an action for damages against her father eleven years after the assaults had ended. The plaintiff based her claim on allegations of assault and battery and breach of fiduciary duty. At trial and upon appeal, her action was held to be statute-barred. La Forest J, for the majority of the Supreme Court, found that the plaintiff's claim, either in assault and battery or breach of fiduciary duty, was not prohibited by the lapse of statutory limitations.[71] Although he determined that a breach of fiduciary duty will circumvent Ontario's Limitations Act,[72] he held that where Canadian jurisdictions have enacted general provisions encompassing actions in Equity, fiduciary duties are caught by those jurisdictions' limitations legislation.[73]

Application of the Statute by Analogy

Where no general provision which encompasses equitable actions exists in a statutory limitations act, a statutory limitation period may only be applied, in appropriate circumstances, by analogy.[74] However, the applicability by analogy must be precise: 'For a limitation period to be applied by analogy, the equitable claim should precisely correspond to one to which a statutory limitation period applies. A vague similarity is not enough.'[75] The only possible analogy to a fiduciary relationship from common inclusions in statutory limitation acts are those sections relating to trusts and trustees. Although trust law is generally applicable by analogy to fiduciary relationships,[76] the preciseness of the analogy depends on the specific type of trust to which the statute refers. Generally, references to trusts in limitation statutes are confined to express or statutory trusts, which are not analogous to fiduciary relations.[77] In any event, Equity rarely limits a purely equitable cause of action by analogy to statutory limitations.

Where the analogy of a statutory limitation period is permitted in concurrent actions in common law and Equity, the courts' equitable jurisdiction is not bound by the statute, but their residual discretion may be employed by the equitable doctrine of laches (la-chéz).[78] Although the courts may bind themselves, by analogy, to the terms of the statute, they may equally choose to ignore the statute altogether. Analogous applications of statutory limitations to equitable actions may also be limited by the presence of any fraudulent concealment of a plaintiff's cause of action by a defendant.[79]

Laches and Acquiescence

The applicability of the doctrine of laches to a breach of fiduciary duty is quite rare. Laches is an equitable doctrine which estops, or prevents, a plaintiff from asserting a right or claim by virtue of the combination of having taken too long to assert that right or claim and the prejudice that would result to the adverse party if the allegation was allowed to proceed after such a delay. It should be noted that mere delay alone is insufficient to ground a defence of laches. The delay must have the effect of demonstrating the plaintiff's acquiescence to the defendant's conduct, thereby implying the waiver of any rights or claims belonging to the plaintiff arising from the defendant's conduct.[80] Acquiescence, in this context, entails the plaintiff's objective knowledge[81] of the existence of and right to bring forth any equitable rights or claims based on certain facts – as opposed to merely having knowledge of the facts, but not knowing that they give rise to any right or claim.[82] The plaintiff, therefore, must know of the existence of the defendant's conduct, the wrongfulness of that conduct, and that the wrongful conduct creates the basis of an equitable action. It should also be noted that acquiescence, on its own, may constitute a defence to a claim of breach of fiduciary duty by virtue of the prospective plaintiff's knowledge of and deemed acquiescence to the wrongful activity: 'In the context of equity, acquiescence may be defined as assent to an infringement of legal rights, expressed or implied from conduct, by which the right to equitable relief may be lost.'[83]

In addition, laches may only be successfully pleaded by a defendant to an equitable proceeding where there is a demonstration of prejudice to the defendant occasioned by the delay in bringing the proceedings caused by the plaintiff's action or inaction.[84] The time from which the reasonableness of any delay is determined is the time at which the plaintiff first acquires sufficient knowledge of the facts which give rise to a cause of action. The determination of whether there has been unreasonable delay sufficient to constitute the basis of a claim of laches is, like all other equitable doctrines, situation-specific. It must, therefore, be made in light of the facts which give rise to the situation leading up to the allegation of delay.

The equitable basis of laches prevents a remedy from being granted where it would be unjust to do so in the circumstances. This premise is consistent with the basis of equitable jurisdiction, which is premised upon the legal maxim *soit droit fait* – let right be done. As La Forest J stated in *M(K) v M(H)*, 'Ultimately, laches must be resolved as a matter of justice as between the parties, as is the case with any equitable doctrine.'[85] Consequently, where a beneficiary asserts a claim against a fiduciary, the doctrine of laches generally will not apply.

194   General Principles of Fiduciary Doctrine

Equitable Fraud

The existence of fraudulent concealment, or other forms of equitable fraud, has a significant impact upon the applicability of statutory limitation periods.[86] Whereas some statutory limitation acts have expressly recognized fraud as a barrier to the commencement of an applicable limitation period,[87] the barrier also exists where it has not been so recognized. As Graeme Mew explains in *The Law of Limitations*, 'Equity will not permit the use of a limitation period as the engine of fraud.'[88] Fraudulent concealment of a cause of action exists where there is conduct which 'having regard to some special relationship between the two parties concerned, is an unconscionable thing for the one to do towards the other.'[89] Where fraudulent concealment of a cause of action exists, a statutory limitation period does not begin to run until the plaintiff may discover, or ought to have discovered, with reasonable diligence, the existence of the cause of action.[90] Although a statutory limitation period cannot run in the face of equitable fraud, laches may still come into play, where appropriate.[91] Just as Equity will not allow fraudulent activity to eliminate a wronged party's right to seek legal redress for that wrong, it will not allow a wronged party to sit on a cause of action to the detriment of the other party or parties involved, notwithstanding the latter's commission of the wrongful act.

Equitable fraud does not exist only in situations where there is an active intent to conceal a cause of action. It may also exist in any situation as a result of the manner in which the act or acts which give rise to a cause of action have been perpetrated.[92] A fraudulent concealment need not amount to deceit or common law fraud to suspend the operation of a statutory limitation period.[93] However, to arrest a statutory limitation, the alleged fraudulent concealment must involve some abuse of a confidential position, intentional imposition, or deliberate concealment of facts.[94] Equitable fraud is a matter of particular relevance to the Crown–Native relationship, which is characterized by the Crown's historical lack of disclosure to Native peoples.[95]

Fiduciary Relations and Equitable/Statutory Bars:
The Underlying Premise of Equity

Allowing fiduciaries to invoke equitable bars, such as laches or acquiescence, to the rights of the beneficiaries whom they are duty bound to serve is repugnant to the essence of fiduciary doctrine and the equitable

A 'Back to Basics' Approach 195

principles which underlie it.[96] Fiduciaries generally possess the ability to conceal, fraudulently or otherwise, the basis of a cause of action from their beneficiaries which may preclude the latter from being able to commence an action for a considerable length of time. It would be inequitable to allow a fiduciary, who has managed to conceal a cause of action for breach of duty from its beneficiary, to escape liability by way of its own actions in camouflaging or hiding the existence of the breach. One possible exception to the general prohibition against fiduciaries invoking laches as a defence may exist in a situation where a beneficiary knows of the existence of a cause of action, but refuses to initiate it, resulting in prejudice to the fiduciary which outweighs the beneficiary's rights.

The invocation of statutory limitation periods as a defence by fiduciaries would also appear to be precluded for the very same reasons. Although, prima facie, when the facts giving rise to a right are known it is presumed that the right is also known, this notion applies only in the absence of a fiduciary relationship or other circumstances which renders it inappropriate or where it would be inequitable to deny the plaintiff relief.[97] A fiduciary's ability to set up a defence of a lapse of a statutory limitation period, laches, or acquiescence in order to escape personal liability also offends the rule against conflict of interest. Such an action is fundamentally inconsistent with fiduciaries' duty to act selflessly and in the best interests of their beneficiaries in the precise manner that a fiduciary is in breach of duty by invoking an exculpatory clause which removes liability for any breach duty.[98]

With the merger of legal and equitable jurisdictions, a statutory limitations act which explicitly states its application to equitable causes of action may attribute time limits to their assertion in judicial proceedings. However, under the general principles established by the Supreme Court of Canada in *M(K) v M(H)*, statutory limitations ought not be implemented where their use would result in the creation or continued existence of unfairness or injustice.

Fiduciary Remedies

The number of potential remedies available to a *cestui que trust* who is the victim of a breach of fiduciary duty is one of the primary reasons for the tremendous popularity of fiduciary arguments. The range of available remedies for a breach of fiduciary duty is far wider than that available in contiguous areas such as breach of confidence and negligent misrepresentation. Moreover, the remedies available for a breach of fiduciary obligation are much more elastic than those available at common law.[99]

In a manner consistent with the situation-specificity of fiduciary doctrine, fiduciary remedies vary according to the nature of the relationship under examination and the type of breach involved.[100] Just as no two fiduciary relationships are identical, no two breaches of fiduciary duty are identical. The wide range of fiduciary remedies exists as a direct result of the multifarious relations that may be described as fiduciary. As Lambert JA explained in the British Columbia Court of Appeal's decision in *Canson Enterprises Ltd v Boughton & Co*: 'The rubric "breach of fiduciary duty" has come to encompass so many different types of liability that it is not now possible to determine the appropriate remedy by defining the wrong simply as a "breach of fiduciary duty." It is necessary, instead, to look through the categorization of the wrong as a "breach of fiduciary duty" to the true nature of the wrong, and to move from there to the determination of the remedy. The nature of the wrong and the nature of the loss, not the nature of the cause of action, will dictate the scope of the remedy.'[101]

Potential remedies which may be invoked upon a finding of a breach of fiduciary obligation include restitutionary, personal, proprietary, and deterrent remedies. These may include equitable remedies – such as constructive trust, injunctions, declarations, prohibitions, rescission, accounting for profits, repayment of improperly used moneys (plus interest), equitable liens, equitable damages,[102] and *in rem* restitution – and/or liability based on negligence, fraud, coercion, undue influence, profiteering, economic duress, negligent misrepresentation, or third party liability. A court may also grant interest on financial proceeds awarded to remedy a breach of fiduciary duty which is payable from the date of the breach.[103] Interest awarded may be ordinary or compounded.

A wronged beneficiary may also obtain the advantage of being able to trace funds, in appropriate circumstances.[104] Exemplary or punitive damages may be awarded against a fiduciary at the court's discretion, particularly where the fiduciary has acted in conflict of interest. Fiduciaries found liable for fiduciary misconduct may have solicitor–client costs awarded against them. Moreover, in situations of potential conflict of interest where a beneficiary cannot unilaterally dismiss a fiduciary – such as with trustees or public officials – and demonstrates grounds for the fiduciary's removal,[105] the beneficiary may seek a court order to remove the fiduciary.[106]

There is also the possibility of a finding of cumulative damages in situations where the fiduciary is liable for damages flowing from more than one action. One such example is a fiduciary's acceptance of a secret commission to act in a manner contrary to the beneficiary's best interests. In such a scenario, the fiduciary is liable to the beneficiary for both the amount of the commission and damages flowing from the breach of duty.[107] The payment of what appears to be double recovery by the beneficiary for the fiduciary's improprieties may be viewed as an improper windfall. However, unless the indecorous fiduciary is not to be fully punished for the breach of duty, there is no other viable alternative which remains faithful to the equitable basis of fiduciary doctrine. This principle was recently affirmed by Morden ACJO in *Olson v. Gullo*: 'I have no doubt that stripping the wrongdoing partner of the whole of the profit, including his or her own share in it, is a strong disincentive to conduct which breaches the fiduciary obligation. Further, as a host of equity decisions have shown for at least two centuries, the fact that this would result in a windfall gain to the plaintiff cannot, in itself, be a valid objection to it.'[108]

Although awards of cumulative damages may appear to give unfair results, this is clearly not so. Awarding cumulative damages ensures that fiduciaries are forced to disgorge the entirety of their profits made while acting against their beneficiaries' interests. It is one of the harsh consequences of the strict adherence of fiduciary doctrine to the requirement of *uberrima fides* and the rule against conflict of interest.

Suppose that the fiduciary F is approached by a third party X who wishes to purchase the beneficiary's B's parcel of land. X intends to resell B's land to a land developer D at a profit. X knows that D is willing to pay $100,000 for the land. X informs F of his plan and offers F $10,000 and a 10 per cent share of any profits from the sale of B's property if F will sell him the property for $60,000. F accepts X's offer and sells X the land for $60,000. X then 'flips' the land by selling it to D for $100,000. In fulfilment of their agreement, X gives F the 'secret profit' of $14,000 ($10,000 + 10% of the $40,000 profit, or $4,000).

From this situation, it may be seen that both F and X have made profits [$14,000 and $26,000 ($40,000 minus the $14,000 to F) respectively] at the expense of B. B's loss is measured by the damage sustained as a result of F's transfer of loyalty to an interest other than B's own. More specifically, B's loss is calculated by the difference between the price B received for the sale of the land ($60,000) and the price obtained by X for the sale of the land to D ($100,000), or $40,000. The secret profit is the means by which F's transfer of loyalty was effected.

If B is awarded a remedy only on the basis of *restitutio ad integrum*, F – while liable for the $40,000 loss suffered by B – retains the $14,000 from X to breach that duty. Because fiduciary laws were promulgated to protect the integrity of socially valuable relationships, F's attempts to profit from the breach of duty to B must also be remediable. This last proposition illustrates the rationale behind cumulative damage awards. Consequently, F must disgorge both the amount of the loss suffered by B as a direct result of the breach and the amount of the bribe paid to F by which F's loyalty was transferred.

Although B is overcompensated for the loss suffered (by gaining $54,000 while suffering a loss of only $40,000), F is not overly punished (by receiving $14,000, yet disgorging $54,000). If F was allowed to keep the $14,000 bribe, F would gain an undeserved advantage by not being forced to personally reimburse B for the full value of B's loss. Under the latter scenario, F is only forced to pay out $26,000 – the $40,000 loss minus the $14,000 bribe – rather than the full $40,000. Moreover, there is no other way that B would be adequately compensated for the loss while F is appropriately punished for the indiscretion. In any event, the $14,000 bribe arguably amounts to unjust enrichment, and F could be forced to disgorge it on that basis. Of course, the courts possess the ability to award punitive damages against F for the breach on top of any other award granted to B. Consequently, F could be found liable in damages to B in excess of $54,000.[109]

There are two purposes behind awarding damages to a *cestui que trust* affected by a breach of fiduciary duty. One is to compensate the *cestui que trust* for any direct loss sustained by the act of breach. The other is to deter fiduciaries from breaching their obligations. The rationale behind awarding cumulative damages is to prevent unscrupulous fiduciaries from benefiting from their positions through acts of breach: 'The real reason for the recovery from the briber is that the latter has wronged the principal by undermining the integrity of his business organization and so sharp is the courts' disapproval of such conduct that they are more prepared to allow the principal to realize a windfall than to forgo the punishment of the wrongdoer. In effect the second recovery fulfills the function of punitive damages with the amount of the bribe serving as an administratively easy method of quantifying the award.'[110] It is therefore more consistent with the equitable basis of fiduciary doctrine to have the *cestui que trust* be overcompensated where a fiduciary commits a breach of duty than to have the fiduciary be insufficiently punished where such a choice has to be made.[111]

Conclusion

The discussion of fiduciary doctrine in this Part offers a functional approach to fiduciary doctrine based on an adherence to the purpose and intent of fiduciary doctrine. Its aim is to replace the categorical approach to fiduciary relations that has hampered the development of fiduciary law as well as providing a sound basis for a contextual analysis of the Crown–Native fiduciary relationship. Because of the complexity of fiduciary doctrine and the confusion surrounding the application of fiduciary law to the Crown–Native relationship, a meaningful discussion of the fiduciary character of the Crown–Native relationship is impossible in the absence of an adequate prior understanding of fiduciary doctrine.

Fiduciary doctrine is not merely a set of loosely fitting or entirely unrelated rules functioning in an ad hoc fashion. Rather, it is a blueprint for the protection and continued efficacy of interdependent societal relations. By animating the theory of fiduciary relations through an examination of the nexus between the rights and obligations arising under their auspices, the interrelationship between the fundamental characteristics and rules of fiduciary doctrine may, themselves, be seen in their proper context. It is only when fiduciary law is truly understood that it may escape from the confusion that now surrounds it.

The Crown's fiduciary obligations to aboriginal peoples are of major significance to the Crown–Native relationship. However, the implications and ramifications of the application of fiduciary doctrine to the Crown–Native relationship have yet to be truly understood by judicial and academic commentators. Part Three will attempt to remedy this deficiency by combining the understandings gained from Parts One and Two to illustrate some of the specific effects of the Crown's fiduciary obligations on the Crown–Native relationship.

PART THREE

The Crown's Fiduciary Duty towards Aboriginal Peoples in Canada

11
The British Crown's Obligations

Although the number of post-*Guerin* cases which consider the fiduciary nature of the Crown–Native relationship continues to increase at a substantial rate, the vast majority of them have done little to enhance the juridical understanding of that relationship. As the *Guerin* decision itself failed to establish a sufficient basis for determining the effects of the Crown's general fiduciary capacity towards aboriginal peoples this is hardly surprising.

Within the limited parameters of the fact situation before it in *Guerin*, the Supreme Court of Canada determine that a fiduciary relationship existed between the Crown and Musqueam band as a result of the nature of their interaction; that the Crown breached its duty by failing to lease the surrendered land in accordance with the band's specified terms; and that the Musqueam band was entitled to a remedy for the breach. In so doing, it answered the pivotal questions of *who* the fiduciary and beneficiary were, *why* the relationship between them was fiduciary in nature, *how* the Crown's actions amounted to a breach of its obligations, and *what* the basis of the remedy awarded was. From the time of its release, however, *Guerin* stood for more than the implementation of fiduciary doctrine to the relationship between the Crown and Musqueam band relating to the latter's surrender of land for leasing purposes. It stood for the general proposition that the Crown plays the role of fiduciary to Native peoples in a wide variety of situations.

Within this larger context, the *Guerin* case did not follow fiduciary doctrine's three-step process. Although it made strong statements about the fiduciary nature of the Crown–Native relationship in general – and detailed some of the reasons why that relationship is fiduciary – *Guerin* neglected to answer a number of fundamental questions which are necessary precursors to a proper understanding of the general fiduciary relationship between the Crown and Native peoples (and which logically flow from the second step of the fiduciary process).[1] Subsequently decided cases have similarly failed to suggest answers to these basic questions. The judiciary's unquestioning adherence to the *Guerin* precedent has only made matters worse. By not recognizing the situation-specificity of fiduciary doctrine, they have fallen prey to applying answers that are relevant only to the facts in *Guerin* to other, unique situations. Not only has this resulted in a number of unsatisfactory judgments, but it has also added to the confusion which permeates the application of fiduciary law to Crown–Native relations.

The only way to rectify the inherent deficiencies in existing Crown–Native fiduciary jurisprudence is to return to the general characteristics and principles of fiduciary doctrine, as outlined in Part Two. Once the courts become better acquainted with the basic premises of fiduciary doctrine they may then apply it to a variety of interdependent relationships, including the *sui generis* relationship between the Crown and aboriginal peoples. Bona fide attempts may then be made to answer the lingering questions that prohibit the development of the juridical understanding of the Crown–Native fiduciary relationship.[2] As the general characteristics and principles of fiduciary doctrine have already been canvassed, it is now possible to proceed to the task of providing answers to the questions left outstanding by *Guerin* and its successors.

Is the British Crown Bound by Fiduciary Obligations to Aboriginal Peoples?

The question of *who* is bound by the Crown's fiduciary obligations to aboriginal peoples – that is, the emanations of the Crown that are responsible for carrying out its fiduciary obligations owed to the Native peoples – is the most vital question left unanswered by judicial and academic considerations of the Crown–Native fiduciary relationship. That no attempts have been made to address this basic question signifies the inherent deficiencies of the present method of descriptive rather than analytical investigation of the Crown–Native relationship which has dominated post-*Guerin* judicial decisions.

In the juridical context, the only direct suggestions as to whether the British Crown is bound by fiduciary obligations to aboriginal peoples may be made by reference to three decisions arising in response to the Canadian government's repatriation of the Canadian constitution in

The British Crown's Obligations   205

1982: *R v Secretary of State for Foreign and Commonwealth Affairs, ex parte Indian Association of Alberta and Others* (henceforth the *Alberta Indian Association* case);[3] *Manuel and Others v Attorney General*;[4] and *Noltcho and Others v Attorney General*.[5]

The Alberta Indian Association *Case*

In the *Alberta Indian Association* case, the Indian Association of Alberta, Union of New Brunswick Indians, and Union of Nova Scotia Indians were concerned that their interests would not be served by the constitutional repatriation process initiated by the federal government. They wanted to ensure that their rights, as well as the Crown's obligations to them – as represented in legislation, proclamations, and treaties – would be protected. Consequently, they sought a declaration from the British secretary of state for foreign and Commonwealth affairs that the British Crown was still responsible for carrying out the treaty and other obligations *vis-à-vis* the aboriginal peoples that it had initiated or agreed to. The secretary of state flatly denied such responsibility. The aboriginal groups then appealed, with leave of the English Court of Appeal, for judicial review of the secretary of state's determination. They sought a declaration that the British Crown was still responsible for carrying out these obligations and that the decision of the secretary of state for foreign and Commonwealth affairs denying any such responsibility was incorrect.

The Court of Appeal unanimously held that the British Crown was no longer responsible for the welfare of aboriginal peoples in Canada. It determined that any responsibility which had been held by the British Crown had been transferred entirely to Canada. A variety of rationales detailing the transfer of the British Crown's obligations to Canada were discussed in the judgments of Lord Denning MR, Kerr LJ, and May LJ. Their judgments do not comment, however, on which personifications of the Canadian Crown – the Crown in right of Canada, the Crown in right of a particular province, or both – are now obliged to fulfil the Crown's historic duty to the aboriginal peoples.

Lord Denning MR based his decision on the initial transfer of powers from Britain to Canada through the British North America Act, 1867, and the gradual and complete devolution of British powers over Canadian affairs to Canada culminating in the Statute of Westminster, 1931. He determined that the transfer of powers by way of this process resulted in a similar transfer of Britain's outstanding obligations to aboriginal peoples to Canada.[6] In addition, he found that the change in the constitutional understanding of the Crown from 'one and indivisible' throughout the Commonwealth to 'separate and divisible' for each self-governing dominion, province, or territory[7] corroborated his finding that the British Crown was no longer under any duty to the aboriginal peoples of Canada. As a result, the content of any duties still owed to the aboriginal peoples under the authority of the single and indivisible Crown or the British Crown became the obligations of either the federal or relevant provincial Crowns.[8]

Kerr LJ agreed with Lord Denning MR's conclusions. He explained that any rights or obligations owed to Native peoples could be binding only upon a governmental representation or emanation of the Crown in the territory in which those rights or obligations existed. Subsequently, be held that all rights and obligations of the Crown, other than those concerning the Queen in her personal capacity, could arise only in relation to a particular government within the Commonwealth.[9] Along this same line of reasoning, May LJ found that the British Crown's responsibility for outstanding obligations to the aboriginal peoples of Canada had 'become the responsibility of the government of Canada with the attainment of independence, at the latest with the Statute of Westminster 1931.'[10] Although he determined that a limited sovereignty over Canada remained with the British Crown after the passage of the Statute of Westminster, 1931, he nevertheless held that this residual sovereignty did not mean that 'any treaty or other obligations into which the Crown may have entered with its Indian peoples of Canada still enure against the Crown in right of the United Kingdom.'[11] Rather, he concluded that any obligation owed by the 'single and indivisible' Crown was now the sole responsibility of the Crown in right of Canada or in right of a particular province.[12]

The House of Lords refused leave to appeal the Court of Appeal's judgment. In delivering the House of Lords' brief reasons for refusing leave, Lord Diplock explained that, as the Court of Appeal had determined, the British Crown no longer possessed any obligations to the aboriginal peoples of Canada. He emphasized that any outstanding obligations owed to the aboriginals were now the responsibility of 'Her Majesty's government in Canada' and that they were to be determined by the Canadian courts.[13]

The *Alberta Indian Association* decision is unequivocal in its finding that the British Crown no longer owes any responsibilities to Native peoples in Canada despite its acknowledgment that the British Crown

The British Crown's Obligations 207

once possessed those same responsibilities. The decision was based on the assumption that the British Crown's transfer of powers to Canada beginning in 1867 was accompanied by a simultaneous wholesale transfer of responsibilities. Once the transaction was completed, the British Crown was no longer burdened by any obligations to Native peoples. However, the Court of Appeal did not discuss the British Crown's fiduciary duty to aboriginal peoples and whether it was also transferred to Canada along with the other powers formerly possessed by the British Crown. This point becomes particularly relevant in light of the premise that fiduciaries may delegate the entirety of their fiduciary powers, but not the entirety of their fiduciary obligations.[14] The fact that the *Alberta Indian Association* case did not discuss the existence or transfer of fiduciary duties from the British Crown to the Canadian Crown should not be altogether surprising, however, given the fact that the case was adjudicated two years prior to the *Guerin* decision.

Manuel v Attorney General; Noltcho v Attorney General

The *Manuel* and *Noltcho* cases were heard together shortly after the decision in the *Alberta Indian Association* case was rendered and its appeal to the House of Lords denied. In the *Manuel* action 124 Indian chiefs, representing themselves and the members of a number of Indian bands, sought declarations which would protect their rights and interests. Although they sought six declarations,[15] the final two were the most important, namely, (1) the British Parliament had no power to amend the Canadian constitution in a manner which would prejudice the Native peoples of Canada without their consent, and (2) the Canada Act, 1982, passed by the British Parliament was *ultra vires*, or in excess of its jurisdiction. In the *Noltcho* action sixty-eight Indian chiefs, in a similar representative capacity, sought declarations which would hold the British Crown liable for outstanding obligations arising under the terms of specified treaties signed between the Crown and the bands named in the action during the period from 1871 to 1907.[16] In response to the two claims, the attorney general of England brought motions seeking that both actions be dismissed as disclosing no reasonable causes of action.

The *Manuel* statement of claim maintained that the aboriginal peoples had special rights which were protected under the Canadian constitution. It insisted that Section 7(1) of the Statute of Westminster, 1931, prevented the Canadian Parliament or the provincial legislatures from altering the constitutional arrangements regarding aboriginal rights that had been established by the terms of the Royal Proclamation of 1763 and a series of nineteenth-century treaties and were included in the British North America Acts 1867 to 1930.[17] Under the new regime, the plaintiffs insisted that their former protection disappeared, as the content of the aboriginal rights included in Section 35(1) of the Constitution Act, 1982, were to be determined in a constitutional conference designed specifically for that function under Section 37(2) of the Act. Moreover, under Part V of the Act, the Canadian constitution was capable of domestic amendment, thereby rendering the protection of aboriginal rights more precarious than they had been previously.[18] Rather than seeking the enforcement of their rights, the plaintiffs in *Manuel* were seeking to preserve the protection of those rights as it existed prior to the passage of the Canada Act, 1982.

The *Noltcho* action alleged that the aboriginal peoples were induced into signing the treaties specified in the claim through assurances by the Crown that the treaties would be permanent in nature. The Crown promised that the treaties would both enure to future generations of Indians and remain binding on the Crown until they were either assigned or abrogated with aboriginal consent. In addition, the statement of claim alleged that, in certain respects, the treaties and warranties attached to them rendered the British Crown a trustee or fiduciary for the Indians.[19] The plaintiff's counsel also argued that the *ratio*[20] of the *Alberta Indian Association* case was obscure and, in any case, fully distinguishable from the present action.

On the basis of the attorney general's motions, Megarry VC held that both actions should be dismissed. The *Manuel* action was dismissed because (1) as an Act of Parliament, the court was bound to obey the Canada Act, 1982, and could not question its validity,[21] and (2) the court had no jurisdiction to make a declaration as to the validity of the constitution of an independent sovereign state. The *Noltcho* action was dismissed on the same basis as the determination made in the *Alberta Indian Association* case. Megarry VC found that that case had correctly determined that any obligations which the Crown had in respect of aboriginal peoples in Canada were the responsibility of the Canadian federal and provincial Crowns and not the British Crown by virtue of the transfer of sovereignty over Canadian affairs. He determined that the British Crown was able to transfer its sovereignty to the Canadian Crown and, along with that transfer, the responsibility for carrying out the obligations it had incurred under the treaties.[22] When the *Manuel* decision was appealed to the English Court of Appeal, it was dismissed on the same

The British Crown's Obligations 209

basis as it had been in the court below. Leave to appeal the decision to the House of Lords was refused.

Interestingly, with regard to the *Noltcho* action, Megarry VC did not dismiss the notion that trusts 'in the ordinary equitable sense' may exist which were binding on the Crown – as distinguished from political trusts, or 'trusts in the higher sense.' He suggested, however, that if any such trusts existed, it would be natural to assume that the Crown, as trustee, should rely on the advice of Canadian ministers instead of British ministers in the execution of those trusts.[23] Although the *Noltcho* action suggested that the British Crown was a trustee or fiduciary for the Indians, which distinguishes it from the *Alberta Indian Association* case, there was no elaboration on the point in Megarry VC's judgment.

Given the pre-*Guerin* positioning of the *Alberta Indian Association*, *Manuel*, and *Noltcho* cases, it remains to be determined whether their precedents apply equally to absolve the British Crown of liability for the fiduciary duty owed to Native peoples. As a result of the drastic changes that have taken place in the juridical understanding of the Crown's obligations to Native peoples since 1982, the English courts' absolution of the British Crown from liability for any obligations owing to the aboriginal peoples of Canada in these cases begs to be considered anew.

The Devolution of the Crown's Powers over Canadian Affairs

The process by which British responsibilities for Canadian affairs, both pertaining to aboriginal peoples and otherwise, were transferred to Canada is not as straightforward as either the *Alberta Indian Association*, *Manuel*, or *Noltcho* decisions present it. The responsibility for fulfilling the Crown's obligations in Canada belonged to the 'single and indivisible' Crown prior to 1867. However, with the establishment of the Dominion of Canada in 1867, the 'single and indivisible' Crown took on a different appearance. As a result of the changes in the political structure of the British Empire in the nineteenth century when the 'single and indivisible' Crown began to divest itself of its colonial holdings, a process of devolution was initiated whereby the 'single and indivisible' Crown's powers and responsibilities[24] for Canada underwent a gradual process of transformation. This devolution of powers and responsibilities included the Crown's fiduciary obligations to the aboriginal peoples of Canada.

Beginning with the passage of the British North America Act, 1867, and the formation of the Dominion of Canada, Canada became more self-governing and, consequently, more responsible for its own affairs. However, the British North America Act, 1867, did not eliminate the entirety of the Crown's responsibility for Canadian affairs. The legislative and executive powers and responsibilities for Canada proceeded through a gradual transformation which was initiated upon Confederation. Initially, they had been ultimately borne by the 'single and indivisible' Crown. At the union they evolved into the joint responsibility of the British and Canadian Crowns. Ultimately, these powers and responsibilities belonged entirely to the Canadian federal and provincial Crowns.

Rather than there being any particular point in time upon which the British Crown divested itself entirely of its responsibilities for Canadian affairs, there was a gradual devolution of executive, legislative, and governmental powers and responsibilities to the Canadian Crown.[25] This period of devolution was marked by a number of different events which indicated both the transfer of increasingly greater degrees of authority from Britain and the increasing independence of Canada. Some of these events included Canada's signature of the Treaty of Versailles in 1919 independently of Britain,[26] the enactment of the Statute of Westminster, 1931,[27] Canada's separate declaration of war with Germany in 1939, and the abolishment of criminal and civil appeals from the Supreme Court of Canada to the Privy Council in 1933 and 1949 respectively. As a result of the political changes in the relationship between the British Crown and Canada which came about as a result of Confederation, British obligations to the aboriginal peoples began to adopt a different character.

The constitutional understanding of 'the Crown' in 1867, as the *Alberta Indian Association* decision indicated, was that the Crown was 'one and indivisible' throughout the Commonwealth. This means that under the aegis of the single and indivisible Crown existed the Crown in right of Britain, the Crown in right of Canada, and so on for each Commonwealth country or dominion. A significant number of the underlying bases of the Crown's general fiduciary obligations to the aboriginal peoples predate the formation of the Dominion of Canada in 1867. Moreover, virtually all of them[28] predate the change in the understanding of the Crown as 'separate and divisible' throughout the Commonwealth recognized at the Imperial Conference of 1926. As the vast majority of the underlying bases of the Crown's fiduciary duty to Native peoples date back to the time when the Crown was single and indivisible throughout the Commonwealth, can the change in the understanding of the Crown in 1926 have any effect upon the Crown's pre-existing fiduciary obligations? The theoretical basis of fiduciary doctrine and the duties, rights, and benefits which it imposes on fiduciaries and beneficiaries bring into question, prima facie, the effect of the change in the constitutional understanding of the Crown from 'one and indivisible' to 'separate and divisible' upon the Crown's pre-existing fiduciary duty. The essence of all fiduciary relationships is that fiduciaries must act with honesty, integrity, and the utmost good faith towards the best interests of their beneficiaries. Consequently, it must be asked whether the evolving transfer of powers over Canada from the single and indivisible Crown to the Canadian Crown was consistent with the aboriginal peoples' best interests. Second, in conjunction with the findings in the *Sparrow*,[29] *New Zealand Maori Council*,[30] and *Eastmain*[31] decisions that the Crown's duty is a purposive one, it must be determined whether the transfer of powers promoted or furthered the best interests of the aboriginal peoples.

Fiduciaries are required to provide full disclosure of their fiduciary activities to their beneficiaries. In the context of the transfer of powers over Canadian affairs, this would entail that the Native peoples be advised about the changes in the ownership of responsibility for Canadian affairs, including any responsibilities owed to the Native peoples. The purposive nature of the Crown's duty may have required it to have consulted the Natives about its intentions prior to their implementation.[32] Fiduciary doctrine also insists that beneficiaries need not inquire into their fiduciaries' activities, but may rely on their fiduciaries' honesty, integrity, and fidelity.[33] Consequently, the aboriginal peoples were not bound to discover the change in the understanding of the Crown from 'single and indivisible' to 'separate and divisible,' even if the change directly affected the fulfilment of the Crown's fiduciary obligations to them by way of a change in the party, or parties responsible for discharging those obligations. In light of these considerations, were the Native peoples' interests, in fact, compromised for the benefit of their fiduciary (or fiduciaries, as the case may have been at a given point in time during the devolution of powers from the single and indivisible Crown) in contravention of fiduciary principles?

The act of transferring powers from the single and indivisible Crown requires greater scrutiny than that provided by the *Alberta Indian Association*, *Manuel*, and *Noltcho* cases. Fiduciary theory insists that whereas fiduciaries may delegate the entirety of their fiduciary *powers*, they may not divest themselves of the totality of their fiduciary *obligations*. Strict adherence to this principle leads to the conclusion that although the single and indivisible Crown may have delegated all of its fiduciary *powers* along with the other powers it transferred, it could not simultaneously transfer the entirety of its fiduciary *obligations* and thereby be relieved of the responsibility of discharging them. This being so, what is the effect of the Crown's residual responsibility for discharging the fiduciary duty owed to aboriginal peoples?

The Effect of the Devolution of the Crown's Powers on Its Fiduciary Duty to Aboriginal Peoples

At this late stage, it is difficult, if not impossible, to pinpoint whether the transfer of powers over Canada was done in good faith and in the best interests of aboriginal peoples. The Canadian Crown's treatment of aboriginal peoples in Canada since 1867 is far from exemplary. The Supreme Court of Canada recognized this fact in its decision in *Sparrow*, where it stated that 'there can be no doubt that over the years the rights of the Indians were often honoured in the breach.'[34] Nevertheless, it remains a matter of speculation as to whether the treatment of the aboriginal peoples would have been any different in the absence of the devolution of powers.

As it is not possible to ascertain how the history of Native affairs would have materialized in the absence of the transfer of powers over Canada, it cannot be absolutely determined whether the Native peoples' interests were compromised by the results of the transfer process. The Canadian Crown had far fewer resources and tangible assets at its disposal to discharge the fiduciary obligations owed to Native peoples than either the single and indivisible Crown or the British Crown. Yet, there does not appear to have been any intention of the Crown to shirk its responsibilities by way of the transfer of powers, and there is no obvious inference that the transfer adversely affected the aboriginal peoples' interests. What is clear is that the Native peoples were never advised of the change in the understanding of the Crown or the transfer of powers over Canadian affairs. Moreover, they were not consulted, even though the transfer directly affected their interests and the fiduciary obligations owed to them.

The Crown's obligation to consult the aboriginal peoples regarding the transfer of powers over Canadian affairs is analogous to the Crown's duty to consult the Huron band prior to extinguishing its treaty rights found by the Supreme Court of Canada in *R v Sioui*.[35] Members of the Huron band had been charged and convicted of cutting down trees, camping, and making fires in unauthorized places in a public park in contravention of the park's regulations. The park was located within territory traditionally occupied by the band. The band members admitted committing the actions that they were eventually convicted of, but claimed that they were practising ancestoral customs and rites which had been protected by a treaty between the band and the Crown signed in 1760.

The Supreme Court determined that the Huron band had the right to practise its ancient customs and rites in the park. It held that the treaty's intent was to enable the band to exercise its customs and rites over the entirety of the territory it had frequented, as long as their performance was not incompatible with the Crown's use of the territory.[36] In reaching its decision, the court paid particular attention to whether the document that the band relied on was, in fact, a treaty within the meaning of Section 88 of the Indian Act.[37] If the document was found to be a treaty, the court had to determine whether the rights it protected had been extinguished by specific documents and events – namely the Articles of Capitulation at Montreal of 8 September 1760,[38] the Treaty of Paris, 1763, and the Royal Proclamation of 1763 – the legislative and administrative history of the Hurons' land; the effect of the long passage of time; and the Huron band's non-use of the treaty. According to the precedent established in *Simon v The Queen*, the onus of proving that a treaty has been extinguished rests with the party alleging the extinguishment: 'Given the serious and far-reaching consequences of a finding that a treaty right has been extinguished, it seems appropriate to demand strict proof of the fact of extinguishment in each case where the issue arises.'[39]

Neither the documents nor the legislative and administrative history relied on by the Crown were found to have presented persuasive evidence that the treaty had been extinguished. Lamer J, as he then was, held that the Articles of Capitulation at Montreal, signed between Britain and France without the consent of the Huron band, could not act to extinguish the band's rights in the separate treaty it had signed with Britain. Because Indian treaties, as indicated in *Simon*[40] and *R v White and Bob*,[42] are solemn agreements between the Crown and Native peoples, the court held that only the band itself could consent to its extinguishment: 'The very definition of a treaty thus makes it impossible to avoid the conclusion that a treaty cannot be extinguished without the consent of the Indians concerned. Since the Hurons had the capacity to enter into a treaty with the British, therefore, they must be the only ones who could give the necessary consent to its extinguishment.'[42]

As Lamer J explained, to enable an agreement between Britain and France to extinguish the rights of the Hurons under a separate treaty

214 The Crown's Fiduciary Duty

'would be contrary to the general principles of law.'[43] He held that the very same reasoning applied to the effects of the Treaty of Paris, 1763, which was also signed between Britain and France without consulting the Hurons. Lamer J also dismissed the Crown's argument that the Royal Proclamation of 1763 extinguished the Hurons' rights under the 1760 treaty because it failed to confirm those rights.[44] Although he incorrectly held that the Proclamation granted certain rights to the aboriginal peoples,[45] Lamer J found that the rights conferred by the Proclamation did not extinguish any other right acknowledged or granted by the Crown under a treaty.[46] Lamer J also determined that the band's non-use of the treaty over a lengthy period of time did not affect its validity or effect.

The *Sioui* decision is particularly important to the issue of the single and indivisible Crown's obligation to consult the aboriginal peoples regarding its transfer of its fiduciary obligations. It suggests that the Crown has a duty to consult the Native peoples prior to engaging in activity which affects the latter's rights. More importantly, though, *Sioui* stands for the proposition that enactments entered into by the Crown without consulting the Native peoples do not extinguish its pre-existing obligations to them without an express indication to do so. This proposition is particularly relevant to a consideration of the effects of the British North America Act, 1867, on the Crown's obligations to the aboriginals, in particular the effect of Section 91(24) of the Act, which grants exclusive legislative authority to the federal Crown over 'Indians, and Lands reserved for the Indians.'

As a federal state, legislative powers and governmental responsibilities in Canada in 1867 were divided between the dominion and provincial governments, primarily by Sections 91 and 92 of the British North America Act, 1867.[47] Amid this division, the responsibility for 'Indians, and Lands reserved for the Indians,' was given to the dominion government under Section 91(24) of the Act. The intention behind Section 91(24) was to transfer responsibility over Indian affairs to the federal Crown. However, the process leading up to the promulgation of the British North America Act, 1867, did not include the aboriginal peoples, nor were they ever consulted about its effects upon their rights. Moreover, nowhere in the Act was there an explicit extinguishment of any pre-existing obligation owed to the aboriginal peoples.

In accordance with the precedent established in *Sioui*, the legislative creation of the dominion of Canada had the effect of giving the federal Crown the responsibility over Native affairs as an addition to the pre-existing fiduciary obligations of the single and indivisible Crown to Native peoples. Because the British North America Act, 1867, did not remove or extinguish these pre-existing obligations, they remained in force. Furthermore, the single and indivisible Crown's pre-existing fiduciary duty to Canada's aboriginal peoples became the jointly held obligation of the British and Canadian Crowns. This occurred as a result of the process of establishing the Dominion of Canada, which transferred the single and indivisible Crown's responsibilities for Canada to the British and Canadian Crowns. The long and the short of the Confederation process was to render the British Crown jointly and severally responsible for the pre-Confederation fiduciary duty of 'the Crown' to Native peoples.[48] In addition, the British Crown may also, prima facie, be held responsible for any post-Confederation fiduciary obligations to Native peoples until such time as it was completely freed of any residual sovereignty over Canada, as the process of transferring responsibility over Canadian affairs was not a *fait accompli* in 1867.

In a manner similar to the precedent established in *Sioui*, the Supreme Court of Canada in *Sparrow* held that the Crown has an obligation to consult with the aboriginal peoples regarding legislative initiatives that have passed the *Sparrow* justificatory test.[49] Although the court only discussed the Crown's obligation to consult the aboriginal peoples with regard to fishing conservation measures, that was because of the facts in issue before the court rather than any intention to limit the Crown's duty to consult.[50] The Crown's duty to consult with the aboriginal peoples is one result of its fiduciary duty to them. Another result is the reading of Section 91(24) of the British North America Act, 1867, in a manner which is consistent with and upholds the honour of the Crown. As the court stated in *Sparrow*, the right of the federal Crown to legislate in respect of 'Indians, and Lands reserved for the Indians' continues in spite of the Crown's fiduciary duty, but that duty requires a justification of any initiative or regulatory scheme that infringes upon or denies aboriginal rights. The requirement of justification was imposed to hold the Crown to a high standard of honourable dealing with respect to the aboriginal peoples of Canada.[51]

As a result of the principles enunciated in *Sioui* and *Sparrow*, Section 91(24) may not be used to deny the continued existence of the British Crown's obligations to the aboriginal peoples. Moreover, in conjunction with fiduciary doctrine's rule against conflict of interest, Section 91(24) cannot be invoked as an exculpatory clause which removes the British Crown's liability for any fiduciary obligations owed to Native peoples.[52]

Therefore, the English Court of Appeal's determination in the *Alberta Indian Association* case that all of the British Crown's obligations to the Native peoples of Canada have been transferred to the Canadian Crown, as well as its reaffirmation in *Noltcho*, is incorrect.

The British Crown's Fiduciary Obligations to Aboriginal Peoples

Not only does the British Crown still possess general and specific fiduciary duties to the aboriginal peoples of Canada, it is liable for breaching those duties in a number of instances. For example, the single and indivisible Crown's failure to provide full disclosure of its actions regarding its transfer of powers over Canadian affairs amounted to a breach of its fiduciary duty to the Native peoples for which the British and Canadian Crowns are liable. Liability also arises from the failure to consult with the Natives about the transfer of powers. As the Native peoples were not consulted of this change despite being directly affected by it, the continuation of the duties and obligations owed to them may not be affected by the consequences arising from any such change.

Had the Natives been consulted about the transfer of powers, the act of transfer would still not have affected the continuation of the fiduciary duties owed to them. Although the party or parties which owed the duties may have changed, the duties themselves still remained and needed to be fulfilled. The changes arising from the transfer of powers upon Confederation also does not affect the aboriginals' right to bring an action for any breach of that duty at any time that a breach is discovered.[53] A cause of action for breach of fiduciary duty exists independently of any considerations as to the quantification and availability of restitution. What may change in certain situations, including that in the present instance, is the range of remedies which may be granted to a wronged beneficiary.

These conclusions are entirely consistent with fiduciary doctrine's principle that fiduciaries may delegate the entirety of their fiduciary *powers*, but not their fiduciary *obligations*. The aboriginal peoples, therefore, remain entitled to rely on the proper discharging of the fiduciary duties owed to them without regard for which emanation of the Crown is now responsible for fulfilling them.[54] In general, fiduciary powers which are transferred by a fiduciary are subject to judicial review where a beneficiary alleges that such a transfer results in a breach of the fiduciary's duties. Yet, as a result of the decisions in the *Alberta Indian Association*, *Manuel*, and *Noltcho* cases, the ability of one or more of the parties

The British Crown's Obligations 217

in those cases to bring an action against the British Crown for breach of fiduciary duty brings into question the applicability of the common law doctrine of *res judicata*.

The doctrine of *res judicata* holds that a final judgment rendered by a court of competent jurisdiction on the merits is conclusive as to the rights of the parties involved and bars re-litigation of the same cause of action or issues in a subsequent action. By not addressing the issue of the British Crown's fiduciary duty to aboriginal peoples in Canada explicitly or implicitly,[55] the *Alberta Indian Association* decision may not act to prevent one or more of the applicants, or the aboriginal nations that they represent, from bringing an action in the English courts alleging the British Crown's breach of fiduciary duty on the basis of *res judicata*.[56] The *Noltcho* plaintiffs would be in a similar position, and for the same reasons, because the issue of the British Crown's fiduciary duty was not decided in that judgment. Of course other aboriginal peoples or groups may still pursue such a course of action against the British Crown if they so choose. There are limiting factors on the pursuit of such a route, though.

Guidelines for Remedying the British Crown's Breach of Its Fiduciary Obligations to Aboriginal Peoples

It has been established that the British Crown remains liable for any breaches of fiduciary duty to Native peoples committed while it retained a degree of residual sovereignty over Canada. However, the practical resolution of a breach of fiduciary duty claim by an aboriginal nation against the British Crown is seriously affected by the former's inability to receive certain remedies from the British Crown which it may obtain from the Canadian Crown. This is due to the complexity of the factual changes in the political structure of the British Empire and the relationship between the British Crown and Canada which occurred as a result of the transfer of powers over Canadian affairs beginning in 1867.

An aboriginal nation's decision of whether to bring a claim of breach of fiduciary duty against the British Crown, on either an individual or jointly held basis with the Canadian Crown, may be significantly influenced by the more limited remedies available against the British Crown. There would be significant jurisdictional obstacles in any attempt to have the British Crown fulfil its duties by encroaching on the exclusive powers over 'Indians, and Lands reserved for the Indians,' reserved to the federal Crown under Section 91(24) of the British North America

Act, 1867. For example, the British Crown could not, at the present, discharge an outstanding obligation under a treaty to set aside a reserve for the use and benefit of an aboriginal Nation because of its lack of sovereignty over the Canadian state.

The issue of Canadian sovereignty would also be questioned by the existence of any remaining obligations owed by the British Crown to Native peoples. The British North America Act of 1867 divided and redistributed powers to the federal and provincial Crowns, although they were subject to the ultimate authority of the Imperial Parliament and the residual prerogative powers of the 'single and indivisible' Crown, and granted virtually complete jurisdiction over Canada to the federal and provincial Crowns.[57] With the promulgation of the Constitution Act, 1982, at the very latest, any residual sovereignty over Canada remaining with the British Crown was extinguished. The factual devolution of powers, therefore, presents significant, if not insurmountable, barriers to the British Crown's fulfilment of the fiduciary obligations owed to aboriginal peoples in matters which cannot be remedied by monetary compensation.

The devolution of powers does not render the continued existence of fiduciary obligations on the part of the British Crown meaningless and incapable of enforcement. The British Crown's obligations towards the aboriginal peoples of Canada, in terms of their enforceability, may be compared to any pre-conquest obligations owed to the Native peoples by the French Crown. The French Crown engaged in the same practices of entering into treaties and various alliances with aboriginal nations as the British themselves had up until the time of conquest. Consequently, the French would have owned similar duties to the Native peoples. Although France's sovereignty over Canada formally ended upon the signing of the Treaty of Paris, 1763, that does not mean that France's obligations to the aboriginal peoples ended in 1763.

As has already been stated, a breach of fiduciary duty is both actionable and remediable once it has occurred and remains subject to the commencement of an action and the awarding of restitution. The passage of time does not forgive a breach of duty, although, in certain circumstances, it may prevent the bringing of an action for breach caused by a lapse of statutory limitations or laches.[58] It may very well affect the availability and quantification of a remedy, though. Like Britain, France would be prevented from setting aside a reserve in Canada in fulfilment of a treaty obligation. However, like Britain, it could conceivably have an award made against it which required monetary compensation to be made to an aboriginal Nation for its breach of duty. What the fact of Britain's and France's present lack of sovereignty over Canada entails is that any restitutionary award made against them for any breach of fiduciary duty is limited to matters which do not involve the exercise of sovereignty over federal or provincial jurisdictions in Canada.

In addition to the more limited range of remedies available against the British Crown, there is the difficulty caused by having to bring a separate action in the English courts in order to seek a remedy for its breach of duty. There also exists the challenge of having to overcome the precedents established in the *Alberta Indian Association*, *Manuel*, and *Noltcho* cases. Although it has been suggested herein that these cases should have no effect on any inquiry into the fiduciary duty of the British Crown, those decisions are consistent with the conventional wisdom that insists that once Britain divested itself of its colonial powers, it also removed its personal liability for matters which pertain only to Canada, including the fiduciary duty to Native peoples.

In practical terms, the British Crown's breach of duty for failing to consult the aboriginal peoples of Canada about the impending transfer of powers over Canada in 1867 was a significant, and actionable, breach of duty. As a result of the situs of the Canadian Crown *vis-à-vis* the British Crown, the primary day-to-day responsibility over Indian affairs would have logically flowed to the former. Owing to the Canadian Crown's inferior resources, this alteration marked a significant change in the ability to carry out the fiduciary obligations owed to the aboriginal peoples. For instance, the Canadian Crown's more limited resources may have meant an inability to conclude land surrender treaties on more favourable terms to the Indians. Regardless, any change in the person or entity owing fiduciary obligations to a beneficiary is a significant alteration in the relationship between fiduciary and beneficiary.

To have prevented any breach of the Crown's duty, the aboriginal peoples should have been consulted prior to the transfer of powers. They should have been provided with the opportunity to be represented at an Imperial conference to discuss their opinions and concerns on the change in understanding of the Crown and the effects that such a change would have on them. This could have been accomplished in a manner similar to the aboriginal peoples' representation and participation in the recent discussions and negotiations between the federal and provincial governments to amend the constitution which led up to the failed Charlottetown Accord. Moreover, it could have been done with little cost or inconvenience to the Crown.

220 The Crown's Fiduciary Duty

At this late date, the only logical remedy for the British Crown's breach of duty would be to award monetary damages against it. It is simply not practicable, or necessarily desirable, to rescind the transfer of powers over Canada. Indeed, such a remedy may not have been practicable in 1867 either, but it would have been seen as more viable at that time, or shortly thereafter, rather than at a point in time more than one hundred years after the fact. If the aboriginal peoples could demonstrate or quantify any losses suffered as a direct result of the transfer of powers in 1867, they would also be entitled to monetary compensation for the amount of those losses, plus interest, either ordinary or compounded, from the date of the wrongdoing. The British Crown could also be made to account for any profits it made as a result of the transfer of powers, plus interest. Moreover, it could be made subject to an order to pay punitive damages as a result of its actions.

Although the British Crown is still potentially liable for any fiduciary duties which it incurred until the removal of its residual sovereignty over Canada, the primary point of de facto responsibility for the fiduciary duty owed to the aboriginal peoples rests with the Canadian Crown. Since the *Guerin* case, Canadian courts have recognized the Canadian Crown's fiduciary duty to the aboriginal peoples. What has yet to be authoritatively determined, however, is whether that duty belongs solely to the Crown in right of Canada, the Crown in right of a province, or to both.

12

The Canadian Crown's Obligations

In the aftermath of the *Guerin* decision, the existence of the Crown's fiduciary duty to the aboriginal peoples is no longer in question. In the majority of post-*Guerin* decisions, judicial attention to fulfilment of the fiduciary duties owed to aboriginal peoples has been directed to the Crown. However, these decisions have not addressed the issue of which emanations of the Canadian Crown – the Crown in right of Canada, the Crown in right of a province, or both – possess fiduciary obligations to the aboriginal peoples. The recognition of provincial fiduciary responsibilities towards the aboriginal peoples is not yet as clear. Whereas the courts have yet to make an explicit determination of the existence of provincial fiduciary obligations, they have provided a variety of hints leading to such a conclusion.

Although the judicial recognition and sanction of the Canadian Crown's fiduciary obligations to aboriginal peoples are a relatively recent occurrence, great insight into ascertaining which emanations of the Crown are responsible for fulfilling those obligations may be derived from some landmark decisions of the late nineteenth and early twentieth centuries, including *St Catherine's Milling and Lumber Co v The Queen*,[1] *Province of Ontario v Dominion of Canada and Province of Quebec: In re Indian Claims* (the *Robinson Treaties Annuities* case),[2] *Ontario Mining Company Ltd v Seybold*,[3] and *Dominion of Canada v Province of Ontario* (the *Treaty No. 3 Annuities* case).[4] In these cases, the courts were faced with determining which levels of government were responsible for discharging treaty obligations owed to Native peoples.

It is important, when considering the judicial determinations made in each of these cases, to be aware of the context within which they were decided, as well as the underlying assumptions of the nature of the

Crown–Native relationship on which they were predicated. When the decisions were made, the Crown–Native relationship was considered akin to that of guardian and ward, albeit without any resultant legal obligations attaching to the Crown. Moreover, the aboriginal peoples were not represented in any of them. Indeed, these cases are determinative only of the rights and obligations of the federal and provincial Crowns, *vis-à-vis* each other, in discharging the obligations owed to aboriginal peoples under the terms of Indian treaties. They do not define the reciprocal rights and obligations of either the federal or provincial Crowns in relation to the aboriginal peoples.

By virtue of its exclusive jurisdiction over 'Indians, and Lands reserved for the Indians,' under Section 91(24) of the British North America Act, 1867,[5] the federal Crown was empowered to enter into treaty negotiations with aboriginal nations across Canada. These negotiations resulted in the formation of numerous treaties, which entailed various obligations to the Native peoples. As a result of the Crown–Native relationship within which they originated, the obligations owed under these post-Confederation treaties – along with the Crown's preexisting obligations stemming from pre-Confederation treaties, and other events and occurrences, as detailed in Chapters 2, 3, and 4 – are all part of the modern Crown fiduciary obligation.

Both pre- and post-Confederation treaties are independent roots of the Crown's modern fiduciary obligations. Because of the factual changes in the Crown's identity and the devolution of legislative and executive responsibilities for Canada to the newly created federal and provincial Crowns in 1867, distinctions must be made between Crown fiduciary duties predating Confederation and those arising after Confederation. In circumstances in which an aboriginal nation is a signatory to a treaty with the Crown, whether the treaty is a pre- or post-Confederation treaty, the Crown owes that nation both general fiduciary duties, which predate Confederation, and more specific fiduciary obligations, which arise from the particular circumstances of the treaty.

The distinction between pre- and post-Confederation fiduciary duties may differentially affect the satisfaction of those duties by the Crown. For example, whether an obligation may be characterized as pre- or post-Confederation is relevant in determining the British Crown's liability. The British Crown would, prima facie, be liable for all *pre*-Confederation duties to Native peoples. It may not be liable for all *post*-Confederation fiduciary obligations, or, because of the gradual devolution of powers to the Canadian Crown and the resultant lessening of its residual sovereignty over Canadian affairs, it may only be liable in part. The liability of the Canadian Crown is also affected by the pre- or post-Confederation nature of a fiduciary obligation. The reason for this is the effects of the British North America Act, 1867, and the assumption of pre-Confederation liabilities under it by the Dominion of Canada by way of Sections 111, 112, 114, and 115.[6]

Whereas the Crown's treaty obligations to the aboriginal peoples were well known in the nineteenth century – even if their fiduciary nature was not – the emanations of the Crown responsible for meeting them were relatively unknown. Over time, as the role of the British Crown diminished in response to the establishment of a stronger governmental presence in Canada,[7] it remained to be determined which personifications of the Crown in Canada were responsible for fulfilling these outstanding obligations. The judicial process of answering this question was initiated in the landmark case of *St Catherine's Milling*.

St Catherine's Milling

The precedent established in *St Catherine's Milling* has had far-reaching consequences that remain to this day. The decision drastically and forever altered the effect of Indian land surrender treaties between the Crown and aboriginal peoples in Canada. Noteworthy for its characterization of the aboriginal interest in land as a 'personal and usufructuary right, dependent upon the good will of the Sovereign,'[8] the decision was also the first major pronouncement on the effect of the constitutional division of federal and provincial powers upon the surrender of lands obtained through Indian treaties.

The *St Catherine's Milling* decision created a lingering and problematic legacy by juxtaposing the federal Crown's acquisition of aboriginal lands and 'extinguishment' of aboriginal title by way of treaty against the provincial Crown's acquisition of a beneficial interest in the land once it had been disencumbered of the aboriginal interest. This element of the case is particularly relevant to the examination of which emanation(s) of the Canadian Crown may be found responsible for discharging the fiduciary obligations owed to aboriginal peoples.

The *St Catherine's Milling* decision centred around a dispute between the province of Ontario and the Dominion of Canada over the ownership of former Indian lands. The lands had been surrendered under Treaty No. 3, a post-Confederation treaty signed in 1873 by the Saulteaux Indians. The St Catherine's Milling and Lumber Company had obtained a licence from the dominion Crown to cut timber on some of the lands that had been surrendered. The Ontario Crown sought to restrain the lumber company from cutting timber on those lands by claiming it owned a beneficial interest in the land based on Section 109 of the British North America Act, 1867.[9] The main issue at bar was which body of the Crown possessed the beneficial interest in the surrendered lands – the federal Crown through the operation of Section 91(24) of the British North America Act, 1867, or the Ontario Crown, by way of Section 109 of the Act.

Considering these sections, the Privy Council found that the federal Crown's Section 91(24) power to enter into treaties and obtain surrenders of Indian lands did not give it any interest in the land once its aboriginal title was extinguished. This conclusion was based on their construction of Section 109 and their understanding of that section's effects in the earlier case of *Attorney-General of Ontario v Mercer*.[10]

In *Mercer* the Privy Council had determined that the legal effect of Section 109 was to exclude all ordinary territorial revenues of the Crown arising within the provinces from the duties and revenues appropriated to the dominion. Section 109 effectively vested the Crown's underlying title to the unsurrendered Indian lands, which were still subject to aboriginal title, in the province in which the lands were located. Once those lands were relieved of any aboriginal interest, the full beneficial interest in those lands became vested in the province.[11]

The Privy Council's finding in *St Catherine's Milling* that 'the Crown has all along had a present proprietary estate in the land, upon which the Indian title was a mere burden'[12] created a difficult situation. It separated the power to enter into treaties and the power to fulfil the terms of those treaties once they had been concluded. The lasting impact of the decision rests exclusive power to obtain a surrender of aboriginal lands and to create reserves[13] in the federal Crown, whereas, after a surrender is obtained, exclusive proprietary and administrative rights over the surrendered lands vest in the Crown in right of the province in which the lands are situated.[14]

The practical result of this division of powers is that although only the federal Crown may create a reserve, it cannot use provincial Crown lands (such as those obtained from First Nations by surrender under a treaty) for that purpose without the cooperation of the province. Consequently, when a treaty provides for the creation of a reserve from lands surrendered under the treaty, the reserve may only be established through the joint effort of the federal and relevant provincial Crowns.

In addition to the implications flowing from the Privy Council's decision, judicial recognition of provincial obligations, with respect to lands surrendered by treaty, may be seen at each stage of *St Catherine's Milling*. At trial, Chancellor Boyd implied that Ontario was bound by the dominion Crown's obligations under Treaty No. 3 because it had received the benefit of the surrendered lands. As he explained in his judgment, 'It would seem unreasonable that the Dominion Government should be burdened with large annual payments to the tribes without having a sufficiency of land to answer, presently or prospectively, the expenditure.'[15] Chancellor Boyd refused to rule on the extent of Ontario's responsibilities to the treaty signatories as it was not made an issue at trial.[16] His statement nevertheless indicates that Ontario, as beneficiary of the surrender of land under the treaty, must also be held responsible for discharging the Crown's obligations under the treaty.

On appeal, Hagarty CJO argued that it would be natural to suppose that the federal and provincial Crowns would have arranged for an equitable distribution of the Treaty No. 3 obligations had the boundaries of Ontario and Manitoba been defined at the time the treaty was signed.[17] He also suggested that the federal and Ontario Crowns should share the financial responsibility to the Indians under the terms of the treaty.[18] Patterson JA, meanwhile, refused to comment on the distribution of treaty responsibilities between the Dominion and Ontario for the same reasons specified by Chancellor Boyd at trial: 'We see that certain outlay was incurred and certain burdens assumed by the Government ... Whether they give rise to any claims or equities between the Dominion and the Province is a matter of policy as to which we have no information, and with which we are not concerned beyond the one question of the effect on the right to the timber.'[19]

The majority of judges of the Supreme Court of Canada did not discuss the issue of who was to bear the responsibilities under the treaty. The dissenting judgment of Strong J, as he then was, however, furthered the earlier reasoning of Chancellor Boyd and Hagarty CJO in explicitly holding that the dominion and Ontario governments were jointly and severally responsible for carrying out the terms of the treaty: '[A]ll the obligations of the crown towards the Indians incidental to their unsurrendered lands, and the right to acquire such lands, and to make compensation therefor by providing subsidies and annuities for the Indians, attach to and may be performed by the Provinces as well as by the Dominion.'[20]

Gwynne J, who also dissented from the majority decision, held that both the beneficial interest in the surrendered lands, and the responsibility for fulfilling the Treaty No. 3 obligations belonged to the federal Crown. The basis for his finding was that the body that obtained the benefits of the surrender was liable for discharging the treaty obligations that had given rise to those benefits.[21] The rationale behind Gwynne J's conclusion, therefore, although leading him to a different result, is nevertheless consistent with those underlying the judgments of Strong J, Hagarty CJO, and Chancellor Boyd.

In delivering the judgment in *St Catherine's Milling* on behalf of the Privy Council, Lord Watson was explicit about Ontario's responsibilities to the treaty signatories. He held that the province was entirely responsible for discharging the annuity obligations incurred under the terms of the treaty: 'Seeing that the benefit of the surrender accrues to her, Ontario must, of course, relieve the Crown, and the Dominion, of all obligations involving the payment of money which were undertaken by Her Majesty, and which are said to have been in part fulfilled by the Dominion Government.'[22]

The results of the considerations of provincial responsibilities at the various stages of *St Catherine's Milling* may consequently be seen to suggest the existence of concurrent federal and provincial fiduciary obligations to aboriginal peoples, at least within the context of Treaty No. 3.

Robinson Treaties Annuities, Seybold, and Treaty No. 3 Annuities

A trilogy of cases, *Robinson Treaties Annuities*,[23] *Seybold*,[24] and *Treaty No. 3 Annuities*,[25] continued the discussion of joint federal–provincial responsibilities for the Crown's treaty obligations to Native peoples that had been started in *St Catherine's Milling*. They each referred to Lord Watson's finding of provincial fiduciary duties in *St Catherine's Milling*. Ultimately, however, they each dismissed any *legal* basis that would oblige provinces to assume or offset the responsibilities incurred by the federal Crown in its negotiations of Indian treaties.

The judgments in these cases reveal that, in arriving at their respective conclusions, the judges either failed to recognize the equitable basis of the provincial duty, as illustrated by Lord Watson in *St Catherine's Milling*, or mischaracterized that basis. Upon closer examination, all three cases may be seen to be consistent with the indications of provincial fiduciary obligations made in the *St Catherine's Milling* decision.

Robinson Treaties Annuities

In the *Robinson Treaties Annuities* case,[26] the Supreme Court of Canada heard an appeal from an arbitration award of 13 February 1895. The arbitration[27] had been authorized to settle the long-standing issue of who was responsible for paying the increase in annuity payments under the terms of the Robinson–Huron and Robinson–Superior Treaties of 1850; the Dominion of Canada, as the successor of the old province of Canada,[28] which had negotiated the treaties, the provinces of Ontario and Quebec which, after Confederation, had reaped the benefits of the lands surrendered under the treaties, or all three.

Both treaties included provisions that guaranteed the aboriginal signatories a particular sum for a perpetual annuity. An identical clause in each treaty provided for the payment of increased annuities if the revenues from the surrendered lands rose sufficiently to allow for the payment of increased annuities to the signatories without resulting in a loss: 'The said William Benjamin Robinson on behalf of Her Majesty, who desires to deal liberally and justly with all her subjects, further promises and agrees that should all the territory hereby ceded by the parties of the second part, at any future period produce such an amount as will enable the Government of this province, without incurring loss, to increase the annuity hereby secured to them, then, and in that case, the same shall be augmented from time to time, provided that the amount paid to each individual shall not exceed the sum of one pound provincial currency in any one year, or such further sum as Her Majesty may be most graciously pleased to order.'[29]

The arbitrators held that Ontario alone was responsible for paying the increase in the annuities because the lands surrendered under the treaties accrued to it.[30] Quebec was absolved of liability because the treaty lands were located within Ontario's boundaries. Ontario appealed the arbitrators' award to the Supreme Court of Canada. Ontario maintained that as the former province of Canada had negotiated the treaties, the federal Crown was solely responsible for discharging any additional debts arising from them. Moreover, it claimed that the obligation for the annuity payments, both the original and any increased amounts, were subsumed under Section 111 of the British North America Act, 1867.[31]

The Supreme Court of Canada, with Gwynne and King JJ dissenting, overturned the arbitrators' award. The majority judgment held that Ontario was liable only for its portion of any increase in the obligations owed under the treaty by the former province of Canada, as it had existed prior to Confederation. Ontario's share of the increase in the annuities was determined to be in proportion to the amount of the surrendered lands situated within its post-Confederation boundaries. The court's decision did not, however, entail provincial responsibility in the manner described in the arbitrators' report.

Instead, the duty imposed on Ontario and Quebec was premised entirely on the fact that the cap placed on the Dominion of Canada's assumption of the pre-Confederation debt of the province of Canada existing at Confederation, under Section 111 of the British North America Act, 1867, had already been surpassed. Under Section 112 of the Act, the dominion's assumption of these pre-Confederation debts was given a limit.[32] Once the outer margin had been reached, the dominion was still obligated to pay the entire debt, but was to be indemnified by Ontario and Quebec for any amount exceeding that point.[33] Contrary to the arbitrators' determination, therefore, the Supreme Court's ruling against the provinces was not based on the provinces' role as successor to the liability belonging to the province of Canada. Strong CJC determined that any increase in the annuity obligations to the Indians, which initially belonged to the province of Canada, was not transferred in whole or in part to Ontario and Quebec upon Confederation, notwithstanding Section 109. Rather, he held that the annuities, both the original and any increased amount, were part of the general debts and liabilities of the former province of Canada and, therefore, became the responsibility of the dominion upon Confederation under Section 111: 'That it was a "liability" though consisting of deferred periodical payments cannot be doubted, and that it was a "debt" though not payable *in presenti* is also clear; it therefore comes within the literal meaning of the 111th section, and we are not at liberty to unravel the arrangements between the two divisions of the old province, upon which it may be assumed the provisions of the Union Act as to the apportionment of assets and liabilities was based in order to arrive at some secondary meaning contrary to the ordinary and natural import of the language of the Act.'[34] Strong CJC based his conclusion largely on the arbitrators' pronouncement. At paragraph XIII of their report, they had determined: 'That all lands in either of the said provinces of Ontario and Quebec respectively, surrendered by the Indians in consideration of annuities to them granted, which said annuities are included in the debt of the late province of Canada, shall be the absolute property of the province in which the said lands are respectively situate, free from any further claim upon, or charge to the said province in which they are so situate by the other of the said provinces.'[35]

Strong CJC relied on the above passage to hold that the increased annuities were a part of the province of Canada's debt existing at Confederation. He also used it to refute the argument that the annuity payments constituted a charge on the lands and were thereby an 'Interest other than that of the Province' under Section 109. It should be noted, though, that the arbitrators' report did not mention the increased annuities under the Robinson treaties being included within the debt of the province of Canada.

Strong CJC contended that it was of no consequence to his findings that, at the time the arbitrators' award was made, the question of who was responsible for paying the increased annuities had yet to be posed.[36] He then attempted to fabricate a concordance between his judgment and the arbitrators' report by stating that, as the arbitrators' award had not been challenged for twenty-five years and may have formed the crux of other dispositions, 'the arbitrators must therefore be taken to have had in mind all the annuities, the original fixed annuities as well as those contingently provided for.'[37] In point of fact, there is no support for this conclusion in the arbitrators' report.[38]

Interestingly enough, in determining that the original annuity payments were part of the general debts and liabilities of the former province of Canada – and, therefore, the responsibility of the dominion Crown by way of Section 111 – and that the increase in the annuity payments was owed by each of the provinces of Ontario and Quebec in proportions that reflected their respective positions within the former boundaries of the province of Canada, Strong CJC's conclusions precisely follow the logic employed by Lord Watson in *St Catherine's Milling*. Save for Section 111's mandated transfer of provincial debts existing at Confederation to the dominion, the provinces of Ontario and Quebec, as successors to the old province of Canada, would have been responsible for paying the original annuity money.

Strong CJC deviated from this rationale in his discussion of the increased annuities. He held that the increase in the annuities was also part of the general debts and liabilities of the former province of Canada existing at Confederation; therefore, it, too, was subsumed under Section 111. A closer examination of the premise upon which the increased annuities were to be awarded demonstrates that Strong CJC's finding is inconsistent with the proper construction of the British North America Act, 1867, and the Robinson treaties.

The Robinson treaties clearly show an intention to provide for two separate annuities. The first annuity – the original amount – was payable on the signing of the treaty by the aboriginal signatories, in a guaranteed sum. The second annuity – the increase – was potentially payable, depending on the revenues generated from the surrendered lands. The first annuity was guaranteed and ascertainable, thereby enabling it to be properly included under Section 111. The second annuity, meanwhile, was entirely contingent upon future events, which may never have come to fruition, and it therefore may never have existed. This uncertainty of the second annuity rendered its classification by Strong CJC under Section 111 as a debt or liability existing at Confederation completely inappropriate.

Strong CJC's inclusion of the second annuity under Section 111 imparted to it a far wider scope than that envisaged by a literal interpretation of either the Robinson treaties or Section 111. The very nature of the basis of the increased annuity made it impossible to determine, other than from year to year, whether it was due and owing. Based on the plain construction of Section 111 of the British North America Act, 1867, moreover, it is difficult to sustain an argument that a future, contingent, and unascertainable liability may be characterized as 'existing at the Union' and, consequently, be transferred to the dominion. At best, Strong CJC's argument that the increased annuities fell under Section 111 may only sustain the proposition that an increased annuity was due and owing to the aboriginal signatories in 1867 for that *particular* year, which ought to be included under the rubric of Section 111.

The other judgments in the case did not adhere to the same foundations as Strong CJC's judgment. Sedgewick J's judgment affirmed Strong CJC's conclusions. An important aspect of Sedgewick J's decision, however, which was not reflected in that of Strong CJC, was his recognition of the equities of the matter before the court: '[T]here is the principle expressed in the maxim *qui sentit commodum sentire debit et onus*. If a person accept anything which he knows to be subject to a duty or charge it is rational to conclude that he means to take such duty or charge upon himself, and the law may very well imply a promise to perform what he has taken upon himself.'[39] Sedgewick J acknowledged that the provinces, by acquiring the benefits of the surrendered Indian lands obtained through the treaties upon Confederation *while in full knowledge of the dominion's outstanding obligations under those treaties*, which it had assumed from the province of Canada, must, in principle, assume responsibility for the payment of the annuities. The provinces were only

The Canadian Crown's Obligations 231

absolved of their liability for the original annuity payments because of the operation of Section 111.

Gwynne J, dissenting, placed the responsibility for making the increased annuity payments squarely on Ontario. He viewed the annuities as a charge upon the lands, which flowed to the province through the operation of Section 109. In this regard, he disagreed with the findings in paragraph XIII of the 1870 arbitration, but sided with its ultimate recommendations:

> And as by the 109th section of the British North America Act the province has become entitled to that fund [from which treaty obligations had been paid prior to 1867], Her Majesty's government of that province must take the same subject to the trust obligation in the interest of the Indians assumed by Her Majesty by the stipulations of the treaties. Her Majesty's government of the province of Ontario must in all reason and justice take the property mentioned in the section subject to the same obligation as to the payment of augmentation of the annuities ... as the late province of Canada would have held them if no union had taken place. This was the unanimous judgment of the arbitrators upon this point. That judgment is not at variance with any principle of law, or any statutory provision; on the contrary it is in perfect accordance with the plainest principles of justice and is not open to any sound legal objection.[40]

King J concurred in Gwynne J's dissent. He insisted that 'Ontario, getting the lands subject to the trust, would have to discharge the burden which before that was upon the province of Canada, now represented by the provinces of Ontario and Quebec.'[41] The trust he referred to was Section 109 of the British North America Act, 1867; the burden was the responsibility of paying the original and increased annuity money, as provided for in the Robinson treaties.

King J also refuted Strong CJC's position regarding the effect of paragraph XIII of the 1870 arbitrators' report and the increased annuity payments under the Robinson treaties: '[T]he matter of the augmentation of annuities was not raised before the arbitrators, and if the views herein stated upon the main point are correct, it is apparent that the two things do not rest entirely upon the same foundations. The finding of the arbitrators that the claim as to the fixed annuities that was brought before them did not constitute a charge upon the lands, is therefore not conclusive as to the matters in question here. Par. 13 is to be read in the light of the contention before the arbitrators, and not as an abstract and general denial of all charges, etc., respecting the annuities, but simply as a denial of the lands being subject to the alleged charge to which it was then claimed to be subject.'[42] It is interesting to note that, on appeal, the Privy Council made no reference to the 1870 arbitrators' report.[43]

Despite the majority's protestations to the contrary, its conclusion in the *Robinson Treaties Annuities* case may be seen to accord with Lord Watson's determination of provincial responsibilities for discharging treaty obligations in *St Catherine's Milling*. The majority's decision differs from Lord Watson's reasoning only in that Section 111 of the British North America Act, 1867, applied in the *Robinson Treaties Annuities* case, but it did not apply in *St Catherine's Milling*, as that case was concerned with a post-Confederation treaty.

In his judgment, Strong CJC attempted to distinguish Lord Watson's dictum in *St Catherine's Milling* by illustrating the differences between its facts and those in the *Robinson Treaties* case: '[I]n the case of *The St Catharines Milling Co v The Queen* ... the Privy Council held that this surrender enured to the benefit of the province of Ontario, and so holding it also decided that Ontario was bound to pay the consideration for which the Indians ceded their rights in the lands. I see no analogy between that case and the present. In the case before us no one doubts that the province of Canada, which acquired the lands, was originally bound to pay the consideration. In the case before the Privy Council the question was, as it were, between two departments of the government of the Crown, and the most obvious principles of justice required that the government which got the lands should pay for them.'[44] Ironically, and in direct opposition to its intended purpose, this passage clearly demonstrates that Strong CJC affirmed Lord Watson's findings in *St Catherine's Milling* within the context in which they arose. His attempt to distinguish on the facts, therefore, Lord Watson's findings in *St Catherine's Milling* from the matter before him in *Robinson Treaties Annuities* was a pointless endeavour. For all intents and purposes, the underlying rationale behind the two cases is the same. Furthermore, both cases would have had similar end results save for the application of Section 111 to *Robinson Treaties Annuities*.

On the dominion Crown's appeal of the matter to the Privy Council, Lord Watson, not surprisingly, affirmed the Supreme Court's majority decision.[45] In accordance with his earlier determination in *St Catherine's Milling*, he held that the province of Canada, and its successors after 1867, were liable for discharging the annuity obligations under the Robinson treaties. Because of the operation of Section 111 of the British North America Act, 1867, however, that responsibility was transferred to

The Canadian Crown's Obligations 233

the federal Crown. Again, the only difference between his decision in the *Robinson Treaties Annuities* case and his earlier findings in *St Catherine's Milling* is that in the former, the operation of Section 111 removed the province's liability, whereas in the latter, section 111 did not apply, so Ontario retained its liability under Treaty No. 3.

Seybold

The issue of provincial responsibility for treaty obligations arose again in *Seybold*.[46] One of the issues in *Seybold* concerned the setting aside and establishment of Indian reserves under the provisions of Treaty No. 3, the same treaty dealt with in *St Catherine's Milling*.[47] Out of the lands surrendered under the treaty for the benefit of the treaty signatories, the federal Crown had set aside reserve lands in 1879. It later sold the reserve lands, without the consent of the province, after obtaining their surrender from the Indians. The vital question in *Seybold*, for present purposes, was whether the obligation to set aside reserves under the treaty rightfully belonged to the federal Crown, the Ontario Crown, or both.

At trial,[48] Chancellor Boyd recognized the difficulty created by the *St Catherine's Milling* decision regrading the establishment of Indian reserves under treaty. He nevertheless determined that Section 91(24) jurisdiction over 'Indians, and Lands reserved for the Indians' gave the federal Crown the right to set aside, and exercise legislative and administrative jurisdiction over, the reserve lands. His ruling directly conflicted with the *St Catherine's Milling* decision, which had clearly separated the two functions. However, at the conclusion of his judgment – and perhaps in recognition of his contradiction of the *St Catherine's Milling* precedent – Chancellor Boyd concluded that it would be preferable to have the treaty reserves allocated 'with the approval and co-operation of the Crown in its dual character as represented by the general and the provincial authorities.'[49]

On appeal to the Divisional Court,[50] Street J also recognized the problems in harmonizing the federal Crown's obligation to establish Indian reserves under the terms of the treaty and the precedent established in *St Catherine's Milling*. To reconcile these incongruous positions, Street J determined that because only Ontario could set aside the surrendered lands for use as a reserve, it was obliged to do so: 'The surrender was undoubtedly burdened with the obligation imposed by the Treaty to select and lay aside special portions of the tract covered by it for the special use and benefit of the Indians. The Provincial Government could not without plain disregard of justice take advantage of the surrender and refuse to perform the condition attached to it.'[51]

A majority decision of the Supreme Court of Canada dismissed the federal Crown's appeal without written reasons.[52] However, Gwynne J, dissenting, insisted that any obligations arising from the treaty must be assumed by Ontario, because it obtained the benefits from the surrender: '[F]or the benefit so obtained by the province by the treaty of surrender the province alone should in justice bear the burthen of the obligations assumed by Her Majesty and the Dominion to obtain the surrender of those lands as was held in the *St Catharines Milling & Lumber v The Queen.*'[53] The federal Crown appealed the Supreme Court's decision to the Privy Council.[54]

The Privy Council determined that the federal Crown's actions in setting aside, and later selling, the reserves were *ultra vires*. In delivering the Privy Council's judgment, Lord Davey stated that Ontario had a duty to fulfil the terms of the treaty. That duty, however, did not exist in a strictly legal sense; rather, it only constituted a moral obligation to cooperate with the federal Crown in setting aside reserves under the treaty: '[T]he Government of the province, taking advantage of the surrender of 1873, came at least under an *honourable engagement* to fulfil the terms on the faith of which the surrender was made, and, therefore, to concur with the Dominion Government in appropriating certain undefined portions of the surrendered lands as Indian reserves. The result, however, is that the choice and location of the lands to be so appropriated could only be effectively made by the joint action of the two Governments'[55] (emphasis added).

Lord Davey's characterization of Ontario's obligations under the treaty is misleading. As a result of the difficulties created by the constitutional division of powers in the British North America Act, 1867, the only way to have ensured that the reserve would be set aside was to have held Ontario and the federal Crown jointly responsible for establishing it. This necessitated that Ontario's duty be declared to be legally binding and not merely an 'honourable engagement.' Otherwise, a guarantee of satisfaction of the treaty promises did not exist, nor did the ability of the aboriginal signatories to legally enforce the treaty obligations owed to them.

It may be argued that negotiations between Canada and Ontario could resolve this dilemma. Indeed, negotiations between Canada and the provinces have resolved problems surrounding the establishment of

The Canadian Crown's Obligations 235

Indian reserves under treaty.[56] If Ontario's responsibility under the treaty in the *Seybold* scenario was not legally binding, however, it was not compelled to reach a settlement with Canada. Indeed, it was not obligated to engage in negotiations with Canada on the issue at all.

Lord Davey's characterization of the nature of Ontario's duty had the potential to create further problems if Ontario made unreasonable demands on Canada for its cooperation in setting aside reserve lands, or simply refused to negotiate altogether. As Ontario was only under an 'honourable engagement' to cooperate with Canada, it was insulated from legal liability for the non-fulfilment of the treaty. Similarly, although legally bound to fulfil the terms of the treaty, Canada could rely on the constitutional division of powers to protect itself from liability for not discharging the treaty promises.

As a result, even if the aboriginal signatories to the treaty successfully concluded a legal action that affirmed their right to receive reserves under the treaty, the judiciary would have been unable to enforce that right. A court could neither compel Canada to unilaterally fulfil the treaty, as Canada does not possess the jurisdiction, on its own, to set aside reserves out of surrendered lands – nor compel Ontario to cooperate with Canada in the setting aside of the reserves, because Ontario was not legally bound by any such obligation.

An analogy may be drawn between this scenario and the proper method of interpreting a statute that explicitly binds *either* the federal *or* a provincial Crown, yet as a result of the constitutional division of powers, implicitly binds *both* Crowns in order to effect its intentions. When such a statute would be frustrated or rendered absurd unless it is read to bind both Crowns, the Supreme Court of Canada has held that the statute must be read to bind both by necessity or logical implication.[57] This concept is also consistent with the principles of interpreting treaties and statutes relating to Indians enunciated by the Supreme Court of Canada in *Nowegijick v The Queen*.[58] In that case, it was held that courts ought to prefer aboriginal understandings of treaties and statues over competing notions if there is a discrepancy regarding the proper construction to be given to a particular phrase or concept.[59]

Treaty No. 3 Annuities

The last case in the trilogy, the *Treaty No. 3 Annuities* case,[60] is noteworthy for the Privy Council's attempt to wrap up the discussion of provincial responsibilities to Native peoples. The issue to be determined was whether the federal or Ontario Crown, or both, were responsible for the payment of annuity moneys to the aboriginal signatories to Treaty No. 3. In accordance with Lord Watson's determination in *St Catherine's Milling*, the federal Crown contended that Ontario was obliged to pay the annuities, because it had obtained the beneficial interest in the lands surrendered under the treaty. Ontario insisted that the federal Crown was solely responsible of the annuity payments, because it had negotiated the treaty.

Burbidge J ruled in favour of the federal Crown at trial. He agreed with Lord Watson's determination in *St Catherine's Milling* that provinces that reaped the benefits of a treaty were responsible for the costs incurred.[61] A majority decision of the Supreme Court of Canada overturned Burbidge J's decision.[62] Idington J determined that Lord Watson's statements in *St Catherine's Milling* regarding Ontario's liability under the treaty were purely *obiter dicta* and, therefore, of no legally binding force or effect.[63] Had Lord Watson's statement been legally binding, Idington J insisted that the *Seybold* case would certainly have explicitly recognized this fact and given effect to it.[64] Curiously, *Seybold* neither explicitly affirmed nor rejected Lord Watson's conclusion in *St Catherine's Milling* on this point.

Idington J also explained that Ontario could not be held responsible for the obligations arising under Treaty No. 3 as it did not have the option of accepting or declining receipt of the beneficial interest in the surrendered lands.[65] Duff J agreed with Idington J, holding that Ontario would only be liable to pay the annuities under the treaty if it had taken *positive* action to derive the benefits it received by way of Section 109.[66] Idington and Duff JJ also dismissed the existence of any equitable grounds on which to base Ontario's responsibility to fulfil the terms of the treaty.[67] In dissent, Davies J, with Girouard J concurring, affirmed the trial judgment on two grounds: Lord Watson's pronouncement in *St Catherine's Milling*, and Strong CJC's affirmation of it in *Robinson Treaties Annuities*.[68] The dissenting judgment in the *Treaty No. 3 Annuities* case is significant, because the disputes in *St Catherine's Milling* and *Treaty No. 3 Annuities* are identical.

When the *Treaty No. 3 Annuities* case was appealed to the Privy Council, Lord Loreburn LC held that there was no legal principle on which to find Ontario legally responsible for fulfilling the payment of the annuity under the treaty.[69] He did not leave the matter entirely without comment, though: 'It may be that, as a matter of fair play between the two Governments, as to which their Lordships are not called upon to

The Canadian Crown's Obligations 237

express and do not express any opinion, the province ought to be liable for some part of this outlay. But in point of law, which alone is here in question, the judgment of the Supreme Court appears unexceptionable.'[70] Entirely *obiter*, Lord Loreburn LC's statement is by no means conclusive on the issue of provincial legal responsibility. It nevertheless recognizes that, as a result of the circumstances created by the constitutional division of powers, the province may well hold obligations to aboriginal peoples independent of those owed by the federal Crown.

Summary and Conclusions

The discussion of *St Catherine's Milling*, and the subsequent trilogy of cases, illustrates the existence of provincial responsibilities for the payment of annuities under pre Confederation treaties as well as joint federal–provincial obligations regarding the setting aside of reserves from lands surrendered under treaty. It also shows the significant distinction between the obligation to pay annuities under a treaty and the obligation to set aside Indian reserves from lands surrendered under it. Because Indian treaties are concrete manifestations of the Crown's fiduciary obligations to aboriginal peoples,[71] these cases demonstrate one basis for the existence of provincial fiduciary duties to Native peoples.

The issue of provincial responsibility in these cases may have been made clearer had the majority of judges rendering decisions not been adversely affected by the issue of privity.[72] As the treaties in question had been negotiated and signed by the federal Crown, the judges found it difficult to find that the provinces could be held liable for obligations undertaken by the federal Crown. This reluctance existed separate and apart from the tangible effect of Section 109 of the British North America Act, 1867, on these situations, which resulted in the provinces receiving the benefits derived from the treaties.

The judges' problem with the privity issues is particularly evident in the *Treaty No. 3 Annuities* case, where Lord Loreburn LC stated: 'In making this treaty the Dominion Government acted upon the rights conferred by the Constitution. They were not acting in concert with the Ontario Government, but on their own responsibility, and it is conceded that the motive was not any special benefit to Ontario, but a motive of policy in the interests of the Dominion as a whole.'[73] Both Idington and Duff JJ voiced similar concerns in the Supreme Court of Canada's determination of the *Treaty No. 3 Annuities* case.[74] What the judges failed to consider was that, at the time that the Robinson treaties and Treaty No. 3

were signed, the constitutional understanding of the Crown was that it was 'one and indivisible' throughout the Commonwealth.[75]

When the British North America Act, 1867, created federal and provincial Crowns in Canada, it did not affect the existing constitutional understanding of the Crown or the nature and extent of its pre-Confederation obligations and responsibilities. It merely divided the powers, responsibilities, and benefits of a single and indivisible Canadian Crown[76] among the newly created federal and provincial Crowns. This division included the Crown's pre-existing fiduciary obligations to Native peoples. Therefore, the allocation of powers in the British North America Act, 1867, did not remove or reduce the Crown's fiduciary obligations to the Natives peoples, but simply redistributed them.[77]

The fact that the Canadian Crown remained single and indivisible prevented it from escaping its obligations to Native peoples by donning a provincial – or federal – Crown 'hat' at its convenience. The Crown could not escape, moreover, liability for adequately discharging its fiduciary duties by virtue of jurisdictional problems, such as those surrounding the establishment of Indian reserves from Indian lands surrendered by treaty: 'Each level of government has an independent constitutional role and responsibility ... Both are, however, subject to the demands of the honour of the Crown, and this must mean, at a minimum, that the aboriginal people to whom the Crown in all its emanations owes an obligation of protection and development, must not lose the benefit of that obligation because of federal-provincial jurisdictional uncertainty.'[78]

Mutual power entails mutual responsibility[79] and it is this mutual responsibility, founded in part on the sharing of legislative and executive powers by the federal and provincial Crowns, that underlies the Crown's fiduciary obligations to aboriginal peoples. If a provincial Crown obtains exclusive proprietary and administrative rights over Indian lands surrendered by treaty, then it must, by necessity or logical implication, also obtain a portion of the fiduciary duties owed to the aboriginal signatories to the treaty.[80] Section 109 of the British North America Act, 1867, is the conduit by which this transfer is effected. Once this transfer takes place, the province is legally bound to cooperate with the federal Crown in fulfilling the terms of the treaty.[81] Brian Slattery has expressed similar sentiments in 'First Nations and the Constitution: A Question of Trust': 'Where the benefiting Province has the exclusive constitutional authority to fulfill the Crown's promises, it cannot take the benefit of the surrender without incurring corresponding fiduciary obligations. Thus, if the Federal Crown has undertaken to set aside

The Canadian Crown's Obligations 239

reserves out of the lands surrendered, this promise binds the Province to which the lands pass, because it alone has the power to carry out the promise.'[82]

Recent Judicial Inferences of Provincial Fiduciary Obligations to Aboriginal Peoples

In opposition to the judicial determinations in the *Robinson Treaties Annuities, Seybold,* and *Treaty No. 3 Annuities* decisions, more recent judicial consideration of provincial obligations indicates a return to the reasoning espoused by Lord Watson in *St Catherine's Milling.*

Smith

In *Smith v R,*[83] the federal Crown, on behalf of the Red Bank Indian band, sought a declaration for possession of surrendered reserve lands that had been squatted on since 1838. In 1895 the band had surrendered reserve lands to the federal Crown to enable them to be sold for the band's benefit.[84] At the time the action was commenced, the surrendered lands had not been sold and remained occupied by squatters.

The Supreme Court of Canada held that the federal Crown could not maintain the action as it no longer possessed jurisdiction over the lands after their surrender. The court did not address the issue of whether the federal or provincial Crowns, or both, were legally responsible for discharging the obligations incurred under the terms of the surrender. It did not, however, leave the issue entirely without comment.

In determining that the band's release of its interests was absolute, Estey J referred to the *Seybold* decision by stating that the effects of the band's release 'might give rise to differences as between the parties to the release.'[85] He suggested that 'if and when such related, but here extraneous, issues arise, the courts concerned may find of interest the comment of Street J in the judgment of the Divisional Court of Ontario in *Ontario Mining Co v Seybold.*'[86] The portion of Street J's judgment quoted by Estey J reads as follows: 'The surrender was undoubtedly burdened with the obligation imposed by the Treaty to select and lay aside special portions of the tract covered by it for the special use and benefit of the Indians. The Provincial Government could not without plain disregard of justice take advantage of the surrender and refuse to perform the condition attached to it.'[87]

Later, in the context of discussing the effects of the Crown's obligations to the band under the terms of the surrender, Estey J commented that 'other consequences could arguably flow from such a transaction' but that they went beyond the court's focus on 'the surrender and its consequences in law in relation to the title to the said lands.'[88] Although Estey J neglected to pursue this line of inquiry,[89] the *Smith* case hints that a provincial Crown may be found liable for discharging the obligations stemming from an Indian land treaty or from the effects of a surrender of Indian reserve lands to the Crown.

Gardner

In *Gardner v The Queen in Right of Ontario*[90] the Eagle Lake band had commenced an action against the federal and Ontario Crowns for their roles in excluding certain lands from the band's reserve allotment under Treaty No. 3. In particular, the band sought a declaration of its right of possession of headlands in the parts of its reserves that were bordered by bodies of water. By agreement with the federal Crown,[91] Ontario had initially undertaken to protect those interests, but effectively reneged on that agreement through its enactment of contrary legislation.[92]

Because of the legislative requirements at the time the band brought its suit, to seek redress against both Crowns, the band was forced to bring concurrent actions in the federal and provincial courts.[93] Ontario insisted that the actions were identical and could not both be maintained. To prevent what it viewed as an abuse of process, Ontario sought to have the Ontario court strike out the band's statement of claim against it. Ontario argued that only the band's Federal Court action against the federal Crown should be allowed to proceed. The basis of its contention was that, as a result of the Indian Act, there was a prima facie privity of contract between the band and the federal Crown.

White J determined that the band could continue the actions concurrently in the federal and Ontario courts. He based his decision on (1) the statutory requirements in existence at the time, (2) his finding that the band had a justiciable claim against the province, and (3) his finding that the province, having promised to uphold the band's interest by agreement with the federal Crown, should have more concern for the band's loss of rights: '[T]he plaintiffs have been deprived of a valuable right which, in part, they paid for by surrendering their aboriginal rights to the Crown in right of Canada. It is unseemly that the Province of Ontario, which in an agreement with the Dominion of Canada, promised to uphold that right, is not solicitous of that right. Perhaps, the

The Canadian Crown's Obligations 241

Province of Ontario should have viewed any imperfection in the plaintiffs' pleading with a more appropriate measure of forbearance.'[94]

The *Gardner* case did not determine Ontario's obligations under the terms of the treaty. The sole matter in issue was Ontario's application to strike out the band's statement of claim. *Gardner* did recognize, however, that Ontario, by virtue of its actions in accepting and later repudiating the protection of the band's rights under the treaty, may possess obligations towards the band based on its enactment of legislation protecting aboriginal interests.[95]

Cree Regional Authority *and* Delgamuukw

The notion of provincial fiduciary responsibilities towards aboriginal peoples was raised again in *Cree Regional Authority v Robinson*[96] and in the trial judgment in *Delgamuukw v British Columbia*.[97] In the *Cree Regional Authority* case, the court implied that provincial Crowns may hold fiduciary obligations towards Native peoples.[98] It determined that in *R v Sparrow*,[99] the Supreme Court of Canada's discussion of fiduciary duties did not distinguish between the federal and provincial Crowns. This led the court to find that 'the provincial authorities are also responsible for protecting the rights of the Native population.'[100]

In the British Columbia Supreme Court's judgment in *Delgamuukw v British Columbia*, McEachern CJBC, as he then was, held that the Crown had a fiduciary duty to allow the plaintiffs to use unoccupied or vacant Crown land for subsistence until the land was dedicated to another purpose.[101] As that duty could only be enforced against the province because of the operation of Section 109 of the British North America Act, 1867, he determined that the province was also bound by the fiduciary duty to the plaintiffs.[102] On appeal, the British Columbia Court of Appeal varied the trial judgment in *Delgamuukw* without comment on this particular issue.[103]

Bear Island

The Supreme Court of Canada's decision in *Ontario (Attorney-General) v Bear Island Foundation*[104] is also noteworthy for its inference of provincial fiduciary responsibility to First Nations. The pivotal issue in the Supreme Court's consideration of *Bear Island* was whether the Teme-Augama Anishnabai people adhered to the Robinson–Huron Treaty, 1850, either expressly or by implication.[105] The Supreme Court's decision suggested that Ontario was bound by fiduciary obligations to the Teme-Augama Anishnabai derived from the Robinson–Huron Treaty, 1850. Although it vaguely stated that 'the Crown ... breached its fiduciary obligations to the Indians,'[106] without stating which emanations of the Crown held and breached those obligations, it also explained that the matters involving the breach of duty 'currently form the subject of negotiations between the parties.'[107]

As discussed in Chapter 6, what is particulary intriguing about the Supreme Court's statement is that the parties involved in the negotiations it mentioned were the Temagami people and the Province of Ontario, but not the federal Crown. By virtue of this circumstance – of which the Supreme Court was eminently aware at the time of its decision – the logical inference to be made is that the court held Ontario responsible for the fiduciary obligations owed to the Temagami people.

Indeed, it is difficult to fathom why the province would be involved in negotiations over the Crown's breach of duty to the Temagami people in the absence of the federal Crown's participation if it were not, itself, bound by a fiduciary duty to the Temagami people. Of more general applicability is the fact that there was nothing unique about Ontario's role in the *Bear Island* scenario which resulted in the Supreme Court's inference of Ontario's fiduciary obligations to the Temagami people.

The events in *Bear Island* (pursuant to which the court found that 'the Crown' had breached its fiduciary responsibilities) are akin to other situations in which lands surrendered by aboriginal peoples under treaties unilaterally negotiated by the federal Crown accrue to the provinces in which the lands are situated under Section 109 of the British North America Act, 1867. The conclusions from the discussion of the *St Catherine's Milling* and trilogy decisions regarding federal and provincial obligations to the aboriginal peoples suggest that the equitable basis of a finding of provincial fiduciary duty is concerned primarily with whether the province reaped benefits under the treaty. In the *Bear Island* scenario, Ontario did reap a benefit by obtaining the beneficial interest in the Indian land surrendered under the Robinson–Huron Treaty, 1850, situated within its boundaries.

Based on these observations, it cannot be claimed that the Supreme Court's conclusions regarding Ontario's fiduciary duty to the Temagami people ought to be restricted to the situation arising in *Bear Island*. The *Bear Island* decision did not, moreover, define or limit Ontario's fiduciary obligation. Accordingly, the Supreme Court's inference of provincial fiduciary responsibilities belonging to Ontario may support the notion of general provincial fiduciary responsibilities to the aboriginal peoples living within their jurisdictional boundaries.

Summary and Conclusions

It is beyond dispute that the relationship between the Crown and Native peoples in Canada far predates the separation of legislative and executive powers established in the British North America Act, 1867. Although this chapter has focused primarily on positive legal rationales for the entrenchment of fiduciary obligations on the federal and provincial Crowns, there is a far more fundamental, and generally neglected, rationale for these conclusions – aboriginal understandings of the Crown–Native relationship, as reflected, in part, in aboriginal understandings of 'the Crown.'

13

Aboriginal Understandings of 'the Crown' and the Nexus between Governmental Power and Fiduciary Responsibility

Traditionally, aboriginal peoples' reference point for the basis of the Crown's fiduciary duty to them in Canada has always been 'the Crown.' It has not been the Crown in right of Britain, the Crown in right of Canada, or the Crown in right of a particular province. This understanding stems from the wording of treaties and of other agreements between the Crown and Native peoples, as well as the explanations provided to the Native peoples by the Crown's own representatives. Based on the accounts of the history and background to many Indian land treaties, no differentiation between the personifications of the Crown were made evident to the Native peoples.[1] From their standpoint, therefore, where the Crown treated with and undertook certain responsibilities towards them, it did so as a unified entity.

Other considerations that have affected the constitutional understanding of the Crown and its responsibilities to aboriginal peoples from the time of contact – including the division by the British North America Act, 1867, of the Canadian Crown into federal and provincial Crowns and the change in the constitutional understanding of the Crown from 'single and indivisible' to 'separate and divisible'[2] – were entirely external to aboriginal understandings of the Crown. The aboriginal peoples were never involved in effecting these changes. Moreover, they were not consulted about them and their effects upon the Crown–Native relationship.

Owing to their situation when these changes were taking place, the aboriginal peoples cannot be expected to have known or fully comprehended the intended effect of these changes without having been informed of them and their effects. In any event, in accordance with fiduciary doctrine, the aboriginal peoples were neither responsible for

Aboriginal Understandings of the Crown   245

discovering the changes in the understanding of the Crown nor was the nature and extent of the Crown's fiduciary duty owed to them lessened in any respect by these changes.[3]

The conflict between aboriginal and non-aboriginal understandings of the Crown is illustrated by the Supreme Court of Canada's decision in *Mitchell v Peguis Indian Band*.[4] The Manitoba government had rebated the Peguis Indian band for moneys the band had paid under an invalid tax imposed on the sale of electricity on Indian reserves. Meanwhile, one of the band's creditors had obtained a garnishing order[5] under the Manitoba Garnishment Act[6] against the rebate. In accordance with the order, the government paid the garnished amount into court. The band sought to have the garnishing order set aside and the moneys paid out of court on the basis that the order was inconsistent with Sections 89(1) and 90(1)(b) of the Indian Act.[7] The band maintained, moreover, that the Manitoba Garnishment Act was not a provincial law applicable to Indians under Section 88 of the Indian Act and, therefore, was not applicable to the matter in issue.[8]

The broad issue before the Supreme Court of Canada was whether the moneys paid to the band could be considered the personal property of a band situated on a reserve and thereby not subject to garnishment under Section 89(1) of the Indian Act. For the purposes of Section 89(1), the definition of personal property situated on a reserve included moneys 'given to Indians or to a band under treaty or agreement between a band and Her Majesty' under Section 90(1)(b) of the act. To determine whether the rebate came under Section 90(1)(b), the court was faced with determining which emanations of the Crown were contained within the phrase 'Her Majesty,' as it was used in Section 90(1)(b).

In principle, all of the members of the Supreme Court of Canada agreed that the use of the phrase 'Her Majesty' in federal legislation could refer to both federal and provincial Crowns. In the particular instance of Section 90(1)(b), however, La Forest J's majority decision held that 'Her Majesty' referred only to the federal Crown. Dickson CJC, dissenting, insisted that the use of 'Her Majesty' in Section 90(1)(b) referred to both federal and provincial Crowns.

Whereas La Forest J's assessment was based on an adherence to the intentions of Parliament in enacting the Indian Act, Dickson CJC concentrated on aboriginal understandings of the phrase 'Her Majesty,' as mandated by the Supreme Court of Canada's decision in *Nowegijick v R*.[9] Relying on *Nowegijick*'s determination that 'treaties and statutes relating to Indians should be liberally construed and doubtful expressions resolved in favour of the Indian,'[10] Dickson CJC held that the definition of 'Her Majesty' in the Section 90(1)(b) of the Indian Act ought to concur with aboriginal understandings of the phrase, which he found included both federal and provincial Crowns: '[T]he Indians' relationship with the Crown or Sovereign has never depended upon the particular representatives of the Crown involved. From the aboriginal perspective, any federal-provincial divisions that the Crown has imposed on itself are internal to itself and do not alter the basic structure of Sovereign–Indian relations.'[11]

The basis of Dickson CJC's conclusion may be found in the historical relationship between the Crown and Native peoples in Canada: 'That relationship began with pre-confederation contact between historic occupiers of North American lands (the aboriginal peoples) and the European colonizers (since 1763, "the Crown"), and it is this relationship between aboriginal peoples and the Crown that grounds the distinctive fiduciary obligation on the Crown.'[12] Because of the pre-Confederation origins of the Crown–Native fiduciary relationship, Dickson CJC held that aboriginal understandings of 'Her Majesty' or 'the Crown' must also be rooted in pre-Confederation realities.[13] Therefore, although the constitutional division of powers upon Confederation may have necessitated the creation of the federal and provincial Crowns in Canada, that change did not affect aboriginal understandings of the Crown. Similarly, it did not affect the fulfilment of the Crown's duty to the aboriginal peoples.[14]

Dickson CJC's adherence to the notion that the provinces share in the Crown's fiduciary duty to Native peoples is reflected in his comments relating to the divisibility of the Crown *vis-à-vis* aboriginal views of the Crown.[15] It is reinforced by his statement that it is possible to 'overemphasize the extent to which aboriginal peoples are affected only by the decisions and actions of the federal Crown.'[16] His discussion of the incidental effects doctrine[17] is also suggestive of provincial fiduciary obligations. Finally, his review of the *Guerin* decision demonstrates that the findings in that case do not prohibit a determination that the Crown's fiduciary duty is shared by the provinces.[18]

La Forest J's majority judgment in *Mitchell* explicitly rejected Dickson CJC's characterization of aboriginal understandings of 'the Crown' as not being reflective of modern circumstances: 'With deference, I question his conclusion that it is realistic, in this day and age, to proceed on the assumption that from the aboriginal perspective, any federal–provincial divisions that the Crown has imposed upon itself are simply internal to itself, such that the Crown may be considered what one might style an "indivisible entity."'[19] His rationale for not holding that Section 90(1)(b) of the Indian Act also encompassed the provincial Crowns is based on his assertion that to include the provinces would grant the aboriginal peoples an advantage which was not justifiable in light of the Crown's historical protection of Indian lands and property, as codified in Sections 87 and 89 of the Indian Act.

Traditionally, only Indian property situated on a reserve was held to be free from taxation or distraint. The *situs*, or location, of the property was, and still is, the determining factor regarding the property's protection under the Indian Act. Section 90(1)(b) statutorily deems any personal property that was given to Indians or an Indian band by Her Majesty as being situated on a reserve and therefore protected. Nevertheless, La Forest J deemed that the Indian Act's protection of Indian property was limited to the personal property promised to Indians in treaties and ancillary agreements by the Crown, in accordance with the latter's historical undertakings.[20] He held that if anything other than a continuation of the Crown's historical practices was envisaged by Sections 87 and 89 of the Indian Act, those sections would have expressly stated such an intention.[21]

La Forest J's interpretation of Section 90(1) in *Mitchell* may be seen to adhere to frozen rights theory, which states that rights exist only in the form that they were exercisable in at a certain point in time and are not capable of modification or change. However, this theory was explicitly rejected by the Supreme Court of Canada in *R v Sparrow*.[22] The majority decision in *Sparrow*, which, ironically, was delivered jointly by Dickson CJC and La Forest J, explained: '[A]n existing aboriginal right cannot be read so as to incorporate the specific manner in which it was regulated before 1982 ... [T]he phrase "existing aboriginal rights" must be interpreted flexibly so as to permit their evolution over time ... Clearly, then, an approach to the constitutional guarantee embodied in s. 35(1) which would incorporate "frozen rights" must be rejected.'[23]

What is intriguing about La Forest J's decision in *Mitchell* is that, despite his emphasis upon the historical origins of the Crown's protection of Indians' personal property, he ignored historical aboriginal understandings of 'the Crown.' Not only are his findings incongruous, but they also contradict two Supreme Court of Canada precedents. His position regarding the Crown's protection of Indians' personal property ignored the Supreme Court's rejection of frozen rights theory in *Sparrow*, which was rendered less than one month before *Mitchell*. Moreover, his determination that aboriginal understandings of the Crown as 'an indivisible entity' do not reflect modern circumstances runs contrary to the precedent established in *Nowegijick*, where aboriginal understandings of words and legal concepts in Indian treaties and statutes relating to Indians are to be preferred over more legalistic and technical constructions.[24]

Modern aboriginal understandings of 'the Crown,' as represented in treaties and through the historical intercourse of governmental authorities and Native peoples in Canada, are founded on understandings passed from generation to generation, and dating back to the various bases of the Crown's fiduciary obligations. They consistently regard the Crown as a *unified whole* with whom treaties were signed and compacts made.[25] La Forest J's characterization of aboriginal understandings of the Crown in *Mitchell*, on the other hand, is reflective of the common law's tendency to attempt to understand aboriginal conceptions exclusively by analogy with common law ideas rather than by viewing them on their own terms.[26]

The problems associated with attempts to understand aboriginal conceptions exclusively by reference to common law ideas is reflected by the growing trend in Canadian aboriginal rights jurisprudence to describe aboriginal rights as *sui generis*.[27] The notion that aboriginal rights do not necessarily correspond to rights comprehensible or recognizable at common law is not an entirely recent phenomenon. It may be traced back to the early nineteenth century, at which time it occupied a prime role in one of the United States Supreme Court's earliest decisions on aboriginal rights, *Johnson and Graham's Lessee v M'Intosh*.[28] In that dispute, resulting from competing claims of ownership of former Indian land,[29] Chief Justice John Marshall did not dispute the validity of the plaintiff's title, which had been purchased from its original Indian owners. He did hold, though, that that title was unenforceable by American courts because it was the creature of a separate legal system and thereby was governed by its laws.

The special, *sui generis* nature of aboriginal rights was later recognized by the Privy Council in *Amodu Tijani v The Secretary, Southern Nigeria*.[30] In that case, Viscount Haldane, commenting on the nature of aboriginal land tenure in West Africa, issued a warning about the judiciary's interpretation of rights that were not formulated within the confines of the common law: 'Their Lordships make the preliminary observation that in interpreting the native title to land, not only in Southern Nigeria, but other parts of the British Empire, much caution is essential. There is a tendency, operating at times unconsciously, to render that title conceptually in terms which are appropriate only to systems which have grown up under English law. But this tendency has to be held in check closely.'[31]

In the Supreme Court of Canada's decision in *Guerin v R*, Dickson J's emphasis on the *sui generis* nature of aboriginal title and of the Crown–Native relationship was also predicated on the necessity to avoid imposing common law formulations to aboriginal concepts.[32] More recently this notion was restated by the dissenting judgment of Isaac CJ in *Apsassin v Canada (Department of Indian Affairs and Northern Development)*. Citing the statements made in *Amodu Tijani* and *Guerin*, Isaac CJ explained that the *sui generis* nature of aboriginal title required that any consideration of the Crown–Native fiduciary relationship, as well as the Crown's concomitant obligations stemming from that relationship, not follow traditional common law precepts.[33] Isaac CJ's sentiments were echoed by Gonthier J in the Supreme Court of Canada's disposition of the *Apsassin* case.[34]

In Canada the courts have overtly described Indian treaties,[35] the Crown–Native fiduciary relationship,[36] aboriginal title,[37] and aboriginal property rights[38] as *sui generis*. The dissenting judgment of Lambert JA in *Delgamuukw v British Columbia* stated that 'all aboriginal rights are *sui generis*.'[39] In making this statement, Lambert JA expanded on the sentiments expressed by Viscount Haldane in *Amodu Tijani*: 'I am satisfied that a jurisprudential analysis of the concepts underlying "rights" in common law or western legal thought is of little or no help in understanding the rights now held by aboriginal peoples and now recognized and affirmed by the common law and by the Constitution ... And it is not only in relation to aboriginal title that trying to describe the title in the terminology of common law tenures is both unnecessary and misleading: trying to describe aboriginal rights in terms of rigorous western jurisprudential analysis may well be equally unnecessary and misleading'[40] All of these cases recognize that aboriginal conceptions and understandings may not always correspond to their common law counterparts.[41] It should not be surprising, then, that aboriginal understanding of 'the Crown' differ from those held by the common law.

If common law views of 'the Crown' differ from aboriginal peoples' traditionally held conceptions, it is incumbent on the Crown to ensure that the former is made evident to the aboriginal peoples. This notion is both consistent with the interpretive principle enunciated in *Nowegijick*[42] and the requirements of fiduciary doctrine. Regardless, any change in the understanding of the Crown may only affect the remedies available for a breach of the Crown's fiduciary duties rather than the nature and extent of those duties or the legal requirement that they be fulfilled. The passage of time does not forgive a fiduciary's breach of duty – although, in certain circumstances, it may prevent the bringing of an action for breach by a lapse of statutory limitations or laches.[43]

As the Crown's general fiduciary duties owed to the Native peoples are a continuation of, or stem from, the duties it owed to them from various pre- and post-Confederation political, military, social, and legal alliances, as well as other historical intercourse between the groups, these duties still exist and are of paramount importance. The determination of which emanation, or emanations, of the Crown must fulfil the duties is a secondary matter, because it only becomes important to determine who owes the duty if the duty is first found to exist. From aboriginal perspectives, the most important concern is to ensure that any obligations that are owed to them are properly fulfilled. Determining which emanations of the Crown owe particular duties becomes relevant where, for example, an aboriginal nation seeks to commence legal action to obtain a remedy for a breach of obligation. It is also relevant where the political concerns of a particular aboriginal nation may affect which emanation of the Crown it may prefer to deal with in situations where such a choice is available.

The totality of the fiduciary obligations owed by the Crown to the Native peoples may be favourably analogized to a pocket watch. The Crown's general fiduciary duty to the Native peoples, like the pocket watch, is a gestalt. Both are comprised of a number of parts which, when assembled together, take on a function which cannot be achieved by the amalgam of its constituent parts taken individually. As the Crown's duty came into existence, it has been divided and redistributed pursuant to the changes in the constitutional understanding of the Crown. Initially, the duty was attached entirely to the single and indivisible Crown. As the single and indivisible Crown's powers were transferred to the British and Canadian Crowns, those duties were also transferred. Ultimately, with the attainment of Canadian independence and the elimination of British residual power over Canadian affairs, the duty was affixed to the Canadian Crown.[44] Individual components of the whole of the Canadian Crown's duty attached to either the federal or provincial Crowns in a manner reflective of the division and redistribution of powers, responsibilities, and benefits under the British North America Act, 1867.

The only constant throughout this process of division and redistribution was the existence of the duty and all of its various components. Doctrinally, the aboriginal peoples may rely on and expect the fulfilment of the fiduciary obligations owed to them by 'the Crown' without having to be aware of which emanation of the Crown is responsible for which duty, or, in specific instances, which Crown is responsible for what parts of each duty.[45] Based on this assertion, Dickson CJC's conclusions in *Mitchell* that any divisions of the Canadian Crown are merely internal to itself and do not affect Crown–Native relations is the correct approach. In a practical sense, however, aboriginal beneficiaries who have suffered a breach of the fiduciary duties owed to them by the Crown ought to inform themselves as to which emanation of the Crown is responsible for that duty prior to seeking a remedy. This process is made far more difficult than necessary at the present time as a result of the absence of cases which explicitly recognize provincial fiduciary responsibilities to Native peoples. To ensure that the proper part is held responsible for any breach of duty that may be found, it would be wise for an aboriginal nation bringing a claim of breach of fiduciary duty to bring it against both the federal and relevant provincial Crowns.

The principle of dividing obligations between the federal and provincial Crowns is not unique to the Crown–Native fiduciary relationship. Another example is the explicit sharing of legislative power – and consequently legislative responsibility – between the federal and provincial Crowns relating to agriculture and immigration under Section 95 of the British North America Act, 1867.[46] The relationship between power and responsibility[47] was expressed by the Supreme Court of Canada in *Sparrow*, where the court stated, in relation to the nexus between Section 91(24) of the British North America Act, 1867, and Section 35(1) of the Constitution Act, 1982, that 'federal power must be reconciled with federal duty.'[48]

Because of the absence of provincial participation in the majority of the events giving rise to the Crown's fiduciary duties towards Native peoples, provincial obligations stem primarily from the federal–provincial distribution of legislative and authoritative responsibilities in Canada. Areas of provincial jurisdiction in the British North America Act, 1867, which have direct effects on aboriginal and treaty rights include Section 92(5) (management and sale of public lands and timber), Section 92(13) (property and civil rights), Section 92A (natural resources), and Section 109 (ownership of lands, mines, minerals, and royalties). The distribution of legislative and authoritative responsibility between the federal and provincial Crowns entails provincial acceptance of both benefits and obligations from the actions of the federal Crown after 1867 and from its predecessors, including the British Crown, prior to 1867.

Provincial obligations also arise from direct provincial actions towards and interaction with aboriginal peoples.

The sharing of legislative responsibility over aboriginal affairs may be seen, for example, in the ability of provinces to pass legislation affecting aboriginal peoples through Section 88 of the Indian Act.[49] Even though legislative jurisdiction over 'Indians, and Lands reserved for the Indians' is an exclusive federal power under Section 91(24) of the British North America Act, 1867, Section 88 of the Indian Act allows for provincial laws of general application to be applied to status Indians[50] by referential incorporation, subject to the terms of Indian treaties, the Indian Act itself, or other federal legislation.[51] In light of the effects of Section 35(1) of the Constitution Act, 1982, however, the constitutional validity of Section 88 is questionable.[52]

Where provinces intrude on the federal Crown's Section 91(24) legislative sphere, they cannot do so without affecting the nature and scope of their own obligations to Native peoples. As Brian Slattery explains: '[S]o long as the Provinces have powers and rights enabling them to affect adversely Aboriginal interests protected by the relationship, they hold attendant fiduciary obligations.'[53] Provinces thereby acquire some measure of the federal Crown's fiduciary responsibility where they pass legislation referentially under Section 88 of the Indian Act, play an active role in the formulation of land agreements concerning the establishment of Indian reserves, or actively participate in the negotiation of Indian treaties and agreements.

The provinces have, for example, passed provincial legislation that directly affects status Indians, including game and wildlife laws. Ontario played an active role in formulating land agreements regarding the establishment of Indian reserves, for instance, when it became involved in the implementation of Treaty No. 3 and Treaty No. 9 reserves. Its role in providing for the establishment of reserves under Treaty No. 3 is illustrated by the sixth clause of An Act for the Settlement of Certain Questions between the Governments of Canada and Ontario Respecting Indian Lands, which states: 'That any future treaties with the Indians in respect of territory in Ontario to which they have not before the passing of the said statutes surrendered their claim aforesaid, shall be deemed to require the concurrence of the Government of Ontario.'[54] Similarly, Quebec's role in negotiating the James Bay and Northern Quebec Agreement[55] and in enacting the provincial legislation necessary for its implementation[56] demonstrates active provincial participation in the negotiation of Indian treaties and agreements.

The line between federal and provincial jurisdictional boundaries is becoming increasingly blurred because of the effects of the Constitution Act, 1982. For this reason, it is likely that provinces will continue to encroach even further upon the federal Crown's Section 91(24) jurisdiction over 'Indians, and Lands reserved for the Indians' without reproach. As Dickson CJC noted in *Mitchell*, the 'fluidity of responsibility across lines of jurisdiction accords well with the fact that the newly entrenched s. 35 of the *Constitution Act, 1982* applies to all levels of government in Canada.'[57] However, if there is to be a point beyond which provincial action that is consistent with or in fulfilment of its obligation to aboriginal peoples is deemed to be *ultra vires*, some judicial definition of that line and of provincial fiduciary responsibilities to the aboriginal peoples is necessary. Otherwise, instances that approach or even cross that line will be difficult, if not impossible to regulate.[58]

Summary

With the passage of the Constitution Act, 1982, provincial governments now have a constitutional responsibility to act in a manner consistent with the furtherance of the aboriginal and treaty rights guaranteed in Section 35(1).[59] In light of the *Sparrow* decision, this arguable entails an obligation to actively and purposively promote or further the rights protected within Section 35(1).[60] This latter notion has since been affirmed by the Federal Court of Appeal in *Eastmain Band v Canada (Federal Administrator)*.[61]

A duty to act purposively, as indicated in *Sparrow*, does not require the Crown to seek prior court approval of legislative or policy initiatives which affect Indians qua Indians. In fact, it requires that provincial Crowns must act, without the need for further judicial direction, where their action is necessary or appropriate to the fulfilment of their fiduciary obligations, including the need to enhance or further Section 35(1) rights: '[I]nitiatives by provincial governments to fulfil their fiduciary obligations need not await the elaboration of section 35 of the *Constitution Act, 1982* into a kind of master treaty framework that will structure First Nations' space in the Constitution. To the extent that provincial governments are in a position to respect and secure existing aboriginal rights, the law declared in *Sparrow* requires them to do so.'[62] If provinces are unsure whether they must act in a specific instance, the purposive nature of their fiduciary duties requires them to make appropriate inquiries.[63] Above all, the purposive nature of the federal and provincial Crowns' fiduciary duties to Native peoples insists that, in light of the historical relationship between the Crown and aboriginal peoples, the

254 The Crown's Fiduciary Duty

Crown must maintain its honour, integrity, and avoid sharp practice in all of its dealings with them.[64]

Under the rubric of Section 35(1) and *Sparrow*'s suggestions as to its proper method of interpretation, a province may exempt aboriginal peoples from certain provincial laws or regulations – from what may otherwise appear to be, on the face of it, neutral legislation – because of the differential impact which those laws or regulations may have upon the aboriginal peoples.[65] This type of activity, however, prima facie amounts to legislation in respect of Indians qua Indians, which falls under the federal government's Section 91(24) jurisdiction. Prior to the existence of the Constitution Act, 1982, there is little doubt that such provincial activity would have been declared *ultra vires*, and thereby rendered void.

After the enactment of the Constitution Act, 1982, the situation changed dramatically. Where a provincial legislative initiative exempts aboriginal peoples in recognition of their aboriginal and treaty rights under Section 35(1), it will be validated by Section 52(1) of the Constitution Act, 1982.[66] Section 52(1) proclaims the Constitution of Canada – including the purposive application of Section 35(1) rights – to be the supreme law of Canada. However, the extent to which a province may act in accordance with the furtherance of Section 35(1) rights before it infringes upon the federal Crown's exclusive jurisdiction over 'Indians, and Lands reserved for the Indians' under Section 91(24) is a point of contention that has yet to be resolved.[67]

In light of the judicial entrenchment of the Crown's fiduciary obligations in *Guerin*; the constitutional responsibility of the federal and provincial Crowns to purposively act to further the aboriginal and treaty rights contained within Section 35(1) of the Constitution Act, 1982; the nexus between governmental power and responsibility; the link between the division or sharing of power and resultant benefits; the inferences of provincial duties owed to aboriginal peoples in the *St Catherine's Milling* and trilogy cases, discussed in Chapter 12, and the more recent judicial suggestions regarding provincial fiduciary responsibilities owed to aboriginal peoples, the notion that provincial Crowns owe fiduciary obligations to the aboriginal peoples is ready for explicit judicial recognition. Whereas Canadian aboriginal rights jurisprudence has yet to authoritatively endorse the existence of provincial responsibilities towards Native peoples, the strong inferences of provincial liability in *Bear Island*[68] and *Cree Regional Authority v Robinson*,[69] for example, indicate that Canadian courts may soon be prepared to move in that direction.

14

Characteristics of the Crown–Native Fiduciary Relationship

Answering the question of which emanations of the Crown are responsible for discharging the fiduciary obligations owed to aboriginal peoples is only the first stage in the process of developing a better understanding of the Crown–Native fiduciary relationship. However, as a result of having made that determination, it is possible to focus attention on some of the other important questions which have remained untouched by judicial decisions in Canadian aboriginal rights jurisprudence.

Is the Crown–Native Fiduciary Relationship Terminable?

In light of the recent discussions and negotiations over the aboriginal right to self-government surrounding the failed Charlottetown Accord,[1] including the federal government's proposal to recognize the aboriginal right to self-government in its amalgam of constitutional proposals[2] and the initial report of the Royal Commission on Aboriginal Peoples,[3] the terminability of the Crown–Native fiduciary relationship is an important matter.

Fiduciary relations do not operate within the same rigid confines and absolute preciseness as do trusteeship duties. Consequently, the duration of a fiduciary relationship cannot be ascertained by reference to trust law. In examining the duration of a trust relationship, it may be seen that a trustee's duties cease upon the closing of the trust. This may occur either as a result of the passage of a prescribed length of time or the attainment of a particular end or purpose, when the terms of the trust have been fulfilled.[4] The prescribed length of the trust is generally established in the trust instrument. In the instance of express trusts, however, a premature closing may come into effect.[5]

256 The Crown's Fiduciary Duty

There are some similarities between the length of trust and fiduciary relationships, though. Like the trust relationship, the duration of a fiduciary relation is situation-specific, being entirely dependent on the particular purpose or goal of the relationship in question. Unlike the trust relationship, the fiduciary relation does not automatically cease upon the attainment of a particular end. In some instances, fiduciary relations do cease upon the attainment of a particular goal, although the fiduciary duties arising from those relations continue indefinitely. Where, for example, two business partners have formally dissolved a one-time business venture and gone their separate ways, their fiduciary relationship in relation to that venture, for all intents and purposes, no longer exists. Nevertheless, the fiduciary duties owed by the partners to each other in relation to that venture continue indefinitely, albeit in a dormant state. Should it subsequently be discovered by partner A that partner B breached his duty to A relating to that venture, the duty resurfaces as the basis of an action for breach of duty by A against B.

If, however, those same partners decide to engage in a series of further ventures after the conclusion of their initial endeavour, the nature of their relationship changes once again. The fiduciary duties which they owe to each other no longer end upon individual ventures. As the nature of their relationship is now an ongoing and continuous one, their duties to each other are similarly ongoing and continuous. The situation-specificity of fiduciary doctrine renders the fiduciary nature of a relationship dependent on the particular characteristics of that relationship. Therefore, whereas the *existence of a trust relationship* creates the operational framework for the intercourse of the parties to it, the *intercourse of the parties* creates the operational framework for the existence of a fiduciary relationship.

A number of issues surround any discussion of the terminability of the Crown's fiduciary duty to Native peoples. The first set of issues revolves around the status of the Crown's duty. It must initially be asked whether the Crown's general fiduciary duty to aboriginal peoples is a permanent one. If it is deemed to be permanent, the question then becomes whether either the Crown or the aboriginal peoples may contract out of it.

As illustrated earlier, the *Sparrow* decision held that the Crown's fiduciary obligation to Native peoples is constitutionally entrenched in Section 35(1) of the Constitution Act, 1982.[6] Any amendment of the rights enshrined within Section 35(1) is subject to the more onerous amending procedure outlined in Section 38 rather than that in Section 43.[7] In the

Characteristics of the Crown–Native Relationship 257

absence of constitutional amendment, the only other way in which the Crown's duty may be removed is with the consent of the aboriginal peoples. Yet, because of the nature and history behind the Crown–Native fiduciary relationship, it would be unseemly to allow the Crown to unilaterally extricate itself from its obligations to the aboriginal peoples without finding itself in breach of its duty.

Although constitutional amendment may eliminate one formalistic basis on which the Crown's obligations are rooted, the Crown's duties predate the enactment of the Constitution Act, 1982, and are entrenched in a number of other sources. For instance, the precedent established in *Guerin* judicially sanctioned the existence of the Crown–Native fiduciary relationship in the absence of any consideration of the effects of Section 35(1), because the Constitution Act, 1982, did not exist at the time that the action was commenced. Therefore, even if it were possible to obtain a constitutional amendment removing the Crown's fiduciary duty to Native peoples from Section 35(1), that action would be insufficient to eliminate the Crown's duty. Assuming, as well, that the *Guerin* precedent were overturned, that occurrence would also not end the Crown's duty. Even in the absence of any positive legal bases on which to ground the Crown's fiduciary obligation, the Crown's duty nonetheless exists on the extralegal plane, just as it existed prior to its judicial recognition in *Guerin*.[8]

As the Native peoples are the sole beneficiaries of the Crown's fiduciary obligations stemming from their relationship, they alone possess the ability to terminate the relationship.[9] Their ability to terminate their fiduciary relationship with the Crown exists independently of their ability to contract out of their rights contained within Section 35(1).[10] By combining the sole ability of Native peoples to terminate at will their fiduciary relationship with the Crown with the concomitant inability of the Crown to escape its fiducial obligations to the Native peoples, the Crown Native relationship may be seen to exist at the pleasure of the aboriginal peoples.

Whereas the Crown's fiduciary duty to the Native peoples exists independently of the Crown's sovereignty, its ability to fulfil that duty would be severely hampered without the concurrent existence of the Crown's sovereignty over Canada. As Chapter 11's discussion of the British Crown's continuing obligations to the aboriginal peoples of Canada indicates, a lack of sovereignty does not terminate the Crown's duty or render it meaningless. Rather, it eliminates the Crown's ability to fully discharge its fiduciary obligations and affects the availability and quantification of a remedy for any breach of duty that it may commit and be found liable for.

Although only the aboriginal peoples may terminate the Crown–Native fiduciary relationship, any continuation of the Crown's fiduciary responsibilities in the presence of the push towards aboriginal self-government raises a second set of issues. Does the transfer of Crown powers or their voluntary relinquishment to the aboriginal peoples reduce the scope of the Crown's fiduciary obligations? In addition, if the Crown's duty may be reduced in scope by the transfer or relinquishment of powers to the aboriginal peoples, to what extent does the Crown retain fiduciary obligations to ensure the smooth transition of those powers?

May the Crown's Fiduciary Obligation Be Reduced in Scope?

What this question asks, essentially, is whether any transfer or relinquishment of powers over Indian affairs directly to Native peoples or organizations is permissible within the scope of the Crown's fiduciary obligation or whether such a transfer constitutes a breach of that obligation. Moreover, along these same lines, does the transfer of previously governmentally controlled or regulated powers to the Native peoples absolve the government of a part of its fiduciary obligations?

In the face of aboriginal self-government negotiations, the ramifications of the transfer of governmental powers to the aboriginal peoples must first be made known. It should be noted, though, that aboriginal self-government exists in many forms. It may be as limited as the ability of aboriginal peoples to determine the make-up of their own band lists or as expansive as complete governmental powers over things and persons aboriginal. In light of this range of possibilities, it would appear likely that different effects would result from a limited transfer of governmental powers – such as those seen in Sections 10(1), 60(1), and 69(1) of the current Indian Act[11] – versus a wholesale transfer of powers from the Crown to the aboriginal peoples.

The questions which arise from a consideration of this issue are vital to the determination of the Crown's role and responsibilities in the face of the evolution of aboriginal self-government. Does the limited transfer of Crown powers to the aboriginals peoples reduce the scope of the Crown's fiduciary obligations? What effect does this limited transfer of powers to the aboriginal have on the nature of the Crown's fiduciary duty to oversee the carrying out of these powers? Does the Crown's duty exist only in respect of powers which it exercises personally? Alternatively, does the complete transfer of powers over things and persons aboriginal result in the termination of the Crown–Native fiduciary relationship? If so, when is it terminated, at the time of de facto self-government (that is, when self-government is first achieved and implemented), or when self-government has been practised and solidly entrenched? What if the Crown is relinquishing or vacating its jurisdiction over a previously controlled area to allow for the exercise of inherent aboriginal powers, such as would appear to be the effect of the federal Crown's phasing out of the Department of Indian Affairs in Manitoba? Finally, must the Crown, by virtue of its fiduciary obligations, oversee the institution of aboriginal self-government mechanisms to ensure that the best interests of the aboriginal peoples are being served?

The essence of the Crown's fiduciary obligation mandates that it act in the best interests of the Native peoples. However, for fiduciaries to act in their beneficiaries' best interests, the fiduciaries must first determine what those interests are. This entails that the fiduciaries must take all necessary steps to inform themselves as to their beneficiaries' best interests, including direct consultation with their beneficiaries. In accordance with the purposive nature of fiduciary doctrine, the Crown must then act to further those interests.[12] The return of legislative or governing powers to aboriginal peoples or the vacating of a jurisdictional area to allow for their exercise of inherent powers would, prima facie, appear to be in the aboriginals' best interests. Consequently, such an action would not only satisfy the Crown's aboriginal duty, but it would also accord with the purposive fulfilment of its obligations.

The current Indian Act provides for the transfer of some previously Crown-controlled activities to Indian bands. Section 10(1) allows a band to assume control over its own membership list as long as it adheres to certain criteria.[13] Under Section 60(1), the governor in council, upon request by a band, may grant to the band the ability to control and manage its own reserve lands.[14] Similarly, Section 69(1) provides for the ability of a band to control, manage, and expend its own revenue moneys.[15] The transfer of these powers by the Crown to the bands to exercise on their own behalf may not completely relieve the Crown of its fiduciary obligations, though.

Unlike the transfer of a duty to another person who is to act in a fiduciary or quasi-fiduciary role, the return of a duty to act on behalf of aboriginal peoples to the aboriginals themselves is a fulfilment of duty rather than a mere transfer of it. Nevertheless, it is insufficient for the Crown to attempt to dispose of its obligations by dumping them unceremoniously on the Native peoples without providing for their harmonious transition to the aboriginal authority. By virtue of the length of time that the Crown has assumed jurisdiction and responsibility for Indian affairs while simultaneously preventing the Native peoples from exercising self-determination, it would be unconscionable to allow the Crown to be instantaneously free of its fiduciary responsibilities without providing for a period of adjustment.

Accordingly, the Crown must be duty-bound to facilitate the transfer of control over certain powers to the aboriginal peoples, to supervise their assumption by the aboriginal peoples during the transition period, and to provide aid where required. This aid may take a variety of forms. It may be advisory in nature, financial, or a combination of both. As no two aboriginal nations are alike, the duration of this transitional period, and the amount of Crown aid required, may only be determined on a case-by-case basis. Moreover, because the Crown–Native fiduciary relationship exists at the pleasure of the aboriginal peoples, this transitional period and the availability of Crown aid may only be terminated when the aboriginal peoples determine that they are no longer required.[16] This unilateral ability of an aboriginal nation to terminate the Crown's transitional duties applies regardless of whether the scope of the powers to be transferred or vacated is limited to the responsibility over band membership lists or if it is as broad as aboriginal self-government. Should the Crown fail to perform this supervisory role, it will be liable for a breach of its fiduciary duty to the same extent and in the same fashion as if it had failed to positively exercise the transferred powers prior to their transfer.

The Purposive Nature of the Crown's Fiduciary Duty

The Supreme Court of Canada indicated in the *Sparrow* decision[17] that the Crown's fiduciary obligation to Native peoples should be purposively applied. The Federal Court of Appeal has subsequently affirmed the purposive nature of the Crown's duty in *Eastmain Band v Canada (Federal Administrator)*.[18] In neither case did the courts explain what this finding means in practical terms. Does the purposive nature of the Crown's duty require it to act positively to further the aboriginal peoples' best interests? If so, is the Crown in breach of its fiduciary obligations if it only acts on behalf of the aboriginal peoples when it is expressly required to – such as in the instance of a band wishing to surrender land?

If the purposive nature of the Crown's duty requires positive activity on its part to promote aboriginal best interests, this renders the Crown's duty *prescriptive* – placing an onus on the Crown, under the watchful eye of aboriginal law, to positively determine or establish what is in the aboriginals' best interests and act accordingly. If, on the other hand, the Crown is not required to actively promote aboriginal interests, the Crown's duty may be described as *proscriptive* – having the courts determine, after the fact, whether particular Crown actions demonstrated fidelity to the aboriginals' best interests. The simplest way to differentiate between these divergent visions is to understand the *prescriptive* vision as being pro-active, whereas the *proscriptive* view may be seen to be passive.

In 'The Fiduciary Principle,'[19] Paul Finn characterized the distinction between the *prescriptive* and *proscriptive*[20] nature of fiduciary relationships in the following terms: 'On one view it is a *prescriptive* notion; its concern is with whether the beneficiary's interests are in fact being served by the fiduciary; and it uses possible effects on those interests as the determinant in settling the fiduciary's responsibilities ... The alternative view sees the fiduciary principle as a *proscriptive* one; it is concerned with the maintenance of fidelity to the beneficiary; and it is activated when the fiduciary seeks improperly to advance his own or a third party's interest in or as a result of the relationship.'[21] Based on his characterizations, Finn concluded that fiduciary obligations cannot be *prescriptive*: 'If a fiduciary's liability was to be determined by reference to whether or not the beneficiary's interests had in fact been served, an often impossible inquiry, more than curious consequences would follow.'[22] These consequences would include the impingement of fiduciary doctrine upon the separate legal spheres occupied by the law of trusts, agency, tort, contract, etc. or, alternatively, their complete replacement by fiduciary law.[23]

Fiduciary theory is quite wide-ranging and, indeed, underlies virtually every aspect of law because of its equitable nature. Correspondingly, it could, potentially, infringe upon or entirely replace the spheres of influence carved out by areas such as contract and tort. However, although fiduciary doctrine does underlie virtually every sphere of law, it acts to complement, not combat or replace, the latter. As Lord Cowper stated in *Dudley v Dudley*, 'Equity therefore does not destroy the law, nor create it, but assist it.'[24] Particular examples of how fiduciary doctrine complements other spheres of law may be found in the doctrines of unconscionability in contract and duty in tort.

An adherence to Finn's vision of fiduciary doctrine as *proscriptive* entails a situation whereby fiduciary doctrine is neither purposive, nor merely passive, but completely inert. As he explained, the fiduciary's duty 'is not, of itself, an independent source of positive obligations which go beyond the exaction of loyalty in relationships.'[25] Paradoxically, the inevitable effect of an inert vision of fiduciary doctrine is the very same impossible inquiry into the actions of fiduciaries which Finn warned about in relation to the *prescriptive*, purposive view.[26] If fiduciary doctrine is truly inert until such time as a breach of duty is proven, then the courts' ability to inquire into fiduciaries' actions at that time to determine whether or not they are in breach of their duties is quite limited and prohibitively difficult.

Fiduciary doctrine is characterized by general principles and characteristics which serve to continuously monitor the actions of a fiduciary. This monitoring of a fiduciary's activities is continuous and is accomplished in a passive, or dormant, state which underlies individual fiduciary relations. This state continues as long as the integrity of these relationships is maintained. When a breach of fiduciary duty is, prima facie, demonstrated to exist, this subterranean monitoring of fiduciaries' actions is activated and brought to the surface.[27] Fiduciary doctrine monitors fiduciaries' positive and passive actions to determine whether they are consistent with their beneficiaries' interests. Accordingly, it captures actions as diverse as a fiduciary's acceptance of a bribe and a fiduciary not purchasing a certain property for a beneficiary in order to acquire it personally.

The theoretical basis of fiduciary doctrine, which is premised around the notion that fiduciaries are bound to act selflessly and in the best interests of their beneficiaries, applies both to situations where fiduciaries are expressly required to act and where fiduciaries have the discretion to act, but where making the positive choice to act results in the fulfilment of their beneficiaries' best interests. If fiduciaries are bound only to consider how to exercise their fiduciary powers when they are required to act, it is possible for them to be in breach of their duties to their beneficiaries in situations where they have the discretion to act, but choose not to. In the example of a fiduciary not purchasing certain property for a beneficiary in order to acquire it personally, it may be seen that a conflict of interest arises if the fiduciary does, in fact, purchase that property for personal gain. Nevertheless, merely by failing to take advantage of the opportunity to purchase the property for the beneficiary, the fiduciary is already in breach of duty for failing to act in the beneficiary's best interests. This result occurs regardless of whether the fiduciary actually purchases the property for personal gain.

A fiduciary's consideration of whether or not to exercise certain powers must be subordinated to the general premise that fiduciaries, on the assumption of their positions, are bound to act in their beneficiaries' best interests. In addition to being required to positively exercise a power where its exercise is in their beneficiaries' best interests, where fiduciaries possess the power to contravene their beneficiaries' best interests, they are bound not to exercise those powers. The *prescriptivist* understanding of fiduciary doctrine shares its ideological foundation with the rule against conflict of interest. Fiduciaries are in conflict of interest not only where they take positive action which contravenes their beneficiaries' best interests – such as where fiduciaries accept bribes in exchange for selling their beneficiaries' property at prices lower than market value[28] – but also where they possess the ability to facilitate their beneficiaries' best interests, but fail to act – as in the example of fiduciaries not purchasing property for their beneficiaries in order to acquire the property for themselves.

The *Sparrow* and *Eastmain* decisions, as well as the decision of the New Zealand Court of Appeal in *New Zealand Maori Council v Attorney-General*,[29] have asserted that the Crown's fiduciary duty to aboriginal peoples should be purposively applied. This entails an obligation on the Crown to act both when expressly called on to do so and where the Crown possesses the discretion to act and acting will further and promote the aboriginals' best interests. In addition to the Crown's fiduciary duty, the purposive method of interpreting Section 35(1) of the Constitution Act, 1982, mandated by *Sparrow* applies equally to the other aboriginal and treaty rights contained within that section.[30] The purposive nature of the Crown's fiduciary duty in *Sparrow* requires the active promotion and furtherance of those rights through direct consultation with the aboriginal peoples.

The existence of Section 35(1) assumes the recognition of aboriginal and treaty rights as important aspects of the Canadian constitutional structure. It is insufficient, however, to merely pay lip-service to the rights in Section 35(1) if they are to have any meaningful place within the constitutional fabric of Canada. There is no reason to constitutionally entrench rights if they are so ill-understood through their lack of definition or articulation that they are rendered incapable of providing any protection whatsoever to the people that they are designed to protect. To enable Section 35(1) rights to perform the protective function intended of them, they must be more clearly understood. To further Section 35(1) rights, therefore, includes the need to remedy the deficient understanding of the rights contained within it, thereby enabling it to protect the special interests of the aboriginal peoples.

The Crown's Duty and Conflict of Interest

The matter of conflict of interest is significant in any discussion of the Crown's fiduciary obligations to Native peoples. By virtue of its fiduciary responsibility, the Crown is duty-bound to act in the best interests of the aboriginal peoples. The rule against conflict of interest insists that the Crown must not benefit from its position as fiduciary, must provide full disclosure of its actions while in its fiduciary capacity – including the obligation to account for profits made while in its fiduciary capacity – and may not compromise or derogate from the Native peoples' interests in favour of its own, or those of a third party. The Crown may be found in conflict of interest even in the absence of malevolent actions merely by deviating from the fiduciary's standard of conduct prescribed by law. In light of the onerous duties imposed on fiduciaries by the rule against conflict of interest, it must be asked how the Crown may maintain fidelity to its fiduciary obligations to Native people while many of its other interests are served by not acting in their best interests.[31]

The rule against conflict of interest may be applied to situations where aboriginal and treaty rights have been extinguished or where they are currently regulated through legislation assented to by the Crown, as those rights are a part of the subject-matter of the Crown's obligations to Native peoples. By abrogating or derogating from an aboriginal or treaty right in favour of its own interests or those of a third party, the Crown is compromising its aboriginal beneficiaries' interests. Therefore, the Crown would, prima facie, appear to be in breach of its duty to the Native peoples where it has either extinguished[32] or continues to regulate[33] aboriginal and treaty rights through actions designed to facilitate or provide for the national interest.

Whereas there are other instances where fiduciaries find it difficult to adhere to their duties to their beneficiaries, or where fiduciaries may be tempted to act in conflict of interest, the situation involving the Crown and its fiduciary responsibilities to the aboriginal peoples is *sui generis*.[34] The Crown's duty to the aboriginal peoples is not its only duty. On a macroscopic level, the Crown also owes a duty to the Canadian population as a whole to act in their collective best interests, or what is better described as the 'national interest.'[35] Consequently, the Crown often finds itself in the difficult situation of having to reconcile each of its duties with its day-to-day activities. Although the reconciling of various fiduciary duties with daily activities is not unique to the Crown,[36] the types of activities and considerations which the Crown is confronted with are unique.

The recent constitutional negotiations leading up to and surrounding the failed Charlottetown Accord are a prime example of the unique situation of the Crown as a fiduciary. The Crown was confronted with reconciling a number of different issues which emanated from some of the multifarious fiduciary obligations that it owes to various elements of the Canadian population. In addition to the recognition of aboriginal self-government, the issues of Senate reform and Quebec sovereignty, among others, were raised. Indeed, the respective concerns of the aboriginal peoples and the Province of Quebec carried some measure of conflict between them. The various personifications and understandings of the Crown and the ability of these understandings to change or be altered over time as a result of the course of historical and political events is yet another unique characteristic of the Crown's fiduciary duties, both in general and, in particular, to the Native peoples. Owing to the number of unique situations which arise as a result of the Crown's role as fiduciary to aboriginal peoples, the potential for conflict of interest is high and the ability to avoid it is oftentimes difficult.

The potential for conflict of interest on the part of the Crown is replicated in a number of areas. One of the most conspicuous of these is the Indian land claims process. In both the Specific and Comprehensive Claims processes,[37] the federal Crown, through its Department of Justice and Department of Indian Affairs, is both the appraiser of a claim's merit as well as its arbiter of fact. The current Specific Claims process, as outlined in *Outstanding Business – A Native Claims Policy*,[38] entails a four-step process.[39] Initially, the claim is presented by the claimant band or bands[40] to the minister of Indian Affairs. The Office of Native Claims reviews the claim at the direction of the minister and then refers all pertinent facts and documents to the Department of Justice for advice on the federal Crown's 'lawful obligation.'

Lawful obligation is defined in *Outstanding Business* as arising in any of the following circumstances: (1) the non-fulfilment of a treaty or agreement between Indians and the Crown; (2) a breach of an obligation arising out of the Indian Act or other statutes pertaining to Indians and the regulations thereunder; (3) a breach of an obligation arising out of government administration of Indian funds or other assets; or (4) an illegal disposition of Indian land. In addition to the above, the Crown will acknowledge claims based on (1) failure to provide compensation for reserve lands taken or damaged by the federal government or any of its agencies under authority, or (2) fraud in connection with the acquisition or disposition of Indian reserve land by employees or agents of the federal government, in cases where the fraud can be clearly demonstrated.[41] On the basis of the Department of Justice's legal opinion, the minister of Indian Affairs accepts claims which are determined to be eligible for negotiation. Where the minister accepts the claim as negotiable in whole or part, the Office of Native Claims is authorized to negotiate a settlement with the claimant.

Where a claim was rejected under this process, no appeal procedure was provided for. The claimant was entitled to present its claim again at a later date for further review if new evidence was located or additional legal arguments produced which had the effect of shedding a different light on the claim. However, in 1992, the federal Indian Claims Commission was created.[42] Its mandate includes a function as an avenue of appeal where a claim under the Specific Claims process has been rejected by the minister:

[T]hat our Commissioners on the basis of Canada's Specific Claims Policy ... by considering only those matters at issue when the dispute was initially submitted to the Commission, inquire into and report upon:
(a) whether a claimant has a valid claim for negotiation under the Policy where that claim has already been rejected by the Minister; and
(b) which compensation criteria apply in negotiations of a settlement, where a claimant disagrees with the Minister's determination of the applicable criteria.

What may be seen from this examination of the Specific Claims process is that the determination of the Crown's lawful obligations is made by the Department of Justice and the minister of Indian Affairs. Clearly, this process illustrates that the Crown is in conflict of interest. The Department of Indian Affairs and the Department of Justice are both appendages of the federal Crown responsible for discharging its duties and obligations. Moreover, as the lawyers of the federal Crown, the Department of Justice is bound, first and foremost, to represent and protect the federal Crown's interests. How is it then possible that these departments may impartially decide on the merits of a particular Indian claim which seeks to reclaim revenue-generating lands from the federal

Crown whose best interests the departments both represent and seek to protect? Quite simply, it is not possible.

The Department of Indian Affairs is directly tied to the Crown's interests. It is responsible for administering the Indian Act, the federal Crown's own legislation which has historically destroyed aboriginal governments and infrastructures while forcing them to become increasingly dependent on the Crown.[43] As Douglas Sanders explains, 'The truth is that the Department is concerned with protecting itself against the Indians. That is understandable, politically, but cannot be reconciled with any trust obligations of the government.'[44] Meanwhile, any claim to impartiality on behalf of the Department of Justice in Canadian aboriginal rights jurisprudence cannot be substantiated by virtue of the fact that if an aboriginal rights issue is the basis of a court action against the federal Crown, the Department of Justice inevitably acts for the federal Crown, not the aboriginal peoples.

In the aftermath of the creation of the Indian Claims Commission, with its seemingly independent, watchdog-like mandate, it appeared as if there would be a greater assurance of impartiality with respect to rejected Specific Claims. However, the commission's limited authority and inability to bind the Crown in its findings ultimately renders it of little use in alleviating the problems caused by the conflict of interest inherent in the Specific Claims process. As Ovide Mercredi and Mary Ellen Turpel explain: 'Under the current policy, the Canadian government still continues to act as lawyer, judge and jury over claims we bring. No matter how you view the Indian Specific Claims Commission, the new Commissioner only has the power to recommend to government, not to reach settlements of disputes. The real control still resides with federal bureaucrats and ultimately with the Minister of Indian Affairs. The policy of control by the federal government has not changed. The paternalism is still there. The only change is the Commission's capacity to review administrative decisions that have been made against the interests of First Nations by bureaucrats.'[45]

What is required to eliminate the Crown's conflict of interest with regard to the Specific and Comprehensive Claims processes is to either broaden the existing mandate of the Indian Claims Commission, in consultation with the aboriginal peoples and their representatives, or to establish a new body which possesses the authority to assess the merits of claims submitted by Indian bands and provide decisions which are binding on the Crown while addressing aboriginal concerns of the deficiencies of the present commission.[46] Such a body could also be given the requisite jurisdiction to engage in binding dispute resolution of contentious matters arising between the aboriginal peoples and the Crown, including the issue of self-government. The vital element required of such a body is that it must possess the authority to investigate and adjudicate these matters and provide decisions which would be binding on all parties involved.

Another potential conflict of interest situation exists with regard to Indian moneys held in trust by the Crown and the Crown's obligations to Native peoples under treaties or other agreements. Under Section 61(1) of the Indian Act,[47] the Governor in Council has complete discretion to determine what uses Indian moneys under this section are to be put.[48] Where, for example, the Crown is obliged to provide enumerated services, such as a schoolhouse or health care, to an aboriginal band by virtue of a treaty or agreement, a conflict of interest situation arises where the Crown pays for these services out of Section 61(1) trust moneys instead of public moneys. Although the Crown must use Indian moneys 'only for the benefit of the Indians or bands for whose use and benefit in common the moneys are received or held,' it may not use Indian moneys to pay for services which it has pledged to provide by way of treaty or agreement. The rule against conflict of interest insists that the Crown must use its own funds, not those of the Indians, to pay for any obligations incurred in its own name.

Perhaps the ultimate conflict of interest on the part of the Crown arose from the inclusion of Section 149A to the Indian Act in 1927,[49] which made the raising of funds for the purposes of commencing legal action against the Crown an offence. This section effectively prevented legal action from being taken against the Crown by Indian bands without any prior determination of whether or not they possessed just claims. By virtue of its ultimate responsibility for Canadian affairs, the effect of Section 149A placed the Crown in an obvious conflict of interest situation.[50] The conflict may be seen to arise from the promulgation of and assent[51] to legislation which had the effect of insulating the Crown from potential liability at the direct expense of its aboriginal beneficiaries' interests.[52] Section 149A was finally repealed in 1951, but had a direct impact on the Crown–Native relationship for twenty-four years. This section also continues to affect aboriginal people's ability to maintain actions against the Crown in the face of 'ultimate limitation periods' and other statutory forms of limitation affecting aboriginal legal actions against the Crown, which continue to run despite this twenty-four-year 'prohibition' on aboriginal legal activity.

The spectre of conflict of interest is also raised by the Crown's duty to promote and protect the Native peoples' interests while simultaneously seeking to obtain surrenders of their lands at the lowest possible cost. This scenario is also a part of the larger rule which forbids fiduciaries from purchasing property under their control from their beneficiaries.[53] Over time the rigidity with which this rule has been enforced by the judiciary has weakened. It has been made subject to certain exceptions, such as where a trustee purchases trust property under the terms of a will, all of which seek to ensure the fair treatment of the beneficiary by the purchasing fiduciary. However, the issue of conflict relating to the Crown's purchase of Indian lands is more deeply rooted in the very heart of the Crown–Native relationship than in virtually any other fiduciary relation.

The Indian Act itself seeks to prohibit, at least in a limited way, the existence of conflict in the purchase of Indian lands. Section 53(3) of the Indian Act prohibits employees of the Department of Indian Affairs, or persons appointed by the minister to manage or sell surrendered Indian lands or to manage, lease, or carry out any other transaction affecting designated lands[54] from purchasing Indian lands without the approval of the Governor in Council.[55] Not surprisingly, there is no provision in the Indian Act, or elsewhere, which prohibits the Crown itself from purchasing Indian lands. Indeed, there are definite problems in the application of this principle of fiduciary doctrine to the Crown–Native relationship.

Under the general principle against fiduciaries purchasing property from their beneficiaries, though, the legitimacy of the Crown's acquisition of Indian lands in Canada is rendered questionable. This principle, at least at first blush, seems to place the Crown in breach of its fiduciary responsibilities to the aboriginal peoples where it obtains Indian lands for its own use,[56] or where it has extinguished or effectively continues to regulate aboriginal and treaty rights. There is also the problem which arises as a result of the Indian Act's requirement, under Section 37, that reserve lands cannot be alienated without first being surrendered to the Crown. How may the Crown obtain a surrender of Indian lands if it is prohibited from acquiring property belonging to its aboriginal beneficiaries? The act of surrender, under current jurisprudence, removes the Indian interest in land, leaving the land subject only to the Crown's complete, perfected title.[57] Therefore, even if only temporarily, the Crown acquires the full interest in Indian lands as soon as it accepts their surrender.

If the Crown cannot obtain such a surrender without breaching its fiduciary duties, does that entail that aboriginal peoples may not alienate their lands at all or does it merely render the operation of Section 37 void? It has been suggested that as a result of these problems, this principle of fiduciary doctrine cannot apply to reserve lands.[58] Another suggestion has been to exclude the rule against conflict of interest from Crown–Native fiduciary relations altogether.[59] Neither of these suggestions are valid solutions to the problem arising as a result of the *sui generis* nature of Crown–Native relations. In fact, the latter is outright dangerous to the interests of aboriginal peoples as the rule provides them with much needed protection against the actions of the Crown. To remove conflict-of-interest guidelines from Crown–Native relations would be tantamount to giving the Crown *carte blanche* to wilfully ignore its fiduciary responsibilities to the Native peoples.

The rule against conflict of interest is a fundamental principle of fiduciary doctrine. Its strict application maintains the integrity of fiduciary relations by providing a significant deterrence to fiduciaries who may be tempted to act indecorously. Whereas the essence of the rule may be simply stated, its precise application is quite complex. The peculiarities of the Crown–Native relationship only serve to further complicate the application of the rule. However, it, like all other fiduciary principles, is susceptible to adaptation to the requirements of specific situations and relationships. One such instance may occur where the Crown has a valid and demonstrated need to obtain Indian lands for public purposes or to regulate aboriginal and treaty rights. The justificatory test instituted for federal legislative initiatives established in *Sparrow* is another example of how the conflict-of-interest rule may be subject to exceptions resulting from the unique position of the Crown as a fiduciary to aboriginal peoples compared with the position of other fiduciaries *vis-à-vis* their beneficiaries.

The permissible range of exceptions under any justificatory test must be consistent with the theoretical basis of the conflict-of-interest rule's general prohibition of fiduciaries' actions which contravene their beneficiaries' interests. The *Sparrow* test, for example, insists that the creation of any limitations to Section 35(1) rights must arise only in circumstances in which they are *absolutely* necessary. The complex regulatory scheme fashioned by the Supreme Court in *Sparrow* is designed to allow only vitally important limitations to Section 35(1) rights to successfully navigate the *Sparrow* test's requirements.[60] Moreover, as the *Sparrow* test recognizes, any such exceptions must remain faithful to the nature of the Crown's fiduciary obligations to the aboriginal peoples.

Although the rule against conflict of interest is adaptable, it is much more harsh and inflexible than most other fiduciary principles. Consequently, it cannot be rendered inapplicable to specific facets of fiduciary relationships or removed from them altogether. As a result of its fiduciary obligations to Native peoples, the Crown must avoid situations where it places itself or is placed in a potential conflict of interest or else risk being found in breach of its duty. Where past conflicts of interest have occurred,[61] the Crown is liable for any breach of its duty to any wronged beneficiary. Where conflicts of interest already exist, such as in the Specific and Comprehensive Claims processes, the Crown must act to eliminate such conflicts by changing the dynamics giving rise to the conflict. In many circumstances, this may require the balancing of competing fiduciary considerations. Nevertheless, the Crown may not favour one fiduciary consideration over another or escape liability for the non-fulfilment of its obligations by citing competing fiduciary responsibilities.[62]

Another way for the Crown to remove a conflict is to eliminate the requirement that a band must make a surrender to the Crown in order to sell or lease its interest in land. The Crown may still make itself a requisite intermediary in the alienation of Indian land interests without the necessity of surrender. For example, it could require that any band wishing to enter into a sale or lease agreement with a private party must submit any such agreement to the minister for approval. More fundamentally, the need for the Crown to continue as a go-between in land transactions between aboriginal peoples and private parties might be reconsidered altogether.

The conflict of interest arising from the Crown's role in the alienation of Indian lands applies equally to the federal Comprehensive Claims process, where bands must relinquish their aboriginal rights in exchange for the rights contained in written claims settlements.[63] This requirement of the Comprehensive Claims process, insofar as it does not serve the best interests of the aboriginal peoples, but acts to their detriment,[64] amounts to a breach of the Crown's fiduciary duty.[65] By requiring a claimant band to surrender its aboriginal rights in exchange for enunciated rights, the band is forced to give up pre-existing rights which are not dependent on recognition by the Crown and that have the potential to be interpreted in an expansive manner[66] in exchange for circumscribed rights that are as expansive as they will ever be. Although the goal of clarifying the rights belonging to an aboriginal group is desirable, the means by which the existing process requires this clarification to take place is unacceptable, and particularly so in light of the Crown's general fiduciary duty to Native peoples and the constitutionalization of aboriginal rights in Section 35(1) of the Constitution Act, 1982.[67] Rather than requiring the aboriginal peoples to relinquish their aboriginal rights, as the current process mandates, the Crown needs to modify or redesign its process to respect existing aboriginal rights and incorporate them into the terms of any agreement reached between the Crown and a claimant band.[68]

The issue of the Crown's ability to escape liability for a breach of its fiduciary obligations by citing competing interests has not been raised often in Canadian aboriginal rights jurisprudence. However, the issue was one of the key aspects of the decision in *Kruger v R*.[69] Although it has not been generally recognized as particularly noteworthy, the *Kruger* case is a prime example of a Crown conflict of interest *vis-à-vis* its fiduciary obligations to aboriginal peoples. For this reason alone, the case deserves closer scrutiny.

15

The Practical Application of Fiduciary Doctrine in the Native Law Context: A Reappraisal of *Kruger v R*

The fact situation in *Kruger* is a prime example of the dilemma raise by the rule against conflict of interest. The federal Crown acquired two parcels of land (Parcel A and Parcel B, as per their designations by the courts) from the Penticton Indian Reserve No. 1 for use as an airport. The Penticton band maintained that the Crown had not properly acquired the two parcels of land, failed to provide them with adequate compensation for the land once it was taken, and pursued other interests ahead of its obligations to the band, thereby breaching its duty to the band. The band commenced an action against the federal Crown for damages for breach of trust and lost revenue. Alternatively, the band claimed damages for the Crown's wrongful taking of the land.

Parcel A had been the subject of extensive lease negotiations between the Department of Transport and the Department of Indian Affairs, acting on behalf of the Penticton Indian band. The Penticton band had surrendered Parcel A for lease according to the terms proposed by Indian Affairs. The Department of Transport objected to the terms of the proposed lease and, instead, expropriated Parcel A in 1938 without obtaining its surrender. Compensation for the expropriation of the land was only paid to the Penticton band in 1941. In 1942 Parcel B was sought by the Department of National Defence for Air in order to expand the air port. The department took possession of Parcel B in 1942, fenced it in, and began work on it even though it had yet to be acquired from the band. After fruitless negotiations over the land, Parcel B was expropriated in 1944. In 1946, as a result of an opinion by the deputy minister of justice that the land could not be obtained by expropriation, but only by surrender, the Department of Transport paid the band $15,000 for the surrender of Parcel B.

The fact situation in *Kruger* juxtaposed the federal Crown's concern as steward of the national interest, represented by its Department of Transport, with its fiduciary responsibility to act in the interests of Indians, represented by its Department of Indian Affairs. The *Kruger* scenario brought about a situation where the Crown was forced to wear its Department of Transport 'hat' in securing the land while simultaneously donning its Indian Affairs 'hat' to selflessly serve the best interests of the affected band. The judicial question to be determined was whether the Crown could successfully wear both hats at once without finding itself in conflict of interest stemming from its duty to the Penticton band.

A trial, the band's action was dismissed. Mahoney J determined that the Crown held title to the reserve lands in question under a legally enforceable trust for the band. He found that the Crown was not in breach of its duty to the band by deciding in favour of expropriating the land for use as an airport. He then held that both parcels of land were eligible for expropriation by the Crown for use as an airport and had been validly expropriated by the Crown for that purpose.

The Federal Court of Appeal upheld the trial judge's disposition of the matter. Urie JA, with Stone JA concurring, acknowledged that when the Crown expropriated the two parcels of land, the same type of fiduciary obligation was created towards the band as would have been created if the lands had been surrendered.[1] The nature of the Crown's obligations to the band was to ensure that the band was properly compensated for the loss of their lands. In accordance with the decision at trial, Urie JA found that the Crown had not breached its obligations to the band. The competing considerations of the Crown, namely, its position as steward of the national interest versus its fiduciary duty to act selflessly in the best interests of the appellants, rendered its actions justifiable under the circumstances: 'From the perspective of the Crown in its Department of Transport incarnation, there were competing considerations ... From these considerations and facts, the question which must be posed is, did the fact that the competing considerations were resolved in respect of both Parcels "A" and "B," with the concurrence of the Indians, on terms which were clearly compromises, not entirely satisfactory to either of the branches of the Crown involved, result in a breach of the Crown's fiduciary duty to the Indians entitling them to the remedies sought in this action? I think not.'[2]

Heald JA divided his consideration of the Crown's actions into the individual situations involving each of the parcels of land. He found that there were competing considerations between the two federal departments regarding Parcel A which resulted in the Crown's conflict of interest *vis-à-vis* its fiduciary obligations to the band. Heald JA based this conclusion on his understanding of fiduciary doctrine's rule against conflict of interest: 'The law is clear that "... one who undertakes a task on behalf of another must act exclusively for the benefit of the other, putting his own interests completely aside" and that "Equity fashioned the rule that no man may allow his duty to conflict with his interest." On this basis, the federal Crown cannot default on its fiduciary obligation to the Indians through a plea of competing considerations by different departments of governments.'[3]

In respect of Parcel B, Heald JA found that the exact same conflict of interest existed.[4] He determined that the negotiations surrounding the proposed surrender of Parcel B were inconsistent with the Crown's fiduciary duty to the band. The Crown failed to provide full disclosure of the pertinent facts, expropriated the land, and rendered no compensation for the taking 'in a timely fashion.'[5] Notwithstanding the presence of the Crown's competing interests, Heald JA concluded that the Crown was in breach of its fiduciary duty to the band by allowing its other interests to compete with those of the band: '[T]he Governor in Council is not able to default in its fiduciary relationship to the Indians on the basis of other priorities and other considerations.'[6] Nevertheless, he dismissed the appeal because of the lapse of the applicable limitations period.[7]

A Critical Analysis of *Kruger v R*

Although the judgments of Urie and Heald JJA in the Federal Court of Appeal's decision in *Kruger* both achieve the same end result, they differ in the manner in which they arrive at their respective conclusions. Urie JA's decision is based on his finding that the Crown was entitled to choose between its competing responsibilities without breaching its duty to the Penticton band. Heald JA disagreed with Urie JA's determination that the Crown did not breach its duty by choosing one of two competing fiduciary obligations. His dismissal of the band's appeal was based purely on procedural grounds. The only commonality in the two judgments is their misunderstanding of fiduciary doctrine; even so, the misunderstandings which plague each judgment are entirely different.

Urie JA's finding that the Crown was not in breach of its fiduciary duty to the band under the circumstances[8] was based on the conduct of individual governmental departments and not on the conduct of the federal Crown as a whole. The Crown's fiduciary duty to Native peoples is not a duty pertaining only to particular governmental departments or agencies, as Urie JA's judgment would appear to indicate. Rather, the duty belongs to the Crown as a whole.[9] Within the context of the *Kruger* scenario, the duty to the band was owed by the federal Crown and its various departments. Urie JA's decision not only ignored this fact, but blatantly contravened the principle of fiduciary doctrine which insists that a fiduciary may not favour one fiduciary consideration over another.[10]

Where the Crown, or any fiduciary, has competing fiduciary responsibilities, it must attempt to balance those duties by seeking ways in which it does not promote one interest at the direct expense of another. Of course, this is not always possible. Nevertheless, a bona fide attempt consistent with the fiduciary standard of *uberrima fides* must be made or else the fiduciary may be found in breach of duty. Any decision made by a fiduciary under these circumstances is subject to judicial review if the courts' intervention is sought by a beneficiary. The judiciary's function in such a situation is to assess whether the Crown, in attempting to balance its duties, acted with *uberrima fides* and maintained fidelity to its duties, even if it did not actually promote or further them as may be required. There is no ideal 'test' which applies to all circumstances of this sort. Although, in some circumstances, the fiduciary may only be required to act with honesty and reasonable prudence, this standard may not be sufficient in all situations.

Heald JA's determination that the existence of competing interests did not vindicate the Crown's breach of duty to the Penticton band is consistent with fiduciary doctrine's insistence that fiduciaries must not allow personal interests or those of third parties to interfere in the performance of their fiduciary obligations. As he explained in his judgment, 'Undoubtedly the Department of Transport had good and sufficient reason for requiring subject lands at an early date for its purposes but that circumstance did not relieve the federal Crown of its fiduciary duty to the Indians.'[11] Nevertheless, by finding that the causes of action in the matter before him could have been discovered had the band exercised reasonable diligence at the time the causes of action arose,[12] Heald JA reluctantly concluded that the band's cause of action was statute-barred.[13] The basis of his conclusion is in error of law, as beneficiaries are under no compulsion or obligation to inquire into the actions of their fiduciaries.[14] Moreover, the effect of statutory limitation periods on beneficiaries in fiduciary relationships is unique to those types of relation-

Practical Application: *Kruger v R* 277

ships and cannot be applied in the same manner as to other situations such as breach of contract.[15]

The Federal Court of Appeal's decision in *Kruger v R* is legitimately open to criticism. It is plagued by key errors of law which arise from its misunderstanding or misconception of fiduciary doctrine. The misunderstanding of fiduciary doctrine evident in the judgments of Urie and Heald JJA questions the authoritativeness of the *Kruger* decision, in particular its handling of the conflict-of-interest question. Indeed, the disposition of the case is wholly inconsistent with fundamental tenets of fiduciary doctrine and the theory proposed herein.[16] Although the *Apsassin* case[17] is also characterized by a conflict of interest, none of the court decisions in *Apsassin* dealt fully with the issue of the Crown's conflict of interest. Consequently, there is a pressing need to correct the mistaken assumptions present in the *Kruger* decision before its skewed notion of fiduciary doctrine becomes an authoritative judicial precedent.

A Reappraisal of *Kruger v R*

The theory of fiduciary doctrine proposed in Chapter 10 suggests that a fiduciary relationship exists when four elements are present. The situation in *Kruger* may be seen to encompass all four:

1 The Crown possessed the ability to affect the interests of the Penticton band, as indicated by its expropriation of part of the band's reserve lands.
2 The band's land interests within the confines of its relationship with the Crown may only have been served – in this instance negatively – through the Crown's actions, as no other party may acquire or expropriate Indian lands.
3 The Crown had an obligation to act in the band's best interests.
4 The band relied on the honesty, integrity, and fidelity of the Crown to fulfil its obligations to act in the band's best interests.

Although the relationship between the Crown and the Penticton band may be viewed as a fiduciary one, it remains to be seen whether the Crown's actions were consistent with its fiduciary obligations to the band.

Based on the further duties imposed on fiduciaries documented in Chapter 10, it may be concluded that the Crown did not fulfil its fiduciary obligations. It failed to act with honesty, integrity, and fidelity in fulfilling the best interests of the Penticton band. The Crown did not further the band's interests, but rather acted against those interests through its method of negotiating leases for the lands, by later expropriating the lands, and, finally, by not offering adequate compensation for taking the lands. The Crown also acted in conflict of interest by (1) benefiting from its position as fiduciary, which enabled it to expropriate the land; (2) failing to provide full disclosure of its activities to the band;[18] and (3) compromising the Penticton band's interests in favour of those of the Department of Transport.

Because of the Crown's failure to fulfil its fiduciary obligations to the band, the Penticton people were unable to enjoy the benefits rightfully belonging to them by virtue of their participation in the fiduciary relationship with the Crown. The band was entitled to rely on the Crown's honesty, integrity, and fidelity to its best interests and was not bound to inquire into the Crown's activities. The band was also able to commence legal action against the Crown once it discovered the cause of action without concern for the application of statutory limitations periods or laches as a result of the Crown's inequitable conduct and the continuous nature of the breach. Furthermore, fiduciary doctrine's reverse onus allowed the band to commence its action by alleging the Crown's breach of duty, placing the onus to discharge the allegation of breach on the Crown. On a finding of a breach of fiduciary duty by the Crown, the band was entitled to remedial aid from the Crown, which was liable for its breach of duty.

The appropriate remedy for the Crown's breach of duty to the Penticton band would have been the value of the loss suffered by the band as a result of the Crown's breach of duty plus the disgorging of any benefits obtained by the Crown from its breach of duty. This would amount to compensatory damages for the monetary value of the land as well as the value of any activities associated with the land.[19] The relevant considerations for determining the amount of compensation due should have included (1) the deprivation of the band's use of the expropriated land for hay and meadow, which eliminated the means of livelihood of many members of the band who were cattlemen; (2) the value of the lands taken, as indicated by Indian Agent A.H. Barber's comment that the expropriated lands were 'some of the best land on the reserve';[20] (3) the Penticton band's loss of income suffered prior to the Crown's acquisition of the land resulting from construction of the airport; (4) the effects of the airport (that is, noise, pollution, etc.) on the band's ability to use and enjoy the rest of its reserve lands; and (5) the disruption of the Penticton band's traditional way of life and its relocation to an area where it could resume that way of life.[21]

In addition to the above, punitive damages for the wilful breach of fiduciary obligations by the Crown, through its Department of Transport,[22] seem appropriate under the circumstances.[23] To justly compensate the band for the Crown's actions and its various losses suffered as a result, the forms of compensation owed to it by the Crown should have included a combination of monetary and punitive damages for the value of the land, loss of income, and the Crown's wrongful actions, as well as expenses for relocation and the purchase of new lands to enable the band to continue its traditional way of life.

The *Kruger* scenario could have been avoided entirely had the Crown taken reasonable steps to accommodate the band's wishes. Prior to expropriating the land, the Crown should have weighed the effects of its desire to expropriate the Penticton band's land with the anticipated effects that the taking of the land would have on the band. A careful consideration of the competing interests and costs involved – in a manner similar to the requirements outlined in the *Sparrow* test – would determine whether the band's land was absolutely needed. This would involve a consideration of the need to build the airport, to build it in that vicinity, and whether it had to be built on the band's land with no other sites being suitable or available in substitution. The Crown's fiduciary duty to the band required it to minimize any detrimental effects on the band. This required determining, before the act of expropriation in each instance, what the detrimental effects to the Penticton people would be and how to either avoid them entirely or minimize their impact. The greater the potential detriment to the Penticton band, the greater the onus would be on the Crown to demonstrate the need to take its lands.

If land in that vicinity was needed and no other land could have been substituted, the Crown was obligated to consult with the band to determine the method by which to adequately and swiftly compensate or otherwise accommodate it for its various losses suffered as a result of the taking of the land. If a voluntary settlement could not be reached, the Crown must have acted in accordance with the importance of its project to build the airport. The cost of compensating the Penticton band should have been directly tied to the importance of the project and the Crown's need to obtain the band's land. As the Crown's fiduciary duty required it to protect and promote the well-being of its beneficiaries, it was obliged to have provided fair and expeditious payment of compensation to the band.

Had the Crown heeded the advice given by the Department of Indian Affairs rather than concentrating exclusively on the Department of Transport's desire to obtain the band's land at the lowest possible price, the entire situation that arose could easily have been avoided. As Heald JA explained in his judgment: 'If there was evidence in the record to indicate that careful consideration and due weight had been given to the pleas and representations by Indian Affairs on behalf of the Indians and, thereafter, an offer of settlement reflecting those representations had been made, I would have viewed the matter differently.'[24]

16

Prospects for the Future

The fiduciary character of Crown–Native relations was fostered by the *sui generis* nature of the relationship from the time of contact through to the present day. The relationship is unusual in a number of respects. From its origins, it has carried a certain antagonistic quality as a result of the intertwined, though often disparate, interests of the parties. The groups were forced into a synergistic relationship despite the adverse nature of their interests resulting from the characteristics of the post-contact period leading up to the British conquest in 1760–1.

The relationship between the Crown and aboriginal peoples arose from the Crown's dependency on the latter. The increasing physical presence of the Crown and the formation of military, political, and economic alliances between the groups balanced out the power relations between them. Over time, the combined factors of disease, war, colonial expansion, and reliance on European manufactured goods took their toll on the Native peoples. These factors, combined with the removal of France as a major player in the North American political and economic scene, resulted in the aboriginals losing their roles as catalysts in the struggle for North American supremacy. Shortly thereafter, they were forced into an increasingly more subordinate position *vis-à-vis* the Crown by virtue of the Crown's colonialist practices.

At various stages in their relationship, each of the groups possessed the ability to affect the other's interests. Moreover, each was entirely dependent on the other for significant periods. During the pre-conquest North American political chess match, the Crown's desire to achieve military and economic supremacy over its European rivals could only be satisfied with the aid of the Native peoples. The military, political, and economic alliances formed between the Crown and Native peoples were concrete manifestations of their interdependency and created their obligations to act in the other's interests. Following the conquest, the aboriginal peoples became dependent on the Crown to protect their lands and rights from increasing non-aboriginal interference. The pre-conquest alliances that had been forged between the groups fell into disrepair as the Crown no longer deemed them to be politically necessary or expedient. It replaced its policy of recognizing aboriginal peoples as sovereign and independent nations with a colonial policy of assimilation and forced dependence.

Even though they may not have trusted each other entirely and often engaged in political subterfuge, both the Crown and the Native peoples placed considerable reliance on each other as a result of the unique circumstances that gave rise to their pre-conquest interdependent relationship. The present-day interaction between the groups is merely the latest incarnation of an evolving historical relationship. The formative years of Crown–Native relations are what give rise to the Crown's general fiduciary duty towards the Native peoples. Whereas the precise nature of this relationship has undergone various changes since its origins, the obligations underlying it have remained constant. Therefore, these obligations must be accounted for in the totality of the relationship from the time of contact, not just in isolated snapshots of it which are frozen at a particular point in time.

Describing the fiduciary nature of the Crown–Native relationship as merely the replication of the hierarchical relationship between the parties created by the Crown's colonialist practices ignores the reason why the relationship became a fiduciary one in the first place. Although the Crown's imposition of the Indian Act and other assimilationist practices on the aboriginal peoples may have created a sufficient basis for a guardian–ward type of fiduciary relation, it ignores the fact that a fiduciary relationship based on mutuality and nation-to-nation relations already existed. In fact, that sovereign relationship had existed for quite some time when British colonialism came into full effect in the nineteenth century.

Chapter 14 has discussed some of the more fundamental characteristics of the Crown–Native fiduciary relationship. In the absence of context, it is impossible to do the same thing for specific fiduciary relations between the Crown and aboriginal peoples. Similarly, it is impossible to delineate the totality of obligations which may arise under specific relationships without a contextual understanding of the participants' interaction. What may be asserted is that the Crown's fiduciary obligations to

Native peoples, in a general or specific context, encompass the range of areas in which the Crown has had and continues to have contact with Native peoples. The Crown's fiduciary obligations to the aboriginal peoples are derived from its responsibilities arising either (1) by the Crown's assumption of responsibility to act in the interests of the Aboriginal peoples of Canada; (2) by way of the Crown's own conduct or actions, such as under treaties or other agreements; (3) as a result of general or specific Crown–Native relations; or (4) by their imposition by the courts. By virtue of the fiduciary nature of its relationship with Native peoples, the Crown is duty-bound to fulfil these obligations and avoid conflicts of interest. Moreover, in accordance with the *prescriptive* understanding of fiduciary doctrine and the functional approach to fiduciary doctrine used herein, these obligations must be fulfilled in a purposive manner.

Implementing a functional approach to fiduciary doctrine eliminates the false impressions about the nature of fiduciary relationships that have been generated by the categorical approach generally used. Indeed, attempts to explain the nebulous fiduciary relation through the use of categories of acceptable classes of fiduciary relationships have often caused, rather than alleviated, confusion. The categorical approach has led many to believe that fiduciary relations are restricted to the paradigms established in their illustrations. Attempting to forge similarities between new and established forms of fiduciary relations, or between corporate and personal fiduciary relations, is not particularly useful or effective because of the tremendous differences between the relationships being compared. The functional approach's focus on the unique circumstances specific to individual fiduciary relationships rather than fashioning a priori assumptions based on generalizations removes the confusion caused by the categorical approach while simultaneously allowing for a contextual appraisal of fiduciary relationships.

By focusing on the entirety of the Crown–Native relationship, for example, the functional approach enables that relationship to be understood both for the duties and obligations that are owed, as well as for the benefits to be received. It allows some of the previously untreated questions relating to the scope of the Crown's duty to be answered. Moreover, as a situation-specific approach, it is reflective of the full extent of the Crown's obligations.

Although the special relationship between the groups has been recognized for quite some time, its precise nature and legal ramifications are just beginning to be understood. The Crown's general fiduciary duty to aboriginal peoples has been demonstrated to be a continuing duty belonging to both the federal and provincial Crowns in Canada.[1] The Crown's duty has also been shown to be generally applicable to the Crown–Native relationship, not just to the surrender of aboriginal lands. More particularly, the Crown's fiduciary duty to the aboriginal peoples may be seen to apply to the following areas (although not limited to them exclusively):

1 Aboriginal lands.
   These should include any lands which Native peoples have an interest in, such as traditional lands, reserve lands (even in situations where a band manages its reserve lands in accordance with Section 60(1) of the Indian Act), treaty land entitlements, and lands surrendered for leasing.
2 Aboriginal moneys.
   The Crown's duty applies, for instance, to the management of Indian band funds and may also apply in situations where a band manages its own funds in accordance with Section 69(1) of the Indian Act.
3 Aboriginal self-government.
   This may include the Crown's obligation to provide funding, administrative services, and supervise the transition to self-government.
4 Aboriginal hunting, fishing, trapping, and agricultural rights.
   This includes wild rice harvesting and may also include the commercial right to hunt and fish.[2]
5 Aboriginal customs, languages, and cultures.
   These may be grouped together with the issue of self-government and may include the requirement that the Crown provide funding in conjunction with the protection of these rights under various treaties and agreements.
6 Resolution of outstanding Native rights claims.
   This includes the Crown's negotiation of such issues (pertaining to both aboriginal and treaty rights) in good faith, avoiding existing and future conflicts of interest, providing funding for aboriginal rights litigation, and creating and/or funding impartial dispute resolution mechanisms.
7 Native health, welfare, and education.
   Provision for these should be as promised under treaties and may include (1) the building of schoolhouses and/or provision of teachers; (2) the provision of hospitals, medical services, or medicines

in accordance with medicine-chest clauses or other provisions; and (3) the provision of adequate housing, sewage, and other waste disposal systems.
8 The range of issues covered by the Indian Act.
The Indian Act was held to codify some of the Crown's fiduciary obligations to aboriginal peoples in *Guerin v R*,[3] *Roberts v Canada*,[4] and *Mitchell v Peguis Indian Band*.[5] These items include provisions dealing with Indian band lists, reserves, surrenders, wills and estates, mental incompetents, minors, and the management of Indian lands and moneys.
9 Aboriginal economic self-sufficiency and development.
This includes Crown obligations arising (1) from the Crown's acquisition of lands, resources, and minerals at the direct expense of its aboriginal beneficiaries; (2) under the terms of treaties whereby the Crown agreed to provide money, tools, livestock, farm implements, and so on to the aboriginal signatories; and (3) from the requirements necessary for the transition to Native self-government.
10 Any other rights which may exist by way of treaty, agreement, statute, constitutional enactment or amendment, Crown practice, or that may be found to exist by the courts.
For instance, in *Eastmain Band v Robinson*,[6] the Crown's fiduciary duty was found to include a duty to follow the Environmental Assessment and Review Process Guidelines Order (EARP guidelines).[7] On appeal, however, the trial decision, including the duty to follow the EARP guidelines, was reversed: see *Eastmain Band v Canada (Federal Administrator)*.[8]

In appropriate circumstances, an aboriginal nation may be entitled to bring a claim for breach of fiduciary duty against the Crown based on its general or specific fiduciary obligations or a combination thereof. The Crown's two-pronged fiduciary duty to Native peoples becomes particularly important where, for example, the Crown entices an aboriginal nation into signing a land surrender treaty under the false threat of being unable or unwilling to protect the nation's land from non-aboriginal encroachment. Historical accounts of the negotiations behind many Indian treaties in Canada and archival research of correspondence in this regard indicate numerous occurrences of this practice.[9] The Crown's negotiation of a treaty under such pretences is a prima facie breach of the Crown's general obligation to act in the aboriginal nation's best interests and the specific obligations contained within the Royal Proclamation of 1763. However, the likelihood of such an argument succeeding in the Canadian courts is minimal at the present time.

Any judicial determination that the Crown acted in breach of its fiduciary duty in such a situation would likely be stunted by a 'floodgates' argument – namely, that by allowing one such claim to succeed, a rash of similar claims would follow. The prima facie breach of the Crown's fiduciary duty in this situation is magnified where an aboriginal nation that had been granted a reserve under a land surrender treaty is coerced into a second surrender of much of their reserve lands under the Crown's false threat of being unable or unwilling to protect those lands. In this latter scenario, however, the floodgates argument may be avoided entirely where the Crown is found to have acted in bad faith.

One example of this latter situation surrounds Treaty No. 72 signed by the Chippewas of Saugeen and Nawash in 1854. Eighteen years earlier, the Chippewas had surrendered 1.5 million acres of their territory to the Crown under Treaty No. 45½ in exchange for a reserve of 450,000 acres. The treaty stipulated that the reserve was to be protected from non-aboriginal encroachment.[10] Shortly after signing the treaty, the Chippewas began complaining to the Crown that their reserve was being encroached upon by squatters and that timber was being cut and removed from it. No action was taken with regard to the complaints. However, in 1854, the Crown sought a further surrender of land from the Chippewas. They were informed by T.G. Anderson, the superintendent of Indian Affairs, that unless they surrendered some of the lands that had been reserved to them under the 1836 treaty, the Crown would not protect those lands from non-aboriginal encroachment as has been promised:[11] 'You complain that the whites not only cut and take timber from your lands but that they are commencing to settle upon it and you can't prevent them, and I certainly do not think the Government will take the trouble to help you while you remain thus opposed to your own interest – the Government as your guardian have the power to act as it pleases with your reserve ... if it is not sold the trees and the land will be taken from you by your white neighbours and your children will then be left without resource.'[12]

As a result of the Crown's position regarding their complaints, the Chippewas surrendered much of their remaining reserve land to the Crown under Treaty No. 72 in October 1854. On closer inspection of the circumstances following the signing of the treaty, it appears that the Crown's failure to protect the Chippewas' lands was based more on its unwillingness rather than any inability to do so. This assertion is corrob-

Prospects for the Future 287

orated by the fact that immediately after the conclusion of Treaty No. 72, the superintendent-general of Indian Affairs issued a notice warning squatters not to trespass on the newly surrendered lands. He also enlisted the aid of the sheriff in the vicinity to police the area and enforce the Crown's exclusive right to the lands. No such actions had been taken prior to the signing of Treaty No. 72.[13]

This situation potentially renders the Crown liable for breaching both its general and specific, Proclamation-based, duties to the Chippewas by entering into either the 1836 or 1854 treaties. In addition to constituting a prima facie breach of these duties, the Crown may also be liable for breaching the specific obligations that it had incurred under the 1836 treaty by entering into the 1854 treaty.[14] Because of its subsequent actions to protect the lands surrendered under Treaty No. 72 from squatters, the Crown appears to have had the ability to have protected them from non-aboriginal encroachment prior to signing the second treaty. Consequently, the Crown's initial failure to protect the lands and later inducing the Chippewas into a further surrender under false pretenses strongly suggests that the Crown may have breached its fiduciary duty.[15] As one author commented on the Crown's activities surrounding the signing of Treaty No. 72, 'The Crown was prepared to use the legal subterfuge of wardship to steal our lands.'[16]

The basis of the breach of fiduciary duty argument against the Crown in this situation is that the Crown assumes a fiduciary duty to aboriginal peoples through the promises it makes in exchange for the surrender of aboriginal lands. Where the Crown incurs specific obligations under a treaty and then seeks to subvert those obligations in a subsequent treaty, it may be found in breach of its general duty to act in its aboriginal beneficiaries' best interests, as well as its specific duties outlined in the Royal Proclamation of 1763 and the terms of the initial treaty. However, by basing the allegation of breach on the specific obligations contained within the initial treaty, the basis of the action is situation-specific and not generally available to other aboriginal groups, thereby eliminating the floodgates argument as a consideration. By eliminating the floodgates argument that a claim of breach of duty based on the Crown's general or Proclamation-based duties unavoidably carries with it, a court's reluctance to rule in favour of a breach of the Crown's fiduciary duty in the situation considered above may be significantly reduced. This is one example of how the general discussion of Crown–Native fiduciary relations contained herein may be rendered applicable to specific situations of potential breaches of the Crown's fiduciary obligations to individual aboriginal groups or bands.

The primary goal of this work has been to further the understanding of the nexus between fiduciary doctrine and the Crown–Native relationship in Canada. To accomplish this end, it has provided guidelines for the application of fiduciary doctrine to that relationship and demonstrated the effects of fiduciary doctrine on it. In so doing, it has departed from the unquestioning application of the *Guerin* precedent to Crown–Native relations that has resulted in the creation and proliferation of a jurisprudentially vacuous fiduciary relationship between the parties.

The inherently flexible and situation-specific principles and characteristics of fiduciary doctrine provide appropriate guidelines to a reasoned and doctrinally sound method of examining the *sui generis* Crown–Native relationship. The binding nature of fiduciary doctrine on the Crown, as well as its greater recognition of the nation-to-nation basis of Crown–Native relations renders it a preferable vehicle for monitoring the parties' interaction than other means, such as international law.[17] Through the application of fiduciary doctrine, certain important elements of the Crown–Native relationship become evident. The rule against delegation – in particular the notion that fiduciaries' may not delegate the entirety of their fiduciary responsibilities – demonstrates that, to varying degrees and extents, the British, federal, and provincial Crowns all possess fiduciary obligations to aboriginal peoples in Canada. The breach of duty on the transfer of powers and responsibilities over Canadian affairs beginning at Confederation stems from the failure to comply with the requirements that fiduciaries not benefit from their positions, provide full disclosure of their fiduciary activities, and not compromise their beneficiaries' interests.

The nature and extent of fiduciaries' responsibilities to their beneficiaries and the requirement that the former act in the latter's best interests prohibit the Crown from unilaterally terminating or reducing the scope of its obligations to the Native peoples, even in the face of aboriginal self-government. The Crown's duty to consult with its aboriginal beneficiaries comes into play where the Crown seeks to transfer or vacate a previously controlled area to allow for the exercise of aboriginal control over various areas of Indian affairs, including self-government. The duty to consult also plays a vital role in satisfying the purposive nature of the Crown's duty. The purposive nature of the Crown's duty renders it responsible for determining the aboriginals' best interests and to actively promote those interests through consultation with the aboriginal peoples. It also requires that the Crown avoid placing itself in situations of conflict of interest and eliminate existing conflicts, such as those resulting from the existing Specific and Comprehensive Claims processes.

Fiduciary doctrine is a vital element of the relationship between the Crown and aboriginal peoples in Canada. It enjoys widespread application within the confines of that relationship and has the potential to expand even further as the relationship continues to evolve. The implications and ramifications of fiduciary doctrine upon the Crown–Native relationship permeate virtually every aspect of the intercourse between the Crown and aboriginal peoples. However, the importance of the Crown–Native fiduciary relationship is not reflected in the current level of understanding by judicial and academic commentators.

This book has suggested a process designed to enhance the understanding of the confluence of fiduciary doctrine and aboriginal rights jurisprudence required by the nature of Crown–Native relations. The historical, political, legislative, and legal background of the relationship and the general premises underlying fiduciary doctrine provide the parameters for clarifying the application of fiduciary doctrine to the Crown–Native relationship. Meanwhile, the application of fiduciary doctrine empowers aboriginal peoples in their relations with the Crown. It is based on the origins of the parties' interaction and reflects the nation-to-nation relationship between them that gave rise to their fiduciary relationship. If the aboriginal peoples were not sovereign nations during the formative years of Crown–Native relations, there would not have been any treaties, compacts, alliances, or agreements between the parties, at least not in the manner and form that they actually took.

During the process of clarifying the precise nature of the Crown–Native fiduciary relationship through examining its historical, political, social, and legal elements, answers to many of the questions which have been ignored by judicial and academic considerations of the Crown Native fiduciary relationship have been proffered to provide a foundation for further discourse in this area. Ultimately, future Canadian aboriginal rights jurisprudence will dictate the direction which this area of law will follow.[18] The discussion herein suggests a basis from which to launch its progression down the path of knowledge and understanding.

The fiduciary relationship between the Crown and aboriginal peoples in Canada is sacred ground on which the participants may trace their paths from the time of contact. It carries the historical relationships, solemn commitments, and mutual obligations between the parties as its fundamental premise. It is reflected in the words, promises, and actions of persons long since deceased and will continue through those of persons yet to be born. Moreover, this overarching relationship is largely responsible for the present status of Canada, both in its triumphs and in its failures.

In accordance with the Supreme Court of Canada's direction in *R v Sparrow*,[19] and the solemnity with which the Crown–Native relationship deserves to be observed, future juridical considerations of the Crown's fiduciary duty to aboriginal peoples ought to adopt a purposive approach to the issues canvassed in this book and those which will inevitably arise on further consideration of the Crown–Native fiduciary relationship. Adopting this approach will enable these examinations to augment or clarify many of the conclusions reached herein by rendering them applicable to the specific circumstances envisaged by particular Crown–Native relationships. It will also foster a growth in the appreciation and understanding of the *sui generis* nature of the Crown–Native fiduciary relationship in a manner consistent with the duty and honour of the Crown and the requirement of *uberrima fides*. This is what is needed if the Crown is to live up to the honour of its solemn commitments, which requires that it act in a manner consistent with their spirit and intent, not just their letter.[20]

APPENDIX 1

Statement of the Government of Canada on Indian Policy, 1969

To be an Indian is to be a man, with all a man's needs and abilities. To be an Indian is also to be different. It is to speak different languages, draw different pictures, tell different tales and to rely on a set of values developed in a different world.

Canada is richer for its Indian component, although there have been times when diversity seemed of little value to many Canadians.

But to be a Canadian Indian today is to be someone different in another way. It is to be someone apart – apart in law, apart in the provision of government services and, too often, apart in social contacts.

To be an Indian is to lack power – the power to act as owner of your lands, the power to spend your own money and, too often, the power to change your own condition.

Not always, but too often, to be an Indian is to be without – without a job, a good house, or running water; without knowledge, training or technical skill and, above all, without those feelings of dignity and self-confidence that a man must have if he is to walk with his head held high.

All these conditions of the Indians are the product of history and have nothing to do with their abilities and capacities. Indian relations with other Canadians began with special treatment by government and society, and special treatment has been the rule since Europeans first settled in Canada. Special treatment has made of the Indians a community disadvantaged and apart.

Obviously, the course of history must be changed.

To be an Indian must be to be free – free to develop Indian cultures in an environment of legal, social, and economic quality with other Canadians.

Foreword

The Government believes that its policies must lead to the full, free and non-discriminatory participation of the Indian people in Canadian society. Such a goal requires a break with the past. It requires that the Indian people's role of dependence be replaced by a role of equal status, opportunity and responsibility, a role they can share with all other Canadians.

This proposal is a recognition of the necessity made plain in a year's intensive discussions with Indian people throughout Canada. The Government believes that to continue its past course of action would not serve the interests of either the Indian people or their fellow Canadians.

The policies proposed recognize the simple reality that the separate legal status of Indians and the policies which have flowed from it have kept the Indian people apart from and behind other Canadians. The Indian people have not been full citizens of the communities and provinces in which they live and have not enjoyed the equality and benefits that such participation offers.

The treatment resulting from their different status has been often worse, sometimes equal and occasionally better than that accorded to their fellow citizens. What matters is that it has been different.

Many Indians, both in isolated communities and in cities, suffer from poverty. The discrimination which affects the poor, Indian and non-Indian alike, when compounded with a legal status that sets the Indian apart, provides dangerously fertile ground for social and cultural discrimination.

In recent years there has been a rapid increase in the Indian population. Their health and education levels have improved. There has been a corresponding rise in expectations that the structure of separate treatment cannot meet. A forceful and articulate Indian leadership has developed to express the aspirations and needs of the Indian community. Given the opportunity, the Indian people can realize an immense human and cultural potential that will enhance their own well-being, that of the regions in which they live and of Canada as a whole. Faced with a continuation of past policies, they will unite only in a common frustration.

The Government does not wish to perpetuate policies which carry with them the seeds of disharmony and disunity, policies which prevent Canadians from fulfilling themselves and contributing to their society. It seeks a partnership to achieve a better goal. The partners in this search are the Indian people, the governments of the provinces, the Canadian community as a whole and the Government of Canada. As all partnerships do, this will require consultation, negotiation, give and take, and co-operation if it is to succeed.

Many years will be needed. Some efforts may fail, but learning comes from failure and from what is learned success may follow. All the partners have to learn; all will have to change many attitudes.

Governments can set examples, but they cannot change the hearts of men.

Canadians, Indians and non-Indians alike stand at the crossroads. For Canadian society the issue is, whether a growing element of its population will become full participants contributing in a positive way to the general well-being or whether, conversely, the present social and economic gap will lead to their increasing frustration and isolation, a threat to the general well-being of society. For many Indian people, one road does exist, the only road that has existed since Confederation and before, the road of different status, a road which has led to a blind alley of deprivation and frustration. This road, because it is a separate road, cannot lead to full participation, to equality in practice as well as in theory. In the pages which follow, the Government has outlined a number of measures and a policy which it is convinced will offer another road for Indians, a road that would lead gradually away from different status to full social, economic and political participation in Canadian life. This is the choice.

Indian people must be persuaded, must persuade themselves, that this path will lead them to a fuller and richer life. Canadian society as a whole will have to recognize the need for changed attitudes and a truly open society. Canadians should recognize the dangers of failing to strike down the barriers which frustrate Indian people. If Indian people are to become full members of Canadian society they must be warmly welcomed by that society.

The Government commends this policy for the consideration of all Canadians, Indians and non-Indians, and all governments in Canada.

Summary

1 *Background*

The Government has reviewed its programs for Indians and has considered the effects of them on the present situation of the Indian people. The review has drawn on extensive consultations with the Indian people, and on the knowledge and experience of many people both in and out of government.

This review was a response to things said by the Indian people at the consultation meetings which began a year ago and culminated in a meeting in Ottawa in April.

This review has shown that this is the right time to change long-standing policies. The Indian people have shown their determination that present conditions shall not persist.

Opportunities are present today in Canadian society and new directions are open. The Government believes that Indian people must not be shut out of Canadian life and must share equally in these opportunities.

The Government could press on with the policy of fostering further education; could go ahead with physical improvement programs now operating in reserve communities; could press forward in the directions of recent years, and eventually many of the problems would be solved. But progress would be too slow. The change in Canadian society in recent years has been too great and continues too rapidly for this to be the answer. Something more is needed. We can no longer perpetuate the separation of Canadians. Now is the time to change.

This Government believes in equality. It believes that all men and women have equal rights. It is determined that all shall be treated fairly and that no one shall be shut out of Canadian life, and especially that no one shall be shut out because of his race.

This belief is the basis for the Government's determination to open the doors of opportunity to *all* Canadians, to remove the barriers which impede the development of people, of regions and of the country.

Only a policy based on this belief can enable the Indian people to realize their needs and aspirations.

The Indian people are entitled to such a policy. They are entitled to an equality which preserves and enriches Indian identity and distinction; an equality which stresses Indian participation in its creation and which manifests itself in all aspects of Indian life.

The goals of the Indian people cannot be set by others; they must spring from the Indian community itself – but government can create a framework within which all persons and groups can seek their own goals.

2 *The New Policy*

True equality presupposes that the Indian people have the right to full and equal participation in the cultural, social, economic and political life of Canada.

The government believes that the framework within which individual Indians and bands could achieve full participation requires:

1. that the legislative and constitutional bases of discrimination be removed;
2. that there be positive recognition by everyone of the unique contribution of Indian culture to Canadian life;
3. that services come through the same channels and from the same government agencies for all Canadians;
4. that those who are furthest behind be helped most;
5. that lawful obligations be recognized;
6. that control of Indian lands be transferred to the Indian people.

Appendices 295

The Government would be prepared to take the following steps to create this framework:

1 Propose to Parliament that the Indian Act be repealed and take such legislative steps as may be necessary to enable Indians to control Indian lands and to acquire title to them.
2 Propose to the governments of the provinces that they take over the same responsibility for Indians that they have for other citizens in their provinces. The take-over would be accompanied by the transfer to the provinces of federal funds normally provided for Indian programs, augmented as may be necessary.
3 Make substantial funds available for Indian economic development as an interim measure.
4 Wind up that part of the Department of Indian Affairs and Northern Development which deals with Indian affairs. The residual responsibilities of the Federal Government for programs in the field of Indian affairs would be transferred to other appropriate federal departments.

In addition, the Government will appoint a Commissioner to consult with the Indians and to study and recommend acceptable procedures for the adjudication of claims.

The new policy looks to a better future for all Indian people wherever they may be. The measures for implementation are straightforward. They require discussion, consultation and negotiation with the Indian people – individuals, bands and associations – and with provincial governments.

Success will depend upon the co-operation and assistance of the Indians and the provinces. The Government seeks this co-operation and will respond when it is offered.

3 *The Immediate Steps*

Some changes could take place quickly. Others would take longer. It is expected that within five years the Department of Indian Affairs and Northern Development would cease to operate in the field of Indian affairs; the new laws would be in effect and existing programs would have been devolved. The Indian lands would require special attention for some time. The process of transferring control to the Indian people would be under continuous review.

The Government believes this is a policy which is just and necessary. It can only be successful if it has the support of the Indian people, the provinces, and all Canadians.

The policy promises all Indian people a new opportunity to expand and develop their identity within the framework of a Canadian society which offers them the rewards and responsibilities of participation, the benefits of involvement and the pride of belonging.

Historical Background

The weight of history affects us all, but it presses most heavily on the Indian people. Because of history, Indians today are the subject of legal discrimination; they have grievances because of past undertakings that have been broken or misunderstood; they do not have full control of their lands; and a higher proportion of Indians than other Canadians suffer poverty in all its debilitating forms. Because of history too, Indians look to a special department of the Federal Government for many of the services that other Canadians get from provincial or local governments.

This burden of separation has its origin deep in Canada's past and in early French and British colonial policy. The elements which grew to weigh so heavily were deeply entrenched at the time of Confederation.

Before that time there had evolved a policy of entering into agreements with the Indians, of encouraging them to settle on reserves held by the Crown for their use and benefit, and of dealing with Indian lands through a separate organization – a policy of treating Indian people as a race apart.

After Confederation, these well-established precedents were followed and expanded. Exclusive legislative authority was given the Parliament of Canada in relation to 'Indians, and Lands reserved for the Indians' under Head 24 of Section 91 of the British North America Act. Special legislation – an Indian Act – was passed, new treaties were entered into, and a network of administrative offices spread across the country either in advance of or along with the tide of settlement.

This system – special legislation, a special land system and separate administration for the Indian people – continues to be the basis of present Indian policy. It has saved for the Indian people places they can call home, but has carried with it serious human and physical as well as administrative disabilities.

Because the system was in the hands of the Federal Government, the Indians did not participate in the growth of provincial and local services. They were not required to participate in the development of their own communities which were tax exempt. The result was that the Indians, persuaded that property taxes were an unnecessary element in their lives, did not develop services for themselves. For many years such simple and limited services as were required to sustain life were provided through a network of Indian agencies reflecting the authoritarian tradition of a colonial administration, and until recently these agencies had staff and funds to do little more than meet the most severe cases of hardship and distress.

The tradition of federal responsibility for Indian matters inhibited the development of a proper relationship between the provinces and the Indian people as citizens. Most provinces, faced with their own problems of growth and change, left responsibility for their Indian residents to the Federal Government. Indeed, successive Federal Governments did little to change the pattern. The result was that Indians were the almost exclusive concern of one agency of the Federal Government for nearly a century.

For a long time the problems of physical, legal and administrative separation attracted little attention. The Indian people were scattered in small groups across the country, often in remote areas. When they were in contact with the new settlers, there was little difference between the living standards of the two groups.

Initially, settlers as well as Indians depended on game, fish and fur. The settlers, however, were more concerned with clearing land and establishing themselves and differences soon began to appear.

With the technological change of the twentieth century, society became increasingly industrial and complex, and the separateness of the Indian people became more evident. Most Canadians moved to the growing cities, but the Indians remained largely a rural people, lacking both education and opportunity. The land was being developed rapidly, but many reserves were located in places where little development was possible. Reserves were usually excluded from development and many began to stand out as islands of poverty. The policy of separation had become a burden.

The legal and administrative discrimination in the treatment of Indian people has not given them an equal chance of success. It has exposed them to discrimination in the broadest and worst sense of the term – a discrimination that has profoundly affected their confidence that success can be theirs. Discrimination breeds discrimination by example, and the separateness of Indian people has affected attitudes of other Canadians towards them.

The system of separate legislation and administration has also separated people of Indian ancestry into three groups – registered Indians, who are further divided into those who are under treaty and those who are not, enfranchised Indians who lost, or voluntarily relinquished, their legal status as Indians; and the Métis, who are of Indian ancestry but never had the status of registered Indians.

The Case for the New Policy

In the past ten years or so, there have been important improvements in education, health, housing, welfare and community development. Developments in leadership among the Indian communities have become increasingly evident. Indian people have begun to forge a new unity. The Government believes progress can come from these developments but only if they are met by new responses. The proposed policy is a new response.

The policy rests upon the fundamental right of Indian people to full and equal participation in the cultural, social, economic and political life of Canada.

To argue against this right is to argue *for* discrimination, isolation and separation. No Canadian should be excluded from participation in community life, and none should expect to withdraw and still enjoy the benefits that flow to those who participate.

1 *The Legal Structure*

Legislative and constitutional bases of discrimination must be removed.

Canada cannot seek the just society and keep discriminatory legislation on its statute books. The Government believes this to be self-evident. The ultimate aim of removing the specific references to Indians from the constitution may take some time, but it is a goal to be kept constantly in view. In the meantime, barriers created by special legislation can generally be struck down.

Under the authority of Head 24, Section 91 of the British North America Act, the Parliament of Canada has enacted the Indian Act. Various federal–provincial agreements and some other statutes also affect Indian policies.

In the long term, removal of the reference in the constitution would be necessary to end the legal distinction between Indians and other Canadians. In the short term, repeal of the Indian Act and enactment of transitional legislation to ensure the orderly management of Indian land would do much to mitigate the problem.

The ultimate goal could not be achieved quickly, for it requires a change in the economic circumstances of the Indian people and much preliminary adjustment with provincial authorities. Until the Indian people are satisfied that their land holdings are solely within their control, there may have to be some special legislation for Indian lands.

2 *The Indian Cultural Heritage*

There must be positive recognition by everyone of the unique contribution of Indian culture to Canadian society.

It is important that Canadians recognize and give credit to the Indian contribution. It manifests itself in many ways; yet it goes largely unrecognized and unacknowledged. Without recognition by others it is not easy to be proud.

All of us seek a basis for pride in our own lives, in those of our families and of our ancestors. Man needs such pride to sustain him in the inevitable hour of discouragement, in the moment when he faces obstacles, whenever life seems turned against him. Everyone has such moments. We manifest our pride in many ways, but always it supports and sustains us. The legitimate pride of the Indian people has been crushed too many times by too many of their fellow Canadians.

The principle of equality and all that goes with it demands that all of us recognize each other's cultural heritage as a source of personal strength.

Canada has changed greatly since the first Indian Act was passed. Today it is made up of many people with many cultures. Each has its own manner of relating to the other; each makes its own adjustments to the larger society.

Successful adjustment requires that the larger group accept every group with its distinctive traits without prejudice, and that all groups share equitably in the material and non-material wealth of the country.

For many years Canadians believed the Indian people had but two choices: they could live in a reserve community, or they could be assimilated and lose their Indian identity. Today Canada has more to offer. There is a third choice – a full role in Canadian society and in the economy while retaining, strengthening and developing an Indian identity which preserves the good things of the past and helps Indian people to prosper and thrive.

This choice offers great hope for the Indian people. It offers great opportunity for Canadians to demonstrate that in our open society there is room for the development of people who preserve their different cultures and take pride in their diversity.

This new opportunity to enrich Canadian life is central to the Government's new policy. If the policy is to be successful, the Indian people must be in a position to play a full role in Canada's diversified society, a role which stresses the value of their experience and the possibilities of the future.

The Indian contribution to North American society is often overlooked, even by the Indian people themselves. Their history and tradition can be a rich source of pride, but are not sufficiently known and recognized. Too often, the art forms which express the past are preserved, but are inaccessible to most Indian people. This richness can be shared by all Canadians. Indian people must be helped to become aware of their history and heritage in all its forms, and this heritage must be brought before *all* Canadians in all its rich diversity.

Indian culture also lives through Indian speech and thought. The Indian languages are unique and valuable assets. Recognizing their value is not a matter of preserving ancient ways as fossils, but of ensuring the continuity of a people by encouraging and assisting them to work at the continuing development of their inheritance, in the context of the present-day world. Culture lives and develops in the daily life of people, in their communities and in their other associations, and the Indian culture can be preserved, perpetuated and developed only by the Indian people themselves.

The Indian people have often been made to feel that their culture and history are not worthwhile. To lose a sense of worthiness is damaging. Success in life, in adapting to change, and in developing appropriate relations within the community as well as in relation to a wider world, requires a strong sense of personal worth – a real sense of identity.

Rich in folklore, in art forms and in concepts of community life, the Indian cultural heritage can grow and expand further to enrich the general society. Such a development is essential if the Indian people are again to establish a meaningful sense of identity and purpose and if Canada is to realize its maximum potential.

The Government recognizes that people of Indian ancestry must be helped in new ways in this task. It proposes, through the Secretary of State, to support associations and groups in developing a greater appreciation of their cultural heritage. It wants to foster adequate communication among all people of Indian descent and between them and the Canadian community as a whole.

Steps will be taken to enlist the support of Canadians generally. The provincial governments will be approached to support this goal through their many agencies operating in the field. Provincial educational authorities will be urged to intensify their review of school curriculae and course content with a view to ensuring that they adequately reflect Indian culture and Indian contributions to Canadian development.

3 *Programs and Services*

Services must come through the same channels and from the same government agencies for all Canadians.

This is an undeniable part of equality. It has been shown many times that separation of people follows from separate services. There can be no argument about the principle of common services. It is right.

It cannot be accepted now that Indians should be constitutionally excluded from the right to be treated within their province as full and equal citizens, with all the responsibilities and all the privileges that this might entail. It is in the provincial sphere where social remedies are structured and applied, and the Indian people, by and large, have been non-participating members of provincial society.

Canadians receive a wide range of services through provincial and local governments, but the Indian people and their communities are mostly outside that framework. It is no longer acceptable that the Indian people should be outside and apart. The Government believes that services should be available on an equitable basis, except for temporary differentiation based on need. Services ought not to flow from separate agencies established to serve particular groups, especially not to groups that are identified ethnically.

Separate but equal services do not provide truly equal treatment. Treatment has not been equal in the case of Indians and their communities. Many services require a wide range of facilities which cannot be duplicated by separate agencies. Others must be integral to the complex systems of community and regional life and cannot be matched on a small scale.

The Government is therefore convinced that the traditional method of providing separate services to Indians must be ended. All Indians should have access to all programs and services of all levels of government equally with other Canadians.

The Government proposes to negotiate with the provinces and conclude agreements under which Indian people would participate in and be served by the full programs of the provincial and local systems. Equitable financial arrangements would be sought to ensure that services could be provided in full measure commensurate with the needs. The negotiations must seek agreements to end discrimination while ensuring that no harm is inadvertently done to Indian interests. The Government further proposes that federal disbursements for Indian programs in each province be transferred to that province. Subject to negotiations with the provinces, such provisions would as a matter of principle eventually decline, the provinces ultimately assuming the same responsibility for services to Indian residents they do for services to others.

At the same time, the Government proposes to transfer all remaining federal responsibilities for Indians from the Department of Indian Affairs and Northern Development to other departments, including the Departments of Regional Economic Expansion, Secretary of State, and Manpower and Immigration.

It is important that such transfers take place without disrupting services and that special arrangements not be compromised while they are subject to consultation and negotiation. The Government will pay particular attention to this.

4 *Enriched Services*

Those who are furthest behind must be helped most.

There can be little argument that conditions for many Indian people are not satisfactory to them and are not acceptable to others. There can be little question that special services, and especially enriched services, will be needed for some time.

Equality before the law and in programs and services does not necessarily result in equality in social and economic conditions. For that reason, existing programs will be reviewed. The Department of Regional Economic Expansion, the Department of Manpower and Immigration, and other federal departments involved would be prepared to evolve programs that would help break past patterns of deprivation.

Additional funds would be available from a number of different sources. In an atmosphere of greater freedom, those who are able to do so would be expected to help themselves, so more funds would be available to help those who really need it. The transfer of Indian lands to Indian control should enable many individuals and groups to move ahead on their own initiative. This in turn would free funds for further enrichment of programs to help those who are furthest behind. By ending some programs and replacing them with others evolved within the community, a more effective use of funds would be achieved. Administrative savings would result from the elimination of separate agencies as various levels of government bring general programs and resources to bear. By broadening the base of service agencies, this enrichment could be extended to all who need it. By involving more agencies working at different levels, and by providing those agencies with the means to make them more effective, the Government believes that root problems could be attacked, that solutions could be found that hitherto evaded the best efforts and best directed of programs.

The economic base for many Indians is their reserve land, but the development of reserves has lagged.

Among the many factors that determine economic growth of reserves, their location and size are particularly important. There are a number of reserves located within or near growing industrial areas which could provide substantial employment and income to their owners if they were properly developed. There are other reserves in agricultural areas which could provide a livelihood for a larger number of family units than is presently the case. The majority of the reserves, however, are located in the boreal or wooded regions of Canada, most of them geographically isolated and many having little economic potential. In these areas, low income, unemployment and under-employment are characteristic of Indians and non-Indians alike.

Even where reserves have economic potential, the Indians have been handicapped. Private investors have been reluctant to supply capital for projects on land which cannot be pledged as security. Adequate social and risk capital has not been available from public sources. Most Indians have not had the opportunity to acquire managerial experience, nor have they been offered sufficient technical assistance.

The Government believes that the Indian people should have the opportunity to develop the resources of their reserves so they may contribute to their own well-being and the economy of the nation. To develop Indian reserves to the level of the regions in which they are located will require considerable capital over a period of some years, as well as the provision of managerial and technical advice. Thus the Government believes that all programs and advisory services of the federal and provincial governments should be made readily available to Indians.

In addition, and as an interim measure, the Government proposes to make substantial additional funds available for investment in the economic progress of the Indian people. This would overcome the barriers to early development of Indian lands and resources, help bring Indians into a closer working relationship with the business community, help finance their adjustment to new employment opportunities, and facilitate access to normal financial sources.

Even if the resources of Indian reserves are fully utilized, however, they cannot all properly support their present Indian populations, much less the populations of the future. Many Indians will, as they are now doing, seek employment elsewhere as a means of solving their economic problems. Jobs are vital and the Government intends that the full counselling, occupational training and placement resources of the Department of Manpower and Immigration are used to further employment opportunities for Indians. The government will encourage private employers to provide opportunities for the Indian people.

In many situations, the problems of Indians are similar to those faced by their non-Indian neighbours. Solutions to their problems cannot be found in isolation but must be sought within the context of regional development plans involving all the people. The consequence of an integrated regional approach is that all levels of government – federal, provincial and local – and the people themselves are involved. Helping overcome regional disparities in the economic well-being of Canadians is the main task assigned to the Department of Regional Economic Expansion. The Government believes that the needs of Indian communities should be met within this framework.

5 *Claims and Treaties*

Lawful obligations must be recognized.
Many of the Indian people feel that successive governments have not dealt with them as fairly as they should. They believe that lands have been taken from them in an improper manner, or without adequate compensation, that their funds have been improperly administered, that their treaty rights have been breached. Their sense of grievance influences their relations with governments and the community and limits their participation in Canadian life.

Many Indians look upon their treaties as the source of their rights to land, to hunting and fishing privileges, and to other benefits. Some believe that treaties should be interpreted to encompass wider services and privileges, and many believe that treaties have not been honoured. Whether or not this is correct in some or many cases, the fact is the treaties affect only half the Indians of Canada. Most of the Indians of Quebec, British Columbia, and the Yukon are not parties to a treaty.

The terms and effects of the treaties between the Indian people and the Government are widely misunderstood. A plain reading of the words used in the treaties reveals the limited and minimal promises which were included in them. As a result of the treaties, some Indians were given an initial cash payment and were promised land reserved for their exclusive use, annuities, protection of hunting, fishing and trapping privileges subject (in most cases) to regulation, a school or teachers in most instances, and, in one treaty only, a medicine chest. There were some other minor considerations such as the annual provision of twine and ammunition.

The annuities have been paid regularly. The basic promise to set aside reserve land has been kept except in respect of the Indians of the Northwest Territories and a few bands in the northern parts of the Prairie Provinces. These Indians did not choose land when treaties were signed. The government wishes to see these obligations dealt with as soon as possible.

The right to hunt and fish for food is extended unevenly across the country and not always in relation to need. Although game and fish will become less and less important for survival as the pattern of Indian life continues to change, there are those who, at this time, still live in the traditional manner that their forefathers lived in when they entered into treaty with the government. The Government is prepared to allow such persons transitional freer hunting of migratory birds under the Migratory Birds Convention Act and Regulations.

The significance of the treaties in meeting the economic, educational, health and welfare needs of the Indian people has always been limited and will continue to decline. The services that have been provided go far beyond what could have been foreseen by those who signed the treaties.

The Government and the Indian people must reach a common understanding of the future role of the treaties. Some provisions will be found to have been discharged; others will have continuing importance. Many of the provisions and practices of another century may be considered irrelevant in the light of a rapidly changing society, and still others may be ended by mutual agreement. Finally, once Indian lands are securely within Indian control, the anomaly of treaties between groups within society and the government of that society will require that these treaties be reviewed to see how they can be equitably ended.

Other grievances have been asserted in more general terms. It is possible that some of these can be verified by appropriate research and may be susceptible of specific remedies. Others relate to aboriginal claims to land. These are so general and undefined that it is not realistic to think of them as specific claims capable of remedy except through a policy and program that will end injustice to Indians as members of the Canadian community. This is the policy that the Government is proposing for discussion.

At the recent consultation meeting in Ottawa representatives of the Indians, chosen at each of the earlier regional meetings, expressed concern about the extent of their knowledge of Indian rights and treaties. They indicated a desire to undertake further research to establish their rights with greater precision, elected a National Committee on Indian Rights and Treaties for this purpose and sought government financial support for research.

The Government had intended to introduce legislation to establish an Indian Claims Commission to hear and determine Indian claims. Consideration of the questions raised at the consultations and the review of Indian policy have raised serious doubts as to whether a Claims Commission as proposed to Parliament in 1965 is the right way to deal with the grievances of Indians put forward as claims.

The Government has concluded that further study and research are required by both the Indians and the Government. It will appoint a Commissioner who, in consultation with representatives of the Indians, will inquire into and report upon how claims arising in respect of the performance of the terms of treaties and agreements formally entered into by representatives of the Indians and the Crown, and the administration of moneys and lands pursuant to schemes established by legislation for the benefit of Indians may be adjudicated.

The Commissioner will also classify the claims that in his judgment ought to be referred to the courts or any special quasi-judicial body that may be recommended.

It is expected that the Commissioner's inquiry will go on concurrently with that of the National Indian Committee on Indian Rights and Treaties and the Commissioner will be authorized to recommend appropriate support to the Committee so that it may conduct research on the Indians' behalf and assist the Commissioner in his inquiry.

6 *Indian Lands*

Control of Indian lands should be transferred to the Indian people.

Frustration is as great a handicap as a sense of grievance. True co-operation and participation can come only when the Indian people are controlling the land which makes up the reserves.

The reserve system has provided the Indian people with lands that generally have been protected against alienation without their consent. Widely scattered across Canada, the reserves total nearly 6,000,000 acres and are divided into about 2,200 parcels of varying sizes. Under the existing system, title to reserve lands is held either by the Crown in right of Canada or the Crown in right of one of the provinces. Administrative control and legislative authority are, however, vested exclusively in the Government and Parliament of Canada. It is a trust. As long as this trust exists, the Government, as a trustee, must supervise the business connected with the land.

The result of Crown ownership and the Indian Act has been to tie the Indian people to a land system that lacks flexibility and inhibits development. If an Indian band wishes to gain income by leasing its land, it has to do so through a cumbersome system involving the Government as trustee. It cannot mortgage reserve land to finance development on its own initiative. Indian people do not have control of their lands except as the Government allows, and this is no longer acceptable to them. The Indians have made this clear at the consultation meetings. They now want real control, and this Government believes that they should have it. The Government recognizes that full and true equality calls for Indian control and ownership of reserve land.

Between the present system and the full holding of title in fee simple lie a number of intermediate states. The first step is to change the system under which ministerial decision is required for all that is done with Indian land. This is where the delays, the frustrations and the obstructions lie. The Indians must control their land.

This can be done in many ways. The Government believes that each band must make its own decision as to the way it wants to take control of its land and the manner in which it intends to manage it. It will take some years to complete the process of devolution.

The Government believes that full ownership implies many things. It carries with it the free choice of use, of retention or of disposition. In our society it also carries with it an obligation to pay for certain services. The Government recognizes that it may not be acceptable to put all lands into the provincial system immediately and make them subject to taxes. When the Indian people see that the only way they can own and fully control land is to accept taxation the way other Canadians do, they will make that decision.

Alternative methods for the control of their lands will be made available to Indian individuals and bands. Whatever methods of land control are chosen by the Indian people, the present system under which the Government must execute all leases, supervise and control procedures and surrenders, and generally act as trustee, must be brought to an end. But the Indian land heritage should be protected. Land should be alienated from them only by the consent of the Indian people themselves. Under a proposed Indian Lands Act full management would be in the hands of the bands and, if the bands wish, they or individuals would be able to take title to their land without restriction.

As long as the Crown controls the land for the benefit of bands who use and occupy it, it is responsible for determining who may, as a member of a band, share in the assets of band land. The qualifications for band membership which it has imposed are part of the legislation – the Indian Act – governing the administration of reserve lands. Under the present Act, the Government applies and interprets these qualifications. When bands take title to their lands, they will be able to define and apply these qualifications themselves.

The Government is prepared to transfer to the Indian people the reserve lands, full control over them, and subject to the proposed Indian Lands Act, the right to determine who shares in ownership. The Government proposes to seek agreements with the bands and, where necessary, with the governments of the provinces. Discussions will be initiated with the Indian people and the provinces to this end.

Implementation of the New Policy

1 *Indian Associations and Consultation*

Successful implementation of the new policy would require the further development of a close working relationship with the Indian community. This was made abundantly clear in the proposals set forth by the National Indian Brotherhood at the national meeting to consult on revising the Indian Act. Their brief succinctly identified the needs at that time and offers a basis for discussing the means of adaptation to the new policy.

To this end the Government proposes to invite executives of the National Indian Brotherhood and the various provincial associations to discuss the role they might play in the implementation of the new policy, and the financial resources they may require. The Government recognizes their need for independent advice, especially on legal matters. The Government also recognizes that the discussions will place a heavy burden on Indian leaders during the adjustment period. Special arrangements will have to be made so that they may take the time needed to meet and discuss all aspects of the new policy and its implementation.

Needs and conditions vary greatly from province to province. Since the adjustments would be different in each case, the bulk of the negotiations would likely be with the provincial bodies, regional groups and the bands themselves.

There are those matters which are of concern to all, and the National Indian Brotherhood would be asked to act in liaison with the various provincial associations and with the federal departments which would have ongoing responsibilities.

The Government proposes to ask that the associations act as the principal agencies through which consultation and negotiations would be conducted, but each band would be consulted about gaining ownership of its land holdings. Bands would be asked to designate the association through which their broad interests would be represented.

2 *Transitional Period*

The Government hopes to have the bulk of the policy in effect within five years and believes that the necessary financial and other arrangements can be concluded so that Indians will have full access to provincial services within that time. It will seek an immediate start to the many discussions that will need to be held with the provinces and with representatives of the Indian people.

The role of the Department of Indian Affairs and Northern Development in serving the Indian people would be phased out as arrangements with the provinces were completed and remaining Federal Government responsibilities transferred to other departments.

The Commissioner will be appointed soon and instructed to get on with his work.

Steps would be taken in consultation with representatives of the Indian people to transfer control of land to them. Because of the need to consult over five hundred bands the process would take some time.

A policy can never provide the ultimate solutions to all problems. A policy can achieve no more than is desired by the people it is intended to serve. The essential feature of the Government's proposed new policy for Indians is that it acknowledges that truth by recognizing the central and essential role of the Indian people in solving their own problems. It will provide, for the first time, a non-discriminatory framework within which, in an atmosphere of freedom, the Indian people could, with other Canadians, work out their own destiny.

Presented to the First Session of the Twenty-eighth Parliament by the Honourable Jean Chrétien, Minister of Indian Affairs and Northern Development (Ottawa: Oueen's Printer, 1969).

APPENDIX 2

The Bull *Romanus Pontifex*, 8 January 1455

Nicholas, bishop, servant of the servants of God. For a perpetual remembrance.

The Roman pontiff, successor of the key-bearer of the heavenly kingdom and vicar of Jesus Christ, contemplating with a father's mind all the several climes of the world and the characteristics of all the nations dwelling in them and seeking and desiring the salvation of all, wholesomely ordains and disposes upon careful deliberation those things which he sees will be agreeable to the Divine Majesty and by which he may bring the sheep entrusted to him by God into the single divine fold, and may acquire for them the reward of eternal felicity, and obtain pardon for their souls. This we believe will more certainly come to pass, thought the aid of the Lord, if we bestow suitable favors and special graces on those Catholic kings and princes, who, like athletes and intrepid champions of the Christian faith, as we know by the evidence of facts, not only restrain the savage excesses of the Saracens and of other infidels, enemies of the Christian name, but also for the defense and increase of the faith vanquish them and their kingdoms and habitations, though situated in the remotest parts unknown to us, and subject them to their own temporal dominion, sparing no labor and expense, in order that those kings and princes, relieved of all obstacles, may be the more animated to the prosecution of so salutary and laudable a work.

...

We [therefore] weighing all and singular the premises with due mediation, and noting that since we had formerly by other letters of ours [through the bull *Dum Diversas*, 18 June 1452] granted among other things free and ample faculty to the aforesaid King Alfonso – to invade, search out, capture, vanquish, and subdue all Saracens and pagans whatsoever, and other enemies of Christ wheresoever placed, and the kingdoms, dukedoms, principalities, dominions, possessions, and all movable and immovable goods whatsoever held and possessed by them and to reduce their persons to perpetual slavery, and to apply and appropriate to himself and his successors the kingdoms, dukedoms, counties, principalities, dominions, possessions, and goods, and to convert them to his and their use and profit – by having secured the said faculty, the said King Alfonso ... justly and lawfully has acquired and possessed, and doth possess, these islands, lands, harbors, and seas, and they do of right belong and pertain to the said King Alfonso and his successors, nor without special licence from King Alfonso and his successors themselves has any other even of the faithful of Christ been entitled hitherto, nor is he by any means now entitled lawfully to meddle therewith – in order that King Alfonso himself and his successors ... may be able the more zealously to pursue and may pursue this most pious and noble work, and most worthy of perpetual remembrance (which, since the salvation of souls, increase of the faith, and overthrow of its enemies may be procured thereby, we regard as a work wherein the glory of God, and faith in Him, and His commonwealth, the Universal Church, are concerned) in proportion as they, having been relieved of all the greater obstacles, shall find themselves supported by us and by the Apostolic See with favors and graces ...

Reprinted from Frances Gardiner Davenport, *European Treaties bearing on the History of the United States and Its Dependencies to 1648*, Vol. 1 (Washington, DC: Carnegie Institution, 1917), at 20–1, 23.

APPENDIX 3

Treaty of Albany, 1664

ARTICLES made and agreed upon the 24th day of September 1664 in Fort Albany between Uhgehando, Shanarage, Soachoenighta, Sachamackas of ye Maques; Anaweed Conkeeherat Tweasserany, Aschanoondah, Sachamakas of the Synicks, on the one part; and Colonell George Cartwright, in the behalf of Colonell Nicolls Governour under his Royall Highnesse the Duke of Yorke of all his territoryes in America, on the other part, as followeth, vizt –

1. Imprimis. It is agreed that the Indian Princes above named and their subjects, shall have all such wares and commodities from the English for the future, as heretofore they had from the Dutch.

2. That if any English Dutch or Indian (under the proteccôn of the English) do any wrong injury or violence to any ye said Princes or their Subjects in any sort whatever, if they complaine to the Governo^r at New Yorke, or to the Officer in Chiefe at Albany, if the person so offending can be discovered, that person shall receive condigne punishm^t and all due satisfaccôn shall be given, and the like shall be done for all other English Plantations.

3. That if any Indian belonging to any of the Sachims aforesaid do any wrong injury or damage to the English, Dutch, or Indians under the proteccôn of the English, if complaint be made to ye Sachims and the person be discovered who did the injury, then the person so offending shall be punished and all just satisfaccôn shall be given to any of His Mat^{ies} subjects in any Colony or other English Plantacôn in America.

4. The Indians at Wamping and Espachomy and all below the Manhatans, as also all those that have submitted themselves under the proteccôn of His Matie are included in these Articles of Agreement and Peace;

In confirmacôn whereof the partyes above mencôned have hereunto sett their hands the day and yeare above written.

GEORGE CARTWRIGHT

THESE ARTICLES following wer likewise proposed by the same Indian Princes & consented to by Colonell Cartwright in behalfe of Colonell Nicolls the 25th day of September 1664.

1. That the English do not assist the three Nations of the Ondiakes Pinnekooks and Pacamtekookes, who murdered one of the Princes of the Maques, when he brought ransomes & presents to them upon a treaty of peace.
2. That the English do make peace for the Indian Princes, with the Nations down the River.
3. That they may have free trade, as formerly.
4. That they may be lodged in houses, as formerly.
5. That if they be beaten by the three Nations above menncôned, they may receive accommodacôn from ye English.

Articles between Col. Cartwright and the New York Indians, 24 September 1664, in Edmund Bailey O'Callaghan, ed., *Documents Relative to the Colonial History of the State of New York*, 11 vols. (Albany: Weed, Parsons, 1853–61), Vol. 3, at 67–8.

APPENDIX 4

Report of the Lords of Trade, 23 November 1761

'Your Majesty, having been pleased to referr unto this Committee a Representation from the Lords Commissioners for Trade and Plantations dated the 11th of this Instant, Setting forth "That they have had under their consideration several letters and papers which they have received from Cadwallader Colden Esqr Lieutenant Governor and late Commander in Chief of Your Majesty's Province of New York in America ...

'"That the Said Lords Commissioners should not upon this occasion take upon them to controvert the general principles of Policy upon which either one or other of these general propositions is founded, but however expedient and constitutional they may appear in the abstract view and consideration of them. Yet they apprehend that when they come to be applied to the present State of Your Majesty's Colonies they will appear in a very different light and be found, the one to be dangerous to their Security and the other destructive to the Interest of the people, and subversive of the Policy by which alone Colonies can be kept in a just dependence upon the Government of the Mother Country.

'"That this is the General Light in which they see these, measures, but as they are in their nature separate and distinct, so they will as the said Lords Commissioners apprehend require a separate and distinct consideration and therefore they humbly offer to Your Majesty what has occurred to them upon each in the order in which they have placed them That it is unnecessary as it would be tedious to enter into a Detail of all the Causes of Complaint which, our Indian Allies had against us at the commencement of the troubles in America, and which not only induced them thô reluctantly to take up the Hatchet against us and desolate the Settlement on the Frontiers but encouraged our enemies to pursue those Measures which have involved us in a dangerous and critical war, it will be sufficient for the present purpose to observe that the primary cause of that discontent which produced these fatal Effects was the Cruelty and Injustice with which they had been treated with respect to their hunting grounds, in open violation of those solemn compacts by which they had yielded to us the Dominion, but not the property of those Lands, It was happy for us that we were early awakened to a proper sense of the Injustice and bad Policy of such a Conduct towards the Indians, and no sooner were those measures pursued which indicated a Disposition to do them all possible justice upon this head of Complaint than those hostilities which had produced such horrid scenes of devastation ceased, and the Six Nations and their Dependants became at once from the most inveterate Enemies our fast and faithful Friends.

'"That their steady and intrepid Conduct upon the Expedition under General Amherst for the Reduction of Canada is a striking example of this truth, and they now, trusting to our good Faith, impatiently wait for the event which by putting an End to the War shall not only ascertain the British Empire in America but enable Your Majesty to renew those Compacts by which their property in their Lands shall be ascertained and such a system of Reformation introduced with respect to our Interests and Commerce with them as shall at the same time that it redresses their Complaints and establishes their Rights give equal Security and Stability to the rights and Interests of all Your Majesty's American Subjects.

'"That under these Circumstances and in this situation the granting Lands hitherto unsettled and establishing Colonies upon the Frontiers before the claims of the Indians are ascertained appears to be a measure of the most dangerous tendency, and is more particularly so in the present case, as these settlements now proposed to be made, especially those upon the Mohawk River are in that part of the Country of the Possession of which the Indians are the most jealous having at different times expressed in the strongest terms their Resolution to oppose all settlements thereon as a manifest violation of their Rights.

'"That the principles of Policy which the said Lord Commissrs have laid down are they apprehend in their nature so clear and uncontrovertible that it is almost unnecessary to add anything further to induce Your Majesty to give immediate Orders for putting a stop to all Settlements upon the Mohawk River and about Lake George until the Event of the War is determined and such Measures taken thereupon, with respect to our Indian Allies as shall be thought expedient, and yet it may be proper to observe that independant of what regards our Connection with the Indians the conduct of those who have in former times been intrusted with the Administration of the Government of New York has in reference to granting of Lands in general been very exceptionable and has held forth a very bad example to their Successors."'

...

'The Lords of the Committee this day took the said Representation into their consideration, and agreeing in opinion with the said Lord Commissioners for

Trade and Plantations do humbly report to Your Majesty that they conceive it advisable that Your Majestys Pleasure should be made known upon the first point of Granting Lands, as well in the Colony of New York as in all other Your Majesty's Colonies on the Continent of America, where such grants interfere with the Indians bordering on those Colonies. ... And therefore that Your Majesty may be graciously pleased to order the said Lord Commissioners to prepare Draughts of Instructions proper to be sent hereupon to the Governors or Commanders in Chief of all Your Majesty's Islands and Colonies in America accordingly, to the end that due obedience be given thereto and the matters complained of so detrimental to the public service, prevented for the future.'

His Majesty taking the said Report into consideration was pleased by the advice of his Privy Council to approve of what is therein proposed and accordingly to order, as it is hereby ordered, that the Lord Commissrs for Trade and Plantations do prepare Draughts of Instructions proper to be sent with respect to the first point of granting Lands, as well to the Governor or Commander in Chief of the Colony of New York, as to the Governors or Commanders in Chief of all other His Majesty's Colonies on the Continent of America where such grants interfere with the Indians bordering on those Colonies. ... And that such Draughts of Instructions be laid before His Majesty at this Board for his Royal Approbation.

Report of the Lords of Trade, 23 November 1761, in Edmund Bailey O'Callaghan, ed., *Documents Relative to the Colonial History of the State of New York*, 11 vols. (Albany: Weed, Parsons, 1853–61), Vol. 7, at 472–6.

APPENDIX 5

Royal Proclamation of 1761

Draft of an Instruction for the Governors of Nova Scotia, New Hampshire, New York, Virginia, North Carolina, South Carolina, and Georgia forbidding them to Grant Lands or make Settlements which may interfere with the Indians bordering on those Colonies.

WHEREAS the peace and security of Our Colonies and Plantations upon the Continent of North America does greatly depend upon the Amity and Alliance of the several Nations or Tribes of Indians bordering upon the said Colonies and upon a just and faithful Observance of those Treaties and Compacts which have been heretofore solemnly entered into with the said Indians by Our Royall Predecessors Kings & Queens of this Realm, And whereas notwithstanding the repeated Instructions which have been from time to time given by Our Royal Grandfather to the Governors of Our several Colonies upon this head the said Indians have made and do still continue to make great complaints that Settlements have been made and possession taken of Lands, the property of which they have by Treaties reserved to themselves by persons claiming the said lands under pretence of deeds of Sale and Conveyance illegally fraudulently and surreptitiously obtained of the said Indians; And Whereas it has likewise been represented unto Us that some of Our Governors or other Chief Officers of Our said Colonies regardless of the Duty they owe to Us and of the Welfare and Security of our Colonies have countenanced such unjust claims and pretensions by passing Grants of the Lands so pretended to have been purchased of the Indians We therefor taking this matter into Our Royal Consideration, as also the fatal Effects which would attend a discontent amongst the Indians in the present situation of affairs, and being determined upon all occasions to support and protect the said Indians in their just Rights and Possessions and to keep inviolable the Treaties and Compacts which have been entered into with them, Do hereby strictly enjoyn & command that neither yourself nor any Lieutenant Governor, Presi-

Appendices 317

dent of the Council or Commander in Chief of Our said ~Colony/Province~ of   do upon any pretence whatever upon pain of Our highest Displeasure and of being forthwith removed from your or his office, pass any Grant or Grants to any persons whatever of any lands within or adjacent to the Territories possessed or occupied by the said Indians or the Property Possession of which has at any time been reserved to or claimed by them. And it is Our further Will and Pleasure that you do publish a proclamation in Our Name strictly enjoining and requiring all persons whatever who may either wilfully or inadvertently have seated themselves on any Lands so reserved to or claimed by the said Indians without any lawfull Authority for so doing forthwith to remove therefrom And in case you shall find upon strict enquiry to be made for that purpose that any person or persons do claim to hold or possess any lands within Our said ~Province/Colony~ upon pretence of purchases made of the said Indians without a proper licence first had and obtained either from Us or any of Our Royal Predecessors or any person acting under Our or their Authority you are forthwith to cause a prosecution to be carried on against such person or persons who shall have made such fraudulent purchases to the end that the land may be recovered by due Course of Law And whereas the wholesome Laws that have at different times been passed in several of Our said Colonies and the instructions which have been given by Our Royal Predecessors for restraining persons from purchasing lands of the Indians without a Licence for that purpose and for regulating the proceedings upon such purchases have not been duly observed, It is therefore Our express Will and Pleasure that when any application shall be made to you for licence to purchase lands of the Indians you do forebear to grant such Licence untill you shall have first transmitted to Us, by Our Commissioners for Trade and Plantations the particulars of such applications as well as in respect to the situation as the extent of the lands so proposed to be purchased and shall have received Our further directions therein; And it is Our further Will and Pleasure that you do forthwith cause this Our Instruction to you to be made Publick not only within all parts of your said ~Provinces/Colonies~ inhabited by Our Subjects, but also amongst the Several Tribes of Indians living within the same to the end that Our Royal Will and Pleasure in the Premises may be known and that the Indians may be apprized of Our determin'd Resolution to support them in their just Rights, and inviolably to observe Our Engagements with them.

Order of the King in Council on a Report of the Lords of Trade, 2 December 1761, in Edmund Bailey O'Callaghan, ed., *Documents Relative to the Colonial History of the State of New York*, 11 vols. (Albany: Weed, Parsons, 1853–61), Vol. 7, at 478–9.

APPENDIX 6

Governor Belcher's Proclamation, Nova Scotia, 1762

His Majesty by His Royal Instructions, Given at the Court of St. James, the 9th day of December, 1761, having been pleased to Signify,

THAT the Indians have made, and still do continue to make great Complaints, that Settlements have been made, and Possessions taken, of Lands, the Property of which they have by Treaties reserved to themselves, by Persons claiming the said Lands, under Pretence of Deeds of Sale & Conveyance, illegally, Fraudulently, and surreptitiously obtained of said Indians.

AND THAT His Majesty had taken this Matter into His Royal Consideration, as also the fatal Effects which would attend a Discontent among the Indians in the Present Situation of Affairs.

AND BEING determined upon all Occasions to support and protect the Indians in their just Rights and Possessions and to keep inviolable the treaties and Compacts which have been entered into with them, was pleased to declare His Majesty's further Royal Will and Pleasure, that His Governor or Commander in Chief in this Province should publish a Proclamation in His Majesty's Name, for this special purpose:

WHEREFORE in dutiful Obedience to His Majesty's Royal Orders I do accordingly publish this proclamation in His Majesty's Royal Name, strictly injoining and requiring all Persons what ever, who may either willfully or inadvertently have seated themselves upon any Lands so reserved to or claimed by the said Indians, without any lawful Authority for so doing, forthwith to remove therefrom.

AND, WHEREAS Claims have been laid before me in behalf of the Indians for Fronsac Passage and from thence to Nartigonneich, and from Nartigonneich to Piktouk, and from thence to Cape Jeanne, from thence to Emchih, from thence to Ragi Pontouch, from thence to Tedueck, from thence to Cape Rommentin, from thence to Miramichy, and from thence to Bay Des Chaleurs, and the environs of

Canso. From thence to Mushkoodabwet, and so along the coast, as the Claims and Possessions of the said Indians, for the more special purpose of hunting, fowling and fishing, I do hereby strictly injoin and caution all persons to avoid all molestation of the said Indians in their said claims, till His Majesty's pleasure in this behalf shall be signified.

AND if any person or persons have possessed themselves of any part of the same to the prejudice of the said Indians in their Claims before specified or without lawful Authority, they are hereby required forthwith to remove, as they will otherwise be prosecuted with the utmost Rigour of the Law.

Given under my Hand and Seal at Halifax this fourth Day of May, 1762, and in the Second Year of His Majesty's Reign.

From Peter A. Cumming and Neil H. Mickenberg, *Native Rights in Canada*, 2nd ed. (Toronto: Indian–Eskimo Association of Canada, 1972), Appendix I, at 287–8.

APPENDIX 7

Royal Proclamation of 1763

Whereas We have taken into Our Royal Consideration the extensive and valuable Acquisitions in America, secured to our Crown by the late Definitive Treaty of Peace, concluded at Paris, the 10th Day of February last; and being desirous that all Our loving Subjects, as well of our Kingdom as of our Colonies in America, may avail themselves with all convenient Speed, of the great Benefits and Advantages which must accrue therefrom to their Commerce, Manufactures, and Navigation, We have thought fit, with the Advice of our Privy Council, to issue this our Royal Proclamation, hereby to publish and declare to all our loving Subjects, that we have, with the Advice of our Said Privy Council, granted our Letters Patent, under our Great Seal of Great Britain, to erect, within the Countries and Islands ceded and confirmed to Us by the said Treaty, Four distinct and separate Governments, styled and called by the names of Quebec, East Florida, West Florida and Grenada ...

And whereas is it just and reasonable, and essential to our Interest, and the Security of our Colonies, that the several Nations or Tribes of Indians with whom We are connected, and who live under our Protection, should not be molested or disturbed in the Possession of such Parts of Our Dominions and Territories as, not having been ceded to or purchased by Us, are reserved to them, or any of them, as their Hunting Grounds. – We do therefore, with the Advice of our Privy Council, declare it to be our Royal Will and Pleasure, that no Governor or Commander in Chief in any of our Colonies of Quebec, East Florida, or West Florida, do presume, upon any Pretence whatever, to grant Warrants of Survey, or pass any Patents for Lands beyond the Bounds of their respective Governments, as described in their Commissions; as also that no Governor or Commander in Chief in any of our other Colonies or Plantations in America do presume for the present, and until our further Pleasure be known, to grant Warrants of Survey, or pass Patents for any Lands beyond the Heads or

Sources of any of the Rivers which fall into the Atlantic Ocean from the West and North West, or upon any Lands whatever, which, not having been ceded to or purchased by Us as aforesaid, are reserved to the said Indians, or any of them.

And We do further declare it to be Our Royal Will and Pleasure, for the present as aforesaid, to reserve under our Sovereignty, Protection, and Dominion, for the use of the said Indians, all the Lands and Territories not included within the Limits of Our said Three new Governments, or within the Limits of the Territory granted to the Hudson's Bay Company, as also all the Lands and Territories lying to the Westward of the Sources of the Rivers which fall into the Sea from the West and North West as aforesaid.

And We do strictly forbid, on Pain of our Displeasure, all our loving Subjects from making any Purchases or Settlements whatever, or taking Possession of any of the Lands above reserved, without our especial leave and Licence for that Purpose first obtained.

And, We do further strictly enjoin and require all Persons whatever who have either wilfully or inadvertently seated themselves upon any Lands within the Countries above described, or upon any other Lands which, not having been ceded to or purchased by Us, are still reserved to the said Indians as aforesaid, forthwith to remove themselves from such Settlements.

And whereas great Frauds and Abuses have been committed in purchasing Lands of the Indians, to the great Prejudice of our Interests, and to the great Dissatisfaction of the said Indians: In order, therefore, to prevent such Irregularities for the future, and to the end that the Indians may be convinced of our Justice and determined Resolution to remove all reasonable Cause of Discontent, We do, with the Advice of our Privy Council strictly enjoin and require, that no private Person do presume to make any purchase from the said Indians of any Lands reserved to the said Indians, within those part of our Colonies where, We have thought proper to allow Settlement; but that, if at any Time any of the Said Indians should be inclined to dispose of the said Lands, the same shall be Purchased only for Us, in our Name, at some public Meeting or Assembly of the said Indians, to be held for that Purpose by the Governor or Commander in Chief of our Colony respectively within which they shall lie; and in case they shall lie within the limits of any Proprietary Government, they shall be Purchased only for the Use and in the name of such Proprietaries, conformable to such Directions and Instructions as We or they shall think proper to give for that Purpose; And we do, by the Advice of our Privy Council, declare and enjoin, that the Trade with the said Indians shall be free and open to all our Subjects whatever, provided that every Person who may incline to Trade with the said Indians do take out a Licence for carrying on such Trade from the Governor or Commander in Chief of any of our Colonies respectively where such Person shall reside, and also give

Security to observe such Regulations as We shall at any Time think fit, by ourselves or by our Commissaries to be appointed for this Purpose, to direct and appoint for the Benefit of the said Trade:

And we do hereby authorize, enjoin, and require the Governors and Commanders in Chief of all our Colonies respectively, as well those under Our immediate Government as those under the Government and Direction of Proprietaries, to grant such Licences without Fee or Reward, taking especial Care to insert therein a Condition, that such Licence shall be void, and the Security forfeited in case the Person to whom the same is granted shall refuse or neglect to observe such Regulations as We shall think proper to prescribe as aforesaid.

And we do further expressly enjoin and require all Officers whatever, as well Military as those Employed in the Management and Direction of Indian Affairs, within the Territories reserved as aforesaid for the use of the said Indians, to seize and apprehend all Persons whatever, who standing charged with Treason, Misprisions of Treason, Murders, or other Felonies or Misdemeanors, shall fly from Justice and take Refuge in the said Territory, and to send them under a proper guard to the Colony where the Crime was committed of which they stand accused, in order to take their Trial for the same.

Given at our Court at St. James's the 7th Day of October 1763, in the Third Year of our Reign.

R.S.C. 1985. App. II, No. 1.

APPENDIX 8

Mi'kmaq Treaty of 1752

Treaty or
Articles of Peace and Friendship Renewed
between
His Excellency Peregrine Thomas Hopson Esquire Captain General and Governor in Chief in and over His Majesty's Province of Nova Scotia or Acadie Vice Admiral of the same & Colonel of One of His Majesty's Regiments of Foot, and His Majesty's Council on behalf of his Majesty.

AND

Major Jean Baptiste Cope chief Sachem of the Tribe of Mick Mack Indians, Inhabiting the Eastern Coast of the said Province, and Andrew Hadley Martin, Gabriel Martin and Francis Jeremiah members & Delegates of the said Tribe, for themselves and their said Tribe their heirs and the heirs of their heirs forever. Begun made and Concluded in the manner form & Tenor following, viz.

1. It is agreed that the Articles of Submission & Agreement made at Boston in New England by the Delegates of the Penobscot Norridgwolk, & St. John's Indians, in the Year 1725 Ratifyed & Confirmed by all the Nova Scotia Tribes at Annapolis Royal in the Month of June 1726 and lately Renewed with Governor Cornwallis at Halifax and Ratifyed at St. John's River, now read over Explained & Interpreted shall be and are hereby from this time forward renewed, reiterated and forever Confirmed by them and their Tribe, and the said Indians for themselves and their Tribe and their Heirs aforesaid do make and renew the same Solemn Submissions and promises for the strict Observance of all the Articles therein Contained as at any time heretofore hath been done.
2. That all Transactions during the late War shall on both side be buried in Oblivion with the Hatchet, And that the said Indians shall have all favour, Friendship & Protections shewn them from this His Majesty's Government.

3. That the said Tribe shall use their utmost Endeavours to bring in the other Indians to Renew and Ratify this Peace, and shall discover and make known any attempts or designs of any other Indians or any Enemy whatever against his Majesty's Subjects within this Province so soon as they know thereof and shall also hinder and Obstruct the same to the utmost of their power, and on the other hand if any of the Indians refusing to ratify this Peace shall make War upon the Tribe who have now Confirmed the same; they shall upon Application have such aid and Assistance from the Government for their defence as the Case may require.
4. It is agreed that the said Tribe of Indians shall not be hindered from, but have free liberty of hunting and Fishing as usual and that if they shall think a Truck house needful at the River Chibenaccadie, or any other place of their resort they shall have the same built and proper Merchandize, lodged therein to be exchanged for what the Indians shall have to dispose of and that in the mean time the Indians shall have free liberty to bring to Sale to Halifax or any other Settlement within this Province, Skins, feathers, fowl, fish or any other thing they shall have to sell, where they shall have the liberty to dispose thereof to the best Advantage.
5. That a Quantity of bread, flour, and such other Provisions, as can be procured, necessary for the Familys and proportionable to the Numbers of the said Indians, shall be given them half Yearly for the time to come; and the same regard shall be had to the other Tribes that shall hereafter Agree to Renew and Ratify the Peace upon the Terms and Conditions now Stipulated.
6. That to Cherish a good harmony and mutual Correspondence between the said Indians and this Government His Excellency Peregrine Thomas Hopson Esq. Capt. General & Governor in Chief in & over His Majesty's Province of Nova Scotia or Accadie Vice Admiral of the same & Colonel of One of His Majesty's Regiments of Foot hereby promises on the part of His Majesty that the said Indians shall upon the first day of October Yearly, so long as they shall Continue in Friendship, Receive Presents of Blankets, Tobacco, some Powder & Shott, and the said Indians promise once every year, upon the said first of October, to come by themselves or their Delegates and Receive the Presents and Renew their Friendship and Submissions.
7. That the Indians shall use their best Endeavors to save the Lives & Goods of any People Shipwrecked on this Coast where they resort and shall Conduct the People saved to Halifax with their Goods, and a Reward adequate to the Salvadge shall be given them.
8. That all Disputes whatsoever that may happen to arise between the Indians now at Peace and others His Majesty's Subjects in this Province shall be tryed in His Majesty's Courts of Civil Judicature, where the Indians shall have the

same benefits, Advantages & Priviledges as any others of His Majesty's Subjects.

In Faith & Testimony whereof the Great Seal of the Province is hereunto appended, and the Partys to these Presents have hereunto interchangeably Set their Hands in the Council Chamber at Halifax this 22nd day of Nov. 1752 in the 26th Year of His Majesty's Reign.

P.T. Hopson		His	
Chas. Lawrence	Jean Baptiste	x	Cope
Benj Green		Mark	
Jno. Salusbury	Andrew Hadley	x	
Willm. Steele	Francois	x	
Jno. Collier	Gabriel	x	

From Peter A. Cumming and Neil H. Mickenberg, *Native Rights in Canada*, 2nd ed. (Toronto: Indian–Eskimo Association of Canada, 1972), Appendix, I pp. 307–8.

Notes

1 Introduction

1 (1984), 13 D.L.R. (4th) 321 (S.C.C.).
2 Use of the term 'the Crown' throughout this book refers to the sovereign power and position of the body which possesses ultimate responsibility for discharging the fiduciary obligations to aboriginal peoples incurred in its name. Where specific emanations of the Crown are referred to, such as the British Crown, the federal Crown, or a provincial Crown, those distinctions are clearly made in the text.
3 The terms 'aboriginal peoples,' 'Native peoples,' and 'indigenous peoples' are used interchangeably herein to refer to the people who are encompassed within the definition of 'aboriginal peoples' in Section 35(2) of the Constitution Act, 1982 – namely the Indian, Inuit, and Métis peoples of Canada. For a more detailed discussion of these terms, see Clem Chartier, '"Indian": An Analysis of the Term as Used in Section 91(24) of the British North America Act, 1867,' (1978–9) 43 *Sask. L. Rev.* 37; Brian Slattery, 'Understanding Aboriginal Rights,' (1987) 66 *Can. Bar Rev.* 727 at n18 and n175; and, generally, Catherine Bell, 'Who Are the Métis People in Section 35(2)?' (1991) 29 *Alta. L. Rev.* 351; Paul Chartrand, '"Terms of Division": Problems of "Outside-Naming" for Aboriginal People in Canada,' (1991) 2:2 *J. Indig. Stud.* 1; Thomas Isaac, "The Power of Constitutional Language: The Case against Using "Aboriginal Peoples" as a Reference for First Nations," (1993) 19:1 *Queen's L.J.* 415. For various legal definitions, see Section 35(2) of the Constitution Act, 1982; Section 2(1) of the Indian Act, R.S.C. 1985, c. I-5, as amended; *Re Eskimo*, [1939] 2 D.L.R. 417 (S.C.C.). Aside from the use of entrenched legal phraseology, such as Indian lands and Indian treaties, where other descriptive terms are used, such as 'Indians,' they refer specifically to those people and not to the aboriginal peoples of Canada generally.

4 Paul D. Finn, 'The Fiduciary Principle,' in Timothy G. Youdan, ed., *Equity, Fiduciaries and Trusts* (Toronto: Carswell, 1989), at 24 (hereinafter 'Fiduciary Principle).
5 The fiduciary concept will be discussed in greater detail in Part Two.
6 A *cestui que trust* is simply another term for a beneficiary of a trust or fiduciary relationship, namely, a person whose beneficial interest in, say, land is held for his or her benefit by another.
7 A trust may have one or more trustees and one or more beneficiaries. There is nothing to prevent trustees from also being beneficiaries of the very trust which they administer as trustees. In addition, a trustee may hold the property of a trust not for any person or persons, but for an object permitted by law, such as a particular charitable purpose.
8 See, for example, *Moore v Royal Trust Co*, [1956] S.C.R. 880; *Standard Investments Ltd v CIBC* (1985), 22 D.L.R. (4th) 410 (Ont. C.A.), rev'g (1983), 5 D.L.R. (4th) 452 (Ont. H.C.).
9 The term 'equitable obligations' refers to responsibilities sanctioned under the authority of Equity, which originated as a separate sphere of legal jurisdiction and was characterized by principles of flexibility, adaptability, fairness, and reason. Equity is now a part of the unified jurisdiction of common law and Equity belonging to Canadian courts.
10 Fiduciary relationships will be discussed in greater detail in Part Two.
11 For suggestions as to the range of the Crown's fiduciary obligations to aboriginal peoples, see Chapter 16.
12 The word 'contact' has been purposely used in place of the more common term 'discovery' to describe the meeting of European and aboriginal peoples. This is because of the historical fact that what is now known as North America was occupied by indigenous peoples who inhabited, hunted, fished, trapped, and farmed the land from time immemorial, well before Europeans were aware of the New World's existence or possessed the ability to travel to its shores. To suggest that any European nation 'discovered' North America presupposes that the continent had previously been completely uninhabited, or, as it is described in legal terminology, *terra nullius* (land belonging to no one). In contrast, 'contact' suggests 'the reciprocity of discovery that followed upon European initiatives of exploration; as surely as Europeans discovered Indians, Indians discovered Europeans': Francis Jennings, *The Invasion of America: Indians, Colonialism, and the Cant of Conquest* (Chapel Hill: University of North Carolina Press, 1975), at 39.
13 Enacted as Schedule B to the Canada Act, 1982, (U.K.) 1982, c. 11, which came into force on 17 April 1982.
14 In particular, which emanations of 'the Crown' owe fiduciary duties to them – the federal Crown, provincial Crowns, and/or a combination of both.

15 This was defeated by referendum on 26 Oct. 1992.
16 The mandate of the Royal Commission on Aboriginal Peoples is reproduced in Schedules I and II of its report, *The Right of Aboriginal Self-Government and the Constitution: A Commentary* (Ottawa: Queen's Printer, 1992).
17 This had existed in the political forum for quite some time previously.
18 (1910), 38 Que. S.C. 268, aff'd (1911), 21 Que. K.B. 316, (1912), 5 D.L.R. 263 (P.C.).
19 On appeal to the Privy Council, it was acknowledged by the seminary that there had been agitation over the land for over 100 years prior to the commencement of the litigation: see (1912), 5 D.L.R. 263 (P.C.), 265. Indeed, partisan literature on the land dispute has existed for more than 100 years: see, for example, J. Lacan and W. Prévost, *An Historical Notice on the Difficulties Arisen between the Seminary of St Sulpice of Montreal and Certain Indians at Oka, Lake of Two Mountains*, 2nd ed. (Montreal: La Minerve Steam Printing Job Office, 1876); Anon., *The Seminary of Montreal: Their Rights and Titles* (St Hyacinthe: Courrier de St Hyacinthe Power Presses, 1880). For concise descriptions of the events leading up to and including the Oka crisis, see J.R. Miller, 'The Oka Controversy and the Federal Land Claims Process,' in Ken Coates, ed., *Aboriginal Land Claims in Canada: An Aboriginal Perspective* (Toronto: Copp Clark Pitman, 1992); *The Summer of 1990*, Fifth Report of the Standing Committee on Aboriginal Affairs, Ken Hughes, MP, Chair, House of Commons, Issue No. 59, May, 1991.
20 Sections 25 and 35 are reproduced in Chapter 4.
21 *R v Secretary of State for Foreign and Commonwealth Affairs, ex parte Indian Association of Alberta and Others*, [1982] 2 All E.R. 118 (C.A.); *Manuel and Others v Attorney General*, [1982] 3 All E.R. 786 (Ch.), aff'd [1982] 3 All E.R. 822 (C.A.); *Noltcho and Others v Attorney General*, [1982] 3 All E.R. 786 (Ch.).
22 See Douglas Sanders, 'The Indian Lobby,' in Keith Banting and Richard Simeon, eds., *And No One Cheered: Federalism, Democracy and the Constitution Act* (Toronto: Methuen, 1983).
23 (1990), 70 D.L.R. (4th) 385 (S.C.C.), at 406.
24 This is entrenched in the federal Indian Act, which was created in 1876 to govern a variety of issues relating to aboriginal peoples and their lands; the Act is discussed in more detail in Chapters 3 and 4.
25 *Statement of the Government of Canada on Indian Policy*, 1969 (Ottawa: Queen's Printer, 1969), at 5: 'The Government believes that its policies must lead to the full, free and non-discriminatory participation of the Indian people in Canadian society. Such a goal requires a break with the past. It requires that the Indian people's role of dependence be replaced by a role of equal status, opportunity and responsibility, a role they can share with all other Canadians.' The White Paper is reproduced here, in its entirety, as Appendix 1.

26 Ibid.
27 See, generally, Harold Cardinal, *The Unjust Society* (Edmonton: Hurtig, 1969).
28 Sally M. Weaver, *Making Canadian Indian Policy: The Hidden Agenda 1968–1970* (Toronto: University of Toronto Press, 1981), at 55.
29 Ibid., at 174.
30 Ibid., at 171.
31 (1973), 34 D.L.R. (3d) 145 (S.C.C.). The *Calder* decision, itself, built on the earlier decision in *R v White and Bob* (1964), 50 D.L.R. (2d) 613 (B.C.C.A.), aff'd (1965) 52 D.L.R. (2d) 481n (S.C.C.).
32 (1888), 14 A.C. 46 (P.C.), aff'g (1887), 13 S.C.R. 577, (1886), 13 O.A.R. 148, (1885), 10 O.R. 196 (Ch); this case will be discussed in greater detail in later chapters.
33 *Calder*, n31 *supra*, at 200, per Hall J; see also the judgment of Judson J in *Calder*, at 152, 156; *R v Koonungnak*, [1963–64] 45 W.W.R. 282 (N.W.T. Terr. Ct.), at 302: 'This proclamation has been spoken of as the "Charter of Indian Rights." Like so many great charters in English history, it does not create rights but rather affirms old rights. The Indians and Eskimos had their aboriginal rights and English law has always recognized these rights.' Note also *United States v Santa Fe Pacific Railroad Company*, 314 U.S. 339 (1941), at 347: 'Nor is it true, as [the] respondent urges, that a tribal claim to any particular lands must be based upon a treaty, statute, or other formal governmental action'; *Cramer v United States*, 261 U.S. 219 (1923), at 229: 'The fact that such right of occupancy finds no recognition in any statute or other formal governmental action is not conclusive.'
34 R.S.C. 1985, App. II, No. 1. The Proclamation is discussed in greater detail in Chapter 2, and reproduced here as Appendix 7.
35 (1888), 14 A.C. 46 (P.C.), at 54. Note also the reference to Lord Watson's finding by Judson J in *Calder*, n31, *supra*, at 152.
36 Refer to the discussion of the purpose and effects of the Royal Proclamation of 1763 in Chapter 2.
37 Note 35 *supra*.
38 Indeed, Judson J's decision in *Calder*, n31 *supra*, at 150, noted that 'Any Canadian inquiry into the nature of the Indian title must begin with *R v St Catharine's Milling & Lumber Co v The Queen*.' Similar sentiments have been expressed subsequent to the *Calder* decision in *Smith v R* (1983), 147 D.L.R. (3d) 147 (S.C.C.), at 224, where Estey J noted that 'The authority of ... [the *St Catharine's Milling*] decision has never been challenged or indeed varied by interpretations and applications,' and, more recently, in *Paul v Canadian Pacific Ltd* (1989), 53 D.L.R. (4th) 487 (S.C.C.), at 504.
39 The ramifications of this exclusion are commented on by John Borrows in 'Constitutional Law from a First Nation Perspective: Self-Government and

the Royal Proclamation,' (1994) 28 *U.B.C. L. Rev.* 1, at 35 n130: 'The fact that First Nations were not represented or called to testify in a case that purportedly decided their rights shows the depth of exclusion that First Nations experienced in getting their perspectives injected into legal discourse. This is highly regrettable given the wealth of testimony available, since the First Nations people who signed the treaty would still have been available to present their understanding.'

40 [1897] A.C. 199 (P.C.), aff'g [1896] 25 S.C.R. 434.
41 [1903] A.C. 73 (P.C.), aff'g (1901), 32 S.C.R. 1, (1900), 32 O.R. 301 (Div. Ct.), (1899), 31 O.R. 386 (Ch.).
42 [1910] A.C. 637 (P.C.), aff'g (1909), 42 S.C.R. 1, rev'g (1907), 10 Ex. C.R. 445.
43 Status Indians are those persons who fulfil the criteria established under the definition of 'Indian' in Sections 6–7 of the current Indian Act, n3 *supra*; see the further discussion in Chapter 3.
44 See George Manual and Michael Posluns. *The Fourth World: An Indian Realty* (Toronto: Collier Macmillan, 1974), for an analysis of the proceedings of the Special Joint Committee.
45 R.S.C. 1906, c. 81.
46 By way of Section 6 of An Act to Amend the Indian Act, S.C. 1926–7, c. 32; Section 149A later became Section 141 of the Indian Act, R.S.C. 1927, c. 98.
47 By the enactment of the revised Indian Act, S.C. 1951, c. 29.
48 See Department of Indian Affairs and Northern Development, *Statement on Claims of Indian and Inuit People* (Ottawa: Queen's Printer, 1973).
49 S.C. 1912, c. 45. Section 2(c) of the Act states: 'That the province of Quebec will recognize the rights of the Indian inhabitants in the territory above described to the same extent, and will obtain surrenders of such rights in the same manner, as the Government of Canada has heretofore recognized such rights and has obtained surrender thereof, and the said province shall bear and satisfy all charges and expenditure in connection with or arising out of such surrenders.'
50 See the *James Bay and Northern Quebec Agreement* (Quebec City: Editeur officiel du Québec, 1976), along with its implementing legislation, the James Bay and Northern Quebec Native Claims Settlement Act, S.C. 1976–7, c. 32, and An Act Approving the Agreement Concerning James Bay and Northern Quebec, S.Q. 1976, c. 46.
51 The Mackenzie Valley Pipeline Inquiry was established to determine the social, environmental, and economic impact of the proposed Arctic Gas pipeline project that was to be built from Prudhoe Bay, Alaska, through the Mackenzie Valley in western Canada.

52 *Northern Frontier, Nothern Homeland: Report of the Mackenzie Valley Pipeline Inquiry* (Ottawa: Supply and Services Canada, 1977).
53 See the definition of comprehensive claims in Chapter 14.
54 Department of Indian Affairs and Northern Development, *In All Fairness – A Native Claims Policy* (Ottawa: Queen's Printer, 1981). This policy was not substantially different than the policy first expressed by the federal government in 1973, however.
55 Department of Indian Affairs and Northern Development, *Outstanding Business – A Native Claims Policy* (Ottawa: Queen's Printer, 1982).
56 See the definition of specific claims in Chapter 14.
57 (1983), 144 D.L.R. (3d) 193 (S.C.C.), at 198. This doctrine was subsequently affirmed on a number of occasions by the Supreme Court of Canada: see *Simon v The Queen* (1985), 24 D.L.R. (4th) 390 (S.C.C.); *Dick v The Queen* (1985), 23 D.L.R. (4th) 33 (S.C.C.); *Derrickson v Derrickson* (1986), 26 D.L.R. (4th) 175 (S.C.C.); *R v Horse*, [1988] 1 S.C.R. 187; *R v Sioui* (1990), 70 D.L.R. (4th) 427 (S.C.C.); *R v Sparrow*, n23 supra; *R v Horseman*, [1990] 1 S.C.R. 901, and; Dickson CJC's dissenting judgment in *Mitchell v Peguis Indian Band* (1990), 71 D.L.R. (4th) 193 (S.C.C.).
58 (1979), 55 C.C.C. (2d) 172 (Ont. H.C.), aff'd (1981), 62 C.C.C. (2d) 227 (Ont. C.A.).
59 See, for example, *R v Sikyea* (1964), 43 D.L.R. (2d) 150 (N.W.T.C.A.), aff'd [1964] S.C.R. 642, where it was held that general federal legislation could remove aboriginal hunting and fishing rights even in the absence of a demonstrated intention by Parliament to do so. See also *R v George* (1966), 55 D.L.R. (2d) 386 (S.C.C.); *Daniels v the Queen*, [1968] S.C.R. 517; *R v Derricksan* (1976), 71 D.L.R. (3d) 159 (S.C.C.).
60 *Indian Self-Government in Canada: Report of the Special Committee* (Ottawa: Supply and Services Canada, 1983). Needless to say, more than a decade later, the issue of aboriginal self-government still remains unresolved. In Frank Cassidy and Robert L. Bish, *Indian Government: Its Meaning in Practice* (Lantzville, BC: The Institute for Research on Public Policy and Oolichan Books, 1989), at 17, the authors point to the following recommendations made in the Penner Committee Report as the most significant:
- that the right of Indian peoples to self-government be explicitly recognized, stated and entrenched in the Constitution of Canada;
- that the federal government pursue constitutional entrenchment of self-government as soon as possible, but in the meantime, introduce and implement an *Indian First Nations Recognition Act* and other legislation that would lead immediately to the maximum possible degree of self-government;

- that Indian governments be recognized as First Nations forming a distinct order of government, with their jurisdiction clearly defined, and their members acting legitimately as the representatives of their peoples in their relationships with Canada;
- that Indian First Nations have the rightful jurisdiction to each determine their own membership as well as full legislative and policy-making powers within the boundaries of Indian lands;
- that a Ministry of State for Indian First Nations, linked to the Privy Council Office, be established to manage and coordinate the federal government's relations with Indian First Nation governments, and the Department of Indian Affairs and Northern Development be phased out within five years;
- that a specialized tribunal be established to decide disputes in relation to agreements between Indian First Nations and other governments;
- that Federal Government funding of First Nations Governments be by direct grant, as nonlimiting as possible, and at rates set by mutual agreements between Indian and the federal governments;
- that a new federal land claims policy, not based on the doctrine of extinguishing aboriginal rights, be established to promote the fair and just resolution of outstanding land claims, on the basis of a recognition of these rights.

61 *Guerin*, n1 *supra*, at 335. In fact, *Calder* had only stated that aboriginal title was not dependent on positive Crown actions or affirmations, although Dickson J's statements are a logical conclusion of the determination made in *Calder*.
62 Ibid., at 356.
63 See, for example, *Kruger v R.* (1981), 125 D.L.R. (3d) 513 (F.C.T.D.), aff'd (1985), 17 D.L.R. (4th) 591 (F.C.A.); *Apsassin v Canada (Department of Indian Affairs and Northern Development)*, [1988] 3 F.C. 20 (F.C.T.D.), aff'd [1993] 2 C.N.L.R. 73 (F.C.A.), rev'd (14 Dec. 1995), file no. 23516 (S.C.C.); *Robert v Canada* (1989), 57 D.L.R. (4th) 197 (S.C.C.); *Paul v Canadian Pacific Ltd*, n38 *supra*; *R v Sparrow*, n23 *supra*; *Delgamuukw v BC* (1991) 79 D.L.R. (4th) 185 (B.C.S.C.); *Ontario (Attorney-General) v Bear Island Foundation* (1991), 83 D.L.R (4th) 381 (S.C.C.).
64 See, for example, Richard H. Bartlett, 'You Can't Trust the Crown: The Fiduciary Obligation of the Crown to the Indians: *Guerin v The Queen*,' (1984–5) 49 *Sask. L. Rev.* 367; Bartlett, 'The Fiduciary Obligation of the Crown to the Indians,' (1989) 53 *Sask L. Rev.* 301; John D. Hurley, 'The Crown's Fiduciary Duty and Indian Title: *Guerin v The Queen*,' (1985) 30 *McGill L.J.* 559; Darlene M. Johnston, 'A Theory of Crown Trust Towards Aboriginal Peoples,' (1986) 30 *Ottawa L. Rev.* 307; William R. McMurtry and Alan Pratt, 'Indians and the Fiduciary Concept, Self-Government and the Constitution: *Guerin* in Perspec-

tive,' [1986] 3 C.N.L.R. 19; James I. Reynolds and Lewis F. Harvey, 'The Fiduciary Obligation of the United States and Canadian Governments Towards Indian Peoples,' unpublished paper (Ottawa: Treaties and Historical Research Centre, 1985); D.P. Emond, 'Case Comment: *Guerin v R*' (1986), 20 E.T.R. 61; Donovan Waters, 'New Directions in the Employment of Equitable Doctrines: The Canadian Experience,' in Timothy G. Youdan, n4 *supra*; Maureen Ann Donohue, 'Aboriginal Land Rights in Canada: A Historical Perspective on the Fiduciary Relationship,' (1990) 15 *Am. Ind. L. Rev.* 369; Phil Lancaster, 'A Fiduciary Theory for the Review of Aboriginal Rights,' unpublished LLM thesis, University of Saskatchewan, 1990.

65 Perhaps not so coincidentally the vast majority of judicial and academic considerations of fiduciary law in the non-Native law context also tend towards the descriptive rather than the analytical. Some recent discussions of fiduciary doctrine by legal commentators have attempted to understand the theoretical basis on which fiduciary doctrine is premised: see, for example, P.D. Finn, *Fiduciary Obligations* (Sydney: Law Book Company, 1977) (hereinafter *Fiduciary Obligations*); Finn, 'Fiduciary Principle,' n4 *supra*; J.C. Shepherd, *The Law of Fiduciaries* (Toronto: Carswell, 1981); Tamar Frankel, 'Fiduciary Law,' (1983) 71 *Cal. L. Rev.* 795; Robert Flannigan, 'The Fiduciary Obligation,' (1989) 9 *Ox. J. Leg. Stud.* 285.

66 The rationale behind the principle of *stare decisis* – which holds that once a court establishes a principle of law to a particular set of facts it will apply that principle to future cases with similar facts and not retry already settled points of law – is to provide law with a sense of stability, continuity, and, most importantly, authority. As Learned Hand J explained in *Spector Motor Service v Walsh*, 139 F. 2d 809 (C.A. Conn. 1944), at 823: '[I]t always gives an appearance of greater authority to a conclusion to deduce it dialectically from conceded premises than to confess that it involves the appraisal of conflicting interests, which are necessarily incommensurable.'

67 See the judgment of Deane and Gaudron JJ in the High Court of Australia's recent decision in *Mabo v Queensland [No 2]* (1992), 175 C.L.R. 1 (H.C. Aust.), an Aboriginal rights case focusing on the question of Aboriginal title, at 120: 'Long acceptance of legal propositions, particularly legal propositions relating to real property, can of itself impart legitimacy and preclude challenge.' Note also the discussion of the effects of precedent in situations where it no longer accords with contemporary notions of justice, at 29, 30, per Brennan J, and at 109, per Deane and Gaudron JJ.

68 This is evidenced by the dearth of analytical examinations – either by the courts or academic commentators – of the Crown's fiduciary obligations to Native peoples beyond the first two years after the *Guerin* decision.

69 See Finn, *Fiduciary Obligations*, n65 *supra*, at 1: '[I]t is pointless to describe a person – or for that matter a power – as being fiduciary unless at the same time it is said for the purposes of which particular rules and principles that description is being used. These rules are everything. The description "fiduciary" nothing.'
70 See also Flannigan, n65 *supra*, at 310: 'It is one thing to describe a relationship as fiduciary in nature. It is a more complex task to specify the content of the obligation in a particular case.' See the discussion of the three-step process of fiduciary doctrine in Chapter 10.
71 Although it need not be restricted to private law contexts. For example, elected public officials have been held to possess fiduciary responsibilities to their constituents regarding their public office duties: see *Toronto (City of) v Bowes* (1858), 14 E.R. 770 (P.C.); *Hawrelak v City of Edmonton*, [1972] 2 W.W.R. 561 (Alta. S.C.), especially 592; aff'd [1973] 1 W.W.R. 179 (Alta. C.A.), but overturned by the Supreme Court of Canada, [1976] 1 S.C.R. 387, by reason of the majority's fundamental misapplication of fiduciary doctrine, which formed the basis of a significant dissent by De Grandpre and Dickson JJ, at 420. Note the criticism of *Hawrelak* in E.I. Jacobs, 'Comment: *Hawrelak v City of Edmonton*,' (1977) 23 *McGill L.J.* 97. Reference should also be made to *Carlsen v Gerlach* (1979), 3 E.T.R. 231 (Alta. Dist. Ct.); *R v Gentile* (1993), 81 C.C.C. (3d) 541 (Ont. Prov. Div.); *Municipal Conflict of Interest Act*, R.S.O. 1990, c. M-50; E.M. Rogers and S.B. Young, 'Public Office as a Public Trust,' (1974) 63 *Georgia L.J.* 1025. John Locke, *Two Treatises of Government*, Peter Laslett, ed., 2nd ed. (Cambridge: Cambridge University Press, 1967), esp. at 385 (para. 149), 399–400 (para. 171).

In the Native law context, elected band chiefs and councillors have also been held to possess fiduciary obligations to their bands. See *Gilbert v Abbey*, [1992] 4 C.N.L.R. 21 (B.C.S.C.); *Joe v John* (1990), 34 F.T.R. 280. See also *Corbiere v Canada*, [1994] 1 C.N.L.R. 71 (F.C.T.D.), where the Federal Court, Trial Division determined that a band's reserve lands and moneys accrue to the benefit of all band members, not just those residing on the reserve, which suggests that the bodies responsible for decisions regarding those assets – the band council and the Department of Indian Affairs – must exercise their authority in a manner which is consistent with the best interests of all band members.
72 The term 'Native law,' although generally well understood for what it encompasses, is somewhat of a misnomer. What is conventionally categorized as Native law is, in fact, the entire sum of common law which applies to Native peoples, not aboriginal legal systems themselves. Nevertheless, there are special circumstances and considerations which must be invoked within existing areas of law where aboriginal peoples are concerned – either as a

result of the special interests and concerns of the aboriginal peoples themselves or because of the effect of specific provisions of the Indian Act – which provides for the existence of Native law as a special enclave within existing realms of law.

73 The public–private distinction in law is one which is filled with controversy. In particular, it has been the subject of substantial debate in relation to the application of the Charter of Rights and Freedoms. For the purposes of our discussion, the categories of 'public' and 'private' law are based solely on the common legal understandings of the terms and are used only to facilitate the understanding of the discussion herein, not to comment on the appropriateness or legitimacy of the public–private distinction *vis-à-vis* the applicability of the Charter.

74 See Dickson J's comments in this regard in *Guerin*, n1 *supra*, at 341. Although Dickson J stated in *Guerin* that fiduciary duties generally arise only in private law contexts, his assertion is incorrect; see n71 *supra*.

75 *Black's Law Dictionary*, 5th ed. (St Paul, Minn: West, 1979), at 1286. See *Guerin*, n1 *supra*, at 343: '[T]he fiduciary obligation which is owed to the Indians by the Crown is *sui generis*. Given the unique character both of the Indians' interest in land and of their historical relationship with the Crown, the fact that this is so should occasion no surprise.'

76 See, for example, the trial judgment in *Apsassin*, n63 *supra*; Patrick Macklem, 'First Nations Self-Government and the Borders of the Canadian Legal Imagination,' (1991) 36 *McGill L.J.* 382.

77 See the discussion in Leonard I. Rotman, 'The Vulnerable Position of Fiduciary Doctrine in the Supreme Court of Canada,' (1995) 23(4) *Man. L.J.* (in press).

78 See n12 *supra*.

79 In spite of all of the changes in the Crown–Native relationship since this period, the formative years of their relationship remain the key to understand the theory behind the nature of the Crown's fiduciary obligations to the aboriginal peoples.

80 See the comments made by Borrows, n39 *supra*, at n105 (27–8): 'The reinterpretation of the fiduciary responsibility on the part of the Crown may shift from being based in the exercise of their discretion on First Nations' behalf (*Guerin v The Queen* ...) to being the result of promises made when the relationship between the parties was established. This is a healthier basis for the relationship because it does not convey a hierarchical confederation of unequal powers but a parallel alliance of mutual support between nation' [references omitted]. Borrows's notion of a more beneficial, or healthier, Crown–Native fiduciary relationship being based on the promises made between the groups when their relationship was established is correct, but it

does not require a 'reinterpretation' of fiduciary doctrine's place within Canadian aboriginal rights jurisprudence, as initiated in *Guerin*. Rather, it merely requires a contextual examination of the nature and extent of that relationship that was not forthcoming either in *Guerin* or in any subsequently decided case on the issue of Crown–Native fiduciary relations.
81 Note 16 *supra*, at 9–10.
82 Dated 24 September 1664, reproduced in Edmund Bailey O'Callaghan, ed., *Documents Relative to the Colonial History of the State of New York*, vol. 3 (Albany: Weed, Parsons, 1853), at 67. Refer to the discussion of the Treaty of Albany in Chapter 2. The text of the treaty is reproduced here as Appendix 3.
83 In 'First Nations Self-Government and the Borders of the Canadian Legal Imagination' n76 *supra*, at 412, Macklem suggests that the use of fiduciary doctrine in aboriginal rights jurisprudence is merely a continuation of the Crown's paternalistic, colonialist attitude towards aboriginal peoples: 'By seeking to ameliorate some of the adverse consequences that flow from the establishment of a legal relationship of inequality ... *Guerin* leaves intact the underlying hierarchical relation between the Crown and First Nations in the context of property entitlements'; see also Macklem, generally, at 410–14. With difference to Macklem's suggestion, rather than adhering to colonialism, the use of fiduciary doctrine in Canadian aboriginal rights jurisprudence refutes the essential premises of colonialism by emphasizing the reciprocal rights, duties, and responsibilities existing within Crown–Native relations.
84 The fact that fiduciary doctrine is a part of English common law does not indicate that the use of fiduciary principles in Crown–Native relations accepts the legitimacy of colonialism and rejects the notion of aboriginal independence. That fiduciary doctrine is a part of the common law actually favours its use over other avenues which are not binding on the Crown. Resorting unreflectively to international law, for example, as a means to assert aboriginal independence merely favours one colonialist system over another. International legal principles originated in the practices of European colonial powers and did not reflect the ideas or aspirations of North American indigenous societies. These principles arose largely as a result of the need to resolve disputes between European nations which desired to colonize the New World in the fifteenth and sixteenth centuries. They provided a dispute resolution mechanism for the amelioration of competing European claims to New World territories through doctrines such as 'discovery,' 'conquest,' 'annexation,' and 'just war.' These profoundly colonialist origins suggest that international law is no better suited to the situation of Crown–Native relationships in Canada than is domestic Canadian law, but that it is based to an even greater degree in assumptions about the inferiority of non-European

nations. See, for example, the comments made by the aboriginal legal scholar Robert Williams Jr, 'Encounters on the Frontiers of International Human Rights Law: Redefining the Terms of Indigenous Peoples' Survival in the World,' (1990) 4 *Duke L.J.* 660, at 664–5: 'Under present, Western-dominated conceptions of international law, indigenous peoples are regarded as subjects of the exclusive domestic jurisdiction of the settler state regimes that invaded their territories and established hegemony during prior colonial eras. At present, international law does not contest unilateral assertions of state sovereignty that limit, or completely deny the collective cultural rights of indigenous people ... Finally, modern international law refuses to recognize indigenous peoples as "peoples," entitled to rights of self-determination as specified in United Nations and other major international human rights legal instruments.'

85 The *sui generis* nature of the Crown–Native relationship and the laws governing that relationship are reflected in the commentary by the Royal Commission on Aboriginal Peoples in *Partners in Confederation: Aboriginal Peoples, Self, Government, and the Constitution* (Ottawa: Minister of Supply and Services, 1993), at 20: 'The doctrine of Aboriginal rights is common law in the sense that it is not the product of statutory or constitutional provisions and does not depend on such provisions for its legal force. Rather, it is based on the original rights of Aboriginal nations, as these were recognized in the custom generated by relations between these nations and incoming French and English settlers from the seventeenth century onward. This overarching body of fundamental law bridges the gap between Aboriginal groups and the general community and regulates the interaction between their legal and governmental systems, permitting them to operate harmoniously, each within its proper sphere. The doctrine is neither entirely Aboriginal nor entirely European in origin but draws upon the practices and conceptions of all parties to the relationship, as these were modified and adapted in the course of contact.'

86 Dickson J acknowledged this point in *Guerin*, n1, *supra*, at 341.

87 See, for example, *Hayward v Bank of Nova Scotia* (1984), 7 D.L.R. (4th) 135 (Ont. H.C.), at 142: '[T]he existence of a fiduciary relationship is determined on a case-by-case basis by a detailed examination of the facts specific to the case.'

88 The situation-specific nature of fiduciary doctrine will be elaborated upon in Part Two.

89 Note 63 *supra*.

90 Ibid., at 384.

91 The significance of the various meanings associated with 'the Crown' and the difficulties which have resulted from their indiscriminate use have been

noted by a number of commentators. For a more detailed discussion of these distinctions, see John T. Juricek Jr, 'English Territorial Claims in North America to 1660,' unpublished PhD thesis, University of Chicago, 1970, and the commentary on it in Geoffrey S. Lester, 'The Territorial Rights of the Inuit of the Northwest Territories,' unpublished DJur Thesis, Osgoode Hall Law School, 1981. Refer also to n2, *supra*.

92 The term 'black-letter' law refers to legal principles stemming exclusively from judicial precedent or legislation without reference to the context in which they originated or how they may require modification in their applicability to different situations.

93 *Guerin*, n1, *supra*.

94 *Guerin*, n1 *supra*; *Roberts*, n63 *supra*.

95 *Sparrow*, n23 *supra*.

96 *Guerin*, n1, *supra*; *Apsassin*, n63 *supra*.

97 Although the legal recognition of aboriginal title is not itself clear after more than 200 years of deliberation.

98 See the discussion of the three-step application of fiduciary doctrine in Part Two.

99 The recognition of aboriginal perspectives by the judiciary appears to be increasing, especially if the Supreme Court of Canada's formulation of its principles of Indian treaty and statutory interpretation in the *Nowegijick* line of cases, n57 *supra*, is an accurate indication of the current judicial climate. This recognition of aboriginal perspectives is not absolute, however, as demonstrated by the Supreme Court of Canada's majority decision in *Mitchell v Peguis Indian Band*, n57, *supra*; *Eastmain Band v Canada (Federal Administrator)*, [1993] 3 C.N.L.R. 55 (F.C.A.); *R. v Howard*, [1994] 2 S.C.R. 299.

100 A wealth of aboriginal perspectives on a number of issues of fundamental importance in aboriginal rights jurisprudence currently exist. They range from general observations to commentaries on more specific topics such as aboriginal self-government. Some of these articles and books may be found throughout the text and in the bibliographic reference.

It should be noted, however, that not all aboriginal perspectives have been incorporated into published works. Many exist only in aboriginal oral histories and traditions.

2 The Politics Underlying the Crown–Native Fiduciary Relationship in Canada

1 As quoted in 'Aboriginal Concepts of Justice,' in A.C. Hamilton and C.M. Sinclair, Commissioners, *The Justice System and Aboriginal People: Report of the*

Aboriginal Justice Inquiry of Manitoba, Vol. 1 (Winnipeg: Queen's Printer, 1991) (hereinafter *Manitoba Aboriginal Justice Inquiry*), at 17.
2 (1984), 13 D.L.R. (4th) 321 (S.C.C.).
3 (1852), 9 U.C.Q.B. 105, at 134.
4 This department is responsible for discharging the federal Crown's obligations to 'Indians and Lands reserved for the Indians,' under Section 91(24) of the British North America Act, 1867 (U.K.), 30–1 Vict. c. 3 – see R.S.C. 1985, App. II, No. 5. Following the passage of the Constitution Act, 1982, the British North America Act, 1867 became known as the Constitution Act, 1867 – see Section 1 of the Constitution Act, 1867. To avoid confusion which may be caused by references to the 1867 Act previous to its name change in 1982, the Act will be described throughout this book as the British North America Act, 1867.
5 (1981), 10 E.T.R. 61 (F.C.T.D.), at 86. Note also Stone JA's judgment in *Apsasin v Canada (Department of Indian Affairs and Northern Development)*, [1993] 2 C.N.L.R. 20 (F.C.A.), at 32, where he summarized the testimony of Dr J.E. Chamberlain, an expert in the field of government policies and administrative practices relating to Indian Affairs in Canada, as stating that: '[D]uring the period from the 1920s to the 1950s, those responsible for Indian Affairs were actuated by the twin principles of protection and advancement. In furtherance of these principles the Crown accepted to protect the Indian of Canada, regarded in a law as minors, from the acts of unscrupulous people and from the results of their own folly, and to advance the Indian people toward self-sufficiency both socially and economically. Government decisions were to be taken in the best interest of the Indian people and government officials were considered to be the best judges of that interest.'
6 The relationship between the British Crown and Native peoples in Canada went through a number of transformations from the time of contact to the present day. These transformations will be discussed in greater detail below.
7 The use of the terms 'guardian' and 'ward' to describe the Crown–Native relationship in Canadian aboriginal rights jurisprudence is too numerous to mention in its entirety, but may be found in the trial decision in *St Catherine's Milling and Lumber Co v The Queen* (1885), 10 O.R. 196 (Ch.) and continued at least until the Supreme Court of Canada's decision in *Francis v The Queen* (1956), 3 D.L.R. (2d) 641 (S.C.C.).
8 See 5 Pet. 1 (U.S. 1831), at 17, where Marshall CJ stated that the relationship of the Cherokee Nation to the United States 'resembles that of a ward to his guardian.' Note also *R v Symonds*, [1847] N.Z.P.C.C. 387 (N.Z.S.C.), at 391.
9 A typical example of this paternalistic attitude, which continued well into the twentieth century, may be seen in *Armstrong Growers v Harris* (1924), 1 D.L.R.

Notes to pages 20-2 341

1043 (B.C.C.A.), at 1046. 'The Indians are wards of the National Government (The Government of Canada) and the statutory provisions are aimed to provide statutory protection to the Indians ... from the rapacious hands of those who ever seem ready to advantage themselves and profit by the Indian's want of business experience and knowledge of world affairs.'

10 (1887), 13 S.C.R. 577, at 649.
11 As quoted by Riddell J in *Sero v Gault* (1921), 50 O.L.R. 27 (H.C.), at 31-2.
12 [1929] 1 D.L.R. 307 (N.S. Co. Ct.).
13 (1985), 24 D.L.R. (4th) 390 (S.C.C.), at 400.
14 (1985), 69 B.C.L.R. 76 (S.C.), at 79.
15 (1990), 70 D.L.R. (4th) 385 (S.C.C.), at 404-6.
16 Ibid., at 404.
17 See, for example, Frances Gardiner Davenport, *European Treaties Bearing on the History of the United States and Its Dependencies to 1648* (Washington, DC: Carnegie Institution, 1917); John T. Juricek, Jr, 'English Territorial Claims in North America to 1660,' unpublished PhD thesis, University of Chicago, 1970.
18 See Francis Jennings, *The Invasion of America: Indians, Colonialism, and the Cant of Conquest* (Chapel Hill: University of North Carolina Press, 1975), at 4.
19 See the bull *Romanus Pontifex*, issued by Pope Nicholas V in 1455, as reproduced in Davenport, n17 supra, at 20, reprinted here as Appendix 2. See also Pope Nicholas V's bull, *Dum Diversas*, of 1452, Calixtus III's *Inter Caetera* of 1456, and Sixtus IV's *Aeterni Regis* in 1481.
20 Through the bull *Inter Caetera*, dated 14 May 1493.
21 For a concise account of these forms of justification, see Brian Slattery, *Ancestral Lands, Alien Laws: Judicial Perspectives on Aboriginal Title* (Saskatoon: University of Saskatchewan Native Law Centre, 1983). Refer also to Slattery, *The Land Rights of Indigenous Canadian Peoples As Affected by the Crown's Acquisition of Their Territories* (DPhil thesis, Oxford University, 1979, reprinted, Saskatoon: University of Saskatchewan Native Law Centre, 1979) (hereinafter *Land Rights*): Geoffrey S. Lester, 'The Territorial Rights of the Inuit of the Northwest Territories,' unpublished DJur thesis, Osgoode Hall Law School, 1981.
22 See Timothy J. Christian, 'Introduction,' in L.C. Green and Olive P. Dickason, *The Law of Nations and the New World* (Edmonton: University of Alberta Press, 1989), at x: 'Indeed, it would be odd if international law did not authorize the expansionist activities of the leading, colonial powers, for the law of nations was little more than a self-serving, crystallization of state practice. One might be forgiven for concluding that a legal analysis of questions of this magnitude is predictably circular, for if it was done it was lawful.'
23 On the use of symbolic acts, reference may be made to Mark F. Lindley, *The Acquisition and Government of Backward Territory in International Law* (London.

Longmans, Green, 1926); F.A. Von der Heydte, 'Discovery, Symbolic Annexation, and Virtual Effectiveness in International Law,' (1935) 29 *Am. J. Int'l Law* 448; Arthur S. Keller, Oliver J. Lissitzyn, and Frederick J. Mann, *Creation of Rights of Sovereignty through Symbolic Acts, 1400–1800* (New York: Columbia University Press, 1938); James Simsarian, 'The Acquisition of Legal Title to Terra Nullius,' (1938) 53 *Pol. Sci. Q.* 111; Myres S. McDougal, Harold D. Lasswell, and Ivan A. Vlasic, *Law and Public Order in Space* (New Haven: Yale University Press, 1963); Juricek, n17 *supra*; L.C. Green, 'Claims to Territory in Colonial America,' in Green and Dickason, n22 *supra*.

24 From Henry S. Burrage, ed., *Early English and French Voyages, Chiefly form Hakluyt, 1534–1608* (New York: Charles Scribner's, 1906), as quoted in Wilcomb E. Washburn, *The Indian and the White Man* (Garden City, NY: Anchor Books, 1964), at 10–11. Other accounts of this occurrence may be found in Juricek, n17 *supra*, at 143–4, quoting Henry P. Biggar, ed., *A Collection of Documents Relating to Jacques Cartier and the Sieur de Roberval*, Publications of the Public Archives of Canada, no. 14 (Ottawa: Public Archives of Canada, 1930), at 64–6, and Brian Slattery, 'Did France Claim Canada upon "Discovery"?' in J.M. Bumsted, ed., *Interpreting Canada's Past*, Vol. 1 (Toronto: Oxford University Press, 1986), at 7–8 (hereinafter 'Discovery'), also quoting Biggar. Note that the Biggar version cites 24 July 1534 as the date of this planting of the Cross.

25 See Juricek, n17 *supra*, at 144, referring to Cartier's erection of the cross: 'Similar strategies were apparently employed by Vasco da Gama in Africa and Samuel de Champlain in Canada again. Any such trickery, if discovered, was sure to discredit an act of possession in the eyes of other Europeans.' Note also Keller et al., n23 *supra*, where the authors state that European nations often performed their symbolic acts in private or, like Cartier, lied to the indigenous inhabitants about the purpose of such acts.

26 For further discussion of this issue, see Brian Slattery, 'Aboriginal Sovereignty and Imperial Claims,' (1991) 29 *Osgoode Hall L.J.* 681 (hereinafter 'Aboriginal Sovereignty'); Juricek, n17 *supra*, at 747–8.

27 Refer to the discussion of the basis of the promulgation of international legal principles in Chapter 1, n84.

28 Note, for example, the reaction of the Peruvian Inca to being told that Spain had been granted a papal commission over their lands in Lindley, n23 *supra*, at 127: 'The Peruvian Inca ... when, hearing of the Pope and his commission, to the Spaniards for the first time, told Pizarro that "the Pope must be crazy to talk of giving away countries which do not belong to him."'

29 See Slattery, 'Aboriginal Sovereignty,' n26 *supra*, at 688.

30 Composed of the Spanish possessions in the Western Hemisphere, which included all of South America (save Brazil), Middle America, Florida, and the majority of land in the United States west of the Mississippi River.

31 See Lesley Byrd Simpson, *The Laws of Burgos, 1512–1513: Royal Ordinances for the Good Government and Treatment of the Indians* (San Francisco: John Howell Books, 1960); Robert A. Williams, Jr., *The American Indian in Western Legal Thought*, (New York: Oxford University Press, 1990), at 86–8.

32 See Vitoria's lecture 'De Jure Belli' in *De Indis et De Jure Belli Relictiones*, Ernest Nys, ed. (Washington, DC: Carnegie Institute, 1917). His view of the necessity to convert the indigenous peoples to Christianity is reflected in the following statement, at 127–8: 'It is through no fault of theirs that these aborigines have for many centuries been outside the pale of salvation, in that they have been born in sin and void of baptism and the use of reason whereby to seek out the things needful for salvation. Accordingly I for the most part attribute their seeming so unintelligent and stupid to a bad and barbarous upbringing, for even among ourselves we find many peasants who differ little from brutes ' Refer also to Thomas Flanagan, 'Francisco de Vitoria and the Meaning of Aboriginal Rights,' (1988) 95:2 *Queen's Quarterly* 421, esp. at 426–8.

33 See n32 *supra*. Although it was initially understood that these lectures were delivered in 1532, it now appears that the actual date of the lectures may have been 1539: see the sources cited in Slattery, 'Discovery,' n24 *supra*, at 25 n120.

34 De las Casas's views are expressed in his treatise, *In Defense of the Indian*, Stafford Poole, trans. (DeKalb: Northern Illinois Press, 1974).

35 See Lewis Hanke, *All Mankind Is One: A Study of the Disputation between Bartolomé de Las Casas and Juan Ginés de Sepúleveda in 1550 on the Intellectual and Religious Capacity of the American Indian* (DeKalb: Northern Illinois University Press, 1974); Hanke, *The Spanish Struggle for Justice in the Conquest of America* (Philadelphia: University of Pennsylvania Press, 1949) (hereinafter *Spanish Struggle*).

36 A number of prominent theorists, including Thomas Hobbes, Hugo Grotius, Samuel von Pufendorf, and John Locke, also published works which analysed the question of indigenous peoples' rights in the face of European colonization. See also the discussion in Williams, Jr., n31, *supra*, Part II.

37 Sir Thomas More, *Utopia*, Paul Turner, trans. (Middlesex: Penguin, 1985), Book 2, at 69–70.

38 Ibid., 'Gilles's Letter to Busleiden,' at 33.

39 This, according to Nonsenso, was of great benefit to all since 'native and colonists soon combine to form a single community with a single way of life, to the great advantage of both parties – for, under Utopian management, land which used to be thought incapable of producing anything for one lot of people produces plenty for two': ibid., Book 2, at 79–80.

40 Ibid., at 80.

344 Notes to pages 25-6

41 As reproduced in Lewis Hanke, *Spanish Struggle*, n35 *supra*, at 51-2.
42 As reflected in Ortiz's argument, n41 *supra*.
43 These were often buttressed by quoting from the works of ancient philosophers such as Plato and Aristotle and the religious writings of St Augustine and Thomas Aquinas.
44 In particular by adopting Aristotle's doctrine of natural servitude. See Aristotle, *The Politics*, Trevor J. Saunders, trans. (Middlesex: Penguin, 1981), at 69 (I. v): 'It is clear then that by nature some are free, others slaves, and that for these it is both just and expedient that they should serve as slaves.' See also Wilcomb E. Washburn, *Red Man's Land / White Man's Law* (New York: Charles Scribner's, 1971), at 8: 'In 1519, Bishop Juan de Quevedo of Tierra Firme (Venezuela) declared to Charles V of Spain that the Indians were slaves by nature in accordance with Aristotle's dictum that some men are by nature inferior.'
45 See, for example, Donald Purich, *Our Land* (Toronto: Lorimer, 1986), at 15: 'Also prevalent, on the part of the Europeans, whether English, Spanish or French, was an ethnocentric attitude that European civilization was the only truly human mode of existence and that any other culture was barbarous and aberrant'; *Re Southern Rhodesia*, [1919] A.C. 211 (P.C.), at 233: 'Some tribes are so low in the scale of social organization that their usages and conceptions of rights and duties are not to be reconciled with the institutions or the legal ideas of civilized society.'
46 See, in particular, Emer de Vattel, *Les Droits des Gens, ou Principes de la Loi Naturelle, appliqués à la Conduite et aux Affaires des Nations et des Souverains*, Charles G. Fenwick, trans. (Washington, DC: Carnegie Institute, 1916); Henry Wheaton, *Elements of International Law*, George G. Wilson, ed. (Oxford: Clarendon, 1936). See also the discussion in Thomas Flanagan, 'The Agricultural Argument and Original Appropriation: Indian Lands and Political Philosophy,' (1989) 22 *Cdn. J. Pol. Sci.* 589.
47 See, for example, Hugo Grotius, *De Jure Praedae Commentarius*, Vol. 1, J.B. Scott, ed. (Oxford: Clarendon Press, 1950); Samuel von Pufendorf, *De Jure Naturae et Gentium Libri Octo*, Vol. 2, J.B. Scott, ed. (Oxford: Clarendon, 1934); Immanuel Kant, *The Philosophy of Law* (Clifton, NJ: Augustus M. Kelley, 1974).
48 See, for example, Christian Wolff, *Jus Gentium Methodo Scientifica Pertractatum*, Vol. 2, Joseph H. Drake, trans. (Oxford: Clarendon, 1934), ch. 2, 89 (s. 168), where he stated that 'whatever a learned and cultivated nation can contribute to make barbarous and uncultivated nations learned and more cultivated, that it ought to do.'
49 R.S.C., 1985, App. II, No. 1, also reproduced in Adam Shortt and Arthur G. Doughty, eds., *Documents Relating to the Constitutional History of Canada, 1759-*

1791 (Ottawa: King's Printer, 1918), Part 1, at 163 (hereinafter *Canadian Constitutional Documents*). There are different versions of the Royal Proclamation of 1763 in existence. Brian Slattery, 'Land Rights,' n21 *supra*, and the Royal Commission on Aboriginal Peoples have suggested that the most accurate printed text of the Proclamation is to be found in Clarence S. Brigham, ed., *British Royal Proclamations Relating to America*, Transactions and Collections of the American Antiquarian Society, Vol. 12 (Worcester, Mass: American Qntiquarian Society, 1911), at 212–18. References to the Proclamation herein, as well as the portions of its reproduced in the Appendices, will refer to the R.S.C. 1985 version, because of its position as the version accepted by the Canadian government. On the notion of the Proclamation as an Aboriginal Bill of Rights, see *St Catherine's Milling and Lumber Co v The Queen* (1885), 10 O.R. 197 (Ch.), at 226; (1887), 13 S.C.R. 577, at 674; *R v White and Bob* (1964), 50 D.L.R. (2d) 613 (B.C.C.A.), at 636, aff'd (1965), 52 D.L.R. (2d) 481n (S.C.C.); *R v Koonungnak*, [1963–4] 45 W.W.R. 282 (N.W.T. Terr. Ct.), at 302; *Calder v Attorney-General of British Columbia* (1973), 34 D.L.R. (3d) 145 (S.C.C.), at 203; *R v Secretary of State for Foreign and Commonwealth Affairs, ex parte Indian Association of Alberta and Others*, [1982] 2 All E.R. 118 (C.A.), at 124–5.

For more detailed discussion of the Proclamation and its effects, see Kenneth M. Narvey, 'The Royal Proclamation of 7 October 1763: The Common Law, and Native Rights to Land within the Territory Granted to the Hudson's Bay Company,' (1974) 38 *Sask. L. Rev.* 123; Jack Stagg, *Anglo-Indian Relations in North America to 1763 and an Analysis of the Royal Proclamation of 7 October 1763* (Ottawa: Research Branch, Indian and Northern Affairs Canada, 1981); Slattery, 'Land Rights,' n21, *supra*; Lester, n21, *supra*; John Borrows, 'Constitutional Law from a First Nation Perspective: Self-Government and the Royal Proclamation,' (1994) 28 *U.B.C. L.* 1.

50 In *Maritime Indian Treaties in Historical Perspective* (Ottawa: Treaties and Historical Research Centre, Research Branch, Corporate Policy, Department of Indian and Northern Affairs Canada, 1983), at 1, W.E. Daugherty described the territorial boundaries of Acadia as 'in its broadest territorial sense ... composed of the present-day Canadian Maritime provinces of Prince Edward Island, Nova Scotia and New Brunswick, as well as the southern shore of the Gaspé and the northern part of the state of the Maine.'

51 As reproduced in Fred L. Israel, ed., *Major Peace Treaties of Modern History 1648–1967*, vol. 1, (New York: Chelsea House, 1967), at 210. Of interest is the interpretation given to this provision in the Treaty of Utrecht by John Graves Simcoe in a letter to Henry Dundas, dated 28 April 1792, in which he wrote about the dispute over British trade with Indian living in the United States:

... I thought it my duty to state to Mr Hammond such a dangerous assumption unwarranted by the definitive construction placed by the Treaty of Utrecht upon the intercourse which Great Britain and France had with the Indians, and considering them as free Nations gave to the subjects of both countries the right of trading with them, and carefully secured to the Indians the liberty, attached to Independant [sic] Nations of carrying their commercial articles to such places in the Dominions of either Nation, as they should prefer, and this Article of the Treaty of Utrecht was never contravened until the year 1756 when the violations of it on the part of France as is generally known ... was the occasion of the War that broke out between Great Britain and France – nor can the claims of the American Indians to the natural privileges of Independent Nations as guaranteed to them by their European Neighbours in the Compact of Utrecht, be more amply expressed and implied than in the General representations of the state of the Indian Department by Sir William Johnson in 1763 to the Lords of Trade that altho' 'fair speeches, promises and the conveniency of trade induced them to afford us and the French a settlement in the Country, yet they never understood such a settlement as Dominion,' and the Indian sense of their own Independency is brought down to so late a period prior to the late war, as the second of February one thousand seven hundred and sixty-nine, when a Seneca Chief in his complaints against the officer Commanding at Niagara, said, as appears by Sir William Johnson's Report, 'We are a free people and accustomed to sell whatever we have to whom and where we like best.' (*Simcoe Papers*, Vol. 1, 140, as cited in Paul C. Williams, 'The Chain,' unpublished LLM thesis, Osgoode Hall Law School, 1982, at 287–8.)

Note that in the book *We Were Not the Savages: A Micmac Perspective on the Collision of European and Aboriginal Civilizations* (Halifax: Nimbus Publishing, 1993), at 66, Daniel N. Paul maintains that the Mi'kmaq nation was not subject to the Treaty of Utrecht:

In 1715 the Micmac laid out in no uncertain terms in spite of British insistence to the contrary, that they did not come under the Treaty of Utrecht. The Micmac informed two British officers who had come to insist that they proclaim George I as their sovereign that they would proclaim no foreign king in their country and would certainly not recognize him as having dominion over their land.

...

At the same meeting the Micmac clarified for the British what their relationship with the French Crown had been and, from their point of view, still was. Since they viewed the French King as a father figure they held him in the highest esteem, because in the Micmac scheme of things fathers

were revered and greatly respected. But they never considered themselves to be subjects of the French King – only his allies.
52 Articles of Capitulation between Their Excellencies Major General Amherst, Commander in Chief of his Britannic Majesty's Troops and Forces in North-America, on the One Part, and the Marquis de Vaudreuil, &c. Governor and Lieutenant-General for the King in Canada on the Other. Montreal, 8 Sept. 1760.
53 As reproduced in *Canadian Constitutional Documents*, Part 1, n49, *supra*, at 33. See also Edmund Bailey O'Callaghan, ed., *Documents Relative to the Colonial History of the State of New York*, 11 vols. (Albany: Weed, Parsons, 1853–61), Vol. 10, at 1117 (hereinafter *NYCD*); Derek G. Smith, ed., *Canadian Indians and the Law: Selected Documents 1663–1972* (Toronto: McClelland and Stewart, 1975), at 1–2; *R v Sioui* (1990), 70 D.L.R. (4th) 427 (S.C.C.), at 456.
54 See also Williams, n51 *supra*, at 73: 'In 1763 the western [Indian] nations were in a state of war with the British, encouraged in part by promises and war belts from the French in Louisiana, in part by their conviction that the British intended to destroy them and take their lands, to cut them out of the fur trade and all other economic benefits. The Royal Proclamation provided reassurances that were needed with respect to the land.'
55 There have been many debates over the precise extent of the geographical boundaries of the Proclamation: see Slattery, 'Land Rights,' n21 *supra*, at 277–81; Lester, n21 *supra*, at 1182–6. In any event, the boundaries marked out by the Proclamation were later altered in the Treaty of Stanwix, 1768, and eventually wiped out altogether by the creation of the United States of America. The Treaty of Stanwix is reproduced in *NYCD*, n53 *supra*, Vol. 8, at 135–7 (with map attached). See also 'Proceedings of Sir William Johnson with the Indians at Fort Stanwix to Settle a Boundary Line,' ibid., at 111–34.

Interestingly, the Royal Proclamation of 1763 and the Treaty of Stanwix were cited some twenty-five years after the latter by John Graves Simcoe as indications that Britain never claimed absolute power or sovereignty over Indian lands not sold or otherwise fairly bestowed to the Crown; see n51 *supra*. The terms of the Proclamation itself, n49 *supra*, at 6, prohibit governing officials in British North America from granting warrants of survey or patents for any lands 'beyond the Heads or Sources of any of the Rivers which fall into the Atlantic Ocean from the West and North West, or upon any Lands whatever, which, not having been ceded to or purchased by us as aforesaid, are reserved to the said Indians.' Meanwhile, the boundaries of the Indian hunting grounds are described as 'all the Lands and Territories not included within the Limits of Our Said New Governments, or within the limits of the Territory granted to the Hudson's Bay Company, as also all the

Lands and Territories lying to the Westward of the Sources of the Rivers which fall into the Sea from the West and North West as aforesaid.'
56 Royal Proclamation of 1763, ibid.
57 For another view that the Proclamation's reserved lands served as a buffer zone between the Thirteen Colonies and Canada, see Clarence W. Alvord, *The Illinois Country, 1673–1818: The Centennial History of Illinois* (Springfield: Illinois Centennial Commission, 1920).
58 This sentiment is echoed by Stagg, n49 *supra*, where he explained one basis of the Proclamation, at 356: '... [P]rotecting lands possessed by Indians was essential to British commercial interests and to the security of British North American colonies ... [T]he benefits of the commercial empire it [Britain] had gained ... could be best accomplished in an atmosphere of inter-racial cooperation rather than of confrontation. To encourage peace on the American colonial frontier, Indians had [to] be provided with some basic guarantee that the land they occupied and hunted upon would not be unilaterally seized or altered in such a way as to deprive them of a livelihood.'
59 It was not until after the promulgation of the Quebec Act, 1774, which preserved and protected French institutions such as the Catholic church, the French language, French civil law, and the seigneury system of land holding under English common law, that Britain ultimately gained full control over Quebec.
60 The restriction on the American colonies' expansionist desires in the Royal Proclamations of 1761 and 1763 (see Appendices) in favour of the protection of Indian interests (as well as Britain's own economic, political, and military interests) was one root cause of the colonies' uprising that eventually led to the American Revolution. See Georgiana C. Nammack, *Fraud, Politics, and the Dispossession of the Indians: The Iroquois Land Frontier in the Colonial Period* (Norman, Okla: University of Oklahoma Press, 1969); at 105: 'Both proclamations were British attempts to provide a sanctuary for the Indians. Indeed, throughout the period from 1664 to the Revolution, there is little question that the Crown's role in attempting to protect the Indians against loss of their lands caused conflict with the colonists and contributed markedly to the colonists' hostility toward the Crown.' It should be noted, however, that the Proclamations were not solely responsible for the American uprising. These Proclamations were only the first in a series of British actions which generated the politics of revolt in the Thirteen Colonies, including the stationing of permanent troops in the colonies and the imposition of revenue-generating legislation designed to fund British efforts to solidify its hold on its North American possessions.
61 Of interest is the fact that the printed copy of the Royal Proclamation that has

survived in the Public Archives of Canada is a copy that was given to the Algonquins and Nipissings and turned over by them to Sir John Johnson, the son of Sir William Johnson, and his successor as superintendent-general of Indian Affairs in Canada, in 1847 in support of a petition in which they outlined their claims to lands in the Ottawa River valley: see Williams, n51 *supra*, at 76.

62 Indeed, the aboriginal rights elements of the Proclamation were never altered and were ultimately enshrined into Canadian constitutional law by Section 25 of the Constitution Act, 1982, the text of which is reproduction here in Chapter 4.

63 Including France, Spain, Portugal, Sweden, and the Netherlands.

64 The actions of some nations, such as France, make it appear that they were far more interested in trade in North American goods through the establishment of New World trading outposts than in establishing and settling permanent North American colonies. The consistently small population of New France attests to this fact.

65 For a time, the mercantile system was quite effective for Britain, as Stagg, n49 *supra*, suggests, at 9: 'With few exceptions, British-sponsored American colonial initiatives harmonized with the objectives of Great Britain: to provide markets for home-manufactured goods, to produce raw materials for the British navy, factories and import companies, and to supply commodities such as tobacco, rice and fish to receptive British markets.'

66 Most of the European seafaring nations with a presence in North America were either already engaged in this practice elsewhere or had initiated plans to begin such a system in North America.

67 Although the following discussion focuses exclusively upon Britain, most European nations that engaged in similar endeavours found similar results.

68 As Francis Jennings explained in *The Invasion of America*, n18 *supra*, at 33: 'The necessity for native alliance was not merely a matter of armed manpower; it was desirable and indeed indispensable because of massive European ignorance. To the European who lacked woodcraft, knew not the native trails, and imagined gothic horrors in every copse, the familiar hunting parks of the Indians were lethal wilderness. The European "settlers," who knew nothing of tillage methods in America and were often revolted at the labor of farming, depended on Indian gardens for subsistence between the deliveries of cargoes from overseas.' Dependence on the Indians for survival was not only confined to the British. W.J. Eccles, *The Canadian Frontier, 1534–1760* (New York: Histories of the American Frontier, 1969), at 24, noted that the French were far more dependent on the Indians than the Indians were on the French.

69 Wilbur R. Jacobs, 'Wampum and the Protocol of Treaty-Making,' in *Dispos-*

sessing the American Indian: Indians and Whites on the Colonial Frontier (New York: Scribner's, 1972), at 160: 'The settlers in all the early colonies learned quickly about the value of Indian maize (corn), squash, and pumpkins and soon adopted native planting and cooking techniques. Tobacco, regarded by the Indians as sacred with particular medicinal properties, was of course also readily planted by the first pioneers.'

70 Ibid., at 161. 'Besides items of food, the settlers borrowed Indian buckskin clothing and Indian canoes, snowshoes, and toboggans. Iroquois-style moccasins survive today ... White pioneers and explorers survived in the wilderness because they mastered Indian techniques of building shelters in the woods or making utensils, weapons, or tools fashioned from wood ... Indian medical cures and skills, many of them lost with the passage of time, have also been of considerable value to those colonials who knew how to use them effectively. Indians had an almost astonishing number of remedies for toothaches, gangrene, ulcers, backaches, headaches, rheumatism, weak or sore eyes, and other complaints. They were also able to perform primitive surgery when required, and their medicine men, sometimes called conjurers, were not far behind modern physicians as successful practitioners in certain areas of psychiatry.'

71 Although Britain may have harboured the desired to completely colonize North America at this time, the Crown's representatives who lived and treated with the Native peoples interacted with them on a sovereign basis, in a manner consistent with the latter's superior military and political strength.

72 See Royal Commission on Aboriginal Peoples, *Treaty Making in the Spirit of Co-existence: An Alternative to Extinguishment* (Ottawa: Minister of Supply and Services, 1995), at 23 (hereinafter *Treaty Making*): '[R]elations between the British and Aboriginal nations, both before and after 1760, were structured less by notions of conquest and discovery than by principles of alliance.'

73 Although it took Britain more than 100 years from the date of the Treaty of Albany, 1664, to fully realize its colonialist ambitions in North America, at the time that these political games were occurring, it was by no means assured that Britain, or any other European nation, would ever be able to colonize North America in the manner that they had envisaged because of the tremendous strength and numbers of the aboriginal peoples. See the further discussion of this point below. Interestingly, within twenty years after defeating the French to remain the largest European colonial power in North America, Britain lost its hold on the thirteen American colonies.

74 Stagg, n49 *supra*, at 1.

75 Also known as the Haudenosaunee (people of the longhouse) and composed of the Mohawk, Oneida, Onondaga, Seneca, Cayuga, and Tuscarora nations.

76 In fact, as Williams, n51 *supra*, points out, at 13, the treaty refers to the Indian treaty signatories as both 'princes' and sachems.' See *NYCD*, n53 *supra*, Vol. 3, at 67, n1 and n3. The Treaty of Albany is reproduced here as *Appendix 3*.

77 The position of the Iroquois *vis-à-vis* Britain was illustrated in an 1889 petition from the former to the governor-general of Canada: 'We remember still that when our forefathers first met with you, when you came with your ship, and our forefathers kindly received you and entertained you and entered into an alliance with you. Though our forefathers were then great and numerous, and your people were inconsiderable and weak, and they knew that, they entered into a Covenant Chain with you and fastened your ship therewith, being apprehensive the bark would break away and your ship would be lost.' See Williams, n51 *supra*, at 210.

78 *NYCD*, n53 *supra*, Vol. 3, at 67. Williams, n51 *supra*, at 97, makes the analogy between the Treaty of Albany's criminal jurisdiction provisions – that where a citizen from one nation harms a citizen from the other, the offender's citizenship determines criminal jurisdiction – and modern provisions for diplomatic immunity.

79 Chief Jean-Maurice Matchewan of the Barriere Lake Indian Government explained the significance of wampum in the following manner: 'Wampum belts were used by Indian nations in eastern North America to record agreements and laws, long before the coming of the white man. Wampum is a cylindrical bead, purple or white in colour, made from the hard shell of the clam. Woven together, the wampum form designs that symbolize actual events. It takes years to make a wampum belt and, once made, it is handed down from generation to generation, along with the memory of what it records.' See 'Mitchikanibikonginik Algonquins of Barriere Lake: Our Long Battle to Create a Sustainable Future,' in Boyce Richardson, ed., *Drumbeat: Anger and Renewal in Indian Country* (Toronto: Summerhill Press, 1993), at 141. In her article 'The Quest of the Six Nations Confederacy for Self-Determination,' (1986) 44 *U.T. Fac. L. Rev.* 1, at 9, Darlene Johnston gave the following explanation of the symbolism of wampum: 'Each design carried with it a universe of meaning. Wampum belts were integral both to spiritual ceremonies and council meetings. Moreover, they were the medium of international communication.' The use of wampum belts to commemorate the treaties entered into between the Iroquois and European nations was a common practice in the seventeenth century. See Robert A. Williams, Jr, 'The Algebra of Federal Indian Law: The Hard Trail of Decolonization and Americanizing the White Man's Indian Jurisprudence,' (1986) *Wisc. L. Rev.* 219, at 291; Jacobs, n69 *supra*, at 41–9.

80 As Williams, n51 *supra*, explains at 277: 'The Six Nations today maintain that

the wampum version of the Treaty of Fort Albany was the first of the Two Row belts.' The significance of the Two-Row Wampum is outlined below.
81 The dealings between the British and the Iroquois as sovereign nations were noted by Sir William Johnson, later superintendent-general of Indian Affairs in British North America, in a speech at the Onondaga Conference attended by the Five Nations in April, 1748: 'Brethren of the five Nations I will begin upon a thing of a long standing, our first Brothership. My Reason for it is, I think there are several among you who seem to forget it; It may seem strange to you how I a Foreigner should know this, But I tell you I found out some of the old Writings of our Forefathers which was thought to have been lost and in this old valuable Record I find, that our first Friendship Commenced at the Arrival of the first great Canoe or Vessel at Albany.' See *Sioui*, n53 *supra*, at 449.
82 The Two-Row Wampum is described in a number of sources: see, for example, Williams, n51 *supra*, at 96: 'The Iroquois tradition is that the Two Row Wampum Belt was made at the same time as this written document [Treaty of Albany]: it provides that the English and the Iroquois will be as two boats on the same river, travelling in the same direction, but parallel, so that neither interferes with the course of the other; it provides that no person from one nation shall cross into the boat of the other.' See also Williams, Jr, n79 *supra*, at 11.
83 Grand Chief Michael Mitchell, Mohawk Council of Akwesasne, 'An Unbroken Assertion of Sovereignty', in Richardson, n79 *supra*, at 109–10. See also Georges Erasmus, National Chief, Assembly of First Nations, 'Twenty Years of Disappointed Hopes,' in Richardson, n79 *supra*, at 1–2: 'All across North America today First Nations share a common perception of what was then agreed [in the Treaty of Albany]: we would allow Europeans to stay among us and use a certain amount of our land, while in our own lands we would continue to exercise our own laws and maintain our own institutions and systems of government.'
84 See *Treaty Making*, n72 *supra*, at 23: 'These early [treaty-making] policies and practices of French and British authorities were rooted in relations based on reciprocity and respect for the autonomy of Aboriginal peoples. Indeed, all the former Aboriginal allies of the French became part of the British network of alliance known as the Covenant Chain, of which the Iroquois were the chief spokespersons.' Whereas the exact date of the commencement of the British–Iroquois Covenant Chain is uncertain, it would appear as though the Treaty of Albany, as the first formal alliance between Britain and aboriginal peoples was, at the very least, a precursor to it; see the statement of Sir William Johnson, n81, *supra*, as well as that of Chief Canasatego in n85 below.

85 Note the statement made by the Onondaga Chief Canasatego in 1744, as quoted by Francis Jennings, *The Founders of America: How Indians Discovered the Land, Pioneered in It, and Created Great Classical Civilizations: How They Were Plunged into a Dark Age by Invasion and Conquest; and How They Are Now Reviving* (New York: Norton, 1993), at 216: 'About two Years after the Arrival of the English, an English Governor came to Albany, and finding what great Friendship subsisted between us and the Dutch, he approved it mightily, and desired to make as strong a League, and to be upon as good Terms with us as the Dutch were, with whom he was united, and to become one People with us: and by his further Care in looking into what had passed between us, he found that the Rope which tied the Ship to the great Mountain was only fastened with Wampum, which was liable to break and rot, and to perish in a Course of Years; he therefore told us, he would give us a Silver Chain which would be much stronger, and would last for ever. This we accepted, and fastened the Ship with it, and it has lasted ever since.' See also, on this point, N. Jaye Frederickson and Sandra Gibb, *The Covenant Chain: Indian Ceremonial and Trade Silver* (Ottawa: National Museum of Man, National Museums of Canada, 1990), at 11; Francis Jennings, *The Ambiguous Iroquois Empire: The Covenant Chain Confederation of Indian Tribes with English Colonies from its Beginnings to the Lancaster Treaty of 1744* (New York: Norton, 1984).

86 Williams, n51 *supra*, at 324. See also Williams, *ibid.*, at 61: 'The chain acts as a symbol which binds the nations together without causing them to lose their individual character ... It is consistent with the unity language of all the other symbols of the Iroquois: the bundles of arrows bound together for strength; the rope which is more powerful than its single strands, and the longhouse itself, many families under one roof.'

87 Ibid., at 65. 'The chain is also designed as a lasting union ... Though it requires care, maintenance and renewal, it is intended to last until the end of the world, like the other symbols of the unity and union of the Confederacy.' See also Frederickson and Gibb, n85 *supra*, at 11: 'Periodic renewal of the covenant was necessary. Formal meetings were held between partners to discuss the details of military support, trade arrangements and land use as Indian and European struggled to control the region. Gifts of wampum, silver, weapons, furs and tools were exchanged as tokens of good will. This became known, in the days of the British–Iroquois covenants as "brightening the Covenant Chain."'

88 Extracted from 'The Honourable William Johnson's second speech to the Sachems and Warriors of the Confederate Nations, Mount Johnson, 24 June 1755,' as reproduced in *NYCD*, n53, *supra*, Vol. 8, at 970.

89 See the Appendices.

90 Union of Nova Scotia Indians, *The Mi'kmaq Treaty Handbook* (Sydney and Truro, NS: Native Communications Society of Nova Scotia, 1987), Preface, i.
91 Ibid. See also Grand Chief Donald Marshall Sr, Grand Captain Alexander Denny, Putus Simon Marshall, of the Executive of the Grand Council of the Mi'kmaw Nation, 'The Covenant Chain,' in Richardson, n79 *supra*, at 82: 'In the Mi'kmaq view, the Mi'kmaq Compact, 1752, affirmed Mikmakik and Britain as two states sharing one Crown – the Crown pledging to preserve and defend Mi'kmaq rights against settlers as much as against foreign nations.'
92 See ibid., at 80: 'The terms of the Treaty of 1725 conform to a pattern that had been established earlier. It was built on the law of Nikamanen [Mi'kmaq international law governing relations with other independent nations]. But it was the first formal treaty between the Wabanaki and the British Crown. For us, it served as a fundamental agreement on the nature of our relations, and it was to be renewed at appropriate intervals.'
93 See L.F.S. Upton, *Micmacs and Colonists: Indian–White Relations in the Maritimes, 1713–1867* (Vancouver: University of British Columbia Press, 1979), at xiii: '[T]he Micmacs were subtle enough to manoeuvre between the two European rivals, treating and trading with the British whenever it was necessary to prompt the French into fresh measures of support.'
94 *Sioui*, n53 *supra*, at 448, 449.
95 Royal Commission on Aboriginal Peoples, *Partners in Confederation: Aboriginal Peoples, Self-Government, and the Constitution* (Ottawa: Minister of Supply and Services, 1993), at 13 (hereinafter *Partners in Confederation*).
96 For an illustration of Iroquois' perspectives on negotiating with the British and French, see Francis Jennings, *The Ambiguous Iroquois Empire*, n85 *supra*; Jennings, *Empire of Fortune: Crowns, Colonies, and Tribes in the Seven Years' War in America* (New York: Norton, 1988); John D. Hurley, *Children or Brethren: Aboriginal Rights in Colonial Iroquoia* (PhD thesis, Cambridge University, 1985, reprinted Saskatoon: University of Saskatchewan Native Law Centre, 1985).
97 In addition to the commonly held notion of Indians as trappers who traded pelts with the Europeans, they were also middlemen who acted as liaisons between Indian trappers and European traders, suppliers of provisions, canoe builders, navigators and guides, interpreters, and providers of transportation. For further reading on the fur trade in Canada, see Harold A. Innis, *The Fur Trade in Canada: An Introduction to Canadian Economics* (Toronto: University of Toronto Press, 1956); W.J. Eccles, 'A Belated Review of Harold Adams Innis's *The Fur Trade in Canada*,' in Bumsted, n24 *supra*; Arthur J. Ray, *Indians in the Fur Trade* (Toronto: University of Toronto Press, 1974).
98 Note 53 *supra*, at 449.
99 See Wilcomb E. Washburn, *The Indian in America* (New York: Harper and

Row, 1975), at 70–1: 'The utility of European firearms, metal knives and fishhooks, iron cooking pots, and similar tools was quickly recognized and these were eagerly sought after by the Indians ... The Indians valued the trader's commodities highly and were willing to exchange what was necessary to obtain them.' See also Jacobs, n69 *supra*, at 77: '[T]he Indians, by the time of Pontiac's uprising in 1763, had become so dependent upon certain tools, weapons, and textiles, that they felt a vital need for them even to continue in the old way of life. It was the gradual decimation of wildlife, especially fur-bearing animals, that made most Indians living adjacent to frontiers of settlement dependent upon whites for commodities that they felt they could not do without.'

100 Upton, n93 *supra*, at xi. Whether the aboriginal peoples who survived the wave of European disease actually lived better than before is a matter of subjective inference which is more complicated than Upton presents it.

101 Dorothy V. Jones, *License for Empire: Colonialism by Treaty in Early America* (Chicago: University of Chicago Press, 1982), at 71, citing Alexander Henry, *Travels and Adventures in Canada and the Indian Territories between the Years 1760 and 1776* (New York: I. Riley, 1809), at 44.

102 The complete text of Minavavana's declaration is reproduced in Borrows, n49 *supra*, at 12–13 [quoting from Wilbur R. Jacobs, *Wilderness Politics and Indian Gifts: The Northern Colonial Frontier, 1748–1763* (Lincoln: University of Nebraska Press, 1966), at 75]. It reads as follows:

Englishman, although you have conquered the French you have not yet conquered us! We are not your slaves. These lakes, these woods and mountains, were left to us by our ancestors. They are our inheritance; and we will part with them to none. Your nation supposes that we, like the white people, cannot live without bread, and pork and beef! But, you ought to know, that He, the Great Spirit and Master of Life, has provided food for us, in these spacious lakes, and on these woody mountains.

Englishman, our Father, the king of France, employed our young men to make war upon your nation. In this warfare, many of them have been killed; and it is our custom to retaliate, until such time as the spirits of the slain are satisfied. But, the spirits of the slain are to be satisfied in either of two ways; the first is the spilling of the blood of the nation by which they fell; the other, by covering the bodies of the dead, and thus allaying the resentment of their relations. This is done by making presents.

Englishman, your king has never sent us any presents, nor entered into any treaty with us, wherefore he and we are still at war; and, until he does these things, we must consider that we have no other father or friend among the white man, than the king of France.

356 Notes to pages 38–9

... [Y]ou have ventured your life among us, in the expectation that we should not molest you. You do not come armed, with an intention to make war, you come in peace, to trade with us, to supply us with necessities, of which we are in much want. We shall regard you therefore as a brother; and you may sleep tranquilly, without fear of the Chipeways. As a token of our friendship, we present you with this pipe, to smoke.

103 Borrows, n49 *supra*, at 13.
104 See ibid., at 15: '[U]til the early 1760s First Nations maintained much of their ability to determine their activities. First Nations' control began to change with the introduction of the Royal Proclamation.'
105 Such as, but not restricted to, the right to hunt, trap, and fish, and includes any rights which fall within those described in Section 25(a) of the Constitution Act, 1982. See the reproduction of Section 25 in Chapter 4.
106 Royal Commission on Aboriginal Peoples, *The Right of Aboriginal Self-Government and the Constitution: A Commentary* (Ottawa, 13 Feb. 1992), at 11. See also *Partners in Confederation*, n95 *supra*, at 19: 'The vision embodied in the *Royal Proclamation of 1763* was coloured by the imperial ambitions of Great Britain, which was seeking to extend its influence and control in North America. Nevertheless, when seen in another light, it has certain points of correspondence with the traditional Iroquois image of the Tree of Peace, as expressed for example by the Onondaga sachem, Sadeganaktie, during negotiations with the English at the city of Albany in 1698: "... all of us sit under the shadow of that great Tree, which is full of Leaves, and whose roots and branches extend not only to the Places and Houses where we reside, but also to the utmost limits of our great King's dominion of this Continent of America, which Tree is now become a Tree of Welfare and Peace, and our living under it for the time to come will make us enjoy more ease, and live with greater advantage than we have done for several years past."' Refer also to the discussion of the Royal Proclamation of 1763 in *Treaty Making*, n72, *supra*, at 24–5.
107 See *R v Koonungnak*, n49 *supra*, at 302: 'This proclamation has been spoken of as the "Charter of Indian Rights." Like so many great charters in English history, it does not create rights but rather affirms old rights. The Indians and the Eskimos had their aboriginal rights and English law has always recognized these rights.'
108 Brian Slattery, 'The Hidden Constitution: Aboriginal Rights in Canada,' (1984), 32 *Am. J. Comp.* 361, at 369. Refer back to the discussion of the Crown's rationale for issuing the Proclamation, *supra*.
109 It is interesting to note, however, that while the Proclamation did not create an Indian interest in land, but merely recognized and affirmed the existence

Notes to pages 39–41   357

of such an interest, the Proclamation emphasized the incongruency between the English common law doctrine of tenures – which holds that all land rights emanate from the Crown – the doctrine of continuity – by which the local law and pre-existing rights of a 'conquered' or 'settled' people are presumed to continue in the absence of any acts to the contrary by a competent authority – and the doctrine of recognition – under which antecedent rights are deemed to be recognized by the Crown where it conducts itself in a manner which indicates its intention to respect those rights. These concepts are described more fully in Slattery, 'Land Rights,' n21 *supra*; Lester, n21 *supra*; Slattery, 'Ancestral Lands,' n21, *supra*. See also *Campbell v Hall* (1774), 1 Cowp. 204, 98 E.R. 1045 (K.B.).

110 As will become evident through the following comparison of some European and aboriginal conceptions, notions of land and its 'ownership' are not universal concepts, but social constructs which are subjectively defined. Notions of 'ownership' and 'property' may exist only within the context of a prescribed set of rules and conventions which are made binding through coercion. Consequently, property laws may be understood as the embodiment of institutionalized cultural norms and practices arising in response to social customs, expectations, and habits

111 'Aboriginal Concepts of Justice,' in *Manitoba Aboriginal Justice Inquiry*, vol. 1, n1, *supra*, at 21, quoting Freda Ahenakew, Cecil King, and Catherine I. Littlejohn, 'Indigenous Languages in the Delivery of Justice in Manitoba,' research paper prepared for the Aboriginal Justice Inquiry, Winnipeg, March, 1990, 23.

112 See also the commentary on common notions of stewardship existing among the Blackfoot and Gitksan and Wet'suwet'en peoples in *Treaty Making*, n72 *supra*, at 10–13 and, more generally, at 2: 'Aboriginal peoples tend to see their relationships to land in terms of an overarching collective responsibility to protect, nurture, and cherish the earth as the giver of life.' Refer also to the statement by Oren Lyons in n119 *infra*.

113 Subject, of course, to any restrictions imposed by law. This concept is illustrated in simple terms in Alan M. Sinclair, *Introduction to Real Property Law*, 2nd ed. (Toronto: Butterworths, 1982), at 8: 'When I state that I am the absolute owner (and we know now what I mean by that statement: "complete owner" insofar as that is legally possible, fee simple owner), I mean no one else has any rights in relation to that property. Within certain limits as set by some governmental body as a town planning commission I can live there, tear it down, turn it into a filling station and generally do as I please with it.'

114 This concept was pioneered by Wesley Newcomb Hohfeld, 'Some Fundamental Legal Conceptions as Applied in Judicial Reasoning,' (1913–14) 23

Yale L.J. 16; Hohfeld, 'Fundamental Legal Conceptions as Applied in Judicial Reason,' (1916–17) 26 Yale L.J. 710; Hohfeld, *Fundamental Legal Conceptions as Applied in Judicial Reasoning and Other Legal Essays*, Walter Wheeler Cook, ed. (New Haven: Yale University Press, 1919). Under Hohfeldian rights analysis, the 'ownership' of land is actually an ownership of powers enforceable under law. In other words, what landowners actually 'own' or possess is not the land itself, but a bundle of rights and powers which, in conjunction with law, allow them to restrict or control others' use of the land.

115 When discussing aboriginal notions of property, it should be noted that there is no such thing as an all-encompassing aboriginal viewpoint, philosophy, or set of beliefs. However, there are certain core elements of most traditional aboriginal societies' conceptions of property, namely, the general inability to 'own' land in the common law understanding of ownership. It is these commonalities which I refer to in the following discussion of aboriginal understandings of property rights.

116 As Vince Forrester, an Aboriginal Australian from the Northern Territory, explains: 'It's impossible in our language to say we own the land. It is the land that owns us. We cannot own it. The land possesses us and it is a sacrilege to talk of owning the land. This idea is diametrically opposed to Western society. The full story of the land is in our music and dance. These are our title deeds to the land.' See Julian Burger, *Aborigines Today, Land and Justice* (London: Anti-Slavery Society, Indigenous Peoples and Development Series Report No. 5, 1988), at 16.

117 [1974] R.P. 38 (Que. S.C.).

118 As detailed in David C. Nahwegahbow, Michael C. Posluns, Don Allen, and Douglas Sanders, 'The First Nations and the Crown: A Study of Trust Relationships,' unpublished research report prepared for the Special Committee of the House of Commons on Indian Self Government, 1983, at 365. Note also the statement made by the nineteenth-century Indian leader Tecumseh, who explained that 'No tribe has the right to sell, even to each other, much less to strangers ... *Sell a country! Why not sell the air, the great sea, as well as the earth*? Did not the Great Spirit make them all for the use of his children?': reproduced in Frederick W. Turner III, ed., *The Portable North American Indian Reader* (New York: Viking, 1974), at 246.

119 See Oren Lyons, 'Traditional Native Philosophies Relating to Aboriginal Rights,' in Menno Boldt, J. Anthony Long, and Leroy Little Bear, eds., *The Quest for Justice: Aboriginal Peoples and Aboriginal Rights* (Toronto: University of Toronto Press, 1985), at 22–3: 'Our aboriginal responsibility is to preserve the land for our children. Everything on and in the land belongs to our chil-

dren. It doesn't belong to us. We have no right to sell it, or give it up, or make a settlement. If we do that we will "settle" our great-grandchildren right out of their aboriginal rights.' See also Leroy Little Bear, 'A Concept of Native Title,' *C.A.S.N.P. Bull.*, Dec. 1976, at 33: 'Ownership does not rest in any one individual, but belongs to the tribe as a whole, as an entity. The land belongs not only to people presently living, but it belongs to past generations and to future generations. Past and future generations are as much a part of the tribal entity as the living generation.'

120 See the references in n49 *supra*.

121 With the notable exception of Alaska, the French islands of St Pierre and Miquelon, and those territories west of the Mississippi which had been ceded to Spain by France.

122 This principle was established by the United States Supreme Court in the landmark case of *Johnson and Graham's Lessee v M'Intosh*, 8 Wheat. 543 (U.S. 1823) and later affirmed in *Worcester v State of Georgia*, 6 Pet. 515 (U.S. 1832). This principle and its explanation in these cases is discussed in Chapter 3.

123 Note 49 *supra*. Compare the Proclamation's statement that 'the several Nations or Tribes of Indians with whom We are connected, and who live under our Protection, should not be molested or disturbed in the Possession of such Parts of Our Dominions and Territories,' with Minavavana's declaration in 1761 that the British 'have ventured your life among us, in the expectation that we should not molest you' in n102 *supra*.

124 See also Borrows, n49 *supra*, at 17–19.

125 This is discussed in Chapters 3 and 4.

126 However, as far back as 1973, the federal Crown publicly recognized its duty towards the aboriginal peoples of Canada in Department of Indian Affairs and Northern Development, *Statement on Claims of Indian and Inuit People* (Ottawa: Queen's Printer, 1973), which sought 'to signify the Government's recognition and acceptance of its continuing responsibility under the British North America Act for Indians and lands reserved for Indians' that it regarded as 'an historic evolution dating back to the Royal Proclamation of 1763.' See *Sparrow*, n15 *supra*, at 405 for its juxtaposition of this statement with the *Statement of the Government of Canada on Indian Policy, 1969*, also known as the 'White Paper,' referred to in Chapter 1 and found in Appendix 1. It should be noted, as the *Sparrow* decision itself indicated, at 406, that the Crown's 1973 *Statement on Claims of Indian and Inuit People* was merely an expression of policy, not of its legal position, and therefore was not binding.

127 Once the Constitution Act, 1982, came into effect on 17 April 1982, all aboriginal and treaty rights in existence on that date could only be abrogated or derogated from with the voluntary consent of the aboriginal peo-

360 Notes to pages 43–5

ples concerned or by constitutional amendment. As will be discussed further in Chapter 6, the Supreme Court of Canada's decision in *Sparrow* subjects legislative infringement of aboriginal rights to an even further limitation.

128 See Frank Cassidy and Robert L. Bish, *Indian Government: Its Meaning in Practice* (Lantzville, BC: Institute for Research on Public Policy and Oolichan Books, 1989), at 13: 'England, France, and then Canada engaged in treaty making for several reasons. At first, the aim was to establish exclusive trading relations. Then the objective was to secure the assistance or neutrality of Indian nations in warfare between the European powers. Eventually, treaties were used as a device for enabling settlement and resource development by non-Indians and to extinguish the land claims of Indian peoples.'

129 Whether these treaties actually involved the 'surrender' of land is a disputed matter, as is the accuracy of the written account of treaties representing the nature of the bargains entered into between the Crown and aboriginal groups. See, for example, Leroy Little Bear, 'Aboriginal Rights and the Canadian "Grundnorm,"' in J. Rick Ponting, ed., *Arduous Journey, Canadian Indians and Decolonization* (Toronto: McClelland and Stewart, 1986), at 243; W.E. Daugherty, *Treaty Research Report: Treaty #3* (Ottawa: Treaties and Historical Research Centre, Indian and Northern Affairs Canada, 1986), at 64; Richard Price, ed., *The Spirit of the Alberta Indian Treaties* (Edmonton: Pica Pica Press, 1987); René Fumoleau, *As Long as This Land Shall Last* (Toronto: McClelland and Stewart, 1976); Harold Cardinal, *The Unjust Society* (Edmonton: Mel Hurtig, 1969), esp. at 28–43. For an account of the Iroquois perspective on early treaties negotiated with European powers, see the sources in n96 *supra*.

130 As reproduced in *Canadian Constitutional Documents*, Part I, n49 *supra*, at 199–200.

131 See Chief Jean-Maurice Matchewan, Barriere Lake Indian Government, 'Mitchikanibikonginik Algonquins of Barriere Lake: Our Long Battle to Create a Sustainable Future,' in Richardson, n79 *supra*, at 173: 'In 1774 Lord Dorchester, the governor, again gave specific reassurances to the Algonquin people with respect to their rights: "All of that which belonged to the King of France belongs to your present Father, the King, but no one can give to another that which does not belong justly to him. That is why if you anciently held the rights to these lands, and if you have not been paid, the rights belong to you still."'

132 Statement by Lord Dorchester, governor of Upper and Lower Canada and commander in chief of His Majesty's forces in North America to the Confederated Indian Nations, 1791, Simcoe Papers, Letterbook 17-1791, as quoted

in Bruce Clark, *Native Liberty, Crown Sovereignty: The Existing Aboriginal Right of Self-Government in Canada* (Montreal: McGill-Queen's University Press, 1990), at 80. See also the comments made by the Union of Nova Scotia Indians in *The Mi'kmaq Treaty Handbook*, n90 *supra*, at 10, relying on another statement made by Lord Dorchester affirming that aboriginal rights were not taken away by the Crown: 'While it was of little comfort to the Mi'kmaq people, in 1793 the Lieutenant Governor of Upper Canada asserted that the Crown's agreements with the indigenous nations prove: "that no King of Great Britain ever claimed absolute or sovereignty over any of your lands or territories that were not fairly sold or bestowed by your Ancestors at public Treaties. They will prove that your natural independency has ever been preserved by your predecessors and will establish that the rights resulting from such independency have been reciprocally and constantly acknowledged in the Treaties."'

133 The exact date of the instructions is unknown, as it was not included in the draft: see *Canadian Constitutional Documents*, Part 2, n49 *supra*, at 814. This document and a related document were discovered among a number of papers under the heading 'Quebec, Dispatches and Miscellaneous, 1786' in the Canadian Archives, C.O. 12, Vol. 18, beginning at 152: ibid., at 812, n1.

134 As reproduced in *Canadian Constitutional Documents*, ibid., Part 2, at 814–15.

135 As reproduced in William M. Malloy, *Treaties, Conventions, International Acts, Protocols, and Agreements between the United States of America and Other Powers, 1776–1909*, Vol. 1 (Washington: Government Printing Office, 1910), at 592–3.

136 Although the war had officially ended with the signing of the Treaty of Ghent (although the treaty was not ratified by the United States Senate until Feb. 1815), the final action of the war came on 8 Jan. 1815, with the decisive defeat of British troops by General Andrew Jackson at the Battle of New Orleans.

137 As reproduced in Malloy, n135 *supra*, at 618.

138 John Leonard Taylor, 'Two Views on the Meaning of Treaties Six and Seven,' in Price, n129 *supra*, at 11.

3 The Incidents of Colonialism

1 As quoted in 'The Inquiry and the Issues,' in *The Justice System and Aboriginal People: Report of the Aboriginal Justice Inquiry of Manitoba*, Vol. 1 (Winnipeg: Queen's Printer, 1991) (A.C. Hamilton and C.M. Sinclair, Commissioners), at 1 (hereinafter *Manitoba Aboriginal Justice Inquiry*).

2 As quoted in J.R. Miller, *Skyscrapers Hide the Heavens: A History of Indian–*

White Relations in Canada (Toronto: University of Toronto Press, 1989), at 207.
3 Britain's earlier policy of recognizing aboriginal peoples as nations is reflected in the instructions from Lord Bathurst to Lt.-Gen. Sir George Prevost, dated 27 Dec. 1814, issued shortly after the signing of the Treaty of Ghent, 1814: 'It is very desirable that any Treaty of Peace which we conclude with Indian Nations or Tribes actually at War with us, should be expressed in terms which denote the Independence of the Nation or Tribe with which we are treating, and you will intimate to the friendly nations that in their Treaties with the United States of America, they ought to adhere as much as Possible to the terms used in their former Treaties with the United States – describing themselves as "Nations" not "Tribes" wherein it had been formerly the practice to so designate themselves.' PAC, M113, 145, cited in Cayuga Arbitration Papers, Great Britain, Reply, Vol. 2, at 364, as cited in Paul C. Williams, 'The Chain, unpublished LLM thesis, Osgoode Hall Law School, 1982, at 294.
4 That is not to suggest that there were no previous treaties which sought the surrender of aboriginal lands. Although such treaties did exist prior to the nineteenth century, they were less prevalent at that time. See the commentary by the Royal Commission on Aboriginal Peoples in its report *Treaty Making in the Spirit of Co-existence: An Alternative to Extinguishment* (Ottawa: Minister of Supply and Services, 1995), at 17: '[T]reaty objectives on the part of Crown representatives alone varied significantly ... and were influenced by a broad range of factors, including the immediate agenda of the government of the day and the particular mandate of the negotiators.'
5 Letter from Lt.-Gov. Adams G. Archibald to the secretary of state for the Provinces, dated 29 July 1871, as detailed in Alexander Morris, *The Treaties of Canada with the Indians of Manitoba and the North-West Territories* (Toronto: Belfords, Clarke, 1880), at 34. See also the discussion of the Crown's actions in obtaining surrenders from the Chippewas of Saugeen and Nawash in Chapter 16.
6 See the discussion in Chapter 2. Note also the comments made by the Royal Commission on Aboriginal Peoples in *Treaty Making*, n4, *supra*, at 29: 'The principle of reciprocity upon which Crown–aboriginal relations had been founded originally was to be discarded by the Crown in its drive to acquire aboriginal territory and absorb aboriginal peoples into the Canadian populace.'
7 See the discussion on this topic in *Treaty Making*, ibid., at 28–9.
8 Sir J. Kempt to Lt.-Gov. J. Colborne, 16 May 1829, *British Parliamentary Papers* (Irish University Press Series), 'Correspondence and other Papers Relating to the Aboriginal Tribes in British Possessions,' 1834, no. 617, at 40–1, as quoted in Miller, n2 *supra*, at 99. See also *Treaty Making*, n4 *supra*, at 28–9.

9 Morris, n5, *supra*, at 288.
10 For example, the Indian Act included a requirement that Indian bands surrender their lands to the Crown if they wished to alienate their lands to a private party. This inclusion in the Indian Act continued the Crown's longstanding practice that had been enshrined in the Royal Proclamation of 1763, but which had earlier origins: see the discussion of this point in Chapter 5, n7 *infra*, and its accompanying text. In addition, the Indian Act contained provisions which gave the Crown control over the management of Indian band funds.
11 S.C. 1876, c. 18.
12 In a great many aboriginal communities, there remains a significant amount of contempt for the Canadian government's imposition of these foreign bodies upon peoples who had their own systems of government in place well before the creation of the Indian Act system or, indeed, prior to the arrival of European people to North America. The extent to which the Indian Act imposes Western ideas of government on aboriginal peoples is reflected by the fact that it contains regulations for the election of chiefs and councillors, including the composition of band councils (s. 74(2)), the eligibility of persons who may be elected to council (s. 75) and to vote in band council electrons (s. 77), and the length of tenure of chiefs and councillors (s. 78). The Act also lists the powers that may be exercised by band councils (ss. 81–6). Section references are to the current Act, R.S.C. 1985, c. I-5.
13 Under Section 2(1) of the current Act, the term 'Indian' refers only to 'a person who pursuant to this Act is registered as an Indian or is entitled to be registered as an Indian.' Note also that until Bill C-31 in 1985, status Indian women who married non-status Indian men or non-Indian men lost their status as a result of such marriages.
14 *Re Eskimo*, [1939] 2 D.L.R. 417 (S.C.C.).
15 Ovide Mercredi and Mary Ellen Turpel, *In the Rapids: Navigating the Future of First Nations* (Toronto: Viking, 1993), at 81.
16 Sections 45–50, 51, and 52 52.5 and the *Indian Estates Regulations*, C.R.C. 1978, c. 954.
17 See *Derrickson v Derrickson* (1986), 26 D.L.R. (4th) 175 (S.C.C.); *Paul v Paul*, [1986] 1 S.C.R. 306; Mary Ellen Turpel, 'Home Land,' (1991) 10 *Cdn. J. Fam. L.* 17.
18 Section 87.
19 Section 89.
20 Mercredi and Turpel, n15 *supra*, at 81.
21 Ibid.
22 Section 2(1).

364 Notes to pages 54–6

23 As now contained in Sections 74 through 80 of the Indian Act.
24 As now contained in Sections 81 through 86 of the Act.
25 Although some aboriginal peoples continue to keep their customary governmental institutions alive and in power, even though, officially, they must adhere to the Indian Act band government system.
26 See, for example, *Logan v Styres* (1959), 20 D.L.R. (2d) 416 (Ont. H.C.); *Isaac v Davey* (1977), 77 D.L.R. (3d) 481 (S.C.C.).
27 R.S.C. 1906, c. 81, as amended by Section 6 of An Act to Amend the Indian Act, S.C. 1926–27, c. 32. See the discussion of this section in Chapters 1 and 14.
28 S.C. 1884, c. 27, s. 3, later Section 114 of the 1886 Act: R.S.C. 1886, c. 43. See also Katherine A. Pettipas, *Severing the Ties that Bind: Government Repression of Indigenous Religious Ceremonies on the Prairies* (Winnipeg: University of Manitoba Press, 1994).
29 Such actions were later made indictable offences: see R.S.C. 1906, c. 81, s. 149. An indictable offence is the more serious classification of criminal offence (the other being summary conviction offences), which, except where otherwise expressly provided for by law, requires every person accused of committing such an offence to be tried by judge and jury: Criminal Code, R.S.C. 1985, c. C-46, s. 471. In 1918, this was changed again from an indictable offence to a summary conviction offence: S.C. 1918, c. 26, s. 7. See note 33, *infra*.
30 This section also made encouraging or assisting in the celebration or performance of these events an offence. See n29, *supra*.
31 Mercredi and Turpel, n15 *supra*, at 27.
32 S.C. 1914, c. 35, s. 8. This new addition was included in the revised Indian Act, R.S.C. 1927, c. 98, s. 140.
33 Indian Act, S.C. 1951, c. 29, s. 123. It should be noted that the only significant changes to these provisions while they remained in force was to make the potlach ban a summary conviction offence rather than an indictable offence: S.C. 1918, c. 26, s. 7. A summary conviction offence is the less serious classification of criminal offence which, except where otherwise provided for by law, carries a maximum penalty of $2,000 and/or six months' imprisonment: Criminal Code, n24 *supra*, s. 787(1).
34 Sinclair, Address, Western Workshop, (Western Judicial Education Centre, Lake Louise, Alberta, 14 May 1990), unpublished, at 9, as quoted in Patricia A. Monture, 'Now that the Door is Open: First Nations and the Law School Experience,' (1990) 15 *Queen's L.J.* 179, at 180. See also Celia Haig-Brown, *Resistance and Renewal: Surviving the Indian Residential School* (Vancouver: Tillacum Library, 1988). Residential schools were incorporated into the *Indian Act* in 1894: S.C. 1894, c. 32, s. 11.

35 Randy Fred, 'Introduction,' in Haig-Brown, n34 *supra*, at 1–2. This quote is also used in the *Manitoba Aboriginal Justice Inquiry*, Vol. 1, n1, *supra*, at 514.
36 As Alan D. McMillan, *Native Peoples and Cultures of Canada: An Anthropological Overview* (Vancouver: Douglas and McIntyre, 1988), at 6, writes: 'In [a] recent survey of native languages ... only three (Cree, Ojibwa, and Inuktitut) were considered to have excellent chances for survival [out of approximately 50 still in existence].' All others were considered endangered, with many listed as 'verging on extinction.'
37 See the discussion in Chapter 2.
38 A similar occurrence, albeit in vastly different circumstances, was contained in a letter from Benjamin Frankin to Peter Collinson, 9 May 1753, reprinted in Leonard W. Labaree et al., eds. *The Papers of Benjamin Franklin*, Vol. 4, (New Haven: Yale University Press, 1961), as quoted in Wilcomb E. Washburn, *The Indian and the White Man* (Garden City: Anchor Books, 1964), at 61–2: 'The little value Indians set on what we prize so highly under the name of Learning appears from a pleasant passage that happened some years since at a Treaty between one of our Colonies and the Six Nations ... the English Commissioners told the Indians, they had in their Country a College for the instruction of Youth who were there taught various languages, Arts, and Sciences; that there was a particular foundation in favour of the Indians to defray the expense of the Education of any of their sons who should desire to take the Benefit of it. And now if the Indians would accept of the Offer, the English would take half a dozen of their brightest lads and bring them up in the Best manner. The Indians after consulting on the proposal replied that it was remembered some of their Youths had formerly been educated in that College, but it had been observed that for a long time after they returned to their Friends, they were absolutely good for nothing being neither acquainted with the true methods of killing deer, catching Beaver or surprizing [*sic*] an enemy.'

Compare this statement with that in Monture, n34, *supra*, at 179: 'When our grandmothers sent their children to school it was with self-sufficiency and mastery over the production of new things in mind. They did not realize that we would never be taught to create the iron cooking pots from the ore of the earth. This is the third generation of our education and our children know less about the production of the stuff of life than our grandmothers. Schools have showed themselves to be ideological processing plants, turning out young people that cannot produce the means to sustain themselves, but who are full from cover-to-cover with the ideological non-sense [*sic*] of European culture.'
39 *Statement of the Government of Canada on Indian Policy, 1969* (Ottawa: Queen's

Printer, 1969) at 5. See also Chapter 1, n25–6 *supra* and their accompanying text; also, Appendix 1.
40 6 Pet. 515 (U.S. 1832), at 546.
41 Ibid., at 544–5.
42 See the discussion in Chapter 1, n84 and its accompanying text.
43 8 Wheat. 543 (U.S. 1823).
44 Ibid., at 573.
45 Ibid.
46 Note 40 *supra*, at 544.
47 See *Campbell v Hall* (1774), 1 Cowp. 204, 98 E.R. 1045 (K.B.); *Re Southern Rhodesia*, [1919] A.C. 211 (P.C.) 233; *Amodu Tijani v The Secretary, Southern Nigeria*, [1921] 2 A.C. 399 (P.C.), at 407; *Oyekan v Adele*, [1957] 2 All E.R. 785 (P.C.), at 788; Brian Slattery, 'The Doctrine at Continuity,' in Slattery, *Ancestral Lands, Alien Laws: Judicial Perspectives on Aboriginal Title* (Saskatoon: University of Saskatchewan Native Law Centre, 1983), at 10–11.
48 (1888), 14 A.C. 46 (P.C.), aff'g (1887), 13 S.C.R. 577, (1886), 13 O.A.R. 148, (1885), 10 O.R. 196 (Ch.).
49 (1990), 70 D.L.R. (4th) 385 (S.C.C.).
50 (1888), 14 A.C. 46 (P.C.), at 54.
51 Ibid.
52 (1887), 13 S.C.R. 577, at 645–6.
53 Note 49 *supra*, at 389: 'This appeal requires this court to explore for the first time the scope of s. 35(1) of the *Constitution Act, 1982*, and to indicate its strength as a promise to the aboriginal peoples of Canada.'
54 Ibid., at 404.
55 For an insightful analysis of these two approaches to aboriginal rights and how they are reflected in the *Sparrow* decision, see Michael Asch and Patrick Macklem, 'Aboriginal Right and Canadian Sovereignty: An Essay on *R v Sparrow*,' (1991) 29 *Alta. L. Rev.* 498. See also Macklem, 'First Nations Self-Government and the Borders of the Canadian Legal Imagination,' (1991) 36 *McGill L.J.* 382; Asch, 'Aboriginal Self-Government and the Construction of Canadian Constitutional Identity,' (1992) 30 *Alta. L. Rev.* 465.
56 Asch and Macklem, n55 *supra*, at 502.
57 By holding that the Musqueam band was an organized society prior to the coming of the Europeans, that fishing was an integral element of their lives from time immemorial – a fact not contested at trial – and that the Musqueam right to fish was 'connected to their physical and cultural survival,' all of which indicates the court's focus upon the 'aboriginality' of the right in question: see *Sparrow*, n49 *supra*, at 398, 402. Note also the focus upon the 'aboriginality' of the right in question in *Sparrow* though the 'preferred means'

exemption in the *Sparrow* justificatory test. This aspect of the *Sparrow* test requires that where a court inquires into whether there is a legislative interference with an aboriginal right, the court must ask whether the effect of the legislation is to 'deny to the holders of the right their preferred means of exercising that right': see *Sparrow*, n49 *supra*, at 411. The *Sparrow* decision will be discussed in greater detail in Chapter 6.

58 See the discussion in Asch and Macklem, n55 *supra*.
59 *St Catherine's Milling*, n50 *supra*, at 58: 'The Crown has all along had a present proprietary estate in the land, upon which the Indian title was a mere burden.'
60 For the use of colonialist theory and assumptions in treaty cases, see, for example, *R v Sylboy*, [1929] 1 D.L.R. 307 (N.S. Co. Ct.); *R v Sikyea* (1964), 43 D.L.R. (2d) 150 (N.W.T.C.A.); *R v Horseman*, [1990] 1 S.C.R. 901. See also the references cited in n17 *supra* regarding matrimonial property.
61 Mercredi and Turpel, n15, *supra*, at 4.
62 As documented in Chapter 2.
63 As the first generally recognized fiduciary law case was *Keech v Sandford* (1726), 25 E.R. 223 (Ch.).
64 The theoretical basis of Equity allows for the settlement of disputes based on principles of flexibility, adaptability, fairness, and reason. As such, it stands in marked contrast to the traditionally rigid, rule-oriented basis of the common law. As Lord Denning MR explained in *Re Vandervell's Trust (No. 2)*, [1974] 1 Ch. 269, at 322, 'Equity was introduced to mitigate the rigour of the law.' See also the explanation given by Lord Cowper in *Dudley v Dudley* (1705), 24 E.R. 118 (Ch.), at 119: 'Now equity is not part of the law, but a moral virtue, which qualifies, moderates, and reforms the rigour, hardness, and edge of the law, and is an universal truth: it does also assist the law where it is defective and weak in the constitution (which is the life of the law) and defends the law from crafty evasions, delusions, and new subtilties [*sic*], invented and contrived to evade and delude the common law, whereby such as have undoubted right are made remediless; and this is the office of equity, to support and protect the common law from shifts and crafty contrivances against the justice of the law. Equity therefore does not destroy the law, nor create it, but assist it.'

Historically, Equity and the common law were parallel systems, but retained their distinctness through their separate jurisdictions until they were merged by the passage of the Judicature Acts of 1873 and 1875: Judicature Act, 1873 (U.K.), 36 & 37 Vict., c. 66; Judicature Act, 1875 (U.K.), 38 & 39 Vict., c. 77. For more background on the origins and history of Equity, see, for example, D.M. Kerly, *An Historical Sketch of the Equitable Jurisdiction of the Court of Chan-*

cery (Cambridge: Cambridge University Press, 1890); G.B. Adams, 'The Origins of English Equity,' (1916) 16 *Columbia L. Rev.* 87; Adams, 'The Continuity of English Equity,' (1916–17) 26 *Yale L.J.* 550; Walter Ashburner, *Principles of Equity* (London: Butterworth, 1902); 16 *Halsbury's Laws of England*, 4th ed. (London: Butterworth, 1976), at 807–12 (para. 1201–7); Sir William Holdsworth, *A History of English Law*, 16 vols. (London: Methuen, 1964).

65 The existence of the Crown's sovereignty does not preclude the existence of aboriginal sovereignty over their lands and peoples. Indeed, the notion of a shared sovereignty does exist within Western legal thought, as evidenced in the distinction between *imperium* and *dominium*. See Sir John Salmond, *Jurisprudence*, 7th ed. (London: Sweet and Maxwell, 1924), Appendix VI, 'International Law,' at 554: '[T]he legal conception of state-territory is distinct from that of state-ownership ... The first conception pertains to the domain of public law, the second to that of private law. Territory is the subject matter of the right of sovereignty or *imperium*, while property is the subject-matter of the right of ownership or *dominium*. These two rights may or may not co-exist in the Crown in respect of the same area. Land may be held by the Crown as territory but not as property, or as property but not as territory, or in both rights at the same time. As property, though not as territory, *land may be held by one state within the dominions of another*.' (Emphasis added)

The distinction between *imperium* and *dominium* has been forgotten or smoothed over, however, as Sir Kenneth Roberts notes in *Commonwealth and Colonial Law* (London: Stevens, 1966) at 625: 'The distinction between these two conceptions has, however, become blurred by the doctrine that the acquisition of sovereignty over a Colony, whether by settlement, cession, or conquest, or even of jurisdiction in territory which remains outside the British dominions, imports Crown rights in, or in relation to, the land itself.'

See also the judgment of Brennan J in *Mabo v Queensland [No.2]* (1992), 175 C.L.R. 1 (H.C. Aust.) at 43–5.

4 The Legislative and Jurisprudential History of the Crown–Native Relationship in Canada

1 David C. Nahwegahbow, Michael W. Posluns, Don Allen, and Douglas Sanders, 'The First Nations and the Crown: A Study of Trust Relationships,' unpublished research report prepared for the Special Committee of the House of Commons on Indian Self-Government, 1983.
2 Although, in all fairness, the terms of reference for the research project indicated that it was to concentrate exclusively on various aspects of the trust relationship between the federal Crown and aboriginal peoples in Canada.

Notes to pages 66-8   369

3 In some circumstances, the use of trust arguments has continued by aboriginal peoples in actions against the Crown. In *Cardinal v R* (1991), 44 E.T.R. 297 (F.C.T.D.), at 316, the court held that although *Guerin v R* (1984), 13 D.L.R. (4th) 321 (S.C.C.) clearly stated that a trust relationship does not, and cannot exist, in the context of a surrender of Indian lands, that does not entail that a trust relationship between the Crown and Native peoples may never exist.
4 Excluding those lands already granted to other British subjects or belonging to other European potentates.
5 R.S.C. 1985, App. II, No. 9. This is discussed in greater detail below. See n20 *infra* and its accompanying text.
6 L.F.S. Upton, *Micmacs and Colonists: Indian–White Relations in the Maritimes, 1713–1867* (Vancouver: University of British Columbia Press, 1979), at 37, notes that at the time of the signing of the Treaty of Utrecht, the aboriginal people of the Maritimes did not view the treaty as rendering them British subjects, or having any effects upon their rights and lands '[T]o quote the Penobscot chief whose words are recorded in the only transcript of an exchange between English and Indians on the morrow of the Treaty of Utrecht: "I have my own kings and governors, my chief and my elders ... I do not wish nevertheless that any stranger erect any fort or establishment on my land. They would embarrass me. I am [strong] enough to occupy the land on my own."'
7 The text of the Royal Proclamations of 1761 and 1763, and Belcher's Proclamation may be found here as Appendices 5, 6, and 7.
8 Discussed in Chapter 2.
9 An Act to Provide for the Instruction and Permanent Settlement of the Indians, S.N.S. 1842, c. XVI.
10 An Act to Regulate the Management and Disposal of Indian Reserves in This Province, S.N.B. 1844, c. XLVII; An Act Concerning Indian Reserves, S.N.S. 1859, c. 14.
11 For further discussion of Crown–Native relations in the Maritimes, see Upton n6, *supra*; Gary P. Gould and Alan J. Semple, eds., *Our Land: The Maritimes* (Fredericton: Saint Annes Point Press, 1980); W.E. Daugherty, *Maritime Indian Treaties in Historical Perspective* (Ottawa: Treaties and Historical Research Centre, Research Branch, Corporate Policy, Department of Indian and Nothern Affairs Canada, 1983); Daniel N. Paul, *We Were Not the Savages: A Micmac Perspective on the Collision of European and Aboriginal Civilizations* (Halifax: Nimbus Publishing, 1993).
12 See Robin Fisher, *Contact and Conflict: Indian–European Relations in British Columbia, 1774–1890* (Vancouver: University of British Columbia Press, 1977); Paul Tennant, *Aboriginal Peoples and Politics: The Indian Land Question in British Columbia, 1849–1989* (Vancouver: University of British Columbia Press, 1990).

13 Nahwegahbow et al., n1 *supra*, at 105; Peter A. Cumming and Neil H. Mickenberg, *Native Rights in Canada*, 2nd ed. (Toronto: Indian–Eskimo Association of Canada, 1972), at 23. The centralization of British Indian policy in Canada mirrored the British goal of establishing a uniform Indian policy throughout its North American colonies. Johnson was appointed as the Indian official for the northern tribes, with a separate official holding responsibility for those tribes in the south: see Cumming and Mickenberg, ibid; 'Lords of Trade to Secretary Fox, 17 Feb. 1756,' in Edmund Bailey O'Callaghan, ed., *Documents Relative to the Colonial History of the State of New York*, 11 vols. (Albany: Weed, Parsons, 1853–61), Vol. 7, at 35.

For greater detail of pre-Confederation Indian legislation, see Nahwegahbow et al., ibid., at 95–145.

14 *Report of the Select Committee on Aborigines, 1837*, Vol. 1, Part 2, (Imperial Blue Book, 1837 nr VII. 425, Facsimile Reprint, C. Struik (Pty) Ltd, Cape Town, 1966), at 75–6. This conclusion was based on the committee's positive adoption of the sentiments included in a dispatch from Sir G. Murray dated 25 Jan. 1830: 'Whatever may have been the reasons which have hitherto recommended an adherence to the present system, I am satisfied that it ought not to be persisted in for the future; and that so enlarged a view of the nature of our connexions with the Indian tribes should be taken as may lead to the adoption of proper measures for their future preservations and improvement; whilst, at the same time, the obligations of moral duty and sound policy should not be lost sight of.'

15 Province of Canada, 'Report on the Affairs of the Indians in Canada,' J.L.A.C., Vol. 6, Appendix T. 24 June 1847, at 360.

16 12 Vict., 1849, c. 9.

17 An Act for the Better Protection of the Lands and Property of the Indians in Lower Canada, 13–14 Vict., 1850, c. 42, s. 1. Another statute setting apart Indian lands in Lower Canada to be managed by the commissioner of Indian lands for Lower Canada under the 1850 legislation, entitled An Act to Authorise the Setting Apart of Lands for the Use of Certain Indian Tribes in Lower Canada, 14–15 Vict., 1851, c. 106, s. 1, was passed the following year. Curiously, the use of the term 'in trust' was dropped, but the use of trust-like terminology remained: '[S]uch tracts of Land shall be and are hereby respectively set apart and appropriated to and for the use of the several Indian Tribes in Lower Canada ... and the said tracts of Land shall accordingly, by virtue of this Act ... be vested in and managed by the Commissioner of Indian Lands for Lower Canada under the Act passed in the Session held in the thirteenth and fourteenth years of Her Majesty's Reign, and intituled [sic], "*An Act for the better protection of the Lands and Property of the Indians in Lower Can-*

ada."' These two statutes later became the subject of contention in *Attorney-General of Canada v Giroux* (1916), 30 D.L.R. 123 (S.C.C.) and *Attorney-General for Quebec v Attorney-General for Canada, Re Indian Lands* (1920), 56 D.L.R. 373 (P.C.), also known as the 'Star Chrome' case.

18 An Act Respecting Management of the Indian Lands and Property, 23 Vict., 1860, c. 151, s. 8. Note also the use of trust terminology in Sections 2 and 3 of the Act.

19 (1901), 32 S.C.R. 1, at 13–14. See also the comments in *R v Morley*, [1932] 4 D.L.R. 483 (B.C.C.A.) at 514. Note, however, the expression to the contrary made by Johnson J.A. in *R v Sikyea* (1964), 43 D.L.R. (2d) 150 (N.W.T.C.A.), at 154. 'It is always to be kept in mind that the Indians surrendered their rights in the territory in exchange for these promises. This "promise and agreement", like any other, can, of course, be breached, and there is no law of which I am aware that would prevent Parliament by legislation, properly within s. 91 of the *B.N.A. Act*, from doing so.' Although Johnson JA's comments in *Sikyea* were entirely consistent with accepted jurisprudence at the time (i.e., that aboriginal and treaty rights could be extinguished by legislation prior to their constitutional recognition and affirmation in Section 35 of the Constitution Act, 1982), in light of the Supreme Court of Canada's statements in *R v Sparrow* (1990), 70 D.L.R. (4th) 385 (S.C.C.) that the federal legislative powers contained in Section 91(24) must be read together with Section 35(1) and that those rights must be construed in a purposive way (see *Sparrow*, at 409, 407 respectively), Johnson JA's comments are no longer appropriate. For further illustration of the inappropriateness of Johnson JA's comments in *Sikyea* when juxtaposed against the Crown's pre-Proclamation undertaking of its special duty towards aboriginal peoples, see the discussion of the two planes of fiduciary doctrine in Chapter 7.

20 Note 5 *supra* (formerly entitled Order of Her Majesty in Council admitting Rupert's Land and the North-Western Territory into the Union).

21 Formerly entitled Order of Her Majesty in Council admitting British Columbia into the Union, dated the 16th day of May, 1871. See R.S.C. 1985, App. II, No. 10.

22 Note 5 *supra*. See Kent McNeil, *Native Claims in Rupert's Land and the North-Western Territory: Canada's Constitutional Obligations* (Saskatoon: University of Saskatchewan Native Law Centre, 1982).

23 Ibid., Schedule B, 2.

24 See Ontario Boundaries Extension Act, S.C., 1912, c. 40; Quebec Boundaries Extension Act, S.C., 1912, c. 45. Note that reciprocal legislation was passed concurrently by the provinces. See *An Act to Express the Consent of the Legislative Assembly of the Province of Ontario to an Extension of the Limits of*

the Province, S.O. 1912, c. 3; An Act Respecting the Extension of the Province of Quebec by the Annexation of Ungava, S.Q. 1912, c. 7.
25 Respectively found in S.C. 1930, c. 29, s. 11, S.C. 1930, c. 41, s. 10, and S.C. 1930, c. 3, s. 10, which were incorporated into the British North America Act, 1930, 20–21 Geo. V., c. 26 (U.K.).
26 S.C. 1876, c. 18.
27 S.C. 1951, c. 29.
28 *Miller v the King*, [1948] Ex. C.R. 372, rev'd (1950), [1950] 1 D.L.R. 513 (S.C.C.) and *St Ann's Island Shooting and Fishing Club v The King*, [1949] 2 D.L.R. 17 (Exch.), aff'd (1950), [1950] 2 D.L.R. 225 (S.C.C.). These cases are discussed in further detail *infra*.
29 See Alexander Morris, *The Treaties of Canada with the Indians of Manitoba and the North-West Territories* (Toronto: Belfords, Clarke, 1880); George Brown and Ron Maguire, *Indian Treaties in Historical Perspective* (Ottawa: Research Branch, Corporate Policy, Department of Indian and Northern Affairs Canada, 1979); Richard Price, ed., *The Spirit of the Alberta Indian Treaties* (Edmonton: Pica Pica Press, 1987); René Fumoleau, *As Long as This Land Shall Last* (Toronto: McClelland and Stewart, 1976); W.E. Daugherty, *Maritime Indian Treaties in Historical Perspective* (Ottawa: Treaties and Research Centre, Research Branch, Corporate Policy, Department of Indian and Northern Affairs Canada, 1983).
30 The same John Beverly Robinson who, as attorney-general of Upper Canada, disparaged the notion of signing treaties with Native peoples: see Chapter 2, n11.
31 (1846), 1 E. & A. 117 (U.C. Exec. Council), at 118.
32 (1858), 15 U.C.Q.B. 392, at 396.
33 One of the earliest of these cases was *Church v Fenton* (1878), 28 U.C.C.P. 384, aff'd (1879), 4 O.A.R. 159, (1880), 5 S.C.R. 239.
34 See, for example, *Attorney-General of Canada v Giroux*, n17 *supra*, where Duff J stated, at 164: 'The Indian interest being, as I have pointed out, ownership is by the terms of the surrender a surrender to Her Majesty in trust to be dealt with in a certain manner for the benefit of the Indians.' See also *Bastien v Hoffman* (1867), 17 L.C.R. 238 (Q.B.); *Re Kane* (1939), [1940] 1 D.L.R. 390 (N.S. Co. Ct.).
35 Such as *Quirt v The Queen* (1891), 19 S.C.R. 510. See also the statement of Taschereau J in *St Catherine's Milling* in Chapter 2, n10 *supra*.
36 Note 34 *supra*.
37 Ibid., at 397.
38 (1905), 9 Ex. C.R. 417.
39 In 1840 the provinces of Upper and Lower Canada were consolidated into the

province of Canada by the Act of Union, 1840 (U.K.), 3–4 Vict., c. 35 – see The Union Act, 1840, R.S.C. 1985, App. II, No. 3 – with all prior debts becoming the responsibility of the newly created province.
40 Section 111 provided that upon Confederation, the Dominion of Canada would absorb and become liable for 'the Debts and Liabilities of each Province existing at the Union.' The amount of the debt absorbed was, however, subject to the limits imposed by Sections 112, 114, and 115 of the British North America Act, 1867.
41 The money was credited by the Department of Indian Affairs to its Indian funds on 29 Aug. 1884 under the authority of an Order in Council dated 30 June 1884, but the money was never actually transferred from the Consolidated Revenue Fund. The Consolidated Revenue Fund was created upon Confederation by Section 102 of the British North America Act, 1867, from all duties and revenues which the pre-Confederation legislatures of Canada, Nova Scotia, and New Brunswick had power of appropriations over at Confederation. These moneys were appropriated for the Public Service of Canada subject to certain charges enumerated in the Act, such as the assumption of the public debts of the pre-Confederation provinces in Section 111.
42 Ontario and Quebec had refused to recognize the validity of the band's claim and to indemnify the federal Crown for the amount of the award. Upon a further review of documents, the band's claim was shown not to be well founded: see n38 *supra*, at 433.
43 Ibid., at 427.
44 See, for example, *Rustomjee v The Queen* (1876), 2 Q.B. 69 (C.A.); *Kinloch v Secretary of State for India in Council*, [1881–2] 7 A.C. 619 (H.L.); *Hereford Railway Co v The Queen* (1894), 24 S.C.R. 1. It should be noted that the political trust doctrine is still evident in modern case law: see *Tito v Waddell (No. 2)*, [1977] 3 All E.R. 129 (Ch.) and the Federal Court of Appeal's decision in *Guerin v R* (1982), 143 D.L.R. (3d) 416 (F.C.A.), which was later overturned upon its subsequent appeal to the Supreme Court of Canada, n3 *supra*. See the discussion of *Guerin* in Chapter 5.
45 Note 38 *supra*, at 438.
46 50–51 Vict., c. 16.
47 Note 38 *supra*, at 441; see also 50–51 Vict., c. 16, s. 15.
48 Note 38 *supra*, at 441.
49 Ibid., at 443.
50 The doctrine of equitable estoppel, or estoppel *in pais*, prevents a party, by virtue of its actions or conduct, from asserting rights which it would otherwise possess.
51 Laches (la-chéz) is an equitable doctrine which estops, or prevents, a plaintiff

374 Notes to pages 78–80

from asserting a right or claim by virtue of the combination of having taken too long to assert that right or claim and the prejudice that would result to the adverse party if the allegation was allowed to proceed after such delay. Laches may only be successfully pleaded by a defendant to a proceeding where there is a demonstration of prejudice to the defendant occasioned by the delay in bringing proceedings caused by the action or inaction of the plaintiff. The doctrine of laches is discussed in greater detail in Chapter 10.

52 The Crown was not held liable for the negligence of its officers prior to May 1953: see the Crown Liability Act, R.S.C. 1970, C-38, s. 24. After that date Crown liability for negligence and in tort was governed by the Crown Liability Act.
53 This term is explained in chapter 1, n9.
54 See n45 *supra*.
55 Specifically in R.S.C. 1970, (2nd Supp.), c. 10.
56 R.S.C. 1886, c. 7, as amended.
57 This was confirmed in Kellock J's analysis of a similar situation in *Miller v The King* (1950), [1950] 1 D.L.R. 513 (S.C.C.), at 522. The *Miller* case is discussed in greater detail *infra*.
58 See also the discussion of this point in David R. Lowry, 'Native Trusts: The Position of the Government of Canada as Trustee for Indians, A Preliminary Analysis,' unpublished report prepared for the Indian Claims Commission and the Union of Nova Scotia Indians, 1973, at 19, where he suggests that there were, indeed, English cases decided prior to *Henry* in which the courts enforced a trust against the Crown.
59 (1935), 5 C.N.L.C. 92 (Exch.).
60 These purposes included: providing rations for the old, sick, and destitute members of the band; furnishing housing, furniture, and clothing for the old and destitute members of the band or houses for young men who took up farming; supplying farming outfits of horses, harness, plows, or other implements for able-bodied members of the band who began farming, as well as cattle and threshing outfits; granting compensation to any Indian who owned buildings or improvements on the land surrendered; and, making interest-free loan advances to able-bodied, returned Indian soldiers who were members of the band to enable them to purchase houses, stables, horses, cattle, or farming implements. Furthermore, on or about 1 Feb. of each year, the interest from all band funds held in trust by the Department of Indian Affairs was to be distributed equally among all band members.
61 For a complete list of the band's objections to charges incurred, see n59 *supra*, at 94–5.
62 By statute, most rights of action are prescribed a maximum range of time

from when the cause of action occurred in which to initiate legal proceedings. Actions which are initiated beyond the maximum time alloted are held to be statute-barred and not maintainable in the courts. The application of statutory limitation periods to claims for breach of fiduciary duty is discussed in Chapter 10.
63 [1948] 3 D.L.R. 797 (Exch.).
64 See Chapter 2, n75.
65 R.S.C. 1927, c. 98 (as amended).
66 Note 63 *supra*, at 797. At the time of the *Chisholm* decision, the minister of mines and resources was also the superintendent-general of Indian Affairs.
67 [1948] Ex. C.R. 372, rev'd (1950), [1950] 1 D.L.R. 513 (S.C.C.).
68 [1948] Ex. C.R. 372, at 376.
69 R.S.C. 1927, c. 34.
70 R.S.O. 1937, c. 118.
71 Note 57 *supra*, at 521, as had been the case with the *Henry* decision, n38 *supra*.
72 Note 57 *supra*, at 521. Kellock J's comments were based on the affirmation of this principle by Baron Atkyns in *Pawlett v Attorney-General* (1668), 145 E.R. 550 (Exch.) and by the Privy Council in *Esquimalt & Nanaimo Railway Co v Wilson*, [1920] A.C. 358 (P.C.). Note also the later commentary on this point by Hall J in *Calder v Attorney-General of British Columbia* (1973), 34 D.L.R. (3d) 145 (S.C.C.), at 221.
73 Note 57 *supra*, at 522.
74 R.S.C. 1927, c. 158.
75 (1880), 15 Ch. D. 67, rev'd on a different point 17 Ch. D. 771 (C.A.), where it was held that money transferred to the Crown by the trustees and executors of the will of a deceased person where no next-of-kin had been discovered was recoverable by the next-of-kin even though, in the interim, the money had been spent by the Crown. This finding stands in direct opposition to the determination made in the *Henry* decision, n38 *supra*, at 441, where Burbidge J held that the Exchequer Court did not possess jurisdiction to hear the Mississaugas of the Credit band's claim – even though he had found that the Crown held the moneys arising from the sale of the surrendered lands in trust for the band – on the basis that the Crown was no longer in possession of the moneys claimed by the band.
76 Note 57 *supra*, at 522.
77 See ibid., at 523, where he noted that the situation created by the surrender of land contained both trust and contract elements.
78 Although see ibid., 524, where Kellock J stated that from the evidence presented before him, it would appear that, at least with respect to the moneys

derived from the surrendered lands, the federal Crown was attempting to exercise some measure of control.
79 [1949] 2 D.L.R. 17 (Exch.), aff'd (1950), [1950] 2 D.L.R. 225 (S.C.C.).
80 The spelling used here reflects that used in the judgment itself.
81 R.S.C. 1906, c. 81.
82 [1949] 2 D.L.R. 17 (Exch.), at 21.
83 Ibid., at 24: 'The statutory authority of the Governor in Council to manage, lease and sell could not be fettered in any such way, nor its authority and duty diverted to anyone named by the surrendering Indians.'
84 As well as holding himself out as having authority to represent and bind the Crown.
85 See n82 *supra*, at 26–7 and the sources cited therein. See the definition of estoppel in n50 *supra*.
86 (1950), [1950] 2 D.L.R. 225 (S.C.C.) at 232.
87 See L.C. Green, 'Trusteeship and Canada's Indians,' (1976–7) 3 *Dalhousie L.J.* 105, at 117.
88 The requirements of the Crown's fiduciary duty to aboriginal peoples in Canada will be discussed in greater detail in the ensuing chapters.
89 At least with regard to the sale, lease, or other disposition of surrendered reserve lands by the Crown, which Section 51 was concerned with, although the Indian Act used similar language in other sections, such as those dealing with the Crown's holding of Indian lands moneys on behalf of Indian bands.
90 The only remaining difference is that a statute such as the Indian Act may be repealed or amended by Parliament, thereby eliminating the legal enforceability of the duties and obligations contained within it.
91 (1989), 57 D.L.R. (4th) 197 (S.C.C.) at 208: 'the provisions of the *Indian Act* which, while not constitutive of the obligations owed to the Indians by the Crown, codify the pre-existing duties of the Crown toward the Indians.' This statement is an elaboration of the earlier commentary by Dickson J, as he then was, in *Guerin*, n3 *supra*, at 340, where he emphasized that the Indian Act confirmed 'the historic responsibility which the Crown has undertaken, to act on behalf of the Indians so as to protect their interests in transactions with third parties.'
92 The term 'equitable obligations' is defined in Chapter 1, n9.

5 The Characterization of the Crown–Native Fiduciary Relationship by the Courts: *Guerin v R*

1 The most prominent early characterization of aboriginal rights as existing at the pleasure of the Crown is seen in the Privy Council's judgment in *St Cathe-*

Notes to pages 88–92 377

rine's Milling and Lumber Co v The Queen (1888), 14 A.C. 46 (P.C.) at 54, where the Lord Watson described the aboriginal interest in land as 'a personal and usufructurary right, dependent upon the good will of the Sovereign.'
2 Ibid.
3 Additionally, the shares in the trust property which the beneficiaries of the trust are to be entitled to must be unequivocal (i.e., the benefit to be obtained from the property by each beneficiary must be ascertained).
4 For a more detailed discussion of the basic legal requirements for the establishment of a trust, see D.W.M. Waters, *Law of Trusts in Canada*, 2d ed. (Toronto: Carswell, 1984) Ch 5; Glanville Williams, 'The Three Certainties,' (1940) 4 *Mod. L. Rev.* 20.
5 It is important to distinguish between the concepts of recognition and affirmation versus that of creation. *Guerin* did not *create* the fiduciary relationship between the Crown and Native peoples in Canada where no such relationship previously existed. Instead, *Guerin* was the first Canadian case which afforded legal protection to the Crown–Native relationship; see Chapter 7 for further discussion of the philosophical underpinnings of this distinction.
6 R.S.C. 1985, c. I-5, s. 37, as amended. Surrenders may only be made to the Crown in right of Canada because of its exclusive jurisdiction over 'Indians and Lands reserved for the Indians,' in Section 91(24) of the British North America Act, 1867.
7 Allowing surrenders of Indian reserve lands only through the Crown is a long-standing practice of the Crown which dates back to the early colonization of North America: see n98 and n99 *infra* and their accompanying text. This practice also existed in other parts of the British Empire: see, for example, *R v Symonds*, [1847] N.Z.P.C.C. 387 (N.Z.S.C.), at 391. Currently, the relevant provisions concerning the surrender of reserve lands are contained within sections 18(1) and 37–41 of the Indian Act, R.S.C. 1985, c. I-5, as amended. For further discussion and analysis of the surrender requirements contained within the Indian Act, see J. Paul Salembier, 'How Many Sheep Make A Flock? An Analysis of the Surrender Provisions of the Indian Act.' [1992] 1 C.N.L.R. 14.
8 This report was made known to the Indian Affairs Branch, as the acknowledgments section of the report indicates that personnel in the Indian Affairs Branch in Vancouver were consulted during the report's preparation.
9 (1984), 13 D.L.R. (4th) 321 (S.C.C.), at 327.
10 Howell confirmed the accuracy of this statement in his testimony at trial, as reflected in the trial judge's statements: (1981), 10 E.T.R. 61 (F.C.T.D.), at 77.
11 [1983] 143 D.L.R. (3d) 116 (F.C.A.), at 428.
12 Ibid., at 430. The trial judge expressed the following view of these statements:

'Anfield's advice as to Howell's opinion on rate of return is, in my view, an overstatement. The band was never given a copy of Howell's letter of May 23, 1957. Nor was the band told, at that time, the golf club proposed to have the right to remove any improvements made to the lands.
13 Note 10 *supra*, at 79–80.
14 Note 9 *supra*, at 354.
15 Note 11 *supra*, at 435.
16 Ibid.
17 Note 10 *supra*, at 87.
18 Note 9 *supra*, at 330.
19 Note 10 *supra*, with additional reasons at (1981), 127 D.L.R.(3d) 170 (F.C.T.D.).
20 The Crown had failed to specifically plead the political trust argument in its statement of defence and declined the opportunity to amend its defence when it was presented with the opportunity.
21 See Chapter 4, n51 for definition.
22 Note 10 *supra*, at 77.
23 Ibid., at 79.
24 Note 11 *supra*, at 432.
25 Note 9 *supra*, at 329.
26 Note 11 *supra*, at 432.
27 Note 10 *supra*, at 82.
28 Ibid.
29 Ibid., at 88.
30 Ibid., at 90.
31 As an equitable doctrine, laches cannot be involved where the party relying on it has acted inequitably. The principles of Equity demand that it will aid only those persons who have not acted unscrupulously. This is reflected by its well-known credos, ' He who seeks, equity must do equity' [see 16 *Halsbury's Laws of England*, 4th ed. (London: Butterworth, 1976), at 874 (para. 1303); Harold Greville Hanbury and Ronald Harling Maudsley, *Modern Equity*, 13th ed., Jill E. Martin, ed. (London: Stevens, 1989), at 27–8; *Davis v Duke of Marlborough* (1819), 2 Swan 108 (Ch.), at 157, per Lord Eldon LC: 'The principle of this court is not to give relief to those who will not do equity'], and, 'He who comes into equity must come with clean hands' [see 16 *Halsbury's Laws of England*, 4th ed., at 875 (para. 1305); Hanbury and Maudsley, *Modern Equity*, 13th ed., at 28; *Fitzroy v Gwillim* (1786), 1 Term Rep. 153 (Ch.), per Lord Mansfield CJ, who said that in an equitable action, a plaintiff must 'come with clean hands according to the principle that those who seek equity must do equity'].
32 See the discussion of the certainty of subject in n3 *supra*. Refer also to the characterization of aboriginal title in *St Catherine's Milling*, n1 *supra*.

Notes to pages 98–100   379

33 R.S.C. 1952, c.149, ss. 37–41.
34 (1935), 5 C.N.L.C. 92 (Exch.).
35 [1948] Ex. C.R. 372; rev'd (1950), [1950] 1 D.L.R. 513 (S.C.C.).
36 (1981), 125 D.L.R. (3d) 513 (F.C.T.D.).
37 Note 11 *supra*, at 442. Le Dain JA did not consider whether the relationship between the Crown and Musqueam band imposed any obligations upon the former.
38 Ibid., at 443.
39 R.S.C. 1952, c. 149, s. 39(1)(c). Le Dain JA explained that even if an Indian Affairs Department official had accepted the oral terms, which he found could not be established by the evidence, the precedent established in *St Ann's Island Shooting and Fishing Club Ltd v The King* (1950), [1950] 2 D.L.R. 225 (S.C.C.) at 232, prevented the governor in council from transferring or delegating its obligations over surrendered lands to departmental officials in the absence of explicit statutory authority to do so, see the discussion of this point in *St Ann's Island* in 'Fiduciaries' Delegation of Authority,' in Chapter 10.
40 (1950), [1950] 1 D.L.R. 513 (S.C.C.).
41 See the discussion of *Miller* in Chapter 4.
42 Note 11 *supra*, at 465.
43 Ibid., at 466.
44 Ibid., at 469.
45 Ibid.
46 Ibid., at 470
47 Ibid. Indeed, earlier in his decision, Le Dain JA cited the statement of Megarry VC in *Tito v Waddell (No. 2)*, [1977] 3 All E.R. 129 (Ch.), at 220–1, to distinguish between the politically based trust and the legally based trust:
    First, the use of a phrase such as 'in trust for,' even in a formal document such as a Royal Warrant, does not necessarily create a trust enforceable by the courts ... Second, the term 'trust' is one which may properly be used to describe not only relationships which are enforceable by the courts in their equitable jurisdiction, but also other relationships such as the discharge, under the direction of the Crown, of the duties or functions belonging to the prerogative and the authority of the Crown.
    ...
    The third is that it seems clear that the determination whether an instrument has created a true trust or a trust in the higher sense is a matter of construction, looking at the whole of the instrument in question, its nature and effect, and, I think, its context. Fourth, a material factor may be the form of the description given by the instrument to the person alleged to be

the trustee. An impersonal description of him, in the form of a reference not to an individual but to the holder of a particular office for the time being, may give some indication that what is intended is not a true trust, but a trust in the higher sense.
48 Note 11 *supra*, at 470–1.
49 The act of state doctrine holds that the Crown cannot infringe the rights of its own citizens by executive action within its own dominions, but only by legislative actions: see *Entick v Carrington* (1765), 19 St. Tr. 1029, 95 E.R. 867 (K.B.); *Walker v Baird*, [1892] A.C. 491 (P.C.); *Attorney-General v Nissan*, [1970] A.C. 179 (H.L.).
50 Note 40 *supra*.
51 The case was heard by the full panel of the Supreme Court; however, Chief Justice Bora Laskin died prior to the rendering of judgment. The *Guerin* judgment was rendered by the remaining eight justices. Upon Laskin CJC's death, his position as chief justice was filled by Dickson J, and, ironically, the vacancy on the Supreme Court was filled by Le Dain J.
52 Note 9 *supra*, at 349.
53 For these reasons, Estey J's judgment in *Guerin* has been routinely ignored in subsequent judicial considerations of the *Guerin* case. Note the dissent to Estey J's argument by Dickson J in *Guerin*, n9 *supra* 343, where he stated that 'not only does the Crown's authority to act on the band's behalf lack a basis in contract, but the band is not a party to the ultimate sale or lease, as it would be if it were the Crown's principal.' See also the discussion in John D. Hurley, 'The Crown's Fiduciary Duty and Indian Title: *Guerin v The Queen*,' (1985) 30 *McGill L.J.* 559, at 564–5; Richard H. Bartlett, 'The Fiduciary Obligation of the Crown to the Indians,' (1989) 53 *Sask. L. Rev.* 301, at 323.
54 Concurred in by Beetz, Chouinard, and Lamer JJ.
55 As he stated, in *Guerin*, n9 *supra*, at 341: '[W]here by statute, agreement, or perhaps by unilateral undertaking, one party has an obligation to act for the benefit of another, and that obligation carries with it a discretionary power, the party thus empowered becomes a fiduciary. Equity will then supervise the relationship by holding him to the fiduciary's strict standard of conduct.'
56 Ibid., at 334.
57 It is a generally accepted principle that the law relating to trustees is applicable by analogy to the law of fiduciaries (with some exceptions): see, for example, *In re West of England and South Wales District Bank, Ex parte Dale and Co* (1879), 11 Ch.D 772, at 778, cited with approval in *Guerin*, n9 *supra*, at 345; *Farrington v Rowe McBridge and Partners*, [1985] 1 N.Z.L.R. 83 (C.A.), at 99; *Canson Enterprises Ltd v Boughton & Co* (1989), 61 D.L.R. (4th) 732 (B.C.C.A.). It should be noted that the status of *Canson Enterprises* as an authority for this

proposition is now uncertain as a result of La Forest J's mistaken understanding of the application of trust law by analogy to fiduciary doctrine in the Supreme Court's consideration of the case, [1991] 3 S.C.R. 534, at 578–80, versus McLachlin J's affirmation of the applicability of trust doctrine, at 546, 549–51. Note also the discussion of the Supreme Court's decision in *Canson Enterprises* as it relates to the issues of contributory negligence and the remoteness of damages in Chapter 10.

58 This finding is largely the result of Dickson J's adherence to the precedent established in *Smith v R* (1983), 147 D.L.R. (3d) 237 (S.C.C.), where the Supreme Court of Canada held that upon surrender, the Indian interest in land disappears. Because Dickson J held, in accordance with *Smith*, that the Musqueam's interest in the reserve lands disappeared upon their surrender, he found that there was no *corpus*, or *res*, upon which to found a trust relationship between the parties. Without a *corpus*, there could be no certainty of subject and, therefore, no trust.

59 Wilson J's judgment was concurred in by Ritchie and McIntyre JJ.

60 See *Guerin*, n9 *supra*, at 356–7, as well as at 359, where she stated: 'It seems to me that the "political trust" line of authorities are clearly distinguishable from the present case because Indian title has an existence apart altogether from s.18(1) of the *Indian Act*. It would fly in the face of the clear wording of the section to treat that interest as terminable at will by the Crown without recourse by the band.'

61 Ibid., at 357–9.

62 Ibid., at 361.

63 See the discussion of the political trust doctrine in Chapter 4.

64 Note 9, *supra*, at 360–1.

65 Ibid., at 361: '[T]he Crown acted in breach of trust when it barrelled ahead with a lease on terms which, according to the learned trial judge, were wholly unacceptable to its *cestui que trust*.'

66 Dickson J bases this conclusion largely on the Supreme Court of Canada's decision in *Smith v R* n58 *supra*, where Estey J characterizes the Indian interest in land as an ephemeral right which disappears on surrender and cannot be transferred to a grantee, whether it be the Crown or an individual: see *Smith*, *supra*, at 250. See also the commentary in Hurley, n53 *supra*, at 572–6; Bartlett, n53 *supra*, at 318–19.

It should be noted that Estey J's characterization of the nature of Indian title in *Smith* is both inconsistent with Dickson J's own definition of aboriginal title in *Guerin* and contrary to precedent. Additionally, Estey J's characterization in *Smith* makes redundant the treaty-making process between the Crown and aboriginal peoples – where the Indian interest in land was transferred, at the Crown's request, by treaty from the aboriginals to the Crown – and ignores the basis of English land law, which insists that the title to land, unless it is an original title, must necessarily be derivative. For a more detailed discussion on this latter point and how it relates to the title of aboriginal peoples, see Kent McNeil, *Common Law Aboriginal Title* (Oxford: Clarendon 1989).

67 Although Dickson J stated, n9 *supra*, at 339, that the nature of aboriginal title does not 'strictly speaking, amount to a beneficial interest,' but is *sui generis*, his statement does not, *ipso facto*, render the Indian interest in land non-beneficial. The point that Dickson J attempts to emphasize in his judgment is that the exact nature of aboriginal title cannot be conclusively determined by analogy with common law concepts of property. As he stated, n9 *supra*, at 339, '... in describing what constitutes a unique interest in land the courts have almost inevitably found themselves applying a somewhat inappropriate terminology drawn from general property law.' This same view was expressed over sixty years earlier by Viscount Haldane in *Amodu Tijani v The Secretary, Southern Nigeria*, [1921] 2 A.C. 399 (P.C.), at 403, where he stated, in discussing the nature of aboriginal title: 'There is a tendency, operating at times unconsciously, to render that title conceptually in terms which are appropriate only to systems which have grown up under English law. But this tendency has to be held in check closely.'

68 Note 9 *supra*, at 336: 'Their interest in their lands is a pre-existing legal right not created by Royal Proclamation, by s.18(1) of the *Indian Act*, or by any other executive order or legislative provision.'

69 Indian lands are inalienable except to the Crown or through the Crown as an intermediary in dealings with third parties, as indicated in the Royal Proclamation of 1763. See n7 *supra*, and nn98–9 *infra*.

70 Note 9 *supra*, at 339.

71 Although Dickson J expressly stated, n9 *supra*, at 339, that there are only two essential features of aboriginal title – its general inalienability and the Crown's obligation to deal with land on the Indians' behalf upon its surrender – implicit in this statement is the fact that aboriginal title is a pre-existing, legal right to property which is not dependent on any action of the Crown but is 'derived form the Indians' historic occupation and possession of their tribal lands': n9 *supra*, at 335. Refer to his commentary on this latter issue, ibid., at 335–9.

72 Note 9 *supra*, at 342. See also 58 *supra* for one basis for his arrival at this conclusion. Note that Dickson J's conclusion that the non-beneficial nature of aboriginal title renders it incapable of constituting the *res* of a trust is disputed by Donovan Waters, 'New Directions in the Employment of Equitable

Doctrines: The Canadian Experience,' in Timothy G. Youdan, ed., *Equity, Fiduciaries and Trusts* (Toronto: Carswell, 1989), at 423, where he suggested that 'A personal interest, less than an equitable estate, is an acceptable beneficial interest for the purposes of a trust. In *Moore v Royal Trust Co*, a mere personal license to live in a particular house was accepted by the Supreme Court of Canada as a valid beneficial interest.' See also *Moore v Royal Trust Co*, [1956] S.C.R. 880.

73 See the discussion in *Guerin*, n9 *supra*, at 360–1.
74 Ibid., at 357.
75 Ibid.
76 Refer to the discussion of the three certainties of trust law *supra*.
77 Note the discussion of this point in Chapter 1.
78 Note 9 *supra*, at 341, per Dickson J: 'It is the nature of the relationship, not the specific category of actor involved that gives rise to the fiduciary duty.' For further elaboration, refer to the discussion entitled 'The Situation Specific Nature of Fiduciary Doctrine,' in Chapter 8.
79 Note 9 *supra*, at 344.
80 Some of these judicial considerations will be discussed in Chapter 6.
81 This misinterpretation of Dickson J's findings in *Guerin* is largely responsible for the stunted growth of fiduciary doctrine within the context of Crown–Native relations in Canada, and it has contributed to the confusion surrounding the implementation of fiduciary doctrine to Canadian aboriginal rights jurisprudence.
82 Note 9 *supra*, at 334: 'The fiduciary relationship between the Crown and the Indians has its roots in the concept of aboriginal, native or Indian title.'
83 Ibid.: 'The surrender requirement, and the responsibility it entails, are the source of a distinct fiduciary obligation owed by the Crown to the Indians.'
84 Ibid., at 340: 'This discretion on the part of the Crown, far from ousting, as the Crown contends, the jurisdiction of the courts to regulate the relationship between the Crown and the Indians, has the effect of transforming the Crown's obligation into a fiduciary one.'
85 Ibid., at 334.
86 Ibid., at 339: 'The Crown is under an obligation to deal with the land on the Indians' behalf *when the interest is surrendered*' (emphasis added).
87 Ibid., at 341–2.
88 Ibid., at 339.
89 Ibid., at 341–2.
90 Namely, the requirement that the Crown must use its discretion over the land to further the interest of the surrendering band.
91 See the Introduction *supra*.

92 On this point, note the comment made by Dickson CJC in *Mitchell v Peguis Indian Band* (1990), 71 D.L.R. (4th) 193, at 209, where he stated, 'On its facts, *Guerin* only dealt with the obligation of the *federal* Crown arising upon surrender of land by Indians ...'
93 Note 9 *supra*, at 339. See also at 339, where Dickson J discussed the relevance of the aboriginal interest in land to the Crown's fiduciary obligation: '... [T]he interest gives rise *upon surrender* to a distinctive fiduciary obligation on the part of the Crown to deal with the land for the benefit of the surrendering Indians.'
94 Ibid., at 340. Note also Wilson J's emphasis on the historic nature of the Crown's duty, at 356–7, where she stated that 'it is the acknowledgment of a historic reality, namely, that Indian bands have a beneficial interest in their reserves and that the Crown has a responsibility to protect that interest.' Note also Wilson J's statement in *Roberts v Canada* (1989), 57 D.L.R. (4th) 197 (S.C.C.) at 208: 'the provisions of the *Indian Act* which, while not constitutive of the obligations owed to the Indians by the Crown, codify the pre-existing duties of the Crown toward the Indians.'
95 R.S.C., 1985, App. II, No. 1, discussed in Chapter 2. For more detailed discussion of the proclamation and its effects, see Kenneth M. Narvey, 'The Royal Proclamation of 7 October 1763. The Common Law, and Native Rights to Land within the Territory Granted to the Hudson's Bay Company,' (1974) 38 *Sask. L. Rev.* 123; Jack Stagg, *Anglo–Indian Relations in North America to 1763 and an Analysis of the Royal Proclamation of 7 October 1763* (Ottawa: Research Branch, Indian and Northern Affairs Canada, 1981); Brian Slattery, *The Land Rights of Indigenous Canadian Peoples as Affected by the Crown's Acquisition of Their Territories* (DPhil thesis, Oxford University, 1979, reprinted, Saskatoon: University of Saskatchewan Native Law Centre, 1979); Geoffrey S. Lester, 'The Territorial Rights of the Inuit of the Northwest Territories,' unpublished DJur thesis, Osgoode Hall Law School, 1981; John Borrows 'Constitutional Law from a First Nation Perspective: Self-Government and the Royal Proclamation,' (1994) 28 *U.B.C. L. Rev.* 1.
96 Note 9 *supra*, at 340, citing the judgment of Lord Watson in *St Catherine's Milling and Lumber Co v The Queen*, n1, *supra*, at 54.
97 See the discussion of the Proclamation in Chapter 2.
98 As quoted in Stagg, n95 *supra*, at 22.
99 See Charles C. Royce, *Indian Land Cessions in the United States, Eighteenth Annual Report of the Bureau of American Ethnology, to the Secretary of the Smithsonian Institute*, Part II (Washington, DC: Government Printing Office, 1896–7), at 571–2 (as quoted in Stagg, n95 *supra*, at 22).
100 Note 9 *supra*, at 340.

101 Such as, but not restricted to, the right to hunt, trap, and fish.
102 As the discussion in Chapter 7 indicates, the Crown's fiduciary obligation to the aboriginal peoples predates the Royal Proclamation of 1763. The Proclamation was merely a concrete recognition and affirmation of the existence of the Crown's pre-existing duty.
103 Sections 25 and 35 are discussed and reproduced in Chapter 2. For more detail on Sections 25 and 35, see Brian Slattery, 'The Constitutional Guarantee of Aboriginal and Treaty Rights,' (1982–3) 8 *Queen's L.J.* 232; Slattery, 'The Hidden Constitution: Aboriginal Rights in Canada,' (1984) *Am J. Comp. L.*, 361; Kent McNeil, 'The Constitutional Rights of the Aboriginal Peoples of Canada,' (1982) 4 *Sup. Ct. L. Rev.* 255; McNeil, 'The Constitution Act, 1982, Sections 25 and 35,' [1988] 1 C.N.L.R. 1; Douglas Sanders, 'The Rights of the Aboriginal Peoples of Canada,' (1983) 61 *Can. Bar Rev.* 314; Kenneth Lysyk, 'The Rights and Freedoms of the Aboriginal Peoples of Canada,' in Walter S. Tarnopolsky and Gérald A.-Beaudoin, eds., *The Canadian Charter of Rights and Freedoms* (Toronto: Carswell, 1982); William Pentney, *The Aboriginal Rights Provisions in the Constitution Act 1982* (LLM thesis, University of Ottawa, 1987, reprinted Saskatoon: University of Saskatchewan Native Law Centre, 1987).
104 Indeed, the nature of the Crown's fiduciary duty as expressed in *Guerin* was considered within the context of the constitutional protection of aboriginal and treaty rights in Section 35(1) of the Constitution Act, 1982, in *R v Sparrow* (1990), 70 D.L.R. (4th) 385 (S.C.C.).
105 Rights *in rem* are rights which are enforceable against the world, as opposed to rights *in personam*, which are rights that are enforceable only against a specific person or persons.
106 See also Brian Slattery, 'First Nations and the Constitution: A Question of Trust,' (1992) 71 *Can. Bar Rev.* 261, where he suggests, at 273, that the range of obligations which exist under the Crown's fiduciary duty include the providing of 'protection to Aboriginal land rights, laws, and powers of self-government, and perhaps also Aboriginal languages and cultures.'
107 See Brian Slattery, 'Understanding Aboriginal Rights,' (1987) 66 *Can. Bar Rev.* 727, at 754: 'The *Guerin* decision, while dealing only with the particular fiduciary relations created by a surrender of Indian lands to the Crown, suggests that a more general fiduciary duty exists that informs and explains those relations.' See also Bartlett, n53 *supra*, at 321–2.

6 Judicial Characterizations of the Crown's Fiduciary Duty after *Guerin*

1 (1984), 13 D.L.R. (4th) 321 (S.C.C.). Refer back to the discussion of the legisla

tive and jurisprudential history of the Crown–Native trust relationship in Chapter 4.
2 This is because of the nature of the considerations germane to the case, not because of any restriction on the scope of the duty; see the discussion in Chapter 5.
3 Of which the Crown's control over aboriginal lands was a later development occurring after the genesis of its fiduciary obligations.
4 Donovan Waters, 'New Directions in the Employment of Equitable Doctrines: The Canadian Experience,' in Timothy G. Youdan, ed., *Equity, Fiduciaries and Trust* (Toronto: Carswell, 1989), at 424.
5 The discussion of post-*Guerin* fiduciary cases herein is not intended to be comprehensive of all cases which discuss the Crown's fiduciary obligations to Native peoples, but focuses upon the more noteworthy decision which are relevant to the analysis herein.
6 (1985), 17 D.L.R. (4th) 591 (F.C.A.), aff'g (1981), 125 D.L.R. (3d) 513 (F.C.T.D.).
7 The *Kruger* case is discussed in greater detail in Chapter 15.
8 (1981), 125 D.L.R. (3d) 513 (F.C.T.D.), at 513.
9 (1985), 17 D.L.R. (4th) 591 (F.C.A.), at 597. See also the comments by Urie JA, at 646: '[I]t is clear that what was said by Dickson J in the *Guerin* case was related to a fiduciary relationship in the context of that case, *i.e.*, where there was a surrender of Indian lands to the Crown on certain terms.'
10 Ibid., at 658.
11 [1988] 3 F.C. 20 (F.C.T.D.), aff'd [1993] 2 C.N.L.R. 20 (F.C.A.), rev'd (14 Dec. 1995), File No. 23516 (S.C.C.). The complete text of the reasons for judgment at trial is reported as *Blueberry River Indian Band and Doig River Indian Band v Canada (Minister of Indian Affairs and Northern Development)* (1987), 14 F.T.R. 161 (F.C.T.D.).
12 Because all persons represented in the *Apsassin* action were either Dunne-Za or Cree by linguistic grouping, they will be collectively referred to herein as the 'Dunne-Ze Cree,' as they were by the Federal Court of Appeal. For a more complete breakdown of the various interests represented in *Apsassin*, see [1993] 2 C.N.L.R. 20 (F.C.A.), at 26.
13 Ibid., at 35–6.
14 Glen's actions contradicted the Department of Indian Affairs' (DIAND) policy against the sale of surplus Indian reserve lands, as indicated in the director's annual reports of 1939 and 1945, as noted in *Apsassin*, n12 *supra*, at 32, per Stone JA, and at 76, per Isaac CJ. This point was not discussed by the trial judge in his reasons for judgment despite its corroboration by expert evidence on governmental policies and administrative practices relating to Indian affairs in Canada.
15 The Veterans' Land Act, 1942, 6 Geo. VI, c. 33.

16 Note that when these negotiations began, DIAND and DVLA were both under the jurisdiction of the minister of mines and resources.
17 An instrument issued by the Crown which grants or confirms the patentee's right to exclusive possession and enjoyment of land.
18 If, indeed, any other duties existed.
19 [1988] 3 F.C. 20 (F.C.T.D.), at 47. In accordance with the *Guerin* judgment, Addy J found that any representations by the Crown to Indians during treaty or surrender negotiations, including those which are not included in the terms of the treaty or surrender, are binding at law.
20 Ibid., at 46.
21 Ibid., at 74: '... [DIAND] was seeking the best price available for the land and was interested in obtaining it immediately in order to purchase substitute reserves closer to the trap lines ... [DVLA] wanted to secure good agricultural land at the lowest possible price in order to allow the veterans to obtain a greater benefit from the purchase.'
22 Ibid., at 75-6.
23 A corporation sole is a corporation consisting of only one person, whose successor becomes the corporation on the former's death or resignation.
24 Under Section 5(1) of the Act.
25 Refer back to the analysis of Dickson J's judgment in Chapter 5.
26 Addy J's understanding of the position of beneficiaries relative to their fiduciaries in fiduciary relationships is based on a fundamental misconception of the nature of fiducial relations. See the discussion of inequality theory in Chapter 9. See also Leonard I. Rotman, 'The Vulnerable Position of Fiduciary Doctrine in the Supreme Court of Canada,' (1995) 23(4) *Man. L.J.* (in press).
27 *Apsassin*, n19 *supra*, at 46-7. It would appear that Addy J either failed to take into account, or simply ignored, the restrictions imposed on status Indians' rights and de facto independence by the Indian Act.
28 Refer back to the distinction between trust and fiduciary law in Chapter 1. Note also the further discussion of the requirement necessary to ground a fiduciary relationship in Chapter 10.
29 [1976] 2 S.C.R. 802. See also the further references given in *Apsassin*, n12 *supra*, at 16, in particular the aboriginal rights case of *Ontario (Attorney-General) v Bear Island Foundation* (1991), 83 D.L.R. (4th) 381 (S.C.C.).
30 *Apsassin*, n12 *supra*, at 68. Refer to the discussion of conflict of interest in Chapters 10 and 15.
31 *Apsassin*, n12 *supra*, at 70. Aside from suffering from the same misunderstanding of fiduciary doctrine as Addy J, Marceau JA failed to recognize that fiduciary obligations may be divided among more than one fiduciary. See the discussion of fiduciary doctrine in Part Two.
32 As a result Isaac CJ found that the negotiations between DIAND and DVLA

over IR 172 amounted to what he described as 'a case of self-dealing in its most elementary form.' *Apsassin*, n12 *supra*, at 88. See also his reasoning, ibid., at 88–93, including the cases cited therein which stand for the proposition that, for the purposes of holding and acquiring land, DVLA was a representative of the Crown.

33 More detailed reasons for Isaac CJ's conclusions in this regard may be seen, ibid., at 84–7.
34 Under Sections 10 and 11 of the Veteran's Land Act, DVLA retained title to each lot until its full purchase price was paid, whereupon, by virtue of Section 5(2) of the Act, a deed conveying a new title to the land was made.
35 In law 'bona fide purchasers for value without notice' are not held responsible for any outstanding debt or obligations in relation to property purchased where they act in good faith and without knowledge of any such encumbrances upon the property.
36 From his consideration of the circumstances, including the Dunne-Za Cree's reliance on the Crown's advice as recently as 1978, Isaac CJ fixed 1975 as the date for the commencement of the statutory limitation period. This date is based on Isaac CJ's statement that this was when the Dunne-Za Cree were advised to seek legal counsel by their District Manager: see *Apsassin*, n12 *supra*, at 976. Note, however, that at 78, Isaac CJ indicated that the Dunne-Za Cree dated their first expression of their legal rights *vis-à-vis* IR 172 in 1977, which they maintained was when they were first advised to seek legal counsel by their district manager. Isaac CJ did not address the issue of laches in his judgment, although it is clear that a party which has committed equitable fraud cannot rely on the equitable defence of laches. See the discussion in Chapter 10.
37 (1992), 96 D.L.R (4th) 289 (S.C.C.), where La Forest J stressed the importance of using a broad, contextual view of the matters in issue and to consider the legislative intent behind statutes of limitation when determining whether parties ought to be precluded from commencing actions to enforce their rights by the passage of time.
38 See the discussion of limitation periods and their application in *M(K) v M(H)* in Chapter 10.
39 See n1 *supra*, at 345.
40 The majority's findings in this regard mirror Addy J's formulation of the nature of the Crown's duty in his judgment at trial.
41 Refer to the discussion in Chapter 10.
42 In particular governmental policy regarding the sale of Indian lands contemporaneous with the surrender of IR 172.
43 See *Apsassin*, n12 *supra*, at 32, 76.

Notes to pages 118–19   389

44 Ibid., at 76
45 (14 Dec. 1995), File No. 23516 (S.C.C.).
46 Ibid., at para. 40: 'I conclude that the evidence does not support the existence of a fiduciary duty on the Crown prior to the surrender of the reserve by the Band.'
47 Ibid., at paras. 33, 35. See the discussion of this point, below.
48 As McLachlin J. stated, ibid., at para. 51: 'The interests and wishes of the Band were given utmost consideration throughout. The choice that was made – to sell the land – possessed the advantage of allowing the Band to get other lands nearer its trap lines. At the time, that was a defensible choice. Indeed, it can be argued that the sale of the surface rights was the only alternative that met the Band's apparent need to obtain land nearer its trap lines. In retrospect, with the decline of trapping and the discovery of oil and gas, the decision may be argued to have been unfortunate. But at the time, it may be defended as a reasonable solution to the problems the Band faced.'
49 Ibid., at para. 46.
50 Ibid., at para. 54: 'While the DIA received a higher appraisal, there were also appraisals giving lower value to the land. In fact, there appears to have been no alternate market for the land at the time, which might be expected to make accurate appraisal difficult. The evidence reveals the price was arrived at after a course of negotiations conducted at arm's length between the DIA and the DVLA.'
51 Ibid., at para. 104: 'The matter comes done to this. The duty on the Crown as fiduciary was "that of a man of ordinary prudence in managing his own affairs": *Fales v. Canada Permanent Trust Co.*, [1977] 2 S.C.R. 302 at p. 315. A reasonable person does not inadvertently give away a potentially valuable asset which has already demonstrated earning potential. Nor does a reasonable person give away for no consideration what it will cost him nothing to keep and which may one day possess value, however remote the possibility. The Crown managing its own affairs reserved out its minerals. It should have done the same for the Band.'
52 Ibid., at para. 111: 'Although the transfer was from one Crown entity to another, it remained a transfer and an alienation of title. ... In summary, the crystallization of the property interest into a monetary sum and the practical considerations negating a duty in the DVLA toward the Band negate the suggestion that the 1948 transfer changed nothing and the real alienation came later.'
53 Ibid., at para. 115: 'Where a party is granted power over another's interests, and where the other party is correspondingly deprived of power over them, or is "vulnerable", then the party possessing the power is under a fiduciary

obligation to exercise it in the best interests of the other: *Frame v. Smith, supra,* per Wilson J.; and *Hodgkinson v Simms, supra.* Section 64 gave to DIA power to correct the error that had wrongly conveyed the Band's minerals to the DVLA. The Band itself had no such power; it was vulnerable. In these circumstances, a fiduciary duty to correct the error lies.'

54 In opposition to McLachlin J's finding to the contrary, ibid., at para. 39, the fact that the band did not entrust the Crown with the power to decide whether it should surrender its interests in IR 172 does not eliminate the existence of the Crown's fiduciary responsibility *vis-à-vis* the band.
55 (1989), 53 D.L.R. (4th) 487 (S.C.C.).
56 (1989), 57 D.L.R. (4th) 197 (S.C.C.).
57 *Paul v Canadian Pacific,* n55 *supra* at 504.
58 Also known as the Campbell River Indian band.
59 Also known as the Cape Mudge Indian band.
60 *Roberts,* n56 *supra,* at 208.
61 (1950), [1950] 2 D.L.R. 225 (S.C.C.). See the discussion of the case in Chapter 4.
62 *Roberts,* n56 *supra,* at 210.
63 (1990), 70 D.L.R. (4th) 385 (S.C.C.).
64 R.S.C. 1970, c. F-14, s. 61(1).
65 Of note is the fact that Sparrow's band, the Musqueam Indian band, is the same band which brought suit against the Crown in *Guerin.*
66 SOR/84-284.
67 Provincial governments may pass legislation affecting aboriginal peoples, subject to the terms of Indian treaties or federal legislation, by way of Section 88 of the Indian Act, R.S.C. 1985, c. I-5, as amended. Rather than having to enact separate federal Indian legislation dealing with a wide variety of matters, Section 88 referentially incorporates provincial legislation of general applicability, where appropriate, into federal law in order to comply with the exclusive legislative authority over 'Indians, and Lands reserved for the Indians' in Section 91(24) of the British North America Act, 1867. See Chapter 13 for further discussion of this issue and its interaction with the Crown's fiduciary duty.
68 *Sparrow,* n63 *supra,* at 389. In reality, the meaning of Section 35(1) should have been clarified to a greater extent prior to *Sparrow.* Section 37.1 of the Constitution Act, 1982, provided for the establishment of constitutional conferences to be held to discuss 'matters that directly affect the aboriginal peoples of Canada,' as detailed in Section 37.1(2). Originally, these conferences were to focus on 'the identification and definition of the rights of those peoples to be included in the Constitution of Canada,' but this clause was eliminated from versions of the constitution after 17 April 1982. See Michael Asch and Patrick

Macklem, 'Aboriginal Right and Canadian Sovereignty: An Essay on *R v Sparrow*,' (1991) 29 *Alta. L. Rev.* 498, at 504. The conferences held under this section ended in 1987 without any further understanding of what aboriginal and treaty rights consist of and what their protection in Section 35(1) entails.
69 *Sparrow*, n63 *supra*, at 406.
70 (1983), 144 D.L.R. (3d) 193 (S.C.C.), which held, at 198, that 'treaties and statutes relating to Indians should be liberally construed and doubtful expressions resolved in favour of the Indian.'
71 (1981), 62 C.C.C. (2d) 227 (Ont. C.A.).
72 *Sparrow*, n63 *supra*, at 408 (reference omitted). See also *R v Agawa* (1988), 65 O.R. (2d) 505 (C.A.) at 524, where, referring to *Guerin* in particular, Blair JA discussed 'the responsibility of government to protect the rights of Indians arising from the special trust relationship created by history, treaties, and legislation.'
73 Note also that the *Sparrow* decision stated, n63, *supra*, at 408, 'The *sui generis* nature of Indian title, and the historic powers and responsibility assumed by the Crown constituted the source of such a fiduciary obligation.'
74 See the discussion in *Sparrow*, n63 *supra*, at 408–9.
75 Ibid., at 409.
76 This insists that it adhere to 'a high standard of honourable dealing with respect to the aboriginal peoples of Canada as suggested by *Guerin v The Queen*': Ibid.
77 Ibid.
78 The *Sparrow* justificatory scheme illustrates the effects of the Crown's fiduciary duty to aboriginal peoples in situations other than the surrender of reserve lands.
79 This is established by Section 52 of the Act.
80 Although rights existing in a democratic society must be balanced with competing rights and interests, due consideration for the manner in which the rights belonging to aboriginal societies have come into conflict with rights belonging to non-aboriginal persons and groups must be factored into any formulaic balancing equation.
81 Named after the case in which the test was first articulated by the Supreme Court of Canada, *R v Oakes* (1986), 26 D.L.R. (4th) 200 (S.C.C.).
82 *Agawa*, n72 *supra*, at 524.
83 Section 35 exists as Part II of the Constitution Act, 1982, entitled, 'Rights of the Aboriginal Peoples of Canada.' Meanwhile, Section 1 of the Charter explicitly states that it applies only to the rights and freedoms which exist *within the Charter*: 'The *Canadian Charter of Rights and Freedoms* guarantees the rights and freedoms set out in it subject only to such reasonable limits

prescribed by law as can be demonstrably justified in a free and democratic society.' The inapplicability of Section 1 to Section 35(1) rights is explicitly recognized in *Sparrow*, n63 *supra*, at 409.
84 For a more detailed explanation of this effect of Section 35(1), see Brian Slattery, 'The Constitutional Guarantee of Aboriginal and Treaty Rights,' (1982–3) 8 *Queen's L.J.* 232, esp. at 243, 264.
85 Refer back to the discussion in Chapter 5. See also the comments made by Heald JA in *Kruger v R*, reproduced at n9 *supra*.
86 See, for example, *R v Joseph*, [1990] 4 C.N.L.R. 59 (B.C.S.C.), at 69; *R v Bombay*, [1993] 1 C.N.L.R. 92 (Ont. C.A.); *R v Jones* (1993), 14 O.R. (3d) 421 (Ont. Prov. Div.), at 431. Note also that in *Agawa*, n72 *supra*, Blair JA held, at 518, that the conclusions reached in the *Sparrow* decision at the British Columbia Court of Appeal level, though dealing only with aboriginal rights, could be applied to the treaty rights issues before him: 'Although *Sparrow* was concerned with aboriginal and not treaty rights, its conclusions can properly be considered in this case.'
87 Note 86 *supra*, at 94. See also *R v Fox*, [1994] 3 C.N.L.R. 132 (Ont. C.A.), at 136.
88 I would like to thank Bob Freedman, of the firm Ratcliff & Company, for his helpful comments and suggestions on this contentious issue. See also the comments by Bruce Wildsmith, 'Treaty Responsibilities: A Co-Relational Model,' (1992) *U.B.C. L. Rev.* Special Edition on Aboriginal Justice 324, at 334.
89 See *Sparrow*, n63 *supra*, at 409, for the court's rationale for its implementation of the *Sparrow* justificatory test.
90 The *Sparrow* test only contemplates valid legislative objectives that have the effect of regulating aboriginal rights.
91 See, for example, *R.W.D.S.U., Local 580 v Dolphin Delivery*, [1986] 2 S.C.R. 573; Katherine Swinton, 'The Application of the Charter of Rights and Freedoms,' In Walter S. Tarnopolsky and Gérald A.-Beaudoin, eds., *The Canadian Charter of Rights and Freedoms* (Toronto: Carswell, 1982); Peter Hogg, 'The Dolphin Delivery Case: The Application of the Charter to Private Action,' (1986–7) 51 *Sask. L. Rev.* 273; Brian Slattery, 'The Charter of Rights and Freedoms: Does It Bind Private Persons,' (1985) 63 *Can. Bar Rev.* 148; Slattery, 'The Charter's Relevance to Private Litigation: Does Dolphin Deliver?' (1987) 32 *McGill L.J.* 905; Allan Hutchinson and Andrew Petter, 'Private Rights / Public Wrongs: The Liberal Lie of the Charter,' (1988) 38 *U.T.L.J.* 278; Roger Tassé, 'Application of the Canadian Charter of Rights and Freedoms,' in Gérald A.-Beaudoin and Ed Ratushny, eds., *The Canadian Charter of Rights and Freedoms*, 2nd ed. (Toronto: Carswell, 1989); Michael Kanter, 'The Government Action Doctrine and the Public/Private Distinction: Searching for Private Action,' (1990) 15 *Queen's L.J.* 33.

92 *Sparrow*, n63 *supra*, at 410. The importance of context in the discussion of aboriginal rights issues has been emphasized on a number of occasions. For example, in *R v Sioui* (1990), 70 D.L.R. (4th) 427 (S.C.C.) at 434–5, where Lamer J, as he then was, stated that any determination of the legal nature of a treaty 'must take into account the historical context and perception each party might have as to the nature of the undertaking contained in the document under consideration,' and, at 460, that 'the treaty essentially has to be interpreted by determining the intention of the parties ... at the time it was concluded.' See also generally *R v George* (1966), 55 D.L.R. (2d) 386 (S.C.C.), at 396–7; *Kruger and Manuel v The Queen* (1977), 75 D.L.R. (3d) 434 (S.C.C.), at 437; *R v Taylor and Williams*, n71 *supra*, at 232; *Sparrow*, n63 *supra*, at 408, 410.
93 *Sparrow*, n63 *supra*, at 411.
94 Ibid. It remains open to question how the aboriginals' 'preferred means' is to be determined and by what standards.
95 Ibid., at 411, 417.
96 Ibid., at 412.
97 Ibid.
98 The determination as to whether a legislative objective is valid is an interpretive question which must be answered in each case within the context in which it arises. The Supreme Court in *Sparrow*, n63 *supra*, at 412, suggested that a 'public interest' justification is 'so vague as to provide no meaningful guidance and so broad as to be unworkable as a test for the justification of a limitation on constitutional rights.' The court does suggest, at 413, that principles of conservation and resource management are valid justifications which are 'consistent with aboriginal beliefs and practices, and, indeed, with the enhancement of aboriginal rights.'
99 As the court stated, n63 *supra*, at 413: 'The special trust relationship and the responsibility of the government *vis-à-vis* aboriginals must be the first consideration in determining whether the legislation or action in question can be justified.'
100 Ibid., at 416.
101 Ibid., at 410, 417–18.
102 Ibid., at 418.
103 Because of the combination of the Crown's fiduciary obligation towards the aboriginal peoples and the court's dictum, n63 *supra*, at 417, that 'the aboriginal peoples, with their history of conservation-consciousness and interdependence with natural resources, would surely be expected, at the least, to be informed regarding the determination of an appropriate scheme for the regulation of the fisheries.' Although the court only discussed the Crown's obligation to consult the aboriginal peoples with regard to fishing conserva-

tion measures, that was because of the facts in issue before the court rather than any intention to limit the Crown's duty to consult. The Crown's duty to consult has since been found to exist, for example, in *Skerryvore Ratepayers' Ass'n v Shawanaga Indian Band* (1993), 16 O.R. (3d) 390 (C.A.) at 400, citing Peter W. Hogg's *Constitutional Law of Canada*, 3rd ed. (Toronto: Carswell, 1992) at 681n.

104 *Sparrow*, n63 *supra*, at 416–17.
105 Ibid., at 417.
106 Ibid., at 410.
107 Ibid., at 407.
108 Although the Federal Court of Appeal affirmed *Sparrow*'s notion of the purposive application of the Crown's fiduciary duty to aboriginal peoples in *Eastmain Band v Canada (Federal Administrator)*, [1993] 3 C.N.L.R. 55 (F.C.A.), citing with approval the judgment in *New Zealand Maori Council v Attorney-General*, [1987] 1 N.Z.L.R 641 (N.Z.C.A.). See the discussion of the *Eastmain* decision *infra*.
109 See the section entitled, 'Is the Crown's Fiduciary Duty Purposive?' in Chapter 14.
110 See, for example, *Bear Island*, n29 *supra*; *Quebec (Attorney-General) v Canada (National Energy Board)*, [1994] 3 C.N.L.R. 49 (S.C.C.); *Apsassin*, n11, *supra*.
111 [1991] 2 C.N.L.R. 22 (F.C.T.D.).
112 Under the Federal Court Act, R.S.C. 1985, c F-7, Rule 475.
113 C.R.C. 1978, c. 963, made pursuant to the Indian Act, R.S.C. 1970, c. I-6, as provided for by the Indian Oil and Gas Act, S.C. 1974–75–76, c. 15.
114 At trial it was agreed that the shortfall in royalties received by the band during the period 1973–7 versus those realized by other bands in Alberta amounted to $994,415.82.
115 *Bruno*, n111 *supra*, at 30.
116 Ibid., at 27 (references omitted).
117 Ibid., at 29 (emphasis added).
118 See the discussion in Chapters 2 and 3.
119 As indicated by the examination of case law in Chapter 4.
120 As the discussion in Chapters 2 and 3 indicates, the Crown's motives *vis-à-vis*. Native people were not always altruistic or wholly directed towards their benefit.
121 The Crown's protection of these non-land interests has been recognized in the Royal Proclamation of 1763 and in pre- and post-Confederation Indian treaties.
122 Refer to the section entitled, 'The Categorical Open-Endedness of Fiduciary Relationships,' in Chapter 8.

Notes to pages 131-3   395

123 [1991] 4 C.N.L.R. 84 (F.C.T.D.).
124 (Quebec City: Editeur officiel du Québec, 1976).
125 James Bay and Northern Quebec Native Claims Settlement Act, S.C., 1976-77, c. 32; An Act Approving the Agreement Concerning James Bay and Northern Quebec, S.Q., 1976, c. 46.
126 SOR 84-467, 22 June 1984.
127 *Cree Regional Authority,* n123 *supra,* at 99.
128 Ibid., at 106.
129 The notion of provincial fiduciary responsibilities towards Native peoples living within their jurisdictional boundaries is considered in Chapters 11 to 13. See also Leonard I. Rotman, 'Provincial Fiduciary Obligations to First Nations: The Nexus between Governmental Power and Responsibility,' (1994) 32 *Osgoode Hall L.J.* 735.
130 [1992] 1 C.N.L.R. 90 (F.C.T.D.), rev'd, *Eastmain Band v Canada (Federal Administrator),* [1993] 3 C.N.L.R. 55 (F.C.A.).
131 [1992] 1 C.N.L.R. 90 (F.C.T.D.), at 101.
132 The EARP Guidelines were held not to apply to the EM1 project because the federal government formally authorized the construction of La Complexe La Grande, of which the FM1 project was one component, when it authorized the construction of the complex in the JBNQA. The federal government affirmed its consent to the project when it adopted the JBNQA into federal law; consequently, the Federal Court of Appeal held that the EARP Guidelines, formulated nine years after the JBNQA, could not apply to halt the EM1's construction while the project underwent an environmental assessment.
133 [1993] 3 C.N.L.R. 55 (F.C.A.), at 74.
134 Ibid., at 63. For further discussion of the Crown balancing its fiduciary obligations to aboriginal peoples with its obligations to the Canadian population as a whole, see Chapters 14 and 15.
135 See n82 *supra.*
136 [1987] 1 N.Z.L.R. 641 (N.Z.C.A.), at 664. The purposive application of the Crown's duty is discussed in Chapter 14.
137 Note 29 *supra.* The *Bear Island* case will be discussed further in Chapter 12.
138 The effect of the cautions was to warn prospective purchasers that the lands in question were the subject of a claim by the Teme-Augama Anishnabai based on their unextinguished aboriginal title.
139 This issue is far more complicated than in its presentation herein. For further elaboration of the issues in *Bear Island* at the pre-Supreme Court of Canada level, see (1984), 15 D.L.R. (4th) 321 (Ont. H.C.); (1989), 58 D.L.R. (4th) 117 (Ont. C.A.); Kent McNeil, 'The Temagami Indian Land Claim: Loosen-

ing the Judicial Straitjacket,' in Matt Bray and Ashley Thomson, eds., *Temagami: A Debate on Wilderness* (Toronto: Dundurn, 1990). Commentary on the Supreme Court's decision may be found in McNeil, 'The High Cost of Accepting Benefits from the Crown: A Comment on the Temagami Indian Land Case,' [1992] 1 C.N.L.R. 40.
140 It is difficult to fathom why the province would be involved in these negotiations in the absence of the federal Crown's presence if it was not, itself, bound by a fiduciary duty to the Temagami people (notwithstanding provincial jurisdiction over those lands via section 109 of the British North America Act, 1867, which is discussed in Chapter 12).
141 See the further discussion of this topic in Chapters 11 through 13.
142 [1992] 2 C.N.L.R. 54 (F.C.T.D.).
143 As Dube J explained ibid., at 61, 'In accordance with the existing practice, a copy of the lease was not sent to the band.'
144 R.S.C. 1927, c. 98.
145 Early in the lease, the band alerted the department to the fact that the reclamation company had been late in its rental payments and had sublet land to local farmers and the Department of Agriculture, in direct violation of the terms of the lease. The band also complained that the terms of the lease were inadequate.
146 A second surrender for the purpose of an absolute transfer of land had been made by the band in 1938 to a local dentist. That surrender was confirmed by Order in Council in 1943. Although a part of the band's action included a claim that the Crown breached its duty to the band regarding this surrender and in allowing the dentist to commence working on the land prior to the execution of the surrender, that aspect of the claim was minor.
147 The band alleged that it was to receive lands outside of its reserve for cutting hay. The band, which primarily raised stock, harvested several hundred tons of wild hay and timothy hay each year. The hay was essential for their cattle and as a revenue source, as they sold hay on the local market.
148 *Lower Kootenay*, n142 *supra*, at 105: 'In my view, the Crown's fiduciary duty was crystallized for the duration of that lease and did not float away after the 1934 surrender, and more so where the proposed surrender was aborted ab initio because of a neglectful omission on the part of the Crown.'
149 Ibid., at 89. See also, at 107, where Dube J stated, 'Having decided to proceed under s. 51, the Crown was duty bound to proceed according to that section.'
150 Citing *Easterbrook v R* [1931] S.C.R. 210, *St Ann's Island Shooting and Fishing Club v The King* (1950), [1950] 2 D.L.R. 225 (S.C.C.), and *The King v Cowichan Agricultural Society*, [1950] Ex. C.R. 448.

Notes to pages 135–6 397

151 *Lower Kootenay,* n142 *supra,* at 108: '[T]he Crown failed in its duty in not informing the plaintiffs, as it was duty bound to do, as soon as it discovered that there was no order in council.'
152 Ibid., at 106: 'Knowing well that the Indians were very reluctant to be locked into a long-term lease, the Crown should at least have secured a more realistic "escalator" clause or a "review" clause and ought not to have bound the band for fifty years to "Depression-era prices" ...'
153 Ibid., at 106: 'The Crown's own public servants quickly realized that the rates set in 1934 were not satisfactory and fair to the Indians. As early as October 31, 1938, or only four years after the surrender, the new Indian Commissioner for British Columbia, Mr D.M. MacKay, wrote to Mr A. Irwin, the local Indian agent, to the effect that the terms of the lease were "Not generous enough" and that the Indians should seek a revision of the terms.'
154 The court found that there was no evidence that the Indians ever claimed or complained about the hay-cutting privileges or that they were part of a surrender or lease or any other agreement binding on the Crown. In any event, the federal Crown had no jurisdiction over the adjacent lands, as they were provincial lands which had been turned over to the Breeders' Association for hay-cutting purposes.
155 [1993] 2 C.N.L.R. 165 (Ont. C.A.).
156 S.C. 1986, c. 1.
157 As reproduced in William M. Malloy, *Treaties, Conventions, International Acts, Protocols and Agreements between the United States of America and Other Powers 1776–1909,* Vol. 1 (Washington, DC: Government Printing Office, 1910), at 592–3. The complete text of Article III of the Jay Treaty, 1794, may be found in Chapter 2.
158 (1956), 3 D.L.R. (2d) 641 (S.C.C.).
159 (1876), 2 Q.B. 69 (C.A.).
160 [1932] A.C. 14 (H.L.).
161 *Vincent,* n155 *supra,* at 176. Whether Indian nations are properly characterized as 'subjects' is a contentious issue which is of considerable importance to aboriginal peoples in Canada and their relationships with the Crown.
162 Namely, that 'treaties and statutes relating to Indians should be liberally construed and doubtful expressions resolved in favour of the Indian': *Nowegijick,* n70 *supra,* at 198. See *Vincent,* n155 *supra,* at 179: '[I]n our opinion the general interpretation principle [in *Nowegijick*] according to which the government has a fiduciary duty towards the Aboriginal peoples is irrelevant to the case at bar.'
163 *Sparrow,* n63 *supra,* at 408.

398 Notes to pages 137-44

164 (1993), 104 D.L.R. (4th) 470 (B.C.C.A.), varying (1991), 79 D.L.R. (4th) 185 (B.C.S.C.).
165 (1991), 79 D.L.R. (4th) 185 (B.C.S.C.), at 482.
166 Ibid.,
167 Ibid., at 490.
168 Further discussion of the effects of Section 109 may be seen in Chapter 12.
169 *Delgamuukw*, n165 *supra*, at 536.

7 The Status of the Crown's Fiduciary Duty

1 (1989), 57 D.L.R. (4th) 197 (S.C.C.).
2 (1990), 70 D.L.R. (4th) 385 (S.C.C.).
3 (1991), 83 D.L.R. (4th) 381 (S.C.C.).
4 (14 Dec. 1995), File No. 23516 (S.C.C.).
5 Such as in *Goodbody v. Bank of Montreal* (1974), 47 D.L.R. (3d) 335 (Ont. H.C.), which is discussed in Chapter 8.
6 See the discussion of the inherent rights approach to aboriginal rights in Canada in Michael Asch and Patrick Macklem, 'Aboriginal Right and Canadian Sovereignty: An Essay on *R v Sparrow*,' (1991) 29 *Alta. L. Rev.* 498, which uses a similar analogy within the context of aboriginal rights in general. The inherent and contingent rights approaches to aboriginal rights are discussed in Chapter 3.
7 (1992), 175 C.L.R. 1 (H.C. Aust.)
8 With the exception of certain parcels of land which had been validly appropriated for administrative purposes inconsistent with the Meriam people's continued enjoyment of their rights and privileges existing under their aboriginal title.
9 Note 7, *supra*, at 59.
10 8 Wheat. 541 (U.S. 1823).
11 Ibid., at 593, 604-5. Note also the discussion of the same point in J.C. Smith, 'The Concept of Native Title,' (1974) 24 *U.T.L.J.* 1, at 13:
> The courts have generally ... referred to native title within the legal system of the dominant society, as a communally held 'usufructuary' interest which is a burden on the legal estate of the crown and is inalienable except to the crown.
> The legal effect of these rulings is that, vis-à-vis the crown or government of the dominant society, the servient society has a legal claim to the land. Vis-à-vis the members of the dominant society, it does not. The rights of the servient society are not in rem. The courts thus have a recognized the property relation as existing between the dominant and servient societies,

but have also recognized that this property relation has not been incorporated into the property system of the dominant society so as to give the servient society property rights against everyone in the legal system.
12 Regarding this important point, the existence of a background document on the history of Canadian Indian policy taken from the office of the assistant deputy minister of Indian affairs during an aboriginal occupation of the Indian Affairs building in Ottawa in 1974, discussed in Paul C. Williams, 'The Chain,' unpublished LLM thesis, Osgoode Hall Law School, 1982, at 308, is particularly intriguing. Under the heading entitled 'Responsibility for a People,' the document reads as follows:

As long as the white population remained small and hence dependent on the natives, relations between Indian and white seemed to be between sovereign powers although all colonial and European governments held to the principle that natives were, in fact, subject peoples, a principle that governed their colonial policies in many other parts of the world.

As the number of colonists increased, this assertion of European sovereignty over the Indians became overt, and gradually the technological superiority of the Europeans, both as a coercive force and as the source of increasing Indian material dependency, enabled them to make good this claim.

If the intent of the parties is irrelevant to the determination of whether a relationship is fiduciary, then the fact that the Crown never intended their relations with the aboriginal peoples to be fiduciary in nature or that 'all colonial and European governments held to the principle that natives were, in fact, subject peoples' is completely irrelevant to the issue of whether the Crown is bound by fiduciary duties to Native peoples. Note the parallels between the first paragraph of this excerpt and Britain's concealed notions of colonialism which only came to fruition by sheer coincidence in Chapter 2. Curiously, if all colonial and European governments held that the Natives were subject peoples, why would the relationships between Europeans and Natives appear as sovereign in their make-up, as the background paper suggests, if they were not so?

13 A wealth of sources document in detail the interdependency of the British–Native relationship in North America. One fine, legally based account which focuses on the relationship of the Iroquois with the British and French from contact to the mid-eighteenth century is John D. Hurley, *Children or Brethren: Aboriginal Rights in Colonial Iroquoia* (PhD thesis, Cambridge University, 1985, reprinted, Saskatoon: University of Saskatchewan Native Law Centre, 1985). A useful historical accompaniment to Hurley is Francis Jennings, *The Ambiguous Iroquois Empire: The Covenant Chain Confederation of Indian Tribes with*

English Colonies from Its Beginnings to the Lancaster Treaty of 1744 (New York: Norton, 1984). See also Darlene M. Johnston, 'A Theory of Crown Trust towards Aboriginal Peoples,' (1986) 30 *Ottawa L. Rev.* 307, at 308.

Reproductions of some accounts of particular historical events may be seen in Virgil J. Voger, ed., *This Country Was Ours: A Documentary History of the American Indian* (New York: Harper and Row, 1972). See also Brian Slattery, 'Understanding Aboriginal Rights,' (1987) 66 *Can. Bar Rev.* 727, at 753-5; Slattery 'First Nations and the Constitution: A Question of Trust,' (1992) 71 *Can. Bar Rev.* 261, at 271-2.

14 *Order of the King in Council on a Report of the Lords of Trade*, 23 Nov. 1761, in Edmund Bailey O'Callaghan, ed., *Documents Relative to the Colonial History of the State of New York*, 11 vols. (Albany: Weed, Parsons, 1853-61), Vol. 7, at 478-9. The Proclamation, and the Report of the Lords of Trade which recommended it, are reproduced here as Appendices 5 and 4 respectively.
15 Note also the conclusions of the *Report of the Select Committee on Aborigines, 1837*, in Chapter 4.
16 S.C., 1876, c. 18.
17 Although this may only amount to an applied fiduciary relationship, depending on the circumstances and nature of the relationship under judicial scrutiny.
18 See Brian Slattery, 'First Nations and the Constitution,' n13, *supra*, at 271-2: 'This relationship is grounded in historical practices that emerged from dealings between the British Crown and Aboriginal nations in eastern North America, especially during the formative period extending from the founding of the colonies in the early 1600s to the fall of New France in 1760. By the end of this period, the principles underlying these practices had crystallized as part of the basic constitutional law governing the colonies, and were reflected in the Royal Proclamation issued by the British Crown on October 7, 1763.'
19 For instance, the Crown's subjugation of the aboriginal peoples would not appear to be consistent with its undertaking to protect the rights and interests of the aboriginal peoples, as outlined in the Royal Proclamation of 1763, or in the terms of the many treaties that it entered into with the aboriginal peoples since 1664.

8 A Re-examination of Fiduciary Doctrine

1 (1726), 25 E.R. 223 (Ch.).
2 *Canadian Aero Services Ltd v O'Malley* (1973), 40 D.L.R. (3rd) 371 (S.C.C.).
3 *Frame v Smith* (1987), 42 D.L.R. (4th) 81 (S.C.C.).

4 *Canson Enterprises Ltd v Boughton & Co* (1991), 85 D.L.R. (4th) 129 (S.C.C.).
5 *Guerin v R* (1984), 13 D.L.R. (4th) 321 (S.C.C.).
6 *McInerney v MacDonald* (1992), 93 D.L.R. (4th) 415 (S.C.C.); *Norberg v Wynrib* (1992), 92 D.L.R. (4th) 449 (S.C.C.).
7 *M(K) v M(H)* (1992), 96 D.L.R. (4th) 289 (S.C.C.).
8 *Hodgkinson v Simms* (1994), 117 D.L.R. (4th) 161 (S.C.C.).
9 See Paul D. Finn, 'The Fiduciary Principle,' in Timothy G. Youdan, ed., *Equity, Fiduciaries, and Trusts* (Toronto: Carswell, 1989), at 24 (hereinafter 'Fiduciary Principle'): 'It is striking that a principle so long standing and so widely accepted should be the subject of the uncertainty that now prevails'; Robert Cooter and Bradley J. Freedman, 'The Fiduciary Relationship: Its Economic Character and Legal Consequences,' (1991) 66 *N.Y.U. L. Rev.* 1045, at 1045–6: 'Legal theorists and practitioners have failed to define precisely when such a relationship exists, exactly what constitutes a violation of this relationship, and the legal consequences generated by such a violation'; Peter D. Maddaugh, 'Definition of Fiduciary Duty,' in *Fiduciary Duties*, Law Society of Upper Canada Special Lectures, 1990 (Toronto: De Boo, 1991), at 16: 'Who is a fiduciary? The answer to this question, despite hundreds of years of litigation on the subject, is not at all clear. The term "fiduciary" is not one used by ordinary people. It is only used by lawyers. This in itself should arouse our suspicions.'
10 Two of the most notorious examples of the misapplication of fiduciary doctrine are *Chase Manhattan Bank v Israel British Bank*, [1981] Ch. 105, and *Goodbody v Bank of Montreal* (1974), 47 D.L.R. (3d) 335 (Ont. H.C.). In each of these cases, fiduciary relationships were found to exist by the courts solely to allow for the equitable tracing of funds rather than because of the fiduciary nature of the relationship between the parties concerned. These cases will be discussed in greater detail *infra*.
11 See *Reading v Attorney-General*, [1949] 2 K.B. 232 (C.A.), aff'd [1951] A.C. 507 (H.L.), discussed *infra*; *Fonthill Lumber v Bank of Montreal* (1959), 19 D.L.R. (2d) 618 (Ont. C.A.), where the defendant bank was held liable for a breach of a 'transmitted fiduciary obligation' arising from its acceptance of money from one of its customers that was properly the subject of a statutory trust owed by the customer to his creditors; *Courtright v Canadian Pacific Ltd* (1983), 5 D.L.R. (4th) 488 (Ont. H.C.), aff'd (1985), 18 D.L.R. (4th) 639n (Ont. C.A.), where a lawyer who failed to disclose his knowledge that he might be charged with a Criminal Code offence to a potential employer and was later arrested and charged after he had been hired by the company as in-house counsel, was held to have breached a fiduciary obligation to the company, even though he was later acquitted of the charge.

12 Such as in the *Chase Manhattan* and *Goodbody* decisions, n10 *supra*, which should have been decided on the basis of unjust enrichment.
13 See Mark V. Ellis, *Fiduciary Duties in Canada* (Toronto: De Boo, 1988), at 1–8: 'It is somewhat ironic that this area – one of the most rapidly expanding and powerful areas of law – is probably one of the least understood.'
14 In fact, one commentator has gone so far as to suggest that the fiduciary argument is one that every litigant should consider: see Malcolm D. Talbott, 'Restitution Remedies in Contract Cases: Finding a Fiduciary or Confidential Relationship to Gain Remedies,' (1959) 20 *Ohio St. L.J.* 320.
15 (1988), 41 D.L.R. (4th) 577 (B.C.C.A.), at 599. See also the comments made by Finn, 'Fiduciary Principle, n9 *supra*, at 10 (discussing in particular the fiduciary's duty of disclosure), and, more generally, at 24–5: 'A compliant judiciary, particulary in some North American jurisdictions, has been prepared on occasion to use the fiduciary principle to provide desired solutions in situations where the law is otherwise deficient or is perceived to be so.'
16 (1987), 11 B.C.L.R. (2d) 361 (S.C.), at 362.
17 *LAC Minerals v International Corona Resources Ltd* (1989), 61 D.L.R. (4th) 14 (S.C.C.), at 26. Refer also to P.D. Finn, *Fiduciary Obligations* (Sydney: Law Book Company, 1977), at 1 (hereinafter *Fiduciary Obligations*): '[T]he term "fiduciary" is itself one of the most ill-defined, if not altogether misleading terms in our law. Yet it retains a large currency being often used as though it were full of known meaning and despite judicial warnings to the contrary.'
18 This phenomenon has even occurred without regard for whether a relationship is properly described as fiduciary: see the discussion entitled, 'The Misapplication of Fiduciary Doctrine,' *infra*.
19 *Hyde v United States*, 225 U.S. 347 (1911), at 391.
20 318 U.S. 80 (1943), at 85–6.
21 Fiduciary remedies will be discussed in Chapter 10.
22 Finn, *Fiduciary Obligations*, n17 *supra*, at 1.
23 Although these premises will be discussed in greater detail herein, they underlie the assertions made throughout this paper in that they shape and inform the understanding and application of fiduciary doctrine according to the theory proposed in Chapter 10.
24 Ernest J. Weinrib, 'The Fiduciary Obligation,' (1975) 25 *U.T.L.J.* 1, at 4. Weinrib's characterization has been cited, with approval, by the Supreme Court of Canada in *Guerin v R*, n5 *supra*, at 340 and in *LAC Minerals*, n17 *supra*, at 61.
25 Eileen Gillese, 'Fiduciary Relations and Their Impact on Business and Commerce,' unpublished paper delivered at Insight conference, 'Trusts and Fiduciary Relations in Commercial Transactions,' 14 April 1988, at 7.

26 As Finn, 'Fiduciary Principle, n9 *supra*, explained, at 26: 'It has been used, and is demonstrably used, to maintain the integrity, credibility and utility of relationships perceived to be of importance in a society. And it is used to protect interests, both personal and economic, which a society is perceived to deem valuable.'
27 See *Nocton v Ashburton*, [1914] A.C. 932 (H.L.), at 963 (per Lord Dunedin): '[T]here was a jurisdiction in equity to keep persons in a fiduciary capacity up to their duty.' See also *Canson Enterprises Ltd v Boughton & Co*, n4 *supra*, at 154 (per McLachlin J).
28 See J.C. Shepherd, *The Law of Fiduciaries* (Toronto: Carswell, 1981), Preface, at v: 'the law of fiduciaries is the legal system's attempt to recognize the more blatant abuses of the trust we place in each other.'
29 This is not to suggest, however, that all fiduciary relationships exist between patently unequal parties; see the discussion of inequality theory *infra*.
30 Weinrib, n24 *supra*, at 11.
31 See the discussion of inequality theory, *infra*.
32 See n26 *supra*; Robert Flannigan, 'The Fiduciary Obligation,' (1989) 9 *Ox. J. Leg.*
supra, at 15; Maddaugh, n9 *supra*, at 26.
33 See also Tamar Frankel, 'Fiduciary Law,' (1983) 71 *Cal. L. Rev.* 795, at 816.
34 [1944] 2 D.L.R. 145 (S.C.C.).
35 Ibid., at 148.
36 The spirit of the defendant's undertaking limited him to disclosure of matters relating only to mineral exploration, not anything of value on the lands in question. See also Maddaugh, n9 *supra*, at 30, who arrives at similar conclusions. Other cases which turn on similar fact situations as *McLeod* include *Tombill Gold Mines Ltd v Hamilton* (1956), 5 D.L.R. (2d) 561 (S.C.C.), and *Pre-Cam Exploration and Development Ltd v McTavish* (1966), 57 D.L.R. (2d) 557 (S.C.C.).
37 Finn, 'Fiduciary Principle,' n9 *supra*, at 46.
38 This accounts for the open-endedness of fiduciary doctrine.
39 *Lloyd's Bank v Bundy*, [1975] 1 Q.B. 326 (C.A.), at 341. See also *Re Craig*, [1971] Ch. 95, at 104. The situation-specificity of fiduciary doctrine was described by Maddaugh, n9 *supra*, at 30 in relation to ascertaining the scope and intensity of particular fiduciary duties owed in specific situations, in the following manner: 'No single test or set of tests will suffice. As in the case of identifying a fiduciary in the first place we must look to the particular relationship that exists between the parties.'
40 Deborah A. DeMott, 'Beyond Metaphor: An Analysis of Fiduciary Obligation,' (1988) 5 *Duke L.J.* 879, at 910.

41 See ibid., at 879; Flannigan, 'Fiduciary Obligation,' n32 *supra*, at 311.
42 This notion has been suggested by DeMott, n40 *supra*, at 879, where she stated that 'Recognition that the law of fiduciary obligation is situation-specific should be the starting point for any further analysis.'
43 See *Tate v Williamson* (1866), 2 L.R. Ch. App. 5 (Ch.), at 60–1: 'The jurisdiction exercised by Courts of equity over the dealings of persons standing in certain fiduciary relations has always been regarded as one of a most salutary description. The principles applicable to the more familiar relations of this character have been long settled by many well-known decisions, but the Courts have always been careful not to fetter this careful jurisdiction by defining the exacts limits of its exercise.'

The open-endedness of fiduciary categorization is well recognized in Canadian jurisprudence. See, for example, *Laskin v Bache & Co* (1971), 23 D.L.R. (3d) 385 (Ont. C.A.), at 392; *Canadian Aero Service Ltd v O'Malley*, n2 *supra*, at 383; *Guerin v R*, n5 *supra*, at 341; *International Corona Ltd v Lac Minerals Ltd* (1988), 62 O.R. (2d) 1 (Ont. C.A.), at 44: 'The circumstances which give rise to such a relationship have not been fully defined nor are they forever closed,' and at 46, referring to the judgment of Dickson J's judgment in *Guerin*, n5 *supra*, at 341; *M(K) v M(H)*, n7 *supra*, at 326, per La Forest J: 'In *LAC Minerals* I stressed the point, which also emerges from *Frame v Smith*, that the substance of the fiduciary obligation in any given case is not derived from some immutable list of duties attached to a category of relationships. In other words, the duty is not determined by analogy with the "established" head of fiduciary duty.'
44 Note 39 *supra*, at 341. See also Ellis, n13 *supra*, at 1–7: 'It is readily apparent that the Courts will not – indeed, cannot – create an exhaustive list of fiduciary categories'; L.S. Sealy, 'Some Principles of Fiduciary Obligation,' [1963] *Camb. L.J.* 119, at 135; Weinrib, n24 *supra*, at 7; J.R.F. Lehane, 'Fiduciaries in a Commercial Context,' in P.D. Finn, ed., *Essays in Equity* (Sydney: Law Book Company, 1985), at 96; Sir Anthony Mason, 'Themes and Prospects,' in Finn, ed. *Essays in Equity*, at 246; Hon. J.R. Maurice Gautreau, 'Demystifying the Fiduciary Mystique,' (1989) 68 *Can. Bar Rev.* 1, at 8.
45 Weinrib, n24 *supra*, at 5.
46 See Shepherd, n28 *supra*, at 21; Finn, *Fiduciary Obligations*, n17 *supra*, at 4; L.S. Sealy, 'Fiduciary Relationships,' [1962] *Camb. L.J.* 69, at 81; Robert Flannigan, 'Fiduciary Obligation in the Supreme Court,' (1990) 54 *Sask. L. Rev.* 45, at 51 (hereinafter 'Supreme Court'); Dennis Klinck, "Things of Confidence": Loyalty, Secrecy and Fiduciary Obligation,' (1990) 54 *Sask. L. Rev.* 73, at 87; Ronald G. Slaght, 'Proving a Breach of Fiduciary Duty,' in *Fiduciary Duties*, n9 *supra*, at 40 'A relationship may be fiduciary in nature for only some specific

purposes or in respect of some specific property, idea or action, or concerning only one of a number of joint undertakings'; *New Zealand Netherlands Society 'Oranje' Inc v Kuys*, [1974] 2 All E.R. 1222 (H.L.), at 1225–6: 'A person ... may be in a fiduciary position quoad a part of his activities and not quoad other parts: each transaction, or group of transactions, must be looked at'; *McInerney v MacDonald*, n6 *supra*, at 423: 'A relationship may properly be described as "fiduciary" for some purposes, but not for others.'

47 Note 17 *supra*, at 29. See also ibid., at 28: '[N]ot every legal claim arising out of a relationship with fiduciary incidents will give rise to a claim for breach of fiduciary duty'; *Guerin*, n5 *supra*, at 341.
48 Frankel, n33, *supra* at 833.
49 See the discussion in 'The Misapplication of Fiduciary Doctrine,' *infra*.
50 Note 8 *supra*, at 219.
51 See the discussion of fiduciary remedies in Chapter 10. Note also the comments made by Sopinka and McLachlin JJ regarding the need to limit the imposition of fiduciary obligations in *Hodgkinson v Simms*, n8 *supra*, at 217: 'The vast disparity between the remedies for negligence and breach of contract – the usual remedies for ill-given advice – and those for breach of fiduciary obligation, impose a duty upon the court to offer clear assistance to those concerned to stay in the former camp and not stray into the latter.'
52 See Finn, 'Fiduciary Principle,' n9 *supra*, at 2, where he states that 'fiduciary law's concern is to impose standards of acceptable conduct on one party to a relationship for the benefit of the other where the one has a responsibility for the preservation of the other's interests.'
53 See the similar sentiments in Flannigan, *Fiduciary Obligation*, n32 *supra*, at 321–2, Ernest Vinter, *A Treatise on the History and Law of Fiduciary Relationships and Resulting Trusts*, 3rd ed. (Cambridge: W. Heffer, 1955), at 2: 'The Court of Chancery has, when the interests of the public generally were concerned ... entertained jurisdiction on grounds of public policy, irrespective of the particular circumstances of the case, to declare void transactions which have taken place under circumstances where, independently of other considerations, from the condition of the parties and the difficulty which must exist of obtaining positive evidence as to the fairness of the transaction, they are particularly open to fraud and undue influence."
54 Note 10 *supra*.
55 See D.W.M. Waters, *Law of Trusts in Canada*, 2nd ed. (Toronto: Carswell, 1984), at 1036.
56 Ibid., at 1037.
57 *Chase Manhattan*, n10 *supra*, at 119, which was based upon Goulding J's

adherence to the precedent established in *Re Diplock*, [1984] Ch. 465, aff'd (*sub nom. Min. of Health v Simpson*), [1951] A.C. 251 (H.L.).
58 See *Re Diplock*, n57 *supra*; *Reading v Attorney-General*, n11 *supra*, at 513–14; *Orapko v Manson Investments Ltd* [1978] A.C. 95 (H.L.), at 104; Waters, n55 *supra*, at 1045.
59 Note 10 *supra*.
60 Ibid., at 340.
61 Ibid., at 339. At the time of the *Goodbody* decision, the judicial recognition of unjust enrichment as an independent cause of action was still in its infancy in Canada: see *Deglman v Guaranteed Trust Co and Constantineau*, [1954] S.C.R. 725. However, the principles of unjust enrichment are now well recognized following the Supreme Court of Canada's decision in *Pettkus v Becker* (1980), 117 D.L.R. (3d) 257 (S.C.C.), thereby eliminating the need for the judicial creation of fiduciary relationships to facilitate the equitable remedy of tracing.
62 Note 11 *supra*.
63 [1949] 2 K.B. 232 (C.A.), at 238.
64 See the discussion in the section entitled, 'Fiduciaries Must Not Benefit from Their Positions,' *infra*.
65 [1951] A.C. 507 (H.L.).
66 Note the commentary by Waters, n55 *supra*, at 405, n24, citing the *Chase Manhattan* and *Reading* decisions: 'It is undeniable that the concept of fiduciary relationship has been stretched in circumstances like these to a degree where it has become meaningless.'

9 Fiduciary Theories

1 See Ernest Vinter, *A Treatise on the History and Law of Fiduciary Relationships and Resulting Trusts*, 3rd ed. (Cambridge: W. Heffer, 1955), at 369: 'Certainty of the law is a desideratum, and the reduction of the borderland to as narrow a tract as possible is one of the aims of this book.'
2 Such as L.S. Sealy, 'Fiduciary Relationships,' [1962] *Camb. L.J.* 69, at 73: 'It is obvious that we cannot proceed any further in our search for a general definition of fiduciary relationships. We must define them class by class, and find out the rule or rules which govern each class.'
3 Such as Stanley M. Beck in 'The Quickening of Fiduciary Obligation,' (1975) 53 *Can. Bar Rev.* 771, at 781: '[C]lear definition is simply not possible, or desirable, when one is dealing with the interaction of human conduct and an infinite variety of ... situations.'
4 For example, P.D. Finn, *Fiduciary Obligations* (Sydney: Law Book Company, 1977) at 1 (hereinafter *Fiduciary Obligations*); Sealy, n2 *supra*, 73; Malcolm D.

Talbott, 'Restitution Remedies in Contract Cases: Finding a Fiduciary or Confidential Relationship to Gain Remedies,' (1959) 20 *Ohio St. L.J.* 320, at 324.

5 See Deborah A. DeMott, 'Beyond Metaphor: An Analysis of Fiduciary Obligation,' (1988) 5 *Duke L.J.* 879, at 879; Robert Flannigan, 'The Fiduciary Obligation,' (1989) 9 *Ox. J. Leg. Stud.* 285, at 311 (hereinafter 'Fiduciary Obligation'). This book falls into this category.

6 See, for example, *Black's Law Dictionary*, 5th ed. (St. Paul, Minn: West, 1979), at 563, where the term 'fiduciary' is described as being: '... derived from the Roman law, and means (as a noun) a person holding the character of a trustee, or a character analogous to that of a trustee'; see also the *Oxford English Dictionary*, 2nd ed. (Oxford: Clarendon Press, 1989), Vol. 5, at 878, where a 'fiduciary' is explained as 'One who holds anything in trust: a trustee.'

7 *Cassell's Latin Dictionary* (New York: Macmillan, 1959), at 247.

8 See D.W.M. Waters, *Law of Trusts in Canada*, 2nd ed. (Toronto: Carswell, 1984), at 712 (hereinafter *Law of Trusts*).

9 For the sake of simplicity, the names of the theories used here reflect their major points of emphasis. They are adapted from the examples used by J.C. Shepherd, *The Law of Fiduciaries* (Toronto: Carswell, 1981), at 51–91.

10 In practice, many judges and scholars subscribe to a combination of one or more of these theories or their derivatives in formulating their own theories of fiduciary doctrine. However, given the variety of characterizations of fiduciary doctrine, no single one of these theories is wholly agreed upon or perceived to be better than others, each is the subject of debate or contention on one or more points. See the remark made by Paul D. Finn in his article entitled 'The Fiduciary Principle,' in Timothy G. Youdan, ed., *Equity, Fiduciaries and Trusts* (Toronto: Carswell, 1989), at 26 (hereinafter 'Fiduciary Principle'): [O]ur present uncertainty is thought to be exacerbated by the lack of a workable and unexceptional definition of a fiduciary. We have no shortage of rival approaches, but none has carried the day.' See also Flannigan, 'Fiduciary Obligation,' n5 *supra*, at 321: 'There have been a number of attempts by commentators recently to explain the basis of the fiduciary obligation ... Unfortunately, there is no consensus.'

11 De facto control may be obtained by virtue of one person's ability to control property whose legal and equitable title belongs to another. Directors of corporations fall under this category by virtue of being able to control a corporation's assets without owning them.

12 De jure control may be obtained in any situation where a person has been assigned legal title or legal control over property whose equitable title remains in another. For example, any trustee who holds property in trust for

the benefit of another exercises *de jure* control over that property as long as it remains subject to the trust.

13 Robert Cooter and Bradley J. Freedman, 'The Fiduciary Relationship: Its Economic Character and Legal Consequences,' (1991) 66 *N.Y.U. L. Rev.* 1045, at 1046. Other 'law and economics' perspectives on fiduciary doctrine include W. Bishop and D.D. Prentice, 'Some Legal and Economic Aspects of Fiduciary Remuneration,' (1983) 46 *Mod. L. Rev.* 289; Kenneth B. Davis, Jr, 'Judicial Review of Fiduciary Decisionmaking – Some Theoretical Perspectives,' (1985–6) 80 *Nw. U. L. Rev.* 1; Henry N. Butler and Larry E. Ribstein, 'Opting Out of Fiduciary Duties: A Response to the Anti-Contractarians,' (1990) 65 *Wash. L. Rev.* 1; Brian R. Cheffins, 'Law, Economics and Morality: Contracting Out of Corporate Law Fiduciary Duties,' (1991) 19 *C.B.L.J.* 28; Frank H. Easterbrook and Daniel R. Fischel, 'Contract and Fiduciary Duty,' (1993) 36 *J. Law & Econ.* 425.

14 See, for example, Richard H. Bartlett, 'The Fiduciary Obligation of the Crown to the Indians,' (1989) 53 *Sask. L. Rev* 301, at 301: 'This paper is founded on the thesis that *the exercise of discretion or power over property*, above and beyond that to which people are usually subject, leads to accountability at law' (emphasis added).

15 A trust may have one or more trustees and one or more beneficiaries. There is nothing to prevent trustees from also being beneficiaries of the trusts that they administer. In addition, a trustee may hold the property of a trust not for any person or persons, but for an object permitted by law, such as a charitable purpose.

16 See, for example, *Moore v Royal Trust Co*, [1956] S.C.R. 880; *Standard Investments Ltd v CIBC* (1985), 22 D.L.R. (4th) 410 (Ont. C.A.), rev'g (1983) 5 D.L.R. (4th) 452 (Ont. H.C.); Peter D. Maddaugh, 'Definition of Fiduciary Duty,' in *Fiduciary Duties*, Law Society of Upper Canada Special Lectures, 1990, (Toronto: De Boo, 1991), at 17: '[A] fiduciary relationship is more than a "trust" relationship, it is a "trust-like" relationship. The technical difference being there is no requirement that a fiduciary hold legal title to property in the wider context.' See also Sealy, n2 *supra*, at 76; Finn, *Fiduciary Principle*, n10 *supra*, at 37: '[I]f a relationship does give one party access to what both parties would reasonably acknowledge to be a thing of value in the circumstances, is there any justifiable reason for allowing the custodian to utilize it disloyally for his own profit and without being accountable therefor, simply because that "thing" does not fall within our conventional conceptions of property?'

17 (1991), 85 D.L.R. (4th) 129 (S.C.C.), at 146. See also Easterbrook and Fischel, n13 *supra*, at 435: 'Most of the relations on the fiduciary list do not involve

Notes to pages 166–7   409

management of property, and those that do have substantial differences in both the nature of the duties and the remedies for breach.'

18 See *Rowe v Grand Trunk Railway Co* (1866), U.C.C.P. 500; *Mitchell v Homfray* (1881), 8 Q.B.D. 587 (C.A.); *Williams v Johnson*, [1937] 4 All E.R. 34 (P.C.); *McInerney v MacDonald* (1992), 93 D.L.R. (4th) 415 (S.C.C.); *Norberg v Wynrib* (1992), 92 D.L.R. (4th) 449 (S.C.C.); Mark V. Ellis, *Fiduciary Duties in Canada* (Toronto: De Boo, 1988), at 10-1 to 10-22; Vinter, n1 *supra*, at 77–85 (doctors / medical advisers – patients); *Huguenin v Baseley* (1807), 33 E.R. 526 (Ch.); *Parfitt v Lawless* (1872), 2 L.R. P. & D. 462; *Allcard v Skinner* (1887), [1886–90] All E.R. Rep. 90 (C.A.); *Morley v Loughnan*, [1893] 1 Ch. 736; Vinter, n1 *supra*, at 16–29 (religious advisers – followers).

19 Note, for example, the comments made by the Hon. Beverley M. McLachlin, 'The Place of Equity and Equitable Doctrines in the Contemporary Common Law World: A Canadian Perspective,' in Donovan W.M. Waters, ed., *Equity, Fiduciaries, and Trusts, 1993* (Toronto: Carswell, 1993), at 42: 'Not only must the first party agree to act on behalf of the other, but the arrangement must have the result of placing the property of the other in the power of the former, thus emulating the classic relationship between trustee and *cestui que trust*.' See also the commentary by Tamar Frankel in 'Fiduciary Relationship in the United States Today,' in Waters, ibid., at 178: 'I believe that judges are likely to refuse to extend fiduciary law to new situations when the new situations do not involve property rights. The reason is that historically fiduciary duties were designed to protect property owners. Hence courts develop fiduciary law by drawing an analogy to new relationships ... [from] property relationships; if the new model does not fit, courts are likely to refrain from applying fiduciary law to the new situations.'

20 It should be noted that reliance is also the basis of other independent heads of obligation, such as negligent misrepresentation, which are not a part of fiduciary doctrine. For a more detailed discussion of the relationship between fiduciary law and some of these other concepts, see Felicity Anne Reid, 'The Fiduciary Concept – An Examination of Its Relationship with Breach of Confidence, Negligent Misrepresentation and Good Faith,' unpublished LLM thesis, Osgoode Hall Law School, 1989; Finn, *Fiduciary Principle*, n10 *supra*.

21 See *Hodgkinson v Simms* (1994), 117 D.L.R. (4th) 161 (S.C.C.).

22 See *Erlanger v New Sombrero Phosphates Ltd*, [1877–78] 3 A.C. 1218 (H.L.)

23 See *McInerney v MacDonald*, *Norberg v Wynrib*, n18 *supra*.

24 See *M(K) v M(H)*, (1992), 96 D.L.R. (4th) 289 (S.C.C.).

25 [1975] 1 Q.B. 326 (C.A.), at 341.

26 R. Meagher, W. Gummow, and J. Lehane, *Equity: Doctrines and Remedies*, 2nd ed. (Sydney: Law Book Company, 1984), at 123. See also R.C. Muir, 'Duties

Arising Outside of the Fiduciary Relationship,' (1964) 3 *Alta. L. Rev.* 359, at 360, who stated that a fiduciary relationship arises 'where one party has dominance, or influence over another party, which dominance is based upon a confidence reposed in him by that other party.'

27 It is also closely related to the inequality theory of fiduciary doctrine, discussed *infra*.

28 See *Filmer v Gott* (1774), 4 Bro. P.C. 230 (H.L.); *Gartside v Isherwood* (1788), 1 Bro. C.C. 558 (Ch.), at 560; Sealy, n2 *supra*, at 69–70; DeMott, n5 *supra*, at 880.

29 Waters, *Law of Trusts*, n8 *supra*, at 405.

30 Shepherd, n9 *supra*, at 58: 'Just as there may be a fiduciary relationship without direct reliance, there may be reliance without a fiduciary relationship.'

31 Many of the ideas discussed in this section are discussed in greater detail in Leonard I. Rotman, 'The Vulnerable Position of Fiduciary Doctrine in the Supreme Court of Canada,' (1995) 23(4) *Man. L.J.* (in press).

32 Note, in particular, McTague JA's explanation of what constitutes a fiduciary relationship in *Follis v Albemarle TP*, [1941] 1 D.L.R. 178 (Ont. C.A.), at 181: 'It seems to me ... that there must be established some inequality of footing between the parties, either arising out of a particular relationship, as parent and child, guardian and ward, solicitor and client, trustee and *cestui que trust*, principal and agent, etc., or on the other hand, that it can be established that dominion was exercised by one person over another, no matter how particular relationship may be categorized.' A more complete discussion of inequality theory, its effects, and how it has been recently applied by the Supreme Court of Canada may be seen in Rotman, n31 *supra*.

33 See, in particular, *Frame v Smith* (1987), 42 D.L.R. (4th) 81 (S.C.C.), esp 99–100 *LAC Minerals v International Corona Resources Ltd* (1989), 61 D.L.R. (4th) 14 (S.C.C.), esp. at 63 (per Sopinka J); *Canson Enterprises v Boughton & Co* (1991), 85 D.L.R. (4th) 129 (S.C.C.); *Norberg v Wynrib*, n18 *supra*; *M(K) v M(H)*, 24 *supra*. Note also Robert Flannigan, 'Fiduciary Obligation in the Supreme Court,' (1990) 54 *Sask. L. Rev.* 45, esp. 62–3 (hereinafter 'Supreme Court'); *Hospital Products Ltd v United States Surgical Corp* (1984), 55 A.L.R. 417 (H.C. Aust.).

34 Note 21 *supra*. For more discussion on the *Hodgkinson* decision and its commentary on the vulnerability component of fiduciary relations, see Rotman, n31 *supra*.

35 See *Burns v Kelly Peters & Associates Ltd* (1988), 41 D.L.R. (4th) 577 (B.C.C.A.), at 600.

36 Ernest J. Weinrib, 'The Fiduciary Obligation,' (1975) 25 *U.T.L.J.* 1, at 6. Refer also to Hon. J.R. Maurice Gautreau, 'Demystifying the Fiduciary Mystique,' (1989) 68 *Can. Bar Rev.* 1, at 5; Tamar Frankel, 'Fiduciary Law,' (1983) 71 *Cal. L.*

Rev. 795, at 810: 'It is important to emphasize that the entrustor's vulnerability to abuse of power does not result from an initial inequality of bargaining power between the entrustor and the fiduciary. In no sense are fiduciary relations and the risks they create for the entrustor similar to adhesion contracts or unfair bargains. The relation may expose the entrustor to risk even if he is sophisticated, informed, and able to bargain effectively. Rather, the entrustor's vulnerability stems from the *structure* and *nature* of the fiduciary relation.'

37 Note 31 *supra*.
38 Hence, for example, the federal Crown's breach of fiduciary duty in *Guerin v R* (1984), 13 D.L.R. (4th) 321 (S.C.C.).
39 Note 18 *supra*, at 501.
40 See Easterbrook and Fischel, n13 *supra*, at 427: 'Fiduciary duties are not special duties; they have no moral footing; they are the same sort of obligations, derived and enforced in the same way, as other contractual undertakings.'
41 Ibid. See also Gautreau, n36 *supra*, at 29: 'There is no difference in principle between contractual duties, duties of care based on the *Hedley Byrne* principal and fiduciary duties. They all involve the same elements. The difference is only in degree. The reliance and vulnerability in a fiduciary situation is normally greater than in other duty situations. Because of this, the duty on the fiduciary is more profound and the law makes available a range of remedies that go beyond mere damage awards. But in the end, fiduciary duties are nothing more than elevated contractual duties or duties of care.'
42 Finn, *Fiduciary Obligations*, n4 *supra*, at 201: '[T]he undertaking may be officiously assumed without request.' See also Austin W. Scott, 'The Fiduciary Principle,' (1949) 37 *Cal. L. Rev.* 539, at 540.
43 Such as entering into a contract or other arrangement or, in the Native law context, the signing of a treaty between the Crown and Native peoples.
44 Note *Huff v Price* (1990), 76 D.L.R. (4th) 138 (B.C.C.A.), at 171, where it was held that in a situation where no previous fiduciary relationship had existed, a fiduciary relation 'grew out of particular elements of the way the structure was managed and manipulated.' See also *M(K) v M(H)*, n24 *supra*, at 324.
45 See Scott, n12 *supra*, at 540; Sealy, n2 *supra*, at 76; Frankel, n36 *supra*, at 820–1; *Lyell v Kennedy* (1889), 14 A.C. 437 (H.L.), at 463, per Lord MacNaghten: 'Nor do I think it can make any difference whether the duty arises from contract or is connected with some previous request, or whether it is self-imposed and undertaken without any authority whatever.'
46 Frankel, n36 *supra*, at 821: 'The courts will look to whether the arrangement formed by the parties meets the criteria for classification as fiduciary, not whether the parties intended the legal consequences of such a relation.'

47 As reflected by the Parol Evidence Rule, which holds that where a written contract exists it alone comprises the terms of the deal between the parties.
48 (1875), L.R. 19 Eq. 462, at 465.
49 See Frankel, n36 *supra*, at 830: 'In the world of contract, self-interest is the norm, and restraint must be imposed by others. In contrast, the altruistic posture of fiduciary law requires that once an individual undertakes to act as a fiduciary, he should act to further the interests of another in preference to his own.'
50 164 N.E. 545 (N.Y.C.A. 1928), at 546.
51 Note 21 *supra*, at 181, 187.
52 DeMott, n5 *supra*, at 879–80.
53 (1879), 11 Ch.D. 772, at 778.
54 See Gareth Jones, 'Unjust Enrichment and the Fiduciary's Duty of Loyalty,' (1968) 84 *L.Q.R.* 472; Sealy, n2 *supra*, at 73, who states that the unjust enrichment theory espoused by Fry J in *Re West of England and South Wales District Bank, Ex parte Dale and Co*, n53 *supra*, 'is really not a definition at all: although it describes a common feature, it does not teach us to recognise a fiduciary relationship when we meet one.'
55 See also Fischel and Easterbrook, n13 *supra*, at 435, where they state that not only is unjust enrichment theory 'perfectly circular,' but that '[t]he description can fit any rule while predicting no outcomes.'
56 Weinrib, n36 *supra*, at 5.
57 Gautreau, n36 *supra*, at 5–6: 'Too often we have permitted the fiduciary concept to drift from its conceptual moorings and to become mixed up with the unjust enrichment concept when the two are really quite distinct.' See also the discussion of the *Chase Manhattan, Goodbody,* and *Reading* decisions in Chapter 8. Cases in which the concept of unjust enrichment is more appropriately applied include: *Fibrosa Spolka Akcyjna v Fairbairn Lawson Combe Barbour Ltd*, [1943] A.C. 32 (H.L.); *Deglman v Guaranteed Trust Co and Constantineau*, [1954] S.C.R. 725; *Pettkus v Becker* (1980), 117 D.L.R. (3d) 257 (S.C.C.); *Sorochan v Sorochan* (1986), 29 D.L.R. (4th) 1 (S.C.C.); *Hunter Engineering Co v Syncrude Canada Ltd* (1989), 57 D.L.R. (4th) 321 (S.C.C.); *Rawluk v Rawluk* (1990), 65 D.L.R. (4th) 161 (S.C.C.); and *Peter v Beblow* (1993), 101 D.L.R. (4th) 621 (S.C.C.).
58 Note the comments by DeMott, n5 *supra*, at 913: 'Unjust enrichment is undoubtedly a useful concept in many situations that raise perplexing questions of fiduciary obligation ... But the principle of unjust enrichment cannot explain as a general matter why some people are under the fiduciary constraint and others are not.'
59 See the discussion in Chapter 8.

Notes to pages 173-8   413

60 See, for example, *Canada Safeway Ltd v Thompson*, [1952] 2 D.L.R. 591 (B.C.S.C.); *Pre-Cam Exploration and Development Ltd v McTavish* (1966), 57 D.L.R. (2d) 557 (S.C.C.); *Canadian Aero Services Ltd v O'Malley* (1973), 40 D.L.R. (3d) 371 (S.C.C.).
61 See *Toronto (City of) v Bowes*, (1858), 14 E.R. 770 (P.C.); *Hawrelak v City of Edmonton*, [1972] 2 W.W.R. 561 (Alta. S.C.), aff'd [1973] 1 W.W.R. 179 (Alta C.A.); rev'd [1976] 1 S.C.R. 387; *Carlsen v Gerlach* (1979), 3 E.T.R. 231 (Alta. Dist. Ct.); John Locke, *Two Treatises of Government*, Peter Laslett, ed., 2nd ed. (Cambridge: Cambridge University Press, 1967), at 385, 399-400; E.M. Rogers and S.B. Young, 'Public Office as a Public Trust,' (1974) 63 *Georgia L.J.* 1025; Municipal Conflict of Interest Act, R.S.O. 1990, c. M-50.
62 See the discussion in 'The Categorical Open-Endedness of Fiduciary Doctrine,' in Chapter 8.
63 DeMott, n5 *supra*, at 915.
64 John D. McCamus, 'The Recent Expansion of Fiduciary Doctrine,' (1987) 23 E.T.R. 301, at 304. See also Weinrib, n36 *supra*; Harold Brown, 'Franchising – A Fiduciary Relationship,' (1971) 49 *Tex. L. Rev.* 650, at 664.
65 Refer back to the illustration of the powers possessed by the fiduciary and beneficiary in the discussion of inequality theory *supra*.
66 Finn, 'Fiduciary Principle,' n10 *supra*, at 46. See also Ronald G. Slaght, 'Proving a Breach of Fiduciary Duty,' in *Fiduciary Duties*, n16 *supra*, at 48.

10 A 'Back to Basics' Approach to Fiduciary Doctrine

1 Although Tamar Frankel, 'Fiduciary Law,' (1983) 71 *Cal. L. Rev.* 795, at 798, has suggested that 'a major reason for recognizing and developing a separate body of fiduciary law is that our society is evolving into one based predominantly on fiduciary relations.' See also Frankel, at 802: 'I submit that we are witnessing the emergence of a society predominantly based on fiduciary relations.'
2 *International Corona Resources Ltd v Lac Minerals Ltd* (1988), 62 O.R. (2d) 1 (Ont. C.A.), at 44 and 46: 'Whether or not fiduciary obligations arise depends on the course of dealings between the parties and the proof of facts which give rise to such obligations.' See also D.W.M. Waters, *Law of Trust in Canada*, 2nd ed. (Toronto: Carswell, 1984), at 407 (hereinafter *Law of Trusts*); Ronald G. Slaght, 'Proving a Breach of Fiduciary Duty,' in *Fiduciary Duties*, Law Society of Upper Canada Special Lectures, 1990 (Toronto: De Boo, 1991), at 38.
3 J.C. Shepherd, *The Law of Fiduciaries* (Toronto: Carswell, 1981), at 127.
4 One may be a fiduciary without directly affecting another's interest. As in the relationship between a corporate director and a shareholder, where the direc-

tor indirectly affects the shareholder's interest by exercising control over the corporation that the shareholder owns a piece of, one's indirect actions may affect another's interests and therefore give rise to a fiduciary relationship in appropriate circumstances: see Paul L. Davies, 'Directors' Fiduciary Duties and Individual Shareholders,' in Ewan McKendrick, ed., *Commercial Aspects of Trusts and Fiduciary Obligations* (Oxford: Clarendon 1992), at 84: 'directors owe legal duties directly to individual shareholders in appropriate situations, and ... judicial decisions have increasingly recognised the force of this point'; Mark V. Ellis, *Fiduciary Duties in Canada* (Toronto: De Boo 1988), at 15–24: 'In most instances, the duty owed to the company [by its directors] is reflective of a similar duty owed to the shareholders, who are in fact the owners of the corporation'; *Coleman v Myers*, [1977] 2 N.Z.L.R. 255 (C.A.); *Goldex Mines Ltd v Revill* (1975), 7 O.R. (2d) 216 (C.A.); *Greenhalgh v Arderne Cinemas Ltd*, [1950] 2 All E.R. 1120 (C.A.); Shepherd, n3 *supra*, at 351–6; Jeffrey G. McIntosh, 'Corporations,' in *Fiduciary Duties*, n2 *supra*, at 207.

It should be remembered that Y's reliance upon X's actions results in an inequality in position of Y *vis-à-vis* X *within the confines of the particular relationship* which does not necessarily extend beyond that relationship. Refer back to the discussion of inequality theory, in Chapter 9.

5 See n4 *supra*.
6 As illustrated in the discussion of contract theory in Chapter 9, a fiduciary relationship may arise as a result of: (1) the parties voluntarily entering into such an arrangement, (2) the unilateral actions of a would-be fiduciary, (3) the nature of the intercourse between the parties, or (4) its imposition by the courts. Moreover, it may arise where neither of the parties intended to create such a relationship.
7 See Chapter 9, n44 *supra* and its accompanying text.
8 'Some Fundamental Legal Conceptions as Applied in Judicial Reasoning,' (1913–14) 23 *Yale L.J.* 16; 'Fundamental Legal Conceptions as Applied in Judicial Reasoning,' (1916–17) 26 *Yale L.J.* 710. See also Hohfeld, *Fundamental Legal Conceptions as Applied in Judicial Reasoning and Other Essays*, Walter Wheeler Cook, ed. (New Haven: New Haven University Press, 1919).
9 See n18 *infra* and its accompanying text.
10 In some instances there may also be third party liability. For example, a corporation may incur liability if corporate fiduciaries, such as directors, breach their fiduciary duties while acting as directors of the corporation. Moreover, where the actions of a fiduciary's appointee results in a breach of the fiduciary's duty to act in the beneficiary's best interests, joint and several liability of both the fiduciary and the appointee may be found.
11 Although this right may be curtailed by the application of provincial limita-

Notes to page 181 415

tion statutes which expressly provide for their application to equitable rights of action. However, where a limitation statute fails to expressly provide for its application to equitable actions, there is no statutory limitation for commencing a claim for breach of duty: see *M(K) v M(H)* (1992), 96 D.L.R. (4th) 289 (S.C.C.); *B(J) v B(R)*, File No. 1862-89, 11 Feb. 1994 (Ont. Gen. Div.). There are serious questions, however, about the ability of statutory limitation periods to apply to beneficiaries in fiduciary relationships when fiduciary doctrine entitles them to rely entirely on their fiduciaries' activities without the need to inquire as to whether the fiduciaries are fulfilling their obligations: see the further discussion of this issue *infra*. Because of the difficulty in discovering a fiduciary breach as a result of the relative positions of beneficiaries *vis-à-vis* their fiduciaries, it would appear inequitable, in many circumstances, to deny beneficiaries the ability to commence legal action against indecorous fiduciaries once the former discovers the existence of the breach.
12 See the discussion in 'The Reverse Onus,' *infra*.
13 See the discussion of contract theory in Chapter 9.
14 The legal concept of *uberrima fides* possesses an entirely separate existence from the concept of good faith in law in that it is an equitable rather than common law duty. That is not to say that *uberrima fides* is not a legally enforceable duty, since the once-separate jurisdictions belonging to law and equity were merged over 100 years ago by way of the British Judicature Acts of 1873 and 1875: Judicature Act, 1873 (U.K.), 36 & 37 Vict. c. 66; Judicature Act, 1875 (U.K.), 38 & 39 Vict. c. 77. The distinction between *uberrima fides* and good faith is made herein because the former is much more onerous than the common law's duty of good faith and requires greater fidelity of a fiduciary to a beneficiary than if ordinary good faith at common law was applicable. Good faith is defined in *Black's Law Dictionary*, 5th ed. (St Paul, Minn: West, 1979), at 623, as: 'An honest intention to abstain from taking any unconscientious advantage of another, even through technicalities of law, together with absence of all information, notice, or benefit or belief of facts which render transaction [*sic*] unconscientious.' *Uberrima fides*, on the other hand, is not merely good faith, but good faith magnified to its highest extreme – i.e., the utmost good faith. It is characterized in *Black's Law Dictionary*, ibid., at 1363, as: 'The most abundant good faith; absolute and perfect candor or openness and honesty; the absence of any concealment or deception, however slight.'

Since fiduciary law is equitable in its origins, the more onerous duty of *uberrima fides* is applicable rather than good faith at common law. In short, *uberrima fides* is a legally enforceable duty whose origins stem from the jurisdiction originally belonging to Equity and is both binding upon fiduciaries and enforceable in a court of law.

An example of *uberrima fides* may be seen in insurance contracts, where a continuing duty of the utmost good faith exists between the insurer and insured due to the nature of insurance contracts and the possibilities which exist therein for *mala fide* activity. See, for example, *Carter v Boehm* (1766), [1558–1774] All E.R. Rep. 183 (K.B.). The seminal case on insurance contracts in Canada is *Fine's Flowers Ltd v General Accident Assurance Co* (1974), 5 O.R. (2d) 137 (H.C.), aff'd (1977), 81 D.L.R. (3d) 139 (Ont. C.A.), where the Ontario High Court of Justice, at 139, described the relationship between insurer and insured as 'a close and continuing relationship.'

15 This standard is objective in that it is determined by the judiciary and is not tailored to the requirements of particular relationships as are many other facets of fiduciary doctrine. See Frankel, n1 *supra*, at 830–1: 'The courts do consider the parties' expectations and professional customs; but in the last analysis, it is the courts that determine the standards.' See also Frankel, 'Continuing Judicial Supervision during the Relation,' ibid., at 821–4; Chapter 8, n53 *supra*.

16 See McLachlin J's comments in *Canson Enterprises Ltd v Boughton & Co.* (1991), 85 D.L.R. (4th) 129 (S.C.C.), at 154, 162.

17 See P.D. Finn, *Fiduciary Obligations* (Sydney: Law Book Company, 1977), at 16 (hereinafter *Fiduciary Obligations*): 'To the extent that he [the fiduciary] has discretions, he can make choices. Equity's concern is to ensure that if and when choices are to be made, they will be made by the fiduciary, and will be made for and in the beneficiaries' interests.'

18 (1958), 12 D.L.R. (2d) 705 (S.C.C.), at 716. See also *Carl B. Potter Ltd v Mercantile Bank of Canada* (1980), 8 E.T.R. 219 (S.C.C.), at 228; Frankel, n1 *supra*, at 824: 'the law entitles the entrustor to rely on the fiduciary's trustworthiness. The entrustor is therefore not required to show that he actually relied on the fiduciary'; Ellis, n4 *supra*, at 2–22, where he comments that judicial findings which place an obligation on beneficiaries to ensure their fiduciaries' fidelity are 'repugnant to the basic duty of utmost good faith owed by the trustee.'

19 This is discussed in 'The Reverse Onus,' *infra*.

20 Fiduciary remedies will be discussed in greater detail at the end of this chapter.

21 Ernest J. Weinrib, 'The Fiduciary Obligation,' (1975) 25 *U.T.L.J.* 1, at 4.

22 By virtue of the power imbalance between beneficiaries and their fiduciaries within the confines of their fiduciary relationships and the latter's control over the former's affairs, unscrupulous fiduciaries are in a position to be able to conceal the existence of a breach of duty or evidence relating to their breach.

23 Although the reverse onus is only one means of determining whether a fiduciary breach has occurred. See Shepherd, n3 *supra*, at 125–37.
24 *Erlanger v New Sombrero Phosphates Ltd*, [1877–78] 3 A.C. 1218 (H.L.), at 1230. See also *Allcard v Skinner* (1886–90] All E.R. Rep. 90 (C.A.), at 93; *Zamet v Hyman*, [1961] 3 All E.R. 933 (C.A.), at 938; Ellis, n4 *supra*, at 1–3 to 1–4; Shepherd, n3 *supra*, at 126–7; Hon. J.R. Maurice Gautreau, 'Demystifying the Fiduciary Mystique,' (1989) 68 *Can. Bar Rev.* 1, at 26–7; Slaght, n2, *supra*, at 42–3.
25 See Robert Cooter and Bradley J. Freedman, 'The Fiduciary Relationship: Its Economic Character and Legal Consequences,' (1991) 66 *N.Y.U. L. Rev.* 1045, at 1048; see also Slaght, n2 *supra*, at 42–3.
26 Ellis, n4, *supra*, at 1–3.
27 This position is expressed in the legal maxim *quod ab initio non valet in tractu temporis non convalescet*, 'That which is bad in its commencement improves not by the lapse of time.' See *Black's Law Dictionary*, n14 *supra*, at 1126. See also *Parfitt v Lawless* (1872), 2 L.R. P. & D. 462, at 468; Ernest Vinter, *A Treatise on the History and Law of Fiduciary Relationships and Resulting Trusts*, 3rd (Cambridge: W. Heffer, 1955), at 11; Ellis, n4 *supra*, at 1–3: 'Even where the fiduciary acts in good faith and in fact reaps a profit for the beneficiary, then, his actions will constitute a breach of fiduciary duty where he places his own interests ahead of, or equal to, the party to whom he owes the duty. The single-mindedness of his intentions must be directed toward the beneficiary to the detriment of his own self-interest.'
28 [1942] 1 All E.R. 378 (H.L.), at 386, per Lord Russell of Killowen. See also at 381, per Viscount Sankey: 'In my view, the respondents were in a fiduciary position and their liability to account does not depend upon proof of *mala fides*.' See also n44 *infra*.
29 See Ellis, n4 *supra*, at 2-20.3, 2-21; see also *Island Realty Investments Ltd v Douglas* (1985), 19 E.T.R. 56 (B.C.S.C.).
30 This section describes the basic rules governing fiduciary relations from which all others are drawn.
31 Refer back to n14 *supra*.
32 The starting point for any discussion of this rule is *Keech v Sandford* (1726), 25 E.R. 223 (Ch.)
33 Robert Flannigan, 'The Fiduciary Obligation,' (1989) 9 *Ox. J. Leg. Stud.* 285 at 299 (hereinafter 'Fiduciary Obligation'). In *Keech v. Sandford*, n32 *supra*, a fiduciary took advantage of an opportunity to renew a lease that his beneficiary could not legally pursue because of a lack of capacity. The fiduciary was found to have breached his duty to his beneficiary since he only obtained the opportunity to renew the lease as a direct result of his fiduciary position: n32 *supra*, at 223–4. See also Gautreau, n24 *supra*, at 17.

418   Notes to pages 185–6

34 As evidenced by the manner in which it was described in *Aberdeen Railway Co v Blaikie Brothers*, n35 *infra*.
35 (1854), [1843–1860] All E.R. Rep. 249 (H.L.), at 252.
36 (1890), 17 S.C.R. 235, at 246. See also Shepherd, n3 *supra*, at 147–51; Paul D. Finn, 'The Fiduciary Principle,' in Timothy G. Youdan, ed., *Equity, Fiduciaries and Trusts* (Toronto: Carswell, 1989), at 199–258 (hereinafter 'Fiduciary Principle); *Bray v Ford*, [1896] A.C. 44 (H.L.), at 51; *Regal (Hastings Ltd v Gulliver*, n28 *supra*, at 381: 'The general rule of equity is that no one who has duties of a fiduciary nature to perform is allowed to enter into engagements in which he has or can have a personal interest conflicting with the interests of those whom he is bound to protect.'
37 Such as in *Reading v Attorney-General*, [1949] 2 K.B. 232 (C.A.), aff'd [1951] A.C. 507 (H.L.), where not only did Reading, the fiduciary, benefit from his breach of duty, but so did the smugglers that he was assisting. Refer to the discussion of this case in Chapter 8.
38 See *Keech v Sandford*, n32 *supra*; *Canadian Aero Services Ltd v O'Malley* (1973), 40 D.L.R. (3rd) 371 (S.C.C.); *LAC Minerals v International Corona Resources Ltd* (1989), 61 D.L.R. (4th) 14 (S.C.C.); *Regal (Hastings) Ltd v Gulliver*, n28 *supra*.
39 See *Ex parte Lacey* (1802), 6 Ves. 625 (Ch.); *Ex parte James* (1803), 8 Ves. 337 (Ch.).
40 Indeed, the passage of time has not dampened the fervency with which the rule against conflict of interest has been enforced by the courts. See *Phipps v Boardman*, [1967] 2 A.C. 46 (H.L.), at 123, where Lord Upjohn warned that 'a person in a fiduciary capacity must not make a profit out of his trust which is part of the wider rule that a trustee must not place himself in a position where his duty and interest may conflict.'
41 *Standard Investments Ltd v CIBC* (1983), 5 D.L.R. (4th) 452 (Ont. H.C.), at 483.
42 The ethical question as to whether fiduciaries may exonerate themselves from conflict of interest liability by disclosing their personal interests to their beneficiaries is the subject of significant debate. For different sides to this debate, see Finn, *Fiduciary Obligations*, n17 *supra*, at 51; Gautreau, n24 *supra*, at 20; Ellis, n4 *supra*, 1–3.
43 See *Bray v Ford*, n36 *supra*, at 51–2: 'It does not appear to me that this rule is, as has been said, founded upon principles of morality. I regard it rather as based upon the consideration that, human nature being what it is, there is danger of the person holding a fiduciary position being swayed by interest rather than duty, and thus prejudicing those whom he was bound to protect. It has, therefore, been deemed expedient to lay down this positive rule.'
44 See Ellis, n4 *supra*, at 1–2 to 1–3: 'It is the fact of a departure from adherence to the beneficiary's best interests, rather than an evaluation of the fidu-

Notes to pages 186–8   419

ciary's motive in the departure, that constitutes a breach of fiduciary duty. It is in this sense that the absence of malice will not validate a repugnant act ... Even where the fiduciary acts in good faith and in fact reaps a profit for the beneficiary, then, his actions will constitute a breach of fiduciary duty where he places his own interests ahead of, or equal to, the party to whom he owes the duty. The single-mindedness of his intentions must be directed towards the beneficiary to the detriment of his own self-interest.' See also n28 *supra*.

45 (1868), 14 Gr. 586 (P.C.).
46 Ibid., at 592.
47 See Finn, *Fiduciary Obligations*, n17 *supra*, at 69: 'When the board exercises a power which affects the rights of the members of differing classes of shares and the company has no real interest how that power is actually exercised, the board has a duty to act fairly as between the classes.'
48 See n4 *supra*.
49 See n37 and n38 *supra*.
50 See *Kruger v R* (1985), 17 D.L.R. (4th) 591 (F.C.A.), per Heald JA.
51 (1984), 13 D.L.R. (4th) 321 (S.C.C.).
52 Note also *Krendel v Frontwell Investments Ltd*, [1967] 2 Q.R. 579 (H.C.), at 584.
53 See also Deborah A. DeMott, 'Beyond Metaphor: An Analysis of Fiduciary Obligation,' (1988) 5 *Duke L.J.* 879, at 922; Robert P. Austin, 'The Role and Responsibilities of Trustees in Pension Plan Trusts: Some Problems of Trust Law,' in Youdan, n36 *supra*, at 128.
54 (1984), 6 D.L.R. (4th) 40 (Alta. Surr. Ct.), at 55.
55 See, for example, *Knox v Mackinnon* (1888), 13 A.C. 753 (H.L.), at 765; *Rae v Meek* (1889), 14 A.C. 558 (H.L.), at 572–3; *Carruthers v Carruthers*, [1896] A.C. 659 (H.L.), at 664, 667; *Wyman v Patterson*, [1900] A.C. 271 (H.L.), at 278, 280–1, 285–6, 287. See also Frankel, n1 *supra*, at 821–2; Tina Cockburn, 'Trustee Exculpation Clauses Furnished by the Settlor,' (1993) 11 *Aust. Bar Rev.* 163, which examines this issue in Australian, Canadian, British, New Zealand, and American jurisprudence.
56 See, for example, *Midcon Oil & Gas Limited v New British Dominion Oil Company Limited* (1958), 12 D.L.R. (2d) 705 (S.C.C.); *Jirna Ltd v Mister Donut of Canada Ltd.* (1973), 40 D.L.R. (3d) 303 (S.C.C.); *Ronald Elwyn Lister Ltd v Dunlop Canada Ltd* (1982), 135 D.L.R. (3d) 1 (S.C.C.) at 15; *Molchan v Omega Oil and Gas Ltd* (1988), 47 D.L.R. (4th) 481 (S.C.C.); Robert Flannigan, 'Fiduciary Obligation in the Supreme Court,' (1990) 54 *Sask. L. Rev.* 45, at 68–70 (hereinafter 'Supreme Court'). These cases are prime examples of modern courts straying from the fundamental principles of fiduciary doctrine, resulting in the confusion that now exists.

57 Assuming that fiduciary law allowed a fiduciary to make use of such a clause.
58 For example, a fiduciary who appoints an agent cannot be relieved of responsibility for the agent's wrongdoing.
59 An early example of this principle may be seen in *Turner v Corney* (1841), 5 Beav. 515 (Ch.), at 517. See also Finn, *Fiduciary Obligations*, n17 *supra*, at 20: 'Any donee of a discretion, who has trust and confidence reposed in his personal judgment in exercising that discretion, cannot delegate it to another in the absence of an express authority to do so.'
60 See Waters, n2 *supra*, at 32; *Turner v Corney*, n59 *supra*.
61 Note, for example, *Canada Safeway Ltd v Thompson*, [1952] 2 D.L.R. 591 (B.C.S.C.).
62 Note 18 *supra*.
63 Ibid., at 228, remembering that trust law is applicable by analogy to fiduciary law, as illustrated in Chapter 5.
64 (1878), 2 O.A.R. 453, at 463–4.
65 (1886), 33 Ch.D. 402 (C.A.), at 410; see also *Re Gabourie; Casey v Gabourie* (1887), 13 O.R. 635 (Ch.); Ellis, n4 *supra*, 2–22, where he commented that judicial findings which place an obligation on beneficiaries to ensure their fiduciaries' fidelity are 'repugnant to the basic duty of utmost good faith owed by the trustee.'
66 See Frankel, n18 *supra*.
67 See also *Midcon Oil & Gas Limited v New British Dominion Oil Company Limited*, n56 *supra*, per Rand J, dissenting.
68 (1984), 10 D.L.R. (4th) 641 (S.C.C.). See also *Central Trust Co v Rafuse* (1986), 31 D.L.R. (4th) 481 (S.C.C.), in which the Supreme Court of Canada held that the reasonable discoverability rule formulated in *Kamloops* applied also to case of professional negligence.
69 Although, there may be enunciated exceptions to the normal application of ultimate limitation periods contained within such the statutes. For example, the proposed new Ontario *Limitations Act (General), 1993* (Bill 99), imposes a 30-year ultimate limitation period for all causes of action. This ultimate limitation period is delayed, however, where the person against whom the claim is made:
   1 Wilfully conceals from the person with the claim the fact that injury, loss or damage has occurred, that it was caused by or contributed to by an act or omission or that the act of omission was that of the person against whom the claim is made, or
   2 Wilfully misleads the person with the claim as to the appropriateness of a proceeding as means of remedying the injury, loss, or damage.

Notes to pages 191–3 421

See also Limitation of Actions Act, R.S.A. 1980, c. L-15, s. 6; Limitation Act, R.S.B.C., 1979, c. 236, s. 6(3)(d), (e). In these situations, the ultimate limitation period commences once the cause of action is reasonably discovered.
70 Note 11 *supra*. Note also *B(J) v B(R)*, n11 *supra*.
71 On the former cause of action, he held that, on the basis of the principle established in *Kamloops v Nielsen*, n68 *supra*, the statutory limitation for incest only begins to run once victims discover the connection between the harm they suffered and their childhood history. See *M(K) v M(H)*, n11 *supra*, at 305, 315.
72 R.S.O. 1990, c. L-15.
73 Note, for example, Limitation Act, R.S.B.C. 1979, c. 236, s. 3(4); Limitation of Actions Act, R.S.A. 1980, c. L-15, s. 4(1)(g); Limitation of Actions Act, R.S.S. 1978, c. L-15, s. 3(1)(j); Statute of Limitations, R.S.P.E.I. 1988, c. S-7, s. 2(l)(g); Limitation of Actions Act, R.S.M. 1987, c. L150, s. 2(l)(n); Limitation of Actions Act, R.S.N.B. 1973, c. L-8, s. 6.
74 See 16 *Halsbury's Laws of England*, 4th ed. (London: Butterworth, 1976), at 837 (para. 934); *Knox v Gye* (1872), L.R. 5 H.L. 656, at 674–5.
75 Graeme Mew, *The Law of Limitations* (Toronto: Butterworths, 1991), at 23.
76 See n 63 *supra*.
77 See *Soar v Ashwell*, [1893] 2 Q.B. 390 (C.A.); *Taylor v Davies*, [1920] A.C. 636 (P.C.). Note also *Guerin v R*, n51 *supra*, at 342–3; *M(K) v M(H)*, n11 *supra*, at 329–30.
78 *M(K) v M(H)*, n11 *supra*, at 332.
79 In *M(K) v M(H)*, ibid., at 333, La Forest J held that the father's fraudulent concealment of his daughter's cause of action prohibited the application of statutory limitations by analogy.
80 See also the formulation of the doctrine of laches in *Lindsay Petroleum Co v Hurd* (1874), L.R. 5 P.C. 221, at 239–40, which was subsequently adopted by the Supreme Court of Canada in *Canada Trust Co v Lloyd* (1968), 66 D.L.R. (2d) 722 (S.C.C.).
81 See *Taylor v Wallbridge* (1879), 2 S.C.R. 616, at 670.
82 Note *Re Howlett*, [1949] Ch. 767.
83 Mew, n75, *supra*, at 25.
84 I.C.F. Spry, *The Principles of Equitable Remedies: Injunctions, Specific Performance and Equitable Damages*, 2nd ed. (London: Sweet and Maxwell, 1980), at 213: 'Laches is established when two conditions are fulfilled. In the first place, there must be unreasonable delay in the commencement or prosecution of proceedings; in the second place, in all the circumstances the consequences of delay must render the grant of relief unreasonable or unjust.'
85 *M(K) v M(H)*, n11 *supra*, at 334.

86 Note, for example, John Brunyate, 'Fraud and the Statute of Limitations,' [1930] 4 *Camb. L.J.* 174.
87 For example, see Alberta's Limitation of Actions Act, n69 *supra*.
88 Mew, n75 *supra*, at 79. See also Michael Franks, *Limitation of Actions* (London: Sweet and Maxwell, 1959), at 237: 'Where the parties stand in a fiduciary relationship to each other it is insufficient for the defendant to show simply that the plaintiff had the means of discovering the fraud: he must prove that the plaintiff's suspicions were aroused and that he determined not to investigate. This general rule that time does not count against the plaintiff until the fraud is or could be discovered applies, not only where the doctrine of laches is alone applicable, but also where the Statute is applied by analogy, and, *semble*, where it applies directly as well.'
89 *Kitchen v Royal Air Forces Ass'n*, [1958] 2 All E.R. 241 (C.A.), at 249.
90 *M(K) v M(H)*, n11 *supra*, at 319; *Guerin*, n51 *supra*, at 345. In *M(K) v M(H)*, the issue of fraudulent concealment was not a basis for judgment since it was raised for the first time at the Supreme Court of Canada level. La Forest J did find, though, that while fraudulent concealment of the cause of action was not available as an independent ground of appeal in that case, it may have an impact on future incest cases.
91 Mew, n75 *supra*, at 27–8: 'No length of time will act as a bar to relief in the case of fraud, whether or not the defendant take steps to conceal its fraud, in the absence of laches on the part of the person defrauded.'
92 *M(K) v M(H)*, n11 *supra*, at 319; 8 *Halsbury's Laws of England*, 4th ed., n74 *supra*, at 413 (para. 919).
93 *Guerin*, n51 *supra*, at 345.
94 8 *Halsbury's Laws of England*, 4th ed, n74 *supra*, at 413 (para. 919).
95 See, in particular, *Guerin*, n51 *supra*, at 345, per Dickson J, and at 362, per Wilson J.
96 In particular, 'He who seeks equity must do equity' and 'He who comes into equity must come with clean hands.' See the references to these notions in Chapter 5 *supra*, note 31.
97 Spry, n84 *supra*, at 214, 413.
98 Refer back to the discussion of the fiduciary's requirement of full disclosure, *supra*.
99 See *Nocton v Ashburton*, [1914] A.C. 932 (H.L.), at 952; Kent Roach, 'Remedies for Violations of Aboriginal Rights,' (1992) 21 *Man. L.J.* 408, at 521–2. For more on fiduciary remedies, see Roach, at 520–7; Ellis, n4 *supra*, at 20-1 to 20-26; John D. McCamus, 'Remedies for Breach of Fiduciary Duty,' in *Fiduciary Duties*, n2 *supra*; The Hon. Mr Justice W.M.C. Gummow, 'Compensation for Breach of Fiduciary Duty,' in Youdan, n36 *supra*; Timothy G. Youdan, 'The Fiduciary Principle: The Applicability of Proprietary Remedies,' in Youdan,

n36 *supra*; Ian E. Davidson, 'The Equitable Remedy of Compensation,' (1982) 3 *Melbourne Univ. L. Rev.* 349; 16 *Halsbury's Laws of England*, 4th ed., n74 *supra*, at 977–89 (para. 1452–64); *International Corona Ltd v Lac Minerals Ltd*, n2 *supra*, at 56–67; Donovan W.M. Waters, 'Lac Minerals Ltd v International Corona Resources Ltd,' (1990) 69 *Can. Bar Rev.* 455.

100 As Cardozo J explained in *Beatty v Guggenheim Exploration Co*, 225 N.Y. 380 (N.Y.C.A. 1919), at 389: 'The equity of the transaction must shape the measure of relief.'

101 (1989), 61 D.L.R. (4th) 732 (B.C.C.A.), at 182, cited with approval by La Forest J in *Canson Enterprises Ltd v Boughton & Co*, n16 *supra*, at 136. See also the reasons given by McLachlin J, ibid., at 156, affirming the analogy between fiduciary and trust damages in *Guerin*, n51 *supra* (see also McLachlin J's discussion of *Guerin*, at 158–61 of *Canson*): 'Differences between different types of fiduciary relationships may, depending on the circumstances, dictate different approaches to damages ... However, such differences must be related in some way to the underlying concept of trust – the notion of special powers reposed in the trustee to be exercised for the benefit of the person who trusts.'

102 These differ from common law damages in that they are not limited by foreseeability or remoteness. See *Caffrey v Darby* (1801), 31 E.R. 1159 (Ch.); J Derek Davies, 'Equitable Compensation: "Causation, Foreseeability and Remoteness,"' in Donovan W.M. Waters, ed., *Equity, Fiduciaries, and Trusts, 1993* (Toronto: Carswell, 1993); Davidson n99 *supra*, at 352: 'Although compensation in Equity will often produce the same results as damages the common law and equitable remedies utilise different rules to achieve the similar goal of compensating a plaintiff for loss suffered ... For example, common law damages in negligence and contract are subject to requirements of foreseeability and remoteness which are not relevant to Equity when it restores property or money lost by breach of an equitable obligation.' An example of equitable damages is compensation for losses sustained as a result of a breach of an equitable obligation.

103 Rather than the date of the beneficiary's knowledge of the breach or the judicial finding of the breach.

104 Tracing funds in equity allows for the following of money by means beyond those available through common law remedies: see Waters, *Law of Trusts*, n2, *supra*, at 1037–53; 16 *Halsbury's Laws of England*, 4th ed, n74 *supra*, at 983–9 (para. 1460–64); Ellis, n4 *supra*, at 20-14 to 20-17. However, relationships have improperly been described as fiduciary merely to allow for the equitable remedy of tracing. see the discussion of the *Chase Manhattan* and *Goodbody* decisions in Chapter 8.

105 Such as the result of irreparable harm to the beneficiary by not removing the

fiduciary, although no past misconduct is necessary to ground an application for a fiduciary's removal. The test used by the courts in this situation is the possibility of conflict not the actual present or past existence of conflict: *Rose v Rose* (1914), 22 D.L.R. 572 (Ont. C.A.); *Re Consiglio Trusts (No. 1)* (1973), 36 D.L.R. (3d) 659 (Ont. C.A.), at 660: 'It is our view that misconduct on the part of a trustee is not a necessary requirement for the Court to act'; see Shepherd, n3 *supra*, at 342, n18.

106 See Shepherd, n3 *supra*, at 342–3; Ellis, n4 *supra*, at 2–3; *Rose v Rose*, n105 *supra*; *Toronto (City of) v Bowes*, (1858), 14 E.R. 770 (P.C.); *Hawrelak v City of Edmonton*, [1972] 2 W.W.R. 561 (Alta S.C.), aff'd [1973] 1 W.W.R. 179 (Alta C.A.), rev'd [1976] 1 S.C.R. 387.

107 See *Alexandra Oil & Development Co v Cook* (1908), 11 O.W.R. 1054 (C.A.), where the Court of Appeal, at 1060, stated that 'A person occupying a fiduciary position of any kind cannot by any possibility be permitted to secretly make to himself a profit in the transactions in which he was concerned in his fiduciary capacity.' See also *Lavigne v Robern* (1984), 51 O.R. (2d) 60 (C.A.), where a shareholder who made a secret profit from the sale of a company he owned jointly with two other shareholders – a sale which he also orchestrated – was forced to disgorge the profit. Since he orchestrated the sale on behalf of himself and the other shareholders in the company, he was deemed to be a fiduciary to the other two shareholders and was forced to disgorge his secret profit gained from his disloyalty. Note also the commentary on this point in Gautreau, n24 *supra*, at 21–4; see also L.S. Sealy, 'Fiduciary Relationships,' [1962] *Camb. L.J.* 69, at 77.

108 (1994), 17 O.R. (3d) 790 (C.A.), at 802.

109 Although this illustration is intended only to demonstrate the dilemma which arises in such a situation, the principles of fiduciary doctrine may also hold X and/or D liable to B if it is determined that they knowingly (i.e., actual or constructive knowledge) assisted in F's breach of duty: see, for example, *Coy v Pommerenke* (1911), 44 S.C.R. 543; *Peso Silver Mines Ltd v Cropper* (1965), 56 D.L.R. (2d) 117 (B.C.C.A.), aff'd (1966), 58 D.L.R. (2d) 1 (S.C.C.); *MacMillan Bloedel Ltd v Binstead* (1983), 14 E.T.R. 269 (B.C.S.C.); Ellis, n4 *supra*, at 12-4.2 to 12-4.3, 18-5 to 18-6, and 20-11 to 20-13; Gautreau, n24 *supra*, at 21.

110 Weinrib, n21 *supra*, at 13–14.

111 The undeserved advantage must go to the beneficiary because only the fiduciary committed a wrongful act: see Sealy, n107 *supra*, at 77: 'a fiduciary is bound to surrender to his beneficiary all "secret profits" received by the fiduciary by reason of his position, whether the beneficiary has a proprietary or even a moral claim to them or not.'

11 The British Crown's Obligations

1 Namely, the application of fiduciary principles to relationships that have been deemed to be fiduciary in nature.
2 The issues raised in this study are by no means exhaustive. The questions below are merely illustrative of the kinds of issues ignored by the courts.
3 [1982] 2 All E.R. 118 (C.A.)
4 [1982] 3 All E.R. 786 (Ch.), aff'd [1982] 3 All E.R. 822 (C.A.).
5 [1982] 3 All E.R. 786 (Ch.). The *Manuel* and *Noltcho* cases, although originating as separate actions, were heard together at trial. Only the *Manuel* decision was heard on appeal.
6 Note 3 *supra*, at 127–9.
7 This principle was recognized at the Imperial Conference of 1926 (Cmd. 2768): ibid., at 128. In his judgment in the *Manuel* and *Noltcho* cases, Megarry VC explained that whereas this change in understanding was recognized at the 1926 conference, how and when the change was made is unknown: n5 *supra*, at 787.
8 Ibid. It should be noted, however, that Lord Denning MR's conclusion is arrived at in spite of his acknowledgment that at the time the British Crown entered into these obligations, the Crown was in constitutional law one and indivisible: n3 *supra*, at 129: '[A]t the time when the Crown entered into the obligations under the 1763 proclamation or the treaties of the 1870s, the Crown was in constitutional law one and indivisible ... But, now that the Crown is separate and divisible, I think that the obligations under the proclamation and the treaties are obligations of the Crown in respect of Canada. They are not obligations of the Crown in respect of the United Kingdom.'
9 Ibid., at 131.
10 Ibid., at 140.
11 Ibid., at 142.
12 Ibid.
13 Ibid., at 143.
14 See 'Fiduciaries' Delegation of Authority,' in Chapter 10.
15 The six declarations, reproduced in the judgment, n5 *supra*, at 790–1, read as follows:
   1 A Declaration that the Parliament of the United Kingdom has transferred sovereignty over Canada to the Dominion of Canada save and in so far as power is reserved to the United Kingdom Parliament by law and by the Statute of Westminster 1931 and the British North America Acts 1867 to 1964.
   2 A Declaration that on the proper construction of the Statute of Westmin-

ster and the British North America Acts no law hereafter made by the United Kingdom Parliament can extend to Canada other than a law made at the request and with the consent of the Dominion of Canada.

3 A Declaration that the words 'Dominion' in the preamble and section 4 of the Statute of Westminster 1931 means in respect of Canada and the people of Canada and 'the consent of the Dominion' means the consent of the people of Canada expressed by (a) the Federal Parliament of Canada (b) all the Legislatures of the Provinces of Canada and (c) the Indian Nations of Canada who have a separate and special status within the Constitution of Canada.

4 A Declaration that on its proper construction the British North America Act 1930 (a) confers on the Indians of the Provinces of Manitoba and British Columbia the rights set out in the agreements scheduled to the Act and (b) imposed restraints on the legislative power of the Parliament of Canada to derogate from such rights.

5 A Declaration that the British North American [sic] Act 1930 can only be amended at the request of and with the consent of the people of Canada expressed by (a) the Federal Parliament of Canada (b) all the Legislatures of the Provinces of Canada and (c) the Indian Nations of Canada.

6 A Declaration that in the premises (1) the United Kingdom Parliament has no power to amend the Constitution of Canada so as to prejudice the Indian Nations without the consent of the Indian Nations of Canada; (2) the Canada Act 1982 is ultra vires.

16 The four declarations sought by the *Noltcho* plaintiffs, reproduced in the judgment, ibid., at 796, read as follows:

(i) A Declaration that each of the Agreements contained in and/or evidenced by the Instruments particularised in the title to this Action and/or the collateral warranties thereto remain in full force and effect; and are binding upon the British Crown; and/or

(ii) A Declaration that the aforesaid Agreements and/or collateral warranties constitute trusts which remain in full force and effect; and are binding upon the British Crown; and/or

(iii) A Declaration that each of the aforesaid Agreements and/or collateral warranties constitute a subsisting Treaty properly so-called made with the British Crown; and/or

(iv) A Declaration that the British Crown is in wrongful repudiation of the said Agreements and/or collateral warranties.

17 Section 7(1) provided that nothing in the act was to be 'deemed to apply to the repeal, amendment or alteration of the British North America Acts 1867 to 1930.'

18 Refer to the discussion of the methods of altering aboriginal rights in Canada in Chapter 6, in relation to the *Sparrow* decision.
19 Note 5 *supra*, at 796. This point is noteworthy, as it arose approximately two years prior to the release of the Supreme Court of Canada's judgment in *Guerin*.
20 The ratio (*ratio decidendi*) is the ground or reason for judgment in a case.
21 Note 5 *supra*, at 793–4.
22 Ibid., at 799: 'I cannot read a promise that the treaty obligation in this case should always bind the British Crown as preventing the British Crown from transferring or altering sovereignty, or as binding the British Crown to carry out obligations when it no longer has the power to do so.'
23 Ibid., at 799.
24 Refer to the discussion in Chapter 13.
25 The ultimate devolution of powers and responsibilities from the 'single and indivisible' Crown to the Canadian federal and provincial Crowns and the emerging independence and sovereignty of Canada is a very complex and contentious issue which cannot be properly entertained within the scope of this work. It is sufficient for present purposes merely to note the transfer of powers, responsibilities, and benefits from the 'single and indivisible' Crown to the dominion and provincial Crowns which occurred gradually over a lengthy period. For a more detailed discussion of this issue, see Brian Slattery, 'The Independence of Canada,' (1983) 5 *Sup. Ct. L. Rev.* 369, in particular the section entitled 'Canadian Independence,' at 390–2, and the sources cited therein, esp. at n61, n66 and n68.
26 The Treaty of Versailles formally marked peace between the Allied nations and Germany following the First World War.
  Note the Supreme Court of Canada' findings in *Reference re Offshore Mineral Rights of British Columbia*, [1967] S.C.R. 816, where the court stated that Canada's sovereignty 'was acquired in the period between its separate signature of the Treaty of Versailles in 1919 and the Statute of Westminster, 1931.' See also *Reference re Amendment of the Constitution of Canada*, [1981] 125 D.L.R. 1 (S.C.C.); Slattery, n25 *supra*, at 390–2; and May LJ's finding of a limited continuing sovereignty of the British Crown over Canada in the *Alberta Indian Association* case, n3 *supra*, at 142.
27 22 Geo. V., c. 4 (Imp.).
28 With the notable exception, for example, of the constitutionalization of the Crown's fiduciary duty in Section 35(1) of the Constitution Act, 1982, which was sanctioned by the Supreme Court of Canada in *R v Sparrow* (1990), 70 D.L.R. (4th) 385 (S.C.C.).
29 *Sparrow*, n28 *supra*.

30 *New Zealand Maori Council v Attorney-General*, [1987] 1 N.Z.L.R. 641 (N.Z.C.A.).
31 *Eastmain Band v Canada (Federal Administrator)*, [1993] 3 C.N.L.R. 55 (F.C.A.), rev'g *Eastmain Band v Robinson*, [1992] 1 C.N.L.R. 90 (F.C.T.D.).
32 See *Sparrow*, n28 *supra*, at 407.
33 See the discussion of beneficiaries' ability to rely on their fiduciaries' fulfilment of fiduciary duties in Chapter 10.
34 *Sparrow*, n28 *supra*, at 404.
35 (1990), 70 D.L.R. (4th) 427 (S.C.C.).
36 Ibid., at 462.
37 R.S.C. 1985, c. I-5, as amended.
38 Referred to in the case as the Act of Capitulation at Montreal.
39 (1985), 24 D.L.R. (4th) 390 (S.C.C.), at 405.
40 Ibid., at 409.
41 (1964), 50 D.L.R. (2d) 613 (B.C.C.A.) 649, aff'd (1965) 52 D.L.R. (2d) 481n (S.C.C.).
42 *Sioui*, n35 *supra*, at 456.
43 Ibid.
44 Ibid., at 457: [T]he silence of the Royal Proclamation regarding the treaty at issue cannot be interpreted as extinguishing it.'
45 The Proclamation merely recognized and affirmed pre-existing aboriginal rights, it did not grant any rights to the Native peoples. See the discussion of *Calder v Attorney-General of British Columbia*, (1973), 34 D.L.R. (3d) 145 (S.C.C.), n43, *supra*, in Chapter 1, as well as the effect of the Proclamation in Chapter 4.
46 *Sioui*, n35 *supra*, at 458.
47 For further discussion of the division of federal and provincial powers, see *The Rowell–Sirois Report*, Donald V.S. Smiley, ed. (Toronto: McClelland and Stewart, 1963).
48 Where more than one fiduciary exists, a beneficiary may bring an action for breach of duty against one or all of its fiduciaries. All fiduciaries are held to be jointly and severally liable for any breach committed by one or more of them against their beneficiaries. A fiduciary not involved in the act of breach cannot be relieved of liability for the breach committed by a co-fiduciary even where the fiduciary in such a situation was completely unaware of the co-fiduciary's actions or the commission of the breach of duty. This rule is tied in with the fiduciary's duty to be fully informed. See, for example, *Canada Safeway Ltd v Thompson*, [1952] 2 D.L.R. 591 (B.C.S.C.).
49 See *Sparrow*, n28 *supra*, at 417.
50 In a manner which is identical to the rationale for not limiting the Supreme Court of Canada's finding of the Crown's fiduciary obligation in *Guerin* to situations involving the surrender of reserve lands.

51 *Sparrow*, n28 *supra*, at 409.
52 Refer back to 'The Requirement of Full Disclosure,' in Chapter 10.
53 Subject, of course, to the discussion of statutory limitations, laches, and acquiescence in Chapter 10.
54 And which would also be liable for any breach of those duties.
55 It is arguable that the *Alberta Indian Association* case implicitly addressed the issue of the British Crown's fiduciary duty by stating that any obligations of the British Crown were transferred to the Canadian Crown. However, because of the unique nature and requirements of the fiduciary obligation, it cannot be presumed that a blanket denial of the British Crown's responsibility to Canada's aboriginal peoples which did not raise the issue of fiduciary duty includes its fiduciary obligations to them.
56 The doctrine of *res judicata* should not be confused with the related principle of *stare decisis*, in which it is open to the parties to a case to dispute the applicability of a judgment in a prior case to their particular fact situation.
57 Subject to some powers reserved to the British Crown, such as the amending of the Canadian constitution.
58 See the discussion of statutory limitations, laches, and acquiescence in Chapter 10.

12 The Canadian Crown's Obligations

1 (1888), 14 A.C. 46 (P.C.), aff'g (1887), 13 S.C.R. 577, (1886), 13 O.A.R. 148, (1885), 10 O.R. 196 (Ch.).
2 [1897] A.C. 199 (P.C.), aff'g [1896] 25 S.C.R. 434.
3 [1903] A.C. 73 (P.C.), aff'g (1901), 32 S.C.R. 1, (1900), 32 O.R. 301 (Div. Ct.), (1899), 31 O.R. 386 (Ch.).
4 [1910] A.C. 637 (P.C.), aff'g (1909), 42 S.C.R. 1, rev'g (1907), 10 Ex. C.R. 445.
5 (U.K.), 30 & 31 Vict., c. 3, reprinted in R.S.C. 1985, App. II, No. 5 (renamed the Constitution Act, 1867). Because a number of the cases cited herein predate the name change of the Act, it will be referred to by its original name to avoid confusion.
6 This issue is dealt with in greater detail in the treatment of the *Robinson Treaties Annuities* case *infra*.
7 For a concise discussion of the devolution of the Crown's duties to the Canadian Crown, see Brian Slattery, 'The Independence of Canada,' (1983) 5 *Sup. Ct. L. Rev.* 369, esp. at 390–2.
8 (1888), 14 A.C. 46 (P.C.), at 54 (hereinafter *St Catherine's Milling*, PC).
9 Section 109 reads: 'All Lands, Minerals, and Royalties belonging to the several Provinces of Canada, Nova Scotia, and New Brunswick at the Union, and all Sums then due or payable for such Lands, Mines, Minerals, or Royal-

ties, shall belong to the several Provinces of Ontario, Quebec, Nova Scotia, and New Brunswick in which the same are situate or arise, subject to any Trusts existing in respect thereof, and to any Interest other than that of the Province in the same.'
10 (1883), 8 A.C. 767 (P.C.).
11 *St Catherine's Milling*, PC, n8 *supra*, at 57.
12 Ibid., at 58.
13 This assertion is based on a straightforward interpretation of the exclusive power vested in the federal Crown over 'Indians, and Lands reserved for the Indians' in Section 91(24) of the British North America Act, 1867, and, more specifically, the power relating to 'Indians,' which exists independently of the power over 'Lands reserved for the Indians,' as determined by the Supreme Court of Canada in *Four B Manufacturing v United Garment Workers of America* (1979), 102 D.L.R. (3d) 385 (S.C.C.), at 398–9. Whereas a province possesses exclusive power over lands surrendered under treaty by way of Section 109, any attempt by a province to set aside an Indian reserve out of those lands would clearly infringe upon the exclusive federal power over Indians – which entails the sole ability to act and legislate in respect of matters that affect Indians *qua* Indians – and, therefore, would be *ultra vires* (beyond its jurisdictional power). Refer to the discussion of the effects of Section 88 of the Indian Act, R.S.C. 1985, c. I-5 on the applicability of provincial legislation to aboriginal peoples in Chapter 14.
14 The Privy Council determined that the British Legislature did not intend to deprive a province of its rights under Section 109 of the British North America Act, 1867, by conferring legislative powers over 'Indians, and Lands reserved for the Indians' upon the Dominion Crown under Section 91(24) of the Act: *St Catherine's Milling*, PC, n8 *supra*, at 59. Indeed, Lord Watson found, at 59, that having the beneficial interest in land accrue to the Crown in right of the province in which the land was located upon its surrender was not incompatible with having legislative control over the same land prior to the surrender reside with the dominion Crown: 'The fact that the power of legislating for Indians, and for lands which are reserved to their use, has been entrusted to the Parliament of the Dominion is not in the least degree inconsistent with the right of the Provinces to a beneficial interest in these lands, available to them as a source of revenue whenever the estate of the Crown is disencumbered of the Indian title.'
15 (1885), 10 O.R. 196 (Ch.), at 235 (hereinafter *St Catherine's Milling, Ch*).
16 Ibid.: 'Whatever equities ... may exist between the two Governments in regard to the consideration given and to be given to the tribes ... is a matter not agitated on this record.'

Notes to pages 225-31   431

17 (1886), 13 O.A.R. 148 at 157 (hereinafter *St Catherine's Milling, OCA*).
18 This is evidenced by his statement that the distribution of the financial responsibilities under the treaty 'could, I presume, be carried out in good faith by arrangement between the two Governments': ibid., at 158.
19 Ibid., at 173.
20 (1887), 13 S.C.R. 577, at 622 (hereinafter *St Catherine's Milling, SCC*).
21 Ibid., at 674-6.
22 *St Catherine's Milling*, PC, n8 *supra*, at 60.
23 Note 2 *supra*.
24 Note 3 *supra*.
25 Note 4 *supra*.
26 [1896] 25 S.C.R. 434.
27 This had been established under Section 142 of the British North America Act, 1867, to determine the 'Division and Adjustment of the Debts, Credits, Liabilities, Properties, and Assets' of Upper and Lower Canada.
28 The dominion was created out of the old provinces of Upper and Lower Canada by the Act of Union, 1840 (U.K.), 3 & 4 Vict., c. 35, reprinted as The Union Act, 1840 in R.S.C. 1985, App. II, No. 3.
29 [1896] 25 S.C.R. 434, at 495 (hereinafter *Robinson Treaties Annuities, SCC*).
30 The accrual occurred by virtue of Section 109 of the British North America Act, 1867.
31 The terms of Section 111 provided that, upon Confederation, the Dominion of Canada would absorb and become liable for 'the Debts and Liabilities of each Province existing at the Union,' subject to the limits on that amount imposed by Sections 112, 114, and 115 of the Act. It was, in essence, a constitutional guarantee that pre-Confederation provincial debts would be paid.
32 The amount of the debt was initially limited to $62,500,000, but was later increased.
33 The province were also obligated to pay interest on that amount at the rate of 5 per cent per annum.
34 *Robinson Treaties Annuities, SCC*, n29 *supra*, at 506.
35 Reproduced, ibid., at 440.
36 Ibid., at 507.
37 Ibid., at 507-8.
38 See the discussion of King J's interpretation of paragraph XIII in relation to this issue at n42 *infra*. In fact, Strong CJC's attempt to rationalize his conclusion with the arbitrators' report reads matters into the report that were neither considered within it nor contemplated at that time.
39 *Robinson Treaties Annuities, SCC*, n29 *supra*, at 533.
40 Ibid., at 525.

41 Ibid., at 548
42 Ibid., at 549–50.
43 [1897] A.C. 199 (P.C.) (hereinafter *Robinson Treaties Annuities, PC*).
44 *Robinson Treaties Annuities*, SCC, n29 *supra*, at 505.
45 *Robinson Treaties Annuities*, PC, n43 *supra*. He also dismissed the notion that the annuity obligations were a charge on the lands, as suggested by the dissenting judgments of Gwynne and King JJ: 'Their Lordships have been unable to discover any reasonable grounds for holding that, by the terms of the treaties, any independent interest of that kind was conferred upon the Indian communities.' Ibid., at 211.
46 Note 3 *supra*.
47 The matters in dispute in *Seybold* were not restricted to resolving who was responsible for fulfilling the obligation to set aside reserves under the treaty, but also addressed other issues such as the ownership of mineral rights. For present purposes, however, discussion of the case herein will be restricted to the former.
48 (1899), 31 O.R. 386 (Ch.) (hereinafter *Seybold, Ch*).
49 Ibid., at 398.
50 (1900), 32 O.R. 301 (Div. Ct.) (hereinafter *Seybold, Div. Ct.*)
51 Ibid., at 303–4.
52 (1901), 32 S.C.R. 1 (hereinafter *Seybold, SCC*).
53 Ibid., at 13.
54 [1903] A.C. 73 (P.C.) (hereinafter *Seybold, PC*).
55 Ibid., at 82–3. Although Lord Davey's 'honourable engagement' did not legally bind the province, it indicated the Privy Council's recognition of existing provincial obligations, notwithstanding that he prefaced his statement with 'Let it be assumed that ...'
56 This is evidenced by some of the agreements between the federal and provincial Crowns regarding Indian lands. See, for example, An Act for the Settlement of Certain Questions between the Government of Canada and Ontario Respecting Indian Lands, S.C. 1891, c. 5; The Ontario Boundaries Extension Act, S.C. 1912, c. 40; The Quebec Boundaries Extension Act, S.C. 1912, c. 45; and An Act for the Settlement of Certain Questions between the Governments of Canada and Ontario Respecting Indian Reserve Lands, S.C. 1924, c. 48.
57 See *Friends of the Oldman River Society v Canada (Minister of Transport)* (1992), 88 D.L.R. (4th) 1 (S.C.C.), at 31–9; *Alberta Government Telephones v Canada (CRTC)* (1989), 61 D.L.R. (4th) 193 (S.C.C.), at 233; *Bombay (Province of) v Bombay (City of)*, [1947] A.C. 58 (P.C.), at 61; Peter Hogg, *Liability of the Crown*, 2nd ed. (Toronto: Carswell, 1989), at 210.

58 (1983), 144 D.L.R. (3d) 193 (S.C.C.).
59 '[T]reaties and statutes relating to Indians should be liberally construed and doubtful expressions resolved in favour of the Indian.' Ibid., at 198. See also *Mitchell v Peguis Indian Band* (1990), 71 D.L.R. (4th) 193 (S.C.C.), at 201: 'Aboriginal understandings of words and corresponding legal concepts in Indian treaties are to be preferred over more legalistic and technical constructions.' This principle of interpretation is consistent with the *contra proferentem* rule in contract law, which holds that any ambiguity in a contract or agreement is to be interpreted against the party that drafted the agreement. See S.M. Waddams, *The Law of Contracts*, 2nd ed. (Toronto: Canada Law Book, 1984), at 345–61.

Earlier cases ascribing to the same interpretive mechanisms as those illustrated in *Nowegijick* include: *Worcester v State of Georgia*, 6 Pet. 515 (U.S. 1832), at 582; *Jones v Meehan*, 175 U.S. 1 (1899); *Robinson Treaties Annuities, SCC*, n29 *supra*, at 535; *R v George* (1966), 55 D.L.R. (2d) 386 (S.C.C.), at 396–7; *Kruger and Manuel v R* (1977), 75 D.L.R. (3d) 434 (S.C.C.), at 437. See also the *Report of the Select Committee on Aborigines, 1837*, Vol. 1, Part 2 (Imperial Blue Book, 1837 nr VII 425, Facsimile Reprint, C. Struik (Pty) Ltd, Cape Town, 1966), at 80. '[A] ready pretext for complaint will be found in the ambiguity of the language in which their agreements must be drawn up, and in the superior sagacity which the European will exercise in framing, interpreting, and in evading them.'
60 Note 4 *supra*.
61 (1907), 10 Ex. C.R. 445, at 496–7 (hereinafter *Treaty No. 3 Annuities, Ex. Ct.*).
62 (1909), 42 S.C.R. 1 (hereinafter *Treaty No. 3 Annuities, SCC*).
63 Statements that are considered to be *obiter dictum* – which, translated literally, means 'a remark by the way' – are those that are incidental or collateral to the issue(s) in contention and, consequently, are of no precedential weight or binding authority in subsequent judicial determinations. The fact that *obiter* comments are not binding, but merely persuasive does not entail that they are unimportant. Indeed, they are often cited and relied on by subsequent courts as the crux of their own determinations.
64 Ibid., at 114–15.
65 Ibid., at 111. Indeed, Ontario received the beneficial interest in the surrendered lands through the operation of Section 109 of the *British North America Act, 1867*, rather than through any positive actions of its own.
66 Ibid., at 126. He also found that Lord Watson's statements in *St Catherine's Mining, PC*, n8 *supra*, were purely obiter and of no legally binding effect: Ibid., at 130–2.
67 Ibid., at 111 (per Idington J), and at 125 (per Duff J).

68 See n44 *supra*.
69 [1910] A.C. 637 (P.C.), at 645 (hereinafter *Treaty No. 3 Annuities, PC*): 'In the present case it does not appear to their Lordships that the claim of the Dominion can be sustained on any principle of law that can be invoked as applicable.'
70 Ibid., at 646.
71 Because of the unique quality of treaties, agreements, and alliances between the Crown and aboriginal peoples, which are built on or stem from the special, *sui generis* relationship between the parties, the obligations assumed thereunder by the Crown are fiduciary in nature; see the discussion in chapter 2.
72 The principle of privity of contract holds that two parties to a contract cannot impose obligations upon a third party who was not privy to the agreement, subject to certain exceptions. See Waddams, n59 *supra*, esp. at 200–4. See also *Dunlop Pneumatic Tyre Co v Selfridge & Co*, [1915] A.C. 847 (H.L.); *Vandepitte v Preferred Accident Insurance Co* [1933] 1 D.L.R. 289 (P.C.); *Greenwood Shopping Plaza Ltd v Beattie*, [1980] 2 S.C.R. 228. Note also the discussion of privity relating to the decision in *Ontario (Attorney-General) v Bear Island Foundation* (1991), 83 D.L.R. (4th) 381 (S.C.C.) in Kent McNeil, 'The High Cost of Accepting Benefits from the Crown: A Comment on the Temagami Indian Land Case,' [1992] 1 C.N.L.R. 40, at 50–4.
73 *Treaty No. 3 Annuities, PC*, n69 *supra*, at 644.
74 See *Treaty No. 3 Annuities, SCC*, n62 *supra*, at 111 (per Idington J), and at 126, and 130–2 (per Duff J). See also the text accompanying n65 and n66 *supra*.
75 See, for example, *Theodore v Duncan*, [1919] A.C. 696 (P.C.), at 706: 'The Crown is one and indivisible throughout the Empire, and it acts in self-governing states on the initiative and advice of its own Ministers in these States.' See also *R v Secretary of State for Foreign and Commonwealth Affairs, ex parte Indian Association of Alberta*, [1982] 2 All E.R. 118 (C.A.), at 127–8, where Lord Denning, MR explained that the change in the constitutional understanding of 'the Crown' as 'single and indivisible' was recognized at the Imperial Conference of 1926 (Cmd 2768) to 'separate and divisible' according to the particular territory in which it was sovereign. See the discussion of the *Alberta Indian Association* case in Chapter 11.
76 The Canadian Crown was, itself, a part of the larger 'single and indivisible' Crown in right of the Commonwealth.
77 See Brian Slattery, 'First Nations and the Constitution: A Question of Trust,' (1992), 71 *Can. Bar Rev.* 261, at 275: 'The rearrangement of constitutional powers and rights accomplished at Confederation did not reduce the Crown's overall fiduciary obligations to First Nations. Rather, these obligations

tracked the various powers and rights to their destinations in Ottawa and the Provincial capitals.'
78 Alan Pratt, 'Federalism in the Era of Aboriginal Self-Government,' in David C. Hawkes, ed., *Aboriginal Peoples and Government Responsibility: Exploring Federal and Provincial Roles* (Ottawa: Carleton University Press, 1989), at 53.
79 See Wesley Newcomb Hohfeld, 'Some Fundamental Legal Conceptions as Applied in Judicial Reasoning,' (1913–14) 23 *Yale L.J.* 16; Hohfeld, 'Fundamental Legal Conceptions as Applied in Judicial Reasoning,' (1916–17) 26 *Yale L.J.* 710; and, Hohfeld, *Fundamental Legal Conceptions as Applied in Judicial Reasoning*, Walter Wheeler Cook, ed. (New Haven: Yale University Press, 1964).
80 See the reference in n57 *supra* and its accompanying text.
81 The province is bound to cooperate to the extent that it is legally or constitutionally able to do so. See Noel Lyon, *Aboriginal Peoples and Constitutional Reform in the 90's* (Background Study No. 7, Constitutional Reform Project, Centre for Public Law and Public Policy, York University, 1991), at 9: 'To the extent that provinces have the constitutional capacity to do things that can affect aboriginal peoples, the Crown in right of a province is no less a successor to the British Crown and is bound by the same fiduciary duty.'
82 Note 77 *supra*, at 275.
83 (1983), 147 D.L.R. (3d) 147 (S.C.C.).
84 In Canada, Indian interests in land cannot be alienated to anyone other than the Crown. This restriction exists as a result of British practice that originated in the early colonization of North America. The most noteworthy indication of the Crown's practice of interposing itself as a requisite intermediary in the sale of aboriginal lands may be seen in the Royal Proclamation of 1763, R.S.C. 1985, App. II, No. 1. Note that this practice also existed in other parts of the British Empire: see, for example, *R v Symonds*, [1847] N.Z.P.C.C. 387 (N.Z.S.C.), at 391. Today, the requirement that surrenders may only be made to the Crown in right of Canada is entrenched in Section 37 of the Indian Act, R.S.C. 1985, c. I-5 and in the exclusive jurisdiction of the Crown in right of Canada over 'Indians, and Lands reserved for the Indians,' in Section 91(24) of the Constitution Act, 1867. For further discussion and analysis of the surrender requirements contained within the Indian Act, see J. Paul Salembier, 'How Many Sheep Make a Flock? An Analysis of the Surrender Provisions of the *Indian Act*,' [1992] 1 C.N.L.R. 14.
85 Smith, n83 *supra*, at 246.
86 Ibid.
87 See n51 *supra* and its accompanying text.
88 Smith, n83 *supra*, at 250.

436 Notes to pages 240–2

89 Undoubtedly as a result of his earlier characterization of these issues as 'extraneous' to the matter before the court: see n86 *supra*.
90 (1984), 45 O.R. (2d) 760 (Ont. H.C.).
91 An Act for the Settlement of Certain Questions between the Governments of Canada and Ontario Respecting Indian Lands, S.O., 1891, c. 3; An Act for the Settlement of Certain Questions between the Governments of Canada and Ontario Respecting Indian Lands, n56 *supra*.
92 The Beds of Navigable Waters Act, S.O. 1911, c. 6; and, An Act to Confirm the Title for the Government of Canada to Certain Lands and Indian Lands, S.O. 1915, c. 12. The latter directly contravenes the agreement between Ontario and Canada established in the 1891 statutes, ibid. See also the discussion of the effects of these statutes in *Ontario and Minnesota Power Co v The King*, [1925] A.C. 196 (P.C.); Angela Emerson, *Research Report on Policy of the Government of Ontario Re: Headland to Headland Question, Treaty #3, 1873–1978* (Office of Indian Resource Policy, Ministry of Natural Resources, 1978); Richard H. Bartlett, *Aboriginal Water Rights in Canada* (Calgary: Canadian Institute of Resources Law, University of Calgary, 1988), at 103–9.
93 At that time the Crown in right of Canada could only be sued in the federal courts, whereas the Crown in right of Ontario could only be sued in the Ontario courts. Section 17(1) of the Federal Court Act, R.S.C. 1985, c. F-7 now provides that the Federal Court, Trial Division possesses 'concurrent original jurisdiction in all cases where relief is claimed against the Crown,' thereby allowing both federal and provincial Crowns to be co-defendants in one action in that court.
94 *Gardner*, n90 *supra*, at 775–6.
95 See the further discussion on this point in Chapter 13.
96 [1991] 4 C.N.L.R. 84 (F.C.T.D.).
97 (1991), 79 D.L.R. (4th) 185 (B.C.S.C.).
98 Refer back to the discussion of the *Cree Regional Authority* case in Chapter 6.
99 (1990), 70 D.L.R. (4th) 385 (S.C.C.).
100 *Cree Regional Authority v Robinson*, n96 *supra*, at 106.
101 Note 97 *supra*, at 482. Refer back to the discussion of *Delgamuukw* in Chapter 6.
102 Ibid., at 536.
103 (1993), 104 D.L.R. (4th) 470 (B.C.C.A.).
104 (1991), 83 D.L.R. (4th) 381 (S.C.C.).
105 See the discussion of *Bear Island* in Chapter 6.
106 Note 104 *supra*, at 384.
107 Ibid.

13 Aboriginal Understandings of 'the Crown' and the Nexus between Governmental Power and Fiduciary Responsibility

1 See, for example, Richard Price, ed., *The Spirit of the Alberta Indian Treaties*, (Edmonton: Pica Pica Press, 1987); René Fumoleau, *As Long as This Land Shall Last* (Toronto: McClelland and Stewart, 1976); John D. Hurley, *Children or Brethren: Aboriginal Rights in Colonial Iroquoia* (PhD thesis, Cambridge University, 1985, reprinted, Saskatoon: University of Saskatchewan Native Law Centre, 1985); Francis Jennings, *The Ambiguous Iroquois Empire* (New York: Norton, 1984); Jennings, *Empire of Fortune* (New York: Norton, 1988); Alexander Morris, *The Treaties of Canada with the Indians of Manitoba and the North-West Territories* (Toronto: Belfords, Clarke, 1880).
2 As described in Chapter 11.
3 As discussed in Chapter 10, a fundamental premise of fiduciary doctrine insists that beneficiaries need not inquire into the actions of their fiduciaries, but may rely entirely on the latter's honesty, integrity, and fidelity to their best interests. As Mark Ellis comments in *Fiduciary Duties in Canada* (Toronto: De Boo, 1988), at 2-22, judicial findings which place an obligation upon beneficiaries to ensure their fiduciaries' fidelity are 'repugnant to the basic duty of utmost good faith owed by the trustee.'
4 (1990), 71 D.L.R. (4th) 193 (S.C.C.). See also the discussion of *Mitchell* from an administrative law perspective in H. Wade MacLaughlan, 'Development in Administrative Law: The 1989–90 Term,' (1991) 2 *Sup. Ct. L. Rev.* (2d) 1 at 13–18.
5 A garnishing order is authorized by statute and allows a debtor's money, property, or receivables (or those which belong to the debtor but are possessed or under the control of a third party, or are owed by the third party to the debtor) to be applied in payment of the debtor's indebtedness to one or more creditors.
6 R.S.M. 1970, c. G20.
7 R.S.C. 1970, c. I-6. Under the current Act, R.S.C. 1985, c. I-5, as amended, these provisions retain the same numbering as under the previous Act.
8 Section 88 allows for provincial laws of general application to be rendered applicable to status Indians – as defined in Section 6 and 7 of the current Act – by referential incorporation, except where they are inconsistent with the terms of the Indian treaties, the Indian Act, or other federal legislation.
9 (1983), 144 D.L.R. (3d) 193 (S.C.C.).
10 *Mitchell*, n4 *supra*, 198. Note also the reference to the problems in the interpretation of Indian treaties in the *Report of the Select Committee on Aborigines*,

1837, Vol. 1, Part 2 (Imperial Blue Book, 1837 nr VII 425 Facsimile Reprint, C. Struik (Pty) Ltd, Cape Town, 1966), at 80.
11 *Mitchell*, n4 *supra*, at 209.
12 Ibid.
13 Ibid.
14 Refer to Chapter 12, n76 and n77 *supra* and their accompanying text.
15 See n11 *supra*.
16 *Mitchell*, n4 *supra*, at 209.
17 This doctrine states that laws in relation to a matter within the competence of one level of government may validly affect a matter within the competence of a second level: see, for example, *Alberta Government Telephones v Canadian Radio-television & Telecommunications Commission* (1989), 61 D.L.R. (4th) 193 (S.C.C.), at 228.
18 *Mitchell*, n4 *supra*, at 209: 'On its facts, *Guerin* only dealt with the obligation of the *federal* Crown arising upon surrender of land by Indians.' See also the discussion in Bradford Morse, 'Government Obligations, Aboriginal Peoples and Section 91(24) of the *Constitution Act, 1867*,' in David C. Hawkes, ed., *Aboriginal Peoples and Governmental Responsibility: Exploring Federal and Provincial Roles* (Ottawa: Carleton University Press, 1989), at 84: 'Although there is no case law on this point, and the Supreme Court in *Guerin* was only dealing with a claim against the federal government, the judgments do not imply a limitation of the duty to the Crown in right of Canada alone.'
19 *Mitchell*, n4 *supra*, at 237.
20 See La Forest J's discussion in *Mitchell*, ibid., at 223–31.
21 Ibid., at 223–4: 'As I see it, if Parliament had intended to cast aside these traditional constraints on the Crown's obligations to protect the property of Indians, it would have expressed this in the clearest of terms.'
22 (1990), 70 D.L.R. (4th) 385 (S.C.C.).
23 Ibid., at 396–7. See also Brian Slattery, 'Understanding Aboriginal Rights,' (1987) 66 *Can. Bar Rev.* 727 at 782, where he stated that the word 'existing' in Section 35(1) suggests that aboriginal and treaty rights 'are affirmed in a contemporary form rather than in their primeval simplicity and vigour.' Slattery's statement was approved by the Supreme Court in *Sparrow*, ibid., at 397. The court's rejection of frozen rights theory in *Sparrow* is also consistent with the precedent it had established in *R v Big M Drug Mart*, [1985] 1 S.C.R. 295, at 343–4, where the majority dismissed the notion of a 'frozen concepts' theory applying to the Charter of Rights and Freedoms by holding that the Charter's guarantee of rights was not confined to the status of those rights when the Charter came into effect. Note, as well, the Supreme Court's rejection of frozen rights theory in the aboriginal rights context in *Simon v R* (1985), 24 D.L.R. (4th) 390 (S.C.C.), at 402–3. See also Brian Slattery, 'The Constitutional

Guarantee of Aboriginal and Treaty Rights,' (1982–3), 8 *Queen's L.J.* 232, at 262: 'The law should be regarded as always speaking, and as applying to new circumstances as they arise.'
24 See Chapter 12, n59, *supra*. It should be noted that while La Forest J agreed with *Nowegijick*'s interpretive principles as they applied to Indian treaties, he held that 'somewhat different considerations must apply in the case of statutes relating to Indians': *Mitchell*, n4 *supra*, at 236.
25 See, for example, Price, n1 *supra*; Fumoleau, n1 *supra*; Morris, n1 *supra*; Harold Cardinal, *The Unjust Society* (Edmonton: Hurtig, 1969).
26 See Price, ibid.; Hurley, n1 *supra*; Francis Jennings, *Ambiguous Iroquois Empire*, n1 *supra*; Jennings, *Empire of Fortune*, n1 *supra*; Morris, ibid.
27 Which means 'Of their own kind or class.' See *Black's Law Dictionary*, 5th ed. (St Paul, Minn: West, 1979) at 1286. The concept of describing aboriginal rights as *sui generis* is described in greater detail in John J. Borrows and Leonard I. Rotman, 'The *Sui Generis* Nature of Aboriginal Rights: Does It Make a Difference?' (forthcoming).
28 8 Wheat. 541 (U.S. 1823).
29 See the discussion of the facts in the *Johnson* case in Chapter 3.
30 [1921] 2 A.C. 399 (P.C.).
31 Ibid., at 402–3.
32 (1984), 13 D.L.R. (4th) 321 (S.C.C.), at 339, 341. Refer back to the discussion of *Guerin* in Chapter 5.
33 [1993] 2 C.N.L.R. 20 (F.C.A.), at 78, 83.
34 (14 Dec. 1995), File No. 23516 (S.C.C.), at para. 8. 'In my view, when determining the legal effect of dealings between aboriginal peoples and the Crown relating to reserve lands, the *sui generis* nature of aboriginal title requires courts to go beyond the usual restrictions imposed by the common law, in order to give effect to the true purpose of the dealings.'
35 See *Simon v R* n23, *supra*, at 404: 'An Indian treaty is unique; it is an agreement *sui generis* which is neither created nor terminated according to the rules of international law.'; *R v Sioui* (1990), 70 D.L.R. (4th) 427 (S.C.C.), at 441.
36 See *Guerin*, n32 *supra*, at 341.
37 See, for example, *Guerin*, n32 *supra*, at 339; *Paul v Canadian Pacific Ltd* (1989), 53 D.L.R. (4th) 487 (S.C.C.), at 505; *Roberts v Canada* (1989), 57 D.L.R. (4th) 197 (S.C.C.), at 207, 208; *Sparrow*, n22 *supra*, at 408; *Mitchell*, n4 *supra*, at 209; *Apsassin*, n33 *supra*, at 78, 83; *Skerryvore Ratepayer's Ass'n v Shawanaga Indian Band* (1993), 16 O.R. (3d) 390 (C.A.), at 400. Refer also to the High Court of Australia's decision in *Mabo v Queensland [No. 2]* (1992), 175 C.L.R. 1 (H.C. Aust.), esp. at 59.
38 These rights include, but are not restricted to, aboriginal cultural property and the right to hunt and fish: see *Sparrow*, n22 *supra*, at 411: 'Courts must be

careful, then, to avoid the application of traditional common law concepts of property as they develop their understanding of what the reasons for judgment in *Guerin* ... referred to as the "*sui generis*" nature of aboriginal rights.'

39 *Delgamuukw v British Columbia* (1991), 104 D.L.R. 470 (B.C.C.A.), at 644.
40 Ibid.
41 See the discussion in Borrows and Rotman, n27 *supra*. Some of the sources that discuss or contemplate differences between aboriginal and non-aboriginal worldviews and ideological conceptions include Leroy Little Bear, 'Aboriginal Rights and the Canadian "Grundnorm,"' in J. Rick Ponting, ed., *Arduous Journey: Canadian Indians and Decolonization* (Toronto: McClelland and Stewart, 1986); Mary Ellen Turpel, 'Aboriginal Peoples and the Canadian Charter: Interpretive Monopolies, Cultural Differences,' (1989–90) 6 *Can. Hum. Rts. Y.B.* 3; Robin Ridington, 'Cultures in Conflict: The Problems of Discourse,' in W.H. New, ed., *Native Writers and Canadian Writing* (Vancouver: University of British Columbia Press, 1990); Robert A. Williams Jr, 'Gendered Checks and Balances: Understanding the Legacy of White Patriarchy in an American Indian Cultural Context,' (1990) 24 *Georgia L. Rev.* 1019; 'Aboriginal Concepts of Justice,' in A.C. Hamilton and C.M. Sinclair, Commissioners, Manitoba Aboriginal Justice Inquiry, *The Justice System and Aboriginal People: Report of the Aboriginal Justice Inquiry of Manitoba: Public Inquiry into the Administration of Justice and Aboriginal People,* Vol. 1 (Winnipeg: Queen's Printer, 1991).
42 Note 9 *supra*.
43 See the discussion of the application of statutory limitation periods and laches to actions for breach of fiduciary duty in Chapter 10.
44 It should be remembered, though, that while fiduciaries may transfer the entirety of their fiduciary *duties*, they may not transfer the entirety of their fiduciary *obligations* to their beneficiaries, as discussed in Chapter 10.
45 Such as in the example of the obligation to set aside an Indian reserve out of lands surrendered under a land surrender treaty, as discussed in Chapter 12.
46 Although it should be noted that the doctrine of paramountcy is explicitly included so that provincial legislation which is repugnant to federal law is rendered null and void to the extent of the repugnancy.
47 See Chapter 12, n79 *supra* and its accompanying text.
48 *Sparrow*, n22 *supra*, at 409.
49 Section 88 reads as follows: 'Subject to the terms of any treaty and any other Act of Parliament, all laws of general application from time to time in force in any province are applicable to and in respect of Indians in the province, except to the extent that those laws are inconsistent with this Act or any

Notes to page 252   441

order, rule, regulation or by-law made thereunder, and except to the extent that those laws make provision for any matter for which provision is made by or under this Act.'
50 See n8 *supra*.
51 The application of Section 88 is a complicated matter. For further consideration of case law dealing with the effect of Section 88, refer to *R v Sutherland* (1980), 113 D.L.R. (3d) 374 (S.C.C.) ('pith and substance' rule); *Kruger and Manuel v The Queen* (1977), 75 D.L.R. (3d) 434 (S.C.C.) (whether provincial laws are of general application and/or impair the status and capacity of aboriginal peoples); *Four B Manufacturing v United Garment Workers of America* (1979), 102 D.L.R. (3d) 385 (S.C.C.) (idem); *Dick v The Queen* (1985), 23 D.L.R. (4th) 33 (S.C.C.); and *Derrickson v Derrickson* (1986), 26 D.L.R. (4th) 175 (S.C.C.) (provincial laws may not interfere with treaty rights); Brian Slattery, *Understanding Aboriginal Rights*, n23 *supra*, at 775–80; Slattery, 'First Nations and the Constitution: A Question of Trust,' (1992) 71 *Can. Bar Rev.* 261 (hereinafter *First Nations*) 282–6; Patrick Macklem, 'First Nations Self-Government and the Borders of the Canadian Legal Imagination,' (1991) 36 *McGill L.J.* 382, at 419–23, 435–45; Bruce Ryder, 'The Demise and Rise of the Classical Paradigm in Canadian Federalism. Promoting Autonomy for the Provinces and First Nations,' (1991) 36 *McGill L.J.* 308, at 371–80.
52 See Slattery, *First Nations*, n51 *supra*, at 284–6, but note also, to the contrary, *R v Alphonse*, [1993] 4 C.N.L.R. 19 (B.C.C.A.) and *R v Dick*, [1993] 4 C.N.L.R. 63 (B.C.C.A.).
53 Ibid., at 274. See also Slattery, *Understanding Aboriginal Rights*, n 23 *supra*, at 755: 'The federal Crown has primary responsibility toward native peoples under section 91(24) of the Constitution Act, 1867, and thus bears the main burden of the fiduciary trust. But insofar as provincial Crowns have the power to affect native peoples, they also share in the trust.'
54 S.C. 1891, c. 5, S.O. 1891, c. 3. Note also the obligations of Ontario and Quebec in the 1912 Ontario and Quebec boundary extension acts: Ontario Boundaries Extension Act, S.C., 1912, c. 40; An Act to Express the Consent of the Legislative Assembly of the Province of Ontario to an Extension of the Limits of the Province, S.O. 1912, c. 3; Quebec Boundaries Extension Act, S.C. 1912, c. 45; An Act Respecting the Extension of the Province of Quebec by the Annexation of Ungava, S.Q. 1912, c. 7, which provide in Section 2a of the federal Ontario Act and Section 2c of the federal Quebec Act: 'That the province of ... will recognize the rights of the Indian inhabitants in the territory above described to the same extent, and will obtain surrenders of such rights in the same manner, as the Government of Canada has heretofore recognized such rights and has obtained surrender thereof, and the said province shall bear

and satisfy all charges and expenditure in connection with or arising out of such surrenders.' These provincially obtained surrenders were subject, however, to the approval of the governor in council (Sections 2b and 2d respectively) and the 'trusteeship of the Indians in the said territory, and the management of ... lands ... reserved for their use, shall remain in the government of Canada)' (Sections 2c and 2e respectively).

55 *James Bay and Northern Quebec Agreement* (Quebec City: Editeur officiel du Québec, 1976), along with its implementing legislation, the James Bay and Northern Quebec Native Claims Settlement Act, S.C. 1976–7, c. 32; An Act Approving the Agreement Concerning James Bay and Northern Quebec, S.Q. 1976, c. 46. Similar situations include Quebec's role in the Cree-Naskapi (of Quebec) Act, S.C., 1984, c. 18 and Ontario's part in negotiating with the Nishnawbe-Aski Nation (NAN) to recognize NAN self-government. Regarding the latter, see the Memorandum of Understanding dated 24 Feb. 1986 between Ontario, the federal Crown, and NAN to enter into negotiations for the purpose of recognizing NAN self-government within the context of Canadian Confederation. This was followed by an Addendum to the Memorandum of Understanding signed on 1 Dec. 1989 and an Interim Measures Agreement dated 12 June 1990 regarding future development adjacent to NAN reserve lands and lands claimed as NAN lands.

See also Morse, n18, *supra*, at 65: 'The Ontario government subsequently obtained a guaranteed role in [Indian treaty] negotiations, first with Treaty No. 9 and its adhesions as well as in the Williams Treaty of 1923. However, this was not truly due to any constitutional imperative, but rather it reflected a federal willingness to include the province and a desire to shift some of the financial burdens onto Ontario's shoulders.'

56 See An Act Respecting Hunting and Fishing Rights in the James Bay and New Quebec Territories, S.Q., 1978, c. 92; The Cree Villages Act, S.Q., 1978, c. 88; An Act Respecting the Land Regime in the James Bay and New Quebec Territories, S.Q., 1978, c. 93.

57 Note 4 *supra*, at 210.

58 Of course, there is always the possibility that agreements between the federal and provincial governments may resolve this potential problem before it arises and without the need for judicial intervention, as with previous intergovernmental agreements discussed above.

59 Note Dickson CJC's comments in *Mitchell*, n4 *supra*, at 210. See also the commentary by the Royal Commission on Aboriginal Peoples in *Treaty Making in the Spirit of Co-existence: An Alternative to Extinguishment* (Ottawa: Minister of Supply and Services, 1995), at 7: '[P]rovincial and territorial government ought to work together with the federal government and Aboriginal nations

to reach agreements that recognize and affirm Aboriginal rights. While Parliament has special responsibilities with respect to "Indians, and Lands reserved for the Indians," the task of achieving lasting co-existence between Aboriginal and non-Aboriginal systems of land tenure and governance also involves provincial and territorial governments. Indeed this task goes to the heart of the future of Aboriginal–Crown relations in Canada, and in this respect all governments – federal, provincial, territorial, and Aboriginal – bear fundamental responsibilities in shaping our future together.'

60 See *Sparrow*, n22 *supra*, at 407: 'The nature of s. 35(1) itself suggests that it be construed in a purposive way.'
61 *Eastmain Band v Robinson*, [1993] 3 C.N.L.R. 55 (F.C.A.).
62 Noel Lyon, *Aboriginal Peoples and Constitutional Reform in the 90's* (Background Study No 7, Constitutional Reform Project, Centre for Public Law and Public Policy, York University, 1991), at 9.
63 Ibid.: 'If there is genuine doubt as to whether aboriginal rights do exist, each provincial government has direct access to its court of appeal, on a reference, for a judicial determination of the matter.' In addition, fiduciaries' responsibilities to act in their beneficiaries' best interests requires them to inform themselves as to what those best interests are, which includes a requirement to consult with their beneficiaries.
64 This is emphasized through the *Sparrow* court's reliance on the precedent established in *R v Taylor and Williams* (1981), 62 C.C.C. (2d) 227 (Ont. C.A.).
65 See, for example, the Ontario Ministry of Natural Resources' Interim Enforcement Policy, dated 28 May 1991, which details the province's relaxed regulation of aboriginal hunting and fishing rights in Ontario.
66 Slattery, *First Nations*, n51 *supra*, at 284 n75, corroborates this notion that a province may pass legislation directed at aboriginal peoples if the effect of the legislation is to grant exemptions to them in recognition of their aboriginal and treaty rights.
67 See n57, and n58 *supra* and their accompanying text.
68 (1991), 83 D.L.R. (4th) 381 (S.C.C.).
69 [1991] 4 C.N.L.R. 84 (F.C.T.D.).

14 Characteristics of the Crown–Nature Fiduciary Relationship

1 This was defeated by referendum on 26 Oct. 1992.
2 *Shaping Canada's Future Together* (Ottawa: Minister of Supply and Services Canada, 1991).
3 *The Right of Aboriginal Self-Government and the Constitution: A Commentary by the Royal Commission on Aboriginal Peoples* (Ottawa: 13 Feb. 1992).

444   Notes to pages 255-61

4 D.W.M. Waters, *Law of Trust in Canada*, 2nd ed. (Toronto: Carswell, 1984), at 961 (hereinafter *Law of Trusts*): 'A trust comes to a close, and the trustee is entitled on a passing of his final accounts to a discharge, when the terms of the trust have been carried out.'
5 Either by virtue of the rules established in the Court of Chancery, most notably the precedent established in *Saunders v Vautier* (1841), 4 Beav. 115 (Ch.) – where it was held that beneficiaries of a trust may terminate the trust because of their equitable interest in the trust *res* – or through the statutory powers of courts to vary or revoke trusts. See Waters, *Law of Trusts*, n4 *supra*, at 962, and, generally, at 961-80, 1055-86.
6 *R v Sparrow* (1990), 70 D.L.R. (4th) 385 S.C.C.) at 408-9. See the discussion of the *Sparrow* case in Chapter 6.
7 See discussion in Chapter 6.
8 See discussion in Chapter 7.
9 Note the similarity between this situation applying to fiduciary relationships and the rule in *Saunders v Vautier*, n5 *supra*.
10 Section 35(1) merely recognizes and protects rights: it does not force their acceptance by the aboriginal peoples. Aboriginal peoples may therefore contract out of Section 35(1) rights if they choose to do so.
11 R.S.C. 1985, c. I-5, as amended; these will be discussed below.
12 See the discussion entitled, 'The Purposive Nature of the Crown's Fiduciary Duty,' *infra*.
13 The band must establish rules for the regulation of the list in accordance with the Act and, once it has indicated its intent to assume control over its membership list, receive the consent of a majority of its electors.
14 Although rights granted under Section 60(1) are subject to revocation at any time by the governor in council via Section 60(2).
15 Either in whole, or in part, subject to the governor in council's approval.
16 In a circumstance where the Crown believes that an aboriginal nation is fully capable of managing its own affairs, yet has not consented to releasing the Crown from its transitional duties, it may make an application to the courts to be relieved of any continuing transitional duties upon the court's concurrence with the Crown's contention. Such an action is quite consistent with a fiduciary's ability to bring a reference as to the fulfilment of its duties before the courts.
17 Note 6 *supra*.
18 [1993] 3 C.N.L.R. 5 (F.C.A.).
19 In Timothy G. Youdan, ed., *Equity, Fiduciaries, and Trust* (Toronto: Carswell, 1989) (hereinafter 'Fiduciary Principle').
20 The use of these terms herein are adopted from Finn, 'Fiduciary Principle,'

Notes to pages 261–4   445

n19 *supra*, although, as will become evident, their meaning within this section is not synonymous with his own characterization of them.
21 Ibid., at 25. See also Felicity Anne Reid, 'The Fiduciary Concept – An Examination of Its Relationship with Breach of Confidence, Negligent Misrepresentation, and Good Faith, unpublished LLM thesis, Osgoode Hall Law School, 1989, at 28; Peter D. Maddaugh, 'Definition of Fiduciary Duty,' in *Fiduciary Duties*, Law Society of Upper Canada Special Lectures, 1990 (Toronto: De Boo, 1991), at 27–8.
22 Finn, *Fiduciary Principle*, n19 *supra*, at 28.
23 The suggestion that fiduciary law may completely replace these separate spheres of influence, albeit in a different context, has also been suggested by J.C. Shepherd, *The Law of Fiduciaries* (Toronto: Carswell, 1981), at 373.
24 (1705), 24 E.R. 118 (Ch.), at 119.
25 Finn, 'Fiduciary Principle,' n19 *supra*, at 28, although he does except what he describes as fiduciary powers – such as those possessed by lawyers in relation to their clients – whereby it is the power held by the former in relation to the latter which results in the relationship being classified as fiduciary rather than a situation whereby powers are given by one party to the other which gives rise to the fiduciary nature of the relationship. For further elaboration on this latter point, see P.D. Finn, *Fiduciary Obligations* (Sydney: Law Book Company, 1977), at 3, 272–3 (hereinafter *Fiduciary Obligations*).
26 See n22 *supra*.
27 See the discussion of fiduciary doctrine in Part Two.
28 Refer back to the illustration in the discussion of fiduciary remedies in Chapter 10.
29 [1987] 1 N.Z.L.R 641 (N.Z.C.A.), at 664.
30 Refer back to the discussion of the justificatory test for legislative initiatives formulated by the Supreme Court in *Sparrow*, n6 *supra*, which is discussed in Chapter 6.
31 See the discussion of conflict of interest in Chapter 10. Note also the comments of the United States Court of Claims in *Three Affiliated Tribes of Fort Berthold Reservation v United States*, 390 F.2d 686 (U.S. Ct. Cl. 1968), at 691: 'It is obvious that Congress cannot simultaneously (1) act as trustee for the benefit of the Indians, exercising its plenary powers over the Indians and their property, as it thinks in their best interests, and (2) exercise its sovereign power of eminent domain, taking the Indian's property within the meaning of the Fifth Amendment to the Constitution ... *Congress can own two hats, but it cannot wear them both at the same time*' (emphasis added). To deal with this situation, the Court of Claims developed what is known as the 'good faith effort' test, which holds that there is no breach of governmental duty where Congress

exercises good faith in its dealings with the aboriginal peoples in question and provides adequate compensation for the taking of aboriginal lands. This test was subsequently endorsed in *United States v Sioux Nation of Indians*, 448 U.S. 371 (1980). For further discussion of the *Fort Berthold* test, see John D. Hurley, 'Aboriginal Rights in Modern American Case Law,' [1983] 2 C.N.L.R. 9, at 37.

32 The past tense is deliberately used here to denote the Crown's inability to extinguish aboriginal and treaty rights which were in existence on 17 April 1982 because of their entrenchment in Section 35(1) of the Constitution Act, 1982. As Brian Slattery explained in 'The Constitutional Guarantee of Aboriginal and Treaty Rights,' (1982–3) 8 *Queen's L.J.* 232, at 243: 'The expression, "aboriginal rights," ... refers to a range of rights held by native peoples, not by virtue of Crown grant, agreement, or legislation, but by reason of the fact that aboriginal peoples were once independent, self-governing entities, in possession of most of the lands now making up Canada ... What [Section 35] does is recognize that some, if not all, of the rights originally vested in native Canadians have survived the process whereby the Crown gained sovereignty over Canadian territories. Insofar as those rights were not lawfully terminated prior to 17 April 1982, they now enjoy the protection of section 35.' See also, ibid., at 262, regarding the protection of treaty rights in Section 35(1).

33 Even in accordance with the principles established in *Sparrow*, n6 *supra*.

34 The following discussion of the unique nature of the Crown's role as fiduciary to aboriginal peoples is not intended to contradict the situation-specificity of fiduciary doctrine, which emphasizes that all fiduciary relationships are *sui generis* and must be treated accordingly. Rather, it is intended for illustrative purposes only.

35 Although this is not the only duty of the Crown, our discussion will be restricted to it. In 'First Nations and the Constitution: A Question of Trust,' (1992) 71 *Can. Bar Rev.* 261, Brian Slattery suggests that the Canadian Constitution as a whole is animated by a general doctrine of collective trust.

36 Indeed, a corporate director possesses various fiduciary duties to the corporation, its employees, and to its various classes of shareholders which must be reconciled with daily operational decisions. For the latter assertion, see the discussion in Chapter 10, n4.

37 The Crown's definition of Specific and Comprehensive Claims, as outlined in the Department of Indian Affairs and Northern Development's booklet entitled, *Outstanding Business – A Native Claims Policy* (Ottawa: Queen's Printer, 1982) (hereinafter *Outstanding Business*), is as follows: 'The term "comprehensive claims" is used to designate claims which are based on traditional Native use and occupancy of land. Such claims normally involve a group of

Notes to pages 265–8 447

bands or Native communities within a geographic area and are comprehensive in their scope including, for example, land, hunting, fishing and trapping rights and other economic and social benefits ... The term "specific claims" ... refers to those claims which relate to the administration of land and other Indian assets and to the fulfillment of treaties.'
38 Ibid. The federal Comprehensive Claims process is detailed *In All Fairness – A Native Claims Policy* (Ottawa: Queen's Printer, 1981).
39 The process is detailed in *Outstanding Business*, n37 *supra*, at 23–4.
40 Only Indian bands, as defined by the Indian Act, are eligible to bring claims under the Specific Claims process, as established under Guideline 2 of *Outstanding Business*.
41 *Outstanding Business*, n37 *supra*, at 20. The numbering of these items corresponds to their numbering in *Outstanding Business*.
42 Pursuant to Order in Council P.C. 1992-1730 (27 July 1992), amending the commission issued pursuant to Order in Council P.C. 1991-1329 (15 July 1991).
43 See the discussion of the effects of the Indian Act on aboriginal peoples in Chapter 3.
44 See Sanders, '"The Friendly Care and Directing Hand of the Government": A Study of Government Trusteeship of Indians in Canada,' unpublished paper, 1977 (on file with author), at 26.
45 Ovide Mercredi and Mary Ellen Turpel, *In the Rapids: Navigating the Future of First Nations* (Toronto: Viking, 1993), at 136–7.
46 Ibid., at 139: 'The Order in Council issued by the Privy Council in 1991 to set up the Indian Specific Claims Commission incorporates a narrow set of criteria from the existing claims policy, further limiting how decisions can be reviewed. We find these terms of reference completely unacceptable for obvious reasons. First, there was no consultation with us. Second, the terms of reference and limitations on compensation are not consistent with legal principles. They violate the concept of equality guaranteed under the Charter of Rights and Freedoms. Third, the terms of reference and limitations on the process represent a serious breach of the federal government's fiduciary obligations to First Nations. Fourth, these limitations tie the hands of the Commission and take away its independence. And finally, the restrictions imposed upon the Commission are inconsistent with then Prime Minister Brian Mulroney's promise that his government is prepared "to go far beyond the status quo."'
47 Note 11 *supra*.
48 Unless, of course, the authority over Indian moneys is managed by a band for itself under Section 69(1).

49 R.S.C. 1906, c. 81, as amended by Section 6 of An Act to Amend the Indian Act, S.C. 1926–7, c. 32; see the discussion of this section in Chapters 1 and 3.
50 Conveniently, it also provided the Crown with immunity from judicial review of its activities relating to or otherwise affecting the aboriginal peoples.
51 Owing to the Crown's powers of reservation and disallowance contained in Sections 55–7 of the British North America Act, 1867. It should be noted that these powers have not been used since 1878. Furthermore, it was agreed at the Imperial Conference of 1930 that they would no longer be used: see Peter W. Hogg, *Constitutional Law of Canada*, 3rd ed. (Toronto: Carswell, 1992), at 302–3; Kent McNeil, 'Envisaging Constitutional Space for Aboriginal Governments,' (1993) 19 *Queen's L.J.* 95, at 117. Nevertheless, bills passed by the Houses of Parliament only become law in Canada after they have received royal assent by the Crown, through its personal representative, the governor-general.
52 The effect of the Crown's actions in this regard are akin to situations where fiduciaries include exculpatory clauses in contracts with their beneficiaries to insulate themselves from liability; see the discussion of this issue in Chapter 10.
53 See, for example, *Ex parte Lacey* (1802), 31 E.R. 1228 (Ch.); *Ex parte James* (1803), 32 E.R. 385 (Ch.). Note also Mark V. Ellis, *Fiduciary Duties in Canada* (Toronto: De Boo, 1988) at 2–9: '[T]he Court enforces such a prohibition on the express premise that public policy seeks to enjoin a person in a position of utmost trust and confidence from following his naturally occurring self-interest, a temptation that must be overcome by operation of a rule of law.'
54 'Designated lands' are defined by Section 2(1) of the Act as 'a tract of land or any interest therein the legal title to which remains vested in Her Majesty and in which the band for whose use and benefit it was set apart as a reserve has, otherwise than absolutely, released or surrendered its rights or interests, whether before or after the coming into force of this definition.'
55 Note also Section 92(1), which prevents full-time Department of Indian Affairs officials and employees from trading or selling goods for profit to an Indian.
56 This is different than the Crown's position as a requisite intermediary in the alienation of Indian lands to a third party, as required by the Indian Act.
57 See *Smith v R* (1983), 147 D.L.R. (3d) 237 (S.C.C.); the *Smith* case is discussed in greater detail in Chapter 13.
58 David R. Lowry, 'Native Trusts: The Position of the Government of Canada as Trustee for Indians, A Preliminary Analysis,' unpublished report prepared for the Indian Claims Commission and the Union of Nova Scotia Indians, 1973, at 38.

59 Michael J. Bryant. 'Crown–Aboriginal Relationships in Canada: The Phantom of Fiduciary Law,' (1993) 27 *U.B.C. L. Rev.* 19, at 43–4, although Bryant concludes, at 44, that 'the conflicts rule in the Crown–aboriginal context should be modified so as to serve the purpose of the imposition of the duty: the safeguarding of aboriginal title and accompanying rights.'
60 Whether the *Sparrow* test is able to accomplish its stated intention is an entirely different matter which remains to be seen through its future application. See also the controversy over the *Sparrow* test's application to treaty rights in Chapter 6.
61 Such as the Crown's traditional practice of using moneys derived from the sale or lease of surrendered lands to pay its own expenses relating to Indian affairs, including paying the salaries of Indian agents: see David C. Nahwegahbow, Michael W. Posluns, Don Allen, and Douglas Sanders, 'The First Nations and the Crown: A Study of Trust Relationships,' unpublished research report prepared for the Special Committee of the House of Commons on Indian Self-Government, 1983, at 290–1; *Dreaver v the King* (1935), 5 C.N.L.C. 92 (Exch.), which is discussed in Chapter 4.
62 Refer back to the section entitled 'Fiduciaries Must Not Compromise Their Beneficiaries' Interest,' in Chapter 10.
63 This topic is discussed in greater detail in Royal Commission on Aboriginal Peoples, *Treaty Making in the Spirit of Co-existence: An Alternative to Extinguishment* (Ottawa: Minister of Supply and Services, 1995).
64 In particular, by requiring a claimant bands to surrender its aboriginal rights in exchange for enunciated rights. See the discussion of this point, below.
65 As the Royal Commission on Aboriginal Peoples commented on this issue, 'Generally speaking, it does not befit a fiduciary to seek to obtain by agreement entitlements it is required by law to protect': n63 *supra*, at 53.
66 For example, aboriginal land rights are inextricably linked with other rights, such as hunting, fishing, and trapping, as well as the right of self-government. Consequently, they are arguably broader than any negotiated land right (based on common law conceptions of ownership) than may be presently obtained in negotiations with the Crown.
67 See n63 *supra*, 68: 'Requiring the extinguishment of Aboriginal title as a precondition of negotiations is out of step with the spirit and purpose of the Royal Proclamation of 1763, the Constitution Act, 1982, and the Crown's fiduciary responsibilities.' As discussed in earlier chapters of this book, the Crown's general fiduciary duty to Native peoples exists within both the Royal Proclamation of 1763 and the Constitution Act, 1982, as well as in a number of other documentable events and sources, such as the Treaty of Albany, 1664, and in specific Indian treaties.

68 An alternative to the existing Comprehensive Claims process, which is based on the principle of recognizing, rather than extinguishing, aboriginal rights, is offered by the Royal Commission on Aboriginal Peoples, ibid., at 59–67. The commission's ultimate recommendations are as follows:
   1 That the federal government not seek to obtain blanket extinguishment of Aboriginal land rights in exchange for rights or other benefits contained in comprehensive agreements;
   2 That the federal government not require partial extinguishment of Aboriginal land rights as a precondition for negotiating comprehensive agreements, and that parties resort to partial extinguishment in the last resort, only after a careful and exhaustive analysis of alternative options;
   3 That the federal government adopt a policy whereby comprehensive agreements can serve as instruments of co-existence and mutual recognition;
   4 That parties strive to identify, as exhaustively as possible, their respective rights by agreement.
   5 That comprehensive negotiations be aimed at
      (a) Crown recognition of Aboriginal rights with respect to land and governance over part of the claim area;
      (b) Aboriginal recognition of Crown rights with respect to land and governance over another part of the claim area;
      (c) co-jurisdiction and co-management of other land within the claim area; and
      (d) the protection of existing third-party interests.
   6 That agreements be worded to allow the Aboriginal rights they recognize to evolve in light of favourable legal developments;
   7 That parties strive for terms that avoid as much as possible conflict between Crown rights recognized by agreement and Aboriginal rights not recognized by agreement;
   8 That agreements provide that, in the event of conflict, Crown rights recognized by agreement and third-party interests protected by agreement take precedence over a party's Aboriginal rights not recognized by agreement;
   9 That agreements impose on parties a duty to bargain in relation to the effects of significant unforeseen legal developments concerning Aboriginal rights not recognized by the agreement. This duty would arise where, but for a Crown right recognized by the agreement, such developments would enure to the benefit of an Aboriginal party. This duty would not arise where a protected third-party interest prevents an Aboriginal party from enjoying the benefit of such a legal development;

10 That governments accept that Aboriginal rights, including rights of self-government, recognized by an agreement are 'treaty rights' within the meaning of section 35(1) of the Constitution Act, 1982;
11 That negotiations be premised on reaching agreements that recognize an inherent right of self-government;
12 That separate negotiations over issues relating to land and issues relating to self-government not be a precondition for entering into negotiations; and
13 That parties establish mechanisms, including mediation and periodic review, to facilitate the resolution of conflict and disputes arising out of their continuing relationship.

69 (1985), 17 D.L.R. (4th) 591 (F.C.A), aff'g (1981), 125 D.L.R. (3d) 513 (F.C.T.D.). Note that the competing interests of the Crown also plays a vital role in *Apsassin v Canada (Minister of Indian Affairs and Northern Development)*, [1988] 3 F.C. 20 (F.C.T.D.), aff'd [1993] 2 C.N.L.R. 20 (F.C.A.), rev'd (14 Dec. 1995), File No. 23516 (S.C.C.), which is discussed in Chapter 6.

15 The Practical Application of Fiduciary Doctrine in the Native Law Context: A Reappraisal of *Kruger v R*

1 (1985), 17 D.L.R. (4th) 591 (F.C.A.), at 647.
2 Ibid., at 654. Note also Urie JA's comments at 648–9: 'There was no breach of the fiduciary obligation of the Crown based on the alleged conflict existing between two of its departments – Mines and Resources, Indian Affairs Branch, and Transport ... Ultimately, a decision had to be taken ... That fact does not mean that there was a breach of fiduciary duty nor that there was a conflict of interest which had to be resolved in their [the Indians'] favour ...'
3 Ibid., at 607–8.
4 Ibid., at 622: 'It is clear, in my view, that the conflict of interest between two departments of the Government of Canada which was so apparent in the dealings with respect to Parcel "A" is equally apparent when the dealings concerning the acquisition of Parcel "B" are scrutinized.'
5 Ibid., at 623.
6 Ibid.
7 Ibid., at 627: 'For all the above reasons, it is my reluctant opinion that the appellants' causes of action herein are statute-barred.'
8 See n2 *supra*, and its accompanying text.
9 See also John D. Hurley, 'The Crown's Fiduciary Duty and Indian Title: *Guerin v The Queen*,' (1985) 30 *McGill L.J.* 559, at 600–1: 'The question of conflict of interest must therefore be decided with reference to the conduct, not of any one department, but of the entire federal government.'

10 See the discussion of this issue in 'Fiduciaries Must Not Compromise Their Beneficiaries' Interest,' in Chapter 10.
11 *Kruger*, n1 *supra*, at 609.
12 Ibid., at 624.
13 See n7, *supra*.
14 See Chapter 10.
15 Ibid.
16 Ibid.
17 *Apsassin v Canada (Minister of Indian Affairs and Northern Development)*, [1988] 3 F.C. 20 (F.C.T.D.), aff'd [1993] 2 C.N.L.R. 20 (F.C.A.), rev'd (14 Dec. 1995), File No. 23516 (S.C.C.); see the discussion of *Apsassin* in Chapter 6.
18 As evidenced through the commencement of airport construction on the land prior to its acquisition by the Crown, the Crown's initiation of procedures to expropriate the land when the Penticton band failed to agree to the Crown's terms, and the evidence presented in *Kruger* which demonstrates that the Penticton people were 'kept in the dark for very large periods of time,' and that their lands were taken from them with no offers of compensation forthcoming in a timely fashion: *Kruger*, n1 *supra*, at 623.
19 To the extent that these may be compensated for either monetarily or otherwise.
20 As expressed in a letter dated 8 July 1940 to the Indian Commissioner for British Columbia: *Kruger*, n1 *supra*, at 598.
21 This factor was recognized and accounted for by the Department of Indian Affairs in a letter to the Department of Transport dated 12 Nov. 1943: Ibid., at 612 and again at 652: 'They are entitled to compensation, in our judgment, for the complete disruption of this Indian community's way of life and for the cost of re-establishing the group where the complete resumption of that way of life may be effected. Owing to their race some opposition to receiving them into available white communities will be encountered and that opposition will be reflected in the price they will have to pay for lands or properties as valuable and as useful to them as those they have been compelled to vacate and give up.'
22 This was illustrated by Heald JA's contrast of 'their rather leisurely approach to negotiations for compensation as compared to their great haste in taking possession and depriving the Indians of their means of livelihood': Ibid., at 622.
23 Especially in light of the Penticton band's reluctance to lease the land to the Crown without adequate compensation, which the Crown was eminently aware of.
24 *Kruger*, n1 *supra*, at 623.

Notes to pages 281–6   453

16 Prospects for the Future

1 Although the British Crown's post-contact obligations to the Native peoples also entail fiduciary responsibility, that responsibility relates only to the period culminating in the removal of its residual authority over Canadian affairs.
2 Aboriginal commercial rights of trapping and agriculture are not disputed matters. On the question of aboriginal commercial fishing rights, see *R v Agawa* (1988), 65 O.R. (2nd) 505 (C.A.); *R v Bombay*, [1993] 1 C.N.L.R., 92 (Ont. C.A.); *R v Jones* (1993), 14 O.R. (3d) 421 (Ont. Prov. Div.); *R v Vanderpeet*, [1993] 5 W.W.R. 459 (B.C.C.A.); *R v Gladstone*, [1993] 5 W.W.R. 517 (B.C.C.A.); *R v NTC Smokehouse Ltd*, [1993] 5 W.W.R. 542 (B.C.C.A.); *R v Lewis*, [1994] 5 W.W.R. 608 (B.C.C.A.). At the time of writing, the British Columbia Court of Appeal fishing rights cases were on appeal to the Supreme Court of Canada.
3 (1984), 13 D.L.R. (4th) 321 (S.C.C.), at 340, 356–7.
4 (1989), 57 D.L.R. (4th) 197 (S.C.C.), at 208.
5 (1990), 71 D.L.R. (4th) 193 (S.C.C.), at 209.
6 [1992] 1 C.N.L.R. 90 (F.C.T.D.).
7 S.O.R. 84-467.
8 [1993] 3 C.N.L.R. 55 (F.C.A.). It should be noted, however, that the appellate decision in *Eastmain*, has no bearing on the applicability of the new *Canadian Environmental Assessment Act* (CEAA) to the Crown's fiduciary duty to Native peoples. For further discussion, see Nancy Kleer and Len Rotman, 'Environmental Protection and First Nations: Changing the Status Quo,' unpublished paper delivered at Canadian Institute Conference, 'Doing Business with First Nations,' 1 and 2 March 1993.
9 See, for example, Alexander Morris, *The Treaties of Canada with the Indians of Manitoba and the North-West Territories* (Toronto: Belfords, Clarke, 1880), at 34, discussed in Chapter 3, n5 *supra*.
10 See n12, *infra*.
11 See John J. Borrows, 'A Genealogy of Law: Inherent Sovereignty and First Nations Self-Government,' (1992) 30 *Osgoode Hall L.J.* 291, at 323: "This tactic ... violated a previous treaty [Treaty No. 45½] between our people and the government that had stated "your Great Father engages for ever to protect you from the encroachment of the whites."'
12 Letter from T.G. Anderson, superintendent of Indian Affairs, 2 Aug 1854 to the Owen Sound and Saugeen Indians: see Borrows, ibid., at 322; PAC, RG 10, Vol. 213, at 126356. Note also the letter from Anderson to the Chippewas of Saugeen dated 16 Aug. 1854, which stated that 'emigrants are coming so thick that I do not believe that the Government will be able to retain for you

all your reserves,' as quoted in Borrows, ibid., at 323, n122; PAC, RG 10, Vol. 541.
13 The discussion in this section has been summarized from information contained in the Public Archives of Canada with regard to Treaty No. 72. See, for example, the *Report on Negotiation Proceedings Regarding Surrender of the Saugeen Tract* from Superintendent General of Indian Affairs L. Oliphant to Lord Elgin, governor-general of Canada, PAC RG 10, Vol. 117.
14 Refer back to n12 *supra*.
15 Other irregularities used by the Crown to secure the surrender of Chippewa lands under Treaty No. 72 may be seen in Borrows, ibid., at 324-7.
16 Ibid., at 324.
17 See the commentary on this point in Chapter 1, n84, and in Chapters 2 and 3.
18 That is not to diminish the important role of direct Crown-Native negotiations within this larger framework. Whereas the course of future Crown-Native negotiations will play a key role in resolving the shape of Crown-Native relations in years to come, they will not be of direct application to the matter of the Crown's fiduciary duty to the aboriginal peoples as understood by the courts.
19 (1990), 70 D.L.R. (4th) 385 (S.C.C.).
20 The 'spirit and intent' of the Crown's solemn engagements is reflected most often in discussions of Crown-Native treaties. See, for example, Grand Chief Donald Marshall, Sr, Grand Captain Alexander Denny, and Putus Simon Marshall, of the executive of the Grand Council of the Mi'kmaw Nation, 'The Covenant Chain,' in Boyce, Richardson, ed., *Drumbeat: Anger and Renewal In Indian Country*, (Toronto: Summerhill, 1993), at 75: 'Treaties are spiritual as well as political compacts that confer binding and solemn obligations on the signatories. The spiritual basis of the treaties is crucial to an understanding of their meaning, since it represents an effort to elevate the treaties, and relations among peoples, beyond the vagaries of political opportunism and expediency. They are intended to develop through time to keep pace with events, while still preserving the original intentions and rights of the parties.'

See also, Indian Chiefs of Alberta, *Citizens Plus* (Edmonton: Indian Association of Alberta, 1970), at 8: 'The intent and spirit of the treaties must be our guide, not the precise letter of a foreign language. Treaties that run forever must have room for changes in the conditions of life.' *R v Horseman*, [1990] 1 S.C.R. 901, per Wilson, J, at 907-143, 917-21.

References

Articles

Adams, G.B. 'The Origins of English Equity.' (1916) 16 *Columbia L. Rev.* 87.
– 'The Continuity of English Equity.' (1916–17) 26 *Yale L.J.* 550.
Aronson, Stephen. 'The Authority of the Crown to Make Treaties with Indians.' [1993] 2 C.N.L.R. 1.
Asch, Michael. 'Aboriginal Self-Government and the Construction of Canadian Constitutional Identity.' (1992) 30 *Alta. L. Rev.* 465.
Asch, Michael, and Macklem, Patrick. 'Aboriginal Right and Canadian Sovereignty: An Essay on *R v Sparrow*.' (1991) 29 *Alta. L. Rev.* 498.
Austin, Robert P. 'The Role and Responsibilities of Trustees in Pension Plan Trusts: Some Problems of Trust Law.' In Timothy G. Youdan, ed., *Equity, Fiduciaries and Trusts*. Toronto: Carswell, 1989.
Barkin, Ira. 'Aboriginal Rights: A Shell without the Filling.' (1990) 15 *Queen's L.J.* 307.
Bartlett, Richard H. 'The Fiduciary Obligation of the Crown to the Indians.' (1989) 53 *Sask. L. Rev.* 301.
– 'You Can't Trust the Crown: The Fiduciary Obligation of the Crown to the Indians: *Guerin v The Queen*.' (1984–5) 49 *Sask. L. Rev.* 367.
Beck, Stanley M. 'The Quickening of Fiduciary Obligation.' (1975) 53 *Can Bar Rev.* 771.
Bell, Catherine. 'Who Are the Métis People in Section 35(2)?' (1991) 29 *Alta. L. Rev.* 351.
Bennett, Gordon. 'Aboriginal Title in the Common Law: A Stony Path through Feudal Doctrine.' (1978) 27 *Buf. L. Rev.* 617.
Berman, Howard. 'The Concept of Aboriginal Rights in the Early Legal History of the United States.' (1978) 27 *Buf. L. Rev.* 637.

Binnie, W.I.C. 'The Sparrow Doctrine: Beginning of the End or End of the Beginning?' (1990) 15 *Queen's L.J.* 217.
Bishop, W., and Prentice, D.D. 'Some Legal and Economic Aspects of Fiduciary Remuneration.' (1983), 46 *Mod. L. Rev.* 289.
Black, Ashley. 'Dworkin's Jurisprudence and Hospital Products: Principles, Policies, and Fiduciary Duties.' (1987) 10 (2) *U.N.S.W.L.J.* 8.
Borrows, John. 'Constitutional Law from a First Nation Perspective: Self-Government and the Royal Proclamation.' (1994) 28 *U.B.C. L. Rev.* 1.
– 'A Genealogy of Law: Inherent Sovereignty and First Nations Self-Government.' (1992) 30 *Osgoode Hall L.J.* 291.
Brant, Dr Clare. 'Native Ethics and Rules of Behaviour.' (1990) 35 *Can. J. Psychiatry* 534.
Brown, Harold. 'Franchising – A Fiduciary Relationship.' (1971) 49 *Tex. L. Rev.* 650.
Brunyate, John. 'Fraud and the Statute of Limitations.' [1930] 4 Camb. L.J. 174.
Bryant, Michael J. 'Crown–Aboriginal Relationships in Canada: The Phantom of Fiduciary Law.' (1993) 27 *U.B.C. L. Rev.* 19.
Butler, Henry N., and Ribstein, Larry E. 'Opting Out of Fiduciary Duties: A Response to the Anti-Contractarians.' (1990) 65 *Wash. L. Rev.* 1.
Carter, Nancy Carol. 'Race and Power Politics as Aspects of Federal Guardianship over American Indians: Land-Related Cases, 1887–1924.' (1976) 4 *Am. Ind. L. Rev.* 197.
Chambers, Reid Peyton. 'Judicial Enforcement of the Federal Trust Responsibility to Indians.' (1975) 27 *Stan. L. Rev.* 1213.
Chartier, Clem, '"Indian": An Analysis of the Term as Used in Section 91(24) of the British North America Act, 1867.' (1978–9) 43 *Sask. L. Rev.* 37.
Chartrand, Paul '"Terms of Division": Problems of "Outside Naming" for Aboriginal Peoples in Canada.' (1991) 2:2 *J. Indig. Stud.* 1.
Cheffins, Brian R. 'Law, Economics, and Morality: Contracting Out of Corporate Law Fiduciary Duties.' (1991) 19 *C.B.L.J.* 28.
Cockburn, Tina. 'Trustee Exculpation Clauses Furnished by the Settlor.' (1993) 11 *Aust. Bar Rev.* 163.
Cohen, Felix. 'Original Indian Title.' (1947) 32 *Minn. L. Rev* 28.
– 'The Spanish Origin of Indian Rights in the Law of the Unites States.' (1942) 31 *Geo. L.J.* 1.
Cooter, Robert, and Freedman, Bradley J. 'The Fiduciary Relationship: Its Economic Character and Legal Consequences.' (1991) 66 *N.Y.U. L. Rev.* 1045.
Cullity, Maurice C. 'Fiduciary Powers.' (1976) 54 *Can. Bar Rev.* 229.
– 'Judicial Control of Trustee's Discretion.' (1975) 25 *U.T.L.J.* 99.
Davidson, Ian E. 'The Equitable Remedy of Compensation.' (1982) 3 *Melbourne Univ. L. Rev.* 349.

Davies, J. Derek. 'Equitable Compensation: "Causation, Foreseeability, and Remoteness."' In Donovan W.M. Waters, ed., *Equity, Fiduciaries, and Trusts, 1993*. Toronto: Carswell, 1993.
Davies, Paul L. 'Directors' Fiduciary Duties and Individual Shareholders.' In Ewan McKendrick, ed., *Commercial Aspects of Trust and Fiduciary Obligations*. Oxford: Clarendon, 1992.
Davis, Kenneth B., Jr. 'Judicial Review of Fiduciary Decisionmaking – Some Theoretical Perspectives.' (1985–6) 80 *Nw. U. L. Rev.* 1.
DeMott, Deborah A. 'Fiduciary Obligations under Intellectual Seige: Contemporary Challenges to the Duty to be Loyal.' (1992) 30 *Osgoode Hall L.J.* 471.
– 'Beyond Metaphor: An Analysis of Fiduciary Obligation.' (1988) 5 *Duke L.J.* 879.
Dewey, John. 'Logical Method and Law.' (1924–5) 10 *Cornell L.Q.* 17.
Donohue, Maureen Ann. 'Aboriginal Land Rights in Canada: A Historical Perspective on the Fiduciary Relationship' (1990) 15 *Am. Ind. L. Rev.* 369.
Easterbrook, Frank H., and Fischel, Daniel R. 'Contract and Fiduciary Duty.' (1993) 36 *J. Law & Econ.* 425.
Eccles, W.J. 'A Belated Review of Harold Adams Innis's *The Fur Trade in Canada*.' In J.M. Bumsted, ed. *Interpreting Canada's Past*, Vol 1. Toronto: Oxford University Press, 1986.
Editors. 'Crown's Fiduciary Obligation toward Native Peoples.' (1985) 1 *Admin. L.J.* 49.
Ellwanger, Kimberley T. 'Money Damages for Breach of the Federal–Indian Trust Relationship after Mitchell II.' (1984) 59 *Wash. L. Rev.* 675.
Emond, D.P. 'Case Comment: *Guerin v R.*' (1986) 20 E.T.R. 61.
Erasmus, George. 'Twenty Years of Disappointed Hopes.' In Boyce Richardson, ed., *Drumbeat: Anger and Renewal in Indian Country*. Toronto: Summerhill Press, 1993.
Finn, Paul D. 'The Fiduciary Principle.' In Timothy G. Youdan, ed., *Equity, Fiduciaries, and Trusts*. Toronto: Carswell, 1989.
Flanagan, Thomas. 'The Agricultural Argument and Original Appropriation: Indian Lands and Political Philosophy.' (1989) 22 *Cdn. J. Pol. Sci.* 589.
– 'Francisco de Vitoria and the Meaning of Aboriginal Rights.' (1988) 95(2) *Queen's Quarterly* 421.
Flannigan, Robert. 'Fiduciary Obligation in the Supreme Court.' (1990) 54 *Sask. L. Rev.* 45.
– 'The Fiduciary Obligation.' (1989) 9 *Ox. J. Leg. Stud.* 285.
Florio, Roger. 'Water Rights: Enforcing the Federal–Indian Trust after *Nevada v U.S.*' (1987–8) 13 *Am. Ind. L. Rev.* 79.
Frankel, Tamar. 'Fiduciary Relationships in the United States Today.' In Donovan W.M. Waters, ed., *Equity, Fiduciaries, and Trusts, 1993*. Toronto: Carswell, 1993.

- 'Fiduciary Law.' (1983) 71 *Cal. L. Rev.* 795.
Gautreau, The Hon. J.R. Maurice. 'Demystifying the Fiduciary Mystique.' (1989) 68 *Can. Bar Rev.* 1.
Gibbens, R.D. 'Causation and Fiduciary Duties.' (1991) 18 *C.B.L.J.* 301.
Gibson, Arrell Morgan. 'Philosophical, Legal and Social Rationales for Appropriating the Tribal Estate, 1607 to 1980.' (1984) 12 *Am. Ind. L. Rev.* 3.
Giles, Jack. 'Fiduciary Duties – The New Reach of Equity.' In Frank E. McArdle, ed., *1987 Cambridge Lectures*. Montreal: Yvon Blais, 1989.
Gormley, Daniel J. 'Aboriginal Rights as Natural Rights.' (1984) 4 *Cdn. J. Nat. Stud.* 29.
Green, Jessie D., and Work, Susan. 'Comment: Inherent Indian Sovereignty.' (1976) 4 *Am. Ind. L. Rev.* 311.
Green, L.C. 'Claims to Territory in Colonial America.' In L.C. Green and Olive P. Dickason, *The Law of Nations and the New World*. Edmonton: University of Alberta Press, 1989.
- 'Trusteeship and Canada's Indians.' (1976) 3 *Dalhousie L.J.* 104.
Griffin, Nicholas. 'Reply to Professor Flanagan.' (1989) 22 *Cdn. J. Pol. Sci.* 603.
Gross, Winifred T. 'Tribal Resources: Federal Trust Responsibility: United States Energy Development Versus Trust Responsibilities to Indian Tribes.' (1981) 9 *Am. Ind. L. Rev.* 309.
Gummow, The Hon. Mr Justice W.M.C. 'Compensation for Breach of Fiduciary Duty.' In Timothy G. Youdan, ed., *Equity, Fiduciaries, and Trusts*. Toronto: Carswell, 1989.
Hammond, R.G. 'Is Breach of Confidence Properly Analysed in Fiduciary Terms?' (1979) 25 *McGill L.J.* 244.
Henderson, James Youngblood. 'Unravelling the Riddle of Aboriginal Title.' (1977) 5 *Am. Ind. L. Rev.* 75.
Henderson, William B. 'Canada's Indian Reserves: The Usufruct in Our Constitution.' (1980) 12 *Ottawa L. Rev.* 167.
Hogg, Peter. 'The Dolphin Delivery Case: The Application of the Charter to Private Action.' (1986–7) 51 *Sask. L. Rev.* 273.
Hohfeld, Wesley Newcomb. 'Fundamental Legal Conceptions as Applied in Judicial Reasoning.' (1916–17) 26 Yale L.J. 710.
- 'Some Fundamental Legal Conceptions as Applied in Judicial Reasoning.' (1913–14), 23 *Yale L.J.* 16.
Hudson, Michael. 'The Fiduciary Obligations of the Crown towards Aboriginal Peoples.' In Frank Cassidy, ed., *Aboriginal Title in British Columbia: Delgammukw v The Queen*. Lantzville, BC: Institute for Research on Public Policy and Oolichan Books, 1992.

Hughes, Camilla. 'The Fiduciary Obligations of the Crown to Aborigines: Lessons from the United States and Canada.' (1993) 16 *U.N.S.W. L.J.* 70.
Hurley John D. 'The Crown's Fiduciary Duty and Indian Title: *Guerin v The Queen*.' (1985) 30 *McGill L.J.* 559.
– 'Aboriginal Rights in Modern American Case Law.' [1983] 2 C.N.L.R. 9.
Hutchinson, Allan, and Petter, Andrew. 'Private Rights / Public Wrongs: The Liberal Lie of the Charter.' (1988) 38 *U.T.L.J.* 278.
Isaac, Thomas. 'The Power of Constitutional Language: The Case against Using "Aboriginal Peoples" as a Reference for First Nations.' (1993) 19(1) *Queen's L.J.* 415.
Jackson, Michael. 'The Articulation of Native Rights in Canadian Law.' (1984) 18 *U.B.C. L. Rev.* 255.
Jacobs, E.I. 'Comment: *Hawrelak v City of Edmonton*.' (1977) 23 *McGill L.J.* 97.
Johnston, Darlene M. 'A Theory of Crown Trust towards Aboriginal Peoples.' (1986) 30 *Ottawa L. Rev.* 307.
– 'The Quest of the Six Nations Confederacy for Self-Determination.' (1986) 44 *U.T. Fac. L. Rev.* 1.
Jones, Gareth. 'Unjust Enrichment and the Fiduciary's Duty of Loyalty.' (1968) 84 *L.Q.R.* 472.
Kanter, Michael. 'The Government Action Doctrine and the Public/Private Distinction: Searching for Private Action.' (1990) 15 *Queen's L.J.* 33.
Kapashesit, Randy, and Klippenstein, Murray. 'Aboriginal Group Rights and Environment Protection.' (1991) 36 *McGill L.J.* 925.
Kelly, Daniel G. 'Indian Title: The Rights of American Indians in Lands They Have Occupied since Time Immemorial.' (1975) 75 *Col. L. Rev.* 655.
Klinck, Dennis. '"Things of Confidence": Loyalty, Secrecy, and Fiduciary Obligation.' (1990) 54 *Sask. L. Rev.* 73.
Lambert, Gail M. 'Indian Breach of Trust Suits: Partial Justice in the Court of the Conqueror.' (1980) 33 *Rutgers L. Rev.* 502.
Large, D.W. 'This Land Is Whose Land? Changing Concepts of Land as Property.' (1973) 1026 *Wisc. Rev.* 1039.
Lehane, J.R.F. 'Fiduciaries in a Commercial Context.' In P.D. Finn, ed., *Essays in Equity*. Sydney: Law Book Company, 1985.
Lester, Geoffrey S. 'Aboriginal Land Rights: Some Remarks upon the Ontario Lands Case (1885–1888).' (1988) 13 *Queen's L.J.* 132.
Lilles, Heino. 'Some Problems in the Adminstration of Justice in Remote and Isolated Communities.' (1990) 15 *Queen's L.J.* 327.
Litman, M.M. 'The Emergence of Unjust Enrichment as a Cause of Action and the Remedy of Constructive Trust.' (1988) 26 *Alta. L. Rev.* 407.
Little Bear, Leroy. 'Aboriginal Rights and the Canadian "Grundnorm."' In J. Rick

Ponting, ed., *Arduous Journey: Canadian Indians and Decolonization*. Toronto: McClelland and Stewart, 1986.
- 'A Concept of Native Title.' *C.A.S.N.P. Bull.* Dec. 1976.
Lurie, Nancy Oestreich. 'Indian Cultural Adjustment to European Civilization.' In James M. Smith, ed., *Seventeenth Century America: Essays in Colonial History*. Williamsburg: University of North Carolina Press, 1959.
Lyon, Noel. 'An Essay on Constitutional Interpretation.' (1988) 26 *Osgoode Hall L.J.* 95.
Lyons, Oren. 'Traditional Native Philosophies Relating to Aboriginal Rights.' In Menno Boldt, J. Anthony Long, and Leroy Little Bear, eds., *The Quest for Justice: Aboriginal Peoples and Aboriginal Rights*. Toronto: University of Toronto Press, 1985.
Lysyk, Ken. 'The Rights and Freedoms of the Aboriginal Peoples of Canada.' In Walter S. Tarnopolsky and Gérald A.- Beaudoin, eds. *The Canadian Charter of Rights and Freedoms*. Toronto: Carswell, 1982.
- 'The Indian Title Question in Canada: An Appraisal in the Light of Calder.' (1973) 51 *Can. Bar Rev.* 450.
- 'The Unique Constitutional Position of the Canadian Indian.' (1967) 45 *Can. Bar Rev.* 513.
Mackenzie, N.A.M. 'Indians and Treaties in Law: Comment on *Rex v Syliboy* (1929), 1 D.L.R. 307.' (1929) 7 *Can. Bar Rev.* 561.
Macklem, Patrick. 'Distribution Sovereignty: Indian Nations and Equality of Peoples.' (1993) 45 *Stan. L. Rev.* 1311.
- 'First Nations Self-Government and the Borders of the Canadian Legal Imagination.' (1991) 36 *McGill L.J.* 382.
MacLauchlan, H. Wade. 'Development in Administrative Law: The 1989-90 Term.' (1991) 2 *Sup. Ct. L. Rev.* (2d) 1.
Maddaugh, Peter D. 'Definition of Fiduciary Duty.' In *Fiduciary Duties*, Law Society of Upper Canada Special Lectures, 1990. Toronto: De Boo, 1991.
- 'Confidence Abused: LAC Minerals Ltd v International Corona Resources Ltd.' (1990) 16 *C.B.L.J.* 198.
Marshall, Grand Chief Donald, Sr., Denny, Grand Captain Alexander, and Marshall, Putus Simon. 'The Covenant Chain.' In Boyce, Richardson, ed., *Drumbeat: Anger and Renewal in Indian Country*. Toronto: Summerhill Press, 1993.
Mason, The Hon. Sir Anthony. 'The Place of Equity and Equitable Doctrines in the Contemporary Common Law World: An Australian Perspective.' In Donovan W.M. Waters, ed., *Equity, Trusts, and Fiduciaries, 1993*. Toronto: Carswell, 1993.
- 'Themes and Prospects.' In P.D. Finn, ed., *Essays in Equity*. Sydney: Law Book Company, 1985.

Massey, Calvin. 'American Fiduciary Duty in an Age of Narcissism.' (1990) 54 *Sask. L. Rev.* 101.

Matchewan, Chief Jean-Maurice. 'Mitchikanibikonginik Algonquins of Barriere Lake: Our Battle to Create a Sustainable Future.' In Boyce Richardson, ed., *Drumbeat: Anger and Renewal in Indian Country.* Toronto: Summerhill Press, 1993.

McCamus, John D. 'Unjust Enrichment: Its Role and Its Limits.' In Donovan W.M. Waters, ed., *Equity, Fiduciaries, and Trusts, 1993.* Toronto: Carswell, 1993.

– 'Remedies for Breach of Fiduciary Duty.' In *Fiduciary Duties,* Law Society of Upper Canada Special Lectures, 1990. Toronto: De Boo, 1991.

– 'The Recent Expansion of Fiduciary Obligation.' (1987) 23 E.T.R. 301.

McClean, A.J. 'The Theoretical Basis of the Trustee's Duty of Loyalty.' (1969) 7 *Alta. L. Rev.* 218.

McDougall, John Lorn. 'The Relationship of Confidence.' In Donovan W.M. Waters, ed., *Equity, Fiduciaries, and Trusts,* 1993. Toronto: Carswell, 1993.

McIntosh Jeffrey G. 'Corporations.' In *Fiduciary Duties,* Law Society of Upper Canada Special Lectures, 1990. Toronto: De Boo, 1991.

McLachlin, The Hon. Beverley M. 'The Place of Equity and Equitable Doctrines in the Contemporary Common Law World: A Canadian Perspective.' In Donovan W.M. Waters, ed., *Equity, Fiduciaries, and Trusts, 1993.* Toronto: Carswell, 1993.

– 'A New Morality in Business Law?' (1990) 16 *C.B.L.J.* 319.

McLeod, Clay. 'The Oral Histories of Canada's Northern People: Anglo-Canadian Evidence Law and Canada's Fiduciary Duty to First Nations: Breaking Down the Barriers of the Past.' (1992) 30 *Alta. L. Rev.* 1276.

McMurtry, William R., and Pratt, Alan. 'Indians and the Fiduciary Concept, Self-Government, and the Constitution: *Guerin* in Perspective.' [1986] 3 C.N.L.R. 19.

McNeil, Kent. 'Envisaging Constitutional Space for Aboriginal Governments.' (1993) 19 *Queen's L.J.* 95.

– 'The High Cost of Accepting Benefits from the Crown: A Comment on the Temagami Indian Land Case.' [1992] 1 C.N.L.R. 40.

– 'The Temagami Indian Land Claim: Loosening the Judicial Straitjacket.' In Matt Bray and Ashley Thomson, eds., *Temagami: A Debate on Wilderness.* Toronto: Dundurn, 1990.

– 'The Constitution Act, 1982, Sections 25 and 35.' [1988] 1 C.N.L.R. 1.

– 'The Constitutional Rights of the Aboriginal Peoples of Canada.' (1982) 4 *Sup. Ct. L. Rev.* 255.

McNeill, Daniel. 'Trusts: Toward an Effective Indian Remedy for Breach of Trust.' (1980) 8 *Am. Ind. L. Rev.* 429.

Miller, J.R. 'The Oka Controversy and the Federal-Land Claims Process.' In Ken Coates, ed., *Aboriginal Land Claims in Canada: An Aboriginal Perspective.* Toronto: Copp Clark Pitman, 1992.

Mitchell, Grand Chief Michael. 'An Unbroken Assertion of Sovereignty.' In Boyce Richardson, ed., *Drumbeat: Anger and Renewal in Indian Country.* Toronto: Summerhill Press, 1993.

Monture, Patricia A. 'Now that the Door Is Open: First Nations and the Law School Experience.' (1990) 15 *Queen's L.J.* 179.

Morse, Bradford. 'Government Obligations, Aboriginal Peoples and Section 91(24) of the *Constitution Act, 1867.*' In David C. Hawkes, ed., *Aboriginal Peoples and Government Responsibility: Exploring Federal and Provincial Roles.* Ottawa: Carleton University Press, 1989.

Muir, R.C. 'Duties Arising outside of the Fiduciary Relationship.' (1964) 3 *Alta. L. Rev.* 359.

Narvey, Kenneth M. 'The Royal Proclamation of 7 October 1763. The Common Law and Native Rights to Land within the Territory Granted to the Hudson's Bay Company.' (1974) 38 *Sask. L. Rev.* 123.

Newton, Nell J. 'Enforcing the Federal-Indian Trust Relationship after *Mitchell.*' (1982) 31 *Cath. U. L. Rev.* 635.

– 'At the Whim of the Sovereign: Aboriginal Title Reconsidered.' (1980) 31 *Hast. L.J.* 1215.

Note. 'Rethinking the Trust Doctrine in Federal Indian Law.' (1984) 98 *Harv. L. Rev.* 422.

– 'Whom Can Indians Trust after *Mitchell.*' (1981) 53 *Col. L. Rev.* 179.

– 'A Remedy for a Breach of the Government–Indian Trust Duties.' (1971) 1 *N.M. L. Rev.* 321.

Ong, D.S.K. 'Fiduciaries: Identification and Remedies.' (1986) 8 *U. Tasmania L. Rev.* 311.

Owen, David P. 'Fiduciary Obligations and Aboriginal Peoples: Devolution in Action.' [1994] 3 C.N.L.R.I.

Pentney, William F. 'The Rights of Aboriginal Peoples of Canada and the Constitution Act, 1982: Part I, The Interpretive Prism of Section 25.' (1988) 22 *U.B.C. L. Rev.* 21.

– 'The Rights of Aboriginal Peoples of Canada and the Constitution Act, 1982: Part II, Section 35: The Substantive Guarantee.' (1988) 22 *U.B.C. L. Rev.* 207.

Pratt, Alan 'Aboriginal Self-Government and the Crown's Fiduciary Duty: Squaring the Circle or Completing the Circle?' (1992) 2 *N.J.C.L.* 163.

– 'Federalism in the Era of Aboriginal Self-Government.' In David C. Hawkes, ed., *Aboriginal Peoples and Government Responsibility: Exploring Federal and Provincial Roles.* Ottawa: Carleton University Press, 1989.

Ridington, Robin. 'Cultures in Conflict: The Problems of Discourse.' In W.H. New, ed., *Native Writers and Canadian Writing*. Vancouver: University of British Columbia Press, 1990.

Roach, Kent. 'Remedies for Violations of Aboriginal Rights.' (1992) 21 *Man. L.J.* 498.

Rogers, E.M., and Young, S.B. 'Public Office as a Public Trust.' (1974) 63 *Georgia L.J.* 1025.

Rotman, Leonard I. 'Provincial Fiduciary Obligations to First Nations: The Nexus between Governmental Power and Responsibility.' (1994) 32 *Osgoode Hall L.J.* 735.

– 'The Vulnerable Position of Fiduciary Doctrine in the Supreme Court of Canada.' (1995) 23(4) *Man. L.J.* (in press).

Ryder, Bruce. 'The Demise and Rise of the Classical Paradigm in Canadian Federalism: Promoting Autonomy for the Provinces and First Nations.' (1991) 36 *McGill L.J.* 308.

Salembier, J. Paul. 'How Many Sheep Make a Flock? An Analysis of the Surrender Provisions of the *Indian Act*.' [1992] 1 C.N.L.R. 14.

Sanders, Douglas. 'Pre-Existing Rights: The Aboriginal Peoples of Canada.' In Gérald A.- Beaudoin and Ed Ratushny, eds., *The Canadian Charter of Rights and Freedoms*, 2nd ed. Toronto: Carswell, 1989.

– 'From Indian Title to Aboriginal Rights.' In Louis A. Knafla, ed., *Law & Justice in a New Land*. Toronto: Carswell, 1986.

– 'The Rights of the Aboriginal Peoples of Canada.' (1983) 61 *Can. Bar Rev.* 314.

– 'The Indian Lobby.' In Keith Banting and Richard Simeon, eds., *And No One Cheered: Federalism, Democracy, and the Constitution Act*. Toronto: Methuen, 1983.

– 'Aboriginal Peoples and the Constitution.' (1981) 19 *Alta. L. Rev.* 410.

Scott, Austin W. 'The Fiduciary Principle.' (1949) 37 *Cal. L. Rev.* 539.

Sealy, L.S. 'Some Principles of Fiduciary Obligation.' [1963] *Camb. L.J.* 119.

– 'Fiduciary Relationships.' [1962] *Camb. L.J.* 69.

Shepherd, J.C. 'Toward a Unified Concept of Fiduciary Relationships.' (1981) 97 *L.Q.R.* 51.

Simsarian, James 'The Acquisition of Legal Title to Terra Nullius.' (1938) 53 *Pol. Sci. Q.* 111.

Slaght, Ronald G. 'Proving a Breach of Fiduciary Duty.' In *Fiduciary Duties*, Law Society of Upper Canada Special Lectures, 1990. Toronto: De Boo, 1991.

Slattery, Brian. 'First Nations and the Constitution: A Question of Trust.' (1992) 71 *Can. Bar Rev.* 261.

– 'Aboriginal Sovereignty and Imperial Claims.' (1991) 29 *Osgoode Hall L.J.* 681.

– 'Understanding Aboriginal Rights.' (1987) 66 *Can. Bar Rev.* 727.

- 'The Charter's Relevance to Private Litigation: Does Dolphin Deliver?' (1987) 32 *McGill L.J.* 905.
- 'The Charter of Rights and Freedoms: Does It Bind Private Persons.' (1985) 63 *Can. Bar Rev.* 148.
- 'Did France Claim Canada upon "Discovery"?' In J.M. Bumsted, ed., *Interpreting Canada's Past*, Vol 1. Toronto: Oxford University Press, 1986.
- 'The Hidden Constitution: Aboriginal Rights in Canada.' (1984) 32 *Am J. Comp. L.* 361.
- 'The Independence of Canada.' (1983) 5 *Sup. Ct. L. Rev.* 369.
- 'The Constitutional Guarantee of Aboriginal and Treaty Rights.' (1982–3) 8 *Queen's L.J.* 232.

Smith, J.C. 'The Concept of Native Title.' (1974) 24 *U.T. L.J.* 1.
- 'The Unique Nature of the Concepts of Western Law.' (1968) 46 *Can. Bar Rev.* 191.

Smith, Lionel D. 'The Province of the Law of Restitution.' (1992) 71 *Can. Bar Rev.* 672.

Swinton, Katherine. 'The Application of the Charter of Rights and Freedoms.' In Walter S. Tarnopolsky and Gérald A.- Beaudoin, eds. *The Canadian Charter of Rights and Freedoms.* Toronto: Carswell, 1982.

Talbott, Malcolm D. 'Restitution Remedies in Contract Cases: Finding a Fiduciary or Confidential Relationship to Gain Remedies.' (1959) 20 *Ohio St. L.J.* 320.

Tassé, Roger. 'Application of the Canadian Charter of Rights and Freedoms.' In Gérald A.- Beaudoin and Ed Ratushny, eds., *The Canadian Charter of Rights and Freedoms*, 2nd ed. Toronto: Carswell, 1989.

Taylor, John Leonard. 'Two Views on the Meaning of Treaties Six and Seven.' In Richard Price, ed., *The Spirit of the Alberta Indian Treaties.* Edmonton: Pica Pica Press, 1987.

Tobias, John L. 'Protection, Assimilation, Civilization: An Outline History of Canada's Indian Policy.' In J.R. Miller, ed., *Sweet Promises: A Reader on Indian–White Relations in Canada.* Toronto: University of Toronto Press, 1991.

Turpel, Mary Ellen. 'Home/Land.' (1991) 10 *Cdn. J. Fam. L.* 17.
- 'Aboriginal Peoples and the Canadian *Charter*: Interpretive Monopolies, Cultural Differences.' (1989–90) *Cdn. Hum. Rghts. Y.B.* 3.

Von der Heydte, F.A. 'Discovery, Symbolic Annexation, and Virtual Effectiveness in International Law.' (1935) 29 *Am. J. Int'l Law* 448.

Washburn, Wilcomb E. 'The Moral and Legal Justifications for Dispossessing the Indians.' In James M. Smith, ed., *Seventeenth Century America: Essays in Colonial History.* Williamsburg: University of North Carolina Press, 1959.

Waters, Donovan W.M. 'Lac Minerals Ltd v International Corona Resources Ltd.' (1990) 69 *Can. Bar Rev.* 455.

- 'New Directions in the Employment of Equitable Doctrines: The Canadian Experience.' In Timothy G. Youdan, ed., *Equity, Fiduciaries, and Trusts*. Toronto: Carswell, 1989.
Weinrib, Ernest J. 'The Fiduciary Obligation.' (1975) 25 *U.T.L.J.* 1.
Wicken, William C. 'The Mi'kmaq and Wuastukwiuk Treaties.' (1994) 43 *U.N.B. L.J.* 241.
Wildsmith, Bruce. 'Treaty Responsibilities: A Co-Relational Model.' (1992) *U.B.C. L. Rev.* Special Edition on Aboriginal Justice 324.
Williams, Glanville. 'The Three Certainties.' (1940) 4 *Mod. L. Rev.* 20.
Williams, Robert A., Jr. 'Gendered Checks and Balances: Understanding the Legacy of White Patriarchy in an American Indian Cultural Context.' (1990) 24 *Georgia L. Rev.* 1019.
- 'Encounters on the Frontiers of International Human Rights Law: Redefining the Terms of Indigenous Peoples' Survival in the World.' (1990) 4 *Duke L.J.* 660.
- 'The Algebra of Federal Indian Law: The Hard Trail of Decolonization and Americanizing the White Man's Indian Jurisprudence.' (1986) *Wisc. L. Rev.* 219.
Willis, John. 'Delegatus Non Potest Delegare.' (1943) 21 *Can. Bar Rev.* 257.
Youdan, Timothy G. 'The Fiduciary Principle: The Applicability of Proprietary Remedies.' In Timothy G. Youdan, ed., *Equity, Fiduciaries, and Trusts*. Toronto: Carswell, 1989.
Zlotkin, Norman K. 'The 1983 and 1984 Constitutional Conferences: Only the Beginning.' [1984] 3 C.N.L.R. 3.

Books

Alvord, Clarence W. *The Illinois Country, 1673–1818: The Centennial History of Illinois*. Springfield: Illinois Centennial Commission, 1920.
Anon. *The Seminary of Montreal: Their Rights and Titles*. St Hyacinthe: Courrier de St Hyacinthe Power Presses, 1880.
Aristotle. *The Politics*. Trevor J. Saunders, trans. Harmondsworth, Middlesex: Penguin, 1981.
Asch, Michael, *Home and Native Land: Aboriginal Rights and the Canadian Constitution*. Toronto: Methuen, 1984.
Ashburner, Walter. *Principles of Equity*. London: Butterworth, 1902.
Axtell, James. *After Columbus: Essays in the Ethnohistory of Colonia America*. New York: Oxford University Press, 1988.
Bailey, Alfred G. *The Conflict of European and Eastern Algonkian Cultures, 1504–1700*, 2nd ed. Toronto: University of Toronto Press, 1969.
Banting, Keith, and Simeon, Richard, eds. *And No One Cheered: Federalism, Democracy, and the Constitution Act*. Toronto: Methuen, 1983.

Bartlett, Richard H. *Indian Reserves and Aboriginal Lands in Canada: A Homeland.* Saskatoon: University of Saskatchewan Native Law Centre, 1990.

– *Aboriginal Water Rights in Canada.* Calgary: Canadian Institute of Resources Law, University of Calgary, 1988.

Beaudoin, Gérald A.-, and Ratushny, Ed, eds. *The Canadian Charter of Rights and Freedoms,* 2nd ed. Toronto: Carswell, 1989.

Berger, Thomas R. *A Long and Terrible Shadow: White Values, Native Rights in the Americas,* 1492–1992. Vancouver: Douglas and McIntyre, 1992.

– *The Second Discovery of America.* Vancouver: Douglas and McIntyre, 1991.

Biggar, Henry P., ed. *A Collection of Documents Relating to Jacques Cartier and the Sieur de Roberval,* Publications of the Public Archives of Canada, No. 14. Ottawa: Public Archives of Canada, 1930.

Black's Law Dictionary, 5th ed. St Paul, Minn: West, 1979.

Blake, Edward. *The Ontario Lands Case. Argument of Mr Blake, QC, Before the Privy Council.* Toronto. Press of the Budget, 1888.

Boldt, Menno. *Surviving as Indians: The Challenge of Self-Government.* Toronto: University of Toronto Press, 1993.

Boldt, Menno, Long, J. Anthony, and Little Bear, Leroy, eds. *The Quest for Justice: Aboriginal Peoples and Aboriginal Rights.* Toronto: University of Toronto Press, 1985.

– *Pathways to Self-Determination: Canadian Indians and the Canadian State.* Toronto: University of Toronto Press, 1984.

Bray, Matt, and Thomson, Ashley, eds. *Temagami: A Debate on Wilderness.* Toronto: Dundurn, 1990.

Brigham, Clarence S., ed. *British Royal Proclamations Relating to America,* Transactions and Collections of the American Antiquarian Society, Vol. 12. Worcester, Mass: American Antiquarian Society, 1911.

Brown, George, and Maguire, Ron. *Indian Treaties in Historical Perspective.* Ottawa: Research Branch, Corporate Policy, Department of Indian and Northern Affairs Canada, 1979.

Brunyate, John. *Limitation of Actions in Equity.* London: Stevens, 1932.

Bumsted, J.M., ed., *Interpreting Canada's Past,* Vol. 1. Toronto: Oxford University Press, 1986.

Burger, Julian. *Aborigines Today, Land and Justice.* London: Anti-Slavery Society, Indigenous Peoples and Development Series Report No. 5, 1988.

Burrage, Henry S., ed. *Early English and French Voyages, Chiefly from Hakluyt, 1534–1608.* New York: Scribner's 1906.

Cardinal, Harold. *The Unjust Society.* Edmonton: Hurtig, 1969.

Cassidy, Frank, ed. *Aboriginal title in British Columbia: Delgamuukw v The Queen.* Lantzville, BC: Institute for Research on Public Policy and Oolichan Books, 1992.

- and Bish, Robert L. *Indian Government: Its Meaning in Practice*. Lantzville, BC: Institute for Research on Public Policy and Oolichan Books, 1989.
Clark, Bruce. *Native Liberty, Crown Sovereignty: The Existing Aboriginal Right of Self-Government in Canada*. Montreal: McGill-Queen's University Press, 1990.
- *Indian Title in Canada*. Toronto: Carswell, 1987.
Coates, Ken, ed. *Aboriginal Land Claims in Canada: An Aboriginal Perspective*. Toronto: Copp Clark Pitman, 1992.
Crawford, James. *The Creation of States in International Law*. Oxford: Clarendon 1979.
Cumming, Peter A., and Mickenberg, Neil H. *Native Rights in Canada*, 2nd ed. Toronto: Indian–Eskimo Association of Canada, 1972.
Daugherty, W.E. *Treaty Research Report: Treaty #3*. Ottawa: Treaties and Historical Research Centre, Indian and Northern Affairs Canada, 1986.
- *Maritime Indian Treaties in Historical Perspective*. Ottawa: Treaties and Historical Research Centre, Research Branch, Corporate Policy, Department of Indian and Northern Affairs Canada, 1983.
Davenport, Frances Gardiner. *European Treaties bearing on the History of the United States and Its Dependencies to 1648*. Washington, DC: Carnegie Institution, 1917.
De las Casas, Bartolomé. *In Defense of the Indians*. Stafford Poole, trans. DeKalb: Northern Illinois Press, 1974.
Department of Indian Affairs and Northern Development. *Outstanding Business – A Native Claims Policy*. Ottawa: Queen's Printer, 1982.
- *In All Fairness – A Native Claims Policy*. Ottawa: Queen's Printer, 1981.
- *Statement on Claims of Indian and Inuit People*. Ottawa: Queen's Printer, 1973.
Dickason, Olive P. *Canada's First Nations: A History of Founding Peoples*. Markham: McClelland and Stewart, 1992.
Eccles, W.J. *The Canadian Frontier, 1534–1760*. New York: Holt, Rinehart and Winston, 1969.
Ellis, Mark V. *Fiduciary Duties in Canada*. Toronto: De Boo, 1988.
Fiduciary Duties, Law Society of Upper Canada Special Lectures, 1990. Toronto: De Boo, 1991.
Finn, P.D. *Fiduciary Obligations*. Sydney: Law Book Company, 1977.
- ed. *Essays in Equity*. Sydney: Law Book Company, 1985.
Fisher, Robin. *Contact and Conflict: Indian–European Relations in British Columbia, 1774–1890*. Vancouver: University of British Columbia Press, 1977.
Franks, Michael. *Limitation of Actions*. London: Sweet and Maxwell, 1959.
Frederickson, N. Jaye, and Gibb, Sandra. *The Covenant Chain: Indian Ceremonial and Trade Silver*. Ottawa: National Museum of Man, National Museums of Canada, 1990.
Frideres, James S. *Native Peoples in Canada: Contemporary Conflicts*, 4th ed. Scarborough: Prentice–Hall, 1993.

Fumoleau, René. *As Long as This Land Shall Last*. Toronto: McClelland and Stewart, 1976.
Gentili, Alberico. *De Iure Belli Libri Tres*. John C. Rolfe, trans. *Classics of International Law*. Oxford: Clarendon, 1933.
Getty, A.L., and Lussier, A.S., eds. *As Long as the Sun Shines and the Water Flows*. Vancouver: University of British Columbia Press, 1983.
Gibson, Charles, ed. *The Spanish Tradition in America*. New York: Harper and Row, 1968.
Goebel, Julius, Jr. *The Struggle for the Falkland Islands*. New Haven: Yale University Press, 1927.
Gould, Gary P., and Semple, Alan J., eds. *Our Land: The Maritimes*. Fredericton: Saint Annes Point Press, 1980.
Green, L.C., and Dickason, Olive P. *The Law of Nations and the New World*. Edmonton: University of Alberta Press, 1989.
Grotius, Hugo. *De Jure Praedae Commentarius*, Vol. 1. J.B. Scott, ed. Oxford: Clarendon, 1950.
Haig-Brown, Celia. *Resistance and Renewal: Surviving the Indian Residential School*. Vancouver: Tillacum Library, 1988.
Hall, William Edward. *A Treatise on the Foreign Powers and Jurisdiction of the British Crown*. Oxford: Clarendon, 1894.
Halsbury's Laws of England, 4th ed. London: Butterworth, 1976.
Hanbury, Harold Greville, and Maudsley, Ronald Harling. *Modern Equity*, 13th ed. Jill E. Martin, ed. London: Stevens 1989.
Hanke, Lewis. *All Mankind Is One: A Study of the Disputation Between Bartolomé de Las Casas and Juan Ginés de Sepúlveda in 1550 on the Intellectual and Religious Capacity of the American Indian*. DeKalb: Northern Illinois University Press, 1974.
– *The Spanish Struggle for Justice in the Conquest of America*. Philadelphia: University of Pennsylvania Press, 1949.
Hawkes, David C., ed. *Aboriginal Peoples and Government Responsibility: Exploring Federal and Provincial Roles*. Ottawa: Carleton University Press, 1989.
Hawley, Donna Lea. *The Annotated Indian Act, 1994*. Toronto: Carswell, 1994.
Hogg, Peter W. *Constitutional Law of Canada*, 3rd ed. Toronto: Carswell, 1992.
– *Liability of the Crown*, 2nd ed. Toronto: Carswell, 1989.
Hohfeld, Wesley Newcomb. *Fundamental Legal Conceptions as Applied in Judicial Reasoning and Other Legal Essays*. Walter Wheeler Cook, ed. New Haven: Yale University Press, 1919.
Holdsworth, Sir William S. *A History of English Law*, 16 vols. London: Methuen, 1964.
House of Commons Special Committee on Indian Self-Government. *Indian Self-*

Government in Canada: Report of the Special Committee. Ottawa: Supply and Services Canada, 1983.

Hurley, John D. *Children or Brethren: Aboriginal Rights in Colonial Iroquoia.* PhD Thesis, Cambridge University, 1985, reprinted, Saskatoon: University of Saskatchewan Native Law Centre, 1985.

Imai, Shin, Logan, Katharine, and Stein, Gary. *Aboriginal Law Handbook.* Toronto: Carswell, 1993.

In all Fairness – A Native Claims Policy. Ottawa: Queen's Printer, 1981.

Indian Self-Government in Canada: Report of the Special Committee. Ottawa: Supply and Services Canada, 1983.

Innis, Harold A. *The Fur Trade in Canada: An Introduction to Canadian Economics.* Toronto: University of Toronto Press, 1956.

Jacobs, Wilbur R. *Dispossessing the American Indian: Indians and Whites on the Colonial Frontier.* New York: Scribner's, 1972.

Jaenen, Cornelius J. *Friend and Foe: Aspects of French–Amerindian Cultural Contact in the Sixteenth and Seventeenth Centuries.* New York: Columbia University Press, 1976.

James Bay and Northern Quebec Agreement. Quebec City: Editeur officiel du Québec, 1976.

Jennings, Francis. *The Founders of America: How Indians Discovered the Land, Pioneered in It, and Created Great Classical Civilizations: How They Were Plunged into a Dark Age by Invasion and Conquest; and How They Are Now Reviving.* New York: Norton, 1993.

– *Empire of Fortune: Crowns, Colonies, and Tribes in the Seven Years' War in America.* New York: Norton, 1988.

– *The Ambiguous Iroquois Empire: The Covenant Chain Confederation of Indian Tribes with English Colonies from Its Beginnings to the Lancaster Treaty of 1744.* New York: Norton, 1984.

– *The Invasion of America: Indians, Colonialism, and the Cant of Conquest.* Chapel Hill: University of North Carolina Press, 1975.

Jennings, R.Y. *The Acquisition of Territory in International Law.* Manchester: Manchester University Press, 1963.

Johnston, Darlene. *The Taking of Indian Lands in Canada: Consent or Coercion.* Saskatoon: University of Saskatchewan Native Law Centre, 1989.

Johnston, Ian. V.B. *Pre-Confederation Crown Responsibilities: A Preliminary Historical Overview.* Ottawa: Treaties and Historical Research Centre, Indian and Northern Affairs Canada, 1984.

Jones, Dorothy V. *License for Empire: Colonialism by Treaty in Early America.* Chicago: University of Chicago Press, 1982.

Kant, Immanuel. *The Philosophy of Law.* Clifton, NJ: Augustus M. Kelley, 1974.

Keller, Arthur S., Lissitzyn, Oliver J., and Mann, Frederick J. *Creation of Rights of Sovereignty through Symbolic Acts 1400–1800*. New York: Columbia University Press, 1938.
Kerly, D.M. *An Historical Sketch of the Equitable Jurisdiction of the Court of Chancery*. Cambridge: Cambridge University Press, 1890.
Knafla, Louis A., ed. *Law and Justice in a New Land*. Toronto: Carswell, 1986.
Lacan, J., and Prévost, W. *An Historical Notice on the Difficulties Arisen between the Seminary of St Sulpice of Montreal and Certain Indians at Oka, Lake of Two Mountains*, 2nd ed. Montreal: La Minerve Steam Printing Job Office, 1876.
Lindley, Mark F. *The Acquisition and Government of Backward Territory in International Law*. London: Longmans, Green, 1926.
Locke, John. *Two Treatises of Government*. Peter Laslett, ed., 2nd ed. Cambridge: Cambridge University Press, 1967.
Malloy, William M. *Treaties, Conventions, International Acts, Protocols and Agreements between the United States of America and Other Powers, 1776–1909*. Washington, DC: Governmental Printing Office, 1910.
Manual, George, and Posluns, Michael. *The Fourth World: An Indian Reality*. Toronto: Collier Macmillan, 1974.
Manypenny, George W. *Our Indian Wards*. Cincinnati Robert Clarke, 1880, reprinted, New York: Da Capo Press, 1972.
McArdle, Frank E., ed., *1987 Cambridge Lectures*. Montreal: Yvon Blais, 1989.
McDouglas, Myres S., Lasswell, Harold D., and Vlasic, Ivan A. *Law and Public Order in Space*. New Haven: Yale University Press, 1963.
McKendrick, Ewan, ed. *Commercial Aspects of Trusts and Fiduciary Obligations*. Oxford: Clarendon, 1992.
McMahon, Matthew M. *Conquest and Modern International Law*. PhD Thesis, Catholic University of America, 1940, reprinted, Millwood, NY: Kraus Reprint, 1975.
McMillan, Alan D. *Native Peoples and Cultures of Canada: An Anthropological Overview*. Toronto: Douglas and McIntyre, 1988.
McNeil, Kent. *Common Law Aboriginal Title*. Oxford: Clarendon 1989.
– *Native Claims in Rupert's Land and the North-Western Territory: Canada's Constitutional Obligations*. Saskatoon: University of Saskatchewan Native Law Centre, 1982.
Mercredi, Ovide, and Turpel, Mary Ellen. *In the Rapids: Navigating the Future of First Nations*. Toronto: Viking, 1993.
Mew, Graeme. *The Law of Limitations*. Toronto: Butterworths, 1991.
Miller, J.R. *Skyscrapers Hide the Heavens: A History of Indian–White Relations in Canada*. Toronto: University of Toronto Press, 1989.
– ed. *Sweet Promises: A Reader on Indian–White Relations in Canada*. Toronto: University of Toronto Press, 1991.

More, Sir Thomas. *Utopia*. Paul Turner, trans. Middlesex: Penguin, 1985.
Morison, Samuel Eliot. *The European Discovery of America*, 2 vols. New York: Oxford University Press, 1971–4.
Morris, Alexander. *The Treaties of Canada with the Indians of Manitoba and the North-West Territories*. Toronto: Belfords, Clarke, 1880.
Morse, Bradford W., ed., *Aboriginal Peoples and the Law*. Ottawa: Carleton University Press, 1985.
Nammack, Georgiana C. *Fraud, Politics, and the Dispossession of the Indians: The Iroquois Land Frontier in the Colonial Period*. Norman, Okla: University of Oklahoma Press, 1969.
New, W.H., ed. *Native Writers and Canadian Writing*. Vancouver: University of British Columbia Press, 1990.
O'Callaghan, Edmund Bailey, ed. *Documents Relative to the Colonial History of the State of New York*, 11 vols. Albany: Weed, Parsons, 1853–61.
Outstanding Business – A Native Claims Policy. Ottawa: Queen's Printer, 1982.
Oxford English Dictionary, 2nd ed. Oxford: Clarendon, 1989.
Paul, Daniel N. *We Were Not the Savages: A Micmac Perspective on the Collision of European and Aboriginal Civilizations*. Halifax: Nimbus, 1993.
Pentney, William. *The Aboriginal Rights Provisions in the Constitution Act, 1982*. LLM Thesis, University of Ottawa, 1987, reprinted, Saskatoon: University of Saskatchewan Native Law Centre, 1987.
Pettipas, Katherine A. *Severing the Ties that Bind: Government Repression of Indigenous Religious Ceremonies on the Prairies*. Winnipeg: University of Manitoba Press, 1994.
Ponting, J. Rick, ed. *Arduous Journey: Canadian Indians and Decolonization*. Toronto: McClelland and Stewart, 1986.
Price, Richard, ed. *The Spirit of the Alberta Indian Treaties*. Edmonton: Pica Pica Press, 1987.
Pufendorf, Samuel von. *De Jure Naturae et Gentium Libri Octo*, Vol. 2. J.B. Scott, ed. Oxford: Clarendon 1934.
Purich, Donald. *Our Land*. Toronto: Lorimer, 1986.
Ray, Arthur J. *Indians in the Fur Trade*. Toronto: University of Toronto Press, 1974.
Reiter, Robert A. *The Fundamental Principles of Indian Law*. Edmonton: First Nations Resource Council, 1990.
Report of the Mackenzie Valley Pipeline Inquiry. *Northern Frontier, Northern Homeland*. Ottawa: Supply and Service Canada, 1977.
Report of the Select Committee on Aborigines, 1837, Vol. 1, Part 2. Imperial Blue Book, 1837 nr VII.425, Facsimile Reprint, C. Struik (Pty) Ltd., Cape Town, 1966.
Richardson, Boyce, ed., *Drumbeat: Anger and Renewal in Indian Country*. Toronto: Summerhill Press, 1993.

- *Strangers Devour the Land*. Toronto: Macmillan 1975.
Roberts-Wray, Sir Kenneth. *Commonwealth and Colonial Law* (London: Stevens, 1966).
Royal Commission on Aboriginal Peoples. *Partners in Confederation: Aboriginal Peoples, Self-Government, and the Constitution*. Ottawa: Minister of Supply and Services, 1993.
- *Treaty Making in the Spirit of Co-existence: An Alternative to Extinguishment*. Ottawa: Minister of Supply and Services, 1995.
- *The Right of Aboriginal Self-Government and the Constitution: A Commentary*. Ottawa, 1992.
- *Shaping Canada's Future Together*. Ottawa: Minister of Supply and Services Canada, 1991.
Royce, Charles C. *Indian Land Cessions in the United States, Eighteenth Annual Report of the Bureau of American Ethnology, to the Secretary of the Smithsonian Institute, Part II*. Washington, DC: Government Printing Office, 1896–7.
Salmond, Sir John. *Jurisprudence*, 7th. ed. (London: Sweet & Maxwell, 1924).
Sauer, Carl Ortwin. *Sixteenth Century North America: The Land and the People as Seen by the Europeans*. Berkeley: University of California Press, 1971.
Scott, James Brown. *The Spanish Origins of International Law, Part 1, Francisco de Vitoria and His Law of Nations*. Oxford: Clarendon, 1934.
Shepherd, J.C. *The Law of Fiduciaries*. Toronto: Carswell, 1981.
Shortt, Adam and Doughty, Arthur G., eds. *Documents Relating to the Constitutional History of Canada, 1759–1791*, 2 vols. Ottawa: King's Printer, 1918.
Simpson, Lesley Byrd. *The Laws of Burgos, 1512–1513. Royal Ordinances for the Good Government and Treatment of the Indians*. San Francisco: John Howell, 1960.
Sinclair, Alan M. *Introduction to Real Property Law*, 2nd ed. Toronto: Butterworths, 1982.
Sioui, Georges E. *For an Amerindian Autohistory: An Essay on the Foundations of a Social Ethic*. Sheila Fischman, trans. Montreal: McGill-Queen's University Press, 1992.
Slattery, Brian. *Ancestral Lands, Alien Laws: Judicial Perspective on Aboriginal Title*. Saskatoon: University of Saskatchewan Native Law Centre, 1983.
- *The Land Rights of Indigenous Canadian Peoples as Affected by the Crown's Acquisition of Their Territories*. DPhil Thesis, Oxford University, 1979, reprinted, Saskatoon: University of Saskatchewan Native Law Centre, 1979.
Smiley, Donald V.S., ed. *The Rowell–Sirois Report*. Toronto: McClelland and Stewart, 1963.
Smith, Derek G., ed., *Canadian Indians and the Law: Selected Documents 1663–1972*. Toronto: McClelland and Stewart, 1975.

Smith, James M., ed., *Seventeenth Century America: Essays in Colonial History*. Williamsburg: University of North Carolina Press, 1959.

Snow, Alpheus Henry. *The Question of Aboriginals in the Law and Practice of Nations*. New York: Putnam, 1921.

Spry, I.C.F. *The Principles of Equitable Remedies: Injunctions, Specific Performance, and Equitable Damages*, 2nd ed. London: Sweet and Maxwell, 1980.

Stagg, Jack. *Anglo-Indian Relations in North America to 1763 and an Analysis of the Royal Proclamation of 7 October 1763*. Ottawa: Research Branch, Indian and Northern Affairs Canada, 1981.

Tarnopolsky, Walter S., and Beaudoin, Gérald A., eds. *The Canadian Charter of Rights and Freedoms*. Toronto: Carswell, 1982.

Tennant, Paul. *Aboriginal Peoples and Politics: The Indian Land Question in British Columbia, 1847–1989*. Vancouver: University of British Columbia Press, 1990.

The Justice System and Aboriginal People: Report of the Aboriginal Justice Inquiry of Manitoba, 2 vols. Winnipeg: Queen's Printer, 1991. (A.C. Hamilton and C.M. Sinclair, Commissioners.)

Turner, Frederick W., III, ed. *The Portable North American Indian Reader*. New York: Viking, 1974.

Union of Nova Scotia Indians. *The Mi'kmaq Treaty Handbook*. Sydney and Truro, NS: Native Communications Society of Nova Scotia, 1987.

Upton, L.F.S. *Micmacs and Colonists: Indian–White Relations in the Maritimes, 1713–1867*. Vancouver: University of British Columbia Press, 1979.

Vattel, Emer de. *Les Droit des Gens, ou Principes de la Loi Naturelle, appliqués à la Conduite et aux Affaires des Nations et des Souverains*. Charles G. Fenwick, trans. Washington, DC: Carnegie Institute, 1916.

Vinter, Ernest. *A Treatise on the History and Law of Fiduciary Relationship and Resulting Trusts*, 3rd ed. Cambridge: W. Heffer, 1955.

Vitoria, Francisco de. *De Indis et De Jure Belli Relictiones*. Ernest Nys, ed. Washington, DC: Carnegie Institute, 1917.

Voger, Virgil J., ed. *This Country Was Ours: A Documentary History of the American Indian*. New York: Harper and Row, 1972.

Waddams, S.M. *The Law of Contracts*, 2nd ed. Toronto: Canada Law Book, 1984.

Washburn, Wilcomb E. *Red Man's Land / White Man's Law*. New York: Scribner's 1971.

– *The Indian and the White Man*. Garden City, NY: Anchor, 1964.

Waters, Donovan W.M. *Equity, Fiduciaries, and Trusts, 1993*. Toronto: Carswell, 1993.

– *Law of Trusts in Canada*, 2nd ed. Toronto: Carswell, 1984.

Weaver, Sally M. *Making Canadian Indian Policy: The Hidden Agenda 1968–1970*. Toronto: University of Toronto Press, 1981.

Wheaton, Henry. *Elements of International Law.* George G. Wilson, ed. Oxford: Clarendon, 1936.
White, Richard. *The Middle Ground: Indians, Empires, and Republics in the Great Lakes Region, 1650–1815.* Cambridge: Cambridge University Press, 1991.
Wildsmith, Bruce A. *Aboriginal Peoples and Section 25 of the Canadian Charter of Rights and Freedoms.* Saskatoon: University of Saskatchewan Native Law Centre, 1988.
Williams, Robert A., Jr. *The American Indian in Western Legal Thought.* New York: Oxford University Press, 1990.
Wolff, Christian. *Jus Gentium Methodo Scientifica Pertractatum,* Vol. 2. Joseph H. Drake, trans. Oxford: Clarendon, 1934.
Woodward, Jack. *Native Law.* Toronto: Carswell, 1989.
Youdan, Timothy G., ed. *Equity, Fiduciaries and Trusts.* Toronto: Carswell, 1989.

Unpublished Materials

Bartlett, Richard H. 'The Existence of an Express Trust Derived from the Indian Act in Respect of Reserved Lands.' Unpublished paper, 1979.
Belgrad, Eric A. 'The Theory and Practice of Prescriptive Acquisition in International Law.' Unpublished PhD Thesis, Johns Hopkins University, 1969.
Borrows, John J. 'A Genealogy of Law: Inherent Sovereignty and First Nations Self-Government.' Unpublished LLM Thesis, University of Toronto, 1991.
Borrows, John J., and Rotman, Leonard I. 'The *Sui Generis* Nature of Aboriginal Rights: Does It Make a Difference?' Forthcoming.
Brans, Dennis M. 'The Trusteeship Role of the Government of Canada.' Unpublished Indian Claims Commission Student Project paper, 1971.
Emerson, Angela. 'Research Report on Policy of the Government of Ontario Re: Headland to Headland Questions, Treaty #3, 1873–1978.' Office of Indian Resource Policy, Ministry of Natural Resources, 1978.
Gillese, Eileen E. 'Fiduciary Relations and Their Impact on Business and Commerce.' Unpublished Paper delivered at *Insight* Conference, 'Trusts and Fiduciary Relations in Commercial Transactions,' 14 April 1988.
Hathaway, G.G. 'The Neutral Indian Barrier State: A Project in British North American Policy, 1754–1815.' Unpublished PhD Thesis, University of Minnesota, 1957.
Hudson, Michael. 'The Rights of Indigenous Populations in National and International Law.' Unpublished LLM Thesis, McGill University, 1985.
Hutchins, Peter W. 'The Legal Status of the Canadian Inuit. Unpublished LLM Thesis, London School of Economics, 1971.
Juricek, John T., Jr. 'English Territorial Claims in North America to 1660.' Unpublished PhD Thesis, University of Chicago, 1970.

Kleer, Nancy, and Rotman, Len. 'Environmental Protection and First Nations: Changing the Status Quo.' Unpublished paper delivered at Canadian Institute Conference, 'Doing Business with First Nations,' 1–2 March 1993.

Lancaster, Phil. 'A Fiduciary Theory for the Review of Aboriginal Rights.' Unpublished LLM Thesis, University of Saskatchewan, 1990.

Lester, Geoffrey S. 'The Territorial Rights of the Inuit of the Northwest Territories.' Unpublished DJur Thesis, Osgoode Hall Law School, 1981.

Lowry, David R. 'Native Trusts: The Position of the Government of Canada as Trustee for Indians, A Preliminary Analysis.' Unpublished report prepared for the Indian Claims Commission and the Union of Nova Scotia Indians, 1973.

Lyon, Noel. 'Aboriginal Peoples and Constitutional Reform in the 90's. Background Study No. 7, Constitutional Reform Project, Centre for Public Law and Public Policy, York University, 1991.

Malbon, Justin E. 'Section 35, Canadian Constitution Act – The Aboriginal Right to Land.' Unpublished LLM Thesis, Osgoode Hall Law School, 1987.

Nahwegahbow, David C., Posluns, Michael W., Allen, Don, and Sanders, Douglas. 'The First Nations and the Crown: A Study of Trust Relationships.' Unpublished research report prepared for the Special Committee of the House of Commons on Indian Self Government, 1983.

Reid, Felicity Anne. 'The Fiduciary Concept – An Examination of Its Relationship with Breach of Confidence, Negligent Misrepresentation, and Good Faith. Unpublished LLM Thesis, Osgoode Hall Law School, 1989.

Reynolds, James I., and Harvey, Lewis F. 'The Fiduciary Obligation of the United States and Canadian Governments towards Indian Peoples.' Ottawa: Treaties and Historical Research Centre, 1985.

Rotman, Leonard I. 'The *Sui Generis* Interpretation of Aboriginal Treaty Rights.' forthcoming.

– Duty, The Honour of the Crown and *Uberrima Fides*: Fiduciary Doctrine and the Crown–Native Relationship in Canada: unpublished LLM Thesis, Osgoode Hall Law School, 1993.

Sanders, Douglas. '"The Friendly Care and Directing Hand of the Government; A Study of Government Trusteeship of Indians in Canada.' Unpublished paper, 1977.

Statement of the Government of Canada on Indian Policy, 1969. Ottawa: Queen's Printer, 1969.

The Summer of 1990. Fifth Report of the Standing Committee on Aboriginal Affairs. Ken Hughes, MP, Chair. House of Commons, Issue No. 59, May 1991.

Turpel, Mary Ellen. 'In *Sparrow* We Trust: Federal and Provincial Fiduciary Responsibilities.' Unpublished paper, 1992.

Williams, Paul C. 'The Chain.' Unpublished LLM Thesis, Osgoode Hall Law School, 1982.

Index

aboriginal land claims
- and dispute resolution, 267–8
- and Indian Claims Commission, 266; deficiencies of, 267, 447 n46
- Comprehensive Claims, 10, 446 n37 (see also aboriginal rights, distinguished from treaty rights, and effect of Comprehensive Claims process); alternative to, 272, 450 n68, and conflict of interest, 265, 267, 271–2, 289, and breach of Crown fiduciary duty, 271, 449 nn65, 67
- Specific Claims, 10, 446 n37; and conflict of interest, 265–7, 271, 289
aboriginal rights. See also *sui generis*, aboriginal rights as; Royal Proclamation of 1763, as recognition and affirmation of pre-existing rights
- and legal positivism, 7–8, 60–1, 62
- bases for refuting, 26
- contingent rights theory, 62–3
- debates over, by Europeans, 24–6
- distinguished from treaty rights, 125; and effect of Comprehensive Claims process, 271–2
- inherent rights theory, 62–3

aboriginal title, 7, 11 (see also *sui generis*, aboriginal title as; Royal Proclamation of 1763, protection of aboriginal lands under); as root of Crown fiduciary duty, 11, 16, 102, 103, 106; nature of, 103–4, 382 nn66–8, 70, 449 n66
acquiescence, 193, 195
Addy, J. 114–15, 116, 117, 118, 135
Alexander VI, Pope, 22
Alfonso V (king of Portugal), 22
American Revolution, 50–1
Anderson, T.G., 286
Anfield, Frank, 89–90, 91–2, 93–4
Angers, J, 80
Archibald, Adams G., 51
Arneil, William, 89–90, 92, 94
Articles of Capitulation at Montreal, 1760, 26, 27, 29, 213
Austin, JA, 125

Bagot Commission, 69
Barber, A.H., 278
Belcher, Jonathan, 67
beneficiaries: duty to inquire into fiduciaries' activities, 182, 190, 211, 244–5, 278, 437 n3; vulnerability

(*see* fiduciary theories, inequality theory)
Bethune, William, 91, 92, 94
Blair, JA, 124, 133
Boyd, Chancellor, 225, 226, 233
Brant, Joseph, 82
Brennan, J, 143
British Columbia Terms of Union, 1871, 70–1
British North America Act, 1867: section 91(24), 70, 72, 123, 145, 214, 215, 217, 222, 224, 233, 252, 253, 254 (*see also* Constitution Act, 1982, section 35(1), and section 91(24) of the British North America Act, 1867); section 92(5), 251; section 92(13), 251; section 92A, 251; section 95, 251; section 109, 138, 224, 228, 229, 231, 236, 237, 238, 241, 242; section 111, 75, 77, 78, 223, 227–31, 232–3; section 112, 223, 228; section 114, 223; section 115, 223
Burbidge, J, 76–8, 236

Cabot, John 22, 48
Cameron, J, 85–6
Cardozo, J, 171
Carleton, Sir Guy. *See* Dorchester, Lord
Cartier, Jacques, 22–3
cestui qui trust. *See* beneficiaries
Charles II (king of England), 67
Charles, Andrew, Jr, 96
Charlottetown Accord, 4, 219, 255
Chisholm, Andrew Gordon, 80–1
Collier, J, 11, 95, 96–7
colonialism, 13, 14, 50, 66; aboriginal responses to, 37–8: and Crown Indian policy, 21–2, 26, 51–3, 282; and Royal Proclamation of 1763, 42, 47; Crown adherence to principles of, 19–20, 26, 29–32, 35, 47–9; effects of, on aboriginal peoples, 50–65, 281
conquest, 22, 23, 58, 64; effect of, 60
Constitution Act, 1867. *See* British North America Act, 1867
Constitution Act, 1982
– section 1, 124
– section 25, 5, 10, 64, 109; content of, 72
– section 35(1), 4, 5, 6, 10, 62, 64, 109, 122–3, 136, 137, 208, 253, 263–4, 272 (*see also* frozen rights); and abrogation of aboriginal and treaty rights, 43; and Crown fiduciary obligation, 123, 129, 136, 140, 256–7, and canons of treaty and statutory interpretation, 136; and Crown–Native fiduciary relationship, 145; and limitation of rights, inapplicability of section 1 test, 124, 391 n83, pre-*Sparrow*, 124, *Sparrow* justificatory test, 124–8; and restraint on sovereign power, 123–4; and section 91(24) of British North America Act, 1867, 251; and section 88 of Indian Act, 252; and struggle for recognition of aboriginal rights, 5; application to all levels of government, 253; as promise to aboriginal peoples, 123; content of, 72, 390 n68; provincial obligations pursuant to, 253–4; purposive nature of, 129, 253, 254, 263
– section 38, 126, 256
– section 43, 126, 256
– section 52(1), 254

Index 479

contact, 4 n12
context, importance of, 4, 12, 15, 16–18, 106, 127, 140, 151, 199, 282, 388 n37, 393 n92
Cooke, P, 133
Cory, J, 119
Covenant Chain, 33–5, 41, 52, 352 n84
Cowper, Lord, 261

Davey, Lord, 234–5
Davies, J, 236
de las Casas, Fr. Bartolomé, 24
de Montesinos, Fr, Antonio, 24
de Sepúlveda, Juan Ginés, 24
Denning, Lord, MR, 205–6
Dickson, CJC: in *Guerin*, 11, 101–2, 103–4, 105, 108, 112, 113, 115, 118, 249, strict interpretation of judgment, 105–8, 109, 121, 123, 125, 129, 130, 138; in *Sparrow*, 21, 246; in *Mitchell*, 245–6, 251, 253
Diplock, Lord, 206
discovery, 22, 23, 58–60, 64
Dorchester, Lord, 44–5
Dube, J, 135
Duff, J, 236, 237

Environmental Assessment and Review Process Guidelines Order, SOR 84–467, 22 June 1984, 132, 133
Equity, 64, 105, 153, 161, 164, 167, 182, 183, 184, 186, 192, 275, 367 n64; and statutory limitation periods, 192, 194–5; maxims, 378 n31, 422 n96
Estey, J, 101, 239–40
Exchequer Court Act, 50–51 Vict, c. 16, 77

fiduciaries. *See also* fiduciary doctrine; fiduciary relations, fiduciary theories
– consultation with beneficiaries in Crown–Native relations, 128, 212–16, 219, 259, 279, 288–9, 393 n103
– delegation of duties, 181, 188–9, 207, 216; and Crown–Native relations, 211–16, 288
– duties, monitoring of, 262
– duty of *uberrima fides*, 159, 180, 181–3, 184, 197, 276, 290, 415 n14
– duty to act in beneficiaries' best interests, 102, 105, 120, 211, 259, 263, 264, 275, 279, 285, 288
– requirement of disclosure, 185, 186, 211, 288

fiduciary doctrine. *See also* fiduciaries; fiduciary relations, fiduciary theories
– and acquiescence, 193, 195
– and Hohfeldian rights analysis, 180–1
– and laches, 118, 190, 192–3, 195 218, 250, 278, 421 n84, 422 n88
– and limitation periods, 181, 190–2, 218, 250, 276–7, 278, 414 n11; and Crown–Native relations, 191, 216, 276; and equitable fraud, 192, 194
– categorical approach to, 151–2, 155, 159–60, 168, 199, 283
– conflict of interest, 114, 116–17, 180, 184, 185–8, 195, 196, 197, 263, 264, 270, 275, 276, 418 n42, 451 n9; and Crown–Native relations, 264 72, 289, 445 n31, and *Kruger v R*, 272–80, elimination of, 271–2, possible exceptions, 270, under Indian Act, 268–9, vis-à-vis land

480 Index

surrender requirements, 268–70, 271
- functional approach to, 158–60, 199, 283
- judicial comfort with, 15–16, 111, 140
- misapplication of, 160–3
- principles of, 14, 261
- purposive nature of, 129, 133, 140, 211, 259, 261–3; and Crown-Native relations, 260–1, 263–4, 283, 288–9, 290
- remedies, 102, 150, 159, 163, 167, 172, 177, 184, 189, 195–8, 216, 258, 278 (*see also* fiduciary relations, between British Crown and aboriginal peoples, remedies for breach of; fiduciary relations, remedies for breach of, in *Kruger v R*)
- reverse onus, 181, 183–4, 278
- situation-specific nature of, 14, 155–7, 179, 196, 204, 256, 283, 288
- theoretical basis of, 152–3, 154–5, 160, 262–3
- three-step application of, 177–84, 203–4
- use in Crown–Native relations, 14, 102
- use not an acceptance of colonialism, 14, 144, 337 nn83–4,
fiduciary relations. *See also* fiduciaries; fiduciary doctrine; fiduciary theories
- as between unequal parties, 12–13, 19–20, 115, 282, 289 (*see also* fiduciary theories, inequality theory)
- as catch-all, 149–50
- as compared to trusts, 3–4, 105, 164–6, 255–6, 408 n16,
- between British Crown and aboriginal peoples, 204–20, 288: remedies for breach of, 217–20
- between Crown and aboriginals (*see also* aboriginal land claims, Comprehensive Claims, and conflict of interest, and breach of Crown fiduciary duty; Constitution Act, 1982, section 35(1), and Crown–Native fiduciary relationship; Indian Act, R.S.C. 1985, c. I-5, and Crown–Native fiduciary relationship; Royal Proclamation of 1763, and Crown–Native fiduciary relationship; *sui generis*, Crown–Native fiduciary relations as); bases of, 12–13, 16, 107, 123, 128–9, 140, 144, 145, 146, 222, 246, 250, 257, 281, 282, 290 (*see also* aboriginal title, as root of Crown fiduciary duty); extent of, 109, 282–3, 284–5, 289; how created, 145–6, 283; planes of, 141–2, 257; reduction in scope, 258–60, 288; terminability, 255–8, 259; types of, 14–15, 222, 285, 287
- between provinces and aboriginal peoples, 131, 132, 134, 138, 205, 206, 208, 220, 221, 226, 238, 241–3, 246, 251–4, 284, 288, 435 n81
- essence of, 211
- evidentiary requirements, 104–5
- general principles governing, 184–9
- increase in arguments in favour of, 150
- intention to enter into, 145, 170, 399 n12
- open-ended nature of, 157
- remedies for breach of, in *Kruger v R*, 278–9

- spirit and intent, 153–4, 290
- types of, 149, 168
fiduciary theories (*see also* fiduciaries; fiduciary doctrine; fiduciary relations): contract theory, 169–71; inequality theory, 167–8, 173, 174, 178, 179; power and discretion theory, 173–4, 178, 179; property theory, 165–6, 174, 179; reliance theory, 166–7, 172, 173, 174, 179; unjust enrichment theory, 171–3, 179; utility theory, 173
Frankfurter, Felix, 150
frozen rights, 247, 438 n23
Fry, J, 172

George III (king of England), 7, 27
Girouard, J, 236
Glen, J. Allison, 113
Gonthier, J, 119, 249
Goulding, J, 161
Grant, William, 93, 96
Guerin, William, 95
Gwynne, J, 70, 225–6, 227, 231, 234

Hagarty, CJO, 225, 226
Haldane, Viscount, 150, 248, 249
Heald, JA, 113, 274–5, 276, 277, 280
Henry VII (king of England), 22, 48
Henry, Alexander, 37
Hohfeld, Wesley Newcomb: method of rights analysis, 40–1, 357 n114. *See also* fiduciary doctrine, and Hohfeldian rights analysis
Holmes, Oliver Wendell, 150
Horton, Robert Wilmot, 20
House of Commons Special Committee on Indian Self-Government (Penner Committee), 10, 66
Howell, Alfred, 90, 91–2, 95

Hudson's Bay Company, 49, 67

Idington, J, 236, 237
Indian Act, 16, 63, 87, 121, 240, 265, 267, 282, 285, 363 n10. *See also* fiduciaries, conflict of interest, and Crown–Native fiduciary relations, under Indian Act
- S.C. 1876, c. 18, 8, 53, 72–3, 145; section 4, 73
- S.C. 1884, c. 27; section 3, 364 n28
- R.S.C. 1886, c. 43; section 114, 364 n28
- S.C. 1894, c. 32; section 11, 364 n34
- R.S.C. 1906, c. 81; section 51, 85–6, 87; section 149, 364 n29; section 149A, 8–9 (*see also* Indian Act, R.S.C. 1927, c. 98, section 141)
  S.C. 1914, c. 35; section 8, 364 n32
- S.C. 1918, c. 26; section 7, 364 n29
- R.S.C. 1927, c. 98, 80, 81, 135; section 51, 134; section 90(2), 81; section 140, 364 n32; section 141, 331 n46
- S.C. 1951, c. 29, 331 n47; section 18(1), 73; section 123, 364 n33
- R.S.C. 1952, c. 149, 97, 101–2, 104, 106: section 18, 99–100, 102; section 37, 379 n33; section 38, 379 n33; section 39, 99, 379 nn38, 39; section 40, 379 n33; section 41, 379 n33
- R.S.C. 1970, c. I-6, 394 n113; section 18, 122; section 89(1), 245; section 90(1)(b), 245–6
- R.S.C. 1985, c. I-5; section 2(1), 54, 363 n13; section 6, 437 n8; section 7, 437 n8; section 10(1), 258, 259; section 18(1), 377 n6; section 37, 269, 270, 377 n6; sections 38–41, 377 n6; sections 45–52.5, 363 n16;

section 53(3), 269; section 60(1), 258, 259, 284; section 61(1), 268; section 69(1), 252, 258, 259, 284; section 74(2), 363 n12; section 75, 363 n12; section 77, 363 n12; section 78, 363 n12; sections 81–6, 363 n12, 364 n24; section 87, 363 n18; section 88, 213, 245, 252, 390 n67, 441 n51; section 89, 363 n19
- and alienation of land, 89
- and Crown–Native fiduciary relationship, 108, 145, 284
- and residential schools, 56–7 (*see also* S.C. 1894, c. 32, s. 11)
- and use of trust/trust-like terminology, 73
- as tool of assimilation, 53–7, 64, 247
- banning traditional aboriginal practices, 55–6 (*see also* Indian Act, S.C. 1884, c. 27, s. 3; R.S.C. 1886, c. 43, s. 114; R.S.C. 1906, c. 81, s. 149; S.C. 1914, c. 35, s. 8; S.C. 1918, c. 26, s. 7; R.S.C. 1927, c. 98, s. 140; S.C. 1951, c. 29, s. 123)
- prohibiting aboriginal access to courts, 8–9, 55, 268 (*see also* Indian Act, R.S.C. 1906, c. 81, section 149A)

Indian Estates Regulations, C.R.C. 1978, c. 954, 363 n16
Indian Oil and Gas Act, S.C. 1974–75–76, c. 15, 394 n113
Indian Oil and Gas Regulations, C.R.C. 1978, c. 963, 129
Indian policy, 66–73 (*see also* colonialism and Crown Indian policy); post-Confederation, 70–3; pre-Confederation, 67–70
Isaac, CJ, 117–18, 249

James Bay hydroelectric project, 9–10
Jessel, MR, 170
Johnson, Sir William, 33, 68, 69
jus gentium. *See* Law of Nations

Kellock, J, 83–4, 99
Kerr, LJ, 205, 206
Kerwin, J, 83, 84
King, J, 227, 231

La Forest, J, 21, 150, 157, 166, 171, 192, 193, 245, 246–8
laches, 78, 97, *See also* fiduciary doctrine, and laches
Lacourciere, J, 161
Lambert, JA, 149, 196, 249
Lamer, J, 213–14
Law of Nations, 22, 23, 60, 64; effects on aboriginal peoples, 23, 58
Laws of Burgos, 24
Le Dain, JA, 98–100, 101, 102, 137
limitation periods, 80, 83, 112, 116, 118, 119–20, 374–5 n62 (*see also* fiduciary doctrine, and limitation periods); and fraud, 97, 118; ultimate limitation periods, 191, 420 n69
Loreburn, Lord, LC, 236–7

Macdonald, J, 21
Mackenzie Valley Pipeline project, 9–10
Mahoney, J, 112, 274
Major, J, 119
Malouf, J, 41
Manitoba Aboriginal Justice Inquiry, 4, 56
Marceau, JA, 116–17
Marshall, CJ, 20, 58, 59–60, 143, 248
May, LJ, 205, 206
McArthur, J, 74

McEachern, CJBC, 137–8, 241
McLachlin, J, 119, 120, 159, 169
Megarry, VC, 208–9
mercantilism, 29, 30
Mercredi, Ovide, 50
Michel, Chief Philip, 19
Minavavana, Chief, 37–8
Morden, ACJO, 197
More, Sir Thomas, 24–5
Mowat, Viscount, 186
Murphy, J, 126
Murray, Gen. James, 43

National Indian Brotherhood, 6
Natural Resource Transfer Agreements, 1930, 71

O'Connor, J, 81, 83
Oka crisis, 4, 5
Ontario Boundary Extension Act, 71
Ortiz, Fr. Tomas, 25

papal bulls, 21, 22, 58; original purpose of, 22
Patterson, JA, 225,
Penzance, Lord, 183
Petition of Right Act; R.S.C. 1886, c. 7, 78; R.S.C. 1927, c. 158, 84
political trust, 20, 74, 95, 98, 99–100, 101, 103, 137–8, 209, 379 n47; definition, 76, 86–7
Portland, Duke of, 83, 84
potlach, 55
precedent, effect of, 11–12, 334 nn66, 67
pre-Confederation Indian legislation, 67–73; and use of trust/trust-like terms, 69–70, 370 n17
property, aboriginal and European understandings of, 39–41

Quebec Boundary Extension Act, 71

Rand, J, 83, 86–7, 121, 182
res judicata, 217
Robinson, CJ. *See* Robinson, Sir John Beverly
Robinson, Sir John Beverly, 20, 74
Robinson, William Benjamin, 227
royal charters, 21, 22, 58
Royal Commission on Aboriginal Peoples, 5, 13, 36
Royal Proclamation of 1761, 67, 145
Royal Proclamation of 1763, 7, 16–17, 29, 43, 50, 61, 67, 81–2, 87, 106, 137, 143, 208, 213, 214, 348 n61, 356 n109 (*see also* colonialism, and Royal Proclamation of 1763; treaties, rights, extinguishment of by Royal Proclamation of 1763), and Crown–Native fiduciary relationship, 73, 108, 144, 145, 285–6, 287; and instructions to General Murray, 7 December 1763, 43–4; as aboriginal bill of rights, 26; as grant of rights to aboriginals, 7–8; as recognition and affirmation of pre-existing rights, 38, 356 n109; background to, 27–9; effect of, 38–9, 41–2, 47; protection of aboriginal lands under, 52, 62, 74, 108–9, 130
Rupert's Land and North-Western Territory Order, 1870, 67, 70–1
Russell, Peter, 83, 84

Sachs, Sir Eric, J, 157, 166
Scott, Duncan Campbell, 50
Sedgewick, J, 230
Select Committee on Aborigines, 69
settlement, 22, 23
Sinclair, J, 56

Sopinka, J, 159
Southin, J, 150
Sparrow, Edward, 92–3
Sparrow justificatory test, 124–8, 270
Sparrow, Ronald, 122
Statement of the Government of Canada on Indian Policy, 1969. *See* White Paper
Statute of Westminster, 1931, 205, 206, 207, 210
Stewart, Alexander, 83
Strayer, J, 130
Stone, JA, 113, 116, 118, 119, 274
Street, J, 233–4, 239
Strong, CJC, 225, 226, 228–30, 231, 232
sui generis: aboriginal rights as, 248–9; aboriginal property rights as, 249, 439 n38; aboriginal title as, 104, 107, 249; Crown–Native treaties as, 249, 439 n35; Crown–Native fiduciary relations as, 12, 146, 249, 264–5, 290, 446 n34; Crown–Native relations generally as, 14, 113, 144, 204, 270, 281, 288, 338 n85
symbolic acts, 22–3, 23–4

Taschereau, J, 20, 61, 83, 185
terra nullius, 58, 59, 60
tracing funds, 161, 196; in Equity, 423 n104
treaties, 64, 74, 212, 289 (see also *sui generis*, Crown–Native treaties as); James Bay and Northern Quebec Agreement, 131–2, 252; Jay Treaty, 1794, 45–6, 136; Robinson-Huron Treaty, 1850, 133, 227–33, 237, 240, 241–2; Robinson-Superior Treaty, 1850, 227–33, 237; Treaty of Albany, 1664, 13, 26, 30, 32–3, 39, 41, 52, 144; Treaty of Ghent, 1814, 46; Treaty of Paris, 1763, 61, 67, 214; Treaty of Utrecht, 1713, 26–7, 29, 67, 345 n51, 369 n6; Treaty of Versailles, 210; Treaty No. 1, 51; Treaty No. 2, 51; Treaty No. 3, 221, 223–6, 233–7, 240–1, 252; Treaty No. 9, 252; Treaty No. 45½, 286, 287; Treaty No. 72, 286–7; and Crown obligations, 205, 206, 207, 218, 221–3; and Crown–Native fiduciary obligations, 73, 87, 208, 222, 238–9; and aboriginal understandings of the Crown, 244; change in nature/intent of, 42–3, 51–2, 144–5; coercion of aboriginals to sign, 51; in British Columbia, 68; interpretation, 10 (*see also* Constitution Act, 1982, section 35(1), and Crown fiduciary obligation, and canons of treaty and statutory interpretation); land surrender, 43, 51–2, 360 n129 peace and friendship, 26, 31, in Maritimes, 34, 41, 43, 67; pre-conquest negotiation of, 36; privity and, 237–9; rights, extinguishment of by Royal Proclamation of 1763, 214
Trudeau, Pierre, 5, 6, 9
two-row wampum, 32–3

Urie, JA, 274, 275–6, 277

Veteran's Land Act, 1942, 6 Geo. VI, c. 33, 113, 115
Vitoria, Francisco de, 24

Watson, Lord, 7–8, 226, 229, 232–3, 236
White, J, 240
White Paper, 6–7, 11, 57–8, 64
Wilson, J, 11, 102–3, 104, 105, 112